Museums in Motion

About the Series

The American Association for State and Local History Book Series addresses issues critical to the field of state and local history through interpretive, intellectual, scholarly, and educational texts. To submit a proposal or manuscript to the series, please request proposal guidelines from AASLH headquarters: AASLH Editorial Board, 2021 21st Ave. South, Suite 320, Nashville, Tennessee 37212. Telephone: (615) 320-3203. Website: www.aaslh.org.

About the Organization

The American Association for State and Local History (AASLH) is a national history membership association headquartered in Nashville, Tennessee, that provides leadership and support for its members who preserve and interpret state and local history in order to make the past more meaningful to all people. AASLH members are leaders in preserving, researching, and interpreting traces of the American past to connect the people, thoughts, and events of yesterday with the creative memories and abiding concerns of people, communities, and our nation today. In addition to sponsorship of this book series, AASLH publishes History News magazine, a newsletter, technical leaflets and reports, and other materials; confers prizes and awards in recognition of outstanding achievement in the field; supports a broad education program and other activities designed to help members work more effectively; and advocates on behalf of the discipline of history. To join AASLH, go to www.aaslh.org or contact Membership Services, AASLH, 2021 21st Ave. South, Suite 320, Nashville, TN 37212.

Museums in Motion

AN INTRODUCTION TO THE HISTORIES, FUNCTIONS, AND ASPIRATIONS OF MUSEUMS

Fourth Edition

Juilee Decker

ROWMAN & LITTLEFIELD
Lanham • Boulder • New York • London

Published by Rowman & Littlefield
An imprint of The Rowman & Littlefield Publishing Group, Inc.
4501 Forbes Boulevard, Suite 200, Lanham, Maryland 20706
www.rowman.com

86-90 Paul Street, London EC2A 4NE

British Library Cataloguing in Publication Information Available

Library of Congress Cataloging-in-Publication Data

Names: Decker, Juilee, author.
Title: Museums in motion : an introduction to the histories, functions, and aspirations of museums / Juilee Decker.
Other titles: Introduction to the histories, functions, and aspirations of museums
Description: Fourth edition. | Lanham : Rowman & Littlefield, [2024] | Series: American Association for State and Local History book series | Includes bibliographical references and index. | Summary: "This book explores the histories and functions of museums while also looking at the aspirations of museums as they shift from their rather simple form of a treasury, storehouse, and tomb to something much more complex and people-centered"— Provided by publisher.
Identifiers: LCCN 2024016994 (print) | LCCN 2024016995 (ebook) | ISBN 9781538155721 (cloth) | ISBN 9781538155738 (paperback) | ISBN 9781538155745 (epub)
Subjects: LCSH: Museums. | Museums—History. | Museums—Philosophy.
Classification: LCC AM5 .D44 2024 (print) | LCC AM5 (ebook) | DDC 069.09—dc23/eng/20240509
LC record available at https://lccn.loc.gov/2024016994
LC ebook record available at https://lccn.loc.gov/2024016995

∞™ The paper used in this publication meets the minimum requirements of American National Standard for Information Sciences—Permanence of Paper for Printed Library Materials, ANSI/NISO Z39.48-1992.

Contents

PART III: MUSEUM ASPIRATIONS

Preface

A book on the history of museums should address museum origins and the middle years that demonstrate the importance of collections (both their keeping and their viewing), as well as the associated research and scholarship, interpretation, engagement, and other activities that demonstrate the expanded roles of museums today. Such a volume might also illuminate the nuances and contours of the pivot away from objects and toward communities and the role of museums within them. This revision of *Museums in Motion* seeks to undertake such a task.

While working on this book, I thought of my students, and their futures in museums: What do they need to know? Histories. Functions. Sure. However, challenges persist in preparing a textbook that coheres with the length of a semester and seeks to cover three areas of discussion, as this book explores the histories and functions of museums while also looking at the current standing of museums and their ongoing efforts toward relevance, resiliency, and future-proofing.

Part I examines the beginnings of museums with chapters dedicated to art and design museums; natural history and anthropological museums; science museums; museums focused on history and the past; and gardens, zoos, and children's museums. Emphasis is on museums in the United States, with some historical framing beyond the United States. Part II explores the primary functions of museums, including conservation, exhibition, interpretation, engagement, and service.

Entirely new to this edition, Part III (Museum Aspirations) features five new chapters, each centered around topics, rather than a museum type or museum function. Each topic is meant to be a micro-narrative and a springboard for a conversation about museums today and their sustainability in the future. They examine museums from the inside (museum workers and their voices, especially, as well as power held by people and institutions) and explore critical issues and contemporary movements facing museums and our society: transparency and openness; labor and equity; belonging and coalition-building; risk-taking and risk aversion; and sustainability and empathy. Undergirding these topics are framing lenses of diversity, equity, and inclusion. On their own, or in conjunction with the chapters in the previous sections of this book, these chapters function as vignettes that aim to guide readers in understanding where, how, and why we need to apply critical lenses to institutions and articulate how doing so helps us to understand this historical moment and, ultimately, how we can realize resiliency and sustainability for museums and those who make their existence possible.

In this way, Part III addresses topics while recognizing COVID-19; the implosion of the museum field through the loss of jobs, restructuring, and institutional closures; and the related impacts on museum studies as an academic field of study at both the graduate and undergraduate level. Part III looks *less* at the work of museums and *more* at the culture, community, and care of museums in its address of critical issues and ways we can move forward.

Advocating for change rather than "death to museums," *Museums in Motion* demonstrates the very premise that museums have been in motion all along, as they have shifted from their rather simple form of a treasury, storehouse, and tomb to something much more complex by deeply considering where museums have come from, where they are today, and where they are going.

Unfortunately, the feature I previously introduced to the third edition, the perspectives offered by working museum professionals, had to be eliminated. I desperately wanted to include these, but I could not, on point of principle. It felt disingenuous for me to write about the crises around work and labor in museums only to ask museum workers to do something for me for free or as a favor, particularly now, post-COVID. It would be unfair of me to ask people to develop content that was going to go into a book that would not be freely available.

Therefore, I talked to colleagues at other institutions, museum workers, and students. I sourced content from books, as well as articles, blogs, social media, podcasts, and other online and virtual resources. I dug in deep and tried to incorporate as many perspectives as possible. Sources are included as the endnotes to each chapter, and I encourage readers to look at these and follow, as well as follow up with, the thought leadership reflected in this book in its entirety. With these museum professionals, practitioners, scholars, and students at the helm, the future for museums is bright. (In addition, see the supplemental book list generated during two Zoom sessions hosted by Museum Studies Network. The list is located in Chapter 14.)

While museums throughout the world are mentioned in this volume, the majority of those beyond the United States are discussed in Part I. It is hoped that all institutions and examples provided throughout the text provide food for thought in navigating all three sections and thinking more broadly, about museums, their histories, their functions, and their aspirations. While this collection of examples and sources is intended as an introduction to the complexities of museum history and practice, it also serves to point out gaps in the literature where further contributions to the dialogue are needed, as beyond the examples cited herein, a vast body of literature exists beyond those mentioned, including numerous online platforms that offer timely dissemination of ideas, such as museum blogs, websites, and podcasts; various forms of social media, including Tumblr, X, Instagram, TikTok, Threads, and other social media; and other avenues.

Just as efforts toward multi-vocality and polyphony in museums are ongoing (consider the of/by/for[1] initiatives) and the objects comprising historic cabinets of curiosities constituted "representativeness of *a larger body* of knowledge,"[2] so, too, do museums today represent larger, and now more diverse and inclusive, bodies of knowledge. All museums play a role in the ecosystem of museum narratives. To continue the framing of museum histories, functions, and aspirations, scholars and practitioners are invited to reach out to offer their stories for inclusion in the next edition of this volume.

Notes

1. The conflation of the words *of*, *by*, and *for* takes its cues from the work of the "OF/BY/FOR ALL" cultural and civic change network established in 2018 by former museum CEO Nina Simon. The words also reference, in the mind of this author, the Gettysburg Address given by President Abraham Lincoln at the cemetery in Pennsylvania on November 19, 1863, in the aftermath of one of the deadliest battles of the U.S. Civil War. Lincoln concluded his brief remarks with a phrase "that this nation, under God, shall have a new birth of freedom—and that government of the people, by the people, for the people, shall not perish from the earth."

2. On documentation of knowledge about objects, see Ramesh Srinivasan, Katherine M. Becvar, Robin Boast, and Jim Enote, "Diverse Knowledges and Contact Zones with the Digital Museum," *Science, Technology, & Human Values* 35(5) 2010: 735–68. Quote appears on page 736, emphasis mine. While the focus of their article is on omissions in tradition museum documentation rather than the history of museums, the article is critical in its framing. In addition, the authors have included citations to the literature of this complex and important topic.

Acknowledgments

Much of the writing with which I am regularly engaged involves case studies, grant writing, and label copy for exhibitions. Stepping away from these parameters to undertake the revision of a museum studies book has afforded me the opportunity to continue my meditation on museums that began as a graduate student in art history and museum studies and continued in and out of my academic and professional career. The opportunity to revise *Museums in Motion* for the previous edition (in 2017) was truly a highlight of my scholarly and teaching pursuits. It gave me an opportunity to bring together narratives of the past and to weave in perspectives from professionals working in museums. I loved inviting people to write first-person perspectives for the book, receiving their contributions, and sharing them in the third edition.

Now the world is changed. And so have museums.

While I have undertaken a number of significant changes in this edition, as outlined in the introduction, I have had to limit my scope and have only been able to explore some of the museums, people, and activities that animate museums (primarily in the United States). Even so, this volume has benefited from the support and input of many—most notably museum professionals, colleagues engaged in the teaching of museum studies, and my students. Knowingly or not, you have shared in my aspiration to revise this volume and, in so doing, have enabled me to bring new thought leadership to the conversation by expanding the discourse to include so many other voices.

Thanks are due to the following colleagues, whose counsel over the past few years has given shape to my visioning as well as the discourse surrounding collections through the journal *Collections*: Cathy Hawks, Smithsonian Institution; Victoria (Tori) van Orden Martinez, Linköping University; and Barbara Wood, National Trust, UK. Their experience, input, perspective, and service to the journal are greatly appreciated and have informed my thinking about museums and archives in countless ways of late.

To colleagues in museum studies programs throughout the United States, I am grateful to share in conversations of theory and praxis, and to envision our work as a springboard for our students' learning and application, as well as our own. Thank you, Harriet Senie, Janet Marstine, Stephanie Brown, Sarah Chicone, Laura-Edythe Coleman, Rosanna Flouty, Jennifer Kingsley, Jessica Luke, Heidi Lung, and Pamela White.

Beyond these cohorts, I am grateful to my students at Rochester Institute of Technology, especially those enrolled in our undergraduate Bachelor of Science museum studies program. In addition, to all students enrolled in my Museums and the Digital Age, as well as my Introduction to Museums courses, I am grateful for their "fresh eyes" on the histories, functions, and aspirations of museums.

In terms of conceptualizing this volume and manicuring its content, form, and context, I want to thank to the initial reviewers of the manuscript proposal. The feedback given and confidence expressed in response to the proposal were particularly helpful as the revision and my new ideas for this volume were beginning to take shape. Thanks are also due to the reviewers from the American Association of State and Local History, who carefully and thoughtfully reviewed the manuscript and provided much-needed perspective on the content and use of the volume.

At the publisher, I would like to thank Charles Harmon and Lauren Moynihan for their support and guidance. In particular, I am grateful that Charles, who approached me about revising the third edition and trusted my vision in completing a more ambitious revision than I had undertaken when translating the second edition into the third. Now, here we are with the fourth edition, with expansion in some areas (all of Part III, for instance) and recission in other areas. I remain grateful to him for this opportunity, which has served as a reminder—time and again—as to how museums have shifted, as Stephen Weil has noted, from being *about something* to being *for somebody*.

A debt of gratitude must be paid to Edward P. Alexander and Mary Alexander, authors of the first and second editions, who laid an amazing foundation on which to build. I remain honored to continue a tradition that they started—conceiving of museums throughout history as vibrant, living, and thriving organizations—and for re-asserting that museums are *in motion*. You'll find notes about each of them at the conclusion of this volume.

Finally, thank you to Greg, my favorite museum companion, who shares my enthusiasm for collections, spaces, and places—and the stories they tell.

There is much to say about the histories and functions of museums as well as what museums can become. I am excited to share this revised edition. I look forward to hearing your thoughts, as well as your suggestions for the fifth edition.

Introduction to Part I

Museum Histories

The 1979 edition of this volume began with these words: "Museums in the United States are growing at an almost frightening rate. If we count the smallest ones with only one person on the staff and he or she without professional training, about five thousand of them exist today, and recently a new one has appeared every 3.3 days."[1] The second edition (2008) estimated the number of U.S. museums at around sixteen thousand. For the third edition, the latest data cited thirty-five thousand active museums in the United States as of 2014. To put this figure into perspective, that number is greater than the sum of Starbucks (approximately eleven thousand) and McDonald's (fourteen thousand) in the United States.[2] Museums in the United States are one-third of the total number of museums worldwide (ninety-five thousand), according to data from the United Nations Educational, Scientific, and Cultural Organization (UNESCO).[3] Approximately 65 percent are located in North America and Western Europe; 33 percent in Eastern Europe, Latin America, and Asia-Pacific states; and less than 1 percent in Africa and the Arab States region.[4]

Globally we are bearing witness to a museum boom, even with the economic downturn of the industry during the COVID-19 pandemic, which temporarily shuttered 90 percent of museums worldwide.[5] For instance, prior to, and now on the other side of, the pandemic, exponential growth of museums has occurred in China. In 1949, amidst the control of the Communist Party, China had twenty-five museums. During the Cultural Revolution of the late 1960s, museums were burned, and collections were dispersed. This period of tumult was followed by a building boom as a means of collecting, displaying, and sharing cultural knowledge and production. That surge continues even with the global financial crises, according to the Chinese Museums Association (2,970 in 2008; 3,866 in 2012; 4,165 in 2013; 5,452, as of 2020).[6] These numbers make for an average of 206 new museums each year. For example, in 2012, 451 new museums opened in China, in contrast to twenty to forty museums built in the United States each year in the decade before the 2008 global financial crisis. New construction is matched by an adoption of policy in 2008 that enacted free museum admission this has, in turn, enabled access to these institutions by those unaccustomed to such experiences.[7] By extension, a greater number of people than ever before are consumers of museums in China.

While the numbers are staggering, so, too, is the work that professionals do in each of these locales where their institutions have the potential to serve as hubs for teaching, learning, and creative inquiry.[8] Where have museums come from? Where are they now? Where are they going? The purpose of this book is to examine the past, present, and future of the museum landscape, with particular attention paid to those institutions in the United States. To be clear, the title of this book indicates that there are *histories* of museums as well as *functions* and *aspirations*. The use of plural nouns is intentional. For as we will see, museums are spaces of multiplicity—from the point of view of the authors or creators of what is on view to the perspectives shared within the museum's walls: museums are intended to be *of*, *by*, and *for* everyone. To begin, let's look at the definition of a museum.

Museums by Definition

When you think of a museum, what image comes to mind? Perhaps you think of a museum that you frequent, such as the nearby art museum, historic house, or zoo. You might even think of your favorite museum—one you have visited online or onsite or one you hope to visit one day. Or perhaps you substitute a metaphor in place of the museum, such as a tomb,[9] a laboratory,[10] a supermarket,[11] a temple, a forum,[12] a veiled vault,[13] or a crucible.[14]

The American Alliance of Museums[15] (AAM), in developing a nationwide museum accreditation program, defines a *museum* as "an organized and permanent non-profit institution, essentially educational or aesthetic in purpose, with professional staff, which owns and utilizes tangible objects, cares for them, and exhibits them to the public on some regular schedule."[16] That definition was met with objection from art centers, children's museums, science centers, and planetariums that have little or no collections. In 1988, the accreditation commission changed the term from "owns and utilizes" to "owns or utilizes" to accommodate those institutions without collections. Today, AAM does not define what museums are; rather, it provides a list of behaviors and capacities of museums, citing their roles as "economic engines" and "community anchors" who serve "the whole public," "partner with schools," "save species," and "improve public health." They are "trusted."[17]

On the other hand, the International Council of Museums (ICOM) has wrestled with the definition over the past eighty years of the organization's history, culminating in the adoption of a new definition at the annual meeting in Prague in August 2022. After several years of deliberation and the involvement of museum professionals and scholars from 126 national committees, ICOM approved a definition that positioned museums as spaces and places that invite communities in, while highlighting the importance of inclusivity and sustainability: "A museum is a not-for-profit, permanent institution in the service of society that researches, collects, conserves, interprets and exhibits tangible and intangible heritage. Open to the public, accessible and inclusive, museums foster diversity and sustainability. They operate and communicate ethically, professionally and with the participation of communities, offering varied experiences for education, enjoyment, reflection and knowledge sharing."[18] While the definition does not impose any mandates upon organizations that call themselves museums, it does frame the work of the only global organization in the museum field, with its forty-five thousand professionals in more than 138 countries. Such language offers a lens through which we can focus our examination and study of the histories and functions of museums and enables us to see how museums are instruments of "soft power" in words of Gail Dexter Lord and Ngaire Blankenberg.[19] Museums are visible displays of cultural power—including art, film, history, music—that are accessible to the public, especially tourists. Tristram Hunt, director of the Victoria and Albert Museum, noted the role of museums, accordingly: "Cultural institutions don't just exert soft power, they equally foster cultural diplomacy through international outreach, knowledge exchange, and creative leadership."[20] In this way, partnerships among and between museums can foster trust and reciprocity as acts of cultural diplomacy. Have museums always served this purpose, in addition to their roles as spaces for showcasing collections, historically? More pointedly, how have individuals and groups defined museums historically and across cultures?

Ancient and Medieval Prototypes

The Latin word *museum* (Greek: *mouseion*) has had a variety of meanings through the centuries. In classical times it signified a temple dedicated to the Muses, the inspirational goddesses of the epic, music, love poetry, oratory, history, tragedy, comedy, the dance, and astronomy. The most famous museum of that era was founded at Alexandria about the third century BCE (Before Common Era, here after BCE) by Ptolemy Soter ("Preserver") or Ptolemy II Philadelphus and was destroyed during various civil disturbances in the third century CE (Common Era, hereafter CE). The Mouseion of Alexandria had some objects, including statues of thinkers, astronomical and surgical instruments, elephant trunks and animal hides, and a botanical and zoological park, but it was chiefly a repository of texts (much like an archive or library)—a kind of institute of advanced study with many prominent scholars in residence.

This original Mouseion was the source for our modern usage of the term *museum*. Its collections were housed in the royal quarter of the city known as the Bruchium. Euclid headed the mathematics faculty and wrote his *Elements of Geometry* there. Archimedes, Appolonius of Perga, and Eratosthenes were only a few of the noted scientists and scholars who lived in the Ptolemaic king's household and made use of the library, lecture halls, covered walks, refectory, laboratories for dissection and scientific studies, and botanical and zoological gardens.[21]

Bearing in mind that *musing* and *amusement* are interrelated and reflect pondering, deep thought, diversion, and entertainment, it is no surprise that *museums* have long been considered *to be places of study* as well as *repositories of collections*. In his examination of museums and their historical construction, literature scholar Didier Maleuvre offers an engaging description of a museum that emphasizes the pondering of objects in an exhibit or collection quite apart from a museum's didactic or teaching emphasis as a site of informal learning.[22]

Though the Greeks and Romans thought of the museum in different terms from those we use today, the ancient world did possess public collections of objects valued for their aesthetic, historic, religious, or magical importance. Greek temples had hordes of votive offerings of gold, silver, and bronze objects; statues and statuettes; paintings; and even bullion that could be expended in case of public emergency. In fifth century BCE Athens, for instance, collections were on display in the Propylaia—a central building flanked with two wings, one of which held the *pinakotheke*, an entry and gathering hall that displayed paintings. The paintings were on planks (Greek: *pinas*), were placed above a marble dado, lighted by two windows from the south, and protected individually by shutters.

The Romans displayed paintings and sculpture in forums, public gardens, temples, theaters, and baths. Roman generals, statesmen, and wealthy patricians often appropriated such objects for their country homes. The emperor Hadrian in the second century CE, at his villa near Tibur (today Tivoli), reconstructed some of the landmarks he had seen in his travels through the empire, for example, the Lyceum and Academy of Athens, the Vale of Tempe in Thessaly, and the Canopus of the Egyptian delta. In a sense, he created an open-air or outdoor museum.[23]

The museum idea was barely kept alive in western Europe during the Middle Ages. Churches, cathedrals, and monasteries venerated relics of religious figures and their followers (including the Virgin Mary, Christ, the apostles, and the saints). These items were embellished with gold, silver, and jewels and were accompanied by manuscripts in sumptuous metal bindings, rich tapestries, and fabrics. These collections of objects were enhanced by material goods brought back from other parts of the world as a result of the Crusades. These collections increased the stores of the Church as well as the palace collections of princes and nobles, thus illustrating what the American museum director and curator Francis Henry Taylor wittily called the "magpiety" of mankind.[24]

From Private Collection to Public Museum

New words appeared in the sixteenth century to express distinctions within the museum concept. The gallery (Italian: *galleria*), a long, grand hall lighted from the side, came to signify an exhibition area for pictures and sculpture. The cabinet (Italian: *gabinetto*) was usually a square-shaped room filled with stuffed animals, botanical rarities, small works of art such as medallions or statuettes, artifacts, and curios. In Germany, these repositories were called *Wunderkammer* (Cabinet of Wonder). Regardless of name, galleries and cabinets rarely were open to the public and remained the playthings of princes, popes, and plutocrats.[25]

The museum went public in the late seventeenth century through the creation of university museums, repositories managed by higher education institutions in support of teaching of research for those affiliated with the university and those in the community. Basel opened the first university museum in 1671, and the Ashmolean Museum received its first collections at Oxford in 1677. The eighteenth century concerned itself with discovering the basic natural laws that formed a framework for the universe and humanity, and intellectuals of the day wished to preserve natural specimens as well as human artistic and scientific creations in museums. The Vatican established several museums about 1750, and the British Museum was formed in 1753, when Parliament purchased Hans Sloane's

Visitors, a kindergarten class from Public School 116, viewing the collection of Arms and Armor, The Metropolitan Museum of Art. Photograph taken in 1913.
Image copyright © The Metropolitan Museum of Art. Image source: Art Resource, NY.

Cast Collection Galleries, Cast Hall; The Metropolitan Museum of Art, photographed in May 1931. View of a visiting class of children.
Image copyright © The Metropolitan Museum of Art. Image source: Art Resource, NY.

The Metropolitan Museum of Art, Great Hall; View of Boy Scouts from California looking at Sphinx of Hatshepsut (31.3.166), photographed August 20, 1935.
Image copyright © The Metropolitan Museum of Art. Image source: Art Resource, NY.

Neighborhood Circulating Exhibition, *European Textiles and Costume Figures*, Walton High School (The Bronx, NY), February 6–April 26, 1939. Teacher from Hunter College with students. The Metropolitan Museum of Art (negative MM8739).
Image copyright © The Metropolitan Museum of Art. Image source: Art Resource, NY.

great collection devoted chiefly to natural science.[26] In 1793, France opened the Palace of the Louvre as the Museum of the Republic. Napoleon confiscated art objects by conquest and devised a grand plan for a unified French museum system as well as subsidiary museums elsewhere. The scheme collapsed with his defeat, but his conception of a museum as an instrument of national glory persisted in France and elsewhere.[27]

Moving from the indoors to out, while ancient the world had its great gardens, and medieval monasteries cultivated and cherished plants and flowers, botanical gardens began to appear at universities—Pisa (1544), Leiden (1587), Montpellier (1593), and Oxford (1621). Scholarly botanists used them for scientific plant study. In addition, herbalists, barber surgeons, physicians, and apothecaries established physic gardens as sources for medicinal treatments rather than simply for study, as in the case of the Chelsea Physic Garden in London (established 1673).[28]

Museums in the United States

As British colonies in North America merged and became the United States, museums evolved alongside the political process as an outgrowth of enlightenment ideals. The Charleston Museum, founded in 1773, collected natural history materials for the "promotion of the Natural History of this Province."[29] Along the Atlantic, small groups of enthusiasts met together to discuss and study objects emerging from the explorations of the new continent. Like their European predecessors, the institutions—philosophical societies, antiquarian groups, museums began with "members." But quickly, the members offered public hours for visitors to gaze upon collections that reflected pursuits from far and away. In addition to providing public access to rare, unfamiliar, and unstudied material, these groups sought financial support from a variety of sources, including paid admissions, making the "entrepreneurial" spirit a special American contribution to museum practice.[30] Charles Willson Peale, the first American museum director to conceive of the museum as a space for curious engagement, established a museum in his home in Philadelphia. The collection moved to Independence Hall and had branches in Baltimore and New York, where Peale mounted specimens of animals, birds, and insects with realistic backgrounds and displayed portraits of nearly three hundred Founding Fathers, painted chiefly by himself or members of his family.[31] In the capital city, the Smithsonian Institution, started in 1846 with the Englishman James Smithson's bequest to the United States "for the increase and diffusion of knowledge." The institution was loath to accept collections and remained chiefly a research institution of pure science. When George Brown Goode joined the Smithsonian in 1873, he launched a campaign to become a national museum devoted to science, the humanities, and the arts.[32] Beyond these efforts, in 1870 three institutions marked the entry of the United States into the museum mainstream with the founding of the American Museum of Natural History, the Metropolitan Museum of Art in New York, and the Museum of Fine Arts in Boston.[33]

By 1900, American museums were becoming centers of education and public enlightenment. This development was natural in a country that prided itself on its democratic ideals and placed deep faith in public education, both as a political necessity and as a means of attaining technological excellence. Two key players in this transition were John Cotton Dana, founder and director of the Newark Museum in Newark, New Jersey, and Benjamin Ives Gilman, secretary of the Museum of Fine Arts in Boston, Massachusetts.

Dana saw museums and libraries as spaces of the everyday rather than the elite. He saw the library—which might be conceived, in some ways, as a museum of thought embodied in the printed word—as a community center where access should be enjoyed by all. He sought to communicate the contents as well as the services to the public so as to encourage use by envisioning the library as:

> a center of public happiness first, of public education next. The necessity of the library, its great value to the community, should be urged by the local press, from the platform, and in personal talk. Include in your canvass all citizens, irrespective of creed, business, or politics; whether educated or illiterate. In getting notices of the library's work in the newspapers, or in securing mention of it from the lecture platform, it is better to deal chiefly in general statements about what the library aims to do and what it has done.[34]

Dana applied this methodology to the museum as well in his calling out "the gloom of the museum" in asking museums and their leaders to extend hours and services and remove the aura of the object, or, in his words, "the sanctity of oil paint" in favor of inquiry and discovery as one might find in a department store. Written more than a century ago, *The Gloom of the Museum* was far-sighted, as evidenced by its rediscovery in the late 1990s, as museums began to understand the need to meet the needs of their communities overall. Throughout that decade and into the twenty-first century, museums have embraced Dana's ideals and have aspired toward accessibility and inclusivity, broader ranges of visitor engagement, and expanded notions of the educational mission.[35]

In contrast, Gilman considered museums as differing by type: "a museum of science . . . in essence a school; a museum of art in essence a temple." For him, works of art communicated directly with their beholders and needed little labeling; art museums were "not didactic but aesthetic in primary purpose." But Gilman wanted art museums to have interpreters to help their visitors see the beauty of their collections. Thus, in 1907, the museum appointed a docent to its staff. Gilman dreamed up this new title, which avoided any reference to "education"; he explained that "a museum performs its complete office as it is at once gardant, monstrant, and docent." Over time, other institutions began to appoint such guides.[36] They frequently refer to the kind of education they provide as "interpretation," or teaching through the use of original objects, emotionally engaging the visitor, and complementing learning through words and verbalization.

Today's Museums

The ancients visited museums, or the "place of the muses," to look upon beauty; to discuss ideas with others; to experiment with natural phenomenon, in essence to be "amused"; and thereby to think deeply and to learn. The eighteenth-century setting for these activities might best be described as a university. From these roots as a center for learning, museums added specimens, historical objects, documents, and artworks, assuming the role as guardian, or "keeper." Brooklyn Museum director Duncan Cameron published the notion that museums occupy two ends of a spectrum, from a "temple" to a "forum" in the early 1970s. A review of museum development, especially in the United States at the beginning of the twenty-first century, reveals that the premodern form of a museum as a site for musing and for discourse or Cameron's forum seems to be on the rise again. The nineteenth-century dominance of collections, the objects within Cameron's temple, has been challenged by those who identify museums to be places for public discussion, engagement, and learning. Today, the balance between the museum as a repository of objects and as a place for learning has tipped back to the ancient forum—though we needn't think of these metaphors as mutually exclusive.[37]

In fact, such a rapid sketch of museum development through the ages gives us a malleable framework of origin stories for the flexible nature of museums today. Wander into a museum, and you may see a variety of activities underway: a group of visitors gathered around an object and engaged in discussion with museum staff facilitating a themed tour; musicians rehearsing for an evening performance; exhibit installers building elements of a temporary exhibit; exhibit co-curators, comprising museum staff and community members, gathered in a meeting room to review suggestions for an upcoming exhibition title; a researcher meeting with conservation staff to see and better understand an object of interest; learning and engagement members exiting the museum to meet with community organizations to arrange literacy training classes at the museum.[38] Beyond the temple, a showroom, a cathedral, a forum, a vessel, a veil, or a crucible, how can we envision the museum? What metaphor comes to mind now—and for our museum of the future?

Without the ability to drill deeply into the story behind every museum in the United States or internationally, this volume considers clusters of museum types—art and design; natural history and anthropology; science; history and its complement museums; gardens and zoos, and children's museums—and situates their emergence alongside broader narratives. Throughout the chapters that follow, the histories of museums demonstrate how the construction of museums lays bare a sense of belonging even as narratives of unbelonging are also part of this construction. Intentionally, in this fourth edition of *Museums in Motion*, greater attention is drawn to presence *and absence* in museum history.

Such recognition of absence has been drawn by museum scholars and practitioners previously. For instance, in reflecting on her experience curating the exhibition *Bridges and Boundaries: African Americans and Jewish Americans*, historian and museum consultant Gretchen Sullivan Sorin wrote (in 2000): "the contents of most history museum storage rooms do not reflect the full record of the nation's past. History museums need to go further to identify artifacts related to groups whose history is not part of the written record."[39] Two decades later, significant attention in the United States, and elsewhere, is being paid to widening the field of vision and to telling more inclusive narratives. These efforts by curators, directors, and every level of museum staff, as well as the communities in which they are situated, have undergirded meaning-making and interpretation of museums more recently.

An example demonstrating how the arc of collections, interpretation, and storytelling can bend toward underrepresented and underserved communities is the creation of the National Museum of

African American History and Culture, the newest Smithsonian Institution on the National Mall. Upon its opening in September 2016 as the only museum "devoted exclusively to the documentation of African American life, history, and culture," its artifacts and the onsite and digital exhibits chronicle slavery, segregation and Jim Crow laws, civil rights, and cultural production. As such, the narratives also reflect the story of America, according to Lonnie G. Bunch, founding director of the museum. "This Museum [tells] the American story through the lens of African American history and culture. This is America's Story and this museum is for all Americans."[40] In a 2016 interview about the opening of the museum, Bunch framed the importance of the duality of museum experiences, as frameworks for understanding. He stated, "This is not a *black* museum. This is a museum that uses one culture to understand what it means to be an American. That, to my mind, is the cutting edge."[41]

Intentionally emphasizing a turn away from narratives of exclusivity and hegemony that have been woven into the history of museums, Bunch authorized an expansion of *the museum* as a concept that foregrounds inclusivity of narratives—a facet absent from the early and middle years of museum-making. Moving away from museums as collections of items gathered by "princes, popes, and plutocrats" and interpretation that reflects a monolithic point of view, museums have become spaces where tangible and intangible heritages are presented, where audiences and communities convene, and where stories are shared. This seismic shift drove the collecting methodology employed by Bunch and his team of curators, who sought to gather artifacts from across the nation to populate the museum. The collecting program—called "Saving African American Treasures"—enabled the team to collect more than thirty-five thousand donations with exhibitions covering subjects around history, community, and culture, such as the Transatlantic slave trade that transformed Africa, Europe, and the Americas; education, institutions, and associations that have strengthened African American communities in the United States.

Such efforts—whether the curation of a single exhibition or the creation of an entire museum—disclose the sharing of authority among museums and their communities through a process that began to take shape in some institutions from 1990 on. As historian Neil Harris suggests: "The museum's position is no longer seen as transcendent. Rather it is implicated in the distributions of wealth, power, knowledge, and taste shaped by the larger social order." Accordingly, American Studies scholar Michael Frisch popularized the term *shared authority* to recognize the role that academic historians and institutions and the public share in meaning making and interpretation. Extending this concept even further, museum professional Nina Simon coined the term *participatory museum* to reflect the collaborative social, and co-creative opportunities that museums offer to their publics.[42] Coming full circle from Gretchen Sullivan Sorin's framing of museums to their enactment by Lonnie Bunch, it seems that now the shared authority, participatory, and co-creation practices are anticipated ways of working. Rather than being unusual, these approaches are becoming expected—both by museum staff and their communities. As we move through these chapters, then, consider where you see shared authority, participation, and the work of museums *in motion*.

Notes

1. American Association of Museums, *America's Museums: The Belmont Report* (Washington, DC: American Association of Museums, 1969), 3, 17–20; American Association of Museums staff, personal correspondence between Mary Alexander and AAM staff, 2006.

2. Christopher Ingraham, "There are More Museums in the U.S. Than There Are Starbucks and McDonalds—Combined," *Washington Post*, June 13, 2014, https://www.washingtonpost.com/news/wonk/wp/2014/06/13/there-are-more-museums-in-the-us-than-there-are-starbucks-and-mcdonalds-combined/.

3. UNESCO cites the number of museums having increased from twenty-two thousand in 1975 to ninety-five thousand today. See UNESCO, "Museums Around the World in the Face of COVID-19," May 2020, https://unesdoc.unesco.org/ark:/48223/pf0000373530.

4. The citations in this paragraph come from UNESCO's report, page 5. Further data may be found here: Statista Research Department, "Leading Countries Worldwide Ranked by Estimated Number of Museums, as of March 2021," May 18, 2022, https://www.statista.com/statistics/1201825/top-countries-by-number-of-museums-worldwide/.

5. UNESCO report, May 2020, 4.

6. Wenyi Zhang, "Number of Museums in China from 2010 to 2020," *Statista*, January 27, 2022, https://www.statista.com/statistics/226450/number-of-museums-in-china/.

7 As vice president of the China Museums Association, An cites "rural migrant workers and urban low-income people" as new audiences for museums, in An Laishun, "Cranking Up the Soft Power Engine of Chinese Museums," in *Cities, Museums and Soft Power*, ed. Gail Dexter Lord and Ngaire Blankenberg (Washington, D.C.: The AAM Press, 2015), 147. See also "Mad About Museums: China Is Building Thousands of New Museums, But How Will It Fill Them?" *Economist* December 21, 2013, http://www.economist.com/news/special-report/21591710-china-building-thousands-new-museums-how-will-it-fill-them-mad-about-museums.

8. IMLS 2014 data for museums is available from "Government Doubles Official Estimate: There are 35,000 Active Museums in the U.S." May 19, 2014. See https://www.imls.gov/news-events/news-releases/government-doubles-official-estimate-there-are-35000-active-museums-us.

9. See Adorno, "Valéry Proust Museum in Memory of Hermann von Grab." *Prisms,* edited by TheodorAdorno. London: Garden City Press: 1967, 175–85. Quote appears on page 175.

10. Alfred H. Barr Jr., American art historian and first director at the Museum of Modern Art (MoMA) in New York, proclaimed that the museum was a laboratory in the catalog celebrating the tenth anniversary of the museum and the inauguration of its new building in midtown Manhattan on W. Fifty-Third Street. See *Art in Our Time: An Exhibition to Celebrate the Tenth Anniversary of the Museum of Modern Art and the Opening of Its New Building Held at the Same Time of the New York World's Fair* (New York: Museum of Modern Art, 1939). See also Hans Ulrich Obrist, *Ways of Curating* (New York: Macmillan, 2014), 70–73.

11. American pop artist Andy Warhol's life-as-art approach led to an exhibition in 1964, *The American Supermarket*, an act and practice that paid heed to the question of art as commodity and commodity as art that featured also in the work of peer artists on the American scene, including Claes Oldenburg, Roy Liechtenstein, James Rosenquist, and others.

12. Brooklyn Museum director Duncan Cameron published the notion that museums occupy two ends of a spectrum from a "temple" to a "forum" in the early 1970s. See Duncan F. Cameron, "The Museum, a Temple or the Forum," *Curator: The Museum Journal* 14:1 (March 1971): 11–24, which also appeared in the *Journal of World History* 14, no. 1 (1972): 189–202. Cameron posits the museum as a place of experimentation and innovation that was complementary to the museum's role as a temple of, and to, learning.

13. The concept of "the veil and the vault" is a design aesthetic proposed by Diller Scofidio + Renfro, in collaboration with Gensler, in the creation of The Broad, Los Angeles' newest museum focusing on contemporary art. The design combines the two key facets of The Broad's mission—exhibition and storage (for use by this institution and others, to which it loans). See The Broad, "Building," http://www.thebroad.org/building, accessed August 9, 2016; see also *The Broad: An Art Museum Designed by Diller Scofidio + Renfro,* edited by Joanne Heyler, Ed Schad et al. (London: Prestel, 2015).

14. I have added the word *crucible* to the list of metaphors in acknowledgment of the challenges museums are facing, much of which have been laid bare as a result of the racial reckoning begun in May 2020 after the death of George Floyd in the United States and the impact of COVID-19 on museum workers, among many others. This notion of the museum as a crucible is informed by the concept of elements interacting and leading to the creation of something new, a distillation or otherwise. The museum-as-crucible acknowledges efforts toward greater transparency in and around museums—in posting salaries with position listings, in labor discussions, and in confronting and addressing the challenges of repatriation, restitution, and decolonization.

15. The American Association of Museums was renamed the American Alliance of Museums in 2012. While the body of this book employs the current name (Alliance), the citations and historical documents incorporates both Association and Alliance; the choice of one over the other is based upon the

name in use at the time of the document, instance, or event cited. The abbreviated form (AAM) is also in use and is consistent with the past and present names of the organization.

16. American Association of Museums, *Museum Accreditation: Professional Standards* (Washington, DC: American Association of Museums, 1973), 8–9. The U.S. Museum and Library Services Act defined a *museum* as "a public or private nonprofit agency or institution organized on a permanent basis for essentially educational or aesthetic purposes, which, utilizing a professional staff, owns or utilizes tangible objects, cares for them, and exhibits them to the public on a regular basis." See http://www.aam-us .org/aboutmuseums/whatis.cfm.

17. American Alliance of Museums, "Museum Facts & Data," 2021, https://www.aam-us.org/programs/ about-museums/museum-facts-data/.

18. International Council of Museums, "ICOM Approves a New Museum Definition," August 24, 2022, https://icom.museum/en/news/icom-approves-a-new-museum-definition/.

19. Gail Dexter Lord and Ngaire Blankenberg, editors, *Cities, Museums and Soft Power* (Washington, D.C.: The AAM Press, 2015).

20. Tristram Hunt, "The Transformational (Soft) Power of Museums: At Home and Abroad," *The Soft Power 30: A Global Ranking of Soft Power*, 2018, 119.

21. George Sarton, *A History of Science: Hellenistic Science and Culture in the Last Three Centuries B.C.* (Cambridge, MA, 1959), 29–34; Germain Bazin, *The Museum Age* (New York: Universe Books, 1967), 16; Alma S. Wittlin, *Museums: In Search of a Usable Future* (Cambridge, MA: MIT Press, 1970), 221; David E. H. Jones, "The Great Museum at Alexandria," *Smithsonian* 2 (December 1971): 53–60; (January 1972): 59–63.

22. Didier Maleuvre, "A Plea for Silence: Putting Art Back in to the Art Museum," in *Museum Philosophy for the 21st Century*, ed. Hugh H. Genoways (Lanham, MD: AltaMira Press, 2006), 167.

23. Bazin, *The Museum Age*, 12–14, 18–23; Wittlin, *Museums: In Search*, 4–7, 12–13; Niels von Holst, *Creators, Collectors and Connoisseurs: The Anatomy of Artistic Taste from Antiquity to the Present Day* (New York: Putnam, 1967), 21–40.

24. Bazin, *The Museum Age*, 29; Wittlin, *Museums: In Search*, 7–8; Francis Henry Taylor, *Babel's Tower: The Dilemma of the Modern Museum* (New York: Columbia University Press, 1945), 11.

25. J. Mordaunt Crook, *The British Museum* (London: Praeger, 1972), 32; Kenneth Hudson, *Social History of Museums: What the Visitors Thought* (Atlantic Highlands, NJ: Humanities Press, 1975), 6; Bazin, *The Museum Age*, 129–30; Holst, *Creators*, 92, 94–96, 103–05; Taylor, *Babel's Tower*, 12–17; Silvio A. Bedini, "The Evolution of Science Museums," *Technology and Culture* 5 (1965): 1–29; Helmut Seling, "The Genesis of the Museum," *Architectural Review* 141 (1967): 103–14.

26. Edward P. Alexander, "Sir Hans Sloane and the British Museum," in *Museum Masters: Their Museums and Their Influence* (Nashville: American Association of State and Local History, 1983), 19–42.

27. Bazin, *The Museum Age*, 141–91; Hudson, *Social History of Museums*, 3–6.

28. Edward S. Hyams and William MacQuitty, *Great Botanical Gardens of the World* (New York: Macmillan, 1969), 16–23, 34–43, 87, 102–03, 107; A. W. Hill, "The History and Functions of Botanic Gardens," *Annals Missouri Botanical Garden* 2 (1915): 185–240.

29. Laura M. Bragg, "The Birth of the Museum Idea in America," *Charleston Museum Quarterly* 1 (1923): 3–13; Barry L. Stiefel, 'Our Museum—Another Handsome Contribution': A Comparative Case Study of the Charleston Museum during its First Formative 150 Years," edited by Juilee Decker, *Collections: A Journal for Museum and Archives Professionals* 11:2 (Spring 2015): 103–14.

30. Joel J. Orosz, *Curators and Culture: The Museum Movement in America, 1740-1870* (Tuscaloosa: University of Alabama Press, 1990), 1–67.

31. Alexander, "Charles Willson Peale and His Philadelphia Museum," in *Museum Masters*, 43–78.

32. Alexander, "George Brown Goode and the Smithsonian Museum," in *Museum Masters*, 277–310.

33. Geoffrey T. Hellman, *Bankers, Bones, Beetles: The First Century of the American Museum of Natural History* (Garden City, NY, 1969); Calvin Tomkins, *Merchants and Masterpieces: The Story of the Metropolitan Museum of Art* (New York: E.P. Dutton, 1970); Walter Muir Whitehill, *Museum of Fine Arts, Boston: A Centennial History*, 2 vols. (Cambridge, MA: Harvard University Press, 1970).

34. John Cotton Dana, *A Library Primer* (Chicago: Library Bureau, 1903), chapter 4, http://standardlibrary .com/authors/d/john_cotton_dana/00015327_a_library_primer/00015327_english_ascii_p001.htm.

35. Written in 1917, *The Gloom of the Museum* was rediscovered by museum professionals in the late 1990s through its issue in an AAM press title. See John Cotton Dana, *The New Museum: Selected Writings by John Cotton Dana*, edited by William A. Peniston, preface by Mary Sue Sweeney Price, and introduction by Stephen E. Weil (Newark: The Newark Museum and the American Association of Museums, 1999). The reference to oil paint appears on page 54; department store on page 57. In addition, Dana supported the concept of branch museums, perhaps inspired by his work in libraries, and called for exhibitions in stores and schools as well as other open spaces.
36. Gilman, *Museum Ideals*, 80–81, 88–102, 279–316; Whitehill, *Museum of Fine Arts*, 1: 293–94.
37. Duncan Cameron, "The Museum, a Temple or the Forum," *Journal of World History* 14, no. 1: 189–204; also in Gail Anderson, ed., *Reinventing the Museum: Historical and Contemporary Perspectives on the Paradigm Shift* (Walnut Creek, CA: AltaMira Press, 2004).
38. Arthur C. Parker, *A Manual for History Museums* (New York: Columbia University Press, 1935), 19.
39. Gretchen Sullivan Sorin, "Why Museums Need to Continue the Discussion about Race in America," *History News* (55:4): 11. *Bridges and Boundaries* was organized in 1992 by the Jewish Museum, New York, in collaboration with the National Association for the Advancement of Colored People. A revisiting of the theme was undertaken in 1999 at UMass Amherst with *Bridges and Boundaries Revisited: African Americans and American Jews.* See https://perma.cc/3ATG-KLV4.
40. National Museum of African American History & Culture, "About" https://nmaahc.si.edu/about/about-museum.
41. Vinson Cunningham, "Making a Home for Black History: The Vision and the Challenges Behind a New Museum on the National Mall," *New Yorker*, August 29, 2016, http://www.newyorker.com/magazine/2016/08/29/analyzing-the-national-museum-of-african-american-history-and-culture.
42. Neil Harris, *Cultural Excursions: Marketing Appetites and Cultural Tastes in Modern America* (Chicago: University of Chicago Press, 1990), 142; Michael Frisch, *A Shared Authority: Essays on the Craft and Meaning of Oral and Public History* (Albany: State University of New York Press, 1990); Nina Simon, *The Participatory Museum* (Santa Cruz, CA: Museum 2.0, 2010).

1

Art and Design Museums

This chapter, as originally conceived by Edward Alexander nearly fifty years ago, reflected a broad definition of "art" museums and approached the institutions as amalgamations of institutional histories, as well as biographies of the individuals who amassed possessions that would become the cornerstones of the collections of these institutions. The narratives were thus simultaneously *histories* and *biographies*. While this chapter retains his classifications, some of the museums described here move past singular time periods or collections of individuals. They aspire toward broader chronological and geographic scope—a framing once referred to as "encyclopedic" because the collections range from Egyptian mummies and material culture to contemporary sculpture and installations. However, this term is now refuted chiefly because it enforces hierarchical notions of classification. The concept of an encyclopedic museum, moreover, centers the attention and value of a work rather on its role and place—as one datapoint in an institution's collection. Rather than seeing the item within its own cultural context, it sees a work of art as representative of one culture across all of time and all of worldwide accomplishment.

The following pages offer a history of art museums, beginning with European examples. While, in many of these narratives, the collector was the animating force behind the creation of art museums, it is important to recognize the role of artists and meaning-makers, without whom the notion of the art or design museum would be impossible, as well as those who supported the collector in commissioning, purchasing, or otherwise acquiring works.

European Collectors, Patrons, and the Earliest Art Museums

Historically royal families or nobles, high clergymen, merchants, or other monied professionals purchased or commissioned paintings, sculptures, and beautiful, functional objects. Developing skills in agile connoisseurship amid court culture, collectors acquired and displayed collections that were proxy for exhibiting power and authority while also crafting aesthetic, intellectual, and political self-identity.

During the fifteenth to eighteenth centuries, wealthy collectors gathered and preserved items that today are found in art museums. On occasion, collectors allowed visitors to see their treasures; the Medici, for example, did so at least as early as the sixteenth century. The arrangements usually were privately made and often required a large tip to a servant.[1] In Rome in 1773, Pope Clement XIV opened the Pio-Clementine Museum; it contained the Vatican collection largely as we know it today.[2] The famed Farnese collection accumulated by Cardinal Farnese (later Pope Paul III) was left to Charles of Bourbon, king of the Two Sicilies, in 1735 and formed the core of the National Museum in Naples; that museum also received much rich material excavated at Herculaneum and Pompeii.[3] The Uffizi Palace at Florence in 1743 secured the Medici collection of paintings under the will of Anna Maria Ludovica, the daughter of Cosimo III. By 1795, the Uffizi had become a true art gallery, with the paintings arranged by schools.[4]

The Habsburg collection in Vienna under Emperor Charles VI in the 1720s had been given elaborate frames and ordered according to overall symmetry and color, with individual paintings cut down or enlarged in size to conform to the arrangement. About 1776, the painter Rosa began to reinstall the collection in the Belevedere Palace. He called in Chretien de Mechel from Basel, who restored the paintings to their original sizes in simple frames, arranged them chronologically according to schools, and produced a catalog. In 1781, the public was admitted three times a week to view the collection.[5]

In France, monarchs Louis XIV, XV, and XVI saw opportunities for display and exhibition in a variety of modalities. Under Louis XIV, the gardens of Versailles were open to the public, and one could easily visit the palace and its paintings if equipped with a plumed hat and sword, which could be rented from the caretaker. Louis XV in 1750 exhibited 110 paintings and drawings in Paris at the Luxembourg Palace, to which the public was admitted twice a week. There was a constant agitation among the intellectuals of the Enlightenment to open a permanent picture gallery, and the Palace of the Louvre was usually suggested as the appropriate place. Denis Diderot, in his *Encyclopédie* (1765), stated that the Louvre ought to rival the famed Mouseion of Alexandria. Thereafter, in 1774, Louis XVI appointed Count d'Angiviller director general of Public Buildings. D'Angiviller moved at once to prepare the royal collection for exhibition and eventually chose for this purpose the great gallery of the Louvre that paralleled the Seine. He had the paintings cleaned, repaired, and reframed, filled in gaps—especially of the Flemish and Dutch schools—and appointed the painter Hubert Robert as keeper of the royal collection. The count created a commission of experts on museum problems. The commission prescribed overhead lighting and, for fire protection, that brick and iron be used wherever possible, as well as fire-resistant walls and a lightning conductor, an innovation popular in that day. But d'Angiviller was indecisive in carrying out the recommendations, and the gallery was not yet open when the French Revolution started.[6]

There were other scattered prototype museums. Basel probably had the first university art collection; in 1661, the city bought the Amerbach Cabinet, which contained some excellent Holbeins; they were exhibited a decade later in the university library.[7] German collections were opened at Dusseldorf, Munich, Kassel, and Dresden about 1750.[8] In 1683, the collection of the Tradescants became the first English museum in its own building, the Ashmolean, at Oxford University, but it was composed chiefly of natural history specimens with little art.[9] Sir Hans Sloane's collection, opened as the British Museum in 1759, contained some miniatures, drawings, and archaeological objects, but was devoted chiefly to natural history. An attempt to bring art into the fold was made by politician and journalist John Wilkes who wanted to join a national gallery to the British Museum in 1777 with the Walpole Collection from Houghton Hall as a nucleus; Parliament refused, and the collection went to Catherine the Great.[10]

Revolution and the Louvre

The Palace of the Louvre in Paris, opened to the public during the French Revolution, may be regarded as the first significant national art museum. While the cataclysm of revolution destroyed some art objects, which were considered hated symbols of the aristocratic regime, the leaders who overthrew the old order argued that the nation's art belonged to all the people of the new society created under the democratic ideals of liberty, equality, and brotherhood. The Louvre was to be the capstone of a system of museums to serve the common man and woman of the new Republic.

The National Museum, a "Monument Dedicated to the Love and Study of the Arts," was opened at the Louvre on August 10, 1793, the first anniversary of the fall of the monarchy. Its Grande Galerie exhibited 537 paintings on the walls and 184 art objects on tables in the middle of the hall. Most of these artworks came from the royal palaces, from churches and religious orders, and from a scattering from the émigrés. In the new decade, in the ten-day period that had replaced the week, the museum reserved five days for artists and copyists, two for cleaning, and three for the general public. So popular were the public days that the crowds of visitors attracted swarms of enterprising prostitutes, and streetlights had to be installed at the approaches.

The pictures were hung frame to frame from floor to ceiling by schools (which were organized by French, Italian, and Northern—Dutch and Flemish—paintings), but within the schools, there were no labels. Thus, the museum was a confusing labyrinth for the untutored visitor. Windows from two sides lighted the hall, and on bright days pictures were exposed to too much sunlight. Fortunately, Hubert Robert, former keeper of the royal collection, was respected in the new order and managed to maintain tolerable standards of housekeeping and conservation. The Louvre was in such bad structural condition that it had to be closed in May 1796, not to open fully again until July 14, 1801. The Grande Galerie was then more rationally arranged on a chronological principle; a few years later, marble columns and statues divided the long vista of the gallery, and overhead lighting was obtained.[11]

Art treasures were taken by Napoleon's armies back to France. Many masterpieces were requisitioned from Antwerp, Brussels, and other cities when Belgium was overrun in 1794. General Bonaparte's Italian campaign of 1796–1797 were political acts that also led to growth of the French national collections of the Louvre, the Bibliothèque Nationale, and the Jardin des Plantes (botanical garden). He took a commission of scholars with him—a mathematician, a chemist, a botanist, two painters, a sculptor, and an archaeologist—to appropriate "goods of artistic and scientific nature" that included books, paintings, scientific instruments, typefaces, wild animals, and natural curiosities from all over Italy. In July 1798, a procession brought the loot of the campaign to Paris: enormous chariots bearing the paintings in huge packing cases, labeled with large letters; massive carts transporting statues decked with laurel wreaths, flowers, and flags; and exotic animals in cages and camels led by their keepers. Military detachments, members of the learned society Institut de France, museum administrators, art professors, and typesetters marched in the parade. The vehicles formed a circle on the Champs de Mars three lines deep around a monument to Liberty, amid the thundering cheers of the packed spectators.[12]

Although the seizure of art removed objects from their original cultural context, French authorities used conservation as justification for their confiscation of the paintings. Many of the seized works (paintings, in particular) were in bad repair, and the conservation staff at the Louvre knew how to clean and restore them. They understood the re-backing process that had been perfected in Italy and France about fifty years earlier and could employ such methods to preserve the works and provide for direct care.[13]

When Napoleon was defeated at Waterloo in 1815, the paintings and art objects he had seized began to flow back to their previous owners. Not all of them returned; some were retained for the Louvre, while most of those taken from churches and monasteries remained in France. But in all, the French museums gave up 2,065 pictures and 130 sculptures. Never again would so many masterpieces of painting and sculpture from across Europe be on view in a single institution. But to what end? Napoleon, indeed, had made works of art and the institution of the museum symbols of French national glory, a concept that would be taken to the extreme in the twentieth century with Hitler and Goering looting the national collections, as well as collections of citizens, as revenge for the humiliation of the Treaty of Versailles. In the twenty-first century, however, conversations are ongoing about restitution and repatriation regarding the works in the Louvre and other national museums. (These topics will be more fully discussed in Section III of this volume.)[14]

A Golden Age for Art Museums: France, England, Germany, Russia

The violent and democratizing changes in European life brought about by both political and industrial revolutions were accompanied by a steady growth of public art museums, and the nineteenth century sometimes is considered the museum's golden age. Parallel with growing nationalism, nearly every country in Western Europe built a comprehensive collection of masterpiece art that extended from ancient times to the present. Usually, a royal collection formed its nucleus, but often the determined efforts of industrial and commercial leaders with able museum directors resulted in a museum taking its place as an important element of urban centers.

As noted above, the Louvre saw rapid growth and soon filled the gaps in its galleries left by the return of the Napoleonic additions through archaeological activity, which yielded Greek vases and bronzes as well as Egyptian collections. Public funds and private gifts—the organization called Friends of the Louvre was formed in 1897—continued to add to its comprehensive holdings.[15]

Great Britain established its National Gallery in London in 1824, although precedents existed. An institution for art instruction and exhibition was established in 1768 (the Royal Academy) while one for connoisseurship was founded in 1805 (the British Institution for Promoting the Fine Arts in the United Kingdom). The National Gallery was unusual in that it did not grow from a royal act nor from subscription as these earlier institutions had. Instead, the purchase of thirty-eight pictures collected by London businessman John Julius Angerstein galvanized the founding of the institution when Sir George Beaumont, himself a collector of note, persuaded the prime minister, Lord Dover, to have the nation pay fifty-seven thousand pounds for the Angerstein pictures. Soon, the present building of the National Gallery was under construction at Trafalgar Square. Its location on "the very gangway of London" represented the founders' interest in making its galleries available to all of London's citizens. The site was the location of the King's Mews before it was redeveloped into public space in the nineteenth century.

All in all, British collectors and artists generously supported the National Gallery, which today represents a comprehensive history of European painting.[16] The British royal family's collections, which are purported to be among the finest collections in "private" hands, are spread among thirteen royal residences, some of which are inhabited and open to the public, such as Windsor Castle, while others are open but not inhabited, such as Hampton Court Palace. In addition, the Queen's Gallery, built in 1962 at the west front of Buckingham Palace is solely devoted to the exhibition of more than four hundred works of art from the Royal Collections.

In Germany, the Hohenzollerns of Prussia backed the creation of one of the world's greatest museum centers in Berlin on a peninsula formed by the Spree and Kupfergraben rivers. This Museum Island, as it was called, contained five museums: the Altes Museum (1830), built around the antiquities and modern painting collections of an eccentric English connoisseur, Edward Solly; the Neues Museum (1855), with Egyptian collections, antique ceramics, and national antiquities; the Nationalgalerie (1876), for modern German art; and the Kaiser Friedrich Museum of Western Art (1904), now the Bode Museum. Most impressive of all was a group of monumental buildings (1907–1930) that contained the Pergamon Museum, with its antiquity Islamic and Middle Eastern collections.[17]

The rise of Hitler brought several disasters to the Museum Island. Ludwig Justi, the long-respected director of the Nationalgalerie, was dismissed, though he refused to leave and was named director of the art library, "degenerate" modern art was removed and in some cases destroyed. In addition, many Jewish staff members were discharged. World War II attacks greatly damaged the Museum Island buildings, and 1,353 paintings were lost. With the fall of the Berlin Wall in 1989, the island assumed a role at the center of Germany's artistic culture. The moving of the national capital to Berlin a decade later added to the island's importance, which continues to this day.[18]

Farther east, Catherine the Great's huge collection in the Hermitage in Saint Petersburg was housed in a palace built by Czar Nicholas I in the 1840s. Its decoration was the result of the work of Berlin museum director and art historian Gustav Friedrich Waagen, who was called in to arrange the pictures and prepare a catalog (1863). Visitors were allowed, but up until 1866, they needed to wear full dress, on the theory that they were visiting the czar and only incidentally the museum. The czars continued to collect great masterpieces, and the coming of the 1917 revolution gave the new Soviet Union control of rich private art collections from throughout the old empire. Museums, historical monuments, and art treasures thus became nationalized.[19]

New Models: Contemporary Art and World's Fairs

A specialized form of art museum collected and exhibited modern art, as, for example, the Luxembourg Palace (1818) in Paris, superseded by the National Museum of Modern Art (1937), which later moved to the Centre Georges Pompidou, or Beaubourg, in 1977; the Neue Pinakothek (1853) in Munich; the Nationalgalerie (1876) in Berlin; and the National Gallery of British Art (established in London in 1897), known today as Tate, has four sites, including two in London, in addition to locations in Liverpool and St. Ives. The focus of these collections is British art from 1500 to the present, as well as international modern and contemporary art from across the globe.[20]

As the nineteenth century was the age of exhibition, the world's fairs offered a space for exhibition of art and design. The earliest of these was held in London in 1851. Known as the Crystal Palace Exhibition, the Great Exhibition at South Kensington was enormously successful, and the profits (some 186,000 pounds) were used to acquire land for a group of museums in this area of London. One of them finally evolved into the Victoria and Albert Museum, which is the world's leading museum of art and design today. In France, a world's fair at Paris in 1855 inaugurated a similar interest in the decorative arts, and the Central Society of Decorative Arts established a museum in 1882, later moved to the Marsan Pavilion of the Louvre. Berlin and Vienna also had such museums.[21]

American Models

The earliest progenitors of the American Art Museum displayed portraits of historical figures (or events) as part of their historical or natural science focus. Pierre Eugène du Simitière and Charles Willson Peale had portraits in their Philadelphia collections in the 1780s, but they regarded them more as historical documents than as works of art. So also did the early historical societies, though the New-York Historical Society (1804) had secured the Luman Reed and Thomas J. Bryan collections of American paintings and European old masters by the 1860s. The society planned a museum of antiquities, science, and art, but failed to raise the necessary funds. The Pennsylvania Academy of the Fine Arts (1805) in Philadelphia not only conducted an art school and held annual exhibitions, but also acquired an outstanding collection of American paintings and sculpture. The Boston Athenaeum (1807), though essentially a library, collected paintings and sculptures that it later turned over to the newly established Museum of Fine Arts. In 1832, Yale built the pioneer American college gallery to house the historical paintings of Colonel John Trumbull. Perhaps the first true and continuing art museum in the country was the Wadsworth Atheneum (1842), founded by American art patron Daniel Wadsworth at Hartford, Connecticut. The use of the term *atheneum* in these examples is significant, as it described cultural institutions where works of art were nestled among other collections, whether literature, history, science, and natural history. Several athenaeums were established in the United States, taking their cues from the ancient Greek premise that such a structure was dedicated to Athena, the goddess of wisdom.[22]

In addition to these brief notations above, the following sections introduce American art museums by location. With more than thirty-five thousand museums in the United States, there are many institutions not mentioned here. A good way to learn more about art museums is to search online, for instance, by exploring the Google Arts & Culture interactive map: https://artsandculture.google.com/partner?tab=map. Or, because museums are tourist destinations, perusing travel guides such as *Fodor's* or *TimeOut* listings, as well as social media communities such as Reddit to locate art museums by time period (Museum of Contemporary Art, Los Angeles); subject focus (portraits in the Museum of Fine Arts, Houston or equine art in the International Museum of the Horse in Lexington, Kentucky); or geographical location.

The Metropolitan Museum of Art

The year 1870 was a landmark year for American art museums, with the establishment of the Metropolitan Museum of Art in New York and the Museum of Fine Arts in Boston. Within the decade, the Corcoran Gallery of Art in Washington, the Pennsylvania (now Philadelphia) Museum of Art, and the Art Institute of Chicago opened for public visitation. Other leading art collections in the United States today include the Detroit Institute of Art (1885); the Brooklyn Museum (1893); the Toledo Art Museum (1901) and Cleveland Museum of Art (1913) in Ohio; and the National Gallery of Art (1937) in Washington, D.C. By the year 2000, there were thirty-five hundred art museums in the United States, half of which had been established after 1970.[23] The combination of private beneficence, city maintenance, and federal tax laws that encouraged private support contributed to this proliferation of art collections held in public trust.

An examination of the Metropolitan and the Museum of Fine Arts reveals the chief forces in the development of comprehensive American art museums. The purposes of the Metropolitan, expressed in Joseph C. Choate's dedication speech of 1880, were twofold: to gather together a more or less complete collection of objects illustrative of the history of art in all its branches, from the earliest beginnings to the present time, which should provide for the instruction and entertainment of the people; and show the students and artisans of every branch of industry what the past has accomplished. Such examples offered inspiration and aspiration for viewers to imitate and exceed such high and acknowledged standards of form and color.[24]

The Metropolitan was greatly influenced by the public museum movement in London, which emerged as a result of the Crystal Palace Exhibition in 1851, as was the Museum of Fine Arts, one of whose founders wrote: "The designer needs a museum of art, as the man of letters needs a library, or the botanist a herbarium." Both museums agreed that few masterpieces were available to them, and in the field of sculpture, they began to gather plaster casts of famed originals. In 1883, the first large money bequest to the Metropolitan was earmarked for the purchase of architectural casts.[25]

The Metropolitan and the Museum of Fine Arts have helped define the scope of a comprehensive art museum. General Louis P. di Cesnola, who became the first director of the Metropolitan in 1879, had been the United States consul on the island of Cyprus; he sold to the Metropolitan two collections of classical antiquities he had excavated. He also sold a smaller accumulation to the Boston museum. J. P. Morgan became president of the Metropolitan in 1904, and by the time of his death in 1913, the museum had acquired important Greek art, made numerous archaeological expeditions to Egypt, secured an outstanding collection of armor, and received the Benjamin Altman bequest of about two thousand masterpiece paintings and Chinese porcelains valued at fifteen million dollars.[26]

In 1924, the president of the Metropolitan, Robert W. de Forest, and his wife, Emily Johnson de Forest, gave the museum its American Wing, which housed colonial and federal period rooms and a distinguished collection of decorative arts. In 1938, the Metropolitan also added to its exhibits The Cloisters, on a lofty site in Fort Tryon Park facing the Hudson River. George Grey Barnard, the sculptor, had begun this collection of architectural elements, sculpture, and decorative arts from medieval cloisters, and John D. Rockefeller Jr. presented the park to the city and paid for erecting, furnishing, and endowing The Cloisters.

During World War II, a collection of musical instruments, acquired as early as 1889, was rejuvenated and beautifully displayed at the Metropolitan; in 1946, the Metropolitan absorbed the ten-year-old Museum of Costume Art and installed it as the Costume Institute, with sixteen thousand items dating from 1690. The Institute now boasts thirty-three thousand objects across seven centuries of fashionable dress and accessories for adults and children comprising collections from the Museum of Costume Art and the Brooklyn Museum Costume Collection (transferred here in January 2009). They are bolstered by a conservation laboratory and a world-renowned research repository, the Irene Lewisohn Costume Reference Library.

Due to robust collecting and the growing need for space, since 1975, the Metropolitan has carried out major expansions of its building, leading to what director Philippe de Montebello calls "museums within the Museum." The phrase refers to real estate, indeed, as well as the breadth and depth within collections holdings across several departments in one institution—as if each unit could stand on its own as a museum. These expansions began with the Temple of Dendur from Egypt (1978); including a wing for the Robert Lehman Collection of three thousand paintings, tapestries, and bronzes; enlarging the American Wing (1980); adding the Michael Rockefeller collection of Asia and Oceania (1982); opening the Lila Acheson Wallace Wing for modern artworks (1987); and installing the Henry R. Kravis Wing of sculpture and decorative arts. In 2016, the Museum extended beyond its Upper East Side location and The Cloisters to include a third iconic site in their repertoire: *The Met Breuer*, an innovative space dedicated to modern and contemporary art, occupying the former space of the Whitney Museum of American Art. Simultaneously, the institution underwent a brand change and became the name by which everyone referred to it—The Met—with three locations—The Met Fifth Avenue, The Met Cloisters, and The Met Breuer. While the third space only lasted four years, it offered more exhibition venue space and conceptually shifted The Met's emphasis to include modern and contemporary art in dialogue with historical works in the collection.[27] According to director and CEO Thomas P. Campbell, the space sought to "provide an unparalleled opportunity to experience modern and contemporary art through the lens of the historical and global Met collection."[28] Such directional shift embodies art critic Calvin Tomkins's assessment that the museum is "a sort of cultural coral reef, always growing and changing."[29]

Returning, perhaps, to collections germane to their ethos as a space for international art across time, The Met is currently undergoing a renovation of its eleven galleries dedicated to Cypriot and West Asian art, including pieces from ancient Iraq, Iran, Turkey, Syria, the Eastern Mediterranean coast, Yemen, and Central Asia. The new galleries, spanning ten thousand years of history and art, are scheduled to open in 2025. They will also, importantly, visually convey the role of Cyprus as a crossroads through the visual and cultural intersections between Cyprus and ancient West Asia represented in these galleries and those of Egypt, Greece, and Rome elsewhere in the museum. Importantly, exhibition design and its tethering to exhibition narrative offers a meta-narrative for visitors: the works are located within a conceptual cultural intersection. The Ancient Near Eastern and Cypriot galleries center cross-cultural collaboration by inviting viewers to gaze across works to see literal and figurative connections between works created in this region.

Museum of Fine Arts, Boston (MFA)

The Museum of Fine Arts, Boston had a host of devoted, well-to-do collectors who worked with knowledgeable curators to build a strong collection. Its East Asian art is the most remarkable of its holdings and is one of the finest collections in the world. Its beginnings came about when, in the 1870s and 1880s, Edward S. Morse and Ernest Fenollosa of Salem and Dr. William Sturgis Bigelow of Boston journeyed to Japan to collect ceramics, statuary, and paintings that eventually went to the museum. Likewise, Chinese, Korean, Indian, and other Near and Far Eastern art were acquired for the collection. The museum also secured Egyptian materials, mainly through Harvard-Boston archaeological expeditions, and it was for a time the leading purchaser of Greek, Roman, and Etruscan antiquities. In addition, a comprehensive collection of European and American paintings was complemented by textiles, American decorative arts, and prints are of quality.

The MFA building on the Fenway opened in 1909 (after its prior residence in Copley Square) with significant expansions in 2010, 2011, and 2013, which have enabled the museum to consolidate its collections while expanding the use of spaces. These include the Art of the Americas Wing, with four levels of American art; the Linde Family Wing, focusing on contemporary art with social and engagement spaces; and renovations and new spaces for European, Asian, and African art.[30]

Art Institute of Chicago (AIC)

Founded as both a museum and a school for the fine arts in 1879, AIC was founded in an era of civic boosterism and rebuilding brought on after the Great Fire engulfed the city in 1871. The AIC found its permanent home in 1893, as part of the construction of the White City proclaimed by architect Daniel Burnham, who was charged with the task of designing a gridded multiplex arena for the World's Fair held in the Windy City that year. A research library was constructed in 1901, to support the curatorial and academic goals of AIC. Eight expansions over the past century have provided gallery and administrative space. The most recent addition was the Modern Wing, which opened in 2009.

Now boasting three-hundred thousand works of art across five thousand years ranging from plaster casts to Chinese bronzes and contemporary design and from textiles to installation art, AIC boasts iconic works, including Grant Wood's *American Gothic*, Edward Hopper's *Nighthawks*, and Georges Seurat's *A Sunday on La Grande Jatte*, a massive pointillist masterpiece made famous in the teen comedy *Ferris Bueller's Day Off* (1986), as well as photographs by Sally Mann and Cindy Sherman, sculpture by Malvina Hoffman and Kiki Smith, and silhouettes by Kara Walker.

Washington, D.C.

Today, Washington, D.C. boasts substantial art collections with the Smithsonian Institution and the National Art Gallery. In the case of the former, French-born British chemist, mineralist, and collector James Smithson (1765–1829) answered the call for a national art collection and research library with his bequest to the nation in 1836. His gift did not result in the creation of the institution bearing Smithson's name until a decade later. During these early years, as the Smithsonian Institution took shape in Washington across myriad interests, the notion of a national art collection became secondary.

However, in the 1920s, when Pittsburgh financier and art collector Andrew W. Mellon joined the Coolidge administration as secretary of the treasury, he began a personal crusade to build a gallery comparable to those in European capitals out of chagrin at the lack of a national art gallery in Washington. Over the next two decades, in addition to building his own private collection, Mellon developed and pursued the creation of a national gallery in Washington. The National Gallery of Art thus emerged from America's own "princely" collections, those of major donors including Mellon's children, Ailsa Mellon Bruce and Paul Mellon, as well as Samuel H. Kress, Lessing J. Rosenwald, and Chester Dale. The initial collection was gifted by Mellon to the nation along with an endowment that afforded construction on the National Mall. Construction began in 1937, and the National Gallery of Art opened in 1941 as a gift to the nation. An addition to the neoclassical marble building designed by John Russell Pope was constructed in the 1970s. Designed by I. M. Pei, the East Building opened in 1978 as the center for modern paintings, drawings, and sculpture. In 1999, the Sculpture Garden opened as a venue for outdoor seating and contemporary sculpture.[31]

In the capital city, the Smithsonian Institution, started in 1846 with the Englishman James Smithson's bequest to the United States "for the increase and diffusion of knowledge," for a time was loath to accept collections and remained chiefly a research institution of pure science. When George Brown Goode joined the Smithsonian in 1873, it began to become a national museum devoted to science, the humanities, and the arts.[32] Comprising twenty museums and galleries and a National Zoo, the Smithsonian museums are home to seventeen collections located in Washington, D.C., with eleven of these located on the National Mall, a green space that serves as center stage for museums, monuments, memorials, and marches. These are considered the nation's museums. Across the Smithsonian's locations, a suite of institutions may be defined as art museums reflecting creative practices across time and geographical reach.

A trio of institutions in D.C. reflect American art. The Smithsonian American Art Museum is the nation's first collection of American art encompassing early American art through contemporary art, photography, Folk and "Outsider" art, and art by Black and Latinx artists. Housed in the first building in the United States intentionally designed as an art museum (the 1858 construction by architect James Renwick Jr.), the Renwick Gallery of the Smithsonian American Art Museum exhibits American contemporary craft. The National Portrait Gallery focuses on visual and performing arts and new media across the centuries from pre-colonial (or precontact) to the present. Of particular mention is the collection of presidential portraits—the only such complete collection of presidential portraits outside of the White House. The most recent paintings on view are the portraits of Barack Obama and Michelle Obama, painted by Kehinde Wiley and Amy Sherald, respectively. The forty-fifth president, Donald Trump, is represented by a photographic print, as the museum awaits dual portraits, which are in the works.[33]

International modern and contemporary art across the centuries may be found in three additional D.C. institutions: the Hirshhorn Museum and Sculpture Garden; the National Museum of Asian Art; and the National Museum of African Art. The Hirshhorn Museum and Sculpture Garden, which opened in 1974, offers three spaces for exhibition: the main building (a cylindrical space designed by mid-century modern architect Gordon Bunshaft), the adjoining plaza, and the sunken sculpture garden. The building itself is testament to modern and contemporary design. Focused collections of Asian art may be found in the National Museum of Asian Art's two galleries: the Freer Gallery of Art—which focuses on Chinese paintings; Indian sculpture; Islamic painting and metalware; Japanese lacquer; Korean ceramics; and American art of the late nineteenth-century aesthetic movement, which sought inspiration in Asian art—and the Arthur M. Sackler[34] Gallery—which focuses on South Asian sculpture; Chinese jades and bronzes; and modern Japanese ceramics. The National Museum of African Art is the only national museum in the United States dedicated to the collection, exhibition, conservation, and study of the arts of Africa. On exhibit are the finest examples of traditional and contemporary art from the entire continent of Africa.

Collections of art, however, are not confined to museums with the words *art* or *design* in their names. For instance, two museums on the Mall bear witness to the significance of artistic expression as part of cultural tradition. The National Museum of African American History and Culture (NMAAHC) is the largest and most comprehensive museum dedicated to examining, documenting, and showcasing the African American story and its impact on American and world history African diaspora culture. Located on the west end of the Mall adjacent to the Washington Monument, the museum opened in 2016 and is the newest Smithsonian on the Mall. Here, art, artifacts, and contexts are presented within their stunning new building—a sheathed glass cube that resembles a beaded crown of Yoruba art, the corona, designed by Ghanaian-British architect David Adjaye. The building, its collections, and its experiences intertwine the histories of enslavement and freedom in the nation's capital.

At the east end of the Mall, near the United States Capitol, the National Museum of the American Indian a presents diverse history and contemporary voices of Native peoples throughout the western hemisphere from the Arctic Circle to Tierra del Fuego. The curvilinear architecture, indigenous landscaping, and outdoor sculpture were created in collaboration with tribal nations and communities to reflect Indigenous culture authentically.

Farther afield from D.C. but still under the Smithsonian banner, in New York City, the National Museum of the American Indian operates a second location at Bowling Green called the George Gustave Heye Center, named after the Wall Street businessman-turned-collector of Native American objects. Heye amassed collections by collecting items on his own, a project he began in 1897 before purchasing collections outright from individuals and institutions. Within twenty years of beginning his pursuit of collections, he opened his own museum in Manhattan in 1922. Initially called the Museum of the American Indian–Heye Foundation, his collection of eight-hundred thousand objects was transferred to the Smithsonian in 1989. Also in New York City, Cooper Hewitt is the nation's only museum dedicated to historic and contemporary design, with a collection of over 210,000 design objects spanning thirty centuries. Located in the landmark Andrew Carnegie mansion and boasting a beautiful public garden, Cooper Hewitt makes design come alive with unique temporary exhibitions and installations of the permanent collection.

Through public-private partnership support, the Smithsonian Institution continues to reflect the heterogeneity of the United States and within this, a space for exhibition of art and design. In 2020, the United States Congress authorized the creation of two additional Smithsonians: the National Museum of the American Latino and the Smithsonian American Women's History Museum, as part of the Consolidated Appropriations Act (2021). The locations for these museums have yet to be decided, though they are expected to be on or near the National Mall. While they are not expressly "art" or "design" museums, they will collect, exhibit, and engage audiences with such collections, as evidenced by previous examples of culturally focused museums.[35]

NYC: MoMA, Whitney, Guggenheim

In the 1930s, New York City emerged as an important center for modern art with three museums. While the paragraphs that follow recount their histories, their journeys are far from over: permanent displays and collections share space with emergent artistic trends and spaces for visitors to come, explore ideas, pose questions, and participate in conversations and experiences—to, ultimately, *make*.

The Museum of Modern Art, familiarly known as MoMA (1929), was founded by Lillie P. Bliss, Abby Aldrich Rockefeller, and Mary Quinn Sullivan, and was conceived as a place devoted to exhibiting and collecting modern art. Over lunch the year prior, the women conceived of a plan to rectify an oversight because "New York alone, among the great capitals of the world, lacks a public gallery where the works of the founders and masters of the modern schools can be seen."[36] They hired a dynamic director, Alfred H. Barr Jr., who sold New Yorkers on French postimpressionism (Cezanne, Seurat, Van Gogh, Gauguin, Picasso, and others) and on Bauhaus modernism, bringing together the visual arts, including architecture, industrial design, film, photography, graphics, and typography. As part of a renovation in 2019, the entire collection was reinstalled, and new spaces allow visitors to make connections with art and its meanings. Two, in particular, invite expanded engagement: the Marie-Josée and Henry Kravis Studio is a space for live and experimental programming, while the Paula and James Crown Creativity Lab is a studio for all where visitors can connect with the artwork, cultures, and environments where artists create.

At about the same time the MoMA trio were hatching their plan, Gertrude Vanderbilt Whitney, assisted by the energetic and witty Juliana Force, crowned their efforts to assist America's modern painters by establishing the Whitney Museum of American Art (1930).[37] The Whitney has emerged as a leader in contemporary art exhibition with its influential biennial exhibitions that reflect one of the latest trends in contemporary art—a temporary exhibition invitational that includes new work by American artists. This notion was introduced as an annual exhibit by Gertrude Vanderbilt Whitney in 1932 to see new artwork created during the previous two years of a particular medium (painting was the focus in 1932–1933; then sculpture, watercolors, and prints for 1933–1934) before returning to painting in 1934–1935; and so on). From 1937, the exhibitions became annual events. In 1973, the exhibitions became biennial events of contemporary American Art, open to all mediums—a format it retains to this day.

The longest-running survey of contemporary American art, the biennials offer a snapshot of the art world curated around a theme while also depositing an exhibition in the timeline of the museum's history, collection, and reputation. As such, these installations have not been without contention. The anonymous feminist collaborative the Guerrilla Girls protested the show in 1987 for its lack of diverse representation as told by the number of women and minorities in the exhibition.[38] In 2017, Dana Schutz's *Open Casket*—a painting of the dead body of Emmett Till, a Black teen in Mississippi lynched in 1955—drew condemnation and protest. The painting by a White artist representing the exploitation of a defining moment in Black history, and the appropriation to the systematic oppression of Black communities in the United States and worldwide, drew extreme criticism. For instance, Hannah Black, a British-born artist, argued that the painting and its anti-Black violence should be removed and, even, destroyed. She mobilized support for this action through an open letter published online.[39] The co-curators of this exhibition instead issued a statement attesting to the role that the biennial and the museum play in allowing artists to explore critical issues such as race relations in the country, without acknowledging the way in which the work by a White artist represents, and profits from, anti-Black violence. Further, the Whitney did not give in to the demands to remove the painting: it remained on view during the biennial. Additional controversies have persisted, such as an association between the institution and the commercial ventures of its board—namely Warren Kanders, who has ties to a company that manufactures tear gas that has been used as a weapon against asylum seekers at the United States-Mexico border. (Kanders eventually stepped down after months of demonstrations about his ties.)[40]

A third institution, the Solomon R. Guggenheim Foundation, was founded in 1937 with a goal of showcasing abstract art of Vasily Kandinsky and others. An outcome of this goal was the creation of the Museum of Non-Objective Painting, which opened in 1939. The Museum was financed by Guggenheim and overseen by Hilla Rebay, who served as the Foundation's curator and the museum's director. The museum operated in rented space of a former automobile showroom–turned–art space. The concept was updated by Peggy Guggenheim's opening of the Art of This Century gallery in 1942. The following year, they commissioned Frank Lloyd Wright to design the permanent home. Opened in 1959, the Solomon R. Guggenheim Museum has become a showspace for modern art on the Upper East Side of Manhattan. This is not the sole Guggenheim art venue. Opened to the public in 1980, the Peggy Guggenheim Collection in Venice, Italy, holds the core personal collection of twentieth-century art owned by benefactress Peggy Guggenheim. New construction was begun in the 1990s to create a Guggenheim Museum in Bilbao, Spain. Upon its opening in 1997, the museum was instantly hailed as an architectural masterpiece. While other Guggenheims (such as SoHo and Las Vegas) came and went, plans are underway to develop another museum in Abu Dhabi.[41]

The Studio Museum, Harlem

Founded in 1968 as a place for artists of African descent to exhibit, but also as a space to be "seen and heard—making themselves a presence in the ongoing cultural conversation—both as individuals and as creators with shared histories and concerns,"[42] the Studio Museum is a legendary art institution that combines making with exhibition and related endeavors. The collections, exhibitions, education, and experiences center on artists who identify as Black Americans, of the African diaspora, and from the African continent. The museum's Artist-in-Residence program builds upon an initial practice of workshops and exhibitions that enabled artists to join together to create and show work. This long-standing studio practice was practical as much as it was conceptual: abstract painter William T. Williams, in conceiving of it, felt it was important to have Black artists working in Harlem and also exhibiting work there. The collection spans seven hundred artists, two hundred years of history, and two thousand works of art across all media. A new, permanent home for the museum is under construction and is slated to open in 2024. The new building—situated on the plot of the museum's original structure, a bank building designed by J. Max Bond Jr., a Black architect. The contemporary space is designed by David Adjaye, who also designed the NMAAHC in Washington, D.C. It will also include a site-specific commission using materials from the former museum by Theaster Gates, a Chicago-based mixed-media artist.[43]

Several other institutions celebrate Black culture, including the Museum of African Diaspora in San Francisco, which has been called "a place of storytelling . . . about people and their experiences, rather than a collection of artifacts." The museum, located in the first three floors of the St. Regis Hotel, anchors their work in four themes: origin, movement, adaptation, and transformation.[44] The museum is also situated in the cultural corridor that includes San Francisco Museum of Modern Art (SFMOMA), the Yerba Buena Center for the Arts, and the Contemporary Jewish Museum. In Los

Angeles are the California African American Museum and the Museum of African American Art, LA. Other institutions include the African American Museum in Philadelphia, the Museum of Contemporary African Diasporan Arts in Brooklyn, and the Harvey B. Gantt Center for African American Arts & Culture in Charlotte, North Carolina, named after the state's first Black mayor.

Art and Architecture

In the nineteenth century, many United States cities built museums to house their artistic treasures to impress citizens and visitors with the community's culture. Often these buildings resembled banks or other civic structures harkening back to classical Greek and/or Roman architecture, reflecting a commitment to protecting the objects. Regardless of the look of the container, one thing is for certain: art museums are at the forefront of transparency of both information and collections as demonstrated by the "open storage," "open study," or "visible storage" movement that has taken hold at public, private, and university museums and renovation or new building projects that support broader viewing of the museum's collections. Such spaces offer an inside look at collections to give a sense of breadth and depth far beyond the number of works exquisitely placed in the other gallery spaces throughout a museum.

The notion of visible storage is relatively new to art museums, making a splash across museums over the past fifty years, but among United States art museums only more recently. The best-known examples of visible art storage are in three NYC institutions, and one in D.C.—all of them initiatives that were funded by the New York–based Henry Luce Foundation and debuted from 1988 to 2004. The first was the Met Museum's Henry R. Luce Study Center for the Study of American Art, which opened in 1988 with more than eighteen thousand items on display—more items in one area than many art institutions have in their entire collections; the New-York Historical Society's installation from 2000, termed a Center for the Study of American Culture (and recently renovated in 2020); the Brooklyn Museum's Visible Storage + Study Center installation, with two thousand items adjacent to the three hundred fifty items on view in the nearby American galleries, which opened in 2001; and the Smithsonian American Art Museum's installation, which opened in 2004. These exhibition-storage spaces are intended to be user-friendly and to encourage close looking. Smaller assemblages have been made by other institutions to copy this aesthetic, as well as its democratizing approach: that art in storage is, still, worthy of exhibition, study, and interest. For instance, university museums have likewise adopted this strategy, as seen at the Johnson Museum of Art at Cornell and the University of Michigan Art Museum. These types of broad experiences are often supplemented by digital ancillaries in the form of apps, websites, and tech stands throughout the museum that offer resources such as a searchable database to enable visitors to find more information about the objects on view as well, as digital interpretive displays.[45]

Beyond a conceptual idea of an "open" vault, is an art museum that has adopted the notion of a "veiled" vault. At The Broad, Los Angeles's newest contemporary art museum, which opened in 2015, the "veil" concept, designed by Diller Scofidio + Renfro, is a building shell whose metal beams appear as a textured fabric that covers but does not hide, just as The Broad Foundation has lent numerous works over its twenty-plus-year history before establishing this permanent home in LA.[46]

Destinations

Art museums have led the way in moving beyond the four walls of a gallery to extend their offerings into new spaces and places—making art museums more than mere repositories: they are destinations. In 2000, the MoMA became the sole corporate member of P.S. (Public School) 1 Contemporary Art Center, founded in 1971 in Long Island City, to broaden its opportunities to support contemporary artists. P.S. 1 has rejuvenated the nineteenth-century school building, and its vast spaces provide contemporary artists with intriguing spaces to show, construct, and build their works (in all dimensions, including sound). The purpose of this space and the partnership with New York's flagship modern and contemporary art institution is "to promote the enjoyment, appreciation, study, and understanding of contemporary art to a wide and growing audience. Collaborative programs of exhibitions, educational activities, and special projects allow both institutions to draw on their respective strengths and resources and to continue shaping a cultural discourse."[47] Another example is North Adams's Mass MOCA (Massachusetts Museum of Contemporary Art), which inhabits more than twenty-five buildings along the streets and industrial alleys of this former mill town, which has become an innovative center for the arts. A broader view has been taken by the Dia Art Foundation, which was founded under the name Lone Star Foundation in 1974, and it has played a role among visual arts organizations nationally and internationally by initiating, supporting, presenting, and preserving art projects, and by serving as a locus for interdisciplinary art and criticism. In terms of sites and locations, Dia is best described as "a constellation of sites, from the iconic permanent, site-specific artworks and installations in New York, the American West and Germany; to an exhibition program that has commissioned dozens of breakthrough projects; to the vast galleries of Dia Beacon; and finally the programs of education and public engagement." At Beacon, Dia presents its permanent collection in this former printing plant situated on thirty-one acres nestled along the banks of the Hudson River. Stars of this self-termed constellation include long-term, site-specific projects in venues across the United States, such as Robert Smithson's *Spiral Jetty* located in Great Salt Lake, Utah, and James Turrell's *Roden Crater*, in Painted Desert, Arizona.[48]

Likewise, Bentonville, Arkansas, has become a hub of art through the creation in this century of several entities—many of them due to the generosity of billionaire heiress and philanthropist Alice Walton, daughter of Sam Walton, founder of Walmart. Chief among these is a sprawling new venue, the Crystal Bridges Museum of American Art, which the *New York Times* proclaimed as being on par with the gifts of the mostly male philanthropists of the nineteenth century. In June 2011, months before the museum opened, critic Carol Vogel proclaimed: "the era of the world-class museum built by a single philanthropist in the tradition of Isabella Stewart Gardner, John Pierpont Morgan Jr. and Gertrude Vanderbilt Whitney may seem to have passed, but Alice L. Walton is bringing it back."[49] The museum is comprised of thirty-five hundred works across five centuries of American art and one hundred twenty acres of nature to situate art. Importantly, admission and parking are free, cementing a commitment to serve guests who may be well-versed in art history and/or may have never visited an art museum before. In the case of the latter, moreover, all field trips for K-12 students are supported by a transportation subsidy and a free lunch for every student in attendance. Their field trips are framed around guided tours that are keyed to K-12 curriculum standards, focusing on four or five works of art that can educate audiences on how to "look at, interpret, and appreciate art."[50] Shortly before the museum opened, this intent was noted in the press, making mention of the museum as having "a serious and real focus on public education."[51]

Public education and access to art are key features of another Walton-funded initiative in Art Bridges, a foundation established in 2017 by Alice Walton to support the creation of collection-based exhibitions allowing access to American art in all regions of the United States. Fulfilling Alice Walton's goal that "everybody deserves access to art," Art Bridges enables institutions to borrow works of art at no cost or to develop exhibitions that might otherwise not be possible without funding in order to bring art to audiences in new ways. The foundation also offers funds to build out programming that mirrors the approaches taken by Crystal Bridges noted above.[52]

Beyond the museum and the philanthropic wing, Walton and company have spawned a second space for contemporary art, food, and music less than two miles away from the museum, in downtown Bentonville. Opened in February 2020, The Momentary cultivates arts and cultural experiences on the premises of a cheese plant repurposed into a contemporary art space. These initiatives have also made Bentonville a hub for contemporary art, as evidenced by the presence of a recent addition to the "21" franchise.

In 2022, the Upcountry History Museum in Greenville, SC hosted the traveling exhibition *Andy Warhol: Endangered Species* organized by Art Bridges with works drawn from the collection of Crystal Bridges Museum of American Art. The ten prints by Warhol are examined through four engaging and multi-disciplinary themes: activism, animals, history and art. The bilingual exhibition (English and Spanish) also featured tactile reproductions and labels in Braille to facilitate learning and engagement. The project was generously funded by Art Bridges Foundation.

Tactile Detail

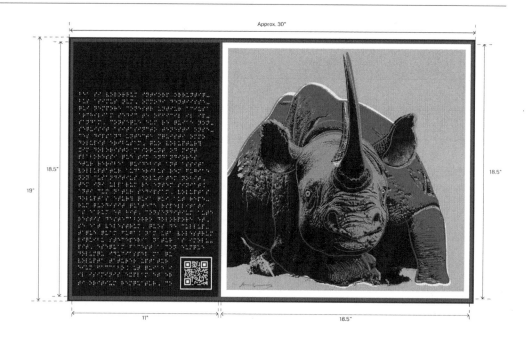

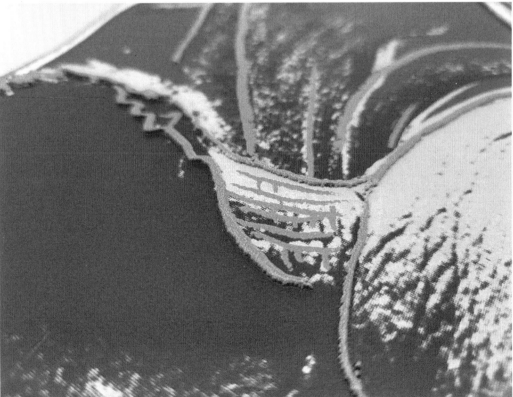

Details of tactile reproductions for exhibition *Andy Warhol: Endangered Species*, organized by Art Bridges. Andy Warhol (1928-1987), Black Rhinoceros, 1983, screen print on paper, 38 x 38 in. Crystal Bridges Museum of American Art, Bentonville, Arkansas, 2015.38.2. © The Andy Warhol Foundation for the Visual Arts / Licensed by Artists Rights Society (ARS), New York / Ronald Feldman Gallery, New York.

"21c" is the nickname of the 21c Museum Hotel, a multiple-venue contemporary art museum developed in 2006 by art collectors and preservationists Laura Lee Brown and Steve Wilson in their hometown of Louisville, Kentucky. The concept was initially developed as a way to combine the interests of Brown and Wilson around contemporary art, while championing new exhibitions, site-specific installations, and programming. These elements are combined with a boutique hotel and a chef-driven restaurant that engages the local community through farm-to-table approaches as well as exhibitions that center local interests. In the case of their first location, Wilson and Brown bought five buildings that were tobacco and bourbon warehouses in the nineteenth century, combined them, and converted them into a museum, ninety-room hotel, and restaurant. This same concept has been brought to their other seven locations, including the aforementioned Bentonville, Arkansas; Lexington, Kentucky; Cincinnati, Ohio; Chicago, Illinois; Kansas City and St. Louis, Missouri; and Durham, North Carolina.[53]

Rather than operating as an institution with hubs at different locations and entirely operating with a single framing lens for that site (such as the Tate outposts or The Met locations mentioned earlier in this chapter), the 21c locations are both independently visioned *and* part of an ecosystem. They are the product of cooperative, shared, and complementary relationships. According to chief curator and 21c museum director Alice Gray Stites, this way of working is unusual: "Think of it as one entity. The

21c, a multiple-venue contemporary art museum-hotel concept developed in 2006 by art collectors and preservationists Laura Lee Brown and Steve Wilson in their hometown of Louisville, Kentucky, has brought art and penguins to Bentonville, Arkansas; Lexington, Kentucky; Cincinnati, Ohio; Chicago, Illinois; Kansas City and St. Louis, Missouri; and Durham, North Carolina. Initially the Red Penguin sculptures by Cracking Art collective were spotted at the 2005 Venice Biennale as part of a public art project. They were purchased by 21c founders and were first exhibited at 21c Louisville in 2006. Thirteen years and several hotels later, each 21c has its own flock of Penguins—each in a color that embodies the singular identity of their city. The Penguins greet visitors throughout the hotel—each in the lobby, elevators, restaurant, guest rooms, and often where you least expect them, driving home the presence of art in every nook and cranny of the museum hotel. *21c Museum Hotel.*

ROBIN KID, aka THE KID, *The State I Am In, In the Consciousness of a Country's Empty Mind*, 2019. Sculpture, silicone, oil paint, various materials. ©ROBIN KID, aka THE KID—All rights reserved—Courtesy the artist for 21c. The bison, as well as other symbolic nationalist imagery on view, evokes the lingering nostalgia for Manifest Destiny, the nineteenth-century cultural doctrine of American dominance that conflates power with progress. The waning of that power, and of the ideals of might and masculinity nurtured by the mythology of the American West, is in Omero Leyva's watercolor *Estampida*. The apparently domesticated bison in ROBIN KID, aka THE KID's lifelike multimedia sculpture, *The State I Am In, In the Consciousness of a Country's Empty Mind*, is being ridden by a tattooed young man wearing branded athletic gear and carrying a baby, with a United States flag draped casually around him. Like many of the figures featured in other works by this aptly named artist, this teenager is both saddled with and astride the weight of ideological inheritance: sitting atop a synthetic bison, his movement into the future has been arrested by the competing mythologies consuming, confounding, and dividing the collective American psyche. On view at 21c Louisville. *21c Museum Hotel.*

Conceptual artist Serkan Özkaya made *David* (inspired by Michelangelo), a double-size, golden replica of Michelangelo's *David*, for the ninth International Istanbul Biennial in 2005. Days prior to the opening of the Biennial, the sculpture collapsed shortly after installation. After the collapse, the artist restored the damaged replica and cast two additional copies, one of which was acquired by 21c Museum in 2010. *21c Museum Hotel.*

David Burns and Austin Young/Fallen Fruit, *The Practices of Everyday Life*, 2016. Burns and Young, who work as the duo Fallen Fruit, explore and transform located geographies and narrative histories at the intersections of public and private spaces. This site-specific commission is inspired by a wide range of definitions of "the public," from the stranger or passerby to the vast public spaces of the internet, and it includes collective histories found in native and creationist mythologies, generational knowledge, and public and private archives. The installation is located in the museum restaurant, Proof on Main, at 21c in Louisville. *21c Museum Hotel.*

exhibitions travel to buildings that are all very different. . . . There's no model. It's exciting—and terrifying."[54] She has also referred to it as "a multi-venue museum . . .with over seventy-five thousand square feet of exhibition space spread across seven cities."[55] As an important ambassador for contemporary art, 21c is seen as a "brand" in the sense that it operates in a certain way with particular standards and outputs in geographical locations that "many New Yorkers and [Los] Angelinos deride as 'flyover country',"[56] in that you don't stop there to see art—you fly over it to get to your art destination. 21c, like Crystal Bridges, are debunking those claims.

For Further Consideration

American art museums have developed differing and sometimes conflicting philosophies about their aims. Benjamin Ives Gilman of Boston insisted that art museums differ from science and history museums in that their collections exist to allow their viewers to experience beauty rather than to convey information. This aesthetic emphasis in a sense meant "art for art's sake," not education. Librarian and museum director John Cotton Dana had a very different idea—to emphasize art in the everyday activities of the community, to make immigrant and minority groups as well as factory workers proud of their culture and their products, to show how even everyday household wares could be well designed; in short, to define the museum as an instrument for community betterment. One should notice that each of these museum innovators with their differing points of view advocates for education as a basic museum purpose. Gilman, though insistent that art objects in themselves were aesthetic rather than educational, organized the first museum docents, offered lectures about art and artists, and generally offered programs for the public that today are part of standard offerings for museum education departments. Such discussions continue today: a fine example of the "arguments" and "perspectives" alive in art museums is revealed in *Whose Muse? Art Museums and Public Trust*, published in 2004. Further discussion of museum purposes, including art museums, may be found in the second section of this book.

For much of the past century, blockbuster exhibitions have been central to the financial support for United States art museums, especially those in large urban centers. They not only attract visitors and increase admissions income and museum shop sales, but they also allow for "cross marketing" to increase tourism citywide. For example, the 1996 Cezanne retrospective exhibition at the Philadelphia Museum of Art attracted more than a half million people in three months. It stimulated "package tours to the city," that included discount airfares, hotel rooms, and even restaurant meals. The city's tourism office estimated that the exhibition had an economic impact on the city of 86.5 million dollars.[57] Yet it is not the size of the exhibition or its comprehensiveness that matters any longer. Dubbing the inaugural show at the Renwick Gallery "art for Instagram's sake," Katharine Schwab remarked that the exhibition *Wonder* capitalized on the promotional power of social media, as it positioned site-specific installations within the walls of the grand 1859 building that sits opposite the White House. In terms of numbers, the exhibition was a blockbuster: it drew more visitors in six weeks than the museum had had in the entire year previous. Such immersive exhibitions have drawn such huge crowds because and in spite of social media. Likewise, *Rain Room* offered a quasi-immersive experience where visitors could walk through a space filled with falling water only to remain dry. The show debuted in 2012 at London's Barbican before making its way to the MoMA and the Los Angeles County Museum of Art.[58] Critics of these displays claim that the attention is on the spectacle and not the art; moreover, the art becomes mediated through the lens of a phone and thus seems to overturn the delight made possible from close viewing and direct experience.

Turning the idea of "experience" on its head, contemporary artists are grappling with the boundaries of experience and, also, the rules of engagement around contemporary art: art collections and art museums are more than repositories or showplaces of works that ought to remain as they were created. British graffiti artist Banksy stretches the idea with *Love Is in the Bin* (2018)—an artwork that shredded upon its sale in 2018 when the auction gavel summoned $1.4 million at auction by Sotheby's Europe. The image of a girl letting go of (or attempting to grasp) a balloon was initially titled *Girl with Balloon*, though the physical presence and its title changed when the shredder built within the frame activated and partially shred the piece. The piece changed hands again in 2021 to the tune of 25.4 million dollars, a record for Banksy.[59]

Moreover, art museums have become sites of protest. In 2022, protests dotted the globe, including scrawling graffiti on artworks, tossing mashed potatoes and tomato soup, and protestors gluing themselves to protective coverings of paintings or the walls nearby. Categorized as "high-profile stunts" by the press, these actions align with climate protests over the past few years and share their aim of disrupting daily life. The actions have led the Association of Art Museum Directors in the United States to issue a statement in October 2022, calling the acts unjustified and misdirected, where "the ends do not justify the means." The following month, as attacks occurred across museums, museum directors worldwide issued a letter that called for a halt to these actions. In addition to calling out the activists, who "severely underestimate the fragility of these irreplaceable objects, which must be preserved as part of our world cultural heritage," the letter pointed to the value of museums as "places where people from a wide variety of backgrounds can engage in dialogue" and "free space(s) for social communication."[60]

As repositories of cultural materials, however, art museums fulfill the aims articulated in the second half of this volume. Like all museums, art museums across the United States promised to address diversity, equity, inclusion, and access (DEIA). They promised to center these notions and make museums about belonging. Two years since the landslide of equity initiatives, spurred on in the wake of the extrajudicial killing of George Floyd in May 2020, open letters from groups and movements were met with public statements by U.S. museums to work toward dismantling systemic racism by listening to communities, improving hiring practices, supporting BIPOC (Black, Indigenous, People of Color) staff, reevaluating workplace culture, offering anti-racism training, and acquiring and exhibiting work from a more diverse range of artists.[61] Commitments by institutional leadership have articulated goals for diversification and governance, staffing and culture, collections and exhibitions, research and publication, and audience engagement.

Small steps can move the needle. For instance, the special exhibition hosted in 2024 at Brooklyn Museum, *Giants: Art from the Dean Collection of Swizz Beatz and Alicia Keys*, is the first major exhibition of these artist-patron's collection, underscores the title of the show with "the renown of legendary artists, the impact of canon-expanding contemporary artists, and [their] monumental works." The exhibition also hopes to encourage "giant conversations" that critique society and celebrate Blackness. Curated by Kimberli Gant, curator of modern and contemporary art at Brooklyn Museum, the show features one hundred pieces, primary large-scale, and a section called "Giant Conversations," which addresses "gender relations, intergenerational knowledge, fantasy and reality, history, language, economies."[62]

Giants is one step, even if a giant one. But what else is to be done?

Consider a 2022 demographic survey from the Mellon Foundation that found that representation by persons of color as museum staff at art institutions has increased by 9 percent since 2015 (from 27 to 36 percent).[63] While gains such as this have been made—and elsewhere, perhaps have been achieved—and meaningful progress has been made toward a fuller representation of women and people of color, we expect, in the twenty-first century that museums—in terms of content and the professionals employed therein—reflect the heterogeneity of the United States. These efforts must be continuous and ongoing in order to fully effect change and to welcome all communities.

Notes

1. Wittlin, *Museums: In Search*, 92-93; Taylor, *The Taste of Angels*, 469; Bazin, *The Museum Age*, 89; Holst, *Creators*, 153-54.
2. Bazin, *The Museum Age*, 166-67; Taylor, *Taste of Angels*, 382-83; Seling, "Genesis of the Museum," 105; Holst, *Creators*, 209-14.
3. Bazin, *The Museum Age*, 163-66.
4. Bazin, *The Museum Age*, 162-63.
5. Bazin, *The Museum Age*, 158-59; Seling, "Genesis of the Museum," 109; Holst, *Creators*, 161-63, 206-09; Hudson, *Social History of Museums*, 28-9.
6. Bazin, *The Museum Age*, 150-56; Bazin, *The Louvre*, 39-45; Taylor, *The Taste of Angels*, 371; Christiane Aulanier, *Histoire de Palais et du Musee du Louvre*, 9 vols. (Paris: Éditions des Musées nationaux, 1947), 64.
7. Bazin, *The Museum Age*, 144.
8. Bazin, *The Museum Age*, 159-60; Taylor, *The Taste of Angels*, 511-25; Holst, *Creators*, 166-67, 169-78, 184-85.
9. Bazin, *The Museum Age*, 144-45; Taylor, *The Taste of Angels*, 414-16; Wittlin, *Museums: In Search*, 46.
10. Bazin, *The Museum Age*, 145-50; Taylor, *The Taste of Angels*, 417-20, 475-76; Holst, *Creators*, 194, 205-06.
11. Bazin, *The Museum Age*, 171-72; Bazin, *The Louvre*, 46-48; Holst, *Creators*, 215-17; Taylor, *The Taste of Angels*, 539; Seling, "Genesis of the Museum," 109; Linda Nochlin, "Museums and Radicals: A History of Emergencies," in *Museums in Crisis*, ed. Brian O'Doherty (New York: George Braziller, 1972), 7-41; Cecil Gould, *Trophy of Conquest: The Musée Napoleon and the Creation of the Louvre* (London: Faber and Faber, 1965), 13-29, 70-71; Wilhelm Treve, *Art Plunder: The Fate of Works of Art in War and Unrest* (New York: John Day, Co., 1961), 139-99; Russell Chamberlin, *Loot! The Heritage of Plunder* (New York: Facts on File), 1983.

12. Bazin, *The Museum Age*, 174; Bazin, *The Louvre*, 48–49; Holst, *Creators*, 217–18; Taylor, *The Taste of Angels*, 544–47; Nochlin, "Museums and Radicals," 13; Gould, *Trophy of Conquest*, 41–66; Victoria Newhouse, *Art and the Power of Placement* (New York: Monacelli Press, 2005), 77–82.

13. Bazin, *The Museum Age*, 176; Gould, *Trophy of Conquest*, 67–69.

14. Bazin, *The Museum Age*, 185–91; Bazin, *The Louvre*, 57–60; Taylor, *The Taste of Angels*, 571–89; Gould, *Trophy of Conquest*, 80–85, 116–35; David Roxan and Ken Wanstall, *The Rape of Art: The Story of Hitler's Plunder of the Great Masterpieces of Europe* (New York, Coward-McCann, 1965); Lynn H. Nicholas, *The Rape of Europa: The Fate of Europe's Treasures in the Third Reich and the Second World War* (New York: Vintage, 1994); Hector Feliciano, *The Lost Museum: The Nazi Conspiracy to Steal the World's Greatest Works of Art* (New York: Basic Books, 1997).

15. Bazin, *The Museum Age*, 201, 204, 207, 209; Bazin, *The Louvre*, 61–85; Holst, *Creators*, 260–61; Marc Fumaroli, "What Does the Future Hold for Museums?" in *Masterworks from the Museé des Beaux-Arts, Lille* (New York: Metropolitan Museum of Art, 1992); Kenneth Hudson, *Museums of Influence* (Cambridge, UK: Cambridge University Press, 1987), 39–64.

16. Frank Herrman, *English as Collectors: A Documentary Chrestomathy* (London: Chatto and Windus, 1972), 263–73; Philip Hendy, "The National Gallery," in *Art Treasures of the National Gallery* (London: Thames and Hudson, 1959), 9–25; Holst, *Creators*, 224–25; Neil MacGregor, "Scholarship and the Public," in *Collections Management*, ed. Anne Fahy (London: Routledge, 1995), 219; Gwen Wright, *The Formation of National Collections of Art and Archaeology*, Studies in the History of Art 47 (Washington, D.C.: National Gallery of Art, 1996); Samson Spanier, "Return to Victorian Splendor," *International Herald Tribune*, September 29, 2005, 24; Christopher Whitehead, *The Public Art Museum in Nineteenth Century Britain: The Development of the National Gallery* (Aldershot, UK: Ashgate, 2005); Kate Hill, *Culture and Class in English Public Museums 1850-1914* (Aldershot, UK: Ashgate, 2005).

17. The Kaiser-Friedrich-Museum was renamed the Bode Museum in 1956 after Wilhelm von Bode, its first curator. The Pergamon Museum was completely closed in October 2023 to visitors. It is expected to be until 2037 (at minimum) as part of a comprehensive renovation.

18. Neil MacGregor, "A Cache of Civilisations," *Financial Times*, November 3, 2006, http://www.ft .com/cms/s/0/0938691a-6a3f-11db-8ae5-0000779e2340.html.

19. Bazin, *The Museum Age*, 214–15, 269; B. B. Piotrovsky, ed., *Art Treasures of the Hermitage* (New York: Portland House, 1990), 15–16; Geraldine Norman, *The Hermitage: The Biography of a Great Museum* (New York: Fromm International, 1997); "The State Hermitage Museum, Leningrad," *Museum* 10 (1957): 97–113; *Museum* 217. The May 2003 issue was dedicated to future plans for Hermitage.

20. Bazin, *The Museum Age*, 217–18; Raymond Charmet, *The Museums of Paris* (New York: Meredith Press, 1967), 5–6; *National Gallery, Millbank [Tate Gallery], Illustrated Guide: British School*, (Glasgow: University Press, 1928), viii–ix; Philip Hendy, "National Gallery," in *Art Treasures of the National Gallery*, 9–25; Newhouse, *Art and the Power of Placement*. Tate, the national collection of British art focusing from 1500 to the present, as well as international modern and contemporary art, has a collection of seventy thousand works. See http://www.tate.org.uk/about/who-we-are/history-of-tate.

21. Bazin, *The Museum Age*, 230–34; Kenneth W. Luckhurst, *The Story of Exhibitions* (London: Studio Publications, 1951), 83–116; Eugene S. Ferguson, "Technical Museums and International Exhibitions," *Technology and Culture* 6 (1965): 30–46; Winslow Ames, "London or Liebnitz?" *Museum News* 43 (October 1964): 27–35; Charmet, *The Museums of Paris*, 11; Victoria and Albert Museum, *Masterpieces in the Victoria and Albert Museum* (London: Victoria and Albert Museum, 1952), iii–iv; Leigh Ashton, "100 Years of the Victoria and Albert Museum," *Museums Journal* 53 (May 1953): 43–47; Bruce Robertson, "South Kensington Museum in Context: An Alternative History," *Museum and Society* 2, no. 1 (March 2004).

22. Leo Lerman, *The Museum: One Hundred Years of the Metropolitan Museum of Art* (New York: Viking, 1969); Calvin Tomkins, *Merchants and Masterpieces: The Story of the Metropolitan Museum of Art* (New York: E. P. Dutton, 1970), 115–20; Stephen Mark Dobbs, "Dana and Kent and Early Museum Education," *Museum News* 50 (October 1971): 38–41; Barbara Y. Newsom, *The Metropolitan Museum as an Educational Institution* (New York: The Museum, 1970); Nathaniel Burt, *Palaces for the People: A Social History of the American Art Museum* (Boston: Little, Brown, 1977) is a readable series of portraits of art museum "characters" from Charles Willson Peale to Thomas Hoving; Joel J. Orosz, *Curators and Culture: The Museum Movement in America, 1740-1870* (Tuscaloosa: University of Alabama Press, 1990); Steven

Conn, *Museums and American Intellectual Life, 1876–1926* (Chicago: University of Chicago Press, 1998); David Carrier, *Museum Skepticism: A History of the Display of Art in Public Galleries* (Durham: Duke University Press, 2006); Richard Rossett, "Art Museums in the United States: A Financial Portrait," in *The Economics of Art Museums,* ed. Martin Feldstein (Chicago, IL: University of Chicago Press, 1991), 129–77; William Hendon, *Analyzing an Art Museum* (New York: Praeger, 1979), 18–33; Alan Wallach, *Exhibiting Contradictions: Essays on the Art Museum in the United States* (Amherst, MA: University of Massachusetts Press, 1998).

23. Barbara Y. Newsom and Adele Z. Silver, eds., *The Art Museum as Educator* (Berkeley: University of California Press, 1978) is a study of art museum practices across the United States; Association of Art Museum Directors, *State of the Nation's Art Museums* (New York: Association of Art Museum Directors, 2004); Cuno, *Whose Muse?*; Didier Maleuvre, "A Plea for Silence: Putting Art Back in to the Art Museum," in *Museum Philosophy for the 21st Century,* ed. Hugh H. Genoways (Lanham, MD: AltaMira Press, 2006), 165–76.

24. Whitehill, *Museum of Fine Arts,* 1:10, 41, 288–301.

25. Laurence Vail Coleman, *The Museum in America: A Critical Study,* 3 vols. (Washington, D.C.: The American Association of Museums, 1939), 1:10, 11, 14–15, 112 and 2:230 and 3:429–32; Walter Pach, *The Art Museum in America* (New York: Pantheon, 1948), 32, 33, 38, 40, 42; Tomkins, *Merchants and Masterpieces,* 38; Burt, *Palaces for the People*; Nancy Einreinhofer, *The American Art Museum: Elitism and Democracy* (London: Leicester University Press, 1997), 144–49. The museum was founded in 1852 as a Museum of Manufactures in London, following the Great Exhibition. The museum was relocated and renamed the South Kensington Museum. It was renamed the Victoria and Albert Museum in 1899.

26. Tomkins, *Merchants and Masterpieces,* 21.

27. The Met Breuer remains a feature on the museum's website, https://www.metmuseum.org/about-the-met/history/met-breuer-archive. The website further explains that the building is in use by the Frick Collection while the Frick's 1914 Carrère and Hastings mansion is under renovation. The temporary relocation to the Breuer is on view through March 2024, with the renovated Frick is slated to reopen in late 2024.

28. The Met, The Met Breuer Press Release, December 1, 2015. http://www.metmuseum.org/press/news/2015/met-breuer-december-update.

29. Walter Muir Whitehill, *Museum of Fine Arts, Boston: A Centennial History,* 2 vols. (Cambridge: Belknap Press, 1979), 1:9–13, 31; Tomkins, *Merchants and Masterpieces,* 23, 70; Weil, "Courtly Ghosts and Aristocratic Artifacts: The Art Museum as Palace," 44–49 offers a discussion of the role of casts at the Metropolitan and the Museum of Fine Arts, Boston; Winifred E. Howe, *A History of the Metropolitan Museum of Art,* 2 vols. (New York: The Metropolitan Museum of Art, 1913, 1946), 1:138–39; Coleman, *The Museum in America,* 1:106–11; Tomkins, *Merchants and Masterpieces,* 39–41. On the expansion, see http://www.mfa.org/about.

30. Howe, *Metropolitan History,* 1:153–56, 180–81, 281–83, and 2:8–14; Tomkins, *Merchants and Masterpieces,* 44, 47, 49–59, 95–182; Whitehill, *Museum of Fine Arts,* 1: chaps. 4, 5, 8 and 2: chaps. 14, 19, 21; Pach, *Art Museum,* 65–68; "Museum of Fine Arts, Boston," *Newsweek,* 1969, 9–15, 162–65; www.mfa.org.

31. David Edward Finley, *A Standard of Excellence: Andrew W. Mellon Founds the National Gallery of Art* (Washington, D.C.: Smithsonian Press, 1973). Major donors to the National Gallery, in addition to Mellon, included: Joseph Widener, Samuel H. Kress, and Chester Dale.

32. Alexander, "George Brown Goode and the Smithsonian Museum," in *Museum Masters,* 277–310.

33. Smithsonian Institution, "America's Presidents," https://americaspresidents.si.edu/.

34. Today more commonly referred to as the National Museum of Asian Art, the Freer and Sackler are positioning themselves as less-tied to their donor identity. This framing as the National Museum of Asian Art has been stated in relation to their collection holdings, but it may be viewed in response to recent accusations by protesters accusing the Sackler family of being a key contributor to the opioid epidemic. The Sackler family owned Purdue Pharma, which created the drug OxyContin, which, through overprescription and negligence, fueled addicted drug usage and, in particular, the opioid crises in the United States Even so, the Sackler name is not unfamiliar in museums, and protests have occurred here since 2018, which is a year prior to the rebranding effort. See Nancy Kenney, "Freer/Sackler Rebrand Its

Identity as the National Museum of Asian Art," *Art Newspaper*, December 5, 2019, https://www.theart newspaper.com/2019/12/05/freersackler-rebrands-its-identity-as-the-national-museum-of-asian-art.

35. House of Representatives Act 133 of the 116th Congress (2019–2020), called the "Consolidated Appropriations Act, 2021," became public law on December 27, 2020. It called for "establish[ing] within the Smithsonian Institution a women's history museum and the National Museum of the American Latino . . . creat[ing] advisory bodies to provide guidance and oversight concerning the development, construction, and administration of the respective museums." See https://www.congress.gov/bill/116th-congress/house-bill/133. The Molina Family Latino Gallery is discussed in Chapter 7, "To Exhibit."

36. Quoted from MoMA's first brochure in 1929. See "Three Women Have a Vision," https://www.moma.org/interactives/moma_through_time/1920/three-women-have-a-vision/.

37. The new location for the Whitney, designed by Renzo Piano Building Workshop and opened in 2016, overlooks the Hudson River and is nestled along the High Line, the city's beloved public art attraction. Located in the Meatpacking District, this new Whitney site "engages the Whitney directly with the bustling community of artists, galleries, educators, entrepreneurs, and residents of the Meatpacking District, Chelsea, and Greenwich Village, where the Museum was founded by Gertrude Vanderbilt Whitney in 1930." See http://whitney.org/About/NewBuilding.

38. The Whitney has recently acquired the group's portfolio of eighty-eight posters and ephemera from 1985 to 2012. See Melena Ryzik, "The Guerrilla Girls, After 3 Decades, Still Rattling Art World Cages," *New York Times*, August 5, 2015

39. The letter was posted on March 21, 2017 and was reposted (the equivalent of being "signed") 1,357 times. See https://blackcontemporaryart.tumblr.com/post/158661755087/submission-please-read-share-hannah-blacks. The letter was circulated on a number of other forms of social media, including Facebook, and is widely available online.

40. Alex Greenberger, "'We Will Come Back': Decolonize This Place Leads Protest at Whitney, Marches to Controversial Board Member's House," *ARTnews*, May 17, 2019, https://www.artnews.com/art-news/news/we-will-come-back-decolonize-this-place-leads-protest-at-whitney-marches-to-controversial-board-members-house-12590/.

41. Other Guggenheim sites include the Guggenheim Museum SoHo, which operated in the 1990s; the Guggenheim Guadalajara (2007–2009), the Guggenheim Hermitage in Las Vegas (2001–2008); Deutsche Guggenheim in Berlin; and the Vilnius Guggenheim Hermitage in Lithuania. See Carol Vogel, "Guggenheim Shrinks in SoHo," *New York Times*, February 5, 1999, http://www.nytimes.com/1999/02/05/arts/inside-art-guggenheim-shrinks-in-soho.html, and "Guggenheim Architecture Timeline," https://www.guggenheim.org/history/architecture.

42. *The Studio Museum in Harlem: 25 Years of African-American Art* (Manlius, NY: Salina Press, 1994), 6; The Studio Museum in Harlem, "A Space to Create," https://studiomuseum.org/creating-space.

43. Gabriella Angeleti, "Studio Museum in Harlem Raises $210M for new David Adjaye Building," *Art Newspaper*, October 28, 2021, https://www.theartnewspaper.com/2021/10/28/studio-museum-in-harlem-marks-milestone-in-construction-of-new-home.

44. "Everything You Need to Know about the Museum of the African Diaspora," *SF Travel*, September 2, 2021, https://www.sftravel.com/article/everything-you-need-know-about-museum-african-diaspora.

45. At the Smithsonian, the Luce Foundation Center for American Art offers 3,300 objects in this first visible art storage in the capital. Hands-on programming, digital interactive including video clips, and contextual information are supported by free Wi-Fi to extend the visitor's experience. The Henry R. Luce Center for the Study of American Art at The Met is organized by material, then form and chronology. See http://www.metmuseum.org/art/libraries-and-research-centers/the-henry-r-luce-center-for-the-study-of-american-art.

46. Travis Diehl, "Veil & Vault: Los Angeles's Newest Museum: The Broad," August 1, 2015, Frieze.com, https://frieze.com/article/veil-vault.

47. See http://momaps1.org/about/affiliation/.

48. On MASS MoCA, see http://www.massmoca.org. The history of Dia is quite complex, involving opening and closing of the Dia Chelsea site, among other shifts and acquisitions. See http://www.diaart.org/contents/page/info/102.

49. Carol Vogel, "A Billionaire's Eye for Art Shapes Her Singular Museum," *New York Times*, June 16, 2011, https://www.nytimes.com/2011/06/17/arts/design/alice-walton-on-her-crystal-bridges -museum-of-american-art.html; Roberta Smith, "Crystal Bridges, the Art Museum Walmart Money Built, Opens," *New York Times*, December 26, 2011, https://www.nytimes.com/2011/12/27/arts/design/ crystal-bridges-the-art-museum-walmart-money-built-review.html.

50. For more on the K-12, college, and afterschool programming, see https://crystalbridges.org/ educators/school-field-trip/. On the early days of the learning and engagement programs, see Nile K. Blunt, "'The Most Unlikely of Places': Opportunities and Challenges of Location at Crystal Bridges Museum of American Art," *Journal of Museum Education* 45:2 (2020): 148-57. The quote comes from Blunt's overview of the challenges of the education division of the museum that includes "programming for guests who may have never visited an art museum before; educating school children who have never before engaged with serious or complex art and art historical concepts; and engaging guests with a collection and exhibitions that are diverse and sometimes controversial." The education division, in this way, adheres to the museum's core mission to "welcome all" by developing and delivering multigenerational programming to educate the public in ways of seeing and understanding art. See page 149.

51. Stated by art historian Michael Conforti, then of the Sterling and Francine Clark Art Institute in Williamstown, Massachusetts, who is quoted in Philip Kennicott, "Crystal Bridges in Arkansas: A World-Class Museum from the Land of Wal-Mart," *Washington Post*, October 1, 2011, https://www .washingtonpost.com/lifestyle/style/crystal-bridges-in-arkansas-a-world-class-museum-from-the -land-of-wal-mart/2011/09/27/gIQAN6OiDL_story.html.

52. See Art Bridges, https://artbridgesfoundation.org/.

53. For more on the musuems, see 21C Musuem Hotel, https://www.21cmuseumhotels.com/blog/. 21c had a location in Oklahoma City that has since been sold to a hotel chain.

54. The quote from Alice Gray Stites appear in Nate Storey, "21c Hotels Brings Contemporary Art to the Heartland," *Surface*, November 1, 2016, https://www.surfacemag.com/articles/21c-hotels-bringing -contemporary-art-hotels-middle-america/. For this chapter, I have conceived of 21c as an ecosystem.

55. "Q&A with 21c's Chief Curator Alice Gray Stites," *21c Museum Hotel*, August 1, 2017, https://www .21cmuseumhotels.com/blog/2017/qa-with-21cs-chief-curator-alice-gray-stites/.

56. The passage about New York and L.A. conceptions of "flyover country" appears in Nate Storey, "21c Hotels Brings Contemporary Art to the Heartland," *Surface*, November 1, 2016, https://www.surface mag.com/articles/21c-hotels-bringing-contemporary-art-hotels-middle-america/.

57. Quoted in Newhouse, *Art and the Power of Placement*, 23; Kevin F. McCarthy, Elizabeth H. Ondaatje, Arthur Brooks, and Andras Szanto, *A Portrait of the Visual Arts: Meeting the Challenges of a New Era* (Santa Monica, CA: RAND, 2005), 32. This volume concludes that blockbusters don't increase audiences; they simply get current visitors to return. Julia Beizer, Susan Breitkopf, and Amanda Litvinov, "Marketing the King: Tut 2 and the New Blockbuster," *Museum News* 84, no. 6 (November–December 2005).

58. Katharine Schwab, "Art for Instagram's Sake," *Atlantic*, February 17, 2016, http://www.theatlantic .com/entertainment/archive/2016/02/instagram-art-wonder-renwick-rain-room/463173/.

59. Sharon Pruitt-Young, "A Half-Shredded Banksy Piece Is Auctioned for $25.4 million, A Record for the Artist," NPR, October 14, 2021, https://www.npr.org/2021/10/14/1046134451/banksy-shredded -auction-sold-record.

60. @MuseumDirectors, Art Museum Directors, November 3, 2022, https://twitter.com/MuseumDi-rectors/status/1588166541820018688. Another statement with many signatories was issued by the German National Committee of the International Council of Museums (ICOM) following an attack on Claude Monet's *Les Meules* at the Barberini Museum in Potsdam, Germany. Climate protesters threw mashed potatoes at the painting on October 23, 2022. See ICOM Germany, "Statement: Attacks on Artworks in Museums," November 2022, https://icom-deutschland.de/de/nachrichten/564-statement -attacks-on-artworks-in-museums.html.

61. Jo Lawson-Tancred, "Two Years Ago, Museums Across the U.S. Promised to Address Diversity and Equity. Here's Exactly What They Have Done So Far," *Artnet*, September 5, 2022, https://news.artnet .com/art-world/museum-dei-plans-2022-2161690.

62. Brooklyn Museum, "Giants: Art from the Dean Collection of Swizz Beatz and Alicia Keys," https:// www.brooklynmuseum.org/exhibitions/giants. The exhibition is on view February 10–July 7, 2024.

Beatz was on the museum's board until 2023, and resigned before the show opened, so as not to fuel suggestions of a conflict of interest. See Will Heinrich, "Swizz Beatz and Alicia Keys Show *Giants* in Brooklyn," *New York Times*, February 7, 2024, https://www.nytimes.com/2024/02/07/arts/design/giants-swizz-beatz-alicia-keys-brooklyn.html; Gant is quoted in Mikelle Street, "Swizz Beatz & Alicia Keys Bring Their Giant Art Collection to the Brooklyn Museum," *W Magazine*, February 22, 2024, https://www.wmagazine.com/culture/brooklyn-museum-swizz-beatz-alicia-keys-collection.

63. Mellon Foundation, "Art Museum Staff Demographic Survey 2022," November 16, 2022, https://mellon.org/news-blog/articles/art-museum-staff-demographic-survey-2022/. Recent reports are available here: https://mellon.org/programs/arts-and-culture/art-museum-staff-demographic-survey/. A survey sponsored by the Black Trustee Alliance for Art Museums compiled responses from more than nine hundred board members (168 Black trustees and 635 White trustees) at one hundred thirty-four North American art institutions. They found that Black trustees are younger, more likely to hold PhDs and professional degrees, and less likely to come from intergenerational wealth, than White board members.

2

Natural History and Anthropological Museums

This chapter presents the historical framing of items gathered from the natural world for their mystery and their capacity to instruct, illuminate, and instill wonder. Perceived as "natural curiosities," these objects were thought, by their early medieval and Renaissance collectors, to have magical powers to promote healing, longevity, fertility, and sexual virility. During the sixteenth and seventeenth centuries, the collections showed signs of becoming the foundations of research centers, since they provided important documents for the scientist—rocks and minerals, fossils and shells, anatomical and botanical specimens, and stuffed animals and fishes from all over the world.[1] Taxonomic displays of collections, first amassed in the Western world as an aid in understanding the framing of Christian doctrine and God's plan, evolved under the influence of humanists and later the impact of naturalist Charles Darwin. In the United States, collections containing human remains were studied by anthropologists associated with natural history museums to reveal the origins of inhabitants of the precontact continent.[2] By the end of the nineteenth century, advances in taxidermy allowed for more "natural" displays of habitat groups, attracting the public to what Charles Willson Peale called "statues of animals with real skin to cover them."[3] Collections grew, halls were renovated and expanded, and educational offerings mushroomed, catering to K-12 students and tourists in the twentieth century. In the twenty-first century, however, natural history collections are being rethought and framed in light of the colonial ideologies and narratives: they are reconsidered through the lenses of authority, control, power, ownership, and restitution. Natural history museums are not the only ones grappling with these questions, as we will continue to see throughout this volume, particularly in Section III (Chapters 11–15).

European Collectors, Patrons, and the Earliest Museums

Many of the holdings of the early museums seem strange indeed to the modern naturalist. The fabulous unicorn's horn, thought capable of foiling poisoners or assassins, was worth a fortune, though no such beast existed. Horns of rhinoceroses or other animals were used for various purposes, as were remains of the sea unicorn (narwhal) and fossils. Giants' bones were found in many a collection, though they actually might be of mammoths, elephants, or fossilized remains. Egyptian mummies were greatly prized, and mummy powder (sometimes a criminal's body treated with bitumen) was sold by apothecaries to staunch the flow of blood or heal bruises and fractures. Human skulls and human skin, derived from unburied corpses, were used for medicinal cures, as were stag and elk antlers. Barnacles were observed to have the shape of small geese and were thought to be born in decayed wood; barnacle geese became another medicinal source used by apothecaries.[4]

In the sixteenth and seventeenth centuries, an astonishingly large number of collections of curiosities were found in every western European country. Around 1550, Conrad Gesner, the Zurich physician sometimes called the "Father of Zoology," had one of the first museums devoted chiefly to natural history; his collection was combined with one belonging to Felix Platter, remnants of which are found today in the Natural History Museum in Basel. Ulisse Aldrovandi had a large museum at

Bologna, which early in the seventeenth century, was joined to one of Ferdinando Cospi and acquired by the City of Bologna.[5]

The seventeenth century saw technical improvements in handling zoological specimens. The use of spirits of wine made preservation in liquid possible; cheap flint glass enabled wet specimens to be viewed more easily; and wax or mercury could be injected into vascular systems so as to exhibit specimens dry. Ole Worm, physician, scientist, and founder of prehistoric archaeology, had a museum at Copenhagen, as did King Christian V. The Amsterdam collections of Bernhardus Paludanus, Frederick Ruysch, and Albert Seba found their way to the Imperial Palace in Saint Petersburg.[6] Important centers of scientific research developed in Italy.[7]

Not merely accumulators, collectors were involved in the construction of knowledge as they gave considerable thought to the classification and arrangement of their treasures. Caspar F. Neickel in his *Museographia*, printed at Leipzig in 1727, recommended six shelves around the room. Natural objects should go on one side with human anatomy, including skeletons and mummies, on the top shelf, and quadrupeds, fishes, and minerals below. Another wall was to hold man-made objects with ancient and modern productions separated. The short end of the room opposite the entrance and lighted by three windows contained cabinets for coins. Portraits of famous men occupied the space above the shelves, whereas Ole Worm's Museum in Copenhagen used three continuous shelves and suspended from the ceiling or mounted on the walls large objects such as stuffed crocodiles, a polar bear, skeletons, arms and armor, and a kayak from the Indigenous Arctic. The cabinet of curiosities gathered by sixteenth-century apothecary Ferrante Imperato and displayed at Paazzo Gravina in Naples, Italy, presented a similar appearance, while an Egyptian mummy at the entrance lured the visitor into the Museo Kircheriano, founded in the seventeenth century by Jesuit father Athanasius Kircher in Rome, Italy.[8]

The Ashmolean Museum

The first public natural history museum was established in England at Oxford University in 1683. Father and son, John Tradescant the Elder and John Tradescant the Younger, may be considered its founders. The elder laid out gardens for several English noblemen and journeyed to Flanders, France, Russia, Algeria, across the Mediterranean, and to Turkey to bring back trees and plants chosen for their beauty and rarity rather than their medicinal qualities. In 1626, he moved to South Lambeth, outside London; his house, known as "The Ark," was filled with his renowned Cabinet of Rarities and surrounded by a fine garden.

In 1656, the younger Tradescant issued *Musaeum Tradescantium*, a catalog of the collection that listed preserved birds, animals, fish, and insects; minerals and gems; fruits; carvings, turnings, and paintings; weapons; costumes; household implements; coins and medals; and beautiful and exotic plants, shrubs, and trees—including Virginia materials, many of them gathered by the son on three trips he made there.[9] While such a collection and its gathering were typical of the period in some ways, the access the Tradescants provided was unusual, for they valued the collection as a tool for education of the general public. Entrance was determined by payment of a fee regardless of status or gender. Hence the catalog, which was issued with the help of fellow collector Elias Ashmole, who received the rarities when the Younger died.

Ashmole gave the collection to Oxford in 1677, but he required the university to put up a special museum building to house the twenty cartloads of the Tradescant accumulation, to which he added books and coins of his own. The museum was on the upper floor, a school of natural science below it presided over by Robert Plot, keeper of the museum and professor of chemistry, and a chemistry laboratory in the basement. The whole was called the Ashmolean Museum. The museum printed regulations on its use in Latin in 1714. Only one group was admitted at a time, and entrance fees were in proportion to the time spent on the guided tours, though groups received a discount.

In terms of locations and collections today, the old Ashmolean building (reestablished in 1924 as the Museum of the History of Science) is still extant today beside the Sheldonian Theatre on Broad

Street in Oxford.[10] The museum completed a significant renovation, reopening in 2009, with new galleries focusing on the art and culture of Africa, opening in 2011.[11] More recently, the museum has begun a teaching engagement program, which centers objects from across the museum as touchstones for conversation, learning, and engagement across the university, in a program called "Agile Objects."[12] A notable effort more recently has been undertaken to "de-colonize" the museum, meaning a long-term initiative aimed at expanding the perspectives presented to move beyond "the dominant cultural group, particularly white colonizers."[13] While both of these examples will be discussed in Sections II and III of this volume, their mention here is to remind us that *the histories of institutions*—like the Ashmolean, and other museums presented here, as well as robust museums throughout the world—*are not fixed*. Rather, they continue from past to present and future.

The British Museum and Natural History Museum

The British Museum was founded by the House of Commons in London in 1753 as a combined national library and general museum that soon became especially strong in collections of antiquities, natural history, and ethnography. In fact, the British Museum might just as readily be included in the previous chapter as an "Art Museum," though it appears here as a Natural History Museum based on its origins. Hans Sloane, eminent physician and observant naturalist and scientist, served as president of the Royal Society, in succession to Isaac Newton, and of the Royal College of Physicians. He was best known for his collection, which was a kind of private museum housed in his home. At his death in 1753, Sloane's natural history collection was enormous—a herbarium of 334 large folio volumes of dried plants; 12,500 vegetable specimens; zoological objects; and stones, minerals, shells, and fossils—without a doubt the finest in the world. Then there were fifty thousand volumes, including seven thousand manuscripts; twenty-three thousand coins and medals; classical, medieval, and oriental antiquities; drawings and paintings; ethnographic objects; and mathematical instruments. Altogether, there were more than eighty thousand objects in addition to the herbarium. Sloane had spent large sums on arranging and cataloging his collections, at least 100,000 pounds.

In his will, Sloane stated that he had made the collection for "the manifestation of the glory of God, the confutation of atheism and its consequences, the use and improvement of physic and other arts and sciences, and benefit of mankind." He wished it to "remain together and not be separate" in the vicinity of London with its "great confluence of people." Parliament decided to meet Sloane's terms, and the British Museum opened in 1759 in Montagu House, a mansion in the Bloomsbury area of London's West End. No admission charge was made, but tickets were required and at least two visits to obtain. By 1803, rules for admission had changed such that one person could apply for up to twelve tickets, thereby redefining the potential audience to include more of the broad public. Uninterested in attracting the wrong sorts, however, rules and expectations of visitors were made clear: "It is expected that Persons who visit the Museum be decent and orderly in their Appearance and Behaviour; the officers being instructed to refuse Admission to, or to cause to withdraw, any one who shall disregard this Caution.—Past Experience has shown the Necessity of this Injunction."[14] By 1810, however, "any person of decent appearance" was admitted without a ticket during restricted hours.[15]

At first there were three departments—Manuscripts, Medals, and Coins; Natural and Artificial Productions; and Printed Books, Maps, Globes, and Drawings. A fourth—Antiquities—was added in 1807, which contained such rarities as the Rosetta stone; the Townley collection of Greek and Roman sculptures, bronzes, and terra cottas; and later, the Portland Vase and the Parthenon Sculptures. Like many collections retrieved from other countries, the question of where these works should be displayed and the possibility of return to their countries and cultures of origin has been a part of public discussion for decades.

In terms of locations and spaces, the collection has been on view in the neo-Grecian building begun by Robert Smirke in 1823 and expanded often since that day.[16] Most significant of these expansions was the separation of the books from the rest of the materials and, as a result, the creation of the independent British Library location (now at St. Pancras) and at the original Bloomsbury site, the Queen Elizabeth II Great Court (aka the Great Court), which was opened by the queen of England in 2000. The glass roof covering the courtyard draws attention to the original circular British Museum Reading Room, a space that now serves as a special exhibition venue. The Court also allows for greater public access to galleries, auditorium space, and classrooms while serving as a connection point to access other portions of the museum as well as a meeting point in the museum.[17] Scholars, explorers, and other travelers on behalf of the British Empire contributed many specimens to the British Museum.[18]

Between 1880 and 1883, the natural history collection was transferred to a twelve-acre site in Kensington; the institution (which became independent in 1963) was known as the British Museum (Natural History) and is now called the Natural History Museum in London. William Flower, its innovative director from 1884 to 1898, divided the collections into a selected and meaningful public exhibition series and a vastly larger reserve or study series for those with special interests (and credentials).[19] Flower believed that scientific research and public instruction were parallel functions of the museum. To this end, he focused on exhibition techniques, especially naturalistic dioramas to display collections. His attention to improving the appeal of specimens led to improvements in basic taxidermy techniques that would further increase the public's interest.

The Natural History Museum's structures consist of a neo-Gothic cathedral to collections built by Alfred Waterhouse in 1881 and the Darwin Centre, a recent addition that enables storage as well as engagement and access to the collections and those who care for some of the millions of insect and plant specimens preserved here, some even collected by Charles Darwin himself. These attributes remain true to Flower's parallel goals of research and instruction as the Centre brings the researchers out of their labs to interact with visitors.

Continental Natural History Museums

The Jardin des Plantes, originally part of the king's garden, was formed in Paris and opened to the public in 1739. Georges-Louis LeClerc, comte de Buffon, its superintendent from 1739 to 1788, used it in writing his thirty-six-volume *Histoire Naturelle*. During the French Revolution in 1793, the Museum National d'Histoire Naturelle was established there. The museum buildings situated in the sixty-acre Jardin des Plantes alongside the Seine provide today's visitors with the opportunity to experience two centuries of natural history museum exhibition techniques. Starting in the Galerie d'anatomie comparee near the park entrance, one can walk by case upon case of articulated skeletons from across the globe. At the other end of the park, however, stands the Grand Galerie de l'evolution opened in 1994. One enters the doors of this impressive nineteenth-century building (designed by Gustave Eiffel) at the lowest level of four floors and is surrounded by steel and glass twenty-first-century exhibition spaces.[20]

The Naturhistoriches Museum in Vienna was founded in 1748, when Emperor Francis I purchased a collection of J. de Ballou of Florence. The museum is housed today in an Italianate building (1881), situated with a twin art museum in a handsome garden. Its collections cover mineralogy, petrography, geology, paleontology, zoology, and botany. Rarities include the finest meteorites in Europe and outstanding prehistory exhibits. While the collection historically included ethnographic materials, including feather ornaments of the Aztecs, they have been transferred to the Museum fur Volkerkunde (1876).[21]

The closest approximation to a natural history museum in Italy today is the Museo di Storia Naturale di Firenze, a cluster of six institutions that are part of the University of Florence, including the Museo Nazionale di Antropologia ed Etnologia; the Museo di Geologia e Paleontologia; and Museo di Mineralogia e Litolgia (which house primarily ethnology and anthropology; geology and paleontology; mineral and lithology collections). Other collections that are part of the museum include a botanical garden, herbarium, and zoo. Tracing its roots to the Medici, the Museo di Storia Naturale opened to the public by Grand Duke Peter Leopold in 1775. It contains wet specimens, live reptiles, and amphibians, mollusks, skeletons, dried bird and mammal skins, mounted specimens, and dioramas. Most unusual of all are wax anatomical models created between 1770 and 1840 in the museum laboratories.[22]

American Beginnings

The first permanent museum in the American English colonies was started in 1773, when the Charleston Library Society decided "to collect materials for a full and accurate natural history of South Carolina." Advertisements were posted to solicit examples of natural products—animal, vegetable, or mineral—and collections were purchased under the advisement of four curators. The society ordered an orrery from David Rittenhouse of Philadelphia and acquired a telescope, camera obscura, hydrostatic balance, and a pair of elegant globes. The earliest collection was destroyed by a fire in 1778, including museum acquisitions and the library's books. It wasn't until the 1790s that interest in reinvigorating the museum resurfaced. Over these years, the Charleston Library Society set about rebuilding its collections and looked to London for inspiration—specifically the British Museum. Early exhibitions during these years were primarily adjunct to the library experience. After a few shifts in its institutional oversight, in 1850 the College of Charleston agreed to house the collection, and the Charleston Museum incorporated in 1915 with its own board of trustees. Since then, the museum has maintained unbroken its historical primacy, leading George G. Simpson of the American Museum of Natural History to deem it, in 1942, "the First Natural History Museum in America."[23]

In Philadelphia, efforts to secure collections were undertaken by Pierre Eugene du Simitiere, the Swiss painter of miniatures who preserved snakes and other natural history specimens in his Curio Cabinet or American Museum, which was opened to the public in 1782. Du Simitiere may have been "the nation's earliest museologist," but far more important was Charles Willson Peale, also of Philadelphia. An accomplished artist, ingenious craftsman, enthusiastic student of nature, and a kind of universal scholar, Peale acquired most of du Simitiere's collection in 1784 to add to some mastodon bones, a preserved paddlefish from the Allegheny River, and paintings of Revolutionary heroes on display in his home. In 1786, he announced that he was forming a museum there: "a Repository for Natural Curiosities," or "the Wonderful Works of Nature," to be arranged according to Linnaean classification. Among other exhibits was a grotto showing snakes and reptiles in their natural surroundings. By 1794, the museum had outgrown Peale's house and moved to the newly completed Philosophical Hall of the American Philosophical Society, which today retains some of its early collections focused on Peale's museum.

Peale was an imaginative and skilled museum director. He developed his own methods of taxidermy and carved larger animals of wood in natural poses to receive the skins. He used arsenic (even though it made him ill) and bichloride of mercury to protect his mounted specimens from insects. He also housed living animals and reptiles in the yard at Independence Hall, the subsequent home of the museum after Philosophical Hall.[24]

Peale's interest in interpreting his "School of Nature" was equally great; he was one of the first to appeal to the general public as well as to the scholar. The Philadelphia Museum and the Baltimore branch developed pioneer systems of gas lighting so as to stay open at night. In addition to a framed catalog after the Linnaean system and an eight-page guidebook, there were lectures, magic-lantern shows, and demonstrations of chemistry and physics (including electricity). Peale's museum, however, received increasingly heavy competition from catch-penny museums and shows devoted solely to entertainment. The City of Philadelphia also took over Independence Hall and charged Peale twelve hundred dollars in annual rent. The result was that the museum began to sacrifice the "rational amusement" of its educational and scientific programs to become more entertaining. By 1820, it featured Signor Hellene, an Italian one-man band who played the Italian viola, Turkish cymbals, tenor drum, Pandean pipes, and Chinese bells. The Peale museums went downhill rapidly after Peale's death in 1827, and the Baltimore and New York ones were soon bankrupt.[25]

Other institutions took root in New York City.[26] John Scudder, who was a naturalist, taxidermist, and youthful curator at John Savage's City Museum there, bought his former employer's ragtag collections and gave his own establishment the designation the "New American Museum," which opened its doors to the public in 1816.[27] Phineas T. Barnum took over Scudder's museum in 1841 and sought to make his fortune by amusing and even bamboozling the public. He never allowed scientific principles to stand in his way. Barnum's American Museum, with more than six hundred thousand accessions, included "industrious fleas," three serpents fed their noonday meals in front of the crowds, two white whales swimming in tanks of salt water, a white elephant from Siam (modern-day Thailand), two orangutans, a hippopotamus ("The Great Behemoth of the Scriptures"), grizzly bears, wolves, and buffalo. In addition, there was a national portrait gallery, panoramas of the Holy Land, and waxwork figures. It is no surprise that Barnum's traveling circus developed from this start.[28]

Despite its emphasis on entertainment, Barnum's American Museum had serious collections of shells, fish, animals, minerals, and geological specimens. When the museum was destroyed by fire in 1865, Barnum talked of building a great new national museum in New York, open to the public without charge. Henry Ward Beecher, Horace Greeley, William Cullen Bryant, and other New Yorkers backed the plan and urged President Andrew Johnson to instruct American ministers and consuls to help collect specimens. Nothing much came of the effort, though Barnum, in union with the Van Amburgh Menagerie Company, set up a New American Museum, which also burned in 1868. His interest in natural history and museums continued, however, and he made gifts of animal skeletons, hides, and other materials chiefly to the Smithsonian Institution, the American Museum of Natural History, and Tufts College. His chief contributions to the museum movement, however, were on the popularization and entertainment side, where his promotional talent and sense of fun were most effective.[29]

Smithsonian Institution

English chemist and mineralogist James Smithson left a contingent bequest to "the United States of America, to found at Washington, D.C. under the name of the Smithsonian Institution, an establishment for the increase and diffusion of knowledge among men." When his heir, a nephew, died unwed and childless, the contingent inheritance became a reality. In 1835, 110 bags of gold sovereigns worth $508,318.46 were shipped to the United States. Smithson had never visited there, and a somewhat startled Congress began to debate what to do with the unprecedented gift.

Proposals were made to use it for a national university, a large museum of natural science, an astronomical observatory, an agricultural experiment station, a normal school for training teachers of natural science, a school for orphaned children, or an agricultural bureau to aid farmers. John Quincy Adams, former president and representative to the legislature, fought hard to keep the fund intact as an endowment for the promotion of science. In 1846, Congress created the Smithsonian Institution, with a board of regents composed of the chief justice of the United States, the vice president, three congressmen, three senators, and six private citizens. The dispute over the use of the money (the income then amounted to about thirty thousand dollars per year) was reflected in the provision that the board erect a building to house a museum with a study collection of scientific materials, a chemical laboratory, a library, an art gallery, and lecture rooms.[30]

The regents chose as their executive or secretary Joseph Henry, one of the leading American scientists of the day, who had done distinguished research in electromagnetism and discovered the principle of the telegraph. Henry thought the increase of knowledge more important than its diffusion; there were "thousands of institutions actively engaged in the diffusion of knowledge in our country," he wrote, "but not a single one which gives direct support to its increase. Knowledge can only be increased by original research, which requires patient thought and laborious and often expensive experiments."[31] Henry passionately argued the merits of pure science and resisted as much as he dared putting Smithsonian income into erecting a large building, acquiring a library, establishing a museum and art gallery, and offering a series of public lectures. He cautiously backed Smithsonian participation in exploring expeditions to the western states, Alaska, and elsewhere; inaugurated an international exchange of scientific publications; and began to publish *Smithsonian Contributions to Knowledge*. And, in what has been called the first crowdsourcing effort within a museum, Henry set up a system of meteorological observations throughout the country, used the telegraph to gather volunteers' data, and created a large weather map that provided new information available to the public daily.[32]

Henry managed to defeat efforts to make the Smithsonian a general copyright library, firing the librarian and transferring the accumulated books to the Library of Congress. He placed the Smithsonian art holdings on permanent loan with the Corcoran Gallery of Art.[33] Henry could not, however, stop the growth of a natural history museum. Spencer Fullerton Baird, a first-rate biologist who became Henry's assistant secretary in 1850, was too clever and too patient for him. Baird thought a United States National Museum would both increase public knowledge of flora and fauna and provide scholars with comparative materials for biological research. Pressure for such a museum came from the exploration of natural resources in the western United States and from Smithsonian participation in international expositions. Both activities brought a stream of specimens and artifacts to Washington.[34]

Baird employed a promising young ichthyologist, George Brown Goode, to arrange Smithsonian and United States Fish Commission exhibits for the Philadelphia Centennial Exposition of 1876. Goode became the leading American museum professional of his day and placed Smithsonian museum activities on a sound scientific basis. He brought back forty-two freight carloads of specimens and objects from the Philadelphia centennial, and after Baird succeeded Henry as secretary, Congress established the United States National Museum in 1879 and provided it with a new home, the present redbrick Arts and Industries Building. Goode argued that they were creating a museum of record to preserve material foundations of scientific knowledge, a museum of research to further scientific inquiry, and an educational museum to illustrate "every kind of material object and every manifestation of human thought and activity." In other words, Goode was determined to collect not only natural history specimens, but also art, historical, and technological objects. The centennial haul included sculpture and graphics, machinery, and decorative arts materials of wood, metal, ceramics, glass, and leather.[35]

Since then, the Smithsonian has grown enormously. Today it consists of nineteen museums, with two new museums in the planning stages, as well as the national zoo and nine research facilities.[36] These museum, education, and research sites house more than 138 million museum objects and specimen, about 80 percent of them in the National Museum of Natural History. This museum has been housed in its own building since 1911 and has sections devoted to anthropology (including what was once the famed Bureau of American Ethnology), botany, entomology, invertebrate and vertebrate zoology, mineral sciences, and paleobiology. The museum has for more than a century led the world in the study, classification, and publication of descriptions of new forms of animals, plants, and fossils. Its huge collections of specimens from all over the globe have permitted systematists to conduct outstanding taxonomic research.[37]

The Smithsonian Institution is a complex mixture of scientific and museum programs. It has been called the "university on the National Mall." Though not entirely an agency of the national government, it receives appropriations from the federal government. According to the Fiscal Year 2022 budget, the Smithsonian's annual budget is approximately $1.06 billion, of which two-thirds is funded through appropriations to support ongoing operations (including Federal staff salaries, collections care, and facilities maintenance) and construction and revitalization of the physical infrastructure, as well as planning and design for future projects.[38] Individual, foundation, and corporate support, along with Smithsonian business ventures, provide the remaining funds. The Smithsonian's vision is to shape "the future by preserving our heritage, discovering new knowledge, and sharing our resources with the world,"[39] thereby demonstrating the institution's leadership in programs and operations that seek to broaden access (particularly through new tools and technologies) and to understand the American experience, particularly history, arts, and culture of all communities in the United States, and unlocking the universe's mysteries as well as understanding the assets and needs of our biodiverse planet.[40]

American Museum of Natural History

American naturalist Albert S. Bickmore[41] was determined that New York City should have a museum of natural history second to none, "affording amusement and instruction to the public" and "teaching our youth to appreciate the wonderful works of the Creator." Bickmore's enthusiasm enlisted the aid of the financial titans of the city, and the state of New York chartered the American Museum of Natural History on April 9, 1869. Bickmore became superintendent of the new institution, which the commissioners of Central Park provided with quarters and exhibit cases on the upper floors of the Arsenal Building in the park.[42]

The American Museum joined with the Metropolitan Museum of Art to secure an arrangement under which New York City provided museum buildings and paid for maintenance and guards, while the boards of trustees furnished collections and the curatorial and educational staffs. President Ulysses S. Grant in 1874 laid the cornerstone of the American Museum's new building on Central Park West, which President Rutherford B. Hayes dedicated three years later. Professor Bickmore resigned as superintendent in 1884 to become curator of a new department of public instruction. He offered schoolteachers a special course in natural history, devised high-quality lantern slides (known as "Bickmore slides"), and soon had reached more than one million persons with his public lectures.[43]

Morris K. Jesup, multimillionaire banker, became president of the American Museum of Natural History in 1881. Jesup attracted wealthy men to support the museum, appointed scholarly curators, and financed museum expeditions, such as Robert E. Peary's expeditions to the North Pole. Jesup liked to see young people in the museum, which he considered a most effective agency "for furnishing education, innocent amusement, and instruction to the people."[44]

Jesup was followed in the museum presidency in 1908 by paleontologist Henry Fairfield Osborn, who developed an ambitious program of fieldwork, scientific research, public exhibition, and engagement. Osborn sensed the public appeal of large fossils, especially those of dinosaurs, and when museum expeditions to the West brought back dinosaur bones, he had the huge skeletons articulated and placed on display. Many scientists considered this innovation radical and vulgar showmanship and insisted that the bones ought to be sorted into drawers and reserved for scientific study. Osborn got Carl E. Akeley, brilliant taxidermist, sculptor, explorer, and inventor, to obtain specimens from which a Hall of African Mammals developed, with twenty-eight habitat groups placed around eight mounted elephants. Further, Osborn developed a well-balanced program of exploration, scientific laboratory work, and exhibition techniques that attracted a large popular audience, including numerous school groups. Publications were of great importance, both the numerous series of scientific reports and the popular, copiously illustrated *Natural History* magazine.[45]

After Osborn's retirement in 1932, the museum secured less flamboyant but more professional administration. Its departments were devoted to astronomy, minerals and gems, paleontology, forestry and conservation, living invertebrates, insects, living fishes, living reptiles, living birds, living mammals, and man and his origins. The museum continued to attract strong financial support from the wealthy and installed the Hayden Planetarium, which offers access to cosmic discovery through exhibits, programs, and online offerings.[46] However, American anthropologist Margaret Mead thought the museum existed for the children and ideally should be planned for twelve-year-olds.

Visiting the museum today, Mead might not recognize some exhibition halls, though she would be thrilled at the evolving approaches taken by the American Museum of Natural History. Over the past two decades, the museum has transitioned narrative messages of the exhibit halls dedicated to particular places into exhibitions that transcend those designations and provide visitors with evidence of the world's complexities and interconnectedness. In addition, opportunities for visitors to connect with content directly (such as the walk-in butterfly conservatory) have been created and, even, improved over time. For example, the Richard Gilder Center for Science, Education, and Innovation, which opened in 2023, enables visitors to see the immediacy of connections to nature through biomimicry as well as expansive approaches to connecting with collections, concepts, and content. Such features engage audiences, such as the insectarium, butterfly vivarium, and floor-to-ceiling collections display of three thousand items from astrophysics to zoology (taking the concept of "open storage" discussed in the previous chapter to new heights, literally!). In addition, the interactive feature *Invisible Worlds* offers a twelve-minute multisensory experience that tells the story of life on earth through the invisible networks that connect all living creatures.

Moreover, a range of experiences across the museum enable visitors to access information on their own terms. The access includes autism-spectrum tours and modes of access and learning geared toward those with mobility challenges, deaf or hard of hearing, and blind or partially sighted guests and offers transcripts, touchable exhibits, and accommodation for service animals. The museum also seeks to connect recent college graduates with pathways to science teaching through the Master of Arts in Teaching (MAT) Earth Science Residency program, a fully paid fellowship program for those interested in STEM education. Established in 2012, the program leverages the museum's unique scientific resources and history of educational leadership to create an environment for learning and application within a natural history museum and with urban partner schools. Graduates leave the program with a degree and specialization in teaching Earth Science for grades 7–12. Indeed, the "natural" in the museum's name has expanded exponentially from the eighteenth-century Enlightenment notions of classifying and creating rational order for the universe to one of inclusion and access, as well as addressing the shortage of qualified teachers in STEM.[47]

Field Museum of Natural History

A third American natural history museum is the result of another world's fair—the World's Columbian Exposition of 1893 in Chicago. Frederick Ward Putnam, curator of the Peabody Museum at Harvard, in 1891 was appointed to head the Department of Anthropology for the exposition, and he urged that the collections shown there become a permanent museum to be known as the Columbian Museum of Chicago.[48] When American entrepreneur Marshall Field, founder of the Chicago-based department store that bore his name, was asked to give money for the proposed museum, he said: "I don't know anything about a museum, and I don't care to know anything about a museum. I'm not going to give you a million dollars." But Edward E. Ayer, an incorporator and the first president, convinced Field that his gift would bring him a kind of immortality, so that he changed his mind and gave one million dollars; other wealthy patrons contributed nearly five hundred thousand dollars. The articles of incorporation of 1893 defined the museum's purpose as "the accumulation and dissemination of knowledge, and the preservation and exhibition of objects illustrating Art, Archaeology, Science and History."[49]

The new museum, opened in 1894 in the Palace of Fine Arts building of the Columbian Exposition in Jackson Park, was generously supported by the elite of Chicago. Marshall Field eventually gave the museum nine million dollars; his nephew Stanley Field was its president for fifty-six years and contributed two million dollars; and his grandson Marshall Field III bestowed another nine million dollars. The museum's name was changed to the Field Museum of Natural History in 1905 and moved into a mammoth white-marble building in Grant Park along the lakeshore in 1921.

The museum has four main departments—anthropology, botany, geology, and zoology—and issues scholarly research publications known as *Fieldiana* in two broad areas (anthropology and life and earth sciences).[50] Its scientific expeditions are numerous; in 1929, seventeen expeditions included Eastern Asia (with Theodore Roosevelt Jr. and Kermit Roosevelt), the Pacific (on Cornelius Crane's yacht, the *Elyria*), West Africa, the South Pacific, the Amazon, Mesopotamia (the Field Museum–Oxford University expedition to Kish), Abyssinia, the Arctic, British Honduras, and the Bahamas.

More recent acquisitions have included the most complete dinosaur skeleton anywhere—a *Tyrannosaurus rex* named "SUE." (The skeleton is ninety percent complete.). Named after the person who discovered it in South Dakota in 1990, the fossil became the center of an intense ownership dispute that resulted in a decision to sell SUE at public auction. The Field Museum acquired the dinosaur in

October 1997 for more than eight million dollars and invested thousands of hours of work to bring the fossil to its fully articulated self. SUE has been on view at the museum since 2000, and it was recently re-installed in the Griffin Halls of Evolving Planet in 2018, with an updated, more accurate portrayal of the *T. rex* skeleton based upon new information uncovered through research. Nearby, interactive media give sensory guidance into the earthly environment sixty-seven million years ago, when SUE roamed the earth, including, sounds of SUE, the feel of its skin, and the smell of a carnivorous dinosaur's breath. SUE's body is also interpreted to better understand dinosaur anatomy.[51]

Other exhibits include Malvina Hoffman's life-sized bronze sculptures of humanity, which she created after traveling the world documenting humankind and returning to the studio to mold and cast 104 works that depict "racial types"—as they were known—to categorize humans.

Commissioned by Museum director Stanley Field, *The Races of Mankind* was on view at the World's Fair of 1933, celebrating the centennial of the city of Chicago. The exhibition was on view for thirty years, and with it came the message that physical differences could be used to categorize

In 1933, the Field Museum opened *The Races of Mankind*. The exhibition featured the work of renowned artist Malvina Hoffman—104 bronze statues of people from around the world—intended as illustrations of "racial types." The Field Museum has undertaken a project to restore 87 of the original 104 sculptures. Half have been reinstalled at the museum in a new exhibition called *Looking at Ourselves: Rethinking the Sculptures of Malvina Hoffman*. The exhibit examines the motivation to create the series, the role they played in the 1933 exhibition, and the persistence of the messaging outlaid therein, as well as current cultural and scientific notions of race. *Courtesy: Field Museum through Google Arts and Culture.*

human beings into races. The museum has re-installed half of the works in a new exhibition, *Looking at Ourselves: Rethinking the Sculptures of Malvina Hoffman*, which examines the motivation to create the series, the role they played in the exhibition, and the persistence of the messaging outlaid therein, as well as current cultural and scientific notions of race. Viewers are asked to consider culture, race, and identity through these bronze types, as well as to recognize that each sculpture was modeled from an actual person—a fact that had been elided over the decades since their debut on June 6, 1933, in the Hall of Man at the Century of Progress Exposition.[52]

Anthropological Museums

Many natural history museums contain antiquities and ethnological materials, as noted with regard to the three American museums we have just discussed. Other museums are devoted primarily to the anthropological field. Below, examples from Netherlands and France are examined before we proceed to the examples from the United States. As each of these examples unfolds, consider how the collections were created and why. Who is represented? And, ultimately, why are human remains present in the museum context at all? Certainly, we have witnessed an "Othering" of cultures beyond one's own—consider Malvina Hoffman's meticulous, curiosity-inspired, and documentary-informed sculptures of humankind discussed above. However, unlike that and museum examples we have seen thus far, anthropological museums are not only reflective of the human experience; they are literal *embodiments* of it. Thus, learning about the history and function of anthropology museums requires an interrogation of colonialism, an awareness and welcome of engagement with source communities, and a hope for the capacity to repair harm through repatriation and restitution initiatives.[53]

As the first ethnographic museum in Europe, the National Museum of Ethnology was founded in 1837 by F. B. von Siebold, who had lived in Japan and gathered an ethnographic collection of some five thousand objects. The museum suffered for a century because of inadequate housing, but slowly it accumulated an important collection of materials from outside the European and classic regions. Transfers from the Royal Cabinet of Rarities, the International Colonial Exhibition held at Amsterdam in 1883, and the National Museum of Antiquities greatly strengthened the museum's holdings. In 1939, it was able to expand its exhibits as a result of acquiring the former building of the University Hospital. Its chief strengths lie in materials from Africa, China, Indonesia, Japan, Korea, Latin America, North America, and Oceania.[54] Today the museum is part of a trio of institutions in Netherlands, which together comprise the National Museum of World Cultures: Wereldmuseum Leiden (formerly the National Museum of Ethnology); the Wereldmuseum Amsterdam (formerly the Tropenmuseum); and the Wereldmuseum Berg en Dal (formerly the Africa Museum). In addition, since 2017, they have joined forces with Wereldmuseum Rotterdam. Among these four institutions, collections bridge past and present particularly though exhibitions of contemporary art: for instance, at Berg en Dal, exhibits showcase works produced in Africa and the diaspora, including North and South America and the Caribbean. Significantly, they recognize the impact of colonialism on their collection, as well as their very existence as institutions. Yet, they attempt to contextualize their past around the objects in their collection and the capacity they have to tell human stories. Ultimately, the museums conflate past and present by conceiving of collections that can make visitors "curious about the vast cultural diversity that enriches the world" and can show visitors that "besides the differences, we are all the same: human."[55]

The Musée de l'Homme (Museum of Mankind or Museum of Humanity) in Paris is an anthropology museum created in 1937 for a World's Fair, the Exposition Internationale des Arts et Techniques dans la Vie Moderne (International Exposition of Art and Technology in Modern Life). It is related to a previous institution, the Musée d'Ethnographie du Trocodéro, which was established in 1878, and to the Muséum national d'histoire naturelle (MNHN), which was founded in 1793, though its origins stem back to the seventeenth-century royal gardens. With the Musée de l'Homme, anthropologist-founder Paul Rivet coined the name for the new museum; he believed that "humanity is an indivisible whole, in space and in time," and that scholarship should break down the barriers of political geography and synthesize the artificial classifications of physical anthropology, prehistory, archaeology, ethnology, folklore, sociology, and philology.[56] The museum has been innovative in its exhibits, using sound ethnography and aesthetic display but subordinating them to the exposition of anthropological theory. It seeks to illustrate the function of the objects against the total background of the culture. The museum seeks to address three themes of the present, past, and future by asking "Who are we? Where do we come from? Where are we headed?"[57]

Over the past decade, however, some of the collections have been transferred to two other museums in France, thus calling into question the role of the Musée de l'Homme. The ethnographic collections were relocated to the new Musée du Quai Branly–Jacques Chirac in Paris and the Museum of European and Mediterranean Civilizations (MuCEM) in Marseille, France. Musée du Quai Branly–Jacques Chirac focuses on Indigenous art and cultures of Africa, the Americas, Asia, and Oceania. (The names in the title refer to French scientist Édouard Branly and the French president, in the tradition of creating museums as monuments to French presidents in recognition of their time in office.) The museum, which opened in 2006, houses collections from a number of institutions, including Musée de l'Homme, and newly acquired additional ethnographic objects, photographs, and documents. The MuCEM also absorbed collections from the Musée de l'Homme, as well as the Museum of Popular Arts and Traditions and other French institutions, to create an emphasis on Mediterranean heritage past and present.

As part of the ongoing debate about the repatriation of cultural heritage, these French institutions have been the focus of discussions about collections building, and in particular the construction of collections through the removal of objects from former French colonies during periods of colonialism. French president Emmanuel Macron commissioned a report (referred to as the "Restitution Report") in 2018, which recommended that "objects that were removed and sent to mainland France without the consent of their countries of origin be permanently returned—if the country of origin asks for them."[58] While some returns have been made, the overall impact is that the international discussion about restitution of looted cultural heritage has been given new momentum, with new activity in this area currently underway among key museums of all types, not solely anthropological museums. (A more detailed account of restitution appears in Section III.)

American Example: Penn Museum

Anthropological and archaeological museums in the United States were framed around excavation and innovation, as well as knowledge construction: *Who are we? What are our origins? Where did we come from? Where are we going?*

A decade after the siting of the World's Fair as the 1876 Centennial Exposition in Philadelphia, the University of Pennsylvania Museum of Archaeology and Anthropology was established in 1887. Called the Penn Museum today, the institution calls upon visitors to "explore our shared humanity," boasting over a million "world wonders" spanning ten thousand years of history that chronicle "an ongoing exploration of the human experience."[59] Penn Museum situates both its history and its current mission around human experience by bridging archaeology with anthropology—by studying objects made by humans with the science of humanity, the museum.

The museum's origins are tied to an expedition to the site of Nippur in modern-day Iraq; the results of that archaeological expedition formed the inaugural exhibition, which opened on December 13, 1889. Over its 150-year history, teams of scientists from Penn Museum have conducted more than three hundred archaeological and anthropological expeditions, which have contributed new knowledge through field research, as well as acquisitions for study. This practice of sponsored excavations throughout the Mediterranean and the Near East was developed by teams in the United States and Europe, thus leading to research and recovery of artifacts that could then be shared with the host countries and research museums. Materials from expeditions that Penn supported are often

‹ ONLINE COLLECTIONS

Download Datasets

Download collection data using the links below. This data is provided 'as-is' — information may be incomplete or outdated. The Creative Commons Attribution 3.0 Unported (CC BY 3.0) license applies to all downloaded datasets. Images are not included.

These files contain metadata about the objects in the Penn Museum collection. See About Collections Search for details on data types and meanings. Some records have more information than others. Images are not included.

Last updated October 28, 2018

- All (379,489 objects)
  - csv (zipped 17.5 MB, unzipped 109 MB)
  - xml (zipped 22.7 MB, unzipped 383.9 MB)
  - json (zipped 20.3 MB, unzipped 215.8 MB)

- African (19,001 objects)

- American (152,757 objects)

- Asian (22,435 objects)

- Egyptian (47, 847 objects)

- European (9,123 objects)

- Historic (2,513 objects)

- Mediterranean (28,081 objects)

- Near East (73,992 objects)

- Oceanian (22,065 objects)

If you have questions, contact digitalmedia@pennmuseum.org

Penn Museum, like many museums, hosts content online. Here, the data portal documents global human history and allows downloads of data regarding a majority of the collection (more than 379,000 items, as of February 2024). *Screencap created February 2024, https://www.penn.museum/collections/objects/data.php.*

supplemented by field notes, bibliographies and research materials, as well as ethnographic information. Thus, their collections are well-documented and offer excellent source material for researchers as well as museum visitors. Because of this, many of the collections in Penn Museum have known *provenience*—that is, the immediate context from which an item was removed, such as its place of discovery and place of origin. Some also have known *provenance*, that is, the ownership of an object from the time of its creation to the present day.[60]

Items not obtained through excavation were purchased from collectors, as well as dealers. In this way, Penn Museum, among other institutions, thus played a leading role in the exchange, study, and display of cultural goods, including art and antiquities. For instance, dealers, such as Loo Ching-Tsai (referred to as C. T. Loo), exported antiques and archaeological pieces from China through his gallery networks in Paris and New York.[61] Loo was the pre-eminent dealer of Chinese artifacts in the United States during the interwar years (approximately 1916–1930s), subject to the whims of collectors' tastes, as well as the abilities of institutions to fund purchases from him. As such, Loo contributed to the culture of illegal acquisition and tomb-robbing, in order to feed a market that he helped to establish. His methods are dubious, through his suggestion that items on the market were "owned by no one" or "accidentally discovered." Today, protections, such as the UNESCO ruling of 1970, are in place and seek to prevent the transfer of goods in this way.[62]

It is important to note, however, that the ability of museums in the United States to display cultural artifacts is part of the beauty of the museum as an institution, surely; it simultaneously discloses the ways in which museums continue to serve as storehouses and tombs—literally and figuratively.

Penn Collections

Penn Museum galleries are framed around geography and cultural perspectives with eleven permanent galleries, as of 2023: Africa, Asia, Egypt, Sphinx, Middle East, Eastern Mediterranean, Etruscan, Greece, Rome, Native American Voices, and Mexico and Central America. In addition, Penn Museum collections may be grouped into three areas: physical anthropology (remains of humans and non-human primates); archaeology (represented by items recovered or discovered through excavation); and ethnology (represented by the tangible and intangible heritage of living people). Material from the physical anthropology collection are available for research only, whereas material from archaeology and ethnology are available for research, curation, and display.

For example, African ethnographic and archaeological items comprise exhibit materials from the Moroccan collection (gathered through personal travels in 1898 and subsequently donated to the museum), the 1936–1937 expedition of Sierra Leone, among several other collections. In 2019, the African galleries were newly renovated and re-installed to feature three hundred objects from twenty-one countries, in an effort to show the diversity of Africa. The re-visioning and re-installation was undertaken by curator Tukufu Zuberi as part of a collaborative effort with African museum directors, curators, and contemporary artists. Situated among the collections are installations of contemporary textiles, sculptures, and mosaics, including a dress designed by Breanna Moore and Emerson Ruffin called *Dress*. This piece was created with artists from Ghana as a two-piece garment made of a white skirt in Ghanian-inspired kente cloth with embroidery and a blue-and-gold bodice inspired by Ethiopian dynastic symbolism.[63]

Penn's physical anthropology collections include a collection of 1,300 human crania (skulls), acquired by the museum in 1966. Known as the Morton Collection, named after the physician who collected them in the nineteenth century, they were gathered as part of an effort to study human differences. Morton's since-disproven work is now understood as a method in helping fuel public thought about enslavement, racial inequality, and its justification. Such collections are still evident across the medical field and museum collections. Thus, Penn's items are part of an ongoing review.[64] To this end, the Museum has moved a collection of fifty-five crania of enslaved individuals from public view to a private classroom: the museum plans to repatriate or rebury these skulls. In addition, the museum has buried the remains of nineteen Black residents of Philadelphia.[65]

Current efforts are underway to rectify past actions beyond the cranial collection, including retention of human remains removed from a fire at the MOVE communal residence in Philadelphia in 1985. Due to an extended investigation, and as a result of the involvement of at least two Penn faculty members (Alan Mann and Janet Monge) to identify remains from the fire, bones of two children were held at the Penn Museum, and later the Princeton Museum, without the knowledge or consent of their living family members.[66] In November 2020, the city of Philadelphia apologized for the "immeasurable and enduring harm" caused by the bombing due to the "cruelty, brutality, and inhumanity of the MOVE Bombing." In 2021, the Penn Museum also apologized for retaining the collections: however, the presence of human remains at Penn discloses more than mere possession. As protestors have cited, the violence of the initial incident "overlaps with the violence of academic institutions keeping the remains of Black people rather than relinquishing those remains for burial."[67]

The Penn Museum has affirmed its commitment "to the ethical stewardship of any and all human remains in [their] care, and to prioritize human dignity as [they] work towards a respectful resolution." Further, the museum has vowed "to be as transparent as possible in the assessment of any credible new evidence that may come to light."[68] The museum returned any remains associated with MOVE to the families in July 2021. Beyond this one example, the museum has received recommendations of several actions by which to do better: reassessing institutional practices on collecting, storing, displaying, and researching human remains; renovating the physical anthropological spaces; hiring a chief diversity officer; and creating a new faculty-curator position to serve bioanthropology and bioarchaeology. While collections are at the forefront of these recommendations, also evident are aspirations of bringing the entire institution into the responsibility of custodial care. Because anthropological and archaeological museums, as all museums, can function as sites of research, constraints must be placed upon the "examination" of human remains. In addition, related research activity must bear in mind Penn's promise of "an ongoing exploration of the human experience," which ought to privilege identity, respect, and dignity over all else.

Related Example: The Mütter Museum

Given the manner through which early athenaeums and natural history museums would have also done double duty as quasi-anthropological museums, one particular institution deserves mention and fuller discussion due to its history as well as its current address of critical issues in museums. The Mütter Museum and Historic Medical Library, part of the College of Physicians of Philadelphia, is a medical history and science museum. Founded in 1787, the College of Physicians is a medical organization, not an actual degree-granting college, and its work is "to advance the science of medicine and to thereby lessen human misery."[69] It has served as a place for the profession, as well as the public, to learn about medicine in myriad ways, including collections. One of these ways is through object-based learning that can come from museum collections. Founded in 1863 by college fellow Dr. Thomas Dent Mütter, the museum displays collections in a "cabinet museum," or "cabinet of curiosity" setting, featuring wax models, antique medical equipment, and anatomical and pathological specimens, including human remains.

As is the case with other institutions with collections that include human remains, the Mütter Museum is undergoing internal discussions around ethical standards and practices. At issue is the nature and manner by which the collections were acquired and how they are displayed. Beginning in late September 2022, with the arrival of a new museum director, a volcanic debate erupted over the ethics of the museum's processes and procedures. To address these questions, the Mütter has begun this process of examination and is in the early stages of an audit of the collections to ensure the accuracy of the records, as well as the provenance, and to ensure the consent and respectful display of human beings. Collections are being scrutinized in terms of the acquisition, display, and interpretation of materials that were acquired since the museum was established more than 150 years ago. Some re-contextualization, which had begun a year earlier, remains in place, pointing to the breadth of work involved. For instance, one of the displays with human skulls was changed so that more context could be added to give details about the human beings, their ages, and cause of death (and ultimately a rationale for their then-legal manner of acquisition). One such label read *Veronica Huber, Salzburg, aged eighteen, executed for murder of her child.* Accompanying it is information that acknowledges the practice of collecting skulls as "discriminatory, non-consensual, and degrading."[70]

Importantly, it is worth noting that in addition to a review of the physical collections, the digital collections are also being reviewed, including museum content on YouTube, again with the lens on ethics and consent. As the museum works through this process, it is inviting feedback from the community, including longtime employees and supporters of the museum. Their work, appropriately called a Postmortem Project, began in October 2023 and is ongoing as of this writing.[71]

Throughout this process, staff at the Mütter, along with their review team, are being guided by the Codes of Ethics from the American Alliance of Museums, the International Council of Museums, and the ICOM Code of Ethics for Natural History Museums. Beyond the questions over human remains and how they should be displayed, there is a broader disc ussion about the future of the museum, and what its role should be.

The Mütter is not alone in this important work. Conversations are being held in other institutions with collections of human remains, including many of those noted earlier in this chapter. For instance, Smithsonian Institution secretary, Lonnie Bunch, announced in August 2023 that the Institution, and in particular, its Natural History Museum, would continue working to repatriate human remains, which has been a work-in-progress for several decades: since the passage of the National Museum of the American Indian Act in 1989 and the related legislation referred to as NAGPRA (Native American Graves and Repatriation Act), the Smithsonian has repatriated the remains of more than five thousand people. While much of the Institution's work has been focused on Indigenous people, beginning in 2023, the Smithsonian established a Human Remains Task Force to develop a policy that addresses the future of all human remains held in their collections.[72]

While the Mütter collections noted above often have the interest of human illness and medical condition at their focus, other collections were gathered with different aims. In the case of the Smithsonian, the head of the anthropology division from 1903 to 1941, anthropologist Ales Hrdlicka, oversaw the acquisition of hundreds of human brains and thousands of other remains. The overwhelming majority of these remains were taken without the consent of the deceased or their family members. Furthermore, Hrdlicka's acquisition of human remains were focused on people of color and Indigenous people to support his scientific (and now debunked) research about race and evidence of White superiority. Secretary Bunch came out with a strong statement against his institution's role in the research and collection of human remains as conducted by Hrdlicka calling it "abhorrent and dehumanizing work . . . carried out under the Smithsonian's name. As secretary of the Smithsonian, I condemn these past actions and apologize for the pain caused by Hrdlicka and others at the institution who acted unethically in the name of science, regardless of the era in which their actions occurred."[73]

As with the Smithsonian, all museums must come to terms with the fact that some actions deemed acceptable at one point are no longer considered so. Complicating this simple statement is the fact that because museums have pasts *and collections that reflect earlier behaviors, actions, and decisions*, institutions have a responsibility to do what is right and to move forward, *ethically*. In this regard, Bunch noted, "the human remains still housed in our collections is certainly illustrative of the Smithsonian's darkest history. This is our inheritance, and we accept the responsibility to address these wrongs to the fullest extent possible."[74]

For Further Consideration

The popularity of world's fairs and their use of dioramas, as well as methods of display that privilege the collector over the collected through placement as well as presumed "Othering," leave us to question whether the heyday of the natural history or anthropological museums has come and gone. As noted throughout in this volume, museum exhibitions are interpretations; and yet, the bringing together of collections and the assertion of control through constructions of knowledge in the form of exhibition content can, ultimately, incite anger, conflict, and controversy. So, too, can the support of museums by philanthropists whose beliefs and actions appear to be at odds with the goals and mission of the institutions they support, as mentioned in the previous chapter. At question here is the American Museum of Natural History and David Koch, both of whom were called into question by an advocacy group, Not an Alternative, who expressed outrage that Koch sits on the Board and regularly funds museum initiatives, even as his corporation, Koch Industries, plays a significant role in the creation of greenhouse gas emissions. Koch also funds actions that obfuscate climate science so as to dim attention to the role his industries play in climate change.

To draw attention to this issue, Not an Alternative organized a pop-up exhibit—*The Natural History Museum*, in September 2014—to "affirm the truth of science" by "looking at the presentation of natural history" and cultivating a mode of inquiry that calls into question the perspectives of "capitalist enterprises, corporate philanthropists, and mainstream political lobbyists" who look at science through their own lenses. In an open letter to museums from members of the scientific community, more than 150 authors cited AAM's Code of Ethics in stating concern between "museums of science and natural history with those who profit from fossil fuels or fund lobby groups that misrepresent climate science." Their call for action is quite clear: "we believe that the only ethical way forward for our museums is to cut all ties with the fossil fuel industry and funders of climate science obfuscation."[75]

The practice of *The Natural History Museum* is one of institutional critique that involves educational events, programming, and critical curation, such as *Mining the HMNS: An Investigation by The Natural History Museum*. *Mining the HMNS* asks questions about museums and sponsorships, investigating the relationship between the Houston Museum of Natural Sciences and its sponsors while examining the immediate environment and air quality of the area, including petrochemical plants and refineries. The exhibition also "highlights the voices and stories that are excluded: those of the predominantly low-income Latino and African-American communities living in the shadow" of these plants.[76] While some museums have committed to divesting of fossil fuel ties, the energy industry is only one industry under attack.

Such calls for museums to divest of fossil fuel ties are only one tentacle of a broader awareness among the public about museums and power. In an age of 24/7 newsfeeds and easy access to the social-media or web-based timelines of an individual or an institution, it is worth asking whether museums should take sponsorship from any companies. And if so, what can museums do to ensure that the ethical values of sponsors match their own? For as much as we can see the extent to which collections can be controlled, contained, restrained, and constrained (think of the cabinets of curiosities mentioned at the beginning of this chapter), museums are not solely about collections and the construction of knowledge through them. Even in the telling of the stories of earth's history and the origins of humankind, a range of possibilities exists: museums are sites of provocation where collections are starting points for narratives built upon, around, and through them. And, in particular, as Section III of this volume reminds us, museums are also sites of convening, discussion, action, and protest.

Notes

1. Paula Findlen, *Possessing Nature: Museums, Collecting and Scientific Culture in Early Modern Italy* (Berkeley: University of California Press, 1994), 398; Eilean Hooper-Greenhill, *Museums and the Shaping of Knowledge* (London: Routledge, 1994).
2. Don D. Fowler, and David R. Wilcox, eds., *Philadelphia and the Development of American Archaeology* (Tuscaloosa: University of Alabama Press, 2003), xii; David Hurst Thomas, "The First American Archaeologist," chap. 3 in *Skull Wars: Kennewick Man, Archaeology and the Battle for Native American Identity* (New York: Basic Books, 2000).
3. Charles Willson Peale, *A Walk through the Philadelphia Museum* (Philadelphia: np, 1892), 6–7.
4. David Murray, *Museums: Their History and Their Use*, 3 vols. (Glasgow: J. Maclehose and Sons, 1904), 1:45–73, includes a bibliography and list of museums in the U.K.; Alma S. Wittlin, *Museums: In Search of a Usable Future* (Cambridge: MIT Press, 1970), 17–22; P. J. P. Whitehead, "Museums in the History of Zoology," *Museums Journal* 70 (1970–1971): 51.
5. Murray, *Museums*, 1:25, 27, 78–80; Wittlin, *Museums: In Search*, 39–53; Whitehead, "Museums in the History of Zoology," 51–52; Silvio A. Bedini, "The Evolution of Science Museums," *Technology and Culture* 5 (1965): 2–6, 11–12; Germain Bazin, *The Museum Age* (New York: Universe Books, 1967), 62, 144; Willy Ley, *Dawn of Zoology* (Englewood Cliffs: 1968), 121–61, 268–73; Giuseppe Olmi, "Science-Honor-Metaphor: Italian Cabinets of the sixteenth and seventeenth Centuries," in *Grasping the World: The Idea of the Museum*, eds. Donald Preziosi and Claire Farago (Hants, UK: Ashgate, 2004).
6. Murray, *Museums*, 1:95–96, 103–104, 115–17; Whitehead, "Museums in the History of Zoology," 52; Bedini, "The Evolution," 2–6; Holger Jacobaeus, *Muséum Regium, seu Catalogus rerum*, Hafniae: literis reg. cels. typogr. Joachim Schmetgen, 1696.
7. At Bologna, the Aldrovandi-Cospi collection was joined by the Instituto delle Scienze of the Conte de Luigi Ferdinando Marsigli. The Medici in Florence collected natural science specimens as well as art. Ferrante and Francesco Imperati had a well-known museum at Naples, while the Jesuit Athanasius Kircher, who considered Noah's ark to have been the most complete natural history museum, was director of the Museo Kircheriano in Rome. Bedini, "The Evolution," 4–6, 11–17; Murray, *Museums*, 1:2, 106–107; Findlen, *Possessing Nature*, 407.
8. Bazin, *The Museum Age*, 115; Wittlin, *Museums: In Search*, 64–65; Bedini, "The Evolution," 25–26; Murray, *Museums*, 1:205–30.

9. Typical rarities in the collection were "unicornu marinum" (narwhal); "dodar, from the Island Mauritius" (the famed, now-extinct dodo); "a cherry-stone, upon one side S. Geo: and the Dragon perfectly cut; and on the other side 88 Emperour's faces"; "Pohaton, King of Virginia's habit all embroidered with shells, of Roanoke"; "Henry the 8 his Stirrups, Haukeshoods, Gloves"; and "Anne of Bullens Nightvayle embroidered with silver."

10. Collections have been scattered—the geological and physical collection to the Clarendon Building, the ethnographic specimens to the Pitt Rivers Museum, and natural history material to the adjoining Oxford University Museum of Natural History. The books and manuscripts were sent to the Bodleian Library. The Ashmolean Museum of Art and Archaeology (1894), now known simply as The Ashmolean, is a general collection of classical through contemporary art, antiquities, works on paper, and numismatics.

11. Robert Theodore Gunther, *Early Science in Oxford*, 15 vols., Oxford, 1923-1967, 1:43-47 and 3:280-333, 46-366, 391-447; Mea Allan, *The Tradescants: Their Plants, Gardens and Museum, 1570-1662* (London: M. Joseph, 1964); Bazin, *The Museum Age*, 141, 144-45; Whitehead, "Museums in the History of Zoology," 54-55; Murray, *Museums*, 1:107-11; Ley, *Dawn of Zoology*, 202-203; Ashmolean Museum, *Treasures of the Ashmolean Museum: An Illustrated Souvenir of Art, Archaeology and Numismatics* (Oxford: Ashmolean Museum, 1970), ii-iii, no. 24; F. J. North, "On Learning How to Run a Museum," *Museums Journal* 51 (April 1951): 4-5; (June 1951): 63-66; D. B. Harden, "The Ashmolean Museum—Beaumont Street," *Museums Journal* 52 (February 1952): 265-70.

12. Jim Harris and Senta German, "Agile Objects," *Journal of Museum Education* 42:3 (2017): 248-57.

13. Rachel Hatzipanagos, "The 'decolonization' of the American Museum," *Washington Post*, October 11, 2018, https://www.washingtonpost.com/nation/2018/10/12/decolonization-american-museum/. Hatzipanagos offers a definition of decolonizing museums.

14. Original Letters and Papers 2 (14 January 1803): fol. 760, as quoted in British Museum, "Chapter IV: The Trustees and Officers of the British Museum: Their Attitudes and Practices During the Administration of Joseph Planta," 6.

15. Edward P. Alexander, "Sir Hans Sloane and the British Museum," in *Museum Masters*, 19-42; G. R. de Beer, *Sir Hans Sloane and the British Museum*, London, 1953, 13-49, 50-95, 108-34, 138-39, 143-53, 160-61; E. St. John Brooks, *Sir Hans Sloane: The Great Collector and His Circle* (London: Batchworth Press, 1954), 13-77, 78-118, 176-201, 209-10, 218-23; Edward Miller, *That Noble Cabinet: A History of the British Museum* (Athens: Ohio University Press, 1974), 26, 36-39, 41, 42-46, 70-71, 74, 77-79, 86-87, 92; J. Mordaunt Crook, *The British Museum* (London: Praeger, 1972), 42-49, 52-54, 65-66; Murray, *Museums*, 1:127-44, 171-72; Kenneth Hudson, *A Social History of Museums: What the Visitors Thought* (Atlantic Highlands: Humanities Press, 1975), 8-10, 18-21, 38, 40; Frank Charlton Francis, *Treasures of the British Museum* (London: Thames and Hudson, 1967), 10; James Britten, *The Sloane Herbarium*, rev. and ed. J. E. Dandy (London: British Museum, 1958); Henry C. Shelley, *The British Museum: Its History and Treasures* (Boston: L.C. Page & Co., 1911), 59-62; Wittlin, *Museums: In Search*, 102-105; Kelly Elizabeth Yasaitis, "Collecting Culture and the British Museum," *Curator* 49, no. 4 (October 2006). Attention to access to the British Museum as part of the larger freedoms of women is carefully paid in Virginia Woolf's fictional account *A Room of One's Own* (1929), which explores women as writers and characters of fiction. In this account, the narrator is denied admission to the library (presumably the British Museum, which functioned as the British Library as well). Woolf writes how she is met by a gentleman who commented that "ladies are only admitted to the library if accompanied by a Fellow of the College or furnished with a letter of introduction." See Rachel Bowlby, *Virginia Woolf: Edited and Introduced by Rachel Bowlby* (London, New York, 1992), quoting pages 7-8 in Woolf.

16. Miller, *That Noble Cabinet*, 74-76, 85-86, 96-108, 111-15, 191-223, 299-320, 327, 336-39, 355-56; Crook, *British Museum*, 62, 66-71, 118, 128, 216, 226-29; Francis, *Treasures of the British Museum*, 22, 25; Hermann Justus Braunholtz, *Sir Hans Sloane and Ethnography* (London: British Museum, 1970), 19-20, 37-45; Hudson, *Social History of Museums*, 39-40.

17. British Museum, http://www.britishmuseum.org.

18. In the fall of 2023, approximately 1,500 items were found to have been stolen, with another 350 items damaged by having gold removed, and another 140 items damaged from tool marks. Some items in the Greek and Roman collections, as well as gems of semiprecious stones and glass dating

from the fifteenth century BCE to the nineteenth century CE, were believed to have been taken by a museum staff person. See Alex Marshall, "British Museum Fires Worker Accused of Stealing Gold and Gems," *New York Times*, August 16, 2023, https://www.nytimes.com/2023/08/16/arts/design/british -museum-theft.html; Alex Marshall, "British Museum Details Extent of Stolen and Damaged Items," *New York Times*, December 12, 2023, https://www.nytimes.com/2023/12/12/arts/design/british -museum-missing-items.html.

19. Miller, *That Noble Cabinet*, 224-44; Crook, *British Museum*, 199-200; Edward Edwards, *Lives of the Founders of the British Museum: With Notices of Its Chief Augmentors and Other Benefactors, 1570-1870*, 1870, reprint (New York: B. Franklin, 1969), 333-36, 487-510, 601-607; Francis, *Treasures of the British Museum*, 14-15, 20-21; Karl P. Schmidt, "The Nature of the Natural History Museum," *Curator* 1 (January 1958): 23; William Henry Flower, *Essays on Museums and Other Subjects Connected with Natural History* (New York: Macmillan, 1898), 15-22, 37-41; James A. Bateman, "The Functions of Museums in Biology," *Museums Journal* 74 (March 1975): 159-64; William T. Stearn, *The Natural History Museum at South Kensington* (London: Heinemann, 1981).

20. Whitehead, "Museums in the History of Zoology," 156; Flower, *Essays on Museums*, 41-47; Rene Taton, ed., *History of Science*, 3 vols. (New York: Basic Books, 1963-1965), 3:325-26; *Museums of the World: A Directory of 17,000 Museums in 48 Countries*, compiled by Eleanor Braun (New York: Bowker, 1973), 78-79; *Guide des Musées de France* (Fribourg: Office du Livre, 1970), 136-37; *Blue Guide: Paris* (London: E. Benn, 1968), 108-10; *Librarie Larousse, Dictionnaire de Paris*, Paris, 1964, 285-86, 358; Murray, *Museums*, 2:93; Hermann Heinrich Frese, *Anthropology and the Public: The Role of Museums* (Leiden: E. J. Brill, 1960), 20, 26-29; Paul Lemoine, "National Museum of Natural History . . . Paris," *Natural History Magazine* (London), 5, (January 1935): 4-19; Bateman, "Museums in Biology," 161; Asma, *Stuffed Animals and Pickled Heads*, 82-86, 170-78; Jacques Maigret, "Aesthetics in the Service of Science: The Grande Galerie de l'Evolution in Paris," *Museum* 48, no. 2 (1996); Michael A. Osborne, "Zoos in the Family," Robert J. Hoage and William A. Deiss, eds., *New Worlds, New Animals: From Menagerie to Zoological Park in the Nineteenth Century* (Baltimore: Johns Hopkins University Press, 1996), 33-38.

21. Flower, *Essays on Museums*, 41-47; *Museums of the World*, 21; Murray, *Museums*, 2: 245-46; Karl Baedeker, *Austria Handbook for Travelers*, 12th ed. (Leipzig: Baedeker, 1929), 103-108.

22. See "Sistema Museale di Ateneo," University of Florence, https://www.sma.unifi.it/?newlang=eng. "La Specola" is the headquarters of the museum. The site is undergoing a multi-year redevelopment (2019-2023) that involves the relocation of several collections, as well as a transition to include more engaging, varied opportunities for learning experiences. For the history of La Specola, see Maria Luisa Azzarol Puccetti, "La Specola, the Zoological Museum of the University of Florence," *Curator* 15 (1972): 93-112; Bazin, *The Museum Age*, 163.

23. Laura M. Bragg, "The Birth of the Museum Idea in America," *Charleston Museum Quarterly* 1 (First Quarter 1923): 3-13; Paul M. Rea, "A Contribution to Early Museum History in America," *American Association of Museums Proceedings* 9 (1915): 53-65; William G. Mazyck, *The Charleston Museum: Its Genesis and Development* (Charleston: Walker, Evans & Cogswell Co., 1908), 5, 28; Hudson, *Social History of Museums*, 31-33; Barry L. Stiefel, "'Our Museum—Another Handsome Contribution': A Comparative Case Study of the Charleston Museum during its First Formative 150 Years," edited by Juilee Decker, *Collections: A Journal for Museum and Archives Professionals* 11:2 (Spring 2015): 103-14; the Simpson quote appears in George G. Simpson, "The First Natural History Museum in America," *Science* N.S., 96:2490 (September 18, 1942), 261-63.

24. Steven Conn, *Museums and American Intellectual Life, 1876-1926* (Chicago: University of Chicago Press, 1998), 35-37, 38-43, 45-47; Joel J. Orosz, *Curators and Culture: The Museum Movement in America, 1740-1870* (Tuscaloosa: University of Alabama Press, 1990), 119-27, 187-95; Fowler and Wilcox, *Philadelphia*; Patricia M. Williams, *Museums of Natural History and the People Who Work in Them* (New York: St. Martins, 1973).

25. William E. Lingelbach, "An Early American Historian," in *Bookmen's Holiday: Notes and Studies Written and Gathered in Tribute to Harry Miller Lydenberg* (New York: New York Public Library, 1943), 355-61; Hans Huth, "Pierre Eugene du Simitiere and the Beginnings of the American Historical Museum," *Pennsylvania Magazine of History and Biography* 69 (October 1945): 315-25; Charles Coleman Sellers, *Charles Willson Peale* (New York: Scribner, 1969), 203-11; Edward P. Alexander, "Charles Willson Peale,"

in *Museum Masters*, 43-78; E. P. Alexander, "Bringing History to Life: Philadelphia and Williamsburg," *Curator* 4 (1961): 61; Hudson, *Social History of Museums*, 33-36; Sellers, *Peale*, 212-17, 219, 221-22, 230, 241, 264-65, 281, 293-301, 303, 333, 335, 340-41.

26. In Philadelphia, at the start of the nineteenth century, the Academy of Natural Sciences convened its first meeting. This group of a dozen or so apothecaries, chemists, and a dentist came together first to socialize and then to collect natural history specimens and to pursue research into natural phenomena. Though slow to open their study collections to the public, they sponsored lectures for members and friends, and by 1839, their library maintained regular public hours. By the time the Philadelphia Peale Museum doors closed in 1850, the Academy of Natural Sciences was open to the public, and in 1866, it welcomed more than thirty-four thousand visitors. In 1868, it displayed the first American dinosaur *Hadrosaurus* from Haddonfield, New Jersey. Sellers, *Peale*, 245, 256, 331, 337, 350-51, 380, 386, 394, 401, 408.

27. Orosz, *Curators and Culture*, 75-80.

28. P. T. Barnum, *Struggles and Triumphs: Or, Forty Years' Recollections of P. T. Barnum Written by Himself* [1869], (New York: A. A. Knopf, 1930), 66-73, 74, 84, 102-103, 105-106, 180-81, 251-252, 392, 406-409; John Rickards Betts, "P. T. Barnum and the Popularization of Natural History," *Journal of the History of Ideas* 20 (1959): 353-68; Morris Robert Werner, *Barnum* (New York: Harcourt Brace, 1923), 43-50, 235-52; Neil Harris, *Humbug: The Art of P. T. Barnum* (Boston: Little, Brown, 1973), 33-57.

29. Barnum, *Struggles and Triumphs*, 465-75, 514-17; Werner, *Barnum*, 302-303; Betts, "Barnum and Popularization," 357-68.

30. Paul H. Oehser, *The Smithsonian Institution* (New York: Prager, 1970), 3-25; Walter Karp, *The Smithsonian: An Establishment for the Increase and Diffusion of Knowledge among Men* (Washington, D.C.: Smithsonian Institution, 1965), 7-19; Geoffrey T. Hellman, *The Smithsonian: Octopus on the Mall* (Philadelphia: Lippincott, 1967), 26-55; Wilcomb E. Washburn, "Joseph Henry's Conception of the Purpose of the Smithsonian Institution," in *A Cabinet of Curiosities: Five Episodes in the Evolution of American Museums*, by Whitfield J. Bell Jr. et al. (Charlottesville: University Press of Virginia, 1967), 106-66; Curtis M. Hinsley, "Magnificent Intentions: Washington, D.C. and American Anthropology in 1846," in *Museum Studies: An Anthology of Contexts*, ed. Bettina Messias Carbonell, London: Blackwell, 2004; Ellis E. Yochelson, *The National Museum of Natural History: 75 Years in the New Museum* (Washington, D.C.: Smithsonian Press, 1985).

31. Washburn, "Joseph Henry's Conception," 106-108.

32. His efforts in this arena became the United States Weather Bureau. See Elena Bruno, "Smithsonian Crowdsourcing since 1849," April 14, 2011, the Bigger Picture, Smithsonian Institution Archives, http://siarchives.si.edu/blog/smithsonian-crowdsourcing-1849.

33. Oehser, *The Smithsonian*, 26-40; Karp, *The Smithsonian*, 19-27; Hellman, *The Smithsonian*, 56-58; Washburn, "Joseph Henry's Conception," 108-66.

34. Oehser, *The Smithsonian*, 40-44; Karp, *The Smithsonian*, 29-43; Hellman, *The Smithsonian*, 89-116; Washburn, "Joseph Henry's Conception," 129-52; James M. Goode, "A View from the Castle," *Museum News* 54 (July-August 1976): 38-45.

35. Oehser, *The Smithsonian*, 44-47; Karp, *The Smithsonian*, 76-80; Hellman, *The Smithsonian*, 94-95, 97, 198; G. Carroll Lindsay, "George Brown Goode," in *Keepers of the Past*, ed. Clifford L. Lord (Chapel Hill: University of North Carolina Press, 1965), 127-40; "A Memorial of George Brown Goode" in *Annual Report of the Board of Regents of the Smithsonian Institution for the Year Ending June 30, 1897: Report of the United States National Museum, Part II*, Washington, DC: Smithsonian Institution, 1901; Robert C. Post, ed., *National Museum of History and Technology, 1876: A Centennial Exhibition* (Washington, D.C.: Smithsonian Institution, 1976), 11-23; Edward P. Alexander, "George Brown Goode and the Smithsonian Museums," in *Museum Masters*, 277-310.

36. The United States Congress passed legislation in December 2020 authorizing the establishment of the National Museum of the American Latino and the Smithsonian American Women's History Museum. Sites for the museums were announced in late 2022, though they require Congressional approval. They are both on undeveloped land administered by the National Park Service: a "South Monument site" across from the National Museum of African American History and Culture, the newest Smithsonian, which opened in 2016, and a "Tidal Basin site" near Maine Avenue, Southwest, with proximity to the

United States Holocaust Memorial Museum. See Peggy McGlone, "Congress Authorizes Smithsonian Museums Focused on American Latinos and Women's History", *Washington Post*, December 22, 2020, https://www.washingtonpost.com/entertainment/museums/smithsonian-museums-latino-womens -history/2020/12/22/4f9211ac-43c6-11eb-b0e4-0f182923a025_story.html; Sarah Y. Kim, "Smithsonian Won't Meet Deadline to Pick Sites for Latino and Women's History Museums," *DCIST*, December 29, 2022, https://dcist.com/story/22/12/29/dc-smithsonian-new-museum-site/.

37. Ellis L. Yochelson, "More than 150 years of Administrative Ups and Downs for Natural History in Washington," *Proceedings of California Academy of Sciences*, vol. 55, su I, art. 6, 113-76; Oehser, *The Smithsonian*, 87-95; Karp, *The Smithsonian*, 44-49; Hellman, *The Smithsonian*, 198-201, 207-208, 215-16; 2003 Collections Statistics, National Collections Program, Smithsonian Institution Archives. Today there are seventeen Smithsonian museums located in the Washington, D.C., area (there are two in New York): the National Museum of American History (1964 as Museum of History and Technology); the National Air and Space Museum (1976); the Steven Udvar-Hazy Center (2004); the National Zoological Park (1887); the Freer Gallery of Art (1906); the National Collection of Fine Arts (1846), today the Smithsonian American Art Museum; the National Portrait Gallery (1962); the Joseph H. Hirshhorn Museum and Sculpture Garden (1966); the Arthur M. Sackler Gallery (1989); the National Museum of African Art (1989); the National Postal Museum (1993); and the Anacostia Neighborhood Museum (1967), today the Anacostia Museum and Center for African American History and Culture. The Cooper-Hewitt Museum (1967) is in New York City, and the National Museum of the American Indian has buildings in both New York (1990) and Washington (2004). Nominal bureaus of the Smithsonian, but with their own boards and financing, are the National Gallery of Art (1941) and the John F. Kennedy Center for the Performing Arts (1958); www.si.edu.

38. Smithsonian Institution, "Smithsonian Fiscal Year 2022 Federal Budget Tops $1 Billion," March 29, 2022, https://www.si.edu/newsdesk/releases/smithsonian-fiscal-year-2022-federal-budget-tops-1 -billion.

39. Smithsonian Institution, "Our Vision," http://www.si.edu/About/Mission.

40. Smithsonian Institution, "Strategic Plan: Four Grand Challenges," http://www.si.edu/About/ Mission.

41. Bickmore studied with Louis Agassiz, founder of the Museum of Comparative Zoology at Harvard.

42. Tony Bennett, *Pasts Beyond Memory: Evolution, Museums and Colonialism* (London: Routledge, 2004), chap. 5; Geoffrey T. Hellman, *Bankers, Bones and Beetles: The First Century of the American Museum of Natural History* (New York: Natural History Press, 1969), 9-28; *Natural History: The Journal of the American Museum* 30 (September–October 1930): 452; Donna Haraway, "Teddy Bear Patriarchy: Taxidermy in the Garden of Eden, New York City, 1908-1936," in *Primate Visions: Gender, Race and Nature in the World of Modern Science* (London: Routledge, 1989).

43. Hellman, *Bankers, Bones, and Beetles*, 28; 35–36; *Natural History* 27 (July–August 1927): 309-91.

44. Hellman, *Bankers, Bones, and Beetles*, 57-115.

45. Hellman, *Bankers, Bones, and Beetles*, 117-206; *Natural History* 30 (September–October 1930): 451-525.

46. Hellman, *Bankers, Bones, and Beetles*, 207-44; Geoffrey T. Hellman, "The Hidden Museum," *New Yorker*, May 19, 1975, 42-74.

47. www.amnh.si.edu.

48. For two years Putnam, and his assistants carried out excavation, collecting, and research from Greenland to Tierra del Fuego that brought anthropological and ethnographic materials to the exposition. Putnam also secured a great collection of minerals, skeletons, mastodon bones, and mounted mammals and birds from Ward's Natural Science Establishment of Rochester, New York.

49. Ralph W. Dexter, "The Role of F. W. Putnam in Founding the Field Museum," *Curator* 13 (1970): 21-26; George A. Dorsey, "The Department of Anthropology of the Field Columbian Museum—A Review of Six Years," *American Anthropologist*, n.s., 2 (1900): 247-65; Field Museum of Natural History, *Annual Report of the Director to the Board of Trustees*, 1960, Chicago: Field Museum of Natural History, 1961; Donald Collier, "Chicago Comes of Age: The World's Columbian Exposition and the Birth of the Field Museum," *Field Museum Bulletin* (May 1969): 2-7; "The Museum's First Million," *Field Museum Bulletin* (August 1970): 13-15.

50. Until December 2010, the Field Museum published four issues, covering each area of the museum. The publications, with articles pertaining to the museum's collections and research, are international in scope and peer-reviewed. See The Field Museum, "Fieldiana," https://www.fieldmuseum.org/science/research/area/fieldiana.

51. The Field Museum, "SUE the T. rex," https://www.fieldmuseum.org/blog/sue-t-rex. The *T. rex*, SUE, was discovered by Sue Hendrickson on a commercial excavation trip north of Faith, South Dakota.

52. The sculptures were put into storage in 1969, and have been returned following conservation and interpretation, which began in 2013. Of the 104 sculptures, eighty-five sculptures were conserved over eighteen months, and fifty were put back on display. See the Field Museum's display information, "'Looking at Ourselves: Rethinking the Sculptures of Malvina Hoffman," https://www.fieldmuseum.org/at-the-field/exhibitions/looking-ourselves-rethinking-sculptures-malvina-hoffman. Two reviews of the show include: Edward Rothstein, "'Looking at Ourselves: Rethinking the Sculptures of Malvina Hoffman' Review: An Exhibition That Goes Out of Its Way to Find Racism Where None Exists," *Wall Street Journal*, March 22, 2016, http://www.wsj.com/articles/looking-at-ourselves-rethinking-the-sculptures-of-malvina-hoffman-review-1458683771; Jennifer Schuessler, "'Races of Mankind' Sculptures, Long Exiled, Return to Display at Chicago's Field Museum," *New York Times*, January 20, 2016, http://www.nytimes.com/2016/01/21/arts/design/races-of-mankind-sculptures-long-exiled-return-to-display-at-chicagos-field-museum.html. The exhibition was on view from January 15, 2016 through January 1, 2017. Google Arts & Culture Exhibition, https://artsandculture.google.com/story/rethinking-the-sculptures-of-malvina-hoffman-the-field-museum/TQUx0COTLheZKA?hl=en.

53. For a brief overview of the scrutiny over ethnographic museums, see the introduction to Alice Stevenson and Alice Williams, "Blind Spots in Museum Anthropology: Ancient Egypt in the Ethnographic Museum," *Museum Anthropology* 45(2022): 96–110, https://doi.org/10.1111/muan.12258. Stevenson and Williams further cite Barbara Kirshenblatt-Gimblett, "Objects of Ethnography," in *Exhibiting Cultures: The Poetics and Politics of Museum Display*, edited by Ivan Karp and Steven D. Lavine, 386–443 (Washington, D.C: Smithsonian Institution, 1991); Elizabeth Hallam and Brian V. Street, editors, *Cultural Encounters: Representing "Otherness"* (London and New York: Routledge, 2000); Laura Peers and Alison K. Brown, editors, *Museums and Source Communities* (London: Routledge, 2003); Viv Golding and Wayne Modest, editors, *Museums and Communities: Curators, Collections and Collaboration* (London: Bloomsbury, 2013); Rodney Harrison, Sarah Byrne, and Anne Clarke, editors, *Reassembling the Collection: Ethnographic Museums and Indigenous Agency* (Santa Fe: SAR Press, 2013); Kylie Message and Andrea Witcomb, editors, *The International Handbook of Museum Studies: Museum Theory* (Malden: Blackwell, 2015);Philipp Schorch and Conal McCarthy, editors, *Curatopia. Museums and the Future of Curatorship* (Manchester: Manchester University Press, 2018);

54. As the twenty-first century opened, the museum adopted a global perspective, seeking to form partnerships and networks with other organizations. One example is the Asian-European Museums Network (ASEMUS), established in 2000, as a cross-cultural network of museums to encourage collections information sharing, including its subproject of the Virtual Collection of Asian Masterpieces (VCM), launched in 2007, with educational and informational content related to more than 2,500 works, 135 museums, and 35 countries. Virtual Collection of Asian Masterpieces, "About the VCM," http://masterpieces.asemus.museum/info/about.nhn. Another more recent initiative that seeks to connect the museum with others is *Sharing a World of Inclusion, Creativity and Heritage: Ethnography, Museums of World Culture and New Citizenship in Europe (SWICH)*, a four-year collaboration among ten museums that looks at "the role that ethnographic and world culture museums can plan in processes of citizenship and belonging in contemporary Europe." In addition to Tropenmuseum, Afrika Museum, and Museum Volkenkunde, Leiden, the partners are: Weltmuseum Wien, Vienna; Musée royal de l'Afrique centrale, Tervuren; Musée des Civilisations de l'Europe et de la Méditerranée, Marseille; Museums of World Culture, Stockholm; Linden-Museum, Stuttgart; Museo Nazionale Preistorico Etnografico Luigi Pigorini, Rome;nMuseum of Archaeology and Anthropology, Cambridge; Slovene Ethnographic Museum, Ljubljana; Museum of World Cultures, Barcelona; Culture Lab–International Cultural Expertise. See http://materialculture.nl/en/projects/sharing-a-world-of-inclusion-creativity-and-heritage-swich.

55. Wereldmuseum Amsterdam, https://amsterdam.wereldmuseum.nl/en/themes/history-wereldmuseum-amsterdam.

56. The history of the Musée de l'Homme extend to 1882 with the collections of the Trocadero Ethnography Museum, which focused on objects that were vanishing before Paul Rivet assumed leadership of that institution and changed the focus from anthropology to ethnology.

57. The Musée de l'Homme, "Presentation," http://www.museedelhomme.fr/en/presentation.

58. Farah Nayeri, "Museums in France Should Return African Treasures, Report Says," *New York Times*, November 21, 2018, https://www.nytimes.com/2018/11/21/arts/design/france-museums-africa -savoy-sarr-report.html. Macron commissioned two academics, the art historian Bénédicte Savoy and the economist Felwine Sarr, to author the report that gave the verdict of restitution, but with little guidance on how to proceed in delivering on this promise.

59. Penn Museum, https://www.penn.museum/.

60. Alessandro Pezzati, Jane Hickman, and Alexandra Fleischman, "A Brief History of the Penn Museum," *Expedition Magazine* 54, no. 3 (December, 2012), https://www.penn.museum/sites/ expedition/a-brief-history-of-the-penn-museum/.

61. Growing interest in purchase of Chinese art and artifacts by European and American collectors coincided with the fall of the Qing Dynasty (1644–1911) and the associated weakening of government supervision of antiquities, with the republic ending thousands of years of imperial rule and transitioning the reverence for imperial objects into one of transaction. As a leading international art dealer, Loo played a significant role in the circulation and reception of Chinese cultural heritage in the United States For more on Loo, see Yiyou Wang, "The Loouvre from China: A Critical Study of C. T. Loo and the Framing of Chinese Art in the United States, 1915–1950," Ph.D. Dissertation, 2007: Ohio University, http://rave .ohiolink.edu/etdc/view?acc_num=ohiou1195498748. As Wang analyzes Loo's strategies and role in the display of Chinese art in America, she concludes that Loo's dealing was "based on America's capitalist and imperialist logic that Chinese antiquities were to be consumed by the rich and the powerful in modern America." As art historian Géraldine Lenain has noted, Loo's life was "full of holes"—meaning gaps in information. The same can be said of the provenance of some of the acquisitions from Loo at Penn and across the United States at anthropological and archaeological museums. See David Pilling, "C. T. Loo: Champion of Chinese Art . . . Or Villain?" *Financial Times*, April 24, 2014, https://www.ft.com/ content/cd747768-cb46-11e3-ba95-00144feabdc0#slide0.

62. See the "UNESCO 1970 Convention on the Means of Prohibiting and Preventing the Illicit Import, Export and Transfer of Ownership of Cultural Property," https://en.unesco.org/fighttrafficking/1970.

63. Jorge Dos Anjos created the sculpture *Wall of Memory for an Ancestral Palace*. Muhsana Ali and Amadou Kane Sy created the mixed-media mosaic *Presence of a Fundamental Absence*. See Kristina García, "Contemporary Art Enhances Penn Museum's African Galleries," *Penn Today*, December 11, 2019, https://penntoday.upenn.edu/news/contemporary-art-penn-museum-africa-sculpture.

64. The cranial collection was built by Morton in the nineteenth century comprised around nine hundred items, which were acquired by the Academy of Natural Sciences of Philadelphia. It added to the collection before its deposit with the university in 1966. See the "Morton Collection Committee: Report on Evaluation Phase," dated April 8, 2021, https://www.penn.museum/sites/morton/Morton CommitteeReport.pdf.

   For more on efforts to review the institution as regarding enslavement institution-wide, see the Penn and Slavery Project, http://pennandslaveryproject.org/, an ongoing initiative established in 2017 as an undergraduate research effort "to uncover the connections between their university and the institution of slavery" with acknowledgment that "Penn's relationship to slavery is complicated, and calls into question our understanding of 'complicity.'"

65. Graham Lee Brewer, "Penn Museum Buries the Bones of nineteen Black Philadelphians, Causing a Disput with Community Members," *AP*, February 15, 2024, https://apnews.com/article/ morton-cranial-collection-penn-museum-bones-repatriation-8b87b5542d9dc18447f791ddfa87f121.

66. Initially known as the Christian Movement for Life and advocating for Black liberation, MOVE is a communal, anti-government movement that was founded in 1972. An early history of the group may be found online: "John Africa's MOVE Organization," http://www.hartford-hwp.com/archives/45a/ index-bb.html, which includes Debbie Africa's essay recounting the preparations to send the children from the home to rural Virginia to escape confrontations locally with the Philadelphia police and city government. See "Memories—Pain of Separation," July 27, 1999, http://www.hartford-hwp.com/

archives/45a/291.html. In May 1985, law enforcement started a fire at the MOVE compound, as noted in newspaper accounts that describe MOVE as "a radical back-to-nature group." See Bill Peterson, "Huge Fire Destroys House of Philadelphia Radicals: Police Helicopter Drops Explosive Device," *Washington Post*, May 13, 1985, https://www.washingtonpost.com/archive/politics/1985/05/14/huge-fire-destroys-house-of-philadelphia-radicals/af4e79f2-68f7-4b03-a017-d5588cb66f8e/. As part of the standoff and fire, five children and six adults were killed by either police gunfire or smoke inhalation; more than sixty homes burned to the ground over two city blocks, thus extending the footprint of the impact beyond MOVE only. Following the events, the remains of all, including children Tree Africa and Delisha Africa were believed to have been buried. Documentation from 1986 associated with the investigation stated that Tree and Delisha had been buried when, in fact, their remains (a pelvic bone and femur) had been held at the Penn Museum and later Princeton University, under the aegis of Mann and Monge. This information was learned only after an online course, "REAL BONES: Adventures in Forensic Anthropology," taught by now-former Penn Museum curator Janet Monge, used the case study of MOVE for one of the course modules. See Krystal Knapp, "Princeton University Takes Down Online Course After Anthropologists' Handling of MOVE Bombing Victim Remains Stirs Controversy," *Planet Princeton*, April 26, 2021, https://planetprinceton.com/2021/04/26/princeton-university-takes-down-online-course-after-anthropologists-handling-of-move-bombing-victim-remains-stirs-controversy/; Krystal Strong, "A Requiem for Delisha and Tree Africa," *Anthropology News*, October 2021, https://www.anthropology-news.org/articles/a-requiem-for-delisha-and-tree-africa/.

67. The quote comes from Abdul-Aliy Muhammad, co-founder of Black & Brown Workers Co-Op, and appears in Hakim Bishara, "Controversy Erupts over Penn Museum's Possession of MOVE Bombing Victims' Remains," *Hyperallergic*, April 22, 2021, https://hyperallergic.com/639910/controversy-penn-museums-possession-of-move-bombing-victims-remains/; Abdul-Aliy A. Muhammad, "Decades after Philadelphia's MOVE Bombing, Penn Museum Still Keeps Secrets on the Remains of 12-Year-Old Girl," *Hyperallergic*, April 20, 2022, https://hyperallergic.com/725976/philadelphia-move-bombing-penn-museum-still-keeps-secrets-on-the-remains/.

68. Penn Museum, "Towards a Respectful Resolution," September 2023, https://www.penn.museum/about-collections/statements-and-policies/towards-respectful-resolution.

69. "About," College of Physicians of Philadelphia, https://collegeofphysicians.org/about.

70. The label copy appeared in Malcolm Burnley, "What the Hell Is Happening with the Mütter Museum?" *Philly Mag*, September 23, 2023, https://www.phillymag.com/news/2023/09/23/mutter-museum-ethics-controversy/.

71. See Mütter Museum at the College of Physicians, "Postmortem Project Town Hall, October 17, 2023," https://www.youtube.com/watch?v=Da0uML0BPy4 . The YouTube series had attracted more than thirteen million views. Upon review, about one-third of the material from the YouTube series has since been made visible again. See Malcolm Burnley, "What the Hell Is Happening with the Mütter Museum?" *Philly Mag*, September 23, 2023, https://www.phillymag.com/news/2023/09/23/mutter-museum-ethics-controversy/.

72. Lonnie Bunch, "Opinion: This is How the Smithsonian will Reckon with Our Dark Inheritance," August 20, 2023, *Washington, Post*, https://www.washingtonpost.com/opinions/2023/08/20/smithsonian-secretary-lonnie-bunch-human-remains/. See also, Nicole Dungca and Claire Healy, "Revealing the Smithsonian's 'Racial Brain Collection'," *Washington Post* August 14, 2023, https://www.washingtonpost.com/history/interactive/2023/smithsonian-brains-collection-racial-history-repatriation.

73. Lonnie Bunch, "Opinion: This is How the Smithsonian Will Reckon with Our Dark Inheritance," August 20, 2023, *Washington Post* https://www.washingtonpost.com/opinions/2023/08/20/smithsonian-secretary-lonnie-bunch-human-remains/.

74. Lonnie Bunch, "Opinion: This Is How the Smithsonian Will Reckon With Our Dark Inheritance," August 20, 2023, *Washington Post,* https://www.washingtonpost.com/opinions/2023/08/20/smithsonian-secretary-lonnie-bunch-human-remains/.

75. An Open Letter to Museums from Members of the Scientific Community, March 24, 2015, http://thenaturalhistorymuseum.org/open-letter-to-museums-from-scientists/.

76. *Mining the HMNS* was on view from March 26 until June 19, 2016. See http://thenaturalhistorymuseum.org/events/mining-the-hmns/.

3

Science Museums

This chapter focuses on museums related to physical science and technology. While this subject, in many ways, may elicit the wonder and awe laid bare in the previous chapter, here the emphasis is on explanation, resolution, and innovation rather than the construction of knowledge as a means of harnessing, defining, and understanding the seemingly unknowable. Under the category of "science museums," then, the focus in this chapter is on artificial curiosities in early collections that also included a range of practical and scientific technology—tools and utensils; locks and keys; lighting devices; clocks and watches; arms, armor, and apparatuses of warfare; musical instruments; globes, astrolabes, and navigational devices; machines, automatons, engines, and mechanical models; telescopes, microscopes, and other optical apparatuses; magnetic and electrical equipment; and scientific or philosophical apparatuses and instruments devoted to mathematics, medicine, astronomy, chemistry, and physics.

While the Industrial Revolution in the eighteenth century and the advent of the World's Fair in the nineteenth increased the recognition of innovation as a product of human cognition and the inevitable rise of museums of technology and science, these institutions, in contrast to natural history museums, sought and exhibited collections relating to technology and the physical sciences. Some of these museums evolved into science centers, with less emphasis on preserving collections for study and for future generations and more attention on educating the public about science and its principles. Melanie Quin outlines four forms of science centers: "scientists' workshop," "technological trade fair," "historical storehouse," and "adventure playground." She suggests that many centers are a combination of these forms.[1]

Moving from classification to their names, the term *science center* has been viewed as more appealing to potential visitors because, historically, the word *museum* suggests stodgy halls with static collections. By contrast, *centers* are seen as sites for activity and engagement.[2] However, some science-centered institutions go by entirely different names, such as the Exploratorium in San Francisco. Other examples include the CuriOdyssey (San Mateo, California); the Exploration Place (Wichita, Kansas); the Imagination Station (Toledo, Ohio); the Sciencenter (Ithaca, New York); and the WonderLab (Bloomington, Indiana).[3] Do not let the names confine your approach to these institutions, however, as science museums/centers/exploratoria are evolving and develop their exhibits and hands-on experiences through one of two historical approaches, or a fusion of them.

Whether the institution is tethered to its history as a collections-based institution or whether it emerged as a science center with the emphasis on interactive exhibitions rather than historical collections, their shared goal is to provide audiences with opportunities for STEM (science, technology, engineering, and math) learning. In this way, science museums serve as "informal science institutions," or ISIs, because they specialize in learning in informal (as opposed to formal, classroom-based) settings. They fulfill an important role in science learning, as noted by the National Science Teachers Association (NSTA): "the learning experiences delivered by parents, friends, and educators in informal environments can spark student interest in science and provide opportunities to broaden and deepen students' engagement; reinforce scientific concepts and practices introduced during the school day; and promote an appreciation for and interest in the pursuit of science in school and in daily life."[4] Science museums are accessible spaces for learning and engagement about science and technology and provide platforms for the public communication of science and technology.[5]

European Collections of Artificial Curiosities

Medieval and Renaissance collectors usually owned abundant artificial curiosities. Jean de France, Duc de Berry, had clocks, mechanisms, and scientific apparatuses. Emperor Rudolph II brought to Prague great instrument makers like Erasmus Habermel and Tycho Brahe, as well as the distinguished mathematician Johannes Kepler. Landgrave Wilhelm IV at Kassel collected instruments and studied mathematics and astronomy, while August I in Dresden used his collection to form a scientific research center in the famed Green Vaults of his palace.[6] Most of the seventeenth-century Italian scientific centers mentioned in the previous chapter had artificial as well as natural curiosities.[7]

Conservatoire National des Arts et Métiers

In the seventeenth century, René Descartes suggested that the French government collect models of inventions for the instruction of artisans, but it was not until 1794 that the revolutionary National Assembly established the Conservatoire National des Arts et Métiers (CNAM).[8] This public depository of machines, inventions, models, tools, drawings, descriptions, and books on the applied arts and trades was housed in the buildings of the old Priory of Saint-Martin-des-Champs in Paris. The machines and models collected by the great engineer and inventor Jacques Vaucanson and by the Academie Royale des Sciences (1666) were the core of the collection which grew rapidly during the last half of the nineteenth century and received much material from the various universal exhibitions. The chief divisions of the collection were physics, electrical industries, geometry, weights and measures, mechanics and machines, transportation, chemical industries, mining and metallurgy, graphic arts, textile arts, arts of construction, and agriculture, and later industrial accident prevention and industrial hygiene. As early as 1819, the conservatoire hired professors to give courses on applying science to arts and industries that, in one year in the 1860s, enrolled 177,000 persons. About 1900, laboratories were established to test scientific apparatuses, building materials, machines, and vegetable substances. The conservatoire also published a six-volume catalog of its holdings, between 1905 and 1910.

Today, CNAM operates primarily as a research institution for the promotion of science and industry akin to an Ivy League in the United States educational system. The museum facet, known as the Musée des Arts et Métiers (Industrial Design Museum) in Paris, exhibits more than 2,400 inventions across seven collections—scientific instruments, materials, energy, mechanics, construction, communication, and transportation. This educational emphasis remains today with CNAM providing courses for students whether enrolled in formal educational programs or informal learning that takes place outside of school. Resources include a central Paris museum and a library rich with materials relating to technology and industrial design. The modern museum, artfully fitted into the ancient Merovingian site, features early aircraft, including the first helicopter; automobiles; the origins of photography; motion pictures; radio and television; radar and the laser; and modern technology to the tune of eighty thousand objects and one hundred-fifty thousand industrial designs. Its displays complement older rarities, such as the ornamental turning lathes Peter the Great presented to the Académie des Sciences, materials on the evolution of the Jacquard loom, apparatuses from Lavoisier's laboratory, Daguerre's early equipment, and a model of the Statue of Liberty designed by Frédéric Auguste Bartholdi.

National Museum of Science and Industry, London

British manufacturers and businessmen were concerned to see that workingmen received practical technical education so as to produce more and better goods. Mechanics' institutes and government schools of design were established in the 1820s and 1830s, and sporadic trade exhibitions were held to show how art and science could be applied to industrial products. The Royal Society of Arts held several such exhibits, imitating those started in France. Henry Cole, versatile artist, musician, litterateur, and civil servant, became convinced that the society should sponsor an international exhibition so as to compare the industrial progress of many nations.[9] Prince Albert, consort of Queen Victoria and president of the society, eagerly embraced the idea, and his support was chiefly responsible for bringing into actuality the Great Exhibition of the Industry of All Nations as the first World's Fair at London in 1851. The "Crystal Palace" exhibition building—1,851 (the date that year) feet long and some 450 feet broad—enclosed eighteen acres that included several large trees. The exposition was an enormous success; in 120 days, it attracted more than six million visitors. When it closed in October, unlike later World's Fairs, it had a surplus—186,000 pounds. The exhibition had beneficial effects on British industrial design and international trade and inspired a series of world's fairs, including a New York Crystal Palace (1853) and the Philadelphia Centennial Exhibition (1876). In addition, regional expositions showcasing art, design, and science were an important part of the exhibition imaginary.[10] Many of these expositions influenced the museum movement; their collections and, in some instances, their buildings were used to house museums.[11]

The royal commissioners, at the urging of Prince Albert, invested the earnings of the Great Exhibition in South Kensington real estate that adjoined the exposition site and eventually helped build a museum complex there. In 1857, the South Kensington Museum of Science and Art opened; it contained much material from the Crystal Palace. Bennet Woodcroft, patent commissioner, who gathered mechanical models in the Patent Office Museum, brought the collection to South Kensington.[12] In 1909, when the building for the Victoria and Albert Museum was completed, the National Museum of Science and Industry (NMSI)—the Science Museum—became independent, opening in its own buildings across Exhibition Road in 1928. The Science Museum developed into one of the greatest museums of science and technology in the world. It collected important historical material relating to power technology, transportation, communication, and manufacturing, creating large "taxonomic" collections of nineteenth-century industrial practices. In the 1960s the museum added important elements of biomedicine to its collecting roster.

Today, the museum offers lectures, demonstrations, films, and special exhibits that strive to tell the story of technological and medical achievement spanning centuries and the globe. As told by their mission: "we aim to inspire visitors with award-winning exhibitions, iconic objects and stories of incredible scientific achievement."[13] The museum has children's programs, including a children's gallery that opened in 1931 with participatory exhibits and engaging programs. More recently, the notion has been to move from the museum to school and home through offerings such as thematic tours, dramatic presentations within exhibitions, IMAX theater presentations, supervised sleepovers, visits to *Wonderlab: The Equinor Gallery*, the interactive space with live science demonstrations, 1:1 contact with Science Explainers, and opportunities to explore across seven interactive zones. These children's programs are especially significant as they reflect current research into how young people learn. They balance current research and children's interests with historical artifacts relating to science and technology.[14]

The Deutsches Museum, Munich

The French and British established the first technical museums, but the Germans devised an even more striking and influential one. Oskar von Miller, an outstanding engineer largely responsible for the Bavarian grid electrical system, was the founder of the Deutsches Museum von Meisterwerken der

Naturwissenschaft und Technic (German Museum of Outstanding Achievements in Natural Science and Technology). As a young man in 1879, von Miller visited the conservatoire in Paris and the Patent Office Museum in South Kensington. In 1903, he presented a plan for a museum to illustrate the development of natural science and technology and the vivid influence of invention and mechanical progress on society.[15] It was endorsed enthusiastically by leading industrialists and scientists, engineering and scientific organizations, the National and Bavarian governments, and the city of Munich. The museum was housed in various existing locations from 1903 until the new museum island building opened its 250,000 square feet of displays to the public until May 6, 1925, the seventieth birthday of its founder.

The Deutsches Museum introduced many innovations in its effort to make science and technology understandable for the general public. Full-scale original or reproduced equipment was on display—for example, replicas of the *Puffing Billy* and *Rocket* locomotives in the Science Museum, the first Siemens electric locomotive (1899), early automobiles by Benz (1885) and Daimler (1886), and Edison's electric-lighting apparatuses (1879). A museum visitor pushing buttons or turning cranks could animate many ingenious scale models. The principles of physics and chemistry were demonstrated, and a dramatic electrical surge generator (1.3 million volts) produced lightning flashes two meters long. The first Zeiss planetarium was installed, as well as realistic reconstructed mines for coal, iron, and salt with full-sized shafts, drifts, and galleries. The museum used period settings, such as an alchemist's laboratory and Galileo's study, as well as dioramas that included a glassblower's workshop and a high-tension power plant.

After extensive post–World War II reconstruction was completed in 1965, the Deutsches Museum retained the traditional chronological presentation of objects of historical interest but pioneered in offering ingenious and exciting exhibits and demonstrations of scientific laws of nature and their application through contemporary technology. It encouraged technological research with a fine scientific library of eight hundred thousand volumes, but its chief purpose was informal education for the masses. A well-equipped auditorium accommodated two thousand persons at public lectures. Attracting more than 1.5 million visitors every year, the Deutsches Museum still has the highest attendance figures of any museum in Germany. In terms of exhibition area, the number and importance of its objects and collections, the breadth of its stated aims and the multiplicity of its activities, it is among the internationally leading scientific and technological museums.[16]

The influence of the Deutsches Museum has been pervasive and extensive across Europe and in the United States. Its display techniques for modern technology emphasize how science works today, and many smaller technical museums have concentrated on this aspect, largely giving up the goal of exhibiting historical development. In the United States, the Smithsonian's Museum of History and Technology (later the Museum of American History); Chicago's Museum of Science and Industry; Henry Ford's Museum in Dearborn, Michigan; and San Francisco's Exploratorium all trace their origins not only to the Deutsches Museum, but also to its founder, Oskar von Miller. His interest in educating the public about science and technology within the museum setting continues to this day in these institutions and many others that embrace the principles of informal learning outlined at the head of this chapter.[17]

American Examples: Philadelphia and Beyond

Franklin Institute Science Museum, Philadelphia

Philadelphia's Franklin Institute, named to honor Benjamin Franklin, was founded in 1824 as a mechanics' institute to dispense information on the useful arts. Located in Independence Hall, it held important industrial exhibitions, awarded prizes, conducted classes and lectures, accumulated a library and a small technological museum with models and natural history specimens, and published a journal. In 1918, it began to develop laboratories, where scientists carried on chemical, biological, physics, and space research. The Franklin Institute opened its Fels Planetarium (only the second planetarium in the United States) in 1933 and a year later its Science Museum.

In the Deutsches Museum tradition, the institute offered visitors interactive exhibitions. The institute's giant-sized, walk-through human heart, complete with sound effects, opened in 1953, providing visitors, especially young ones, an appreciation for the role of that organ in the health of us all. Today, the Franklin Institute Science Museum's exhibitions, including a recently refurbished planetarium with exhibitions relating to space and space exploration, focus on technology, science, and medicine, and, in the tradition of Benjamin Franklin, human inventiveness.[18]

The Philadelphia Centennial & the Smithsonian Institution's Technology Museums

The Philadelphia Centennial Exposition of 1876 was a six-month extravaganza paying tribute to the hundredth anniversary of the Declaration of Independence and offering five huge main buildings devoted to industrial exhibits, machinery, agriculture, horticulture, and art, together with 250 smaller structures. These were scattered through 233 acres of the broad reaches of Fairmount Park. There were some thousands of exhibitors, including those from forty-one foreign governments. Machinery Hall was especially impressive, with its great seven-ton Corliss engine started up by President Grant and Dom Pedro II, emperor of Brazil, and furnishing power to fourteen acres of clattering machinery that included printing presses, typecasting machines, envelope makers, and pin-forming machines amid huge Krupp cannons, car wheels, water pumps, boats, and locomotives.[19]

Many national and state governments donated their centennial exhibits to the Smithsonian, and this flood of materials led to the erection of a National Museum Building (today the Arts and Industries Building) completed in 1881. The Smithsonian regents in 1924 appealed to Congress unsuccessfully for a "Museum of Engineering and Industry." At last, in 1955, Leonard Carmichael, the institution's seventh secretary, persuaded Congress to appropriate funds for a new National Museum of History and Technology which opened in 1964 (its name changed in 1980 to the National Museum of American History).

At the Museum of History and Technology, the chief science and technical displays included military ordnance, graphic arts, photography, musical instruments, farm machinery, road vehicles, American merchant shipping, bridges and tunnels, heavy machinery, electricity, tools, timekeepers, record players, typewriters, locks, physical sciences, medical sciences, manufactures, textiles, petroleum, nuclear energy, coal, iron, and steel. Full-scale original objects—including a railroad engine built into the building—meticulously built scale models, period rooms and shops, visitor-activated demonstrations, and motion pictures are used in interpreting these subjects.

The above example of a hybrid science + technology + history museum sought to address the gulf between history and technology and to reveal the presence of science and technology in the nation's development by developing exhibitions about technology with historical topics. In addition, emphasis is on the role of invention and innovation through science and technology in American history, with the founding of the Jerome and Dorothy Lemelson Center for the Study of Invention and Innovation in 1994. The Lemelson Center is situated in the eponymous Hall on the first floor of the Smithsonian National Museum of American History, where it draws upon the Smithsonian's vast collections of artifacts and archival materials to communicate ideas about science, technology, and the history of invention. In addition, the dynamic space called Spark!Lab provides opportunities for children, families, and adults to learn about the invention process, inventors and intentions in American history, and innovations that are changing the world today. The original Spark!Lab opened in 2008, ultimately giving rise to the SparkLab Network in 2011, which enables institutions to purchase a two-year membership to access exhibition, experiments, and science and innovation-framed content to use at their own institutions. Such a novel idea for a science museum calls to mind the innovative approach to art exhibitions described earlier in Chapter 1 with the 21c Museum Hotel concept.[20]

National Air and Space Museum

Before the creation of the Smithsonian's Museum of History and Technology, the institution's Arts and Industries Building displayed the famed Wright Brothers' *Flyer* (1903), Samuel Pierpont Langley's *Aerodrome Six*, Charles Lindbergh's *Spirit of St. Louis*, Robert Goddard's first successful rocket, and numerous other examples of air and space equipment until the National Air and Space Museum on the National Mall was completed in 1976. Today, it houses many of the icons of flight, including those mentioned above as well as newer spacecraft. In addition to this aeronautical and space hardware are materials that relate to man's centuries-old fascination with traveling in and through the air around us. There's even a "moon rock" for visitors to touch. On the National Mall visitors enjoy engaging permanent and temporary exhibitions, an IMAX theater, along with a planetarium show. The museum is also home to the Center for Earth and Planetary Studies (CEPS), the scientific research unit and the hub for the Planetary Image Facility with hard-copy images from the earliest space travel of the 1960s through the most recent missions.

The National Air and Space Museum has a second location, in Chantilly, Virginia, near Washington Dulles International Airport, called the Udvar-Hazy Center. Opened in December 2003, its hangar-sized buildings permit the display of many more artifacts, including a Lockheed SR-71 Blackbird, a Concorde, the Boeing B-29 Superfortress *Enola Gay*, and the Space Shuttle *Discovery*. In addition to the artifacts on display, the Center has an IMAX theater as well as an observation tower that yields 360-degree views of the nearby airport. In addition, the center serves as the site for preservation work—which can be observed by visitors. The museum has numerous online, onsite, and downloadable resources to enable parents and teachers to connect their children with the STEM learning and creativity afforded through science and space exploration.[21]

As part of a multi-year renovation that began in 2018, all twenty-three exhibitions in the museum will be reimagined with new presentation spaces and attractions. While the collections hold more than 44,000 aviation artifacts, 17,000+ space-related artifacts, and 4,700+ works of art, some are more notorious than others. In 2015, the museum launched a successful crowdfunding campaign on the platform Kickstarter to raise funds to conserve Neil Armstrong's *Apollo 11* spacesuit and Alan Shepard's *Mercury* spacesuit for exhibition. Called "Reboot the Suit," the campaign involved more than nine thousand contributors who, in the process of pledging funds, shared memories of this garment that enabled Armstrong on his mission in 1969. Because the goal of five hundred thousand dollars was reached within just five days, the museum employed the development officer's dream of tacking on a "stretch" goal by asking for an additional two hundred thousand dollars for Shepard's suit. The funds raised were put toward conservation, research, and the fabrication of a mannequin and display for the new exhibition, *Destination Moon*. The exhibition features iconic objects from the Museum's unrivaled collection of *Mercury*, *Gemini*, and *Apollo* artifacts, including the crowd-funded, preserved space suits as well as spacecraft. The exhibit demonstrates the science, technology, and perseverance required to go to the moon, as well as the persistence to return, even today.[22]

The aforementioned crowdfunding campaign enabled the Smithsonian to underscore the power of objects to make connections with their audience while tapping in to the potential of technologies and the web to reach unknown potential donors.[23] But soaring to new heights metaphorically or physically is nothing new for the Air and Space Museum.

To celebrate the fiftieth anniversary of the flight of *Apollo 11*, the museum soared to new heights by creating an onsite experience like no other. Over three days in July 2019, the museum illuminated the nearby Washington Monument with a full-sized projection of the *Saturn V* rocket that sent *Apollo 11* into orbit on July 16, 1969. Making use of the sheer quantity of documentation available about the mission to share the story of the American spaceflight that landed humans on the moon, the program "Apollo 50: Go for the Moon" consisted of a seventeen-minute show that combined full-motion projection mapping of archival footage and audio and visual recordings to re-create the launch of *Apollo*

Apollo 50: Go for the Moon was a free-admission, public commemoration of the fiftieth anniversary of *Apollo 11*, the first lunar landing. In July 2019, the Washington Monument was transformed by archival footage and media. The project was commissioned by the Smithsonian National Air and Space Museum in partnership with the National Park Service. The event was was created by 59 Productions, an experience design firm based in the U.K.

Apollo 50: Go for the Moon, *created by 59 Productions and commissioned by the Smithsonian's National Air and Space Museum. Photo by Evelyn Hockstein.*

11 and tell the story of the first moon landing. The show unfolded just outside the museum's front doors on the National Mall with the mapping of the 363-foot *Saturn V* rocket projected onto the east side of the Washington Monument with additional supporting screens, to include a forty-foot-wide re-creation of the famous Kennedy Space Center countdown clock. The remarkable event was shown multiple times over those days and coincided with the return of Armstrong's space suit to public view at the museum, for the first time in thirteen years, after being conserved.[24]

The Museum of Science and Industry, Chicago

Continuing this tradition of World's Fair connections, the Museum of Science and Industry's history is tied to the fair held in Chicago in 1933, though its origins may be rooted two decades earlier. In 1911, Julius Rosenwald, head of Sears, Roebuck and Company in Chicago, took his family to Munich, where he met the enthusiastic von Miller. Rosenwald continued visiting him through the years, and in 1921, he told the Chicago Commercial Club "that Chicago should have . . . a great Industrial Museum or Exhibition" with "machinery and working models illustrative of as many as possible of the mechanical processes of production and manufacture."[25] By 1926, the museum was incorporated, Rosenwald had given it three million dollars, and the Chicago South Park Board had earmarked 3.5 million dollars of a bond issue to renovate for its use the crumbling Palace of Fine Arts, a building left from the Columbian Exposition of 1893 and once used by the Field Museum of Natural History. In June 1933, during the Chicago centennial World's Fair dubbed "A Century of Progress," the museum managed to open partially, featuring a simulated coal mine complete with operating mine "cage elevator," shaft, mine train, and working face of a coal seam.

By 1940, the museum board elected as its president Lenox R. Lohr, who had successfully managed "A Century of Progress" and had since been serving as president of the National Broadcasting Company. Lohr combined the qualities of the hard-driving, tough businessman and the imaginative promoter. He did everything he could to build attendance, which in 1939 was about 470,000; he believed that if it could reach a million, then more industry would be attracted to design and install significant technological displays. He thought 90 percent of the exhibits should be devoted to the present, only 10 percent to the past, and that 10 percent of the total should change each year. In exchange for a company's planning and erecting an exhibit, the museum would guarantee to show it for at least five years; would charge the company a fixed yearly fee that would reimburse the museum for operating, maintaining, and demonstrating it; and would give the company credit with an appropriate and discreet label. The museum would have full control of the exhibit to see that it met its standards of truthfulness, clarity, and educational purpose. This was, essentially, a world's-fair approach to the technical museum and required no curators, but excellent public relations and promotion.

Today the museum boasts fourteen acres of inquiry, "400,000 square feet of hand-on exhibits designed to spark scientific inquiry and creativity," making it the western hemisphere's largest science museum.[26] Here, science is defined in a multitude of subject areas, from chemistry, design, energy, and engineering to innovation, life sciences, manufacturing, space, technology, and transportation. Exhibits include *You! The Experience*, which examines the human body as well as people's experiences, choices, personalities, and environment. One of the exhibits includes a thirteen-foot tall, animated heart beating in real time and showing interior and exterior activity; another features iStan, a computerized mannequin and human patient simulator. Other exhibits include a model railroad, a submarine, and a mine shaft, in addition to examinations of sustainable futures.[27]

The Henry Ford, Dearborn, Michigan

At the start of the twentieth century, automobile industrialist Henry Ford began to accumulate vast stores of cultural and industrial Americana, including historic American buildings. He arranged his collections at Dearborn, Michigan, into two sections—an outdoor, or open-air, historical village similar to the Scandinavian folk museums, and an indoor museum extending behind a reproduction of Philadelphia's Independence Hall, Carpenter's Hall, and Old City Hall. Together, these facilities, known as Greenfield Village, would show the story of progress through displays while the village would show use—two sides of the same coin, as Ford wished to show "the history of our people as written into things their hands made and used," and he argued that "a piece of machinery, or anything that is made is like a book, if you can read it."[28]

Construction on the first buildings at Greenfield Village began in 1928 and came to include craft and early machine shops, as well as the cycle shop of the Wright brothers, the re-creation of the New Jersey lab where Thomas Edison invented his electric lighting system, and other birthplaces and buildings associated with ingenuity. Most important of all in showing technological development was the Mechanical Arts Hall, an eight-acre teakwood expanse with serried rows of machines and apparatuses devoted to agriculture, domestic arts, lighting, power, machinery, communications, and transportation. All objects are full-scale, most of them original, but with a few reproductions.

By the mid-1930s, the Village shops were staffed by people demonstrating traditional craft skills—including glassblowers, blacksmiths, and potters. Though his museums contained many historical, architectural, and decorative arts materials, they were especially rich in important American and British items of industrial development. The twelve-acre museum contained a vast collection of largely uninterpreted artifacts that may have given the ordinary visitor visual and intellectual indigestion, but we are indebted to Ford for recognizing their value as historical evidence. Today, modern exhibition techniques have transformed the setting and its objects into comprehensible and valuable evidence of mainly British and American inventiveness. This section of the Henry Ford is most like a traditional science and technology museum, while the village area, with its blend of museum types, reflects history museum traditions and practices akin to living history museums as addressed in the following chapter.[29]

The museum also has partnerships with the Ford Motor Company's Dearborn Truck Plant in partnership with the United Auto Workers Union. Together, they have created the "Ford Rouge Tour" to give a five-pronged experience away from the museum but on the site of the historic Rouge Factory. The site has been transformed from a brownfield to a sustainable manufacturing setting that enables museum visitors to have "awe-inspiring encounters with America's celebrated manufacturing past, present and future, plus a look into the sheer scale of a working auto factory."[30]

Museum of Science, Boston

Emerging from a nineteenth-century natural history society in Boston, the Museum of Science, Boston is tied to the post–World War II years, when the museum's leaders expanded the scope of the "society" to encompass science and technology in addition to natural history. This change was made manifest when the museum relocated from Boston's Back Bay to the shores of the Charles River, forming a science park. Progress continued throughout the decades. With its 1951 expansion, the museum sought to address all the sciences within a single building. Subsequent additions—including an IMAX theater; the Charles Hayden Planetarium, the most technologically advanced digital theater in the region, offering evening astronomy activities; a 4D Theater which combines 3D features with extrasensory elements, such as weather effects, to give an immersive experience; flight simulators, which afford 360-degrees of pitch; and the butterfly garden which enables observation of the four stages of the butterfly life cycle.[31]

Science Centers

Museums of science and technology emerged from the traditional enlightenment museum form, simply changing the exhibitions from those of natural objects to man-made phenomenon but continuing the overall purpose to aid visitors in understanding the world around them. Perhaps more than any other museum space, science centers hold particular importance as they play a central role in the public understanding of science and offer engaging contexts for informal learning that are many times immersive and high-tech, as well as hands-on. The earliest science centers opened their doors in the 1930s, at the height of public appreciation for the contributions of science (and technology) to daily comforts. These centers, in many instances, emerged from international expositions where a nation's technological muscle was on display.

Scholars John Bettlestone, Colin H. Johnson, Melanie Quin, and Harry White have traced the lineage of science museums across two lines: the grand museums, such as London's Science Museum and Deutsches Museum, Munich, and Chicago; and the hands-on approach developed in North America during the height of the space race.[32] As Sheila Grinell has noted, "In the late 1960s, after the decade of reform in science education that followed *Sputnik*'s launch in 1957, several institutions opened that elaborated on the concept of interactivity. The Exploratorium in San Francisco and the Ontario Science Center near Toronto eschewed historical and industrial collections in favor of apparatuses and programs designed to communicate basic science in terms readily accessible to visitors." The premise was that engagement through experience would serve to stimulate original thinking about science.[33]

Today, the range of exhibits include didactics + interactives—so-called didacteractive—as part of an enabling or empowering exhibit that may have multiple outcomes as a result of the high level of creative contribution.[34] With more than 1,400 science and technology centers worldwide, the range of opportunities and contexts is incredible, though a commonality is their focus on informal learning, as described by the Association of Science and Technology Centers. Founded in 1973, the ASTC supports global science engagement. It "creates strategic opportunities, develops intellectual capital, and assembles resources to support our members in realizing their missions and engaging their communities." The organization's alliances and partnerships, publications, and professional development champion informal learning, the building block of the museum experience, by supporting the work of science centers, nature centers, museums, zoos, botanical gardens, and children's museums.[35]

The ASTC is keenly transparent about its core values in a commitment to science and to equity and justice. In valuing the role of science in museum work, the ASTC holds its membership to a science commitment, which reads: "ASTC and its members agree that science is a human endeavor that uses scientific methods, observations, and experimentation to develop explanations of the natural world; scientific theories are grounded in and compatible with evidence internally consistent, and demonstrably effective in explaining a wide variety of phenomena; science is based on scientific methods, scientific observation, experimentation, and many thousands of peer-reviewed publications; and the development of technology has always, and continues to, depend on scientific research and human ingenuity."[36] In addition, the museum has established a "Call to Action and Commitment to Advance Equity and Justice" to invite members to work together to learn, share, and take action in their communities.[37]

Science and technology museums are inheritors of the extended subject area broadly known as STEM (Science, Technology, Engineering, and Math) that includes engineering and math. Other extensions include STEAM, with the addition of Art; SHTEAM, with the additions of History and Art; and STREAM, with the addition of Reading and Arts. While these fields have been around for a long time, their acronyms are a recent addition, and their presence and, even, frequency of use indicates the ways in which our environments indicate the value and strength of interdisciplinary learning. In fact, recent funding opportunities from the National Science Foundation (NSF) pay heed to the connections between STEM learning and museums. The NSF issued a series of grants to support museum projects under the special initiative called "Advancing Informal STEM Learning," which research on the design, development, and impact of STEM learning opportunities and experiences for the public.

The NSF also supports a number of museum exhibits, including *Race: Are We So Different?*—a traveling exhibition that looks at the science, history, and lived experience of race and racism in the United States—and a number of exhibits at specific institutions. Projects such as these demonstrate how the successful integration of arts-based and interdisciplinary programs serve to recognize and value different approaches to learning in science-based disciplines.[38] In addition, during the early days of the COVID-19 pandemic, the NSF promoted their support of STEM resources at museums by publicizing online learning opportunities and resources informed by research, evaluation, and best practices of museums.[39]

Exploratorium, San Francisco

Oskar von Miller's Deutsches Museum personally influenced founders of other science and technology museums (as mentioned above, Henry Ford and Julius Rosenwald) and more recently physicist Frank Oppenheimer, creator and founder of the Exploratorium in San Francisco. From his position as a professor at the University of Colorado, Oppenheimer envisioned a new sort of museum that addressed the interests of learners and their curiosity about the world around them. He called it a Museum of Science, Art, Industry and Craft (MOSAIC), generically, "an xploratorium," a place where visitors could understand the world by exploring it themselves. Oppenheimer acknowledged that a visit to the Deutsches Museum sparked his thinking about how museums could "teach" their visitors.

In 1968, the Exploratorium opened in the abandoned buildings of the Pan-American Exposition in San Francisco.[40] The early exhibitions were "works in progress" that captured the imagination of the few visitors who found their way to the door. Youthful explainers within the exhibit spaces offered explanations and guidance to visitors when asked. Oppenheimer stated the Exploratorium's purpose: "It should be a place where people come both to teach and to learn."[41] Today, the Exploratorium and Oppenheimer's vision of the dynamic role museums can play in engaging their visitors are models for other institutions worldwide. The Exploratorium pronounces its broadest service by stating that they "create tools and experiences that help you to become an active explorer: hundreds of explore-for-yourself exhibits, a website with over 50,000 pages of content, film screenings, evening art and science events for adults, plus much more. We also create professional development programs for educators, and are at the forefront of changing the way science is taught. We share our exhibits and expertise with museums worldwide." Truly, the onsite and online, as well as takeaways, are critical to the Exploratorium's practice.[42]

Onsite, the center offers six main galleries with interactive exhibits alongside an observation area called *Exhibit Workshop*, where visitors can look at exhibits in the making.[43] The museum also offers teaching and learning tools that provide museum professionals across the world with simple ways to illustrate scientific principles, whether in community-based children's museums or larger regional science centers. The resources include the websites (and microsites within the Exploratorium's main site); a learning commons for educators alongside a digital library of PDFs, movies, podcasts, and other media; publications focusing on formative evaluation, arts integration, and more focused topics; downloadable apps that can be used as teaching tools; and descriptions and instructions on how to build mini-versions (aka "snacks") of Exploratorium exhibits.[44] In addition, the Exploratorium is seen as the prototype for more than one thousand hands-on, participatory institutions worldwide.[45]

For Further Consideration

Today's science museums trace the trajectory of museum history in their own evolution from being about something to being for somebody. Melanie Quin, quoted earlier in this chapter, chronicled the inward, private nature of these institutions in cadence with their subject, calling science "a slow, often tedious, business, with most experiments being controls designed to show that in certain conditions nothing happens." At that time, she questioned the role of science museums, as an extension, asking, "Is it simply that science museums seldom attempt explanations because explaining is not their traditional aim? Or have they found it impossible to present ideas in a museum context? Are the concepts and principles underlying appearances just too hard to present without the kind of background knowledge instilled over years, in courses in schools and universities? We may need somewhat separated, more thoughtful 'Explanatories.'"[46]

However, the lines between expert and public have blurred considerably across all museum fronts. This is not to suggest that expertise, credentialing, and experience do not matter, but an acknowledgment that we can learn in community. We are, in fact, stronger together.

Consider that the Exploratorium launched its website in 1993—truly early in the post-internet revolution. In thinking of the connections between the web and science centers, in 2001, Rob Semper wrote of the internet as a valuable extension of a science center's visitor's "browsing" behavior. He reported that science centers were using their websites for connecting with audiences and to support membership, admissions, public information, and exhibition promotion. He described the Exploratorium as becoming a "giant production studio for the web." In contrast, in 2006, Jim Spadaccini explained how those Exploratorium beginnings remained unfulfilled. He suggested that the museums must "embrace user-created content . . . the science center 'audience' could be seen as potential collaborators and, in some cases, even content experts." Spadaccini's claim meant the need to embrace two-way communications through the web, which challenges the idea of museums "as authoritative sources of information."[47]

This notion of public activity and browseability is taken further through the citizen-scientist (aka #citsci and Science 2.0) movement. In fact, in looking at the history of science museums, we can observe that the notion of contributing scientists as individuals who actually made their living doing something else is actually quite old, as is the notion of collaboration and networking (even in a pre-social-media world). The newish movement, accelerated through the internet and social media, enables the public to gather useful data for researchers—as in counting or identifying bees, birds, and

Academy in Action exhibit, West Hallway View. Photo by Nicole Ravicchio © 2024 California Academy of Sciences. All rights reserved.

fish in one's region—while also giving citizens—in the form of schoolchildren and adults—the ability to contribute to something greater. For example, eBird, launched by the Cornell Lab of Ornithology as an internet-based citizen-science project, enabled birders to report sightings and observations. Other examples of human computation exercises include FoldIt, which helps predict protein structures, and GalaxyZoo, which identifies galaxies out of celestial images.[48] A website offers listings of more than 1,600 formal and informal research projects and events that include agriculture, astronomy, climate, geography, nature, and more. A second type of "crowdsourcing" involves efforts to connect online visitors with collections and to tap their expertise, time, and interest to contribute to the identification or transcription of collections for public use. For instance, the the Smithsonian Institution's Transcription Center (SITC) demonstrates the capacity of "the crowd" to utilize a website and web application to access digitized records. Collections include digitized diaries, photo albums with captions, field notes journals, specimen labels, and lab experiment logs. The SITC also houses numerous other collections, beyond science, as well.[49]

These moves toward anchoring science learning in the everyday while contributing to a collective endeavor is a return to Joseph Henry's gathering of meteorological data that, in the case of the new work, impacts scientific research, particularly in the fields of biology, conservation, and ecology which have been the primary fields utilizing citizen science.[50] They are also part and parcel of a broader shift in museums, which will be more fully addressed in Sections II and III of this book in the discussions around "shared authority" and how museums are moving away from didactic, directed delivery of content. In tours and other experiences, museums are shifting away from being the sole voice. They are moving away from being "the sage on the stage" with confidence, status, and privilege, and moving toward models of multi-vocality where audiences, visitors, and guests can contribute to shared learning. Museum staff and the institution at large might move from being "the sage on the stage" to the "guide on the side." This phrasing is used in museum education and interpretation and higher education to acknowledge parallel shifts toward "student-centered" and "audience-centered" techniques for learning, thus affirming the close relationship between meaning-making and multi-vocality.[51]

Notes

1. Melanie Quin, "Aims, Strengths, and Weaknesses of the European Science Centre Movement," in *Towards the Museum of the Future: New European Perspectives*, eds. Roger Miles and Lauro Zavala (London: Routledge, 1994), 40.

2. John G. Beetlestone, Colin H. Johnson, Melanie Quin, and Harry White, "The Science Center Movement: Contexts, Practice, New Challenges," *Public Understanding of Science* 7, no. 1 (January 1998): 5–26; Kenneth Hudson, *Museums of Influence* (Cambridge: Cambridge University Press, 1987), 88–112.

3. Victor Danilov, *America's Science Museums* (New York: Greenwood Press, 1990), 291; Howard Learner, *White Paper on Science Museums* (Washington, D.C.: Center for Science in the Public Interest, 1979); Victor J. Danilov, *Science and Technology Centers* (Cambridge: MIT Press, 1982).

4. Quoted in Lori Walsh and William Straits, "Informal Science Learning in the Formal Classroom: Creating a Quality Partnership with Informal Science Institutions," *Science and Children* 51:9 (July 2014): 54–58. Quote from the NSTA is dated 2012 and appears on page 55.

5. See the academic and professional organization in the field of science communication called the Public Communication of Science and Technology Network, https://www.pcst.network/about/overview/.

6. Silvio A. Bedini, "The Evolution of Science Museums," *Technology and Culture* 6, no. 1 (Winter 1965): 1–29, especially the table on pages 2–6; Germain Bazin, *The Museum Age* (New York: Universe Books, 1967), 37–39, 75–76, 86–87, 144.

7. For instance, Aldrovandi, Cospi, and Marsigli at Bologna; the Medici brothers, Grand Duke Ferdinand II and Leopold, with their Academia del Cimento (of the Experiment) in Florence; Ludovico and Manfredo Settala, father and son, in Milan; and the Jesuit Kircher in Rome. Martha Ornstein Bronfenbrenner, *The Role of Scientific Societies in the Seventeenth Century*, 3rd ed. (Chicago: University of Chicago Press, 1938), 77–90, 219. So did Ole Worm and Christian V in Denmark and the Tradescants and the Royal Society (1662) in London. The Society for the Encouragement of Arts, Manufactures, and Commerce (now the Royal Society of Arts), founded in 1754, eventually placed its collection of models in the Science Museum. The Teyler Stichting (Foundation) established at Haarlem in 1778 had the chemist and electrical experimenter Martin van Marum as its first director and still contains his great electrostatic machine of 1784. See Bedini, "The Evolution," 18–20; Ornstein, *The Role*, 112–15; Eugene S. Ferguson, "Technical Museums and International Exhibitions," *Technology and Culture* 6 (1965): 30–46, especially 32, 45; Bazin, *The Museum Age*, 144–45.

8. Among the founding members of the Conservatoire was Henri Jean-Baptiste Grégoire, often called Abbé Grégoire.

9. Edward P. Alexander, "Henry Cole and the South Kensington Museum," *Museum Masters: Their Museums and Their Influence* (Nashville: American Association of State and Local History, 1983), 141–75.

10. For instance, the Southern Exposition was an annual event held from 1883–1887 in Louisville. See "Louisville's Southern Exposition," *Filson Historical Society*, http://filsonhistorical.org/galleries/louisvilles-southern-exposition/.

11. Kenneth W. Luckhurst, *The Story of Exhibitions* (New York: Studio Publications, 1951), 83–116; Christopher Hobhouse, *1851 and the Crystal Palace* (New York, 1937), 1–9, 24–40, 43–61, 150–65; Hector Bolitho, *Albert, Prince Consort* (Indianapolis: Bobbs-Merrill, 1964), 117, 119–20, 125–28; Ferguson, "Technical Museums," 30, 32–33, 35–39; Lord Amulree, "The Museum as an Aid to the Encouragement of Arts, Manufactures, and Commerce," *Museums Journal* 39 (November 1939): 350–56; Kenneth Hudson, *A Social History of Museums: What the Visitors Thought* (Atlantic Highlands: Humanities Press, 1975), 41–47.

12. Woodcroft preserved important historic equipment, including a Necomen type of atmospheric engine (1791); the Boulton and Watt rotative beam engine (1788); Arkwright's cotton-spinning machine (1769); Symington's marine engine (1788); and the locomotives *Puffing Billy* (1813) and Stephenson's *Rocket* (1829). The collection eventually went to the South Kensington Museum.

13. Science Museum, "About Us," http://www.sciencemuseum.org.uk/about-us.

14. Science Museum, "About Us," http://www.sciencemuseum.org.uk/about-us and https://www.sciencemuseum.org.uk/see-and-do/wonderlab-equinor-gallery.
15. Alexander, "Oskar von Miller and the Deutsches Museum," in *Museum Masters*, 341–75.
16. Richards, *Industrial Museum*, 20–32, 70–110; Ferguson, "Technical Museums," 30, 41–42; Karl Bassler, "Deutsches Museum: Museum of Science and Technology," *Museum* 2 (1949): 171–79; "Heavy Current Electrotechnology: A New Department of the Deutsches Museum," *Museum* 7 (1954): 161–66; three articles by Hermann Auer: "The Deutsches Museum, Munich," *Museum* 20 (1967): 199–201; "Problems of Science and Technology Museums: The Experience of the Deutsches Museum, Munich," *Museum* 21 (1968): 128–39; and "Museums of the Natural and Exact Sciences," *Museum* 26 (1974): 68–75. See also "Oskar von Miller," *Museums Journal* 34 (June 1934): 76–79; Richards, *Industrial Museum*, 33–45, 111; Gunter Knerr, "Technology Museums: New Publics, New Partners," *Museum International* 288, no. 4 (October–December 2000): 8–13; http://www.deutsches-museum.de.
17. "Technisches Museum fur Industrie und Gwerbe, Wien," *Museum* 5 (1952): 98; http://www.tmw.at. The Technical Museum of Vienna used materials accumulated during the International Exposition held there in 1873 and the 1908 Jubilee of Emperor Franz Joseph to build support for the museum. It was greatly influenced by the Deutsches Museum, and when it finally opened in 1918, it used many of von Miller's vivifying exhibition techniques. Its dynamic director, Ludwig Erhard, used consultants from most of Austria's trade organizations to build the museum's collections.
18. One enthusiastic reporter wrote: "Surely here, and not in literature, science, or art, is the true evidence of man's creative power; here is Prometheus Unbound." Federal, state, and city funds underwrote the cost of the fair to supplement concession fees and admission revenue from more than eight million visitors. Bruce Sinclair, *Philadelphia's Philosopher Mechanics: A History of the Franklin Institute, 1824-1865* (Baltimore: Johns Hopkins University Press, 1974), 39–41, 93–96, 100–103, 259–61; I. M. Levitt, "The Science Teaching Museum of the Franklin Institute, Philadelphia," *Museum* 20 (1967): 169–71; Robert W. Neatherby, "Education and the Franklin Institute Science Museum," *Museums Journal* 64 (June 1964): 50–58; Ferguson, "Technical Museums," 34–35; Brooke Hindle, "Museum Treatment of Industrialization: History, Problems, Opportunities," *Curator* 15 (1972): 216; Victor J. Danilov, "Under the Microscope," *Museum News* 52 (March 1974): 37–38; International Committee, *Museums of Science and Technology, Guidebook*, 1974, 145–54; http://www.fi.edu.
19. Charles S. Keyser, *Fairmount Park and the International Exhibition at Philadelphia* (Philadelphia: Claxton, Remsen & Haffelfinger, 1876), 1–82; Lynne Vincent Cheney, "1876: The Eagle Screams," *American Heritage* 25 (April 1974): 15–35, 98–99; Luckhurst, *Story of Exhibitions*, 52, 124–25, 136–37, 175, 190, 202, 206; Paul H. Oehser, *The Smithsonian Institution* (New York: Prager, 1970), 49–57, 189–90, 193–94, 196–97; Geoffrey T. Hellman, *The Smithsonian Institution: Octopus on the Mall* (Philadelphia: Lippincott, 1967), 97–98; Walter Karp, *The Smithsonian Institution: An Establishment for the Increase and Diffusion of Knowledge among Men* (Washington, D.C.: Smithsonian Institution, 1965), 55–69, 75–93; Gene Gurney, *The Smithsonian Institution: A Picture Story of Its Buildings, Exhibits and Activities* (New York: Crown, 1964), 7–22, 62–97, 99–102; National Museum of History and Technology, *Exhibits in the Museum of History and Technology: An Illustrated Tour* (Washington, D.C.: Smithsonian Institution, 1968), 40–41, 45–51, 60–63, 74–127; O'Dea and West, "Editorial," 150–57; Frank A. Taylor, "The Museums of Science and Technology in the United States," *Museum* 20 (1967): 158–63; *Museums Journal* 27 (April 1927): 327; *Museums Journal* 28 (December 1928): 204; *Museums Journal* 48 (November 1948): 174; Robert P. Multhauf, "A Museum Case History: The Department of Science and Technology of the United States Museum of History and Technology," *Technology and Culture* 6 (Winter 1965): 47–58; Bernard S. Finn, "The Science Museum Today," *Technology and Culture* 6 (Winter 1965), 74–82. One centennial park visitor was Dom Pedro II, last emperor of Brazil. He loved museums, technology, and education. He was a collector and spent a good deal of time at the Smithsonian.
20. The original Spark!Lab closed in 2012 in preparation for the renovation of the Museum's west wing. Today, the Draper Spark!Lab has the look and feel of an inventor's work space. See https://invention.si.edu/try/sparklab. Regarding the network, the cost, at the time of writing, for purchasing a two-year membership in SparkLab is $40,000. See https://invention.si.edu/node/11457/p/464-how-join and https://affiliations.si.edu/sparklab/.

21. Michal McMahon, "The Romance of Technological Progress: A Critical Review of the National Air and Space Museum," *Technology and Culture* 22, no. 2 (1981): 281–96; Michael Wallace, *Mickey Mouse History and Other Essays on American Memory* (Philadelphia: Temple University Press, 1996), 288–91; see http://airandspace.si.edu; and https://airandspace.si.edu/visit/educators.
22. See https://airandspace.si.edu/exhibitions/destination-moon.
23. Marina Koren, "The Smithsonian Raises $700,000 on Kickstarter to Save Neil Armstrong's Spacesuit," *Atlantic*, August 18, 2015, http://www.theatlantic.com/technology/archive/2015/08/smithsonian-neil-armstrong-spacesuit-museum/401663/.
24. Meilan Solly, "Watch the *Apollo 11* Anniversary Show That Was Projected onto the Washington Monument," *Smithsonian Magazine*, July 10, 2019, https://www.smithsonianmag.com/smart-news/life-sized-apollo-11-rocket-will-be-projected-washington-monument-commemorate-50th-anniversary-moon-landing-180972590/; https://airandspace.si.edu/go-for-the-moon.
25. Herman Kogan, *A Continuing Marvel: The Story of the Museum of Science and Industry* (Garden City: Doubleday, 1973), 9–11, 18–19, 30, 43, 45–55, 71, 87, 89, 95, 98–101, 111–13, 115, 117–20, 124–29, 131–33, 134, 138–43, 145-57, 162–63, 174, 185, 194–95, 197–99, 205.
26. Museum of Science and Industry, Chicago, "About the Museum," http://www.msichicago.org/explore/about-us/about-the-museum/.
27. Lenox Riley Lohr, "Publicity and Public Relations," *Museum* 4 (1951): 229–33; Daniel M. MacMaster, "The Museum of Science and Industry, Chicago," *Museum* 20 (1967): 167–68; Hindle, "Museum Treatment," 206–19; Ferguson, "Technical Museums," 42–46; Danilov, "Under the Microscope," 37–44; *International Committee, Museums of Science and Technology, Guidebook*, 1974, 169–76; and the museum's exhibit sites, including http://www.msichicago.org/visit/plan-your-visit/ and http://www.msichicago.org/explore/whats-here/exhibits/you-the-experience/.
28. Ford stated this at the museum's dedicated in 1929. It is reprinted in Hugh McCann, "Museum Traces History of Wheels," *New York Times*, April 2, 1972, 228, https://timesmachine.nytimes.com/timesmachine/1972/04/02/91324459.html?pageNumber=228.
29. Henry Ford Museum Staff, *Greenfield Village and Henry Ford Museum* (New York: Crown Publishers, 1972), 6–25, 46, 50–53, 70–91, 98–103, 142–217; *Greenfield Village and Henry Ford Museum, Selected Treasures* (Dearborn: Edison Institute, 1969), 4, 6; William Greenleaf, *From These Beginnings: The Early Philanthropies of Henry and Edsel Ford, 1911-1936* (Detroit: Wayne State University Press, 1964), 71–112; Allan Nevins and Frank Ernest Hill, *Ford: Expansion and Challenge, 1915-1933* (New York: Charles Scribner's Sons, 1957), 497, 500–506; Ferguson, "Technical Museums," 42; Hindle, "Museum Treatment," 210–11; https://www.thehenryford.org/history-and-mission/creating-our-campus/.
30. Henry Ford, "Ford Rouge Factor Tour Highlights," https://www.thehenryford.org/visit/ford-rouge-factory-tour/highlights.
31. Museum of Science, http://www.mos.org/.
32. For instance, the Ontario Science Centre opened in Toronto in 1969 to celebrate Canada's centennial and sought to take science out of the laboratory and put it in the hands of visitors to the museum. Currently, the museum is housed in an architectural complex of three extremely innovative, though aged, buildings. Over the past six decades, it has welcomed more than fifty million visitors. In early 2023, the premier of the province of Ontario, Doug Ford, announced plans to relocate the museum to a smaller, newer, and custom-built facility on the Toronto waterfront. That plan has been met with some opposition. See Ontario Science Center, "Relocation," https://www.ontariosciencecentre.ca/about-us/ontario-science-centre-relocation.
33. Sheila Grinnell, *A New Place for Learning Science: Starting and Running a Science Center* (Washington, D.C.: Associate of Science-Technology Centers, 1992), 6–7.
34. John G. Beetlestone, Colin H. Johnson, Melanie Quin, and Harry White, "The Science Center Movement: Contexts, Practice, Next Challenges," *Public Understanding of Science* 7(1998): 5–26; quoted material from 7–8.
35. ASTC, "About ASTC," https://www.astc.org/about/.
36. ASTC, "About ASTC," https://www.astc.org/about/.
37. ASTC, "Advancing Equity and Justice," https://www.astc.org/about/equity/.

38. National Science Foundation, "Now Showing: Film, TV, Museums, and More," https://www.nsf.gov/news/now_showing/museums/skyline.jsp.
39. See NSF, "National Science Foundation-Funded Projects with Online Learning Products & Resources," March 29, 2020, https://www.informalscience.org/news-views/national-science-foundation-funded-projects-online-learning-products-resources.
40. The Exploratorium moved from the Palace of Fine Arts to Pier 15 on the waterfront of the Embarcadero. Construction began on the new site in 2010 and the museum held its grand opening at the new location in 2013. See http://www.exploratorium.edu/piers/.
41. Frank Oppenheimer, "A Rationale for a Science Museum," *Curator* 11, no. 3 (1968): 206.
42. Exploratorium, http://www.exploratorium.edu/about-us.
43. Exploratorium, "Designing Teaching and Leaning Tools," http://www.exploratorium.edu/education/designing-teaching-learning-tools.
44. Edward P. Alexander, "Frank Friedman Oppenheimer," in *The Museum in America: Innovators and Pioneers* (Walnut Creek: AltaMira Press, 1997), 117–32; Hilde S. Hein, *The Exploratorium: The Museum as Laboratory* (Washington, DC: Smithsonian Press, 1990); Sally Deunsing, "Exporting the Exploratorium: Creating a Culture of Learning," *ASTC Dimensions*, November–December 1999, 3–7. Linda Dackman, "Invisible Aesthetic: A Somewhat Humorous, Slightly Profound Interview with Frank Oppenheimer," *Museum* 150 (1986): 120–22.
45. This trajectory is communicated in the website sharing the new beginning for the museum as part of its construction and move in 2013. See http://www.exploratorium.edu/piers/.
46. Melanie Quin, "The European Science Centre Movement," in *Towards the Museum of the Future*, 47.
47. Rob Semper, "Nodes and Connections: Science Museums in the Networked Age," *ASTC Dimensions*, November–December 2001; Jim Spadaccini, "Museum and the New Web: The Promise of Social Technologies," *ASTC Dimensions*, July–August 2006; Leo Tan and R. Subramaniam, *E-Learning and Virtual Science Centers* (Hershey, PA: Information Science Publishing, 2004). To return to the notion of "browsing" behavior, these two authors suggest that science centers especially need to approach the web as they do their onsite exhibition spaces and programming; simply stated, it is merely browsing in a different venue.
48. C. Wood, B. Sullivan, M. Iliff, D. Fink, and S. Kelling, "eBird: Engaging Birders in Science and Conservation." *PLoS Biology* 9(12):e1001220; http://ebird.org/content/ebird/news/rba; http://fold.it/portal/info/science.
49. For more on the Transcription Center, see *Collections: A Journal for Museum and Archives Professionals* 12:2 (June 2016), edited by Juilee Decker, guest edited by Meghan Ferriter and Christine Rosenfeld, https://journals.sagepub.com/toc/cjxa/12/2.
50. The listing of citsci projects is here: http://scistarter.com/about.html. Citing Follet and Strezov's study, which reports that the first article published using citizen science appeared in 1997, in 2007, six papers were presented at the Ecological Society of America meeting. And, since this time, peer-reviewed citizen science articles have increased. See Ria Follett et al., "An Analysis of Citizen Science Based Research: Usage and Publication Patterns," *PLOS (Public Library of Science) ONE*, 2015, doi:10.1371/journal.pone.0143687; Christopher Kullenberg et al., "What Is Citizen Science? – A Scientometric Meta-Analysis," *PLOS (Public Library of Science) ONE*, 2016, doi: 10.1371/journal.pone.0147152; both of which were cited in Jennifer Grigg, "Examining New Trends in Citizen Science," Phys.org, February 2, 2016, http://phys.org/news/2016-02-trends-citizen-science.html.
51. Alison King, "From Sage on the Stage to Guide on the Side," *College Teaching* 114:1(Winter, 1993): 30–35.

4

History, Place, and the Past

This chapter examines a range of museums that present history in myriad ways. They might focus on explaining the past through material culture shown in context with objects on view; storytelling framed around embodied experiences in immersive settings; and place-based narratives that bear witness to a community or cultural group, an event or tragedy that occurred at a site, or other respectful commemorations. As a type of museum, history museums emerged from two of the types of museums addressed in previous chapters—art and design and natural history museums. Yes, in some ways, they move beyond these origin stories, as museum scholar Ellis Burcaw notes: "All museums are history museums in the sense that all preserve objects pertaining to past events and situations."[1] A national census of history-focused organizations (if we use a broader terminology than *merely* museum) was conducted by the American Association for State and Local History (AASLH) to reveal that there are more than 21,588 history organizations in the United States Although this reflects a staggering number, the census fully acknowledges that the count is conservative and may reflect the "floor rather than a ceiling" in terms of how many history-centering organizations exist.[2]

To take a step back and center the concepts of history, place, and their intersection with museums and memory institutions, this chapter is organized around three categories of history-focused museums based upon the emphasis of the education, interpretation, and engagement the museum delivers—whether that focus is on collections, structures/sites, or commemoration. These distinctions are made for the sake of "lumping" together all museums that address history and the past around a cluster of approaches, rather than "splitting" them into a series of categories too numerous to list.[3] To be clear, the boundaries between these three frames of reference that form categories around collections, sites/structures, and commemoration are, in fact, blurred, and their introduction here is not meant to confine, restrict, constrain, or judge. The categories are simply a method to help frame the narrative for the purposes of an introduction to history museums writ large.

The first section examines European precedents for history museums and the primacy of object-based collections, such as the Muse Jovianum and industrial and decorative arts museums. The second section explores institutions that privilege structures and sites, such as open-air museums, historic houses, sites of conscience, and memorial museums. The third section describes preservation and commemorative practices that have led to the creation of organizations, such as historical societies, and have also directed national campaigns that have impacted the delivery of exhibitions and programs of local, regional, state, and national museums around milestone anniversaries of historic events, including the bicentennial (and forthcoming semiquincentennial) of the founding of the United States and the sesquicentennial of the American Civil War.

In simplest terms, history museums are physical places we can enter, examine, and explore in order to learn about the past and to frame our own understandings of the past in the present. What will become apparent in this chapter is how the designation of "history museum" has myriad instantiations and how one museum might actually fulfill the goals of more than one type of history museum. This overlapping of aims has, in fact, been broached in each chapter prior to this one: some art collections also housed objects of a natural history sort. In those cases, the blurring was across the boundaries of that museum type (and across chapters, if you will). Here, there is the added complication in that the term *history museum* can mean many things. History museums are historical societies and organizations that offer broader framing around a community or culture, an event, or an organization. History museums include an historic house that presents an environment in which to view such collections and to learn about the history in the spaces where it was lived. History museums are open-air or outdoor museums that offer a compilation of historic structures, arranged around a theme, chronological framing, or other idea and staffed with costumed interpreters. History museums are memorial museums, a new category developed in the late twentieth century, that give extended opportunities for reflection as well as research through associated libraries and archives.[4] History museums are historic grounds that are selected for preservation and amplified through interpretation. In the interest of "lumping," then, this chapter frames all the museums in it as related in their interest in examining and presenting the past and using it as an opportunity to reflect on our world today and to make a better tomorrow.

History Museums and Collections

Early European Historical Collections

History museums emerged in the eighteenth century from natural history museums, with their focus on taxonomic collections that revealed human negotiation with and manipulation of the natural and built environment. In the nineteenth century, history museums adapted exhibit styles from art museums and presented objects from the past as exemplars of design and human accomplishment. Today, history museums collect and preserve objects of the past and use them to convey historical perspective and inspiration.

Museum Jovianum

The history museum emerged from those devoted to natural history and art. It was, at first, a spin-off from the art collection. Paolo Giovio, bishop, humanist, and scholar, was the best known of the early collectors of likenesses of famous men. At his residence in Como about 1520, he began to assemble 280 portraits in four categories—deceased poets and scholars, living poets and scholars, artists, and political leaders, including military commanders, statesmen, popes, and monarchs. The living members of this cult of glory were represented by portraits painted from life, but the others were represented by busts one and a half feet high painted on canvas and based upon what sources Giovio could find. This assemblage came to be known as the Museum Jovianum: it was considered one of the marvels of the age. (It bears mention that Giovio revived and brought into general use the word *museum*.) Also attesting to the museum's significance, Cosimo de Medici sent Christofano dell' Altissimo to Como to make copies of Giovio's portraits for the Medici collection in Florence after the collector died. This type of historical collection was also kept alive through the books of engravings of the portraits that appeared in Florence (1551), Paris (1552), and Basel (1557).[5]

As a kind of history museum, the Museum Jovianum became enormously popular with noble and wealthy collectors in the sixteenth and seventeenth centuries. Catherine de Medici, wife of the French Dauphin (later Henri II), in her Paris residence had 551 portrait drawings, many of them set in paneled walls. Her Enamel Cabinet paired thirty-two portraits with thirty-two Limoges enamels, and her Mirror Cabinet contained another eighty-three portraits mounted with 119 Venetian-looking glasses.[6] Paul Ardier, lawyer and secretary of defense, filled a long gallery of his Château de Beauregard in the Loire Valley with 327 portraits organized and displayed around the kings of France; this Gallery of Portraits can still be viewed in the chateau today. About 1600, the Gonzagas had a special room containing the likenesses of "the most beautiful women in the world," and Catherine the Great later bought the *Cabinet of Muses and Graces* for her Peterhof palace.[7]

The concept of the Museum Jovianum may have appealed to antiquarians, but rows of portraits, often uniform in size, did not constitute an exciting exhibition technique. Nevertheless, it had American versions. Du Simitiere's small museum at Philadelphia in 1782 exhibited many of his drawings of Revolutionary military leaders and statesmen; some of his works were engraved and published in French, Spanish, and English editions. Peale's Philadelphia Museum displayed 269 portraits and paintings, most of them by Peale and his family and of Revolutionary leaders and the Founding Fathers. From 1817 until his death in 1834, John Henri Isaac Browere sought unsuccessfully to establish a national gallery by modeling busts of famous Americans, most of their faces delineated from life masks made by a secret process of applying thin coats of quick-drying grout to the greased subject. Alexander Hamilton, Thomas Jefferson, Marquis de Lafayette, John Adams, John Quincy Adams, James and Dolley Madison, James Monroe, Martin Van Buren, and Henry Clay are some of the twenty-one busts or masks that have survived.[8] The early American historical societies also collected portraits, and as late as the 1850s, Lyman Copeland Draper of the State Historical Society of Wisconsin was forming a frontier historical art gallery composed chiefly of portraits of pioneers and Indians; he thought "the noblest aim of Art . . . the illustration or perpetuation of great events in history." While many portrait collections have dispersed, the National Portrait Gallery of the Smithsonian Institution in Washington has become a modern American Museum Jovianum with more than twenty-two thousand depictions in a variety of media that feature presidents and first ladies, citizens and soldiers, artists and scientists, orators and movie stars.[9]

Depictions of politicians, inventors, and other individuals can only perfunctorily communicate the history of a nation. Thus, the National Museum of American History (NMAH) was created on the heels of the nation's bicentennial, in 1980, as a reincarnation of the Museum of History and Technology.[10] Today NMAH is well known for its thematic exhibitions ranging from the inaugural gowns of the First Ladies to iconic displays featuring Dorothy's ruby slippers from *The Wizard of Oz*, Muhammed Ali's boxing gloves, and a piece of Plymouth Rock. Beyond fragments and personal objects, the museum also displays architectural structures: the exhibit *Within These Walls* presents a reconstructed Georgian-style, timber-framed house that is the means of telling the story of the five families who lived in it when it stood in Ipswich, Massachusetts, from the mid-1760s through 1945.[11]

Exciting new exhibits have been installed recently including *Entertainment Nation/Nación del espectáculo*, an expansive bilingual exhibition highlighting museum collections with a lens on entertainment, with approximately two hundred objects on view, including Indiana Jones's fedora; the stopwatch from the television program *60 Minutes*; John Coltrane's saxophone; Prince's "Yellow Cloud" guitar; Captain America's red, white, and blue shield; and Mia Hamm's 1996 Olympic soccer jersey. The museum curators present these items in conversation with one another in hopes that by doing so, viewers can see how "entertainment played a key role in shaping the nation at any given time in the nation's past." Museum director Anthea Hartig categorized this exhibit's purpose as helping visitors to "understand the power of entertainment as a force for change" and part of the museum's mission to "use history to empower people to create a more just and compassionate future." In addition to the onsite exhibition, the museum is rolling out an entire exhibition platform with content from the onsite experience, as well as online digital programming, and supporting K-12 curriculum. *Entertainment Nation* is the largest long-term bilingual exhibition on the National Mall and has a projected life span of twenty years to allow for swapping in-and-out of collections, graphics, and interactives.[12]

More generally, the museum has developed a comprehensive digital engagement plan that encompasses the websites with online exhibitions and collections access, blogs, educational materials for teachers and students, and social media. Through these initiatives, the museum aims to leverage collections and stories while encouraging "visitors to be more involved, thoughtful citizens." In this way, the museum has demonstrated how history extends beyond the four walls of an historic house or site to meet visitors where they are.[13]

Industrial and Decorative Arts Collections

A precursor of the history museum was the museum of industrial or decorative arts. After the Great Exhibition of 1851 in London, the South Kensington Museum (today the Victoria and Albert Museum, or the V&A) was founded with industrial and decorative art from the Crystal Palace. Its exhibits were organized under the technical classification system, by which ceramics, glassware, metalwork, enamels, and the like were placed together, often in separate rooms, arranged chronologically or by patterns. Nearly everything was on display (today we call this system "visible storage," as discussed in Chapter 1). This kind of exhibit may have satisfied scholars and connoisseurs intent upon examining large numbers of examples and craftsmen looking for sources of inspiration for their own work, but crowded exhibits and heavy glass cases crammed with objects did little to engage or educate the general public.[14] (See Chapter 1 for further discussion of the Victoria and Albert Museum origins.)

A group of German museum curators conceived a new arrangement for such material. The Germanisches Museum at Nuremberg in 1856 purchased an old Carthusian monastery and installed there six original rooms ranging from one of a Tyrolean peasant (fifteenth century) to those of Nuremberg patricians (seventeenth century). By 1888, the museum had many such rooms following this culture history arrangement, so that one could imagine that he was walking through several centuries of German history. At the turn of the century, the Swiss Landesmuseum in Zurich had sixty-two such rooms, and the Bavarian Museum in Munich offered seventy-six period galleries and rooms.

The role and attitude of the nineteenth-century-museum visitor in relation to museum objects changed in a dramatic way, especially in history museums (and, to some degree, in natural history museums, too). No longer did visitors expect to stroll past portraits of the famous and cases of precious objects. The actual setting of the experience fundamentally changed a museum visit. Ethnographic clusters of "folk," displays of costumes on mannequins, and even whole room settings of objects removed the separation of the viewer from the object in significant ways. As will be revealed, the outdoor museum changed the dynamic further. First, visitors encountered spaces "inhabited" by wax figures. And museums in Holland, Denmark, and Sweden welcomed visitors into display spaces, complete with a person to add to the visitor-object exchange so as to incorporate a third dimension—that of the narrative.[15]

History Museums and Structures/Sites

This section addresses institutions that have a special significance based upon the location of their structure. They include open-air museums, historic houses, sand sites of conscience, and memorial museums. Larger sites, perhaps with or without structures, but still framed through an interpretive lens, are discussed in the final sections of this chapter, "Sites of Conscience" and "History Museums and Commemoration."

Open-Air or Outdoor Museums

European international expositions in the nineteenth century featured national displays that promoted technological achievements, agricultural products, and unique qualities. Folk objects were on display at the 1878 *Exposition Universelle* in Paris. The following Paris fair, in 1889, showcased people, their objects, and ways of life: people brought from faraway lands were living in reconstructed houses, wearing traditional dress, practicing arts, and playing Indigenous music. A Colonial Exhibition at Amsterdam in 1883 displayed an Indonesian Kampong, and two years later, this outdoor village was given to the Rijksmuseum voor Volkenkunde at Leiden, where it attracted large crowds before damage from the harsh winters led to its closing in 1891. These popular exhibitions used ethnographic techniques, linking history museums to natural history and anthropological museum practices, and provided viewers with an engaging sense of culture and history. Such exhibition of folk objects and the inclusion of individuals from these communities was a "fresh museum concept" according to Bernard Olsen, founder of the Danish Folk Museum. Olsen noted that these materials were associated with a "class" whose life and activities were heretofore unexamined.[16] Olsen and others carried out such displays without evidencing the lack of consent of those being treated no better than the objects on view. (Further discussion of such "Othering" is discussed in Chapter 2 and in Section III.)

This drive to see and to understand cultures and forms from faraway places persisted beyond the fairs. In fact, in the last quarter of the nineteenth century, the Scandinavians developed a new kind of museum devoted to folk culture, ethnography, and social history. Scholar, teacher, and folklorist Artur Hazelius of Stockholm was father of the idea. Hazelius was distressed to see the Industrial Revolution threaten the pleasant, coherent, and distinctive ways of living found in the different regions of Sweden and, indeed, all of Scandinavia. He determined to collect and preserve the furniture, furnishings, implements, costumes, and paintings of yesteryear. In 1873, he opened in Stockholm his Museum of Scandinavian Folklore (later called *Nordiska Museet*, or Nordic Museum). As his collection grew, he was offered entire buildings and other materials too bulky to show indoors. As a result, he acquired seventy-five acres on a rocky bluff at an old fortification (Skansen) overlooking Stockholm Harbor and started an open-air, or outdoor museum there in 1891. At Skansen, Hazelius amassed buildings moved from various parts of Scandinavia—today, some 150 structures dating from the Middle Ages to the twentieth century that include farmhouses, a manor house, barns, outbuildings, cottages, shops, a church, and craftsmen's workshops. Hazelius and his successors added attractive gardens and typical farm crops to set off the buildings, as well as authentic furniture and furnishings for the interiors. Costumed interpreters contextualize the culture, traditions, and life of the former inhabitants. Orchestras and musicians perform onsite, and restaurants and bars serve period food throughout the year.[17]

Museums focusing on multiple structures reconstructed as if a village, along with demonstration of historic trades, and skills, such as farming, cooking, and sewing, offered a new format and context for museums. These sites employ living history as a form of re-creation of the site as well as contextualization of it. Above, Anneliese Meck, former associate director of DEAI at Genesee Country Village & Museum in Mumford, New York, demonstrates candle making.
Photo taken by Elizabeth Lamark, Courtesy of Genesee Country Village & Museum.

Museum interpretation can be enhanced by interpreters demonstrating skills and trades at Genesee Country Village & Museum in Mumford, New York, a sprawling museum complex with an art gallery, nature trails, historic base ball field, and historic village. Jamison Taylert demonstrates skills of a blacksmith inside of the museum's blacksmith shop, an early nineteenth-century shop relocated from Elba, New York, to the museum campus.
Photo taken by Matt Wittmeyer, Courtesy of Genesee Country Village & Museum.

Hazelius used the idea of heritage and understanding of the past as a steadying influence in the face of the violent changes of modern life. He offered a new approach in museum exhibition, for he wished "to place the historical objects in their functional context . . . against the background of their entire cultural environment." He re-created the life of older periods, stimulating the sensory perceptions of the visitors and giving them a memorable experience. As they walk about the carefully restored environment of another day, their thoughts and emotions help bring the place to life.[18] Haze-lius's ideas served as inspiration for other open-air museums in Scandinavia and beyond.

U. S. Outdoor Museums and Historic House Sites

The first large American outdoor museum organized on the Scandinavian model and moving historical structures to a central location was Greenfield Village at Dearborn, Michigan, dedicated by Henry Ford in 1929.[19] Along with Greenfield Village, Plimoth Patuxet (formerly known as Plimoth Plantation)[20] and Williamsburg,[21]among other outdoor museums in the United States, employ living history as a form of re-creation of the site as well as contextualization of it. Throughout the description and discussion that follows, attention should be paid to the ways in which the living history techniques employed at these sites involve a range of theatrical techniques, including first-, second-, and third-person strategies that seek to enliven the museum experience.

While part of the entire "Henry Ford" campus discussed in Chapter 3's address of "Science Museums," here the attention is on Greenfield Village, where Ford aimed to recenter the attention of historians and the public away from politics and wars. Contemptuous of book learning, big ideas, and windy

Actor David Shakes portrays Frederick Douglass in the historic Brooks Grove Methodist Church, which dates to 1844. The church is one of sixty-eight historic structures moved to create the historic village at Genesee Country Village & Museum.
Photo taken by Elizabeth Lamark, Courtesy of Genesee Country Village & Museum.

generalizations, Ford's anti-intellectual attitude led him to assert: "Most history is more or less bunk." Still, he was interested in his own kind of history, and he said about Greenfield Village: "When we are through, we shall have reproduced American life as lived; and that, I think, is the best way to preserve at least a part of our history and tradition. For by looking at things people used and that show the way they lived, a better and truer impression can be gained than could be had in a month of reading."[22]

By 1936, the 240 acre "village" contained more than fifty buildings, including a traditional New England green with a church, town hall, courthouse, post office, and general store; the Scotch Settlement schoolhouse Ford attended as a boy; the Plymouth, Michigan, carding mill to which Ford's father took wool; Noah Webster's house; William Holmes McGuffey's (of McGuffey Readers fame) Pennsylvania log-cabin birthplace; a five-hundred-ton stone Cotswold Cottage; and John Bennet's jewelry shop from Cheapside, London, which has been repurposed as a sweetshop. Ford did not intend that his village would actually represent the life of a specific historical place; rather he conceived of the village *in toto* as a museum with the buildings as specimens. Ford turned the buildings of Greenfield Village into enormous museum objects and thus created a new context for them.[23]

Many outdoor museums of this general type developed in the first half of the twentieth century, including Plimoth Patuxet and Old Sturbridge Village in Massachusetts; Mystic Seaport in Connecticut; the Farmers' Museum in Cooperstown, New York; Shelburne Museum in Vermont; and Old World Wisconsin in Wisconsin. Establishing and sustaining such museum complexes requires clear definition of purpose supported by historical research to re-create an authentic, historically justifiable community that engages with visitors in a way that sustains interest in the past and its intersections with our present human condition.[24]

History, Place, and the Past

Established in 1947, Plimoth Patuxet is a re-creation of the seventeenth-century settlement in Massachusetts. While consisting of reproduction dwellings and public buildings based on careful research into both the site and the era, the site's major contribution to history museum practice is its interpretive approach of using staff to represent the actual early inhabitants of the colony. The research efforts led by anthropologist James Deetz included not only understanding what the site should look like, but also seeking to reproduce for visitors an authentic experience. Later, adaptations of the English language were used onsite to align with the vernacular that emerged in seventeenth-century Massachusetts.

Plimoth Patuxet and other living history sites sought to engage visitors with "characters" from the past to further intensify the experience. Such "first-person" interpretive approaches would affect interpretive practices across the country and, in the case of outdoor museums, became a springboard for discussions about social history. Moreover, this additional level of context furthers the level of engagement beyond the idea of simply moving disparate old buildings into a pleasant parklike setting. The context shifts from interpretation to living history.[25]

An exemplar of interpretation and *in situ* learning may be found at Colonial Williamsburg, the pre-served and restored capital of eighteenth-century Virginia. Perhaps the best-known outdoor museum in the United States, Colonial Williamsburg has expanded the historic-house concept to include the major part of a colonial city, over three hundred acres and eighty-eight original eighteenth-century buildings with carefully furnished interiors open to the visiting public. As a living historic district, it has hundreds of houses, shops, and public outbuildings occupied by residents of Williamsburg or rented to tourists.

Colonial Williamsburg was founded in 1926, when John D. Rockefeller Jr. decided to finance the dream of W. A. R. Goodwin, rector of Bruton Parish Church, to bring the colonial capital back to life. The town plan was virtually intact, and some eighty-five original buildings still stood. They were provided with authentic outbuildings; gardens based on American and English precedents were developed; and some important buildings were reconstructed when enough evidence was available. Historical, architectural, archaeological, and curatorial researchers worked together to obtain a high degree of authenticity. As the project matured, careful attention was given to its education program or interpretation. Well-trained costumed guides and working craftsmen convey life on the scene with period dining, military drills, music, dancing, plays, fireworks, and many other activities that appeal to the visitor and encourage participation. Emphasis is placed on using the historical environment as a primary resource in conjunction with inquiry-based learning.

This type of environment, however, faced challenges in the 1970s, as the public was less inter-ested in prescribed enactments and grew more interested in accurate historical context that was interpreted with the visitor present. According to scholar David B. Allison, "History has already lost its relevance to much of the public." Citing Rosenzweig and Thelen's essential work on the "past" as opposed to "history," Allison points out that "most Americans care deeply about their own personal connection with history—their genealogy and family stories—but that they are turned off by how museums and formal educators present history. . . . They strip history of its vibrancy and relevance by deemphasizing relatable human stories and . . . [use] outmoded educational theories and techniques that may once have worked but are now as dead as the people that they try to each about."[26] Those who enliven history—those "outsider" history-makers—offer much to the history of living history and museums through their embrace of re-creation as well as contextualization.[27]

Although most American outdoor museums may be classified as history museums or historic sites that include political, economic, and social history contexts, the outdoor museum, as a concept, has been classified as a folk museum or ethnographic park. This treatment is due to the fact that the outdoor museum was "more than a new idea of museum arrangement," more than combining the pleasant atmosphere of the picnic with the serious museum visit. Its most important contribution "was the conception that the greatness of a country, the strength of its industries, the beauty of its art, have firm roots in that country's own history."[28]

More recently, however, living history sites are coming to terms with the realities of their past. In 2020, Plimoth Plantation announced a name change to Plimoth Patuxet in order to reflect the Indigenous language name for the region. Moreover, the dropping of the word "plantation" diminished the association with Black enslavement and, instead, prioritized the historical reenactments of both the seventeenth-century English colony (referred to as Plimoth in the original spelling, rather than Plymouth) and the Wampanoag tribe. Even so, there is more work to be done in terms of telling fuller narratives onsite. While the name change is a start, expansion of the Wampanoag exhibition, beyond a single homesite, would allow for broader representation and storytelling, in comparison to multiple sites comprising an entire village designated for the stories of the English colonists.[29]

At Colonial Williamsburg, expanded programming allows for multiple narratives to be told, rather than simply those of the monied class, working class, or trades. For example, a suite of events and experiences enables visitors to learn more about the free and enslaved Black people of Williamsburg. On a visit to Colonial Williamsburg today, for instance, some tours offer highlights focused on Black artists and artisans. Some structures, by their mere existence, can also draw attention to Black experiences, such as the First Baptist Church, one of the country's earliest Black congregations, and Williamsburg Bray School, the oldest extant building dedicated to the education of Black children in the United States. Costumed interpretation presents the lives of Black individuals in Williamsburg, such as James Armistead Lafayette, an enslaved Virginian who won his freedom for his service as a double agent in the American Revolution, and Gowan Pamphlet, an enslaved tavern worker who founded the aforementioned Baptist Church.

While the previous two examples disclose ways that attention is drawn to developing fuller narratives in living history museum settings, a third example bears mention here: the framing of plantation museum sites in the South and the persistent presence of multiple buildings onsite, typically cabins for the enslaved. An exceptional example of interpretation of this sort is Whitney Plantation in Wallace, Louisiana, which centers the stories of enslaved people while exploring and laying bare the horrors of enslavement. (By contrast, other plantations and their ancillary structures offer only eclipsed perspectives.) As African American studies scholar Stephen Small has noted in his examination of how plantation museums reveal contemporary struggles in storytelling around enslavement, such sites tie together representations of elite Whites and marginalized Blacks in past and present terms. They can disclose what the institutions choose to present about the past and what they, ultimately, choose not to include in their narratives about the past. These competing presentations are what Small refers to as "social forgetting and social remembering."[30]

Returning to the example of Whitney Plantation, writer, poet, and scholar Clint Smith has commented on the compression of past in present on this very site and its environs. He noted that the descendants of the enslaved still live in the surrounding areas amid "the intergenerational poverty that plagues many formerly enslaved communities nearly a century and a half after emancipation."[31] In thinking about the role of history museums, open-air museums, historical interpretation, and the task set before museums to communicate ideas through narrative embodiment, storytelling, and meaning-making at these sites, we might pause to reflect on how we think museums can appropriately communicate an awareness of the nuances and contours of such conflations of past and present.

United States Historic Houses

As we move from the examination of open-air museums in the United States to the historic houses/house museums, attention can be drawn to a museum type that scholar Charlotte Smith has referred to as the "Great Man" genre.[32] However, as fuller narratives are being told at open-air museums, so, too, are enriched stories becoming a part of the historic house narrative framing. An example of this expanded universe—beyond that of the "Great Man"—may be found at Monticello, Thomas Jefferson's home in Charlottesville, Virginia. Designed by the statesman and built over forty years as a home with an ornamental landscape, farm, and garden with orchards and vineyards, as well as a plantation,

Monticello was, in Jefferson's words, his "essay on architecture." While Jefferson died deeply in debt, stewardship of the house was the result of non-relatives who worked to restore and preserve the house until it was sold to the newly formed Thomas Jefferson Foundation in 1923.

Today, guided tours are offered of the twenty-one-room home along with outdoor tours focusing on Jefferson's interests in gardening, botany, and agriculture, and the enslaved persons whose labor made the management of the estate possible. While the house and gardens are standard fare at institutions of this sort, the perspectives of the enslaved persons—in fact, truly, the actual acknowledgment of their existence—came only following DNA test results in 1998 that determined Thomas Jefferson fathered children with an enslaved person, Sally Hemings, years after the death of Jefferson's wife.[33]

This new discovery furthers our understanding of Jefferson and, importantly, the 130 individuals who lived and worked on Mulberry Row, the industrial hub of Jefferson's five thousand-acre plantation. While these narratives are referenced only briefly in the general house tour, two additional opportunities provide context about the enslaved people at Monticello. A daily offering, "Slavery at Monticello," tells of the experiences of enslaved people who lived and labored, there as does a free app by the same name. Released in 2015, the app offers archival photographs and map features alongside commentary and narration by descendants of the enslaved community that lived at Monticello. The content is fully functional onsite and off, although the visitors to the house who are using the app will have an enhanced experience as Beacon technology alerts them to curated content as they near particular locations onsite.

As part of a multi-year effort to restore Monticello as Jefferson knew it, "and to tell the stories of the people—enslaved and free—who lived and worked" there, a second tour, "From Slavery to Freedom," is a longer, small-group, interactive experience that takes visitors through the home and gardens and along Mulberry Row to the Burial Ground for Enslaved People, before concluding with a facilitated dialogue on race and the legacies of slavery in the United States The title of this tour and dialogue experience takes its cues from the eponymous history book, written by John Hope Franklin in 1947, which has been continuously reprinted.[34]

In addition, onsite at Monticello, new signage just past the visitor center parking outlines the location of the Burial Ground, where more than twenty graves have been confirmed as part of an archaeological project undertaken in 2000-2001. Graveyards such as these are "considered the first black institutions in North America, and were expressions of the separateness that slavery created."[35] Expanded online content also discloses the range of resources focusing on enslavement at Monticello.[36] Such archaeological and historical research, and reinterpretation, offers an important example of the possibilities of multi-vocality, expanded narratives, and enhanced experiences at plantation and historic house sites in the United States Museums are cautioned, however, not to fall into the trappings of nostalgia, as Clint Smith witnessed on hist visits to Monticello, among other sites in the United States.[37]

In contrast to Monticello, Mount Vernon, Washington's plantation in Virginia, serves not only as a historic home, but also a monument to the first outstanding American historic preservationist, Ann Pamela Cunningham of South Carolina.[38] Various proposals had been made for Mount Vernon—that it serve as a summer residence for the president, that it be an old soldiers' home, a model farm, or an agricultural college. Private speculators suggested converting the mansion into a resort hotel or using the estate as a factory site. Neither the federal government nor the commonwealth of Virginia would agree to acquire it, but Cunningham was determined to "save American honor from a blot in the eyes of the gazing world" and to establish a shrine where "the mothers of the land and their innocent children might make their offering in the cause of greatness, goodness, and prosperity of their country." In 1856, Virginia chartered the Mount Vernon Ladies' Association of the Union. The Association raised two hundred thousand dollars to buy the plantation and began preservation work on the mansion on February 22, 1860. Extravagant schemes were suggested, such as taking the house down piece by piece and replacing it with a marble-faced replica, but Cunningham declared that the Association would "preserve with sacred reverence" Washington's house and grounds "in the state he left them."

An historic house more focused on everyday experiences may be found in the Lower East Side Tenement Museum (LESTM) in Lower Manhattan, New York, a type that Smith calls a "Social History" house museum, which emerged as an outgrowth in the field of history where effort is made to give disenfranchised members of society a voice. The museum, created by Ruth Abram, a social and civil rights activist, is sited in a five-story building built in 1863 and home to nearly seven thousand working-class immigrants until 1935. After the zoning laws changed and it could not sustain residential inhabitants, the street-side structure was a saloon, butcher shop, and clothing store, while the other floors were untouched. Abram, along with Anita Jacobson, discovered the building and its potential in 1988. In transitioning the building into a museum, they have also uncovered more than two thousand items that provide material cultural evidence of an immigrant past.[39] From 1988 until 1992, Abram and Jacobson began working to transform the tenement into a museum. To date, six of the apartments have been restored.

The museum preserves and interprets the narratives of immigrants, migrants, and the working class through personal narratives and by using the domestic space as a platform for social issues, such as race, ethnicity, class, and human rights. Through their work, the museum aims to "build an inclusive and expansive American identity and believe that the exploration of our complex history—one with moments of both inclusion and exclusion—helps prepare us to recognize and discuss today's complex issues with empathy and nuance." In this way, LESTM seeks to connect history to contemporary life and, ultimately, action.[40]

Each of these historic house examples shows a different way of establishing the presence of the past in contemporary museum experiences. Whereas Monticello has been the product of personal-turned-private foundation support, Mount Vernon illustrates reliance on private voluntary organizations like the Ladies' Association, and the Lower East Side Tenement Museum is a national historic site that has grown from the efforts of two historians and activists who teamed up with other preservationists to form the Lower East Side Preservation Coalition. In these latter two cases, importantly, amateur efforts led by women have been effective endeavors that have helped advance women's agency in cultural and social reform.[41]

Sites of Conscience

The term *sites of conscience* refers to "a place of memory—such as a historic site, place-based museum or memorial—that prevents this erasure from happening in order to foster more just and humane societies today." They are places that provoke as well as instill memories, however traumatic, and enable visitors to make connections between the past and the present. These organizations, institutions, and sites expand the definition of history museums and, in this way, are consciously and publicly striving to serve the public, as Elaine Heumann Gurian suggests, by "blurring" the boundaries between museums, memory work, and public service agencies. These institutions have foregrounded social change by advancing advocacy as part of their work.

The framing of Sites of Conscience, while new to the museum space, was codified in December 1999, around international interest and "the obligation of historic sites to assist the public in drawing connections between the history of our site and its contemporary implications. We view stimulating dialogue on pressing social issues and promoting humanitarian and democratic values as our primary function." The founding members were: the Lower Eastside Tenement Museum (New York), the Gulag Museum at Perm 36 (Russia), District Six Museum (South Africa), Liberation War Museum (Bangladesh), Workhouse (England), Project to Remember (Argentina), Slave House (Senegal), Terezin Memorial (Czech Republic), and the United States National Park Service.

Today, the International Coalition is "the only global network of historic sites, museums, and memory initiatives that connects past struggles to today's movements for human rights."[42]

The coalition moves beyond the walls of the museum to fill the spaces left by a history without context and fulfill needs acknowledged by Duncan Cameron, who charged that "by failing to provide meaningful interpretation of the collections museums [we] are, by that omission, guilty of misrepresentation, distortion of fact and encouragement of attitudes towards cultures other than our own which are dangerous and destructive."[43]

Within this call for situational context, a new type of museum was spawned in the late twentieth century, that of the memorial museum. In the United States, the earliest of these include the United States Holocaust Memorial Museum (dedicated in 1993) and the Oklahoma City National Memorial & Museum (memorial dedicated in 2000; museum dedicated in 2001). More recently were formed the 9/11 Memorial & Museum (memorial dedicated in 2011; museum dedicated in 2014), and the Legacy Sites in Montgomery, Alabama (The Legacy Museum, the National Memorial for Peace and Justice, and the Freedom Monument Sculpture Park), which bear witness to racial injustice at the sites where these events occurred and encompass the Atlantic slave trade to mass incarceration and the current crisis of police violence against Black people. All these institutions are a hybrid of history museums and interpretation sites that foreground historical context and place-based significance, respectively. They also memorialize and bring attention to place by being situated on the site of a tragedy, thus doubling their agency as both museums and sites of mourning.

9/11 Memorial & Museum, New York, New York

Such institutions combine ritual, veneration, and memorialization along with the gathering of collections to tell the story of the event to which the museum is tied. For instance, the 9/11 Memorial Museum displays the survivors' staircase (a fragment of stairs that many used to escape the wreckage), steel beams from the Twin Towers that became a surface for messages and prayers, and other architectural elements. All these were incorporated into the narrative of the museum, as "tangible links to the destruction and evidence of survival," while personal objects, embodiments of those whose lives were lost, are presented in great number and scale. As such, the 9/11 Memorial & Museum presents a context for the reenactment of this tragic event that touched the lives of so many, rather than an interpretation of an historical past. In this instance, and the other examples of memorial museums in the United States and elsewhere, museums also have the capacity to function as contemporary history museums and sites of advocacy and engagement—building upon the aims of the Sites of Conscience discussed above.

Such institutions face challenges, too, as public art scholar Harriet F. Senie has observed. Senie remarks on the entangled narratives and consequences brought on by such museums and memorials—sites where heroes and victims are conflated and "where critical space is devoted to the valorization of the latter." In discussing these sites, Senie notes the lack of context and individuation as well as the problematics of narrativization, or the lack thereof. "Since most visitors do not know the dead personally, however, and similar narratives are often used to describe each person, the overall effect is to render them all but indistinguishable. Such a homogenized composite does little to honor them; it conveys a kind of uniformity reminiscent of high school yearbooks. Concurrently, the focus on civic victims has created a misleading linkage of the distinct tragic events that led to their respective deaths."[44]

The Legacy Sites, Montgomery, Alabama

In contrast to the approaches taken in three address of specific tragedies, the Legacy Sites recognize and address long, and ongoing, injustices and their persistence today. Three locations comprise the Legacy Sites: The Legacy Museum, the National Memorial for Peace and Justice, and the Freedom Monument Sculpture Park. Together the sites offer an immersive, site-specific, yet also translatable, journey through the tragedy, and yet also the persistence, of racial injustice from the Atlantic slave trade to mass incarceration and the current crisis of police violence against Black people.

The Legacy Sites in Montgomery, Alabama (The Legacy Museum, the National Memorial for Peace and Justice, and the Freedom Monument Sculpture Park) bear witness to racial injustice at the sites where these events occurred and encompass the Atlantic slave trade to mass incarceration and the current crisis of police violence against Black people. At the National Memorial for Peace and Justice at the end of the pathway (above, foreground), 801 monuments, just like those in the memorial proper, are replicas that are to be retrieved by the counties where lynchings occurred. Behind the replicas stands the monument where the iconic pillars of six-foot monuments were constructed of Cor-ten steel with the names of the victims and places of their deaths and dangling from beams just as lynched bodies dangled from trees in the past. *Photo by author, taken August 2021.*

The first of these sites, the Legacy Museum, is located on the site of a cotton warehouse where Black people were forced to work in bondage. Here, the Museum tells the story of enslavement in the United States as the starting point for the narrative that follows. The exhibitions discuss laws, as well as individual acts, that caused oppression, racial terrorism and segregation, and its legacy in the form of mass incarceration, an era that legal scholar Michelle Alexander has called "The New Jim Crow." (The Jim Crow laws were enacted at local and state levels that legitimized anti-Black racism in the United States from the late nineteenth century until the passage of the Civil Rights Act of 1964 and the Voting Rights Act of 1965.) [45] As columnist Danté Stewart wrote upon his visit to the museum: "Every room offered a historical journey, from enslavement to modern-day mass incarceration, and summoned the history of White violence against Black life. Each also stirred an unshakable belief in Black dignity. . . . We saw heads of the formerly enslaved, sculpted with reverence [by Kwame Akoto-Bamfo's *Nkyinkyim Installation*]. We heard voices telling the stories of children who began their lives under the safe covering of a parent, only to be robbed of that peace. We saw scenes brought to life by a painter's heart and hand, displaying the many iterations of Blackness and its power."[46]

History, Place, and the Past

At the second site, on Caroline Street, is the National Memorial for Peace and Justice, which features an installation of more than eight hundred Cor-ten steel beams that identify and recognize more than 4,400 Black people killed in racial terror lynchings in the United States from 1877 until 1950. The site has three areas to guide the visitor experience here, and as well as a companion experience to the museum visit. The first of these is the walk to the monument, which interprets the history of African Americans from the middle passage through Reconstruction. The second is the aforementioned monument, where the iconic, six-foot pillars bear the names of the victims and the places of their deaths. Each beam dangles just as lynched bodies dangled from trees in the past. After this, visitors encounter the third area—the walk from the monument, which interprets the African American experience since 1950. At the end of the pathway, the memorial creates space for authorizing the past and challenging the communities who have done such harm in the past to admit and authorize truth and reconciliation. An additional 801 replica monuments, just like those in the memorial proper, serve as invitations. Each has the county, state, victim's names, and dates of death: they are on offer to be retrieved by the counties where the lynchings occurred. According to Sia Sanneh, a senior attorney who worked on the project, "We hope over the years the entire landscape of America will change as these markers are claimed."[47] In order to do so, the Monument Placement Initiative requires that communities have a public location for placing the monument and, importantly, demonstrate their commitment to racial reconciliation.

The third site, the Freedom Monument Sculpture Park, is made up of seventeen acres "along the very river [Alabama River] where tens of thousands of enslaved people were trafficked, breathtaking art and original artifacts invite an immersive, interactive journey and provide a unique view into the lives of enslaved people" and to honor the lives of ten million Black people enslaved in America.[48] Uniting these sites is soil. Soil undergirds the experiences: as soil from the lynching sites across the country are exhibited in the museum and onsite at the memorial, and the soil along the banks of the Alabama River which situates a monument honoring enslaved people in the United States.[49]

The International African American Museum, Charleston, South Carolina

Like the 9/11 Memorial & Museum, in honing in on a particular location, and the Legacy Sites, in framing past and present through the lens of enslavement, the International African American Museum (IAAM) in Charleston, South Carolina, is situated on Gadsen's Wharf, the disembarkation point of up to 40 percent of enslaved persons who were transported to the United States The newest museum among those discussed in this chapter, IAAM opened in June 2023, and its first installation consisted of galleries, a theater, a genealogy resource center, and a memorial garden. The permanent exhibition galleries demonstrate how enslaved and free Africans shaped economic, political, and cultural development across these themes: Transatlantic Experience, Atlantic Worlds, South Carolina Connections, Gullah Geechee, American Journeys, Carolina Gold, and African Roots. The special exhibition space provides another opportunity for reflecting on past and present. The inaugural special exhibition was a traveling exhibition organized by the Smithsonian called *Men of Change: Power, Triumph, Truth*, which tells his(stories) of Black men in the United States woven together over several themes: catalysts, community, fathering, imagining, myth-breakers, and storytellers. Vignettes share stories of celebrities, including Muhammed Ali, James Baldwin, Ta-Nehisi Coates, LeBron James, Kehinde Wiley, and many others.[50]

According to Malika N. Pryor, the museum's chief learning and engagement officer, the museum centers past and present in a tightly woven matrix of perseverance: "What we endeavor to do as visitors move through IAAM is to center the people who lived because they chose to. Our exhibitions are a curatorial prism, infracting light to create multiple colors that are engaging and dancing with the concepts of people, place, space and time—triangulating continental Africa, the United States and the greater Diaspora. Starting today, what we look forward to our visitors doing is choosing, just as our ancestors chose, sometimes just one step, one foot in front of the other."[51]

As sites of conscience, the 9/11 Memorial & Museum, the Legacy Sites, and the International African American Museum have an additional purpose: they authorize opportunities for reflection, healing, and recovery in addition to the rather traditional aims of museums as places of learning and knowledge construction. In the case of the second and third of these, the institutions, further, work alongside communities to amplify voices that have been ignored or marginalized from museum practices and inspire advocacy and action, thus realizing a vision of addressing past trauma as part of the path of change for the future.

History Museums and Commemoration

This section addresses an approach to interpreting the past that focuses on the significance of an event that warrants recognition and commemoration in the present. Unlike sites of conscience that call to mind trauma, the institutions engaged in this type of history work are focused on preservation (of sites, as well as stories and ideas) and commemoration (the carrying of those stories forward to the present). The commemoration is the spark that drives historical interpretation efforts on a local, regional, and national level. The efforts may result in activities such as costumed interpreters onsite, but they may also result in a wave of activity carried out by history museums seeking to share in the commemorative activities whose aims are to remember, commemorate, and understand the past in the present. This section addresses the earliest such commemorative activity conducted by historical societies and, relatedly, the emergence of public history as an academic discipline, before moving on to address the commemoration of the nation's centennial and bicentennial of the American Revolution, in 1876 and 1976 respectively, and other events that have born their imprint on the work of history museums. It is important to note that celebrations and commemorations of the United States as a nation have, to a great extent, elided the presence of those who were inhabitants of the land we now call our nation. Moreover, United States settler colonialism relies on Indigenous dispossession and genocide, as well as anti-Blackness and enslavement. As we move toward 2026, history organizations have opportunities to cast the net more widely and to weave together the many threads of narratives that reflect more voices, as explained below.

United States Historical Societies and Lineage Societies

As noted in the earlier chapters of this volume, the first permanent museum in the American English colonies was the Charleston Library Society, founded in South Carolina in 1773. Related, the historical society has been a staunch backer of the history museum in the United States. The founders of the first societies—the Massachusetts Historical Society (1791) at Boston, the New-York Historical Society (1804), and the American Antiquarian Society (1812) at Worcester, Massachusetts—were driven by a zeal for learning, love of country, and lineage. They had unlimited faith in the power of knowledge and reason and were determined to preserve the story of their defeat of the powerful British Empire and to point out the factors that caused the American genius for self-government to flower.

With their broad aspirations and enthusiastic energy, the early historical societies often embarked upon programs too ambitious and too widely dispersed. Thus, the New-York Historical Society collected animal, vegetable, and mineral specimens; productions of "the American Continent and the adjacent Islands"; coins and medals; European old-master paintings; artifacts of the Plains and South American Indians; Egyptian rarities, including three large mummies of the sacred bull Apis; as well as documents, paintings, and objects of New York origin and interest. Eventually, the society narrowed its field of collection to New York and began to dispose of materials outside that scope.[52]

By 1876, the centennial of American independence, seventy-eight historical societies existed in the country, about half of them with museums. Today there are thousands of them, ranging from very small to very large (with budgets from $0 to the millions), as the lines between historical societies and museums continue to blur, as noted in the 2022 AASLH census of history organizations.[53] Some of the earliest societies—for example, the Massachusetts Historical Society and the American Antiquarian

Society—had limited membership; still, the general trend has been to admit anyone with the proper interest and willingness to pay dues. The earliest societies were all entirely private in finance and control, but starting in the 1850s, Wisconsin and others in the Midwest received state appropriations. Their ideal became to serve everyone in the state, and programs broadened; the imaginative efforts of Reuben Gold Thwaites of the State Historical Society of Wisconsin to reach both learned and popular audiences illustrate this development.[54] Many societies no longer limit themselves to the scholarly activities of library, research, and publication; instead they now also promote museums, the marking of historic sites, historic preservation, school tours and clubs, and a host of other programs appealing to all ages. Their central museums often have expanded to include a chain of historic houses, preservation projects, and outdoor museums. As part of its central function, the historical society sometimes institutes educational, cultural, and community-oriented programs similar to those carried on directly by art or science museums, and state historical societies have often helped promote and assist local historical societies in counties and municipalities.

Historic house preservation and museum construction in the United States is tied to the development of lineage societies such as the Daughters of the American Revolution (DAR), the Sons of the Revolution, and the Colonial Dames, for instance, all of which drew upon narratives about the American Revolution and, by extension, George Washington and the colonists. For instance, members of the DAR are united in their lineal descent from patriots of the American Revolution. The membership is dedicated to historic preservation, education, and patriotism, with an emphasis on restoring and maintaining historic sites, as well as gravesites, memorials, and monuments.[55] The DAR have worked to preserve more than 250 historic houses in the United States.[56] Among these was the home of Susan B. Anthony in Rochester, New York, which today is part of the multi-building campus of the National Susan B. Anthony Museum and House. Susan B. Anthony (1820-1906) was a member of the Irondequoit Chapter of the DAR; another member of that chapter, Martha Taylor Howard, worked to preserve the house and to establish it as a memorial to Susan B Anthony, thereby connecting revolutions of two different sorts.[57]

Other organizations, such as the United Daughters of the Confederacy (UDC), championed ladies' memorial associations and were interwoven with Confederate veteran groups formed in the late 1860s to honor Confederate soldiers. The efforts of these groups and individuals—many of whom were associated, for instance, with groups such as the Sons of Confederate Veterans (SCV) and the United Daughters of the Confederacy (UDC)—led to a robust period of monument and memorial construction in the 1890s–1930s. This was framed within the context of the myth of the "Lost Cause" of the American Civil War, which subscribed to the belief that the effort of the treasonous rebellion by Confederates was a noble fight to defend states' rights rather than preserve slavery. That is, the efforts of Confederate leaders and soldiers, therefore, was viewed as a heroic, if a *lost*, cause. By the turn of the century, the Lost Cause was firmly established as a central focus of the work of the UDC, including its monument, historic house, and museum activity.[58]

Even as the DAR and UDC reflect divergent interests and histories of the United States that are at odds with one another, the importance of their efforts toward preserving historic sites and structures of importance, as well as imprinting the collective memory about people of the past, cannot be overstated. As such, the impact of lineage societies and their tethering to institutional histories can be cause for celebration, as well as concern. What beliefs do these societies espouse? Whom are they recognizing as integral to their work? What ideals do the namesakes of their historic homes and sites embrace? Questions such as these are starting points for understanding individual ideology as well as institutional genealogy, the latter as a topic taken up in Chapter 15 of this volume.

National Efforts

Another factor impacting the state and status of history museums in the United States was the commemoration of the nation's bicentennial of the American Revolution, in 1976—a grandiose effort by societies, organizations, and (even) Congress for patriotic exhibits that expressed nationalism and national unity. Just as the centennial spurred the creation of historic houses and sites, the national bicentennial in 1976 stimulated preservation activities in communities across the country.[59]

The American Revolution Bicentennial Commission (ARBC) and the American Revolution Bicentennial Administration (ARBA) sought activities across a range of arenas—including sports, education, arts, history, construction, and otherwise commemorative activities, as well as exhibitions—that could enlist the interest of all Americans and would promote national unity. As Charles Mathias, the senator from Maryland who introduced the legislation on July 4, 1966, that led to the first Bicentennial Commission (ARBC) and the subsequent creation of the ARBA, noted a decade later: "Celebration of our 200th birthday as revolutionary freedom fighters, therefore, fades quickly in light of present struggles to reignite the eroded faith and sensitivity of our citizenry. What the Bicentennial offers us is an appropriate time to dedicate all our energies to forging new principles based on our historic values, principles which should fully reflect the challenges of our times and tile realities we wish to experience in our third century."[60]

Through word and image, exhibitions were expected "to tell a story in literary form, to win an audience, and to point out moral lessons from the past."[61] For instance, *The World of Franklin and Jefferson*,[62] which charted the role of these two in their commitment to independence and freedom, toured throughout the United States and Europe from 1975 until 1977. This and other exhibitions, such as *USA '76: The First Two Hundred Years* and *A Nation of Nations*, relied upon themes of unity and progress to promote loyalty to the federal government,[63] even as confidence in the government and ratings of the nation by the public continued to fall over the decade of the 1970s in response to civil unrest, high inflation and unemployment, Watergate, and involvement in the Vietnam War.[64] Put simply, exhibitions countered the reality of the social, economic, and political environment across the nation.

Moving away from the curatorial machine on the national level to the grassroots activities on the local level, the Bicentennial begat a sense of discovery and celebration in local heritage and history.[65] As Barbara W. Sommer has recounted, "Many of these newly founded organizations had missions that included managing reference libraries, museums, and in some cases, historic sites or small publication programs."[66] They are part of their communities and work with and through them as institutions of local history. In this way, history museums, national initiatives, and regional societies reinforce interest in the past.

Commitment to reflection, commemoration, and preservation has been carried out by the National Park Service, created in 1916 as part of the United States Department of the Interior. The NPS enacted more than a century of federal advocacy and funding into history and the historic preservation movement with the Historic Sites Act of 1935, which declared "a national policy to preserve for historic use historic sites, buildings, and objects of national significance for the inspiration and benefit of the people of the United States." This policy was greatly expanded by the National Historic Preservation Act (NHPA) of 1966, which established the National Register of Historic Places (NRHP), now boasting more than one million properties consisting of individual structures and those that are part of historic districts.[67] The Park Service also developed trailside museums and visitor centers for its numerous archaeological and historical properties as part of the Mission 66 initiative, which brought over one billion dollars of infrastructure and architecture improvements to parks over a ten-year period (1956–1966) in celebration of the fiftieth anniversary of the NPS, and the decade leading up to the Bicentennial of independence from Britain, discussed above.[68]

American Civil War Sesquicentennial (2011–2015)

Additional events of national interest have spawned significant activity in history museums. For instance, the sesquicentennial of the American Civil War (2011–2015) brought attention to the rehabilitation of the topographic, landscape, and cultural features of a number of park sites, particularly those associated with the activity and engagements of this conflict (1861–1865).[69] Greater attention was also paid to unraveling the mystic chords of memory to give a new birth to the historic landscapes and to reimagine exhibits to complement these interpretations. In his charge to his staff, NPS chief historian Robert K. Sutton commanded them to expand the narratives that unfold through interpretation and engagement at these sites: "In the aftermath of national trauma, we as a Nation (consciously or unconsciously) have assigned the rights of memory to a few select groups. In the aftermath of the Civil War, we accorded these rights to the veterans on both sides of the conflict. They, in turn, fostered a swift but incomplete reconciliation—one that pasted over but did not extinguish lingering bitterness, one that was based on selective memory, and forged, in part, at the expense of liberty for free blacks and newly freed slaves. . . .As a result, large segments of the population fail to see the war's relevance. The NPS has failed to find ways to engage large segments of Americans in ways that demonstrate how the war is relevant to them." Pointing out that historical scholarship has evolved, and spurs debate as well, the NPS entered into a new phase of storytelling, a century since its founding, that acknowledged history as the subject of continual debate, rather than etched in stone.[70]

For the sesquicentennial, from 2011–2015, restorations, rehabilitation, and renovations as well as onsite, commemorative events, were held across the country as diverse perspectives were developed to expand the narratives beyond strategies and tactics and, perhaps, draw in new audiences. In addition, the Civil War sesquicentennial gave museums across the nation the opportunity to cull from their collections to create exhibitions and programs associated with this war or its contexts. For instance, the Charleston Museum exhibited clothing, uniforms, accessories, quilts, and coverlets in 2011 as part of *Threads of War: Clothing and Textiles of the Civil War*; The Met exhibited more than two hundred photographs in the summer of 2013 for *Photography and the American Civil War*; the Library of Congress exhibited *The Last Full Measure: Civil War Photographs from the Liljenquist Family Collection* in 2011; and the National Portrait Gallery put on seven exhibitions online and onsite that focused on Civil War portraiture and related objects from 2012 through 2016.[71]

National Semiquincentennial (2026)

Methods of interpreting the past continue to evolve as we move further from the Bicentennial of the United States and the sesquicentennial of the American Civil War and closer toward the semiquincentennial of the United States in 2026. In addition to the promotion and coordination efforts of the United States Semiquincentennial Commission,[72] national organizations such as the American Association for State and Local History (AASLH), the National Council on Public History (NCPH), the Association of African American Museums, the Association of Tribal Archives, Libraries, and Museums, and others have developed guidance for those working to engage audiences interested in history and the past. Important to these approaches are the questions: What are we commemorating? And, relatedly, why?

The AASLH has produced a guide, *Making History at 250: The Field Guide for the Semiquincentennial*, that offers themes, ideas, goals, and information to guide history-framed museum work and to put these organizations at "the center of important conversations in their communities, allowing meaningful dialogue, informed debate, and mutual understanding to replace rancorous partisan conflict."[73] Key to this vision and, as we have seen, the work of history museums writ large, is incorporating perspectives into the crafting and interpretation of stories and for inviting the publics—that is, communities at large and individuals as the fullest expression of a heterogenous group—to participate in the making of history. In this way, the initiative chiefly articulates the difference between history and the past—between the prescribed narrative as told by an elite few and the events that transpired and were witnessed by individuals who reflect a multitude of perspectives. The goal is to engage in open conversations about what history is, to craft narratives about the past, and to reify what the United States can be through the inclusion of multiple perspectives and sources that have heretofore been excluded, marginalized, or unstudied.

For Further Consideration

Such efforts call to mind the movement in history museums in the United States that was in step, in the mid-twentieth century, with the academic social history movement that sought to better understand the American past from the perspective of the "bottom up"—those participants who were unlettered whose existence may not be as well-documented in collections or scholarship. In addition, the emergence of the field of public history, in the late 1970s, brought historians and other humanities scholars outside of the academy where they sought employment that would enable them to engage with the public often and directly.[74] Together, these shifts in direction brought intellectual changes to history museums. But, as evidenced in this chapter, more needs to be done.

Audiences are ready to rise to the challenge—in fact, they have been ready; we—as practitioners, scholars, and researchers—have lagged. Nearly forty years ago, Roy Rosenzweig and David Thelen argued in *The Presence of the Past*: "The most significant news of this study is that we [historians] have interested, active, and thoughtful audiences for what we want to talk about. The deeper challenge is finding out how we can talk to—and especially *with* [emphasis added]—those audiences." Historian Eric Foner, in an interview for *Museum News*, echoed Rosenzweig's position from the perspective of history exhibitions and scholarship: "But I think they [museums] don't give enough credit to the audience for being able to tackle complicated ideas, so there is frequently a tendency towards oversimplification. . . . I think that we owe it to visitors to give them the most up-to-date, complex history that we can, and that's where museums have sometimes fallen down in the past. The history presented has been over-simplified and too bland."[75]

Such calls are to engage in conversation and make the museum a space that can be a community garden (metaphorically), where ideas can seed, sprout, and bloom. The opening up of conversation and transparency about the work of history is also an invitation for letting go. By sharing authority and embracing what amounts to user-generated content, is part of the broader movement within museums to "let go" of their authority in favor of inclusion and participation, as further discussed in Sections II and III. The invitation to share, the expansion of narratives, and the multivocality of how museums cultivate audiences and engage them is a form of crowdsourced content, similar to the citizen-science projects mentioned in the previous chapter. Such efforts provide much-needed service to our institutions and "can result in deep and sustained engagement among virtual museum visitors" that may also contribute to their own personal goals, such as lifelong learning.[76]

Viewed within the context of the racial reckoning in the United States and more broadly, after the extrajudicial killing of George Floyd in 2020, history organizations and, truly, all museums have become the site of a range of activities—from conversations, exhibitions, and events, to protests, open calls for change, and action. In the United States, calls for social injustice have played out in our museums, as well as in town squares, boulevards, university quadrangles, and administrative edifices. Such grassroots initiatives have made clear how history seeps into our environments and is embodied in historic houses, collections, and narratives about the past that intrude into daily life in immediate, persistent, and anxious ways. The naming of institutions after enslavers and Confederates, for instance, is challenged, as are the collections in museums (such as items owned by these individuals, portraits and busts of them, and other likenesses), as well as indoor and outdoor statuary such as monuments and memorials. In these ways, historic houses, their collections, and museums are constructs that can (and have) framed the past in terms of nostalgia. History (and other) museums offer visible representations of entitlement, possession, control, and authority. They provide a view of the past through lenses that enable us to view memory, race, and the legacies of war, power, and subjugation.

Yet history museums also offer the opportunity to pose and answer questions about what history is (as opposed to nostalgia), whose stories are told as part of that history (and whose stories need to be sought out), whose memory matters, and ultimately how history is made.

Today, and in the future, history museums can frame the past in terms of memories and the fullest range of lived experiences. History organizations—like those described here—and sites of conscience are places that provide opportunities to peek at the past and to use the past as a platform on which to build a better tomorrow. In these ways, history museums—whether lumped together into the categories offered here or split into an atomized list that reflects the unique nature of each institution and the communities it serves—offer insight into who we are, what we value, and where we want to go in the future.

Notes

1. G. Ellis Burcaw, *Introduction to Museum Work*, 3rd ed. (Walnut Creek: AltaMira Press, 1997), 63.
2. American Association of State and Local History, "2022 National Census of History Organizations," https://www.aaslh.org/census/.
3. The terms *lumping* and *splitting* are used in any discipline where categorization is required, though methods may be at odds. The earliest documented use of the term was by naturalist and evolutionary biologist Charles Darwin in 1857; and later it was used by paleontologist George Simpson regarding the classification of mammals. Lumpers define terms broadly; splitters make precise categorizations. I was first turned on to these words through an article by Kiersten F. Latham, "Lumping, Splitting and the Integration of Museum Studies with LIS," *Journal of Education for Library and Information Science*, 56:2 (Spring 2015): 130–40.
4. For the third edition of this volume, the term history museum was expanded from the previous two editions to include historic houses, interpretation sites, sites of conscience, and memorial museums.
5. Niels von Holst, *Creators, Collectors and Connoisseurs* (New York: Putman, 1967), 92, 106; Francis Henry Taylor, *The Taste of Angels: A History of Art Collecting from Rameses to Napoleon* (Boston: Little, Brown, 1948), 77–8; Germain Bazin, *The Museum Age* (New York: Universe Books, 1967), 56–58; Alma S. Wittlin, *Museums: In Search of a Usable Future* (Cambridge: MIT Press, 1970), 37.
6. Taylor, *The Taste of Angels*, 193; Bazin, *The Museum Age*, 65–67.
7. Bazin, *The Museum Age*, 102–104; Holst, *Creators*, 92.
8. Most of the busts are in the collection of the Fenimore Art Museum (formerly the Fenimore House, New York State Historical Association) in Cooperstown, New York. See David Meschutt, *A Bold Experiment: John Henri Isaac Browere's Life Masks of Prominent Americans* (Cooperstown: New York State Historical Association, 1988).
9. Bazin, *The Museum Age*, 230; Hans Huth, "Pierre Eugene du Simitiere and the Beginnings of the American Historical Museum," *Pennsylvania Magazine of History and Biography* 69 (October 1945): 315–25; Charles Coleman Sellers, *Charles Willson Peale*, 213, 264–65, 303, 334–44; John H. Demer, "The Portrait Busts of John H. I. Browere," *Antiques* 110 (July 1976): 111–17; Edward P. Alexander, *The Museum: A Living Book of History* (Detroit: Published for the Detroit Historical Society by Wayne State University, 1959), 4–5, 7–8; Edward P. Alexander, "An Art Gallery in Frontier Wisconsin," *Wisconsin Magazine of History* 29 (March 1946): 281–300; the National Portrait Gallery, http://npg.si.edu/about-us; Bazin, *The Museum Age*, 225; Ned J. Burns, "The History of Dioramas," *Museum News* 17 (February 15, 1940): 8–12; E. V. Gatacre, "The Limits of Professional Design," *Museums Journal* 76 (December 1976): 95; Sellers, *Peale*, 205–11; Oliver W. Larkin, *Art and Life in America* (New York: Holt, Rinehart, and Winston, 1949), 112–13.
10. Here's how the Smithsonian's annual report describes the basis for the change: "The fundamental mission is clear: to interpret histories of the peoples of the United States primarily through evidence inherent in material artifacts. Science and technology has provided many of those artifacts, the ways in which they reflect social history is an important part of their story. Therefore, without diminishing our traditional emphasis upon technology, we have been reordering our staff not only to elucidate the recent effloresence of research into America's social history but also to participate actively in expanding the frontiers of such knowledge."

    Moreover, attention should be drawn to the importance of the new building for the National Air and Space Museum, which opened on July 4, 1976, in celebration of the bicentennial, as well as the renovation of the Arts and Industries Building in order to re-create the Centennial Exposition of Philadelphia, held in 1876. See http://siarchives.si.edu/history/general-history.

11. The National Museum of American History, "Popular Exhibitions and Event Spaces," http://american history.si.edu/museum/special-events/event-spaces.

12. Smithsonian Institution, "Smithsonian Entertainment Exhibition to Showcase Pop Culture," December 7, 2022, https://americanhistory.si.edu/press/releases/entertainment-exhibition-showcase-pop-culture. The exhibition opened on December 9, 2022. See "Entertainment Nation," https://www.youtube.com/watch?v=AvQEMI3BNVI.

13. The National Museum of American History, "Department of New Media," http://americanhistory.si.edu/about/departments/new-media.

14. Victoria and Albert Museum, http://www.vam.ac.uk; Victoria Newhouse, *Art and the Power of Placement* (New York: Monacelli Press, 2005), 267. In addition, the central gardens surrounding the 145 galleries reopened in 2005 offer a space for refreshment, relaxation, and exhibition.

15. Mark B. Sandberg, *Living Pictures, Missing Persons: Mannequins, Museums and Modernity* (Princeton: Princeton University Press, 2003), 208-31.

16. Connections between the American and Scandinavian concept of folk may be found in Gerard C. Wertkin, *Encyclopedia of American Folk Art* (London: Routledge, 2004), xxxii–xxiii.

17. http://www.skansen.se/en/artikel/annual-festivities. Attendance figures were gathered from Skansen homepage, 2008.

18. The museum's 20th-century collection of houses reflects Norwegian urban design as it has changed decade by decade. Hermann Heinrich Frese, *Anthropology and the Public: The Role of Museums* (Leiden: E.J. Brill, 1960), 11, 12; P. H. Pott, *National Museum of Ethnology, Leiden, 1837-1962* (The Hague: The Museum, 1962), 4-5; Mats Rehnberg, *The Nordiska Museet and Skansen* (Stockholm: Almqvist & Wiksell, 1957); Bo Lagercrantz, "A Great Museum Pioneer of the Nineteenth Century," *Curator* 7 (1964): 179-84; Lorwerth C. Peate, *Folk Museums*, Cardiff, 1948, 15-21; Peter Michelsen, "The Outdoor Museum and Its Educational Program," in *Essays to Be Presented at the Seminar on Preservation and Restoration, September 8-11, 1963* (Williamsburg: National Trust for Historic Preservation in the United States for Colonial Williamsburg, 1963); *Historic Preservation Today* (Charlottesville: University of Virginia Press, 1966), 201-17 and also comment by E. P. Alexander, 218-24; F. A. Bather, "The Triumph of Hazelius," *Museums Journal* 16 (December 1916): 136; Holger Rasmussen, ed., *Dansk Folkemuseum und Frilichtsmuseet*, Copenhagen, 1966, 7-10; *The Sandvig Collections: Guide to the Open Air Museum* (Lillehammer: Gjøvik, 1963); Reidar Kjellberg, "Scandinavian Open Air Museums," *Museum News* 39 (December 1960–January 1961): 18-22; Peter Holm, "The Old Town: A Folk Museum in Denmark," *Museums Journal* 37 (April 1937): 1-9; Adelhart Zippelius, *Handbuch der europaischen Freilichtmuseen*, Koln, 1975; Alexander, "Artur Hazelius and Skansen," in *Museum Masters*, 239-76; Sandberg, *Living Pictures, Missing Persons*, 123, 148-53; Tony Bennett, *The Birth of the Museum: History, Theory and Politics* (London: Routledge, 1995), 110-14; Kenneth Hudson, *Museums of Influence* (Cambridge: Cambridge University Press, 1987), chapter 6 (Skansen).

19. Other examples that combine historic preservation with outdoor museum functions include: Old Salem (North Carolina), a Moravian community; Conner Prairie (Indiana), a Midwest frontier settlement; Columbia (California), a mining town; and Colonial Williamsburg (Virginia).

20. This institution was known as Plimoth Plantation until July 2020, when the new name was implemented, with the alternative spelling of the Massachusetts colony's name and the Wampanoag name for the land where the English settlers landed in 1620. The name change coincides with events marking the four hundredth anniversary of the landing of the *Mayflower* in what is now the town of Plymouth. See Theresa Machemer, "Massachusetts' Plimoth Plantation Will Change Its Name," *Smithsonian Magazine*, July 16, 2020, https://www.smithsonianmag.com/smart-news/massachusetts-plimoth-plantation-change-its-name-180975323/.

21. Raymond B. Fosdick, *John D. Rockefeller, Jr.: A Portrait* (New York: Harper, 1956), 272-301; Edward P. Alexander, *The Interpretation Program of Colonial Williamsburg* (Williamsburg: Colonial Williamsburg, 1971), 1-46; Edward P. Alexander, "Restorations," in *In Support of Clio: Essays in Memory of Herbert A. Kellar*, eds. William B. Hesseltine and Donald R. McNeil (Madison: State Historical Society of Wisconsin, 1958), 195-214; Richard Handler and Eric Gable, *The New History in an Old Museum: Creating the Past in Colonial Williamsburg* (Durham: Duke University Press, 1997); Henrietta Wexler, "The Way Things Really Were," and Tracey Linton Craig, "A Hard Row to Hoe," *Museum News* 69 no. 1 (January–February 1988); Michael Wallace, "Mickey Mouse History: Portraying the Past at Disney World," in *Mickey Mouse*

History and Other Essays on American Memory (Philadelphia: Temple University Press, 1996), 13–16; Irvin Haas, *America's Historic Villages and Restorations* (New York: ARCO Publishing, 1974); Jay Anderson, *Time Machines: The World of Living History* (Nashville: American Association of State and Local History, 1986); Candace Tangorra Matelic, "Through the Historical Looking Glass," *Museum News* 59, no. 2 (March–April 1980): 36–45; James Deetz, "A Sense of Another World: History Museums and Cultural Change," *Museum News* 59, no. 3 (May–June 1980): 40–45; David Peterson, "There Is No Living History, There Are No Time Machines," *History News* (September–October 1988): 28–30; Hudson, *Museums of Influence*, chapter 7 (Colonial Williamsburg); and David B. Allison, *Living History: Effective Costumed Interpretation and Enactment at Museums and Historic Sites* (Lanham: Rowman & Littlefield/AASLH, 2016).

22. William Greenleaf, *From These Beginnings: The Early Philanthropies of Henry and Edsel Ford, 1911–1936* (Detroit: Wayne State University Press, 1964), 71–112; Allan Nevins and Frank Ernest Hill, *Ford: Expansion and Challenge, 1915–1933* (New York: Charles Scribner's Sons, 1957), 497–506, 614; *Guidebook of Greenfield Village* (Dearborn: Edison Institute, 1957), 1; Greenfield Village and the Henry Ford Museum; Alexander, "Restorations," 201–204; "The Henry Ford, America's Greatest History Attraction Brings the American Experience to Life," press release, January 28, 2003; The Henry Ford, http://thehenryford .org; Wallace, *Mickey Mouse History*, 9–13; See discussion in Chapter 4 of the Henry Ford name change (2003).

23. Steven Conn, *Museums and American Intellectual Life, 1876–1926* (Chicago: University of Chicago Press, 1998), 158.

24. Museums focusing on living history, farming, and agricultural history offered a new format and context for museums. Their governing body, ALHFAM (the Association for Living History, Farm and Agricultural Museums), was established initially as the Association for Living Historical Farms and Agricultural Museums in 1970, before changing the name in 1998. See http://www.alhfam.org/Our-History. Other associations of interest include the First-Person Interpreters Professional Network (FPIPN).

25. Plimoth Plantation, http://www.Plimoth.org; Warren Leon and Margaret Piatt, "Living-History Museums," in *History Museums in the United States*, 64–97.

26. David B. Allison, *Living History: Effective Costumed Interpretation and Enactment at Museums and Historic Sites* (Lanham: Rowman & Littlefield/AASLH, 2016), chapter 1 (p. 16 in ebook). Allison cites Roy Rosenzweig and David Thelen, *The Presence of the Past: Popular Uses of History in American Life* (New York: Columbia University Press, 1998).

27. Benjamin Filene, "Passionate Histories: 'Outsider' History-Makers and What They Teach Us," *Public Historian* 34 no. 1 (2012): 11–33.

28. Bather, "The Triumph of Hazelius."

29. Theresa Machemer, "Massachusetts' Plimoth Plantation Will Change Name," *Smithsonian*, July 16, 2020, https://www.smithsonianmag.com/smart-news/massachusetts-plimoth-plantation-change-its -name-180975323/.

30. While Small interrogates a focused selection of three museum sites in Natchitoches, Louisiana (Oakland Plantation, Magnolia Plantation Complex, and Melrose Plantation), his investigation is worthy of examination here. See Stephen Small, *In the Shadows of the Big House: Twenty-First-Century Atebellus Slave Cabins and Heritage Tourism in Louisiana* (Jackson, MS: University Press of Mississippi, 2023).

31. Clint Smith, *How the Word Is Passed: A Reckoning with the History of Slavery Across America* (New York: Little, Brown and Company, 2021).

32. Charlotte Smith, "Civic Consciousness and House Museums: The Instructional Role of Interpretive Narratives," *Australasian Journal of American Studies* 21:1 (July 2002): 74–88, especially 74.

   In terms of historic house "firsts," the first historic house was established at the Jean Hasbrouck House, George Washington's headquarters in Newburgh, New York. The house was originally called a "Memorial House" and was used as a museum to the history of the Huguenot settlement in the area. Nearly three hundred years old (as determined by the dendrochronology of some beams, which appear to have been cut in 1721), this Dutch stone house underwent partial restoration in 2007. It is one of several properties in this Huguenot settlement in the Hudson River Valley. On the notion of the "memorial," see http://www.hasbrouckfamily.org/houses.htm; New York State Legislature, *Assembly, Select Committee on the Petition of Washington Irving and Others to Preserve Washington's Headquarters in Newburgh*, No. 356, March 27, 1839, 1–5.

33. Daniel P. Jordan, "Statement on the TJMF Research Committee Report on Thomas Jefferson and Sally Hemings," January 26, 2000; downloaded from https://www.monticello.org/sites/default/files/inline-pdfs/jefferson-hemings_report.pdf.

34. John Hope Franklin, From Slavery to Freedom: A History of American Negroes (New York: A.A. Knopf, 1947; 8th ed. Boston: McGraw-Hill, 2000). It bears mentioning that the book is noted for its interjection of Black history within American history. The book is also credited with playing an important role in the creation of African-American (or Black) Studies as an academic discipline.

35. The quote regarding the burial ground was taken from Charley Miller and Peter Miller, Monticello: The Official Guide to Thomas Jefferson's World (Washington, D.C.: National Geographic Society, 2016) and may be found at https://www.monticello.org/site/plantation-and-slavery/honoring-ancestors. Information on the Mountaintop Project may be found at https://www.monticello.org/site/visit/mountaintop-project-revealing-jeffersons-monticello.

36. Monticello, "Slavery at Monticello Tour," https://www.monticello.org/visit/tickets-tours/slavery-at-monticello-tour/.

37. Clint Smith, How the Word Is Passed: A Reckoning with the History of Slavery Across America (New York: Little, Brown and Company, 2021).

38. Richard Caldwell, A True History of the Acquisition of Washington's Headquarters at Newburgh, by the State of New York, Salisbury Mills (NY: Stivers, Slauson & Boyd, 1887), 7–41; Charles B. Hosmer Jr., Presence of the Past: A History of the Preservation Movement in the United States before Williamsburg (New York: Putnam, 1965), 35–37; Alexander, "Anne Pamela Cunningham," in Museum Masters, 177–204; Michael Wallace, "Preserving the Past: Historic Preservation in the U.S.," in Mickey Mouse History; John A. Herbst, "Historic Houses," in History Museums in the United States, 98–114; Patricia West, Domesticating History: The Political Origins of America's House Museums (Washington, D.C.: Smithsonian Institution Press, 1999), 1–37; Rosanne Pavoni, "Towards a Definition and Typology of Historic House Museums," Museum International 53, no. 2 (2001): 16–21; Karen Zukowski, "The Importance of Context," in Conservation in Context: Finding a Balance for the Historic House Museum, ed. Wendy Claire Jessup (Washington, D.C.: National Trust for Historic Preservation, 1995), 5–19.

39. Bill Schulz, "Some Surprising Relics at the Tenement Museum," New York Times, November 6, 2015, http://www.nytimes.com/2015/11/08/nyregion/some-surprising-relics-at-the-tenement-museum.html.

40. For the museum's mission, see Lower Eastside Tenement Museum, "About Us," https://www.tenement.org/about-us/. Joelle Jennifer Tutela, Becoming American: A Case Study of the Lower East Side Tenement Museum, Ph.D. dissertation, City University of New York, 2008; Ruth Abram, "A Museum Grew in Me," Horizons of Culture & Life, Summer 1991, 12; and Lower Eastside Tenement Museum, A Tenement Story History of 97 Orchard Street and the Lower Eastside Tenement Museum (New York: Lower Eastside Tenement Museum, 1999).

41. Gerald W. Johnson, Mount Vernon. The Story of a Shrine (New York. Random House, 1953), 8–11, Hosmer, Presence of the Past, 44–62.

42. See https://www.sitesofconscience.org/.

43. Cameron, "The Museum, a Temple or the Forum," 196.

44. Harriet F. Senie, "The Conflation of Heroes and Victims: A New Memorial Paradigm," in A Companion to Public Art, edited by Cher Krause Knight and Harriet F. Senie (Chichester: Wiley, 2016), 107–20.

45. Jim Crow was a Black minstrel character developed by Thomas Dartmouth Rice, who, after traveling to the South, created a Black stage character with that name in 1830. Rice would have to don "blackface"—by darkening his skin with shoe polish, greasepaint, or other mediums—as a manner of developing song and dance that was, ultimately, an assertion of power, control, and denigration. In the modern context, Alexander asserts that "mass incarceration is, metaphorically, the New Jim Crow." See Michelle Alexander, The New Jim Crow: Mass Incarceration in the Age of Colorblindness, (New York: The New Press, 2010).

46. Danté Stewart, "Opinion: My Kids Need to Know That Black Is Brilliance. So We Go to Museums," Washington Post, February 12, 2023, https://www.washingtonpost.com/opinions/2023/02/12/black-history-month-children-museums/.

47. DeNeen L. Brown, "'Lynch Him!': New Lynching Memorial Confronts the Nation's Brutal History of Racial Terrorism," *Washington Post*, April 24, 2018, https://www.washingtonpost.com/news/retropolis/wp/2018/04/24/lynch-him-new-lynching-memorial-forces-nation-confront-its-brutal-history-of-racial-terrorism/.

48. Equal Justice Initiative, "Freedom Monument Sculpture Park," https://legacysites.eji.org/about/monument/.

49. The common thread of soil is my observation, based upon the little I know about the third site, as yet, and only having visited the museum and memorial in 2022.

50. Information on the exhibition *Men of Change* may be found at the Smithsonian: https://menofchange.si.edu/exhibit/men-of-change/, and Shantay Robinson, "How Black Men Changed the World," *Smithsonian Magazine*, March 14, 2022, https://www.smithsonianmag.com/smithsonian-institution/how-black-men-changed-the-world-180979710/.

51. IAAM, "International African American Museum Opens to the Public," June 28, 2023, https://iaamuseum.org/news/international-african-american-museum-opens-to-the-public/.

52. Kevin M. Guthrie, *The New-York Historical Society: Lessons from One Non-Profit's Long Struggle for Survival* (San Francisco: Jossey-Bass, 1996).

53. The second edition of this book listed fifteen thousand societies. The number ten thousand came from Debbie Ann Doyle, "The Future of Local Historical Societies," *Perspectives on History: The Newsmagazine of the American Historical Association*, December 2012, https://www.historians.org/publications-and-directories/perspectives-on-history/december-2012/the-future-of-the-discipline/the-future-of-local-historical-societies. The fourth edition refers to the AASLH's 2022 National Census of History Organizations, which identifies 21,588 history organizations: https://www.aaslh.org/census/. For an understanding of the blurring of the lines between the the classifications, see pages 15–17 of the report, which states, "In particular, many organizations described as historical societies in fact steward and exhibit collections and many include a museum. When we look at the specific activities of different history organizations, the lines between these various institution types tend to blur." In terms of lineage societies, the Hereditary Society Community of the United States of America identified more than three hundred in the United States as of 2006. See Loretto Dennis Szucs and Sandra Hargreaves Luebking, *The Source: A Guidebook to American Genealogy* (Provo, UT: Ancestry, 2006), 897, https://archive.org/details/sourceguidebook00lore/.

54. Edward P. Alexander, "Ruben Gold Thwaites," in *The Museum in America: Innovators and Pioneers* (Walnut Creek: AltaMira Press, 1997), 85–100. Regarding The Valentine, in the 1980s the board changed its name to the Valentine Richmond History Center, seeking to extend its public appeal, and now, it is simply known as The Valentine. For its history, see "About Us," http://thevalentine.org/about/history-mission.

55. The National Society of the Daughters of the American Revolution, see https://www.dar.org/national-society/what-we-do. The organization was founded in 1890, and it incorporated in 1896 by an Act of Congress. They have 190,000 members and 3,000 chapters.

56. See Victor J. Danilov, *Women and Museums: A Comprehensive Guide* (Lanham: AltaMira Pres, 2005).

57. See Jennifer M. Lloyd, "Martha Taylor Howard and the Campaign to Preserve the Susan B. Anthony House," *Rochester History* 80:2 (Spring 2023).

58. On the UDC, see Karen L. Cox, *Dixie's Daughters: The United Daughters of the Confederacy and the Preservation of Confederate Culture* (Gainesville: University Press of Florida, 2019); Gaines M. Foster, *Ghosts of the Confederacy: Defeat, the Lost Cause, and the Emergence of the New South* (New York: Oxford University Press, 1987). Some of the chapter houses where UDC members met have been named to the National Register of Historic Places. See, for instance, the Agnes Lee Chapter House in Decatur, Georgia. https://www.hmdb.org/m.asp?m=197673.

59. William C. Everhart, *The National Park Service* (New York: Praeger, 1972), 33, 74–79, 249–60; U.S. Council of Mayors, *With Heritage So Rich: A Report on Historic Preservation* (New York: Random House, 1966), 204–208; American Association of Museums, *The Official Museum Directory, 1977: United States and Canada* (Washington, D.C.: American Association of Museums, 1976), 849–71; National Alliance of Preservation Commissions, http://napc.uga.edu; National Register of Historic Places, Title 36: Section

60.3, "Parks, Forests, and Public Property, Chapter One, Part 60," https://www.nps.gov/nr/regulations.htm#603.

60. The long quote appeared in a prepared statement by Mathias to the Special Subcommittee on Arts and Humanities as regarding Bicentennial Era Programs, 1976, which met on Friday, April 9, 1976.

    In addition, as recorded in Hartje, Mathias stated, "We believe not only that the revolution was the most important event in our history but, even more, that the ideas and ideals of the revolution are as real and relevant today as they were two hundred years ago." See Robert G. Hartje, *Bicentennial USA: Pathways to Celebration* (Nashville, TN: The American Association for State and Local History, 1973), 19. Hartje was director of the Bicentennial Project of AASLH.

61. Robert G. Hartje, *Bicentennial USA: Pathways to Celebration*, (Nashville, TN: The American Association for State and Local History, 1973), 239.

62. *Franklin & Jefferson*, prepared by Charles and Ray Eames' Office, was the final exhibition by Eames Office. Former Office staff member Jeannine Oppewall reported the significance and joy of the work when she stated, "I actually got up in the morning and considered who was important to put on a timeline about the history of ideas and America during the revolution. Who else gets to do that for a living!" British *Vogue* reported high praise in terms of design and delivery of animated history when it noted, "The layout and visual impact are staggering: one wants to spend days studying the documents, photographs, and artifacts that bring the period vividly to life."

    See "The World of Franklin & Jefferson," http://www.eamesoffice.com/the-work/the-world-of-franklin-jefferson/.

63. See Colleen C. Griffiths, *In Service of Society: Conflicts of Curatorship in 1976 Bicentennial Museum Exhibitions*, thesis, University of North Carolina at Wilmington, 2010. Griffiths examines these three exhibitions as exercises in curatorial authority "to create unifying narratives of nationalism" (iv). See also Tammy S. Gordon, *The Spirit of 1976: Commerce, Community, and the Politics of Commemoration* (Amherst: University of Massachusetts Press, 2013).

64. Pew Research Center, "How Americans View Government: Deconstructing Distrust," March 10, 1998. In his Foreword to this report, director of the Pew Research Center for the People and the Press Andrew Kohut asked, "At what point does such profound distrust of government become dangerous, threatening our ability as a society to address the pressing issues of the day?"

65. See Jane R. Glaser and Artemis A. Zenetou, *Museums: A Place to Work—Planning Museum Careers* (New York: Routlege for The Smithsonian Institution, 1996). Glaser and Zenetou chart trends in museum work, provide an overview of positions, and track growth in the profession.

66. Barbara W. Sommer, *Practicing Oral History in Historical Organizations* (Practicing Oral History Series) (Walnut Creek: Left Coast Press, 2015), chapter 1.

67. The National Historic Preservation Act of 1966 articulates a process that requires each federal agency to consider historic buildings in funding and the granting of permits. The goal is to minimize potential harm and damage to historic properties by considering the effect a project may have on an archaeological or historic site. Under Section 106, "Protection of Historic Properties," federal agencies must alert State or Tribal Historic Preservation Officers (SHPO or THPO) and local governments, and members of the public to determine whether their work is slated to be sited on, or may impact, a historic site. Section 106 requires a review of the site in order to inventory and identify historic properties, for the assessment of adverse effects (if any), and for the resolution of said effects. While the process may involve disagreement between parties, the aim is (ultimately) to minimize risk and harm to historic properties and to identify solutions to avoid, minimize, or mitigate any adverse effects on historic properties. U.S. General Services Administration, "Section 106: National Historic Preservation Act of 1966," https://www.gsa.gov/real-estate/historic-preservation/historic-preservation-policy-tools/legislation-policy-and-reports/section-106-of-the-national-historic-preservation-act.

68. "Mission 66. Modern Architecture in the National Parks," http://www.mission66.com.

69. Information about battlefield preservation and restoration may be found at the National Park Service and Civil War Trust sites for each location.

70. Robert Sutton (et al.), *Holding the High Ground: A National Park Service Plan for the Sesquicentennial of the American Civil War*, May 2008.

71 https://www.charlestonmuseum.org/news-events/?s=threads+of+war; http://www.metmuseum.org/exhibitions/listings/2013/photography-and-the-american-civil-war; https://www.loc.gov/exhibits/civil-war-photographs/; http://npg.si.edu/exhibit/cw/npgcivilwar.html.

72. The commission was established in 2016 as the Congressionally appointed body in charge of promoting and coordinating the United States Semiquincentennial. See https://america250.org/.

73. The goals of the initiative are to: "make history relevant to every American, every day; tell inclusive stories about the American past; increase funding for history; enhance the public's engagement with history collections; and emphasize the importance of history education." See American Association for State and Local History (AASLH), "Commemorating America's Semiquincentennial," https://aaslh.org/programs/250th/. The themes are: Unfinished Revolutions; Power of Place; "We the People"; American Experiment; and Doing History.

74. The National Council on Public History reports that by the late 1970s, these practitioners wanted a professional organization that would address their concerns and interests. The establishment of the NCPH in 1979 met this need. The term *public history* was coined by Robert Kelley of the University of California, Santa Barbara. See Indiana University, Ruth Lilly Special Collections and Archives, "National Council on Public History Records, 1977–2002," http://www.ulib.iupui.edu/collections/general/mss021.

75. Taylor, *A Common Agenda for History Museums*; Roy Rosenzweig and David Thelen, *Presence of the Past: Popular Uses of History in American Life* (New York: Columbia University Press, 1998), 189; Eric Foner, "The Historian in the Museum," *Museum News* 85, no. 2 (March–April 2006): 46–47; Susan A. Crane, "Memory, Distortion and History in the Museum," in *Museum Studies: An Anthology of Contexts*, ed. Bettina Messias Carbonell (London: Blackwell, 2004); Starn, "A Historians Brief Guide," 68–98.

76. Crowdsourcing is discussed as a lifelong learning effort in Meghan Ferriter and Christine Rosenfeld, "Focus Issue: Exploring the Smithsonian Institution Transcription Center," *Collections: A Journal for Museum and Archives Professionals*, edited by Juilee Decker 12:02 (Spring 2016).

5

Gardens, Zoos, and Children's Museums

Unlike the previous chapters—where objects are often prized for their rarity, value, and/or place in a historical continuum—here, the collections are vastly different. Further, whereas gardens and zoos anchor their activities around living collections and research, conservation, and the dissemination of knowledge around species, habitat, and sustainability, children's museums are wildly diverse in collections and eschew constraints of Linnean taxonomy. Moreover, children's museums differ from all other museums because their very name specifies the audience, not the collections. However, all three of the museum types addressed in this chapter frame health and well-being, curiosity, and wonder in a tightly woven matrix of learning, discovery, and play. With this in mind, the discussion in this chapter brings together gardens, zoos, and children's museums as unique institutions that are united in their approach to informal and experiential learning as critical ways to engage visitors.

Botanic gardens, zoos, and children's museums fit into the definition of a *museum* adopted by the American Alliance of Museums. They are organized, permanent, and nonprofit in form; essentially educational or aesthetic in purpose; have a professional staff; and own, utilize, and conserve tangible objects, which they exhibit to the public on some regular schedule. They also have their own discrete areas of collecting that reflect plant and animal species, their care, and conservation, as well as the range of human activity, particularly that of children past and present around daily life, as well as creative enrichment and play. Regardless of the collection type, these museums emphasize the collections for their utility in education and interpretation as means to engage, intrigue, and inform their visitors about plants, animals, and children. In addition, by looking at the purpose of garden, zoo, and children's museum collections and their employ to the service of education, it is easy to realize a shared methodology for learning and engagement that privileges informal and experiential learning to a greater extent than the museums discussed thus far. Third, unlike the topics of several of the previous chapters—art, science (including natural history), and history—the subject of this chapter is not keyed directly to an area of elementary and secondary education. That is, gardens, zoos, and children's experiences are not directly reflected in subject areas that children learn in a K-12 school. Rather, they are areas that are ripe for exploration within and across many subjects. Finally, by prioritizing informal, as opposed to structured, learning, and experiential, as opposed to passive, learning, these museums embrace and fully reflect the learning styles and interests of their primary audiences: children. This is not to suggest, of course, that gardens, zoos, and children's museums are *only* for children. Like all museum types discussed thus far, they are for everyone!

This chapter offers a brief history of gardens, zoos, and children's museums. The first two sections have European antecedents, while the third reflects a briefer history, as children's museums are an American invention. While the historical framings are brief, the intent is to show the range of examples across each museum type and to show their importance historically and today.

Botanic Gardens

Prior to delving into the history of botanic gardens, a few statements about word use are in order. The terms *botanic* and *botanical*, in reference to gardens, may be used interchangeably. Botanic gardens are open to the public, as are "public gardens," which simply open to the public without the interest in collection, research, and learning. The latter, however, are beyond the scope of this volume. Thus, when the word *garden* appears on its own, the meaning of "botanic garden" is implied.

The First Botanical Gardens

Humankind has long enjoyed and appreciated the aesthetic, medicinal, and economic uses of plants and has mixed these purposes for organizing a garden with the purely scientific and botanical ones. While the gardens of Emperor Shennong in China (2800 BCE), of the king of Thebes or of Thutmose III at the Temple of Karnak in Egypt (both about 1500 BCE), and of Aristotle in Greece or the Mouseion at Alexandria (fourth century BCE) may not have been true botanical gardens, they contained exotic plants, both beautiful and useful. Similarly, the gardens of herbs and medicinal plants of the early monasteries such as Saint Gall (ninth century), or even medieval gardens and later the physic gardens, such as Chelsea (1673), had many botanical features. The Mexican gardens of Istapalan and Chalco encountered by Cortez and his followers were closer to true botanical gardens, for the Aztecs had made considerable study of medical botany.[1]

There is a long-standing dispute over whether the first European botanic garden was situated in Padua or Pisa. The senate of the Venetian Republic ordered the garden at Padua in May 1545, and its original layout remains largely intact. Francesco Bonafede was its founder, Giovanni Moroni drew the plan, and Luigi Squalerno (commonly called Anguillara) was its first prefect. It was attached to the University of Padua, which had had a Chair of Simples (medicinal plants) since 1533, and in 1591, it issued the first garden catalog.[2] The Pisa garden may have been in existence in July 1545, but it was moved to the site it occupies today in 1595. It was founded by physician and botanist Luca Ghini. At Pisa, the arrangement was geometric with separate sections for bulbs and poisonous, prickly, odoriferous, and marsh plants, and an arboretum was added to the garden in 1841. The prefect gave lectures on simples and actual demonstrations on living plant specimens in the garden.[3]

Another famed early botanic garden, Hortus Botanicus, was established in Leiden in 1587. The university there decided that a botanical, rather than an apothecary, garden was better suited for the development of its medical faculty, and it persuaded the great botanist Charles de l'Ecluse (Carolus Clusius) to become its second prefect, (1593–1609). The Leiden garden had a succession of able directors, including Hermann Boerhaave, (1709–1730), with whom Linnaeus studied. He published a catalog of the garden, but perhaps more significantly, he introduced the tulip to Holland and the potato to Europe.[4]

Other sixteenth-century gardens were established at Zurich, Bologna (1567); Leipzig, Montpellier (1593); Heidelberg (1597); and Copenhagen (1600), and by 1700, there were twenty such gardens in Europe, usually connected with universities. Interest in close observation and taxonomy caused scientific botany to thrive as an adjunct to the medical schools in the universities at a time when the development of other sciences was being hampered by medieval tradition. The Oxford Botanic Garden (1621) boasted a "Nursery of Simples" and "a Professor of Botanicey"; its conservatory was heated by a four-wheel fire basket of burning charcoal hauled back and forth by a gardener.[5]

The private garden of the Tradescants was contemporary with Oxford, and the Chelsea Physic Garden was founded at London in 1673 by the Society of Apothecaries. Hans Sloane purchased a site for it in 1722 on the condition that it present fifty well-dried and preserved specimens of distinct plants to the Royal Society each year until two thousand had been given. Philip Miller, whom the naturalist and classifier Linnaeus called "the Prince of Gardeners," authored the *Gardeners Dictionary* (1731), which soon ran through eight editions, a knowledge base that endowed him to serve as head gardener at Chelsea in 1723. By Miller's day, botanical gardens were found throughout Western Europe, including one on the Apothecary Island in Saint Petersburg (1714).[6]

European botanical gardens evolved into distinct types over the centuries. The sixteenth and seventeenth centuries saw medicinal gardens that provided university medical faculties with plant material. Colonial gardens emerged in the seventeenth and eighteenth centuries with growing fascination for the new plant materials from Europe's far-flung colonies. Linnaean gardens developed in the eighteenth century and affected nineteenth-century gardens, as well, with a focus on the taxonomy of plants, both native and colonial in origin. Civic gardens reflected the growing urbanization of Europe and the United States in the nineteenth and early twentieth centuries. To complement civic gardens, specialist gardens focused on plant materials of specific types and emphasized research and conservation. Today, the sanctuary garden reflects the need to protect plant material from degradation and extinction.[7]

The Royal Botanic Gardens at Kew

In the 1750s, Augusta Saxe-Gotha, dowager princess of Wales, began to develop her nine acres in Kew House, west of London, as a botanical garden. She was assisted in this work by William Kent, the landscape architect, and by Lord Bute (John Stuart, third earl of Bute), a keen and knowledgeable botanist. Saxe-Gotha's son, George III, in 1772 inherited Kew and joined to it his Richmond Lodge garden; thus, the name "the Royal Botanic Gardens of Kew."[8] The cultivation of the garden varieties was managed by King George III's chief botanical advisor, Joseph Banks, just home from a 'round-the-world trip with Captain Cook on the *Endeavour*. He sent collectors across the empire. By the time the king and Banks died in 1820, some seven thousand new plants had come to Kew from overseas.

After the passing of George III and Banks, the Royal Gardens deteriorated before their transfer from the personal property of the Crown to the Commissioners of Woods and Forests. Thus, Kew became a national institution and expanded considerably over the following decades to become a great center for botanical exchange, resulting in the delivery of many exotic plants within the British Empire and beyond. For instance, Cinchona plants (from which quinine is derived) came to Kew from Peru, to be grown and sent to India. Cork oaks from Portugal were developed for South Australia, tobacco for Natal in Eastern Africa, and Chinese tea for Assam. Coffee, allspice, cinnamon, mango, tamarind, cotton, ginger, and indigo went around the world in Wardian cases from the nurseries and forcing houses of Kew.[9] Today Kew has the largest herbarium in the world, with some seven million dried specimens, adding thirty thousand specimens each year.[10]

American Botanic Gardens

During the colonial period, John Bartram, plantsman and plant explorer, collected native species at his farm near Philadelphia as early as 1728. Bartram's cousin, Humphrey Marshall, in 1773 established a similar garden at West Bradford in Chester County, near Philadelphia. Robert and William Prince started a nursery at Flushing, Long Island, in 1737, and four generations of their family continued the business until 1867; for a time they called part of it the Linnaean Botanic Garden in honor of the Swedish botanist who developed binomial nomenclature. A most important early venture was the Elgin Botanic Garden of 1801, which occupied twenty acres in New York City on the present site of Rockefeller Center. Its founder was David Hosack, prominent physician and professor of botany and *materia medica* (medical materials) at Columbia College, who considered the garden a valuable adjunct to his teaching. By 1811, however, he was compelled to sell it to the state of New York, which eventually turned the property over to Columbia College. The college allowed the garden to deteriorate and disappear.[11] Today there are over five hundred botanical gardens in the United States. The oldest of these is the United States Botanic Garden, which is rooted in George Washington's vision, more than two hundred years ago, for a national garden that would "demonstrate and promote the importance of plants to the young nation."[12]

Missouri Botanical Garden

The Missouri Botanical Garden, of seventy-five acres, was organized at St. Louis in 1859. Henry Shaw, a native Englishman, came to St. Louis in 1819 and made a fortune in merchandising. George Engelmann, a German immigrant physician and botanist, urged Shaw to transform his estate into a botanical garden, and Asa Gray of Harvard and Joseph Hooker, later director at Kew, supported that idea. Engelmann refused the directorship of the garden because it was too far out of town (now about twenty minutes from the center of the city), and Shaw, from 1859 to 1889, served as director of what is often still called "Shaw's Garden."[13]

The Missouri Botanical Garden has an herbarium (including the Bernhardi collection of more than five million specimens), a library, an orangery (the Linnaean House which is the oldest continuously operating display conservatory in the United States) built in 1850, conservatories for American and South African desert plants, two rose gardens, outstanding collections of the flora of Panama and of water lilies (developed by George H. Pring), and beneficial arrangements with local colleges and universities for training gardeners. Perhaps its most spectacular feature is the Climatron, a Buckminster Fuller geodesic dome, built in 1960, eighty feet high and 175 feet in diameter. The Climatron controls air and humidity so as to provide different climatic environments for the plants grown there.[14]

Huntington Botanical Gardens

The Huntington Botanical Gardens in San Marino, California, was established in 1903, when Henry E. Huntington, the railroad magnate, acquired an estate there and decided to develop a library and art gallery with encircling gardens. The garden opened to the public in 1928. William Hertrich, an Austrian-trained botanist, was superintendent. Twelve gardens contain fifteen thousand plant varieties, alongside sculpture, palms, and herbs.[15] Twenty-first-century garden additions include the largest Chinese-style garden outside China and the Rose Hill Conservatory for Botanical Sciences, which emphasizes programming for schoolchildren. In addition, the California Garden, with nearly fifty thousand native and dry-climate plants, reflects the local climate as well as both the agricultural and elegant estate history of the 207-acre Huntington grounds.[16]

Longwood Gardens

Longwood Gardens, at Kennett Square, Pennsylvania, contains plants chosen for beauty and display, and thus it does not constitute a true botanical garden. The garden covers a thousand acres and includes an arboretum established about 1800 by Joshua and Samuel Pierce. In 1906, Pierre S. Du Pont, prominent industrialist of the Du Pont Company and General Motors, bought the tract to save the arboretum from destruction. In 1921, he established the gardens as a permanent public institution. He conceived of Longwood as a cultural center devoted primarily to horticulture, but also to architecture, music, and drama. Thus, Longwood has gardens, conservatories, fountains, a singing-chimes tower, a pipe organ, and an open-air theater. The outdoor gardens include the old arboretum, varied wildflowers, and more formal sections that focus on rock, topiary, rose, and water lily plantings—many of which mark the influence of the Italian and French gardens, including Fontainebleau. The conservatories cover about four acres and vary from desert to tropical rainforest. Longwood has supported many activities of value to American horticulture. It has cooperated with the United States Department of Agriculture in sending plant explorers to the far reaches of the world, and it has supported the American Horticultural Society's project to computerize all plant species in American botanical gardens.[17] Longwood also seeks to be a leader in horticulture education and leadership through the Longwood Fellows program, a thirteen-month residential learning experience that trains professionals seeking pragmatic leadership development.[18] This program is geared toward those who wish to become public horticulturalists—a new professional akin to the public historian. Longwood serves as an exhibition venue also. One of the most exciting of these displays was *Making Scents: The Art and*

Longwood Gardens at Kennett Square, Pennsylvania, covers a thousand acres and includes an arboretum established about 1800 by Joshua and Samuel Peirce. Longwood has gardens, conservatories, fountains, a singing-chimes tower, a pipe organ, and an open-air theater. Conservatory photo taken by Afever, June 2022. *CC BY 4.0 https://creativecommons.org/licenses/by/4.0, via Wikimedia Commons.*

Passion of Fragrance (2010), which explored the mystery, artistry, and science of the sense of smell. Visitors were able to participate by making their own fragrance combination after learning about the combinations of plants and flowers that make up iconic perfumes of today and yesteryear.[19]

Chicago Botanic Garden

Tracing its roots to the Chicago Horticultural Society, founded in 1890, the Chicago Botanic Garden embraces the society's motto "city in a garden" by hosting shows, including the World's Columbian Exposition Chrysanthemum Show held in conjunction with the World's Fair in 1893. The garden's modern history began anew when the Society created and managed a new garden, with a groundbreaking in 1965 and debut in 1972. With 365 acres, twenty six gardens, and four natural areas, the Chicago Botanic Garden is the largest of any United States botanic garden, and it sees more than one million visitors annually, including programs for schoolchildren and teachers. The garden has a library onsite with more than 110,000 volumes, including media of all types as well as the archives of the Chicago Horticultural Society.

The garden is part of an entire Learning Campus that provides opportunities to stimulate the senses and inspire wonder in the horticultural experience. It serves as a "living laboratory" for the study of nature and provides real-world encounters with materials while also encouraging an understanding of the environment and conservation. The Learning Campus includes several components that provide contact between visitor and collections. Features include in-ground and raised beds, habitats, tools, and materials for use by learners of all ages "to get their hands in the Garden's soil and to experience the joy of nurturing a plant on the Garden grounds." An aquatic garden offers opportunities to collect water samples, evaluate the quality of the water, and look closely at aquatic creatures, while areas of "hiding places," "climbing places," "resting places," and rolling hills are situated among a canopy of trees, understory plants, and flowers. Chicago Botanic has carefully taken interest in nature play and learning places as a way of offering places where all ages and abilities can engage with nature.[20]

Hart Island Project

An unusual nature space is coming into focus at Hart Island, outside of New York City—a site originally purposed as a penal colony, this potter's field where the city has long buried its unclaimed dead. Among the first to be buried on Hart Island were Civil War veterans, though in the late twentieth century, those who died from AIDS-related illnesses were buried on Hart Island. Throughout, those without means have been buried here, a practice undertaken by inmate burial crews, which have since been replaced by contracted laborers. In 2021, the management of the site was transferred from the Department of Corrections to the Department of Parks & Recreation to facilitate its transition to a garden and public park. According to Melinda Hunt, the founder of the nonprofit Hart Island Project, the goal is to transition the site into a space of respect and dignity, in contrast to its origin story of penal control. While more than a million people are buried on the 131-acre strip of Long Island Sound off the coast of the Bronx, in the coming years, the site will be transformed, with education and engagement opportunities such as nature classes and guided tours. Further public access will help "change the narrative."[21] While not a traditional garden, by definition, as we have examined above, the initiative deserves mention because it defies categorization. It seems to be, in many ways, a site of conscience, as it grapples with memory and the past, and yet it is also very keenly tied to the present and future. Moreover, it is situated as an opportunity for public engagement and learning through nature exploration and play. Maybe it is, ultimately, just a park—but given the site's history and the presence of individuals and groups seeking to reclaim the lost historical narratives of those buried here, it seems that it could, ultimately, be *more than* a park.

Health and Well-Being

Keenly gardens and other outdoor museum spaces, such as zoos, fulfill an important role in connecting us to the natural world. Because of the increasingly sedentary, screen-filled lives of those of us in the digital age, journalist Richard Louv warned of *nature deficit disorder*, a phrase he coined to describe the physical, social, and psychological costs of alienation from nature. Further, Louv noted the benefits and rewards and understanding nature—an area where, perhaps, gardens can assist: "The future will belong to the nature-smart—those individuals, families, businesses, and political leaders who develop a deeper understanding of the transformative power of the natural world and who balance the virtual with the real. The more high-tech we become, the more nature we need." Such a call for action may be enough to prompt positive change in us, and in the museums that form our cultural landscape.[22] While Louv defined this term in 2005, his work has continued to frame the good of nature and the outdoors in contrast to our increasingly insular, digital worlds: "Today, children and adults who work and learn in a dominantly digital environment expend enormous energy blocking out many of the human senses in order to focus narrowly on the screen in front of their eyes."[23] Through access to the outdoors, gardens and zoos can provide opportunities for learning and restorative experiences in nature.

Zoos

Humankind has always been interested in the other animals of the world as sources of food and clothing, as companions or pets, and as strange and curious phenomena. Scholars suggest that from their beginnings, zoos required two basic elements: "wealth and leisure. There had to be enough money (to pay for food and housing and keepers) so that keeping animals in parks and cages did not interfere with the other luxuries of the owners of the zoos and parks. There also had to be sufficient leisure for enjoying the exhibits."[24] In fact, the domestication of animals goes back many millennia.

The First Zoos

Queen Hatshepsut of Egypt, in the fifteenth century BCE, had an extensive palace menagerie that she stocked with monkeys, leopards, birds, wild cattle, and a giraffe; she sent an animal-collecting expedition through the Red Sea to what is today Somalia. By 1000 BCE, the Assyrians fancied leopards and lions. King Solomon maintained herds of cattle, sheep, deer, and horses, as well as flocks of fowl; he traded with King Hiram of Tyre to obtain apes and peacocks or parrots. About that time, Emperor Wen Wang established a zoological garden in China. After 700 BCE the Greeks were setting up menageries, and Aristotle describes three hundred separate species in his *History of Animals* (fourth century BCE). The Mouseion at Alexandria possessed animals, and the Romans had aviaries and menageries, some of the latter with bulls, elephants, rhinoceri, hippopotami, lions, bears, leopards, tigers, and crocodiles to be used in gladiatorial combats. Charlemagne had three small zoos in the eighth century. In 1230, Henry III had a menagerie in the Tower of London; Marco Polo saw Kublai Khan's great animal collection in the fourteenth century; and Cortez visited Montezuma's zoo at Tenochtitlan, Mexico in 1519.

Holy Roman Emperor Francis I established the first great modern zoo at Schonbrunn in Vienna in 1752, with a rococo pavilion where his wife, Maria Theresa, could breakfast while watching the animals. He sent collectors to America, and his son opened the zoo to the public in 1765. Other zoos were started at Madrid and at the Jardin des Plantes in Paris during the eighteenth century; the latter received animals from the Menagerie du Parc founded by Louis XIV at Versailles.

Thomas Stamford Raffles, an English administrator who founded Singapore, was an animal lover and an admirer of the Jardin des Plantes zoo. He began the Zoological Society of London in 1826. Its royal charter called for the "advancement of zoology and animal physiology, and the introduction of new and curious subjects of the animal kingdom." The zoo, situated at one end of Regent's Park, opened first to society members in 1828 and to the public in 1846 with two llamas, a leopard, kangaroos, a Russian bear, emus, cranes, and other birds in suitable dens, aviaries, and paddocks. In 1931, it opened a five-hundred-acre branch thirty miles from London at Whipsnade, in Dunstable, Bedfordshire, the first wild-animal park in the world, and it displays and breeds large groups of animals. Today the London Zoo is the world's oldest scientific zoo with 756 species and 17,480 individuals.[25] Other outstanding European zoos are found in Antwerp, Amsterdam, Berlin, Munich, Frankfurt, Cologne, and Zurich.[26]

A revolution in zoo construction took place between 1902 and 1907, when Carl Hagenbeck, an animal dealer, set up his own zoo in Stellingen, a suburb of Hamburg. Beginning with a flat plain, Hagenbeck built an artificial, mountainous-like terrain with carefully constructed moats to contain the animals and with none of the customary cages and iron bars. This open-enclosure zoo was the prototype of the present spacious wild-animal parks that leading zoos in the world are beginning to acquire to supplement their city-restricted locations. In addition to revolutionizing zoo exhibitions, Hagenbeck's collecting practices added breeding of threatened species to zoo functions. Not only was Hagenbeck an innovator in zoo practices, but he also loved the animals he collected and developed techniques for training them with gentle methods using simple rewards of food tidbits instead of torture with whips and red-hot irons. Outside Hamburg, visitors can enjoy Hagenbeck's zoo today.[27]

The definitions of *menagerie* and *zoo* have changed over time. To review the evolution of menageries and zoos is to detect a changing purpose for these gardens or parks. In the eighteenth century, Europe's menageries made taxonomic collections (not unlike natural history collections) with specimens arranged in cages by "type." In addition to studying the differences among the specimens, the princely collectors of these menageries often sought the exotic to dazzle their guests. Zoological gardens emerged as more "sophisticated" menageries with an emphasis on natural settings for the specimens. Their purposes were education, research, and conservation (or protection of species).

With the global threats to flora and fauna, conservation parks (or bioparks) emerged with immersion exhibits that allowed visitors to be "among the animals" and emphasized natural habitats and conservation. Today's zoological parks encompass conservation parks, aviaries, herpetariums, safari parks, insectariums, butterfly parks, and even endangered species rehabilitation centers. National parks and wildlife reserves are extending even further the boundaries of zoos.[28]

Early American Zoos

The Philadelphia Zoological Garden (1854) is the oldest chartered zoo in the United States, though the tiny Central Park Menagerie in New York was the first actually to exhibit animals. Other prominent mainstream zoos are found in Chicago's Lincoln Park (1868), the National in Washington (1889), Milwaukee County (1892), New York's Bronx (1895), Saint Louis (1913), San Diego (1916), Fort Worth (1923), Detroit (1928), and Brookfield near Chicago (1934). The Arizona-Sonora Desert Museum at Tucson (1952) specializes in animals of the American desert despite its name. The public's attitudes toward United States zoos can be categorized in this way: zoos as jails (1865–1900), zoos as art galleries (1900–1950), and zoos as conservation facilities, with an emphasis on public education supplemented by natural-looking, immersive environments for the animals and visitors in a re-created theme, habitat, or landscape.[29]

Following the designs of the London Zoo, the Philadelphia Zoological Garden in Fairmount Park opened its exhibits to the public in 1874 in anticipation of the Centennial Exhibition, planned for 1876. Many other zoos resulted from similar international expositions around the world. The Philadelphia Zoo included in its offerings the first children's zoo in the United States, a phenomenon quickly adopted by other zoological parks. Today the Philadelphia Zoo welcomes nearly a million family visitors each year. In addition to its animal collections, the carefully preserved Victorian-era buildings and forty-three acres of gardens attract and charm its visitors.

The New York Zoological Society, formed in 1895 and opened to the public in 1899, adopted a plan radical for its day. Instead of showing native and foreign animals in cramped pens and paddocks, it tried to place them in large free-range enclosures and natural surroundings. William Temple Hornaday, the first director, was a strong and energetic leader who served for more than thirty years until his retirement at age seventy-two in 1926. He chose a new site for the zoo in the southern Bronx covering 250 acres. New York City purchased the land, constructed roads and buildings, and provided maintenance and keepers, while the society paid for animals and the curatorial and educational staff. The society also took over the Aquarium at Castle Clinton on the Battery in 1902 and operated it there until 1941; it reopened on Coney Island in 1957. Hornaday refused to employ the Hagenbeck system of moats, because he did not want to keep the public sixty or seventy feet away from the animals. He thought a zoo existed "to collect and exhibit fine and rare animals" and to enable "the greatest possible number of people to see them with comfort and satisfaction."

Hornaday, in addition to serving as the first director of the Bronx Zoo, chaired the American Bison Society and led its effort to protect these vanishing North American animals. Of the fifty million bison once in the United States, only one thousand remained, and Hornaday set about making sure that the zoo bred and protected them. In fact, at the start of the twentieth century, the Bronx Zoo shipped fifteen bison to Oklahoma, helping to return them to their original homes. Today, the origin of many bison can be traced back to the Bronx Zoo program. In addition to bison, the zoo also protected snow leopards, first exhibiting them in 1903. Under the leadership of the New York Zoological Society (later the Wildlife Conservation Society), the Bronx Zoo helped to form the Species Survival Program (SSP), which coordinates zoo breeding efforts for endangered species worldwide. What started with American bison extended to many other species.

In 1926, W. Reid Blair succeeded Hornaday at the Bronx Zoo and at once began experimenting with barless, moated parks; built a separate Ape House; and improved the educational program. This early effort at working with schools grew into a program that now serves millions of school children each year. A real change of direction came in 1940, when Fairfield Osborn, son of Henry Fairfield Osborn, became president of the board. He believed that a zoo's chief function was the protection of animals as part of the whole environment—forests, soils, waters, and wildlife. With these changes of purpose came many experiments in better exhibition techniques that included experiences for visitors to see animals in context through affordances such as an aerial tramway and butterfly garden. The recent *Congo Gorilla Forest* exhibit immerses visitors in the atmosphere of the forest, placing them nose-to-nose with gorillas—through glass, of course, while the seabird aviary (replacing the original aviary that opened with the zoo in 1899) is a sixty-foot-tall walk-through adventure.

The zoo boasts nineteen exhibits and invites visitors to enjoy additional "experiences," such as a movie at the 4D theater. A few exhibits have been inspired by recent movies, such as *Dinosaur Safari* (hinting to the craze of *Jurassic Park*) and *Madagascar!*, which have drawn attention due to their connections with blockbuster films. Advocacy is also part of the zoo's remit and is evidenced through programs such as their origami elephant papercraft, which draws attention to the loss of elephants due to ivory poaching. In fact, the zoo garnered attention for their collection of 78,564 paper pachyderms in 2016, drawing recognition by the *Guinness Book of World Records* as the largest display of origami elephants.[30]

Further, the WCS (Wildlife Conservation Society), the organization that oversees the Bronx Zoo management, has expanded field conservation operations to nearly sixty nations and all of the world's oceans; has supported the creation or expansion of more than 240 protected areas; and has provided over four hundred million visitors with "immersive, memorable experiences" at the Bronx Zoo and the four New York City wildlife parks (Central Park Zoo, Prospect Park Zoo, Queens Zoo, and the New York Aquarium). The SSP program, aka the "animal dating service," assists many zoos in breeding programs worldwide. The vision of the zoo, as outlined in its 2020 strategy, speaks to the broader aims of zoos, botanic gardens, and museums, which see part of their mission as social responsibility and having a foot in the past as well as the present and the future. The WCS aims "to maintain its historic focus on the protection of species while developing an ambitious plan to engage with a rapidly changing world."[31]

The National Zoological Park in Washington, D.C., established by Congress in 1889 and joined to the Smithsonian Institution a year later, was formed with the purpose of "the advancement of science and the instruction and recreation of the people." The zoo emerged in Rock Creek Park in the city's center thanks to the efforts of Hornaday, Smithsonian secretary Samuel Langley, and landscape architect Frederick Law Olmsted. The founders sought not only to display exotic animals, but also to provide a refuge for those species that were vanishing from the American landscape (especially bison and beaver). In 1975, the zoo opened the thirty-two-hundred-acre Conservation and Research Center in Front Royal, Virginia, to serve as a refuge for vanishing wildlife. This facility allows the zoo to pursue its dual functions of scientific research and conservation and public exhibition of animals. The National Zoo is a leader in training zoo professionals from around the world through its zoological medicine residency training and professional conservation programs. The zoo's formal mission statement reflects its commitment to the public and to professional training: "We save species. We provide engaging experiences with animals and create and share knowledge to save wildlife and habitats."[32]

Moving from outdoor spaces of botanic gardens and zoos to children's museums, the focus of health and well-being shifts from the care and conservation of plants and animals to the curiosity and wonder of children.

Children's Museums

Children's museums were devised as spaces intent upon serving the needs and interests of young people. The earliest children's museums established in the United States were the Brooklyn Children's Museum (1899), the Boston Children's Museum (1913), and the Children's Museum of Indianapolis

(1925). All of them were shaped by the progressive education movement and were championed by women who assumed leadership roles (an unusual circumstance in the early twentieth century).[33]

Even as children's museums have their primary audience in their name, their audience is far broader. The names of these institutions also vary: Port Discovery (Baltimore, Maryland), Please Touch Museum (Philadelphia, Pennsylvania); The DoSeum (San Antonio, Texas); EdVenture (Columbia, South Carolina); and the Thinkery (Austin, Texas). As Elaine Heumann Gurian, former exhibit center director of the Boston Children's Museum, explains: "I do not like *museum* because we are more than a museum, and I do not like *children's* because we are not a museum for children only."[34] Gurian is not alone in this attitude, and children's museums have adopted names designed to attract visitors, not to turn away some as "too old." But the names also remind us not to constrain what such museums are to their communities.

As noted at the outset of this chapter, children's museums are a distinctive American institution. The Brooklyn Children's Museum (1899) was the first one in the world; today they are found worldwide and number in the hundreds, with most in the United States. The Association of Children's Museums (ACM), a professional member organization for the children's museum field, counts among their roster 470 institutions in fifty states and sixteen countries.[35] But why and how did they emerge as a distinct type of museum?

American educator reformer and theorist John Dewey was especially influential in outlining the educational needs of children and a rationale for creating spaces for children to learn and to exploit opportunities for learning by doing. Dewey's stance took into account current thinking that identified and defined the qualities of "childhood" as a distinctive stage in human development; thus, his "model" school plan included a museum for students within its walls.[36] Some American museums created museum-schools, where docents lectured to students and supervised them in conducting experiments in laboratory-like spaces, and local school systems assigned teachers to work in the museum. The overarching principle was that "play" is a child's "work."

In addition to museum schools, precursors to children's museums may be found in "children's galleries." The children's gallery in the Smithsonian Institution was created in 1900–1901 by aeronautical engineer Samuel Pierpont Langley, Smithsonian secretary from 1887 to 1906. With the notion that "Knowledge Begins with Wonder," he oversaw the installation of exhibits in the Smithsonian Institution Building with cases designed at a lower height for children and without the usual scientific labels, asserting, "We are not very much interested in the Latin names, and however much they may mean to grown-up people, we do not want to have our entertainment spoiled by its being made a lesson."[37] The guiding principle for the room's exhibitions was, in his words, "to attract, amuse and only incidentally, to instruct."[38] Langley's focus on the room's development was so strong that he referred to himself as its "honorary curator," in addition to being secretary of the institution. The children's room opened in the south tower of the Smithsonian Institution Building (the castle) in 1901 and remained in place with few changes until 1939, when the space was filled by an exhibition to orient the public to all the Smithsonian's programs.[39] Children's galleries, with aims similar to those exemplified by Langley's efforts, were created in other institutions across the United States.

Brooklyn Children's Museum

The Brooklyn Institute of Arts and Science opened the first building designed to serve children in December 1899. Curator William Henry Goodyear proposed the idea as a means to use museum collections currently in storage. In 1900, a Brooklyn Children's Museum flyer addressed "To Our Young Friends" invited children in: "The management wishes you to use these collections to your own profit and pleasure, at all times. . . . Boys and girls, like yourselves, often find odd and curious animals, or plants, or minerals, about which they would love to learn something. Come to the Museum and bring them with you; someone will be found here who can tell you about them. . . . When you visit the Museum do not fail to ask the attendants to show or to explain to you any objects that may attract you.

Interior view, Children's Room in the South Tower of the Smithsonian Institution Building, or Castle. Stenciled over the door to the garden was a quote paraphrased from Aristotle that reads, "Knowledge begins in wonder." According to Smithsonian documentation, "The natural history displays were conceived by Secretary Samuel P. Langley (1887–1906) and were intended to inspire children to study the natural world. Cases were specifically designed to suit a child's height and all Latin labels were replaced with poetic inscriptions. To enhance children's interest in natural history, Langley had live birds and fish placed in the room. Grace Lincoln Temple designed the decorative scheme of the room, which featured a stenciled Celtic wall frieze of stylized birds and an elaborate painted ceiling of a leaf-covered trellis with birds peering down." See https://siarchives.si.edu/collections/siris_arc_401577.
Image courtesy United States National Museum Photographic Laboratory, Smithsonian Institution, Smithsonian Institution Archives, Record Unit 95, Box 41, Folder 08, Image No. SIA_000095_B41_F08_003.

The attendants are here for that purpose: they are glad to have you ask questions." The flyer closed with an invitation to seek out the librarian, "Miss Draper," with questions.[40] The concept centered support of various classroom subjects particularly along the lines of "nature study."[41]

In 1902, a young woman trained as a teacher and interested in sharing with children her love of biology and nature joined the museum staff. Assistant curator and subsequently curator in chief (or director), Anna Billings Gallup brought to this new type of museum her love of learning and of children and her commitment to making the museum serve children's interests and needs. She often followed young visitors around the museum exhibits to see what caught their fancy. She sought to create "an attractive resort for children."[42] Gallup explains the children's museum concept as a welcoming space for children, created and existing for them.[43] Under her leadership the museum thrived, expanding its program offerings and reaching out to the community as John Cotton Dana did at the Newark Museum, only Gallup's audience was young people.[44]

Brooklyn seems to have done it all: worked with teachers, science clubs, Boy and Girl Scouts, and the Americanization School (designed to teach immigrants English following World War I), as well as engaged children as both teachers (for the younger ones) and learners. Their collections served the children; they rejected the rare and fragile, collecting instead objects and specimens that children could use, handle, and experiment with. Gallup was renowned for simply opening exhibit cases to allow visitors to look closely and to handle objects.

With this one example, it is clear that children's museums could not simply be a few galleries within museums or extensions of them: they exist as their own institutions. They also operate as "third places"[45] that are neither home (first place), nor school or work (second place), where ideas are shared, relationships are built, and fun times are possible. Moreover, children's museums as third places resist the compartmentalization and categorization of museums' Linnean past. They offer places beyond home and school for experiential learning, interaction with objects, and inquiry, whether alone or together.[46]

The Brooklyn Museum served as inspiration for other institutions to include spaces exclusively for children in their museums and launched the creation, in the early twentieth century, of other children's museums in the United States In addition, the personal leadership of Brooklyn's Anna Billings Gallup fostered the emergence of other children's museums. Gallup welcomed visitors to Brooklyn and gave speeches about the museum to professional groups and civic organizations, especially reaching out to women's groups and individuals with interest in replicating the Brooklyn Museum in their own communities.

The growth of these two enterprises—children's galleries and children's museums—fostered the creation, in 1938, of a specific division (called the "Children's Division") of the museum accrediting body, American Association of Museums (now American Alliance of Museums), or AAM. As a charter member of the organization in 1906, Gallup was a respected museum professional: it was through her leadership and intervention that the division was created to extend the organization's services to museums that aim to reach children.

Children's Museum, Boston

Whereas the Brooklyn Children's Museum emerged from an established museum, Boston's origins lie in two arenas: first, nature study along the lines of Gallup's expertise, and second, a group of science teachers who had shared teaching collections among their classrooms. They both have ties to Ann Billings Gallup. Gallup attended the second meeting of the American Alliance of Museums in 1907, where she presented a paper "The Work of a Children's Museum." Also at that meeting was Delia I. Griffin, who presented her paper, "The Educational Work of a Small Museum," which focused on her work as director of the Fairbanks Museum in St. Johnsbury, Vermont. The two women shared an interest in nature study and access to collections.

Meanwhile, the Boston Science Teachers' Bureau was organizing collections to be used in classroom teaching. By 1909, the teachers had coordinated the collections effort, and by 1913, they organized a museum focusing on exhibitions and programs to engage and educate children (called the Children's Museum at the time). Delia Griffin was hired as curator of the museum. Serving teachers and children emerged as coequal goals for the new museum. The museum has remained true to these origins not only by serving teachers, but also by promoting exchange among teachers and fellow museum professionals to educate children, whether in the museum or classroom. Charles J. Douglas, president of the Children's Museum, described the museum at a 1920s AAM meeting: "It is a teaching organization which uses museum exhibits and apparatus as tools. It is not on account of these exhibits, mainly, that thousands of children come to us with enthusiasm and delight. No . . . They are drawn to us because here a meaning is put into these things, and natural phenomenon [are] made understandable."[47] As Griffin later noted, the goal of the museum was to train the "plastic minds of children to observe accurately and think logically."[48]

From 1962 to 1985, Michael Spock played a role in Boston similar to that of Brooklyn's Anna Billings Gallup. Spock led Boston's museum with a firm commitment to children, along with a democratic view of how the organization should operate to serve both audience and staff. It is intriguing to note that the museum had no separate "Education Department;" rather, its staff was organized to serve (educate) its young visitors. Of special importance in Boston was the exhibition development process that relied on visitors' participation to create the final product. Elements of exhibits would be created with materials that could be modified or even disposed of if they were found to be ineffective. In 1981, exhibit center director Elaine Heumann Gurian reported: "We think we are 65% right in the first installation of any exhibition, which means we are about 35% wrong. . . . We go through a process of observation, tryout, more observation, revision. . . . Modification of techniques is constant."[49] In the spirit of Brooklyn's Gallup, Boston's children gained an important sense of ownership of the museum.

Over time, the Children's Museum staff embraced novel and sensitive exhibition topics. Their respect for the interests and concerns of children are reflected in two important exhibitions: *What's Inside?* focused on explaining how objects work, complete with a toilet cut in half to expose its inner workings, and *What If I Couldn't?* focused on the impact of disabilities on everyday activities. Each of these exhibitions addressed the human condition from the perspective of a child. They addressed in the most sensitive ways those questions that young people sometimes are discouraged from asking.[50]

Boston's influence, like that of Brooklyn before it, has extended beyond children's museums to the broader museum profession. Michael Spock and his staff, like Gallup before them, actively participated in AAM activities and reached out to museum professionals. The museum's staff helped to establish the American Association of Youth Museums in 1964, today the Association of Children's Museums (ACM), the leading organization of children's museums in the world.

The Children's Museum of Indianapolis

The foundation of the Children's Museum of Indianapolis, like the earlier two examples, are also associated with Anna Billings Gallup. Ideas were percolating among philanthropists and women reformers, notably the Indianapolis Progressive Education Association (PEA), which founded a school that subscribed to the principles of Marietta Pierce Johnson's "Organic School Model." This model drew upon John Dewey's ideas about learning by doing. Daughters of wealthy socialite Mary Stewart Carey, Martha Carey and Mary Carey Appel, were among the founders of this school, and they fostered their mother's interest in the cause and children's education. Her interest was blooming such that in 1925, Mary Stewart Carey paid a visit to the Brooklyn to visit the Children's Museum while on vacation in New Jersey. She returned to Indianapolis determined to create for her city an institution to meet the needs of the city's children. The new museum in Indianapolis took a path that seems akin to today's participatory practice. Civic activist Carey created "Museum Week" in December 1925, when she personally solicited objects, over a period of a week, from the public for a new museum. Not only did she write to teachers and other adults, but she sent individual letters to children, seeking gifts to place in the museum that would be meaningful to Indianapolis' citizens. Her requests were taken so seriously that the new museum had to move twice in its first year to accommodate its growing collections. Through the process, the museum collected stuffed fish, Italian tiles, artworks, and souvenirs from abroad.[51]

Between 1925 and 1976, the museum occupied a series of large houses in Indianapolis, including founder Carey's; each time moving to ever-larger quarters to meet the growing demands for its programs. Today, The Children's Museum is the largest children's museum in the United States, with visitation exceeding a million each year.[52] With its 472,900 square-foot facility situated on twenty-nine acres, its collections total more than one hundred twenty thousand objects representing three broad domains: natural science, world cultures, and the American experience.[53]

The Children's Museum has made its immediate community a priority through exhibits, resources, and programming. While the usual fare of dinosaurs, mummies, and outer space are regular features of the museum, additional exhibits enable visitors to come into contact with the world around them in meaningful, age-appropriate ways. The exhibit *Take Me There: Greece* encourages cultural appreciation through hands-on learning and activities that are fully sensory. Visitors board a scaled version of aircraft before touching down in a Disney-like world with local markets, a bakery, and houses set in make-believe Athens and Corinth. The experience promotes learning and interest in contemporary cultures.

The exhibit *The Power of Children: Making a Difference* tells the stories of Anne Frank, Ruby Bridges, Ryan White (who was from Indiana), and Malala Yousafzai. Live performances, as well as sound and light shows, in the exhibition space communicate the stories of youngsters who changed the world. Visitors can walk around the large exhibit and immerse themselves in four areas, each with a full-size replica of spaces that were important to the journeys of these heroes: Anne Frank's annex, Ruby Bridges's classroom, Ryan White's bedroom, and Malala Yousafzai's home. The exhibits communicate the power of using words, actions, voice, and education, just as Anne wrote about her experience in hiding during the Holocaust; Ruby became one of the first Black students to attend a school that used to be only for White children; Ryan spoke out to help calm fears about AIDS; and Malala supported the right of girls to education. The museum invites visitors to acknowledge the power they have by asking them to make a promise by thinking of ways to change their communities.

A third space, unlike the two discussed above, is temporary rather than permanently installed. Entitled *Stories from Our Community*, the venue's content changes to reflect community interests. On view in the summer of 2023, *The Art of Protest* focused on public art in Indianapolis created by the Eighteen, a collective of Indianapolis-area visual artists who created the Black Lives Matter mural on Indiana Avenue downtown, the historic hub of the city's Black culture. Created in August 2020 as part of the George Floyd protests across the United States, the mural features colorful interpretations of each letter and symbol in the messaging of the hashtag #BlackLivesMatter.[54] The museum situated the narrative about the mural around the works of each artist, reflecting on their own artistic practice, independent of this mural's creation. In addition, a smaller replica of the letters and symbols of the mural are exhibited with information about the mural, as well as question for visitors to consider when looking at the art and thinking about the mural and its purpose. Nearby, video interviews with the members of the collective explain the artistic process and describe the creation of the mural. In this exhibition, the wall panel asks visitors to think about stories as the process and product of museums and the connections to the community: "Storytelling helps communities to share their history, traditions, and ideas." While this kind of exhibition might seem to be more "at home" in an art gallery, its placement at the Children's Museum signals the way in which this particular museum, and all museums, can have the capacity to connect communities through storytelling.[55]

Such exhibition practice, steeped in community, are underscored by other instances where the Children's Museum demonstrates what it means to be a community resource. Through its extension outdoors, the Sports Legends Experience consists of twelve outdoor sports experiences and an indoor exhibit. Though seasonal, the outdoor experiences allow children to engage in a wide range of physical activities and exercise—while, also, decreasing the threat of nature-deficit disorder. Children can learn about sports and physical fitness by trying their hand at ball sports (baseball, basketball, football, soccer, tennis) and golf, hockey, and racing. The exhibit also includes interactive displays that teach children about the history and science of sports. Through such a bold, broad education and engagement practice geared toward its immediate community, The Children's Museum of Indianapolis has demonstrated its role as a vital resource to its community.[56]

Play

As noted at the head of this chapter, these gardens, zoos, and children's museums frame health and well-being, curiosity, and wonder through experiences of learning, discovery, and play. They are united in their approach to informal and experiential learning as critical ways to engage visitors. They have welcomed these ways of learning, including self-directed play, where children "can follow their interests, explore the unknown, link outcomes with choices, conquer their fears, and make friends." More broadly, play has important links to developing key skills that serve as "a foundation for life-long success, including critical thinking, communication, problem solving, and collaboration. Often referred to as 21st century skills, these capabilities complement core subject matter knowledge and are highly valued in a world that is increasingly complex, competitive, and interconnected."[57]

While great attention has been paid to children's museums and play, these are not the only museums that can emphasize play as a way of learning and engaging at the museum. While certainly it would be inappropriate to take a priceless painting off a wall of museum and "play" with it, play can be incorporated into the experiences visitors have at museums. The same is true at other museums. An information brief about the power of play in children's museums, published by the Association of Children's Museums in 2023, in fact points to this capacity of play and learning beyond children's museums. Play enables joyful discovery, assertion of agency, skill development, social-emotional learning, innovation and creativity, as well as cross-cultural empathy and collaboration.[58] Surely all museums want to bring these possibilities to their audiences, as well.

For Further Consideration

To wrap up the discussion of the three museum types addressed in this chapter, it is helpful to recall the devices of framing health and well-being, curiosity, and wonder, as well as learning, discovery, and play. Gardens, zoos, and children's museums center informal and experiential learning as critical ways to engage visitors. They have fully realized the activities and strategies of museums more broadly over the past three decades in moving away from being *about something* and toward being *for somebody*. Gardens, zoos, and children's museums have positioned themselves as unique among museums. Gardens and zoos have living collections, and children's museums are keyed to a focused audience; whereas art and design, natural history and anthropology museums, science museums, and history organizations do not primarily center either of these attributes. Gardens, zoos, and children's museums also have intentional, social roles.

For instance, recent research by Jocelyn Dodd and Ceri Jones (2010) has identified seven areas where botanic gardens are demonstrating a greater social role, relevance, and responsibility by: broadening audiences; enhancing relevance to communities and, by extension, meeting their needs; educating their audiences; conducting research that has socioeconomic impact locally and globally; contributing to public and political debates on the environment; modeling sustainable behavior; and changing attitudes and behaviors.[59] The same can be said of socially relevant zoos. For instance, the exhibition *One Cubic Foot*, an initiative of the Seneca Park Zoo Society (Rochester, New York) involved photographer and environmentalist David Liittschwager's documentation of the nearby Genesee River as an example of the biodiversity of ecosystems. The Genesee River, once one of the nation's most polluted rivers, is undergoing a renaissance; as this is documented in the portrait of biodiversity captured by Liittschwager's recording of everything within one cubic foot of the water within the equivalent of a twenty-four-hour period in August 2015. The photographs were, in turn, put on exhibit at the area contemporary art center for exhibition and an artist talk in the spring of 2016. Liittschwager's work provided fertile ground for scientific research and knowledge, as well as a heightened awareness of the value of the river as a thriving ecosystem.[60] Such noticeable actions, accounts on blogs, and conservation-centered exhibitions on zoo grounds are beginning to play a role in asserting citizen awareness or action.[61]

Children's museums have the capacity to be socially relevant as well. For instance, in December 2000, a full-service public library branch was established inside the Children's Museum of Indianapolis—the first of its kind, which has now spawned other museums to follow suit in providing some measure of library services. Dubbed "InfoZone," the library branch has more than ten thousand books, in addition to computers and printers available for use for all. In addition, the museum's interest

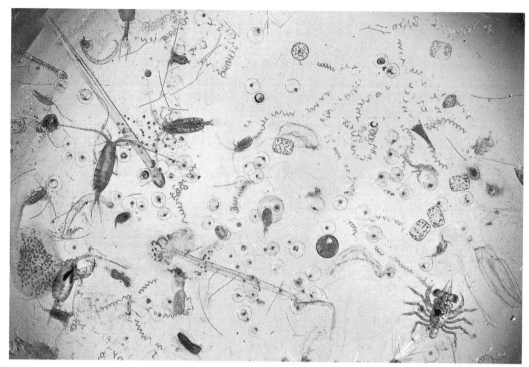

David Liittschwager, *One Dip of a Hand Net, 2006.* Liittschwager's photography of nature up-close has been featured in zoos and museums. In particular, the exhibition *One Cubic Foot* examines the biodiversity of ecosystems, waterways, and aquatic culture. This particular image was made onboard the NOAA ship *Oscar Elton Sette* off Kona, September 20, 2006. It shows marine microfauna with diverse planktonic organisms, ranging from photosynthetic cyanobacteria and diatoms to many different types of zooplankton, including both holoplankton (permanent residents of the plankton) and meroplankton (temporary residents of the plankton, e.g., fish eggs, crab larvae, worm larvae). It reflects just a bit of the highly diverse life forms that one finds in the planktonic realm.
Courtesy of David Liittschwager.

in providing accessible, positive learning environments for children and families has spawned the "Access Pass Program," which enables families to visit the museum (and other participating cultural attractions in the city) for two dollars per person/per visit so the cost of admission is not a barrier to access. The museum has also partnered with surrounding neighborhoods and foster family programs to provide free membership to the museum.

As this examination of the history of gardens, zoos, and children's museums thus illustrates, exhibits and programming have seamlessly extended beyond their immediate subjects to include awareness of their audience's physical, intellectual, spiritual, and emotional needs. As such, they evidence ways in which they can foster social inclusion, community cohesion, and lifelong learning that parallel the initiatives of museums overall. Thus, in many ways children's museums, zoos, and gardens *are the quintessential museums* for the twenty-first century. At these places, visitors can learn, engage, and play through onsite encounters with collections—whether living specimen, reproductions of a tactile or digital nature, or teaching materials. Regardless of the means of dissemination of this content, gardens, zoos, and children's museums do fulfill every function of museums, the subject to which our attention turns next.

Notes

1. Marilyn Hicks Fitzgerald, *Museum Accreditation: Professional Standards* (Washington, D.C.: American Association of Museums, 1973), 8; Arthur W. Hill, "The History and Functions of Botanic Gardens," *Annals Missouri Botanical Gardens* 2 (1915): 185-240; Edward S. Hyams and William MacQuitty, *Great Botanical Gardens of the World* (New York: Macmillan, 1969), 12-13; Edward S. Hyams, *A History of Gardens and Gardening* (New York: Praeger, 1971), 9-125; George H. M. Lawrence, "The Historical Role of the Botanic Garden," *Longwood Program Seminars* 1 (1968-1969): 43-44; Howard S. Irwin, "Botanical Gardens in the Decades Ahead," *Curator* 16 (1973): 45-55; Ulysses Prentice Hedrick, *A History of Horticulture in America to 1860* (New York: Oxford University Press, 1950), 3-4; Donald Wyman, "The Arboretums and Botanical Gardens of North America," *Chronica Botanica* 10 (Summer 1947): 405-408.
2. Hyams and MacQuitty, *Great Gardens*, 18-22; Hill, "History and Functions," 191-92, 194, 225; Lawrence, "Historical Role," 34-35; Andrew Cunningham, "The Culture of Gardens," in *Cultures of Natural History*, eds. N. Jardine, J. A. Secord, and E. C. Spray (Cambridge: Cambridge University Press, 1996), 38-56.
3. Hyams and MacQuitty, *Great Gardens*, 23; Hyams, *Gardens and Gardening*, 126-28; Hill, "History and Functions," 192-95, 226; Lawrence, "Historical Role," 34; J. D. Hunt, *Garden and Grove: The Italian Renaissance Garden in the English Imagination 1600-1750* (Princeton: Princeton University Press, 1996); Universiteit Leiden, Hortus *botanicus*, "Get Married in the Hortus," https://hortus.leidenuniv.nl/en/venue-hire/.
4. Hyams and MacQuitty, *Great Gardens*, 34-43; Hyams, *Gardens and Gardening*, 128-30; Lawrence, "Historical Role," 34-35; Candice A. Shoemaker, ed., *Encyclopedia of Gardens: History and Design*, Chicago Botanic Garden, vol. 2 (Chicago: Fitzroy Dearborn, 2001), http://www.nationaalherbarium.nl.
5. Anthony Wood, *The History and Antiquities of the University of* Oxford (Oxford: J. Gutch, 1796), 896; Hyams and MacQuitty, *Great Gardens*, 23, 82-85, 102-103; Hill, "History and Functions," 192, 194, 197-201, 233; Lawrence, "Historical Role," 34; William C. Steere, "Research as a Function of a Botanical Garden," *Longwood Program Seminars* 1 (1968-1969): 43-47.
6. Hyams and MacQuitty, *Great Gardens*, 107-108; Hill, "History and Functions," 197, 203-206; Lawrence, "Historical Role," 35; Steere, "Research as a Function," 44. On the Wardian case, see Kenneth Lemmon, *The Golden Age of Plant Hunters* (London: Dent, 1968), 54, 183-84, 217; Shoemaker, *Encyclopedia of Gardens*, vol. 3, 1417.
7. Rinker, *Weight of a Petal.*
8. W. B. Turrill, *The Royal Botanic Gardens, Kew: Past and Present* (London: Herbert Jenkins, 1959), 18-34; Mea Allan, *The Hookers of Kew, 1785-1911* (London: Michael Joseph, 1967), 36, 151; Ray Desmonds, *Kew: The History of the Royal Botanic Gardens* (London: Harvill Press and Royal Botanic Gardens, Kew, 1998); Hyams and MacQuitty, *Great Gardens*, 104-105, 108-109; Hyams, *Gardens and Gardening*, 250-51; Hill, "History and Functions," 206-207, 235; on Capability Brown Festival, see http://www.capabilitybrown.org/.
9. Turrill, *The Royal Botanic Gardens, Kew*, 20-32, 86-89; Allan, *Hookers*, 36, 77-79, 88-89, 105-106, 109-10, 138-41, 146-52, 178-79, 200-201, 205-206; Hyams and MacQuitty, *Great Gardens*, 108-10; Lawrence, "Historical Role," 35-36; Hill, "History and Functions," 207-209.
10. Kew Royal Botanic Garden, "Herbarium," http://www.kew.org/kew-science/collections/herbarium.
11. Hedrick, *History of Horticulture*, 71-72, 85-92, 207-209, 423-24; Joseph Ewan, ed., *A Short History of Botany in the United States* (New York: Hafner Pub., Co, 1969), 2-5, 33-34, 38-39, 132-33; Christine Chapman Robbins and David Hosack, *Citizen of New York* (Philadelphia: American Philosophical Society, 1964), 26, 4-99, 195-97; Hyams, *Gardens and Gardening*, 209.
12. United States Botanic Garden, "About Us," https://www.usbg.gov/about-us.
13. Hyams and MacQuitty, *Great Gardens*, 148-52; Carroll C. Calkins, ed., *Great Gardens in America* (New York: Coward-McCann, 1969), 242-51; Ewan, *A Short History*, 43-44; Wyman, "The American Arboretums and Botanical Gardens," 437-38.
14. Soderstrom, *Recreating Eden.*
15. Hyams and MacQuitty, *Great Gardens*, 156-63; Calkins, *Great American Gardens*, 272-81; Wyman, "The American Arboretums and Botanical Gardens," 422-23; William Hertrich, *The Huntington Botanical Gardens, 1905-1949* (San Marino: Huntington Library, 1949).

16. The Huntington, "The Huntington Botanical Gardens," http://huntington.org/webassets/templates/general.aspx?id=17082.

17. Hyams and MacQuitty, *Great Gardens*, 142–47; Hyams, *Gardens and Gardening*, 312; Calkins, *Great American Gardens*, 168–75; Wyman, "The American Arboretums and Botanical Gardens," 447–48; *Longwood Gardens, A Visit to Longwood Gardens*, 8th ed. (Kennett Square, PA: The Gardens, 1970); *Longwood Gardens, Fountains of Longwood Gardens* (Kennett Square, PA, 1960: The Gardens); Lanning Roper, "Longwood Gardens: A Twentieth Century American Pleasure Ground," *Royal Horticultural Society, Journal* 82 (May 1957): 1–9.

18. Program components include program content, local and regional immersion, a cohort project, and field placement. Longwood Gardens, "Longwood Fellows," http://longwoodgardens.org/education/longwood-fellows.

19. On the exhibition, see Sharon Loving and Richard Stamelman, "Longwood Gardens: The Making of *Making Scents*," *Collections: A Journal for Museum and Archives Professionals*, edited by Juilee Decker, 8:3 (Summer 2012), 199–220.

20. Information about the garden's history may be found online at Chicago Botanic Garden, http://www.chicagobotanic.org/ and https://www.chicagobotanic.org/education/campus. Information about the new renovations and the Learning Campus may be found in Katherine A. Johnson, Eileen Prendergast, and Jennifer Schwarz Ballard, "An Outdoor Museum Perspective on Education and Audience Engagement," in *Collections Care and Stewardship: Innovative Approaches for Museums*, edited by Juilee Decker (Lanham, MD: Rowman & Littlefield, 2015), 11–26.

21. Corey Kilgannon, "A Potter's Field as a Public Park?" *New York Times*, March 26, 2023, Section MB, 1. Hunt states that the city should stop using park enforcement officers as mandatory escorts and add a few essentials such as a free-roaming park with a minimum of structural improvements, including a welcome center, bathrooms, benches, and some vending machines to improve and expand visitation.

22. For information on nature deficit disorder and creating and managing natural places of wonder, see Richard Louv, *Lost Child in the Woods: Saving Our Children from Nature Deficit Disorder* (Chapel Hill: Algonquin Books, 2005); Richard Louv, *The Nature Principle* (Chapel Hill, Algonquin Books, 2011); Cheryl Charles, "Battling the Nature Deficit with Nature Play: An Interview with Richard Louv and Cheryl Charles," *American Journal of Play* 4:2 (Fall 2011): 137–49.

23. See Jill Suttie, "How to Protect Kids from Nature-Deficit Disorder," *Greater Good Magazine* September 15, 2016, https://greatergood.berkeley.edu/article/item/how_to_protect_kids_from_nature_deficit_disorder.

24. Harry Gersh, *The Animals Next Door: A Guide to Zoos and Aquariums of the Americas* (New York: Fleet Academic Editions, 1971), 1–14; R. J. Hoage, Anne Roskell, and Jane Mansour, "Menageries and Zoos to 1900," in *New Worlds, New Animals: From Menagerie to Zoological Park in the Nineteenth Century*, eds. Robert J. Hoage and William A. Deiss, (Baltimore: Johns Hopkins University Press, 1996), 8–15; John C. Coe, "The Evolution of Zoo Animal Exhibits," in *The Ark Evolving: Zoos and Aquariums in Transition*, ed. Christen M. Wemmer (Washington, D.C.: Smithsonian Institution, 1995), 96–102.

25. London Zoo, "About Us," https://www.zsl.org/. Beyond the scope of this brief entry, read about actions of zoo staff and their relationship with the public. See zookeeper Colette Gibbings's account of going completely disposable and plastic-free for thirty-one days. See Colette Gibbings, "Conservation: My Plastic Free Month," *ZSL*, July 20, 2016, https://www.zsl.org/blogs/conservation/my-plastic-free-month.

26. James Fisher, *Zoos of the World: The Story of Animals in Captivity* (Garden City: Natural History Press, 1967), 21–57; Bernard Livingston, *Zoo: Animals, People, Places* (New York: Arbor House, 1974), 15–35, 71, 233; Gersh, *The Animals Next Door*, 1–14; *International Zoo Yearbook* 14 (1974): 257–327; Wilfrid Blunt, *The Ark in the Park: The Zoo in the Nineteenth Century* (London: Hamish Hamilton, 1976), 10, 16–31; Bob Mullan and Gary Marvin, *Zoo Culture* (Urbana: University of Illinois Press, 1999); Michael Osborne, "Zoos in the Family: The Geoffroy Saint-Hilaire Clan and Three Zoos in Paris," in *New Worlds, New Animals*, 34–36; Harriet Ritvo, "The Order of Nature: Constructing the Collections of Victorian Zoos," in *New Worlds, New Animals*, 43–50.

27. Edward Alexander, "Carl Hagenbeck and His Stellingen Tierpark," in *Museum Masters*, 311–39; Rothfels, *Savages and Beasts*, 199; John C. Coe, "The Evolution of Zoo Animal Exhibits"; Wemmer, *The*

Ark Evolving, 105–109; Fisher, *Zoos of the World*, 138, 164–69; Livingston, *Zoo*, 137, 152; Gersh, *Animals Next Door*, 14–15; Herman Reichenbach, "A Tale of Two Zoos: The Hamburg Zoological Garden and Carl Hagenbeck's Tierpark," in *New Worlds, New Animals*, 51–62; http://www.hagenbeck.de.

28. Vernon N. Kisling Jr., ed., *Zoo and Aquarium History: Ancient Animal Collections to Zoological Gardens* (Boca Raton: CRC Press, 2001); Heini Hediger, *Man and Animal in the Zoo: Zoo Biology*, trans. Gwynne and Winwood Reade (London: Routledge, 1969).

29. *International Zoo Yearbook* 14 (1974): 257–327; Livingston, *Zoo*, 236, 239–40, 280–82; Gersh, *Animals Next Door*, 15–16, 70, 78, 85, 95–96, 111, 115, 120–21, 135, 141, 148–49; Andrew Rowan and Robert Hoage, "Public Attitudes Towards Wildlife," in *The Ark Evolving*, 32–60; John C. Coe, "The Evolution of Zoo Animal Exhibits," in *The Ark Evolving*, 102–105; Vernon N. Kisling Jr., "The Origin and Development of American Zoological Parks to 1899," in *New Worlds, New Animals*, 109–26; Clark DeLeon, *America's First Zoostory: 125 Years at the Philadelphia Zoo* (Virginia Beach: Donning, 1999); Elizabeth Hardouin-Fugier, *Zoo: A History of Zoological Gardens in the West* (London: Reaktion, 2002); http://www.PhiladelphiaZoo.org.

30. Danny Lewis, "World's Largest Herd of Origami Elephants Takes Over the Bronx Zoo," *Smithsonian Magazine*, November 18, 2016, https://www.smithsonianmag.com/smart-news/worlds-largest-herd-origami-elephants-takes-over-bronx-zoo-180961161/.

31. Alexander, "William Temple Hornaday," in *The Museum in America*, 189–204; William Bridges, *Gathering of the Animals: An Unconventional History of the New York Zoological Society* (New York: Harper & Row, 1974), 16–17, 20–38, 57–60, 99–122, 223–30, 387–88, 412, 414, 440–86, 505; Livingston, *Zoo*, 263–79; American Association of Zoological Parks and Aquariums, *Zoos and Aquariums in the Americas* (Wheeling, WV: np, 1974), 97; "Elephant and Tiger and Rhinoceros Roaming the Bronx? Preposterous!" *New York Times*, August 17, 1977; Coe, "The Evolution," 109; John Fraser, "Museums and Civility," *Curator* 47, no. 3 (July 2004): 252–55; Jeff Hayward and Marilyn Rothenberg, "Measuring Success in the 'Congo Gorilla Forest' Conservation Exhibition," *Curator* 47, no. 3 (July 2004): 261–82; Jacob E. Osterhout, "The Bronx Zoo Turns 110: Here are 110 Things You Need to Know About This NYC Favorite," *Daily News*, November 13, 2009, http://www.nydailynews.com/new-york/bronx/bronx-zoo-turns-110-110-nyc-favorite-article-1.417057; New York City Department of Parks & Recreation, "History of the Bronx Zoo," https://www.nycgovparks.org/about/history/zoos/bronx-zoo; for vision 2020, see https://www.wcs.org/about-us and https://www.wcs.org/our-work/2020-strategy.

32. In the second edition of this text, the mission read: "We are the nation's zoo, providing leadership in conservation science. We connect people with wildlife through exceptional animal exhibits, explore solutions through science-based programs, build partnerships worldwide, and share our discoveries." The shift from discovery to knowledge sharing, engagement, and saving of species is indicative of the trend more broadly in museums toward participatory engagement. For information about the history of the National Zoo, see Helen Lefkowitz Horowitz, "The National Zoological Park: 'City of Refuge' or Zoo?" in *New Worlds, New Animals*, 126–35, Heather Ewing, "The Architecture of the National Zoological Park," in *New Worlds, New Animals*, 151–64.

33. The Detroit Children's Museum was founded in 1917, though is not discussed in this volume. For more on the four children's museums, see Jessie Swigger, "The First Four: Origin Stories of the First Children's Museums in the United States," *Association of Children's Museums*, March 8, 2019, https://childrensmuseums.org/2019/03/08/the-first-four-childrens-museums/.

34. Gurian, "Adult Learning," 275.

35. Association of Children's Museums, "History of ACM," https://childrensmuseums.org/about/history/. Today known as the Association of Children's Museums, this organization began in 1962 as the American Association of Youth Museums before changing names twice (Association of Youth Museums and then the Association of Children's Museums).

36. George E. Hein, "John Dewey and Museum Education," *Curator* 47, no. 4 (2004): 413–27.

37. Smithsonian Institution, "Online Exhibition: The Children's Room in the Smithsonian Institution Building," https://www.si.edu/HHP/exhibitions/childrens-room.

38. Smithsonian Institution Archives, Record Unit 55, file 17, Smithsonian Institution, assistant secretary in charge of the United States National Museum, Records.

39. Smithsonian Institution Archives, Record Unit 55, file 17; LeBlanc, "The Slender Golden Thread"; Smithsonian Institution Architectural History & Historic Preservation Division, "The Children's Room in the Smithsonian Institution Building: Knowledge Begins in Wonder," https://www.si.edu/ahhp/childrens roomintroduction.

40. Brooklyn Institute of Arts and Sciences flyer, 1900, Smithsonian Institution Archives, Record Unit 55, file 17.

41. Jessie Swigger, "The First Four: Origin Stories of the First Children's Museums in the United States," *ACM*, March 8, 2019, https://childrensmuseums.org/2019/03/08/the-first-four-childrens-museums/.

42. Cassandra Zervos, *Children's Museums: A Case Study of the Foundations of Model Institutions in the United States*, thesis, Pennsylvania State University, 1990, 36.

43. Edward P. Alexander, *The Museum in America: Innovators and Pioneers* (Walnut Creek: AltaMira Press, 1997), 140.

44. Alexander, *The Museum in America*, 140.

45. *Third place* was defined by sociologist Ray Oldenburg in 1989 and popularized more recently by Starbucks CEO Howard Schultz as the desired feeling for their cafés. See Ray Oldenburg, "The Great Good Place: Cafés, Coffee Shops, Bookstores, Bars, Hair Salons, and Other Hangouts at the Heart of a Community" (New York: Marlowe, distributed by Publishers Group West, 1999 [reprint of 1989]).

46. On Gallup and Louise Connolly, who worked in education at Newark, see George E. Hein, "Progressive Education and Museum Education: Anna Billings Gallup and Louise Connolly," *Journal of Museum Education* 31, no. 3 (2006): 161–73.

47. Adelaide B. Sayles, *The Story of the Children's Museum of Boston* (Boston: George H. Ellis Press, 1937), 27.

48. Jessie Swigger, "The First Four: Origin Stories of the First Children's Museums in the United States," *ACM*, March 8, 2019, https://childrensmuseums.org/2019/03/08/the-first-four-childrens-museums/.

49. Elaine Heumann Gurian, "Adult Learning at Children's Museum of Boston," in *Museums, Adults and the Humanities*, ed. Zipporah Collins (Washington, D.C.: American Association of Museums, 1981), 194.

50. Gurian, "Adult Learning," 289–91.

51. On the Careys, see Jessie Swigger, "The First Four: Origin Stories of the First Children's Museums in the United States," *ACM*, March 8, 2019, https://childrensmuseums.org/2019/03/08/the-first-four-childrens-museums/; more generally, see Zervos, *Children's Museums*, 94–95.

52. As of 2014, visitation was 1.2 million per year. See "The Children's Museum Ranked Among the Most Visited Museums in North America!" November 11, 2014, https://www.childrensmuseum.org/content/children%E2%80%99s-museum-ranked-among-most-visited-museums-north-america.

53. Children's Museum of Indianapolis, "About," https://www.childrensmuseum.org/about.

54. Children's Museum of Indianapolis, "Stories from Our Community: The Art of Protest," https://www.childrensmuseum.org/exhibits/stories.

55. Description of the exhibitions at the Children's Museum of Indianapolis are based upon the author's visit to the museum in June 2023.

56. Children's Museum of Indianapolis, "Community Programs," https://www.childrensmuseum.org/content/community-programs.

57. Boston Children's Museum, "The Power of Play," http://www.bostonchildrensmuseum.org/power-of-play.

58. K. T. Todd, "Information Brief: The Power of Play in Children's Museums and Elsewhere," *ACM*, July 17, 2023, https://childrensmuseums.org/2023/07/17/powerofplay-brief/.

59. Jocelyn Dodd and Ceri Jones, "Redefining the Role of Botanic Gardens: Towards a New Social Purpose" (Richmond [UK]: Botanic Gardens Conservation International [BGCI], 2010).

60. Seneca Park Zoo, "One Cubic Foot," http://senecaparkzoo.org/citizen-science/; YouTube videos illustrate the process and results. See parts 1, 2, 3: https://youtu.be/oVcKfwad3po; https://youtu.be/_CGyGZS2zRk; https://youtu.be/RzpeMFaEsEw.

61. See Colette Gibbings, "Conservation: My Plastic Free Month," *ZSL*, July 20, 2016, https://www.zsl.org/blogs/conservation/my-plastic-free-month.

Introduction to Part II

Museum Functions

Limitations are present throughout this volume, because such books are constrained by a number of variables (an interest in covering a broad swathe of chronology without being too granular in attempt; a reasonable number of chapters keyed to the length of a semester or other educational construction of time; and the primary geographic emphasis of the United States and Europe, particularly England, France, and Scandinavia). This middle third is also limited by the number of verbs that animate the chapter titles and the corresponding text, so as to suggest the variety of functions while not expanding these to an unreasonable breadth. Museums are not required to undertake every function listed; and yet many institutions do so in an effort to meet the needs, interests, and desires of their communities—the audiences whom they serve. Likewise, the final third of the volume will be limited by the number of topics it will address—always aware that each institution is unique, as are its challenges.

To _____

To mirror the first and third sections of this volume, the number of functions in this edition of the book has been decreased to five. The functions are identified and discussed as follows: to conserve, to exhibit, to interpret, to engage, and to serve. Unstated in the list of functions is "to educate," as articulated in the Belmont Report (1968).[1] In addition, "To Collect" has been removed. This is not to question whether museums do not need objects, as has been proffered by Steven Conn,[2] but rather, to authorize the address in the final third of the book, where discussions around ownership, repatriation, and decolonization are centered.

It is no easy task to articulate museum functions around five actions, each of which corresponds to a chapter in this section. Do these actions relate to the metaphors that have been used to describe museums—such as a tomb,[3] a laboratory,[4] a supermarket,[5] a temple, a forum,[6] or a veiled vault[7]? Or do they reflect on museum histories, the proffering of education and knowledge construction aptly framed in J. Mordaunt Crook's examination of museums, which called "the modern museum . . . is a product of Renaissance humanism, eighteenth-century enlightenment and nineteenth-century democracy."[8] It seems that twenty-first-century museums boldly undertake activities that hold their collections in public trust, that educate, and also that tap into the unmet needs of their publics and reflect their communities.

Operationally, they do all these things by extending beyond their boundaries physically and conceptually and by facilitating multimodal literacy.[9] Museums present their audiences with online and onsite learning opportunities. They provide spaces for immersive, hands-on activities that provide audiences with the opportunity to be creative, to wonder, to play, to problem-solve, and to partici-pate.[10] In developing analog and digital opportunities onsite and online, museums offer opportunities to develop skills and ways of knowing. These literacies might be expanded conceptually to reveal a multiplicity of literacies as narratives that join together *ways of knowing* with *ways of doing* onsite and online as part of the museum experience. They offer different ways of seeing the world around us, of constructing knowledge, and of making meaning.

And, as a final thought before moving on to the chapters comprising Section II, consider fram-ing your reading by contemplating what *you* conceive as the functions of museums. When I posed this question to my students recently, one of them (an interior architecture student) remarked that museums *inspire*. I asked if she would accept "to educate" as a substitute, questioning if *educate* and *inspire* were one and the same. She resisted and went on to explain that when she seeks inspiration, she looks at the environment around her—including the tangible collections on our campus. She noted the specific importance of the Vignelli Center for Design Studies,[11] which holds the extensive archive of designers Massimo and Lella Vignelli (think the traditional New York City subway map or the paper fold-out National Park Service maps), in her practice. Social media tools and online lurking are other-wise important in building out a visual vocabulary, but collections *inspire*. They moved her to act, to design, to create, to fulfill an unrealized vision. Other students have suggested other verbs: *celebrate, provocate, honor, expand, immerse, connect, challenge*. Each of these requires a pause, a shift in thinking about what museums are, and what they do.

While I have resisted my inclination to include "to inspire" or any of the other verbs, due to the limits of space, perhaps the fifth edition of *Museums in Motion* will include these functions, in addition to many others.

Notes

1. American Association of Museums, America's Museums: The Belmont Report: A Report to the Federal Council on the Arts and the Humanities (Washington, D.C.: AAM, 1968).
2. Steven Conn, *Do Museums Still Need Objects?* (Philadelphia: University of Pennsylvania Press, 2010). See especially chapter 1, with the question of objects (pp. 20-57), and chapter 2, which asks about possession: "Whose Objects? Whose Culture? The Contexts of Repatriation," pp. 58-85.
3. See Adorno, "Valéry Proust Museum in Memory of Hermann von Grab," *Prisms*, edited by Theodor Adorno. (London: Garden City Press, 1967), 175-85. Quote appears on page 175.
4. Alfred H. Barr Jr., American art historian and first director of the Museum of Modern Art (MoMA) in New York, proclaimed that the museum was a laboratory in the catalog celebrating the tenth anniver-sary of the museum and the inauguration of its new building in midtown Manhattan on West Fifty-Third Street. See Art in Our Time: An Exhibition to Celebrate the Tenth Anniversary of the Museum of Modern Art and the Opening of Its New Building Held at the Same Time of the New York World's Fair (New York: Museum of Modern Art, 1939). See also Hans Ulrich Obrist, Ways of Curating (New York: Macmillan, 2014), 70-73.
5. American pop artist Andy Warhol's life-as-art approach led to an exhibition in 1964, The American Supermarket, an act and practice that paid heed to the question of art as commodity and commodity as art. It is also featured in the work of peer artists on the American scene, including Claes Oldenburg, Roy Lichenstein, James Rosenquist, and others.
6. Brooklyn Museum director Duncan Cameron published the notion that museums occupy two ends of a spectrum, from a "temple" to a "forum," in the early 1970s. See Duncan F. Cameron, "The Museum, a Temple or the Forum?" Curator: The Museum Journal 14:1 (March 1971): 11-24, which also appeared in Journal of World History 14, no. 1 (1972): 189-202. Cameron posits the museum as a place of experimentation and innovation that was complementary to the museum's role as a temple of, and to, learning.
7. The concept of "the veil and the vault" is a design aesthetic proposed by Diller Scofidio + Renfro, in collaboration with Gensler, in the creation of The Broad, Los Angeles' newest museum focusing on

contemporary art. The design combines the two key facets of The Broad's mission—exhibition and storage (for use by this institution and others, to which it loans). See The Broad, "Building," http://www .thebroad.org/building, accessed August 9, 2016; see also The Broad: An Art Museum Designed by Diller Scofidio + Renfro, edited by Joanne Heyler, Ed Schad et al. (London: Prestel, 2015).

8. J. Mordaunt Crook, *The British Museum* (London: Praeger, 1972), 32.

9. Carey Jewitt and Gunther Kress, editors, *Multimodal Literacy* (New York: Peter Lang, 2003). See also https://multimodalstudies.wordpress.com/what-is-multimodal-literacy/.

10. See Alex Freeman, Samantha Adams Becker, M. Cummins, E. McKelroy, C. Giesinger, B. Yuhnke, "Makerspaces: Time to Adoption Horizon: One Year or Less," *NMC Horizon Report: 2016* (Austin, Tex.: The New Media Consortium, 2016), 38.

11. Interestingly, when recounting this discussion with the archivist of the Vignelli, she indicated that inspiration is part of their mission: "The Vignelli Center for Design Studies collects, preserves and makes accessible the primary source materials produced by Massimo and Lella Vignelli along with other design exemplars for historical research, education, and creative inspiration. The Center fosters design excellence by working with students, designers, educators, and the public around the world through educational programming, providing design history resources, and creating design solutions to meet human needs with the Vignelli legacy of Modernist values and philosophy at its core." Jennifer Whitlock, personal interview and follow-up email conversation, September 30, 2016.

6

To Conserve

Not until the twentieth century did museums clearly realize that one of their chief functions, as well as an all-important duty, was to pass on their collections in pristine condition to succeeding generations. Such a responsibility assumed a burden of care that might involve repairing collections in order to prolong their lifespan. These earliest attempts at care were called *restoration*—borrowing from the core principle "to restore," as in, returning to an original state. Such activities were intended to repair works or to slow the degradation of materials. As scientists learned to slow the degradation of museum materials, a new profession of scientifically knowledgeable "conservators" began to replace the artists and craftsmen commonly known as "restorers." The term *conservation* was adopted to broaden the range of activities undertaken relative to collections.

Thus, *conservation* encompasses a range of actions taken by museum professionals toward the long-term preservation of cultural property. These activities include: examination, documentation, treatment, and preventive care. They support and are supported by research and education. The goal with all conservation activities is to remain true to the maker's intent. *Restoration*, on the other hand, is essentially a type of conservation work in that it aims to modify the condition of an item with the goal of bringing it closer to its original, maker-intended state. A third facet, *stabilization*, refers to conservation efforts that seek to minimize deterioration (rather than restoring).[1]

In the United States, individuals undertaking such conservation activities are referred to as *conservators*. In Europe, the preferred term for these professionals is *conservator-restorer*, acknowledging the duality of the role in caring for collections. Two governing bodies for these professionals include the American Institute for Conservation (AIC, founded 1972), which represents 3,500 individuals and allied professionals working in more than forty countries worldwide. The organization brings together expertise from science, art, and history to foster the treatment, research, collections care, and education/training of professionals working toward the preservation of cultural heritage. The organization also advocates for sustainable practices to fight the impacts of the climate crises, preserve heritage at risk, and improve the field of conservation. In addition, the AIC partners with the Foundation for Advancement in Conservation (FAIC) to promote preservation and protection of cultural heritage.[2] The European Confederation of Conservator-Restorers' Organisation (ECCO/established 1991) represents six thousand professionals in twenty-three countries. The organization began hosting a "European Day of Conservation-Restoration" in 2018 to bring attention to Europe's cultural history; to engage users of social media, especially youth; and to highlight themes important to the preservation of cultural heritage. Both of these organizations articulate professional standards, publish guidelines for education and practice, and foster the exchange of knowledge through research, publication, and presentation on areas of relevance to the field.

In addition, a number of other national and regional organizations, such as the Canadian Conservation Institute (founded 1972), an agency within the Department of Canadian Heritage, advances and promotes conservation. Along with its sister agency, the Canadian Heritage Information Network (CHIN), these entities offer conservation and collections management resources to the Canadian museum community. Whether documenting, managing, sharing information about, and otherwise caring for collections or lending expertise in conservation science, treatment, and preventive conservation, CHIN and CCI support the national and international collections communities.

The Fédération Française des Professionnels de la Conservation-Restauration (French Federation of Conservator-Restorer, established 1992) supports conservation professions in the preservation of cultural heritage.[3] In addition, intergovernmental organizations, such as ICCROM (International Centre for the Study of the Preservation and Restoration of Cultural Property), provide training to mid-career professionals and play a key role in drafting guidelines for cultural heritage protection.[4]

Surveys and Data

In August 2004, the first comprehensive survey of condition and preservation needs of all United States collections held in the public trust was conducted. The survey was distributed to more than 14,500 museums, historical societies, archives, libraries, and archaeological repositories and scientific research centers, asking institutions to report on all aspects of conservation and preservation. The resulting publication, *A Public Trust at Risk: The Heritage Health Index Report on the State of America's Collections*, published in 2005 by Heritage Preservation with funding from the Institute of Museum and Library Services (IMLS), involved more than three thousand museum professionals from institutions large and small across the United States and offered the only such holistic data to date. The report drew attention to the 4.8 billion artifacts being cared for nationally while also reporting that United States collections are visited 2.5 billion times per year. Not only are collections large and broad, they are of interest and seemingly valued.

But are institutions doing enough to care for their collections in perpetuity? Are the staff equipped to do what they can to preserve cultural heritage?

The Heritage Health Index Report (2005)[1]

- Eighty percent of the surveyed institutions have no paid staff responsible for collections care.
- Seventy percent of institutions have not assessed collections conditions or needs.
- Thirty percent of collections are in "unknown" condition.
- Eighty percent of institutions do not have adequate environmental controls in place.
- Sixty-five percent of collections suffer from improper storage conditions, with 26 percent of institutions lacking environmental controls entirely.
- Eighty percent of institutions do not have a plan to protect collections in case of emergency.

1 Heritage Preservation, *A Public Trust at Risk: The Heritage Health Index Report on the State of America's Collections* (Washington, D.C.: Heritage Preservation, 2005).

The study grew from the President's Committee on the Arts and the Humanities, which issued a report in 1997 that looked at conditions affecting the arts and their future health. Heritage Preservation then initiated discussion about a national collection-needs assessment at its annual meeting two years later (Charting a New Agenda for a New Century), which set the stage for the Heritage Health Index.

The second HHI, called the Heritage Health Information Survey Report, was collected in 2014 and released in 2019. Framed around five research questions that could be investigated at collecting institutions through the Institute for Museum and Library Services, the HHI examined the following:

1. What is the current state of tangible cultural heritage collections?
2. To what extent have institutions prioritized collection preservation?

3. To what extent have institutions developed emergency plans and trained staff to implement these plans to protect collections?
4. To what extent have institutions assigned staff responsibilities in caring for collections?
5. What is the current state of the preservation of digital collections?

These five questions are interrelated, and their answers reveal information about collections at present, their condition, and their retention and preservation.

The data was gathered from 1,714 institutions representing 31,290 archives, museums, libraries, historical societies, and scientific collections of more than 130 billion items across the nation. The collections are comprised of photographic images (36 percent); unbound materials (33 percent); and historic, ethnographic, archaeological, natural science, and art objects (representing about 23 percent of all materials), in contrast to the numbers of recorded sound and moving-image items as a portion of the collections (less than 0.2 percent each).[5] Further, the data highlights the need for collections preservation and illuminates the challenges collecting institutions face. The data above were not entirely updated in the new report; however, it did reflect change over the ten-year span.

Comparison Data from the Heritage Health Index (2019)[1]

- Incidence of damage from improper storage and light exposure decreased by 30 percent.
- Eighty-six percent of institutions had assigned collections care to personnel, over 78 percent reported in 2004.
- Forty-five percent of organizations reporting had conducted a collections assessment, which was a 50 percent increase over 2004.
- Forty-two percent of organizations were engaged in more emergency planning, an increase from 20 percent in 2004.
- Forty-nine percent of organizations placed funds on collections preservation, up from 23 percent in 2004.

---

1 See IMLS, "Heritage Health Information Survey (HHIS) Report: A Snapshot of Facts and Figures," 2019, www.imls.gov/hhis.

Having data doesn't mean we understand what to do with, or how to care for, collections. While there is no one-size-fits-all approach to caring for collections, the purpose of this chapter is to outline desirable museum principles and practices to care for objects, concluding with more generalized discussions of professional conservation concerns. Where there is mention of conservators, it should be understood that this title refers to a trained, accredited conservation professional while also recognizing that many museums are not in the position to have a full-time person with such credentials on staff. However, the American Institute for Conservation (AIC) provides advice and guidance in hiring conservation professionals for particular (often grant-funded) projects. Additionally, the collections community (comprised of conservators, registrars, collections managers, and others who work directly with collections and provide for their safekeeping and long-term care) is one that aims to help one another in caring for our collections *in toto*. In fact, a number of resources are available that are keyed to the "lone arranger"—often the only person responsible for caring for collections in the local historical society or museum.[6] Today, online resources do offer an incredible amount of information—much of which has been vetted, even authorized, by reputable organizations. The American Institute of Conservation, for instance, provides good, helpful information about collections care. Moreover, email and listservs have changed the way that information and access to professionals, such as conservators, can be obtained.

As far as day-to-day operations within museums and collections without conservation staff, appropriate preservation activities are carried out by a wide variety of staff, from the director to volunteers. No museum aspires to fame through a botched restoration such as that done by Cecilia Giménez, an elderly parishioner-turned-amateur-restorer who attempted to improve the condition of a fresco of Christ painted around 1930. An unremarkable work on its own, the small painting in the Sanctuary of Mercy Church in Borja, Spain, bore the brunt of restoration that disfigured the face of Christ to such a degree that it became known as *Monkey Christ* and has become both an internet phenomenon and a tourist attraction. With visits to the town escalating from six thousand to ten times that, interest in the work and its story facilitated attention by the local authorities, who opened an interpretation center dedicated to the story of the painting in March 2016.[7] While this example witnessed a remarkable outcome, the condition of the work remains compromised and serves as a reminder that *all museums and collections professionals* aspiring to protect the objects should strive to meet the basic standards described here.

The Nature of Museum Objects

A conservator is interested in the materials of which museum objects are made—not primarily their aesthetic form, but their molecular and atomic composition and structure. These objects range from the quotidian detritus of life to those made from the finest materials to adorn their owner or for public display. The conservator wants to know about their condition—how much they have deteriorated and how they can be stabilized for a long future. In doing this work, he or she is dealing with four chief classes of substances: organic materials, metals and their alloys, siliceous and equivalent materials, and easel and mural paintings. Harold J. Plenderleith, former keeper of the British Museum research laboratory, authored *The Conservation of Antiquities and Works of Art: Treatment, Repair, Restoration* (1962), the classic reference for scientific museum conservation. In the revised second edition (1971), A. E. A. Werner, then the keeper of the laboratory, collaborated with Plenderleith to include updated information as well as content regarding museum lighting and atmosphere pollution. These volumes remain valuable basic reference tools. In addition, more recent publications and other resources issued by the American Institute for Conservation and the Getty Conservation Institute (established 1985) and other organizations and institutions, have enriched our understanding of the nature of museum objects and how we should care for them.[8]

With regard to non-living collections in art and design museums, science centers, history and place-based museums, and children's museums the following descriptions apply. (Living collections and those relating to animal materials will be discussed below.) Organic materials include hides, leather, parchment, paper, bone, ivory, textiles, and wood. They are of animal or vegetable origin, are carbon-based, and have cellular structure. They are susceptible to deterioration by light, variations in humidity and temperature, dryness or brittleness, and excessive humidity (dampness) that produces molds, mildew, and other biological reactions.

Gold, silver, lead, tin, copper (and its alloys, including bronze), iron, and steel are the chief metals. They are inorganic, much more stable than organic materials, and little affected by light, temperature variations, or biological reaction. They differ in their resistance to deterioration from variations in humidity and from impurities in the air or the ground. Gold is the only metal that remains virtually intact under all conditions. The others, including bronze, suffer from corrosion that may produce a patina or incrustation that ultimately transforms the metal into the mineral ore from which it was extracted. Silver exposed to air tarnishes and, if underground for a long period, may take on a patina. Copper and iron are easily oxidized in air and especially in the ground. Copper and bronze show brown, blue, or green patinas, and iron can be completely transformed into rust.

Siliceous (silica-containing) materials and their equivalents consist of natural stone, bricks, pottery and other ceramics, and glass. Natural stone varies in its resistance to deterioration. Granite and basalt are relatively impervious, but limestone and sandstone are vulnerable to industrial sulfur fumes, automobile emissions, temperature and humidity variations, saline efflorescences, and cryptomatic vegetation (molds and mosses). Bricks and pottery, both of clay, are similar to natural stone in their resistance. If baked at higher temperatures, they are equivalent to stone of average resistance; if baked at low heat or air-dried, they correspond to soft natural stone. Ceramics fired at high temperatures have great resistance to deterioration, but water with salt in solution can produce efflorescences in them. High humidity can dull the transparency of normally stable glass and lead to crizzling with a multitude of small cracks or fissures.

Easel and mural paintings are complex chemical compounds that contain in their various layers both organic and inorganic materials. The outer layer of varnish is completely organic; the paint layers and ground or coating are usually a combination of organic and inorganic; the support, if wood or canvas, is organic, or if metal or a wall substance, inorganic. Adhesives used between the layers are organic. Varnish, which normally lasts only twenty to fifty years before losing its elasticity, also turns yellow. Mediums or vehicles of oil or distemper in the paint layers become brittle and subject to dampness, while the ground or foundation is susceptible to high humidity. Soft wood and canvas supports of easel paintings attract insects and are distorted by dampness; saline efflorescences and mold attacks murals. Decay also weakens the adhesives between layers and results in unsticking and blisters. These categories of objects may, of course, be combined in ways that make their care more complicated.

In terms of the individual who cares for the particular item, think of the item type. For instance, paintings conservators treat paintings while textile conservators treat tapestries, carpets, quilts, and the like. The most diverse of the group are objects conservators who care for three-dimensional works of art, such as pottery, furniture, glass, and sculpture. By extension, objects conservators deal with the broadest range of materials—stone, wood, clay, glass, and plastic, which may be coupled with other organic and inorganic materials, including paint. On the other end of the spectrum, conservators who treat specialized collections, such as musical instruments, deal with the narrowest range of materials.

As noted above, botanical gardens and zoos have their own special concerns regarding the professional standards of care for living collections. Botanical garden herbariums carefully preserve dried plants and seeds, allowing gardens to exchange species. Today these simple practices are complemented with international seed banks protecting species' DNA, sometimes in cooperation with botanical gardens or even international governmental initiatives. Norway's effort to freeze DNA samples on the island of Svalbard reflects heightened international concerns. The zoos' Species Survival Plans (SSPs) are a cooperative approach to maintaining biodiversity, a special form of conservation. The SSPs form an international matrix for "matchmaking" to ensure the maximum amount of biodiversity within zoos. The fundamental elements include good animal care in terms of nutrition, social systems, mating systems, reproductive and parental influences, environmental factors, medical health, and reproductive biology and genetics. With the vanishing of wild animals of so many types, zoo populations form the future for many species. In the basic sense, they are the ultimate conservators.[9]

Threats to Collections and Collections Care

Given the range of collections and the materials comprised, threats to collections vary widely. Referred to as "agents of deterioration," they refer to natural as well as human interventions that can negatively impact the life cycle of collections.[10] The list was first proposed as nine threats by conservator Stefan Michalski in 1987. Of the agents, the first five—physical force, thieves (and vandals and displaces), fire, water, and pests—have been deemed of widespread concern throughout the world, according to the Canadian Institute for Conservation, while the others are of particular concern to museums.[11]

Over the years, a number of lists have appeared with varying numbers (either nine or ten traditionally). In 1994, Robert Waller, then at the Canadian Museum of Nature, proposed the addition of "curatorial neglect" to recognize that collections can be threatened, even if neglected.[12] (See "Agents of Deterioration" Table.) That term has undergone review as well and, more recently, has been redefined by Waller and Cato as *dissociation* which takes on a broader dimension, a philosophical—as

Fire is one of the Agents of Deterioration that threatens collections. Bernard Kapel, librarian, removing works of art during a fire at the Museum of Modern Art, New York. April 15, 1958. AP/Wide World Photos. (AP131) Location: The Museum of Modern Art/New York, NY/U.S.A.
Photo Credit: Digital Image © The Museum of Modern Art/Licensed by SCALA/Art Resource, NY.

opposed to a tangible, measurable—one. Dissociation "results from the natural tendency for ordered systems to fall apart over time" and results in "loss of objects, or object-related data, or the ability to retrieve or associate objects and data." The damage from such deterioration may impact the legal, intellectual, and cultural aspects of an object, whereby Waller and Cato refer to this as the "metaphysical agent" of deterioration. Moreover, the impact of such dissociation may result in greater and further loss in terms of the value of the collection as a whole.[13]

As evident from the list above, the environment has a powerful influence on objects, which tend to establish equilibrium with their surroundings. Whenever the environment changes, the objects are likely to suffer. Thus, when archaeologists open a tomb, objects apparently in perfect condition may shrink or warp and sometimes even turn to dust. The changes in the relative humidity and temperature of the atmosphere cause such deterioration.

An example from the collections of the Qin Shi Huang Mausoleum Museum in Xi'an, Shaanxi Province illustrates this point. The museum is charged with the task of managing the assets of forty years of careful and extensive excavation of the site where more than eight thousand figures—many of them terra-cotta warriors—surround the tomb of the first emperor of China, Qin (died 210 BCE). The figures convey realism in their poses, facial expressions, and clothing and looked even more life-like through the multicolored paint and lacquer that adorned them. These colors were extracted from natural materials, including stone, gems, and animal materials, which were then applied over a layer

Table 6.1.   Initial list of the "Agents of Deterioration," along with a refined listing with specifics regarding water and radiation. Note the addition of *dissociation*, which replaced the term *curatorial neglect*, which was added to the list by Robert Waller around 1994.

Initial List, as identified by Stefan Michalski, 1987	Current list, as appearing on the Canadian Conservation Institute website, last updated 2017[1]
Physical forces (neglect, catastrophe)	Physical forces
Criminals (vandals, thieves)	Thieves and Vandals
Fire	Fire
Water	Water
Pests	Pests
Contaminants	Pollutants
Radiation (ultraviolet, light)	Light—Ultraviolet, and Infrared
Incorrect temperature (fluctuations, too high)	Incorrect Temperature
Incorrect relative humidity	Incorrect Relative Humidity
(damp, mold; above/below a critical value; above 0 percent relative humidity; fluctuations)	Dissociation

1 The initial list is drawn from presentation by Stefan Michalski at an IIC-Canadian Group conference in 1987 as "Preventive Conservation: A Wall Chart" and published by Michalski at the ICOM-CC Dresden conference in 1990; it is available here: https://www.icom-cc-publications-online.org/2673/An-Overall-Framework-for-Preventive-Conservation-and-Remedial-Conservation. Michalski's list included refinements for several of the terms. For the full listing of agents and explanations, see https://www.canada.ca/en/conservation-institute/services/agents-deterioration.html. Regarding dissociation, see Robert Waller and Paisley S. Cato, "Dissociation: Ten Agents of Deterioration," November 19, 2015, https://www.canada.ca/en/conservation-institute/services/agents-deterioration/dissociation.html.

Table compiled by the author, based upon sources utilized in this chapter.

of lacquer coating (also natural). However, most of these colors disintegrated as they were exposed to the dry air of their post-discovery environment. (The site was uncovered in 1974 and excavated that year, as well as in 1985 and 2009, ongoing). One study showed that once exposed, the lacquer beneath the paint began to curl after fifteen seconds and flake in four minutes—statistics that bear witness to the importance of environment to the life and sustainability of an object.[14]

Charged with the care of objects for perpetuity, museums therefore need to provide a stable environment. The *Heritage Health Index Report* suggests that museums begin their conservation efforts with the most basic environmental conditions for their objects. Even with the most limited resources, museums can establish conditions so that they "do no harm" to artifacts. A critical element to maintain this most basic standard is that storage areas, while out of the public view, are central to the ongoing conservation/preservation needs of collections. Clean, dry, temperature-controlled spaces are fundamental to caring for objects. Although complex, expensive conservation practices may be out of the reach of many museums, careful storage practices and appropriate lighting for works on view and on display are certainly within reach.[15]

Temperature and Relative Humidity

So while the agents of deterioration noted earlier address many threats to the environment, the most easily understood are relative humidity and temperature of the collections environments and exposure to light of the varied objects in their collections. The first two qualities are closely related; in fact, relative humidity is defined as the ratio of the amount of water vapor present in the air to the greatest amount possible at the same temperature. Consider a more familiar example: heating your home in the winter. Increasing the temperature of a building reduces the humidity markedly and may result in too dry an atmosphere, while lowering the temperature may raise the humidity so much that it reaches the dew point and water condenses on walls and objects. A temperature of 60 to 75 degrees Fahrenheit is comfortable for museum visitors year-round. At that temperature, the relative humidity should not fall below 50 percent, or organic materials such as paper, parchment, and leather will become brittle; canvas will go slack; and textiles and the adhesives used in making furniture will dry out and deteriorate. Similarly, if the relative humidity exceeds 65 percent, mold and mildew will grow on glue, leather, and paper; wood will swell and canvases tighten; and oxidation of metals will increase. The ideal relative humidity for most museum objects at temperatures of about seventy degrees Fahrenheit is 50 to 65 percent. To put it simply, professionals refer to the 70/50 rule, meaning an approximate temperature of 70 degrees Fahrenheit with 50 percent relative humidity (RH).

Environmental monitoring is a critical piece of collections care for museums. The origins of recording of conditions relative to a collections environment may be traced to the invention of the hygrothermograph, a device that records temperature and relative humidity. Thermographs have their roots in the Kew Gardens, where honorary director Francis Ronalds began using photography to record natural phenomena, including temperature, in visual form.[16] Still in use today, such devices produce visual readings onto graph paper slid onto a roll. Since the 1990s, however, data such as temperature and humidity may be recorded digitally through use of a small, wall-installed device that serves as a preservation environment monitor, aka *a datalogger*. This compact, battery-run device is placed in the room where monitoring is required. The data is retrieved by inserting a portable memory card (flashdrive) into the device, which then writes all the data to a file. This file can be received, manipulated, and interpreted by collections and conservation staff in order to understand the current and past environment and to make any adjustments to care for the collections. Additional developments in environmental monitoring include wireless solutions that rely on Wi-Fi, Bluetooth, and low-range radio waves, rather than memory cards and, further, enable remote access to environmental monitoring.[17]

Measuring and understanding this data, tracking it longitudinally, and acting on any inconsistencies is critically important in the care of collections, as the variation of a stable environment can be most damaging. Every museum should strive to obtain such climate control for its entire buildings, but especially for its exhibition and storage spaces. Contaminated air may blacken lead pigments, tarnish metals, or bleach out or stain materials. As conservator Nathan Stolow observed, crowded galleries can also produce high levels of carbon dioxide and ammonia that are damaging to objects.[18] In instances where controlling the conditions of large spaces becomes impossible, museums can create "microclimates" for objects. These can be individual areas within a room or actual cases that allow for closer control of the conditions for the objects. They can be as simple as covering the glass of an exhibit case with fabric that the visitor removes to see the object and replaces afterward, or as complicated as individual controls for the case's internal atmosphere.

Lighting

A third important part of the museum environment is lighting, which poses risks in terms of fading or darkening or other discoloration. Strong light or ultraviolet rays damage watercolors, paintings, paper, textiles, and other materials, usually by fading or embrittlement. Natural light is especially destructive because of ultraviolet radiation, and it should be controlled by blinds, curtains, or special glass. Incandescent bulbs give off heat, which must be lessened in museum cases. The ultraviolet emissions of fluorescent tubes can be reduced to safe levels by covering the bulbs with sleeves that retard photochemical degradation by blocking ultraviolet radiation. Too much light intensity from spotlights or too high a general illumination should also be avoided.[19]

Thus, by addressing the most basic environmental conditions for their objects, museums can establish conditions that "do no harm" to artifacts. Negligence may result in exposure of objects to excessive light, heat, or humidity, as well as infestations of pests or accidents that result in the physical destruction of the object. Attending to all these measures, however, takes time and money. Though it may be difficult to raise money for such purposes, air-conditioning and regular control of the environment in the long run are more important for a museum than the acquisition of million-dollar objects.

Conservation-Related Tasks

At the start of the twentieth century, international purchases of artworks flourished. The traffic flowed from Europe west to the United States. Art dealers in European capitals sought artworks and offered them to American industrialists intent on adding luster to their surroundings and prestige. New art was appreciated and consumed by women who had gained agency as connoisseurs who were educated and thus became patrons.[20] Dealers promoted restoration practices to attract buyers and make a sale. Restorers worked to make the object more attractive; their interests lay in sales and not in the integrity of the work. From these beginnings emerged in the mid–twentieth-century professional conservation practices overseen by museums with responsibilities for protecting cultural artifacts for the public good. In the twenty-first century, the role of conservation has become even more complex, with museums recognizing that objects document the past and that their modification or restoration should be rare and guided by the "intent" of their maker.[21] In addition, new tools and technologies have facilitated new, less-invasive methods of collections care.

The conservator we know today has developed since the mid–twentieth century. He or she emerged from a tradition of restoration and aesthetics where the restorer took an empirical approach to treating works—what might be defined as the earliest forms of conservation. In these instances, the professional knew certain practical treatments to use on deteriorating art and historical objects and with skilled hands applied them; the conservator would frequently describe himself or herself as an artist. Charles Willson Peale, for example, made himself sick using arsenic to preserve his specimens.[22] The conservator uses knowledge of science (especially chemistry and physics) to examine objects and artifacts, to determine appropriate treatments to maintain them in stable condition, or to restore them to a previous condition. Within the museum, he or she is responsible for establishing and maintaining environmental conditions to protect the object, whether in storage, on display, or in transit.

Given that *conservation* is a blanket term that refers to the long-term preservation of cultural property and cultural heritage and may include activities such as examination, documentation, and treatment, the conservator has two classes of duties. As an advisor on collections care, the conservator can establish institutional practices that protect objects, and thereby avoid the necessity for restoration. Today, this is called *preventive conservation*. A second role begins with inspection of a museum's holdings in cooperation with the curator and other collections staff and assignment of priorities for objects that need *treatment*; this often becomes a continuing responsibility with periodic inspections of records.

Guiding Principles

When treating a work in a museum's collection, the conservator observes several guiding principles. One of these is to examine the objects to be worked on, using the latest scientific methods, in *order to understand, as thoroughly as possible, the nature of the object* at this moment in time and to determine the prognosis of the deterioration and any alterations. Such examination would also include the identification and calculation of risks to the object and/or collections—a term called *conservation risk assessment*. Defined by conservator and heritage professional Robert Waller, *risk assessment* aims to "quantify all risks to collections; useful estimates can be obtained of the relative magnitudes of most risks."[23] Further, Waller developed a cultural property risk analysis model, using the Canadian Museum of Nature as a case study, to guide priorities for resource allocation.[24] What these kinds of activities

SUNY Buffalo State University is home to the Patricia H. and Richard E. Garman Art Conservation Department. The images that follow show the work done in the graduate program in the dual M.A. and M.S. program in Conservation of Art and Cultural Heritage and Conservation Science and Imaging. Various mediums and methods are shown including objects, paintings, paper, and library/archives/book conservation. *Courtesy Patricia H. and Richard E. Garman Art Conservation Department at SUNY Buffalo State University.*

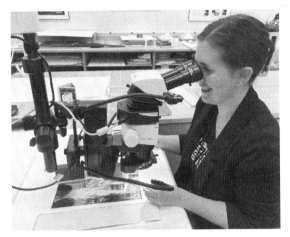

make clear is the value of and connections between preventive conservation, conservation research, and long-term collections care.

A second principle requires the conservator *to make as few changes as possible and to keep any changes reversible in the future.* For example, fifty years ago a restorer might have decided that a polychrome wood sculpture was so worm-eaten that it would be acceptable to replace a considerable portion with new wood, shaped and painted as nearly like the original as could be made. A more conservative kind of restoration—say, fumigation of the statue to stop worm damage and minimum repainting with soluble paint—would have preserved it for the better treatment that could be given now. Regardless of the approach taken, a detailed written and visual account of everything discovered about the object, good or bad, and every step taken in repairing or restoring it should become part of the museum record for the object. If further work is needed in the future, judgments can be made based upon this record.

Another of the conservator's rules is *not to use conjecture in restoration or reconstruction of objects*. If he or she cannot find out by research what the actual appearance was, restoration should not proceed. Another pitfall is to use today's taste in restoring an object. For example, the H. F. Du Pont Winterthur Museum acquired an early-nineteenth-century wooden sculpted man's bust with several bad cracks; it had been cleaned down to the wood. In restoring it, the question arose whether to paint it a stone color or to use a natural finish that would show off the wood grain. Modern taste would have dictated the latter course, but research into the early-nineteenth-century practice and faint traces of paint led to painting it the stone color.

Put simply, conservation must be guided by careful research that includes acceptable practices of the discipline as well as the fundamental cultural context of the object. Conservator Miriam Clavir argues that: "Conservation is more than a set of physical preservation techniques, it is also an interpretive activity which involves a complex of artistic, scientific and historical ideas which influence the approach to treatment whether they are acknowledged or not."[25]

Four Roles of Conservators

Four roles have expanded for conservators. The first is involved with protecting *the museum's environment* from insects and other pests that can harm the objects. "Integrated pest management" (IPM) seeks to protect the collection, and even the museum environment, by using natural approaches and compounds that will get rid of the pests, but not harm the environment, either inside or outside the museum. Some large museums actually have integrated pest managers on staff who keep up with the latest "natural" solutions to protecting collections areas.[26]

Second, conservators also are often involved in the *creation of institutional emergency plans*, with detailed instructions on how to protect the collections in times of fire, flood, or other disaster. Conservators not only assist in creating the plans, but also in carrying out special "triage" activities as a museum staff responds to disasters. Often conservators assemble disaster "carts" that hold items for use in protecting or stabilizing collections in case of emergencies. In the 1980s, there was a national emphasis on creating operative disaster plans for museums across the country. The Getty Institute's *Building an Emergency Plan* identifies thirty recent disasters affecting cultural institutions around the world, ranging from fires, floods, earthquakes, hurricanes, and volcanic eruptions to wars and terrorist bombings from 1981 to 1997.[27] The recent experiences of museums during extreme weather conditions, such as hurricanes and floods, are overall disasters that impact museums, as well as the people in their communities. The American Institute for Conservation has an emergency committee that supports the function and role of the National Heritage Responders (NHR). The NHR responds to the needs of cultural institutions and the public during emergencies and disasters through coordinated efforts with first responders, state agencies, vendors, and the public.[28]

Third, conservators are involved in *decisions and activities related to special exhibitions*. Large-scale, once-in-a-lifetime exhibitions attract visitors, promote scholarly research, and increase public enlightenment. They usually involve borrowing materials from several museums, and a curator plays a significant role in deciding when objects in his or her care should be lent. Working in consultation with museum registration and collections management staff, the curator carefully considers the dangers to which such exhibits expose objects and the gains afforded by such opportunities. Can they stand the jolting and jarring of travel and the changes in humidity and temperature they are sure to encounter? Can they be properly packed for transport? Will the borrower provide careful handling, dependable environmental control, and protection against fire, vandalism, and theft? These practical questions will help the curator, conservator, and collections team decide whether the proposed exhibit is important enough to justify the risks to the objects in his or her care.[29]

Some objects will be too delicate or fragile to stand any shipping. Others may be allowed to travel only occasionally to exhibits of exceptional importance with strictly specified conditions of packing, handling, and protection during transit and on exhibition. In another category will be placed objects sound, stable, and structurally strong enough to be included in traveling exhibitions. Once the decision has been made to lend objects, arrangements must be made for their packing, transport, exhibition, repacking, and return travel.[30] Transport should be carefully planned. Upon arrival, the objects, still within their packing cases, should be allowed to "rest," reaching equilibrium in their new setting. (Consider our earlier example of the terra-cotta warriors' fate upon coming into contact with their new environment!)[31] Ideally that atmosphere is the same whether in a storage area or gallery.

Fourth, conservators are STEM experts in their communities, as object conservation has stepped out of the office and lab spaces of museums and entered the galleries. In 1996, the Walters Art Museum in Baltimore, Maryland, dedicated major gallery space to revealing to visitors the tasks performed by the museum's conservators. The objects on view reflected the care and attention of the conservator to the object and its context. Some of the exhibition cases included scientific instruments and explained their use by conservators. The purpose of the exhibition was to alert visitors to the role of conservation, the importance of the decisions made by the conservator, and on another level, the investment of the museum as a public institution in caring for objects for public benefit.

As the twenty-first century opened, the original *Star-Spangled Banner*—not the anthem of the "broad stripes and bright stars," but the actual United States flag from the War of 1812—required conservation. The National Museum of American History placed the work-in-progress on view as an exhibition. Visitors could watch the conservators as they treated the flag that flew over Fort McHenry and inspired Francis Scott Key to write the song that became the national anthem of the United States. By observing what was being done and reading the surrounding label texts, viewers could understand the decision-making process for restoring and conserving the object to protect it for future generations and learn a bit about the science of conservation.

Evidence of broader, long-standing commitments to conservation, education, and public engagement may be seen in the 2006 launch of the Lunder Conservation Center at the Smithsonian American Art Museum. On the museum's third floor, visitors can watch conservators work through glass walls of several labs and studios, reflecting the types of materials being treated (frames, objects, works on paper, and other mediums).[32]

At Penn Museum, a glass-enclosed conservation lab, *In the Artifact Lab*, offered a view of a range of artifacts at varying stages of treatment from 2012 through 2023. Over these years, visitors have been able to watch collections specialists examine, research, clean, repair, and document coffins, mummies, and other specimen from ancient Egypt. Visitors were given the opportunity to ask questions of the team from the Penn Museum Conservation Department, as all this took place in the space of an exhibition. Collections surrounded the conservation lab, enabling visitors to make connections between what they observe in the lab and what they see in the exhibit cases. A website recounts the Lab's eleven-year-run.[33] Given the Penn Museum's history (founded in 1887 as an archaeology and anthropology research museum), this university museum has the grand responsibility to care for approximately one million objects, making it an appropriate setting for a space that is part-exhibition, part-laboratory, and part-classroom.[34] While the lab has closed, the conservation work is ongoing, of course, though behind closed doors.

Other examples of conservation in plain sight may be found with online materials, such as the George Eastman Museum's 3D tour of their conservation lab, with keyed information available upon access. In addition, the Museum's YouTube channel delves into conservation and related collections topics.[35] In addition, institutions such as the University of Kansas collaborated internally between the University of Kansas's (KU) Spencer Museum of Art and KU Libraries during the early days of COVID-19 to create digital content that could center collections as an antidote to social isolation. This joint effort demonstrates how the constraints of physical distancing as a preventive health measure also delivered preventive conservation strategies to apply to collections at home. The goal of this joint effort in 2020 was to "sustain a sense of community with Friends of the Museum and Friends of the

Libraries by triangulating among institutional collections, examples from staff members' homes, and the invitation for Friends to share their collections." The synergy between collections care and community care—as in museum professionals, as well as audiences whom they serve, is worth underscoring as we continue to think about the role of museums in their communities.[36] In fact, given this range of examples from the past twenty years, perhaps conservation practices are becoming part of the visitor's expectation rather than being seen as a supporting function carried out in labs and offices out of public view.[37]

Another example comes from Harvard Art Museum. Its recent conservation treatment of murals by American Modernist painter Mark Rothko reveals powerful capabilities at the intersection of science, engagement, and exhibition. From November 2014 through July 2015, *Mark Rothko's Harvard Murals*—a display of six paintings, related drawings, and a digital projection—disclose the intersections between art, science, and technology. The genesis of the exhibition included five canvases formerly on view in a penthouse dining room in one of the campus buildings. On display in the 1960s and 1970s, they entered storage in 1979. Since their creation in 1962 and installation in 1964, they suffered irreversible damage from light. For this new display, the paintings were exhibited alongside a camera-projection system that included custom-made software-enabling digital projection technology to restore the appearance of the murals' original rich colors.

The task of restoring the color was no easy challenge, as conservators of today have no chemical means to restore the faded crimson backgrounds without intervening in an irreversible manner (which is not acceptable practice) or without altering the material of the murals by overpainting (also unacceptable practice). At Harvard, the conservation team tackled this problem by undertaking a complex series of actions, whereby the conservation scientists reconstructed what the paintings looked like when they were originally installed; they then replicated this effect digitally through the projection of compensation images (representing the current condition of each work being subtracted from the target, intended image). This compensated image, when projected onto the faded paintings, digitally returns their lost color.[38] As a result, the paintings were on view for the first time alongside related studies and a sixth mural that was intended to be displayed with the other five but was never exhibited.

While reversible, noninvasive, and technically innovative, this combination of art, science, and technology offers a third option for conservation in the twenty-first century (beyond preservation and restoration), and that is *presentation*. For here, the digital project restores the visual appearance of works of art in a case where traditional methods could not be used. Moreover, the trace of the artist's hand is always present, as no additive or subtractive measures were used as related to pigments and materials used by Rothko. Third, the effect was stunning and all-the-while able to be silenced. In fact, once per day the projectors were shut off so visitors could see the Rothkos in their present state, without the addition of light.[39] And while technically complicated and expensive to run, preserve, and document, such measures offer opportunities for us to see works in a new light—literally—and for collections professionals to expand their toolbox and to think more broadly about how to see their works with fresh eyes.

Protection and Public Access

Historian and archaeologist Alessandra Malucco Vaccaro argues: "Striking a balance between the demands of conservation and the rights of the public is one of the most difficult challenges, but it is also the most urgent to undertake in order to secure the future of the past."[40] The caves at Lascaux in southwestern France are a perfect example of these conflicting demands. Four teenagers discovered the fifteen-thousand-year-old paintings 250 meters belowground in late 1940. With the end of World War II, the entry was expanded, and visitors began to arrive at the rate of more than one thousand a day. After little more than twenty years of such visitation, the paintings began to show damage from the elevated levels of carbon dioxide—due to the increased human presence in the caves. In the spring of 1963, the caves were permanently closed to the public, and the atmosphere was returned to its earlier levels. In 1979, Lascaux was added to the UNESCO World Heritage Sites list. The following year, the Dordogne Tourism Department created a replica of the cave, duplicating both its contours and its ancient images. This replica opened to public viewing in 1983 (Lascaux 2) and featured 90 percent of the original paintings set into the same hill as the original cave. Meanwhile, mold began to infect the original cave (and continues to do so). A third Lascaux, a mobile reconstruction, began an international tour. In the summer of 2016, Lascaux 4 opened as the only full and exact replica of the original Lascaux (aka the Montignac-Lascaux International Parietal Art Center/Lascaux Parietal Art International Centre). This site is constructed in a different cave and offers a new facsimile as well as a theater that uses screens, objects, light, and sound to re-create the atmosphere and environments effectively. In addition, a 3D interactive cinema, screen-based art gallery, and temporary exhibition space will bring greater attention to the nearby caves by providing a fuller understanding of its context then and now.[41]

Throughout these iterations and the subsequent deterioration of the caves, serious scholarly attention was paid to rethinking public access to prehistoric sites, of which there are 147 Paleolithic sites and twenty-five decorated caves in this region (the Vézère Valley). And the decision has been made to improve access through another iteration while continuing to research, study, and improve the conditions of Lascaux 1 and 2.[42]

Sustainability and Metrics

Concerns about sustainability have stimulated a reexamination of many areas of museum practice, including environmental guidelines. In 2008, the International Institute for Conservation (IIC) began a series of discussions entitled "Dialogues for the New Century: Discussions on the Conservation of Cultural Heritage in a Changing World." The first of these, held at The National Gallery (London) in September 2008, "Climate Change and Museum Collections," explored the subject of climate change and its potential effects on cultural heritage, aiming to fill a gap in knowledge and awareness by museum professionals of the work between climate change and museum collections (notwithstanding the built environment). Using an analogy familiar to scientists and conservation professionals—a spectrum—Jerry Podany, president of the IIC, asked his audience of museum professionals to visualize

> On one end are informed and enlightened people who know what this challenge is and who are struggling to find ways to address it. . . . Over on the other end of this spectrum are the uninformed, the stubborn and even those who are sceptical about the very existence of climate change and its effects. Scattered along our spectrum and clustered surprisingly close to the end populated by the uninformed, are many conservation and museum professionals who, through no fault of their own, remain unaware of the challenges that museums are about to face. They believe that their collections are, after all, safely tucked within the walls of their museums, safe from any climate threat. They ask, "What could be the problem?"[43]

Speakers at the symposium, and many others, agree that as the climate becomes more extreme or unstable, collections are at risk. They call for museums to be proactive in several ways, including collaboration among conservators and scientists, curators, and collections professionals, to model the links between damage and the environment as well as the environment and energy. Another measure is to understand what damage may be occurring to collections outright by using algorithms (called *Preservation Metrics*) to "integrate the effects of dynamic environmental changes over time" which can then "yield some insight into what it means, for example, for a collection to experience more frequent and intense periods of heat and humidity than it has been accustomed to."[44] Methods such as these present new ways of managing, understanding, and forecasting the museum environment—actions that are in the interest of and the responsibility of museums.

Cultural Heritage at Risk in the United States and Worldwide

Issues facing cultural heritage conservation and preservation (2023)[1]

- Climate crisis and environmental impact
- Collection care and preventive conservation
- Digital technology: Research and practice
- Diversity, equity, inclusion, and accessibility
- Education, professional development, and leadership
- Engagement, communication, and storytelling
- Field investment, infrastructure, and sector health
- Philosophy and ethics in conservation
- Science and materials

1 National Endowment for the Humanities and the Foundation for the Advancement in Conservation, *Held in Trust: Transforming Cultural Heritage Conservation for a More Resilient Future*, 2023, https://www.culturalheritage.org/about-us/foundation/programs/held-in-trust.

In closing, it is important to note that the needs of museums are long-term, persistent, and critical as far as collections care and preservation. The conservation organizations described earlier in this chapter were established after sustained discussion on both national and international levels about nature conservation and the preservation of cultural properties.

Consider the response to the wave of destruction brought on by World War II. In the years following the war, conferences and delegations discussed the matter of cultural property during times of conflict. In 1948, Article 27 of the "Universal Declaration of Human Rights" identified the protection and promotion of culture as a human right imperative. The text reads:

1. Everyone has the right freely to participate in the cultural life of the community, to enjoy the arts and to share in scientific advancement and its benefits.
2. Everyone has the right to the protection of the moral and material interests resulting from any scientific, literary or artistic production of which he is the author.[45]

It further notes, at the conclusion, that no one has the right, in turn, to "engage in any activity or to perform any act aimed at the destruction of any of the rights and freedoms set forth herein." Both the production and the persistence of culture are, therefore, human rights, according to U.N. standards.[46]

In May 1954, an intergovernmental conference was held at The Hague. Now referred to as the "Hague Convention on the Protection of Cultural Property in the Event of Armed Conflict," the resolutions set forth established that all signatories "must protect and respect civilians and civilian property, including their cultural heritage." Further, the preamble to the convention authorized a joint responsibility to protect one's own culture and that of others: "any damage to cultural property, irrespective of the people it belongs to, is a damage to the cultural heritage of all humanity, because every people contributes to the world's culture."[47]

Shortly thereafter, in 1956, delegates to the UNESCO (United Nations Educational, Scientific, and Cultural Organization) General Conference came together in New Delhi determined to establish an international center focused on the preservation and restoration of cultural property. Their aim was "to increase awareness and scientific knowledge about the conservation and restoration of cultural heritage and offer a place where specialists could come together, share their experiences, and compare and debate ideas."[48] The UNESCO convening gave the opportunity for countries to outline their pledge to protect world heritage and called upon states/countries to report on their commitment to the conservation of natural and tangible cultural heritage. Meanwhile, international efforts were put toward saving artifacts and architecture in Upper Egypt, near the border with Sudan. From 1959–1968, the rock-cut temples of Abu Simbel were relocated so they would not be submerged by the reservoir of the Aswan Dam. Since that time, attention has also been paid to conserving and safeguarding non-mobile artifacts, including Venice and its lagoon; the ruins at Moenjodaro, Pakistan; and the Borobudur Temple Compounds in Indonesia.

Even so, and unfortunately, tragedies can strike beyond the bounds of pledges to protect cultural heritage. For instance, in 2018, the National Museum of Brazil (Museu Nacional-UFRJ) in Rio de Janeiro was engulfed in flames, as a result of either an electricity issue or an open fire that spread throughout the 122-room building. Catastrophe resulted in the significant loss of the structure, as well as the decimation of collections, including 92.5 percent of its archive and more than twenty million items. Brazilian president Michel Temer called the losses "incalculable," stating "the loss of the National Museum is incalculable for Brazil. Today is a tragic day for our country's museology. Two hundred years of work, research, and knowledge were lost. The value of our history cannot be measured now, due to the damage to the building that housed the Royal Family during the Empire. It is a sad day for all Brazilians."[49] As of 2022, a portion of the building has been repaired, a few exhibits re-installed, and progress made as the museum looks toward 2027, when it is expected to fully reopen.[50]

Combating the threats to collections is no easy task. Conservators and those working in preservation and cultural heritage more broadly may seek guidance from the International Centre for the Study of the Preservation and Restoration of Cultural Property (ICCROM). Formed in 1959 at the height of robust international activity around cultural heritage preservation, ICCROM's mission taps in to five areas of activity: information, research, cooperation, advocacy, and training. The Centre manages a library with conservation literature in more than sixty languages, organizes meetings to develop methods and approaches that meet international ethical standards, serves as a liaison and partner with organizations in member countries, plays an advisory role to the UNESCO World Heritage Convention (established 1972), and administers capacity-building programs throughout the world. The organization is active in the salvage of heritage in emergency situations today—a legacy that extends back to the rescued temples of Abu Simbel in Egypt in 1966, noted above. That year, ICCROM began to train museum collections professionals in methods appropriate for disaster situations. Over the past forty years, ICCROM courses have involved nearly seven thousand professionals. They have also partnered with member states to support their local work in safeguarding heritage within their borders and beyond.

Although, collections are at risk internationally, even so it is important to acknowledge the role of advocacy by international organizations regarding access to cultural heritage. In 2001, UNESCO adopted a "Universal Declaration on Cultural Diversity," which states that "respect for the diversity of cultures, tolerance, dialogue and cooperation, in a climate of mutual trust and understanding are among the best guarantees of international peace and security."[51] Evidence of the reach of these intergovernmental organizations demonstrates the reality of cultural heritage is at risk—even in our museums. How can the museum community rise to the challenge to serve our own collections, as well as those of our fellow institutions worldwide?

While conservation is a relatively young field in the United States, that does not mean the need is not severe. In fact, the National Endowment for the Humanities (NEH) and the Foundation for the Advancement in Conservation (FAIC) issued a call to action in 2023. Their combined report, *Held in Trust*, was the result of a four-year collaboration to disentangle the issues facing cultural heritage conservation and preservation. It began with the question, "What would it take to move the field of conservation from surviving to thriving?" The report offers actionable steps that can be taken by cultural institutions, practitioners, and communities over several areas.[52]

Each of these topics has a time frame and outcomes, many of which advocate for partnership, collaboration, and sustainability. The project is about collections, as well as the institutions and individuals who care for them, while also looking at who, what, when, where, and why the preservation and conservation of tangible and intangible cultural heritage work is done. It was funded as part of the *More Perfect Union* initiative and part of the upcoming semiquincentennial of the United States. The report is, ultimately, a useful tool to understand what it means for museums "to conserve" and how that work is not to be undertaken by conservators alone.

Protecting Collections under Attack

Conservators and conservation-related collections care professionals perform critical service in times of need. Their work is important, now more than ever. Together, all of us have a responsibility to protect collections, especially when they are under intentional threat. As Neil Brodie, director of the Illicit Antiquities Research Centre at Cambridge (UK), has noted: There are three ways in which wars threaten cultural materials: the most obvious is damage from military attack, but another threat is removal of materials for profit, to fund the war or for propaganda purposes, with the final means perhaps the most disturbing, that of destroying cultural materials to erase cultural or religious symbols within a society.[53] The invasion of Iraq in 2003 brought significant turbulence upon the museum collections there.[54] In 2014, mosques and shrines throughout Iraq were destroyed by ISIL (Islamic State of Iraq and the Levant), actions the director-general of United Nations Educational, Scientific, and Cultural Organization (UNESCO), Irina Bokova, has called "a form of cultural cleansing." In the wake of active terrorist activity in the Middle East, UNESCO and a number of museum officials have condemned the deliberate destruction of cultural heritage. According to then-director Bokova, such acts are war crimes against the people of these countries where the objects were created and are held, as well as against the global community.[55] (The topic of trade, cultural goods, and protection of heritage is also addressed in Chapter 11.)

Surely, the function of a museum is to conserve or care for its collections. That is easy to understand when objects are housed in a museum, with adequate conditions and no threats imposed by agents of deterioration. Inevitably, threats present themselves—whether natural or human interventions that can negatively impact the life cycle of collections. While museums, alliances, and cultural organizations have sought an end to the destruction of cultural heritage, as well as illicit trafficking and related misconduct as a result of extremist political activity, more must be done, in order to ensure, *and insure*, museums for the future. Otherwise, the museum functions addressed in the following chapters (to exhibit, to interpret, to engage, and to serve) have nothing on which to build, and they have no purpose, relative to collections.

Notes

1. H. J. Plenderleith and A. E. A. Werner, *The Conservation of Antiquities and Works of Art: Treatment, Repair, Restoration* (London: Oxford University Press, 1971); Nicholas Stanley Price, M. Kirby Talley Jr., and Alessandra Malucco Vaccaro, eds., *Historical and Philosophical Issues in the Conservation of Cultural Heritage* (Los Angeles: Getty Conservation Institute, 1996); Marcia Lord, "Editorial," and Gael de Guichen, "Preventive Conservation: A Mere Fad or Far-Reaching Change?"; Giorgio Torraca, "The Scientist in Conservation," *Getty Conservation Institute Newsletter* 14, no. 3 (1999); Graeme Gardiner, "Prevention Rather Than Cure: Preservation versus Conservation," *Museum International* 46, no. 3 (1994): 54–56; R. J. Barclay, "The Conservator: Versatility and Flexibility," *Museum International* 45, no. 4 (1993); "Conservation and Preservation Issue," *Museum News* 68, no. 1 (January–February 1989); Gregory J. Landrey et al., *The Winterthur Guide to Caring for Your Collections* (Winterthur: Henry Francis Du Pont Winterthur Museum, 2000); Getty Conservation Institute, http://www.getty.edu/conservation/; American Institute for Conservation, "About Conservation," http://www.conservation-us.org/about-conservation/faqs#.V5YwK46DBHA. The "AIC Definitions of Conservation Terminology" is available online: http://cool.conservation-us.org/waac/wn/wn18/wn18-2/wn18-202.html.
2. See AIC/FAIC, https://www.culturalheritage.org/.

3. Patrick Boylan, "The Conservator-Restorer," *Museum International* 39, no. 4, 1987; Eleonore Kissel, "The Restorer: Key Player in Preventative Conservation," *Museum International* 51, no. 1 (1999). For the AIC, see http://www.conservation-us.org/. For the CCI, see http://canada.pch.gc.ca/eng/1455565479898. The CCI was created in 1972 and became a Special Operating Agency of the Department of Canadian Heritage in 1992. For the French Federation of Conservator-Restorer, see http://www.ffcr.fr/; for the European group, see European Confederation of Conservator-Restorers' Organisation, see http://www.ecco-eu.org/.

4. International Centre for the Study of the Preservation and Restoration of Cultural Property, http://www.iccrom.org/; see also http://www.iccrom.org/about/what-is-iccrom/.

5. See IMLS, "Protecting America's Collections: The HHIS Report," 2019, https://www.imls.gov/publications/protecting-americas-collectionss. Data was collected in 2014 from 1,714 respondents and extrapolated to reflect the collections and practices, as well as the challenges and opportunities facing more than thirty-one thousand collecting institutions in the United States.

6. The term *lone arranger* is borrowed here from the Society of American Archivists's notion of one who works alone in an archive. See "Lone Arrangers Roundtable," http://www2.archivists.org/groups/lone-arrangers-roundtable#.V5VEDo6DBHA; and the blog of Linda Clark Benedict, retired "lone arranger" archivist at a small liberal arts college, Hobart and William Smith Colleges in Geneva, New York: https://lcb48.wordpress.com/.

7. "Spanish 'Monkey Christ' Woman to Appear in Music Video," April 14, 2014, http://www.bbc.com/news/blogs-news-from-elsewhere-27020725; on the interpretation center, see Aitor Bengoa, "El eccehomo de Borja ya tiene quien lo explique," March 16, 2016, http://cultura.elpais.com/cultura/2016/03/16/actualidad/1458155898147342.html.

8. Plenderleith and Werner, *The Conservation of Antiquities and Works of Art*. The Getty Conservation Institute offers up-to-date information on conservation approaches on their website, www.getty.edu/conservation.

9. Melissa Fay Greene, "Breeding Zoo Stock," *Museum News* 68, no. 1 (January–February 1989): 58–59; Nigel Rothfels, *Savages and Beasts: The Birth of the Modern Zoo* (Baltimore: Johns Hopkins University Press, 2002), 199.

10. The nine agents of deterioration were first proposed as "Preventive Conservation: A Wall Chart" by Stefan Michalski at the 1987 conference of the International Institute of Conservation-Canadian Group. The list was first published by Stefan Michalski at the ICOM-CC Dresden conference in 1990. Although Charlie Costain is frequently credited for ideating the list, he states that by the time he wrote an article about the list in 1994, the information had already been in use, and the poster widely distributed for six or seven years. For this corrective note, see his post to the Conservation Distribution List dated April 25, 2003, https://cool.culturalheritage.org/byform/mailing-lists/cdl/2003/0507.html. Lists and contexts for the Agents appear in: Charlie Costain, "Framework for Preservation and Museum Collections," Ottawa. Canadian Conservation Institute Newsletter 14 (1994): 1 4; Stefan Michalski, "A Systematic Approach to Preservation: Description and Integration with Other Museum Activities," in *Preventive Conservation Practice, Theory and Research: Preprints of the Contributions to the Ottawa Congress*, September 12–16, 1994, edited by Ashok Roy and Perry Smith (London: International Institute for Conservation of Historic and Artistic Works, 1994), 8–11; Carolyn L. Rose and Catherine A. Hawks, "A Preventive Conservation Approach to the Storage of Collections," in *Storage of Natural History Collections: A Preventive Conservation Approach*, edited by Carolyn L. Rose, Catherine A. Hawks, and Hugh H. Genoways (Pittsburgh: Society for the Preservation of Natural History Collections, 1995), 1–20; Robert R. Waller, "Risk Management Applied to Preventive Conservation," in *Storage of Natural History Collections: A Preventive Conservation Approach*, edited by Carolyn L. Rose, Catherine A. Hawks, and Hugh H. Genoways (Pittsburgh: Society for the Preservation of Natural History Collections, 1995), 21–27.

11. The wall chart, produced by the CCI, indicates all ten agents, as noted here: https://www.canada.ca/en/conservation-institute/services/preventive-conservation/framework-preserving-heritage-collections.html. Earlier versions of the chart did not include the final element. For the full listing of agents and explanations, see https://www.canada.ca/en/conservation-institute/services/agents-deterioration.html.

12. Regarding risk management and assessment, see Robert R. Waller, "Conservation Risk Assessment: A Strategy for Managing Resources for Preventive Conservation," in *Preventive Conservation Practice, Theory and Research: Preprints of the Contributions to the Ottawa Congress*, September 12–16, 1994, edited by Ashok Roy and Perry Smith (London: International Institute for Conservation of Historic and Artistic Works, 1994), 12–16. Here Waller proposed the addition of "curatorial neglect" as the tenth agent.

13. R. Robert Waller and Paisley S. Cato, "Dissociation," Ten Agents of Deterioration, November 19, 2015, https://www.canada.ca/en/conservation-institute/services/agents-deterioration/dissociation.html.

14. Zhou Tie, "New Developments in the Conservation of the Polychromy of the Terracotta Army," in *Monuments & Sites III: The Polychromy of Antique Sculptures and the Terracotta Army of the First Chinese Emperor*, ICOMOS, 2011.

15. *A Public Trust at Risk*; the following websites are very helpful in answering basic conservation inquiries: the Canadian Conservation Institute, http://www.cci-icc.gc.ca; the Getty Institute, http://www.getty.edu/conservation/about/index.html; and the American Institute for Conservation, http://www.culturalheritage.org/.

16. Beverley F. Ronalds, "Sir Francis Ronalds and the Early Years of the Kew Observatory," *Weather: A Publication of the Royal Meteorological Society*, 71:6 (June 2016): 131–34, doi:10.1002/wea.2739.

17. Based at Rochester Institute of Technology, IPI began development of the Preservation Environment Monitor (PEM) in 1995, specifically for use in cultural institutions. After years of field testing, the PEM became available for sale in July 2000. Over three thousand units were sold to over five hundred institutions in the United States and abroad. PEM2 was introduced in 2008 and is currently in use. See Image Permanence Institute, https://www.imagepermanenceinstitute.org/environmental/pem-datalogger and https://www.imagepermanenceinstitute.org/environmental/pem2-datalogger. The data can be monitored, managed, and analyzed in eClimate Notebook, a web-based tool also offered by IPI. See https://www.eclimatenotebook.com/. A new environmental-monitoring platform, Conserv, offers a wireless sensor that feeds data into Conserv's cloud storage repository for real-time temperature, humidity, and light levels; data analysis; threshold alerts; and integrated pest management. With Conserv, wireless and non-wireless sensors are used; the latter are LoRaWA (low-power, low-frequency radio waves) to communicate over long distance it enables a network of physical devices with sensors that can collect, process, and exchange data over a network. Here, the wireless data loggers are connected to a gateway, which is in charge of forwarding the data to a cloud server.

18. Nathan Stolow, *Conservation and Exhibitions: Packing, Transport, Storage and Environmental Consideration* (London: Butterworth, 1987), 173; Karen Motylewski, "A Matter of Control," *Museum News* 69, no. 2 (March–April 1990).

19. In terms of recent work in the field of conservation, when guidelines for museums were first explored sixty years ago, color science had determined that a measurement of fifty lux (one lux equaling one lumen or measurement per square meter). was enough to ensure that viewers were seeing the full range of color. Further research in the 1980s revealed that older individuals, with less crisp vision, need more light to see subtleties of color that might be apparent in works in museums. And, more recently, research has sadly revealed that humans' ability to discriminate large patches of color falters as we age. Therefore, museums are at a crossroads of wanting to protect their collections (and perhaps be sustainable and energy-conscious) while meeting the needs of visitors desiring to see nuances of works. On lighting, see Stefan Michalski, "Agent of Deterioration: Light, Ultraviolet and Infrared," Canadian Heritage (Government of Canada), updated January 15, 2016, http://canada.pch.gc.ca/eng/1444925073140.

20. *Vogue* editor Frank Crowninshield reported "It was, without doubt, the women who reacted most spontaneously to the works seen at the Armory [Show, 1913, New York]." He noted that Louisine Havemeyer and Bertha Honore Palmer were the first patrons of Impressionists in Boston, New York, and Chicago, and Sarah Sears "instituted the rage for Cezanne in America." Other women patrons include Abby Aldrich Rockefeller, Gertrude Stein, Etta Cone, Claribel Cone, and Lillie P. Bliss. See Crowninshield, "The Scandalous Armory Show of 1913," *Vogue*, September 15, 1940: 68–71; 114–16.

As Meyer Shapiro has noted, "Women . . . were among the chief friends of the new art, buying painting and sculpture with a generous hand. Art as a realm of finesse above the crudities of power appealed to the imaginative, idealistic wives and daughters of magnates occupied with their personal fortunes. . . . At this moment of general stirring of ideas of emancipation, women were especially open to manifestations of freedom within the arts." See Meyer Schapiro, "Rebellion in Art," in Daniel Aaron, ed, *America in Crisis: Fourteen Crucial Episodes in American History* (New York: Knopf, 1952), 202–42.

21. Clavir, *Preserving What Is Valued*; Meryle Secrest, *Duveen: A Life in Art* (New York: Knopf, 2005), 219, 252, 376–77; Jonathan Ashley-Smith, "The Ethics of Conservation," in *Care of Collections*, Simon Knell, ed.

22. Edward P. Alexander, "Charles Willson Peale," in *Museum Masters: Their Museums and Their Influence* (Nashville: American Association of State and Local History, 1983), 60.

23. Robert Waller, "Conservation Risk Assessment: A Strategy for Managing Resources for Preventive Conservation," in *Preventive Conservation Practice, Theory and Research: Preprints of the Contributions to the Ottawa Congress*, September 12–16, 1994, edited by Ashok Roy and Perry Smith (London: International Institute for Conservation of Historic and Artistic Works, 1994), 12–16.

24. Robert R. Waller, "Cultural Property Risk Analysis Model: Development and Application to Preventive Conservation at the Canadian Museum of Nature," Ph.D. dissertation, Göteborg: Acta Universitatis Gothoburgensis, Institute of Conservation, Göteborg, Sweden, 2003.

25. Clavir, *Preserving What Is Valued*, 41; Sherman E. Lee, *Past, Present, East and West* (New York: George Braziller, 1983), 37; James Cuno, ed., *Whose Muse? Art Museums and Public Trust* (Princeton: Princeton University Press, 2004), 32–35; Tony Bennett, "Out of Which Past?" *The Birth of the Museum: History, Theory and Politics* (New York: Routledge, 1995).

26. Stolow, *Conservation and Exhibitions*, 23; David Pinniger, *Pest Management in Museums, Archives and Historical Houses* (London: Archetype Publications, 2001); David Pinniger and Peter Winsor, *Integrated Pest Management: Practical, Safe and Cost-Effective Advice on the Prevention and Control of Pests in Museums* (London: Museums and Galleries Commission, 1998); Lynda, Zycherman, ed., *A Guide to Museum Pest Control* (Washington, D.C.: Association of Systematics Collections, 1988); Mary-Lou Florian, *Heritage Eaters* (London: James and James, 1997).

27. *Building an Emergency Plan: A Guide for Museums and Other Cultural Institutions* (Los Angeles: Getty Conservation Institute, 1999); K. Sharon Bennett, ed., *SEMC Disaster Response Handbook* (Charleston: South East Museums Conference, 1999); *Field Guide to Emergency Response* (Washington, D.C.: Heritage Preservation, 2006); "Recovering from Disaster," *History News* 61, no. 2 (Spring 2006). This is a special issue with a comprehensive resource list, including internet aid.

28. On the NHR see https://www.culturalheritage.org/resources/emergencies/national-heritage-responders.

29. Rebecca A. Buck and Jean Allman Gilmore, *The New Museum Registration Methods* (Washington, D.C.: American Association of Museums, 1998).

30. The whole transaction must be covered by written agreements and by insurance. The exhibition team, thus, expands to include security, registrar, designer, and architect, and it assumes the following duties: evaluation of conditions, establishment of environmental controls for each object, assessment of safety (in transport, especially), monitoring storage and gallery conditions, and coordination with designers and architects to ensure safety and special conditions for each object on view. Once again, many museums will assign such a role to a staff member, regardless of his or her title and normal responsibilities. Trained packers should do the packing, unpacking, and repacking of loans, because at these points the damage to objects is most likely. Packing material should be stored in the same atmospheric conditions as the exhibition spaces. Those who did the unpacking should also do the repacking, and the same materials should be used. See Stolow, *Conservation and Exhibitions*, 2.

The packing process can be as elaborate as the situation requires. If the distances involved are short, the objects may be taken by car or van with abundant padding and careful separation, but without special cases. Caroline Keck's *Safeguarding Your Collection in Travel* shows the small museum how to instruct a carpenter to build a solid, watertight, shock-absorbing case in which objects can be "floated," with inner cushioning provided by some of the new plastic foam materials. A reliable commercial packing firm may also be used, though its work should be carefully supervised. A larger museum will have its own trained packing staff. In instances of important international exhibitions of extremely rare objects, as Nathan Stolow points out, conservators and preparators know how to build ideal containers with preconditioned packing materials or silica gel panels that will maintain about the same humidity and temperature the objects enjoy in their "home" museum. See Caroline K. Keck, *Safeguarding Your*

Collection in Travel (Nashville: American Association for State and Local History, 1970); Stolow, *Conservation and Exhibitions.*

31. If a carefully checked and reliable moving company is used, the lending and receiving museum staffs should supervise the loading and unloading. The transportation should be direct, without layovers or transshipments. For extremely rare objects, a museum staff member should accompany the shipment, going and coming. Even the conditions of the packing materials, if they are to be reused, should be kept in near-constant conditions. The installation of borrowed materials is the responsibility of the curator of the borrowing museum; he should see that they have the same protection as those of its "home" museum.
32. Smithsonian American Art Museum, "Lunder Conservation Center," https://americanart.si.edu/lunder/index.cfm.
33. Penn Musuem, "In the Artifact Lab," https://www.penn.museum/sites/artifactlab/.
34. Penn Museum, "In the Artifact Lab: Conserving Egyptian Mummies," http://www.penn.museum/exhibitions/special-exhibitions/in-the-artifact-lab. For the beginnings of the lab, see http://www.penn.museum/sites/artifactlab/2012/10/.
35. See George Eastman Museum, "Conservation Laboratory Tour," https://www.eastman.org/360-conservation-lab-tour; and YouTube Channel, https://www.youtube.com/@GeorgeEastmanMuseum.
36. Adina Duke and Jacinta Johnson, "A Curiosity of Cabinets: Collections Care as Community Care," *Collections*, edited by Juilee Decker, 17:2 (2021): 148–58, https://journals.sagepub.com/doi/full/10.1177/1550190620980838.
37. Joyce Hill Stoner, "Conservation Center Stage," *Museum News* 76, no. 3 (May–June 1997).
38. In technical terms: "Having established a target image for each mural, the scientists proceeded to capture highly precise images of the paintings in their current condition. Through a complex set of digital calculations, scientists subtracted the perfectly aligned current condition images from their corresponding target images in order to create a 'compensation image.' These images represent a precise map of the missing color in each panel. The perfectly aligned (registered) compensation images projected onto the faded canvases virtually return their lost color." See Harvard Art Museums, "Digital Restoration," http://www.harvardartmuseums.org/tour/art-science/slide/515.
39. Each day at 4 p.m., the projectors are turned off. http://www.harvardartmuseums.org/visit/exhibitions/4768/mark-rothkos-harvard-murals.
40. Malucco Vaccaro, "The Emergence of Modern Conservation Theory," in *Historical and Philosophical Issues*, 206.
41. Information on Lascaux's condition and its UNESCO status may be found here: http://whc.unesco.org/en/soc/3291. Information on Lascaux 3 and 4 may be found here:
"Rendex-vous at Lascaux II, in Montignac," http://us.france.fr/en/discover/lascaux-montignac-dordogne; "Lascaux," http://us.media.france.fr/en/node/3420.
42. UNESCO, "Prehistoric Sites and Decorated Caves of the Vézère Valley (France)," http://whc.unesco.org/en/soc/930/.
43. David Saunders, "Climate Change and Museum Collections," in *Conservation*, 53:4 (2008): 287–97.
44. Using the term *damage function* which has been used by geologists, May Cassar (University of London) calls for collaboration and modeling in "Climate Change and the Collection Environment," IIC, "Climate Change and Museum Collections," September 17, 2008. On IPI's preservation metrics, see James M. Reilly, "Climate Change and the Care of Museum Collections," IIC, "Climate Change and Museum Collections," September 17, 2008.
45. Authorized as a common standard for all people and nations, the UDHR was authorized at the General Assembly of the United Nations in Paris in 1948. See United Nations, "Universal Declaration of Human Rights," https://www.un.org/en/about-us/universal-declaration-of-human-rights, Article 27.
46. See United Nations, "Universal Declaration of Human Rights," https://www.un.org/en/about-us/universal-declaration-of-human-rights, Article 30.
47. See UNESCO, "1954 Convention for the Protection of Cultural Property in the Event of Armed Conflict," https://en.unesco.org/protecting-heritage/convention-and-protocols/1954-convention.
48. See Alexander, Alexander, and Decker, *Museums in Motion*, 3rd edition, 246.

49. See https://twitter.com/MichelTemer/status/1036418286534238208.

50. Gabriella Angeleti, "After a Devastating Fire in 2018, the National Museum of Brazil Unveils the First Stage of Its Restoration Project," *Art Newspaper*, September 2, 2022, https://www.theartnewspaper.com/2022/09/02/after-devastating-fire-in-2018-the-national-museum-of-brazil-unveils-the-first-stage-of-its-restoration-project.

51. United Nations, "Universal Declaration on Cultural Diversity," November 2, 2001, https://www.ohchr.org/en/instruments-mechanisms/instruments/universal-declaration-cultural-diversity.

52. National Endowment for the Humanities and the Foundation for the Advancement in Conservation, *Held in Trust: Transforming Cultural Heritage Conservation for a More Resilient Future*, 2023, https://www.culturalheritage.org/about-us/foundation/programs/held-in-trust.

53 Neil Brodie, "Stolen History: Looting and Illicit Trade," *Museum International* 55, nos. 3–4 (2003)."

54. See Matthew Bogdanos, "Casualties of War: The Looting of the Iraq Museum," *Museum News* 85, no. 2 (March–April 2006) for a discussion of the impact of the U.S. invasion on Baghdad.

55. In a statement released on April 18, 2016, in reference to the destruction of two gates at Mesqa and Adad, as well as the ramparts of Ninevah (Mosul), Bokova stated, "These deliberate destructions are a war crime against the people of Iraq, whose heritage is a symbol and medium of identity, history and memory. These destructions are linked to the suffering and violence on human lives, and weaken the society over the long term. They are also attacks against the humanity we all share, against the values of openness and diversity of this region, as the cradle of civilizations," http://whc.unesco.org/en/news/1483.

7

To Exhibit

Before diving into the substance of this chapter, it is important to note that the reason this chapter follows the one on conservation is conceptual. For if we assume that museums have collections and intend to share them for the purposes of education, among other reasons, we acknowledge implicitly two undergirding principles not expressly addressed in this middle section of the book, First, before collections can be exhibited, they must exist. And to exist in perpetuity, they must be cared for. Hence, the series of museum functions begins with care ("To Conserve") and now shifts to exhibition ("To Exhibit").

Exhibition assumes organization, be that conceptual (such as a checklist or framing around classification principles), or literal (such as display in a room or storage space). In the former category, as early as the seventeenth century, "rules" for organizing natural history collections were set down and exchanged among collectors.[1] The organization was matched by a system of classification developed in the eighteenth century by the Swedish botanist, zoologist, and scientist Carl Linnaeus. Once organized and called by name, though, how should a collection be displayed?

The Italian *studiolo*, or cabinet room, with its cosmos in miniature, emerged as an expected setting for fine and decorative objects. Here the written word and the material objects surround the visitor and provide a setting for intellectual retreat with books, works of art, and specimen displayed on shelves and hung from the ceiling. While the display varied from cabinet to cabinet, once inside, collectors knew what to expect when traveling to see other collectors' objects.

Emerging from these displays for the *cognoscenti* were arrangements of objects seeking to advance understanding. Displays evolved into exhibits: the purpose became public education and the expansion of the audience. In the eighteenth century, Charles Willson Peale's museum in Philadelphia offered displays that took on a rhetorical mode, appealing to a patriotic audience seeking knowledge from a collection of "all that is likely to be beneficial, curious or entertaining to the citizens of the new world." Given the size of this task, Peale also appealed to his public to contribute to such an endeavor and, in turn, to create a national museum.[2]

Several forces contributed to the changed attitudes toward exhibitions. Perhaps strongest has been the steady democratization of Western society, which transformed museums into cultural and educational institutions serving the general public. Also important was the influence of world's fairs that demanded less-cluttered exhibits, often with large objects that could be easily seen and walked around, as well as dramatic displays to attract and hold popular attention. In the twentieth century, United States theme parks built on these traditions, further pressuring museum displays to modify traditional visual storage showcases and seek more popular appeal. Additionally, the rise of department stores, with compelling, sales-producing arrangements of goods, influenced museum exhibition design.[3] Museums have added multimedia elements and brought "explainers," "facilitators," "communicators," and interpreters into galleries. In the twenty-first century, museum websites have offered another dimension to exhibitions—virtual experiences that encompass both exhibition and engagement.

This chapter and the chapters that follow ("To Interpret"; "To Engage"; and "To Serve") discuss elements of museum interpretation and facets of engagement. Together, these three chapters provide a full picture of the landscape of interpretation, engagement, and action in twenty-first-century museums. In addition, many books, websites, and other resources offer guidance, chief among them *The Manual of Museum Exhibitions* (3rd Edition), edited by Maria Piacente, which offers guidance from development and design to implementation framed around five interrogative adverbs—*why, where, what, who,* and *how*—each of which comprises a section of the volume. In it, the chapters and numerous case studies support the many facets of interpretive planning, the design and content coordination, and the fabrication and installation that enable exhibitions to realize connections between the visitor, the object, and the stories they tell. In addition to the *Manual,* other resources may be gleaned from the notes for this chapter.

Kinds of Exhibits

An exhibit may be defined as a showing or display of materials for the purpose of communication with an audience. Museums may display objects against stark backgrounds, alone, or sometimes with unobtrusive written labels offering the visitor the most basic information (artist, maker, date of production, and museum catalog number). The objects on display may be organized in many ways—by type, by chronology, by theme, or in isolation—or they may foreground a didactic message for visitors. The artwork, the artifact, or the object dominates. Such a process seems simple, but why and how does a museum place the objects or artwork within the exhibit? One nineteenth-century example in Berlin reveals the complexity of these decisions and how an institution's interpretive messages change. In the mid-nineteenth century, academically trained art historians—a first in museum history—designed Berlin's Old Masters Painting Gallery exhibitions, balancing three competing principles: aesthetics, historical perspectives, and systematic organization. The overall guiding principle for the galleries' design was the public's appreciation for paintings. The museum placed its most important works in the main galleries, with lesser works along the periphery. The exhibition's interpretive function guided not only the artwork placement, but also the basic design of the building housing them. Interestingly, within fifty years, another principle dominated, that of placing the objects within their historical settings—not actual period rooms, but spaces that evoked the artistic ambience of the assembled artworks. So the interpretation and the exhibitions changed. In discussing the impact of exhibition installations, museum director and curator Walter Hopps states: "the values change in a room when one picture is moved: it's like the way a dinner party changes according to the guests."[4] In the tradition of "lumping" together exhibition practices, museums create three chief types of exhibits—permanent, temporary, and online.

Permanent Exhibitions

Permanent exhibitions are displays that showcase masterpieces and iconic objects—such as the Georges Seurat's *A Sunday Afternoon on the Island of La Grand Jatte* (Art Institute of Chicago); the *Apollo* suits specially created for the space program (Smithsonian); or SUE, the *T. rex* who roamed the continent sixty-seven million years ago (the Field Museum). The challenge for museums is balancing the interests and demands of an audience with the needs of the collections and, in turn, balancing the amount of time that items are studied, repaired, or on loan to another museum. In addition, permanent exhibitions refer to thematic or chronological displays that present a narrative of the institution and its history. Such displays include the permanent exhibition *The Holocaust* at the United States Holocaust Memorial Museum in Washington, D.C. This exhibit presents a narrative history over galleries on three floors that include nine hundred artifacts. The exhibition chronicles the rise of the Nazi Party in 1933; the outbreak of World War II in 1939; policies toward the Jews, from persecution to mass murder; the rescue and resistance efforts; and the aftermath of the Holocaust. In addition, the recurring theme is individual responsibility toward fellow human beings in danger.[5] Because all of the items on view are owned by the museum or are on long-term loan, the exhibition may remain intact for an extended amount of time, notwithstanding instances when individual objects or audio/visuals may be swapped in or out of the exhibition or as needed to care for the collection.

Georges Seurat's *A Sunday on La Grand Jatte—1884* is permanently installed in the Art Institute of Chicago. The work featured prominently in the 1980s movie hit *Ferris Bueller's Day Off* and is now one of more than forty thousand works from the Art Institute that are available through their website free of charge through "open access."

Georges Seurat, A Sunday on La Grand Jatte—1884, 1884-1886, oil on canvas, Art Institute of Chicago, Helen Birch Bartlett Memorial Collection. https://www.artic.edu/artworks/27992/a-sunday-on-la-grande-jatte-1884.

A second example of a permanent exhibition is, actually, simply a long-term exhibition that uses materials from the permanent collection of a museum, whether or not iconic, with perhaps a few items on long-term loan. The exhibition is not intended to be permanent, both out of concern for collections but also because of the likelihood of repeat visitors. Therefore, the exhibition may be "refreshed" every few years. For instance, the National Museum of American History developed a new display for the new millennium, *Within These Walls*. Since its debut in 2001, the exhibit of a single house relocated from Ipswich, Massachusetts, tells the stories of five families and two hundred years of their history.[6] The exhibit remains on view and still attracts crowds who feel a connection to it, regardless of how similar this single house is to their own lived experience.

Temporary Exhibitions

Temporary exhibitions are part of the exhibit practice. Temporary exhibits on special themes may feature objects from the museum's collection brought from storage or their usual display places, perhaps supplemented by loans from other museums and collectors. They perform many functions, as explained below, with several examples.

Museums have collections; they store and care for them; they put them on view for visitors to learn about them, and the context of which they are a part, through exhibitions. At their core, such exhibitions attract visitors with interests relating to the exhibit theme. Throughout the earlier part of this volume, numerous examples of exhibitions were given to explain museum history. A less-traditional example of such a temporary exhibition was an installation at the Museum of Sex in New

Visitors encounter *Félix González-Torres Untitled* (LA), 1995, on view at RIT City Art Space, Rochester, New York, in 2021–2022. Filling a corner of the gallery with apple-green candies ready for the taking, the gallery offered a visitor-driven art experience while simultaneously asking complex questions surrounding identity, community, and representation—all amid the challenge of the COVID-19 pandemic. City Art Space worked closely with Rochester-area partners such as Out Alliance, Rochester's LGBTQ+ equality and community enhancement organization, and individuals connected to LBGTQ+ rights and activism to shape and inform the content of their virtual offerings. The first program discussed how González-Torres's candy spills have been interpreted. Generous support for this project provided by Art Bridges.
Félix González-Torres (1957–1996), Untitled (LA), *1991, green candies in clear wrappers, endless supply, original weight: 50 lbs. Jointly owned by Art Bridges and Crystal Bridges Museum of American Art. Photo Credit: John Aäsp.*

York City, where a cataclysm of sights and smells introduced visitors to artist Portia Munson's work *The Pink Bedroom*, where pink objects were arranged on and around a bed with an intangible compendium of aromas. In its iterations since 1994, the installation has explored girlhood and femininity. Here, the work also took on a sensory mode, with a signature scent created by Marissa Zappas, a Brooklyn perfumer—all within the context of the museum itself. Thus, if not drawn in by the subject, the sight and smell of the temporary exhibition (spring 2023) could attract visitors.[7]

Temporary exhibits offer museums an opportunity to attract visitors to return to a space because of continued interest or to see what's new. An example is the Molina Family Latino Gallery (MFLG), which is housed within the Smithsonian National Museum of American History (NMAH). The Gallery is the first long-term iteration of Congress' authorization to create an additional Smithsonian, the National Museum of the American Latino (NMAL), to "advance the representation, understanding and appreciation of Latino history and culture in the United States." Although the physical building is still in its planning stages, the Molina Gallery serves as a temporary, though long-term, exhibition

space. Inside the NMAH's Molina Gallery, temporary exhibits focused on Latino history and culture drive home the message that Latino history is United States history. The first exhibition in MFLG is *¡Presente! A Latino History of the United States*, which examines four themes to help visitors connect history to the present-day experiences and identities of United States Latinos: Colonial Legacies, Wars of Expansion, Immigration Stories, and Shaping the Nation. Each section has an introduction area with a single object; wall case(s) with objects, text, and graphics; and several interactives. In this space, objects are changed out approximately twice per year for purposes of collections care, but also to allow the visitors to experience new stories and objects.[8]

Temporary exhibits also allow museums to modify and expand their interpretive messages, perhaps as a result of new scholarship or as an effort to attract participation through co-creation and co-curation or through attendance by new audiences. Exhibits of this type might involve loans from collecting institutions or community members. Or exhibits might involve displays obtained from a museum that develops and travels shows from their collections or displays created by an exhibition service.

Temporary exhibitions may also be curated with the express purpose of traveling to other venues, many times those from which the exhibition was curated. Examples include *Tattoo*, a collection of more than 170 objects related to the worldwide practice of inking one's flesh. The exhibition began at the Musée du Quai Branly—Jacques Chirac in Paris, whose collections focus on objects belonging to Indigenous cultures, and it has traveled to the Field Museum (2016–2017). By connecting past with present, "the exhibition includes a thoughtful exploration of a new generation of practitioners who are creating new forms of expression, while drawing upon the great ritual and artistic practices of the past."[9]

An exhibition of another form has been developed with attention to crowds and desires more so than collections, spaces, and places. This other form of temporary exhibition, termed a "blockbuster," has gained prominence in the United States since the 1970s. The Metropolitan Museum's 1974 *Treasures of Tutankhamen*, shortened to *King Tut*, traveled to six venues, with crowds totaling eight million. *Van Gogh's Van Goghs: Masterpieces from the Van Gogh Museum* was an exhibit at the Los Angeles County Museum of Art in 1999. From the summer of 2014 through the spring of 2015, at three venues in London, Chicago, and Paris, *David Bowie Is* drew record-number crowds to see three hundred costumes, photos, film clips, artwork, and other documents of the multifaceted artist's life and work.[10]

On a much smaller scale than the traditional blockbuster show, though still wildly-sought- after, are tickets to hyped exhibitions on view in a multitude of locations simultaneously or in sequence over many months and venues. Such was the case that ushered in a condition called "Kusama fever," which took hold internationally in 2017 as an expression of the burning desire to visit one of Yayoi Kusama's *Infinity Mirror Rooms* in person. While modest in their outlay as single spaces that offer enclosed illusions of infinite space, the installations were located in Washington, D.C., Singapore, Seattle, Toronto: the list goes on. The demand to see them was "unprecedented," leading museums to take up new methods of dealing with the demand. The Broad (in Los Angeles), for instance, set up a virtual queue system that enabled visitors to sign up on a wait list on an iPad in the lobby before awaiting an automated text message alerting them that their time had come. Visitors could then enjoy the other aspects of the museum instead of waiting in line.[11]

While COVID-19 shuttered museums and canceled numerous exhibitions, the notion of blockbuster shows, with crowds crammed into small galleries, seems very likely to return to the museum experience. Exhibitions such as these are intended to gain maximum public impact, often assembling artworks or objects of international fame. Often the museum shop and restaurant will also follow the exhibit theme with items for sale and special menus. Convention and visitors' bureaus, as well as partner hotels to museums, offer "package tours," which included exhibition tickets, discounts at local eateries, and amenities at the hotel. In these ways, such exhibitions—whether permanent or temporary, large or small—also contribute to the local economy. Beyond the impact and interest for the visitor, it is important to know that the creation of such exhibitions draws on new scholarship and international teams of scholars and often furthers the enrichment of our understanding of the subject at hand.

Online Exhibitions

Online exhibitions have been the result of artistic practice since the 1990s,[12] but they have only taken hold in museums since the turn of the century. Early in this period, duplications of the onsite exhibit experience were avoided, out of fear that audiences would stay at home, and not venture to the museum. Thus, online exhibitions were merely pages of content that sought to encourage a museum visit, or web content was viewed as an enhancement to the onsite exhibition by providing space for ancillaries and additional content that could exist online and beyond the life of the exhibition. Online exhibitions also have become a means of display by registering collections that are not assembled onsite. In this way, they become exhibition spaces in their own right.

In defining principles of online exhibit design, Marc Tinkler and Mark Freedman, of Plumb Design, forecast—in 1998—its future based upon the principles of onsite design. They saw such displays as more than simply "putting collections online"; rather, they can be curated, educational, and thought-provoking opportunities for visitors to experience.[13] In fact, many of the attributes of exhibitions—such as the "choreography of the viewer's experience," the interaction between viewer and work, as well as the need to adopt a seamless experience that does not overwhelm the visitor—are shared whether onsite or online.

Moreover, digital exhibitions can facilitate experiences that may not be possible otherwise. For instance, through partnerships with organizations worldwide, Google Arts & Culture aims to "preserve and bring the world's art and culture online so it's accessible to anyone, anywhere."[14] Founded in 2011, Google Arts & Culture creates free tools and technologies for museums and other cultural institutions to use to share their collections by providing a platform for hosting and a method for controlling, managing, and accessing digital files (such as images of collections, video, and other media) to create online exhibitions for all. The exhibitions may be published to the platform, to an app, or to a website.[15] Recent exhibitions include *H-1B*, created by Smithsonian Asian Pacific American Center in the fall of 2015 to mark the twenty-fifth anniversary of the H-1B visa, which permits employment of non-United States citizens with exceptional skills, such as training in STEM fields, on a temporary basis. This exhibition existed only online,[16] whereas an exhibition from the National Susan B. Anthony Museum and House offers a supplement to an onsite visit by providing the opportunity to view together more than one hundred items that are unable to be viewed altogether upon a visit to the historic property. Moreover, because photography is limited while taking a tour of the house, the digital exhibition offers some visual record of one's visit.[17] In addition, virtual exhibitions can pay tribute. For instance, several institutions in the United States, Canada, England, and India collaborated to create an online exhibition a year after a 7.8 magnitude earthquake hit Nepal. Conceived and organized by the Rubin Museum of Art and launched in 2016, *Honoring Nepal: People, Places, Art* recognizes the loss of life and destruction and honors "Nepal and its legacy by highlighting the people, places, and art that make this culture unique in the world."[18]

While onsite, online, or any combination of the two formats can offer richer potential for creating exhibitions that connect with viewers in myriad ways, aggregated content held in exhibition platforms such as Google Arts & Culture has been shown to affirm colonial and other biases, as Inna Kizhner *et al.* have shown. Their data from 2019 reveal the following:

- The majority of the content features works held in collections in the United States;
- The majority of the content features art from the twentieth century;
- Only 7.5 percent of the content is from institutions beyond the United States, the UK, Netherlands, and Italy;
- Few African cultural institutions have contributed to the platform, and by extension, very little African culture is reflected in the content on the platform; and
- Artworks from capital cities dominate the collections, while art from provinces is underrepresented.[19]

This slim representation of the world's art and culture stands in stark contrast to the vision of the program's director, Amit Sood, who stated, in 2016, that Google Arts & Culture would offer viewers "without real access to arts and culture" the opportunity to gain access through technology.[20] According to Kizhner and colleagues, Google Arts & Culture is, in fact, an example of "digital cultural colonialism," which reinforces the conventional traditions of art collection and interpretation, privileging a majority culture, in this case the United States (82 percent of the collections holdings at that time), followed by the UK (5.8 percent of the total); the Netherlands (1.7 percent), and so on.

With a different effect—one of greater access than the artist may have intended—viewers on the Google Arts & Culture platform are afforded the opportunity to see more than what would be possible if viewing the works in person. This suite of applications known as "Art Camera" offers viewers the opportunity to "discover all the details you might have missed"—thereby assuming visitors had, in fact, seen the works in person, or online, but in not as great of detail as on this platform. Witnessing high resolution images of more than one billion pixels, viewers can take a closer look by zooming in, to better see the details of works and sites (in particular, ceilings!), all in a process of discovery by screen rather than close observation and honed skills of visual acuity. Moreover, the brushstrokes become so enlarged that their distinct figures have lost shape: without the context of the entirety, the artistic process, and the product, are compromised.[21]

Such biases, and features, demonstrate how digital tools that seek to provide greater access can, in fact, reinforce stereotypes. It is the task of museums, as institutions, to do better than their aggregated platforms: they must maintain focus on the visitor.

Museum—Object—Visitor

Museums create interpretive programming as a means of connecting the content with its audiences. To this end, museums have begun providing visitors with "experiences" within their galleries designed to help them understand the object and its context. In 1992, Kenneth L. Ames describes the exhibition experience this way: "Exhibitions are primarily nonverbal, sensory experiences. People may read the words we write, but they are more likely to get caught up in the multisensory experience we try to provide."[22] Case in point: *The Pink Bedroom* described above, or the Longwood Gardens exhibitions described in Chapter 5. Consider, too, the nineteenth-century diorama—whether in a natural history or history museum—which sought to place objects within their "natural" settings, thereby increasing visitors' understanding of their context or meaning. In science centers, visitors often push buttons to make machines or models "work." Other types of museums adapted these "hands-on" experiences to their exhibits. In some museums, visitors even encounter representations of individuals from the past, come to "tell a story" to those in the gallery.

This deconstructing of the museum exhibit case is the result of a variety of influences, some intentional and others inadvertent.[23] Children's museums, since their inception in the nineteenth century, have sought to engage the observer with items to touch, technological processes to try, and even clothing to try on. The 1970s efforts to create children's rooms (galleries) within museums brought these techniques into mainstream museum exhibitions. In addition, international expositions, which have garnered attention since 1851, as well as amusement parks—both of which are intended to entertain and amaze—influenced museum developers and designers and affected visitors' expectations of exhibitions.[24]

Other initiatives, such as inventive exhibition strategies, have enabled new experiences to emerge. For instance, the temporary installation of the Schmidlapp Gallery in the Cincinnati Art Museum in 2011 fostered both private and social experiences focused on works of art. For this installation, eighteen of the more than sixty thousand works were selected as an introduction to the museum. But this was no mere hanging of pictures on a line from one end of the gallery to the other: instead, the long, narrow gallery was transformed into a near-sacred space with side alcoves, one for each work, draped with black tassel-like cording, enabling visitors to enter one of these "chapels" and "truly concentrate on some of the great works of art" in the collection, to "lose yourself in them, and learn a great deal from a concentrated experience."[25] The installation was amplified with theatrical lighting in each space and labels that glowed, in order to facilitate reading with ease. Looking back at the installation now, with another decade of museum experiences in the rearview mirror: would this focused, quiet, and reflective experience, resonate today?

For the past decade, the trend has been toward repositioning the role of the object and the authority of the museum in a triangulation between museum as an authority, viewer as participant, and object and/or idea being shared. Over the years, cultural institutions, including museums, have developed a more participatory approach that enables them to reconnect with their public (and, truly, their *publics*, as evidence that the audiences are neither homogenous nor monolithic). Along with the call for participation, some museums have been adopting a less absolute role when it comes to creating and interpreting their content, to the extent that museums and their publics engage in discourse. Visitors and participants can play a role in exhibition creation, interpretation, and dissemination in ways that were never possible before. In a fine arts museum, what might this look like? It could possibly involve visitor-curated content making its way into an exhibition; station, or stations within a gallery where placards pose questions of visitors—asking, perhaps, what a work means to them or asking which work is a favorite—alongside a stack of Post-it Notes for visitors to have their say; or images of visitors to a gallery posted to social media with the museum's hashtag (such as #ManusxMachina for the exhibition *Manus x Machina: Fashion in an Age of Technology* on view at The Met during the summer of 2016). While exhibitions emerged from a responsibility to display knowledge construction for private-turned-public audiences to see, they have become sites of engagement and critical thinking for all.

In terms of the broader picture, a frequent point made about this overall shift in museums is likening it to the shift in internet communication. As we have moved beyond the world of an internet that generated results to encounter web 2.0 as a platform with user-generated content, so, too, have we moved into what museum theorist and practitioner Nina Simon has called Museum 2.0.[26] In describing this shift, Simon proclaims the emergent practices of the twenty-first century by, in fact, connecting them with threads of scholarship and practice from the past century. Simon's plea for audience-centered institutions may be seen as a renewal of the work of John Cotton Dana, Elaine Heumann Gurian, and Stephen Weil. Meaning-making as a co-creative, if not independent, endeavor takes its cues from George Hein, John Falk, and Lynn Dierking. And, the point that "users' voices can inform and invigorate both project design and public-facing programs" builds upon the work of Kathleen McLean, Wendy Pollock, and the design firm IDEO.[27] In calling for a participatory cultural institution, Simon seeks "a place where visitors can create, share, and connect with each other around content." In the very basic of terms, content need not mean an *object*. Building upon Weil's notion that museums should be *for something* rather than solely *about something*, museums are instruments of community, engagement, and social change.[28] Thus, in the museum of the twenty-first century, the deconstructing of the museum exhibit case has born the construction of communities within the space of the museum—and beyond it.

Creating the Exhibition

The chief components of a museum exhibition's development are (a) a concept (message) or storyline, (b) objects to be displayed, (c) the setting which might include custom-built elements and layout within a museum building, and (d) "front end" evaluation studies or audience research. Regardless of whether an exhibition is onsite, online, or some measure of the two, all four of these factors should be considered.

Depending on a museum's staff size, the concept may emerge from an individual curator's, researcher's, or even collector's investigations, or it may reflect a discussion of how to attract more visitors. Today's exhibitions typically result from a team effort. Whether ideas or objects are the exhibition's starting point, the clarity of the concept profoundly affects the final product. Though this discussion of exhibition elements begins with "the idea," another element—the objects—can just as readily be the starting point for a museum exhibition. Regardless of which comes first, it is the melding of the objects with the ideas that forms the basis for an interpretive exhibition and makes it more than simply a display of items from a museum's storage rooms. Onsite exhibitions, moreover, factor into the concept and design process of the museum's spaces and how they can be used to engage visitors and further the exhibitions' intent. In addition, consideration should be given to audiences beyond the primary, intended audience. Who else will be interested in this exhibition? What might they want to know?[29]

Not all museum spaces are equal, and the exhibit design process should acknowledge early on the impact of the exhibition environment. At the United States Holocaust Memorial Museum in Washington, D.C., even the elevators that take visitors to the exhibit entry contribute to the interpretive message by evoking a sense of confinement and "transport." Careful attention to identifying an exhibition's potential audience, especially through direct research, guides exhibition developers' decisions from central themes and messages to object placement and design.

Numerous books have been written as manuals to guide exhibition design. Before addressing exhibition development steps, a word about exhibition teams is necessary. The days of the single curator conceiving and installing an exhibition are remnants of the past, thus making it critically important for museum professionals to realize the need and value of working collaboratively.[30] An exhibit team might include a curator; a designer; an educator; a subject specialist, such as an historian or scientist; and in some instances, the museum's development officer.[31] Moreover, as museums see their roles as part of the community where they reside, exhibit teams may include members of the public as co-curators, content experts, and knowledge bearers.

The Concept

The exhibit starts with a concept, an idea, or a point of view that is developed in one of two ways. First, it may be stated as a theme, and through careful study and research, analyzed and divided into subthemes. Then objects can be sought and arranged in exhibit units to elucidate the story. A second approach begins with a collection of objects, and from them a theme and subthemes are developed. Often both approaches are used simultaneously. In addition, exhibition devices or online ancillaries may be included as part of the visualization and planning.[32]

Developing a clear exhibition concept with subthemes and exhibit units obviously requires intensive research, akin to writing an authoritative essay on the subject of the exhibition. Thus, the traditional methods of historical and scientific research are employed with careful examination of primary sources. In a small museum, the curator or even the director may do the whole job—research, exhibition design, and installation. In a larger institution, a research assistant may assemble the scholarly materials, a curator the objects, and a designer the presentation plan. The audience for the exhibit should be defined and preferably sampled, if not fully included in the exhibition preparation. In the former case, members of the team identify and contact prospective audience(s) to discover what they want to know about the subject and how they respond to certain emerging exhibit concepts and designs. In the latter, members of the team invite participation from the community to work alongside them to create one element of an exhibition, or its entirety. An example of such an effort is the Rochester Museum & Science Center's *Changemakers: Rochester Women Who Changed the World* exhibition, which was on view in 2020 and remains an online exhibit. *Changemakers* was framed around the opportunity to celebrate the centennial of woman suffrage in the United States while highlighting the women who have advocated for change and equality in myriad ways. Women who were the focus of the exhibit were nominated and selected by more than fifty community curators reflecting individual perspectives, as well as that of eleven organizations, and three Diversity, Equity, and Inclusion consultants not affiliated with the museum. Together the team shared authority with the museum staff in decision-making, content expertise, and diverse perspectives to "more inclusively, authentically, and accurately represent all of the women featured in *The Changemakers*—particularly Black women, Indigenous women, and other women of color."[33]

These practices of community co-creation and co-curation are far from the monolithic museum practices of yesteryear and the one-to-many model of a staff person at a museum who directly engages with the public, as defined by Elizabeth Merritt, founding director of the Center for the Future of Museums at the American Alliance of Museums. In 2018, Merritt noted that museums and cultural organizations need to be relevant to their full communities, which may take shape in the form of hiring "community engagement curators" (CECs) "to engage local communities in an open dialogue about their needs, elevate the museum's connection to local communities, and effect meaningful change through educational programming." Merritt also notes that the position would best be served beyond single occurrences, "to ensure that community voices are heard—not just in a single exhibit or program, but as part of a sustained collaboration."[34]

But what could be accomplished if museums were pushed beyond working with community curators, and instead, focused on expanding the museum as a place where exhibition teams routinely thought beyond the walls of the institution? Museums have the capacity to, and have demonstrated that they can, move beyond the transactional interaction of one staff person at the institution with a broad, diverse audience to embrace audiences and invite them in—as visitors, co-creators, and staff.

Selecting the Objects

George Brown Goode of the Smithsonian Institution described exhibitions this way: "An efficient educational museum may be described as a collection of instructive labels, each illustrated by a well-selected specimen."[35] As the exhibit team crafts the exhibition's purpose and themes, they must also turn their attention to the objects that will help visitors understand their messages. Frequently, the narrative script has a parallel document, the object list that identifies specific objects to be used. Careful object-based research should guide the process. As noted earlier in the discussion of temporary exhibitions, objects may need to be borrowed from other institutions to complement the museum's collection.[36]

With today's understanding of the need to care for museum objects, exhibit elements may be designed to protect the items on display. For example, a delicate object may require special conditions or a "microclimate." This may be as sophisticated as a sealed case with special temperature and humidity controls or as simple as a black cloth that visitors pick up when viewing the object and return to cover it when they step away. As the exhibit team works, it must address these needs. This process becomes even more demanding if the objects will be on view for a long time or if they are to travel to other museums.

Alternatively, online exhibitions present opportunities to bring together collections that may be impossible to assemble in a single venue. When serving as a record of and enhancement to onsite exhibitions, online exhibitions can provide space for additional educational, interpretive, and engagement ancillaries to supplement the onsite experience.

Creating the Layout

As the exhibit script is developing, the designer joins the team to consider space requirements. First and foremost, the museum building itself, whether historic house or art museum with expansive gallery spaces, will affect basic design considerations. In addition to the concept of the exhibition and the needs of its objects, the exhibition team must address the visitors' needs as they move both into and within the exhibition spaces. In the United States, with the passage of the Americans with Disabilities Act (ADA) in 1990, public museums must provide access to all visitors regardless of ability.[37] As an extension of Title III of the ADA, the Department of Justice has begun to address accessibility of websites, including exhibition sites, referred to as the 2010 ADA Standards for Accessible Design.[38] Are images posted with written descriptions for screen readers to decipher? Can the site be navigated with a keyboard rather than a mouse? Are captions included for audio content? Moving beyond mere access to inclusion, museum design should consider the "full range of human diversity with respect to ability, language, culture, gender, age, and other forms of human difference." Such design consideration should be given when planning an onsite as well as an online exhibition.[39]

As an exhibit team begins to map out the placement of objects, supporting materials, and exhibit "furniture" in the museum, they must address a series of questions. Equally, these questions should be considered when drafting a website. How do you introduce or orient visitors to the exhibit's concepts? Does the exhibit design, and perhaps its messages, suggest a single pathway through its spaces? Or, if the exhibition has "subthemes," how are they differentiated from the main theme? How do you accommodate visitors with different levels of interest or knowledge? Does the exhibit need spaces within it to accommodate groups of visitors (especially school groups)? How and where do you place audiovisual elements—computer touch screens, video or audio elements, even small theater spaces—to give visitors a break in their progress through the exhibition spaces? How do groups of visitors comfortably use interactive elements? How does one participate, offer feedback, and contribute to the exhibition? Simple comment notebooks, talkback boards, digital kiosks, and hashtags, as noted earlier, are spaces where visitors can register their reactions. While these engagement opportunities have usually been relegated to the final room of an exhibition, they are now interspersed within the space of an exhibition to invite conversation, contribution, and collaboration throughout the experience.[40]

Choosing Design Techniques

For many years, museums presented their exhibits in rectangular or square rooms, utilizing the four walls and floor for pictures and cases. This arrangement could become monotonous and dull and has sometimes been called "the tyranny of the rectangular room". Instead, modern designers have embraced curved, angled, or screen walls; movable panels; varied divisions; angles; and platforms "to reduce the sheer acreage of floors." Such devices add appeal and change of pace, thus diminishing museum fatigue and boredom.[41] In the twenty-first century, however, exhibition design techniques have pushed boundaries even further, to move beyond the physical space of the gallery and the objects contained within. Traditionally, exhibited objects are on display in cases—wall or table types, usually rectangular or square, and freestanding. Otherwise, objects are shown without cases, protecting them by suspending them out of reach or by placing them so that a platform or pebbled surface reminds the visitor of the distance between him or her and the item on view. For a variety of reasons, a replica of an object might be on display. For instance, in January 2016, the American Museum of Natural History in New York put on view the *Titanosaur*, a cast of a 122-foot-long dinosaur that lived in the Patagonia approximately one hundred million years ago. Lifelike in appearance and shocking in proportion, the neck and head of the dinosaur extend beyond the gallery's walls to the elevator banks.[42]

In addition, 3D-printed objects have become part of exhibition protocol, as a framework or as an outcome. At the Museum of Design Atlanta (MODA), 3D printers greet visitors to the gallery and gift shop, enabling everyone to watch an object emerge from pixels and bits. The printers are an apt accessory to the active, design-thinking that MODA encourages and promotes through its exhibitions, events, and conversations—all of which originate from the maker space in the foyer of the museum. Other institutions share this interest in maker culture, the maker movement, and maker faire events, which, by their very nature of reproduction, seemingly assert a return to materiality.[43]

As part of the inaugural exhibition at the newly renovated Renwick Gallery in Washington, D.C., a life-size 3D-printed sculpture draws attention in the Octagon Room, where a replica of Hiram Powers's *Greek Slave* was on view, alongside videos of the scanning and printing processes that gave way to this contemporary reproduction. The mere presence of a newly made replica is a brilliant means of underscoring the original artist's concerns and fears about illegal reproduction and copying of his work. Originally cast in 1843, this critically acclaimed work was prized for its lifelikeness and was replicated in both marble and plaster. (Nearby, the Smithsonian's American Art Museum owns the original plaster from which replicas were made.) Also on view with the 3D-printed *Greek Slave* is the patent application made by Powers in 1849 to protect his work from illegal reproduction[44]; though certainly he never dreamed the possibility of the Renwick and the Smithsonian team scanning and releasing a point cloud of the sculpture for all to see, understand, and—if desired—create for themselves.

Such interventions in the space of the gallery speak to the broader activities that are part of the twenty-first-century digital culture and are made possible by the convergence of several trends and fields that integrate technology and making from outside of the museum to the spaces within it. In addition to the types of replicas, reproductions or similar types of objects are an important part of the demonstration spaces at science and children's museums, as well as the hands-on exploration areas in many museums—regardless of type.

Given twenty-first-century viewing practices and the needs and interests of the viewer (discussed in the following chapters), objects of wonder—whether authentic, reproductions, or digital images—certainly take their cues from exhibition displays of yesterday, including the diorama—which began as a life-size exhibit with three-dimensional specimens or objects in the foreground amid realistic surroundings, often with a curved, painted background. The habitat groups of natural history museums showed animals in a proper setting. American taxidermists and designers William Temple Hornaday and Carl Akeley set the standard for dioramas at the end of the nineteenth century (see Chapter 2).[45]

Multimedia options provide opportunities for museums to assist visitors in placing the exhibition and its objects in a broader context. Monitors, kiosks, and virtual-reality gear in galleries offer visitors related or expanded content at a touch or a click. Screens within the galleries allow visitors to learn more about an object, its history, techniques used in its creation, and other information. They can also set the stage for the exhibition and orient visitors to what they will experience in the galleries, or at historic sites around the property.

Moving from the fixed to the portable, exhibition design may include voiced or captioned guidance in the form of audio commentary to provide greater context and details too cumbersome for an exhibit label or extended wall text. Frequently referred to as "audio tours," these guides originated with special exhibitions, as in 1952's *Vermeer: Real or Fake* at the Stedelijk Museum in the Netherlands. Intended as a means of providing tours for foreign visitors visiting the temporary exhibition,[46] the guide provided a portable device to visitors, which enabled them to connect wirelessly to a closed-circuit device and listen to the content in their native language. While this model required geographical constraint to the area of the radio network, the goal of the Stedelijk's tour is similar to the multimedia of the late twentieth and twenty-first centuries: to allow for an enhanced experience in front of the object. In the intervening years—some fifty years of audio guides ostensibly—the initiatives and direction of these guides have changed: from audio-only to multimedia experiences, and from narrative flow—much like the space of the museum itself—to free-choice learning.

Audio and multimedia tours also offer expanded content beyond what might be expected. Building upon the Stedelijk's model, taped acoustaguide formats exploded in the early 2000s, with device-specific models requiring museums to purchase hardware for use by visitors, to delivered content to personal devices where museums experimented with technology from iPods to messages broadcast to personal cell phones. For instance, the Cleveland Museum of Art's *Art Conversations Audio Tour*, launched in 2010 in conjunction with the reopening of the 1916 galleries of the museum, offered a highlights tour of the permanent collection. Accessible by smartphones via the web or through museum-provided iPod touch (portable audio file/MP3) devices, the tour offers expanded content from local artists, curatorial staff of the museum, and international scholars.[47] Viewers are also empowered by the devices they bring with them into the gallery space, such as tablets and smartphones. While not part of the exhibition design, per se, the BYOD (Bring Your Own Device)[48] approach impacts the ways in which content can be delivered, which, in turn, impacts the exhibition's design onsite and online.

In addition, apps are increasingly developed for museums as part of the overall education and engagement road map for the entire collection or as a discrete endeavor for a single show. For instance, the Cleveland Museum of Art launched an exhibition-focused app, *Art and Stories from Mughal, India*, in the summer of 2016. The app features a multimedia tour that takes the conversational tone of their previous audio tour to an entirely new level. It "is like walking through the exhibition with the curator telling you her favorite stories." In addition, the Mughal app provides users with an audio glossary for pronouncing names and terms as an educational tool, and for engagement, the app features curated content for sharing on social media by including one hundred facts for sharing—one for each painting in the show—peppered with the hashtag #CMAMughal.[49]

Returning to the original aims of the Stedelijk's audio tour, and significantly expanding it as well, The Met launched its first audio guide in app form in 2014. The guide provides tours in ten languages, and it spans more than three thousand audio and video messages, including a tour for kids. The app and guide identify its chief purposes as education and engagement by telling visitors they can "get the whole story. Engage with thousands of artworks in the galleries and select exhibitions."[50] Apps have even been created in advance of museums themselves, as is the case of the app for the National Museum of African American History and Culture, the newest addition to the Washington Mall. The app exploring the planned museum's site and collections—featuring augmented reality—was launched in 2013, three years in advance of the museum's opening in September 2016.[51]

By selecting to use digital tools such as these, visitors take control of their own education, interpretation, and engagement threads—much more of which will be addressed in Chapters 8 and 9.

While it may seem as though these expanded options for exhibition and museum-visitor-object triangulation are contributing to the deconstruction (or destruction) of the traditional exhibition cases and designs, the onsite and online exhibition environments, as well as apps, share the same interests: conceptual framework and narrative, awareness of and aim to reach the audience, and engagement. In writing about the onsite exhibition design process, emeritus professor and gallery director Tom Klobe states, "An analysis of how the material to be presented can best be understood by visitors—and of how the installation design can enhance the intended visitor response—is integral to a conceptual approach to planning and design. Exhibitions, after all, are addressed to the visitors. *The goal is to make the art or the collection accessible to viewers.* It must encourage visitors to gather, from their experience, a greater understanding of and appreciation for what they are seeing (emphasis added)."[52] The same could be said of online exhibitions.

Labels

Labels are a basic means by which a museum transforms a collection of objects into a storytelling exhibition that communicates effectively with its chosen audience. They must attract the viewer's attention; convey information about the objects on display in a concise, yet understandable way; and by successfully provoking curiosity, motivate the visitor to look at the whole exhibition.

There are several types of labels. The main label, often called a *text panel* because of its size and prominence, briefly and clearly introduces the themes of the exhibit. This label will be prominently placed and may consist of artwork and text; it is similar to the title page of a book. A secondary topic label (sometimes called a *case label*) will be used for the exhibition's subthemes; though not so prominent as the text panel, its headline will have large letters, and its subhead, while brief, will be long enough to give the gist of the subtheme. These labels are essential to understanding the exhibition and will carry its overall message to viewers who do no more than read them and look at the objects. Other explanatory labels, longer and of smaller type size, give facts, figures, and explanations for interested viewers and specialists, but they can be ignored by less-interested visitors. Caption labels also are usually supplied for most individual objects; they briefly give the chief facts, such as name of the object, maker, date, and place of origin.

Exhibit and evaluation consultant Beverly Serrell offers rules for creating quality labels based on research and recommendations from researchers and colleagues: careful visitor orientation (both spatially and in terms of content) keeps visitors' attention; more visitors read shorter labels than longer ones; labels next to an object will be read more than labels with numerical keys to a group of objects; labels with concrete, visual references will cause visitors to read-look-read-look; visitors will read interesting labels aloud, increasing social interactions and engaging children, too.[53]

Conceptually, label writing involves two distinct processes—literary composition and visual appearance. On the literary side, the purpose is to translate the detailed knowledge, and often the jargon of the curator, into a short, straightforward explanation using language readily understood by the non-specialist. Some labels ask questions and seek engagement from the audience. The best of these ask questions that visitors ask themselves. In another category are labels for interactive, participatory, and hands-on exhibits. Such labels need to respond to and serve the design and the way it is used by visitors.[54] Several types of interactive models can be used to connect engagement in a task and understanding the experience at hand.[55] Content aside, the second requirement of a label is legibility, which may include lettering, typefaces, spacing, and color selection. Here is where the expertise of an exhibition designer and institutional standards, as well as inclusive design, provide needed guidance. Even with all the ancillaries and opportunities beyond written text that abound within and beyond the gallery, labels remain the basic means of enabling viewers to understand exhibitions. Guidebooks, catalogs, and the aforementioned multimedia apparatuses help, but there remains no satisfactory substitute for a well written, visually attractive label.[56]

Launched in the summer of 2021, The Fralin's Little Museum of Art was inspired by a desire to engage with the community during the museum's closure due to COVID-19 and to provide an opportunity to highlight the artwork of local and student artists. This miniature museum consists of six galleries, each measuring approximately one foot square, and showcases tiny works on a rotating basis. At the close of each exhibition, the artwork is moved to the Free Little Museum Store. In the spirit of the Free Little Libraries, the public can take a piece or swap with one of their own, sharing art throughout the community. The Little Museum of Art is on view twenty-four hours a day.
Photo by Coe Sweet.

Before concluding this chapter, it is worth mentioning a modest, relevant, and equally important format of exhibition. Developed at the Fralin Museum of Art at the University of Virginia, the Little Museum project takes its cues from the Little Free Library initiative. The library program is an international movement in more than 120 countries that seeks to provide barrier-free access to books.[57] The museum equivalent is a space with six galleries, each one foot by one foot. Since 2021, the museum has hosted one exhibition per month in their Little Museum, ranging from art of all mediums (except video, although there's hope for that to be solutioned soon!). While art is the primary focus for the exhibitions, other types of exhibitions, including science and botanical displays, have been installed. The exhibit space is located directly outside of the museum and is open 24/7 for the entire campus and community. Like the libraries, the museum has a "free exchange" opportunity for individuals to take or swap a piece, sharing art throughout the community.[58] Such a novel approach shows how college campuses can be also sites of exhibitions in new, innovative, and accessible ways.

All the examples throughout this chapter, in framing what it means *to exhibit*, underscore the core of museum work: storytelling. Storytelling undergirds interpretation, engagement with audiences, and the manner through which museums serve their communities, as described in the following three chapters: "to interpret," "to engage," and "to serve." It is also the starting point for the following chapter.

Notes

1. Giuseppe Olmi, "Science Honour-Metaphor: Italian Cabinets of the Sixteenth and Seventeenth Centuries," in *Grasping the World: The Idea of the Museum*, eds. Donald Preziosi and Claire Farago (Hants: Ashgate, 2004), 129–56; Paula Findlen, *Possessing Nature: Museums, Collecting and Scientific Culture in Early Modern Italy* (Berkeley: University of California Press, 1994).
2. Charles Willson Peale, "To the Citizens of the United States of America," in *Dunlap's American Daily Advertiser*, Philadelphia, January 13, 1792.
3. Neil Harris, "Cultural Excursions: Marketing Appetites and Cultural Tastes in Modern America," *Museum News* 69, no. 5 (September–October 1990).
4. Rudiger Klessmann, *The Berlin Museum* (New York: Abrams, 1971), 58. "Wilhelm von Bode invented a 'Berlin Style' of his own in the Kaiser Friedrich Museum exhibitions rooms. His Italian interiors in particular, with their delicate blending of color and material and their harmonious arrangement of pictures and sculptures, frames and chests, have been widely admired and frequently imitated"; the Hopps quote appears in Victoria Newhouse, *Art and the Power of Placement* (New York: Monacelli Press, 2005), 10.
5. United States Holocaust Memorial Museum, "Overview of Museum Collections," https://www.ushmm .org/research/research-in-collections/overview.
6. Smithsonian, "Smithsonian Tells 200 Years of History through One House," April 20, 2001, http:// amhistory.si.edu/house/resources/forthepress.asp. See also the exhibition website: http://amhistory.si .edu/house/home.asp.
7. Trey Taylor, "The Loss of Innocence Is in the Air," *New York Times*, April 23, 2023, ST1.
8. On the Molina Family Latino Gallery, see Jenarae Bautista and Sarah Elston, "The Molina Family Latino Gallery: A PEAS Case Study," forthcoming in *Collections*, edited by Juilee Decker (publication date: 2024).
9. Field Museum, "Tattoo," https://www.fieldmuseum.org/at-the-field/exhibitions/tattoo. The exhibition was on view from October 21, 2016 through April 30, 2017.
10. Kevin F. McCarthy, Elizabeth H. Ondaatje, Arthur Brooks, and Andras Czanto, *A Portrait of the Visual Arts: Meeting the Challenges of a New Era* (Santa Monica: RAND, 2005), 32. The origin of the blockbuster phenomenon is much older. The City of Manchester, England, hosted *Art Treasures of the United Kingdom* in 1883 that attracted more than a million visitors in four months. In addition to building temporary exhibition space, the city added a special train station to its railroad lines to move visitors to the exhibit hall; Randolph Starn, "A Historian's Brief Guide to New Museum Studies," *American Historical Review* 110, no. 1 (February 2005): 94; Newhouse, *Art and the Power*, 25. On Bowie, see Judy Fayard, "From Jeff Koons to Henri Matisse's Cut-outs, Catch the Art Shows You Missed," *Wall Street Journal*, November 20, 2014, http://www.wsj.com/articles/ blockbuster-cultural-exhibitions-on-the-move-to-new-cities-1416523935.

11. Elena Goukassian, "How Long Do You Have to Wait to Get into a Kusama *Infinity Room*? We Found Out," *Hyperallergic*, January 22, 2018, https://hyperallergic.com/421316/kusama-infinity-room-wait-times/.

12. It's worth noting that museums have existed virtually in the form of digital surrogacy, stemming from artistic practice in the early 1990s. Artist Jeffrey Shaw created *The Virtual Museum* (1991) as a digital reproduction of the exhibition space at Brucknerhaus in Linz, Austria, where a large monitor on a motorized platform enabled a seated visitor (and others in the room) to meander through four other virtual spaces. The direction is guided by the sitter's body weight, which moves the chair. Shaw's work is described here: https://digitalartarchive.at/features/featured-artists/featured-artist-jeffrey-shaw .html, and, may be viewed here: Media Art Net, "Jeffrey Shaw, The Virtual Museum," http://www .medienkunstnetz.de/works/the-virtuel-museum/, accessed November 14, 2023.

13. Marc Tinkler and Mark Freedman, "Online Exhibitions: A Philosophy of Design and Technological Implementation," *Museums and the Web 1998: Proceedings*, http://www.museumsandtheweb.com/mw98/ papers/tinkler/tinkler_paper.html.

14. Google Arts & Culture, https://about.artsandculture.google.com/.

15. Google Cultural Institute is an outgrowth from Google Art Project, which was launched in 2011 and brings together works of art from around the world presenting them with incredibly high-definition photography, Street View, and other interfaces that are simply not possible in a face-to-face encounter. At a time when museums were reluctant to release any digital images of works in their collections, Google Art Project featured seventeen museums in nine countries with one thousand images in 2011; by April 2012, those numbers had grown to thirty thousand artworks and Street View for forty-six museums. The project also expanded to include non-Western content. "In other words, the Art Project is no longer just about the Indian student wanting to visit the Metropolitan Museum of Art in New York. It is now also about the American student wanting to visit the National Gallery of Modern Art in Delhi." See Amit Sood, "Going Global in Search of Great Art," https://googleblog.blogspot.fr/2012/04/going-global-in -search-of-great-art.html.

16. *H-1B*, https://www.google.com/culturalinstitute/beta/u/0/exhibit/QRdMk4sZ.

17. National Susan B. Anthony Museum & House, https://www.google.com/culturalinstitute/beta/u/0/ exhibit/wwISTw3PopLIJQ.

18. *Honoring Nepal: People, Places, Art*, https://www.google.com/culturalinstitute/beta/u/0/exhibit/ gQKiSTOiApY_Jw. The virtual exhibition included contributions by the British Museum, Freer and Sackler Galleries, LIFE Photo Collection, Dr. Bhau Daji Lad Mumbai City Museum, Los Angeles County Museum of Art, Nepal's Children Art Museum, Newark Museum, and the Royal Ontario Museum; it was conceived and organized by the Rubin Museum of Art.

19. Melissa Terras, "New Paper: Digital Cultural Colonialism: Measuring Bias in Aggregated Digitized Content Held in Google Arts and Culture," *Melissa Terras: Adventures in Digital Culture*, January 18, 2021, https://melissaterras.org/2021/01/18/new-paper-digital-cultural-colonialism-measuring-bias-in -aggregated-digitized-content-held-in-google-arts-and-culture/, which cites Inna Kizhner, Melissa Terras, Maxim Rumyantsev, Valentina Khokhlova, Elisaveta Demeshkova, Ivan Rudov, Julia Afanasieva, "Digital Cultural Colonialism: Measuring Bias in Aggregated Digitized Content Held in Google Arts and Culture," *Digital Scholarship in the Humanities* 36, 3 (September 2021): 607–40, https://doi.org/10.1093/ llc/fqaa055.

20. Amit Sood, "Every Piece of Art You've Ever Wanted to See—Up Close and Searchable," *TED*, February 2016, "https://www.ted.com/talks/amit_sood_every_piece_of_art_you_ve_ever_wanted_to_see _up_close_and_searchable.

21. The Art Camera hub is here: https://artsandculture.google.com/project/art-camera; "12 Artworks You'll Love to Zoom Into," https://artsandculture.google.com/story/hAXhy-4s3wl8KA; "10 Astonishing Ceilings You Can See Up Close," https://artsandculture.google.com/story/kAXBsfwsy8zFJg.

22. Kenneth L. Ames, Barbara Franco, and L. Thomas Frye, eds., *Ideas and Images: Developing Interpretive History Exhibits* (Nashville: American Association for State and Local History, 1992), 319; Jane Bedno and Ed Bedno, "Museum Exhibitions: Past Imperfect, Future Tense," *Museum News* 78, no. 5, 38–43; Elaine Heumann Gurian, "Noodling Around with Exhibition Opportunities," in *Civilizing the Museum* (New York: Routledge, 2006), 150–61.

23. Harris, "Cultural Excursions"; Neil Harris, "Exhibiting Controversy," *Museum News* 74, no. 5 (September–October 1995); Pere Alberch, "The Identity Crisis of Natural History Museums at the End of the Twentieth Century," in *Towards the Museum of the Future: New European Perspectives*, eds. Roger Miles and Lauro Zavala (London: Routledge, 1994); Charles Saumarez Smith, "Museums, Artefacts and Meaning," and Philip Wright, "The Quality of Visitors' Experiences in Art Museums," in *The New Museology*, ed. Peter Vergo (London: Reaktion Books, 1989); Ivan Karp and Steven D. Lavine, eds., *Exhibiting Cultures: The Poetics and Politics of Museum Display* (Washington, D.C.: Smithsonian Institution Press, 1991); Luke, *Museum Politics*.

24. International expositions continue to expose visitors to technological advances, often in ways that may be adapted by museums. U.S. theme parks, from Anheuser Busch's Busch Gardens with its European themes, to Universal Studios' joint venture with Disney in Florida, provide families with not only museum-like exhibits, but also experiences that range from hair-raising roller-coaster rides to musical performances.

25. The quotes are from Cincinnati Art Museum Director Aaron Betsky's description of the exhibition process for Schmidlapp Gallery, *Cincinnati Art Museum*, November 15, 2011, https://www.cincinnatiartmuseum.org/about/blog/schmidlapp-gallery/. I did see and share this experience with students on at least two occasions in 2011. See one such blog post here: http://gcva.blogspot.com/2011/11/core-strength.html.

26. See Nina Simon, *The Participatory Museum* (Santa Cruz: Museum 2.0, 2010).

27. See Nina Simon, *The Participatory Museum*, ii.

28. Stephen E. Weil, "From Being about Something to Being for Somebody: The Ongoing Transformation of the American Museum," *Daedalus*, 128:3 (Summer 1999): 229-58.

29. Joseph Wetzel, "Three Steps to Exhibits Success," *Museum News* 50 (February 1972): 20; Lothar P. Witteborg, "The Temporary Exhibit in Science Museums," in *Temporary and Travelling Exhibits* (Paris: United Nations Educational, Scientific and Cultural Organization, 1963), 15-29.

30. Ames, Franco, and Frye, *Ideas and Images*, 190; see Cindy Robinson and Warren Leon in *Ideas and Images* for a discussion of exhibit team challenges, 211-32; *Museum News* 70, no. 2 (March–April 1991), this issue is on museum exhibition techniques; Steven Lubar, "The Making of 'America on the Move' at the National Museum of American History," *Curator* 47, no. 1 (January 2004): 19-51; Lisa C. Roberts, *From Knowledge to Narrative: Educators and the Changing Museum* (Washington, D.C.: Smithsonian Institution, 1997), 86-88; Elaine Heumann Gurian, "Let's Empower All Those Who Have a Stake in Exhibitions," in *Civilizing the Museum* (New York: Routledge, 2006), 162-66.

31. David Dean, *Museum Exhibition: Theory and Practice* (London: Routledge, 1994), 157; Mary Ellen Munley, "Education Excellence in American Museums," *Museum News* 65, no. 2 (December 1986): 51-57. In the United States, exhibition development teams emerged in the late 1970s as the result of several influences. The National Endowment for the Humanities' growing support for interpretive exhibitions nationwide required museums to include scholars or specialists in the humanities. Museums often drew on university scholars to supplement their staff and meet NEH standards. At the same time, the children's museums exhibit process involving teams, led by the Boston Children's Museum's active professional outreach, raised professional awareness of the value of teams in exhibit development. By the 1980s, the Kellogg Foundation supported a nationwide project to support museums, creating exhibits with teams and assessing their value at the end of the process. Both the financial support and professional attention to teams increased their use by museums of all sizes and disciplines.

32. Roberts, *From Knowledge to Narrative*; Ames, Franco, and Frye, *Ideas and Images*; Arminta Neal, *Help! for the Small Museum: A Handbook of Exhibit Ideas and Methods* (Boulder: Pruett Press, 1969), 21-27.

33. Rochester Museum & Science Center, "The Changemakers: Credits," https://rmsc.org/changemakers/credits/, accessed September 20, 2023.

34. Elizabeth Merritt, "Community Curating: A Macro to Micro View," March 13, 2018, Center for the Future of Museums Blog, https://www.aam-us.org/2018/03/13/community-curating-a-macro-to-micro-view/, accessed August 12, 2023.

35. George Brown Goode, *Annual Report of the Board of Regents of the Smithsonian Institution for the Year Ending June 30, 1889*; Neil Harris, "Museums, Merchandising, and Popular Taste: The Struggle for Influence," in *Material Culture and the Study of American Life* (New York: Norton, published for the Henry

Francis du Pont Winterthur Museum, 1975); Edward P. Alexander, "George Brown Goode," *Museum Masters: Their Museums and Their Influence* (Nashville: American Association of State and Local History, 1983), 277–310.

36. In preparing the object list, the collections manager, curator, or registrar will locate a potential object to review its condition and appropriateness for display. In addition to selecting appropriate artifacts, the team must address the needs of the objects to be displayed. As the exhibit develops, curators and conservators may discover that an object needs conservation, or it may require special conditions for display.

37. According to the ADA National Network, which is funded by the Department of Health and Human Services, within the context of the ADA, *disability* is "a legal term rather than a medical one," and as such, the ADA's definition of *disability* is different from how disability is defined under some other laws. "The ADA defines a person with a disability as a person who has a physical or mental impairment that substantially limits one or more major life activity. This includes people who have a record of such an impairment, even if they do not currently have a disability. It also includes individuals who do not have a disability but are regarded as having a disability. The ADA also makes it unlawful to discriminate against a person based on that person's association with a person with a disability." See https://adata .org/faq/what-definition-disability-under-ada.

38. The accessibility standards, called the 2010 Standards for Accessible Design (the 2010 Standards), establish minimum criteria for accessibility in design and construction. See ADA, https://www .ada.gov/2010ADAstandards_index.htm.

39. Sina Bahram, "Make Your Website Accessible Before You Are Forced To: An Inclusive Design Approach Avoids Costly Legal Issues and Reaches New Visitors," *Museum*, July/August 2016: 17–18. On inclusive design, see Inclusive Design Research Centre, Ontario College of Art & Design University, "What Is Inclusive Design?" http://idrc.ocadu.ca/index.php/about-the-idrc/49-resources/online -resources/articles-and-papers/443.

40. John Beetlestone, Colin H. Johnson, Melanie Quin, and Harry White, "The Science Center Movement: Contexts, Practice, Next Challenges," *Public Understanding of Science* 7, no. 1 (January 1998): 5–26; Mary Alexander, "Do Visitors Get It? A Sweatshop Exhibit and Visitors' Comments," *Public Historian* 22, no. 3 (Summer 2000): 85–94; Stephen T. Asma, *Stuffed Animals and Pickled Heads: The Culture and Evolution of Natural History Museums* (Oxford: Oxford University Press, 2001), 234; Sharon Macdonald, "Accessing Audiences: Visiting Visitor Books," *Museum and Society* 3, no. 3 (November 2005): 119–36.

41. Victoria Newhouse identifies and discusses five core decisions for displaying art as "the length, texture, and color of walls, the choice of frames for paintings and pedestals for sculptures, how labeling is best handled, the space's scale, the quality of light, and how the works are placed in relation to each other." See Newhouse, *Art and the Power*, 214; Ned J. Burns, *National Park Service Field Manual for Museums* (Washington, D.C.: U.S. Government Printing Office, 1941), 72–78, 85–86; Asma, *Stuffed Animals and Pickled Heads*, 234–36.

42. American Museum of Natural History, "The Titanosaur," http://www.amnh.org/exhibitions/the -titanosaur/.

43. Liz Neely and Miriam Langer, "Please Feel the Museum: The Emergence of 3D Printing and Scanning," Museums and the Web 2013: Portland, OR, http://mw2013.museumsandtheweb.com/paper/ please-feel-the-museum-the-emergence-of-3d-printing-and-scanning/.

44. Menachem Wecker, "The Scandalous Story Behind the Provocative 19th-Century Sculpture *Greek Slave*, *Smithsonian*, July 4, 2015, http://www.smithsonianmag.com/smithsonian-institution/scandalous -story-behind-provocative-sculpture-greek-slave-19th-century-audiences-180956029. An interesting part of the exhibition, curated by Karen Lemmey, lies beyond the 3D printing and its ancillaries. The presence of a life cast of a forearm and hand matches the left arm and hand of *Greek Slave*, suggesting that Powers employed this method when working on the sculpture. While understood today as offering lifelikeness, life casts were considered a shortcut that enabled artists direct access to the body rather than forcing them to translate a subject (a body in life, in 3D) into a sketch and then into a 3D form again.

45. Full-scale groups are expensive and take up much exhibition space. Karen Wonders writes: "It was the scenic attraction of dioramas which led the American Museum of Natural History (AMNH)

to devote such a large percentage of the museum budget toward the creation of monumental diorama halls. As a result, during its diorama heyday, the AMNH had a larger exhibition staff than that of the Metropolitan Museum of Art, its sister institution across Central Park. In justifying this expenditure, the director of the American Museum of Natural History in 1937 is reported to have declared: 'They buy their art; we must *make* ours.'" Karen Wonders, *Habitat Dioramas: Illusions of Wilderness in Museums of Natural History* (Uppsala, Sweden: Acta Universitatis Upsaliensis, 1993), 76; Edward P. Alexander, "Carl Ethan Akeley" and "William Temple Hornaday," in *The Museum in America: Innovators and Pioneers* (Walnut Grove: AltaMira Press, 1997).

46. Loïc Tallon, "About that 1952 Sedelijk [*sic*] Museum Audio Guide, and a Certain Willem Sandburg," *Musematic*, May 19, 2009, http://musematic.net/2009/05/19/about-that-1952-sedelijk-museum-audio-guide-and-a-certain-willem-sandburg/.

47. The selected works include the bronze of Marcus Aurelius, Egyptian paintings on the coffin of Nesykhonsu, an Ejagham headdress, and a Byzantine processional cross. In the case of the cross, content on the audio guide focuses on the historical perspective of the art. In addition, "listeners will also learn how processional crosses are still used today. Both a former priest and parishioner from the Saints Constantine and Helen Greek Orthodox Cathedral in Cleveland provide perspectives on processional crosses and what they mean within the church." Cleveland Museum of Art, "Museum's Art Conversations Take Audio Tours to a New Level," July 13, 2010, https://www.clevelandart.org/blog/2010/07/13/museum%E2%80%99s-art-conversations-takes-audio-tours-a-new-level.

48. *BYOD* was coined in 2009 by tech company Intel in reference to bringing one's own device to work. See James Gardner, "Everything You Need to Know About BYOD," *iMeetCentral by PGI*, March 13, 2013, https://imeetcentral.com/everything-you-need-to-know-about-byod. The term has migrated to education, where students bring whatever device they have to class to use as an educational tool.

49. Christopher Moore, "5 Reasons Why You Should Download the CMA Mughal App," Cleveland Museum of Art Blog, July 20, 2016. The app also features an list of related events and gallery tours as well as museum information. Interestingly, the museum news listing about the app includes a reference to its staying power, beyond the exhibition; "The Cleveland Museum of Art's CMA Mughal app will be available throughout the exhibition Art and Stories from Mughal India, which runs July 31 to October 23, 2016, and beyond."

50. The languages are: English, Spanish, Portuguese, French, Italian, Japanese, Chinese, Korean, German, and Russian. The Met, "Audio Guide," http://www.metmuseum.org/visit/audio-guide.

51. Smithsonian Institution, NMAAHC App, https://itunes.apple.com/us/app/view-nmaahc/id626274903?mt=8.

52. Tom Klobe, *Exhibitions: Concept, Planning and Design* (Washington, D.C.: The AAM Press, 2012).

53. Beverly Serrell, *Exhibit Labels: An Interpretive Approach*, 2nd edition (Lanham, MD: Rowman & Littlefield, 2015), 2. Serrell identifies "ten commandments" of label writing, while Bitgood points to sixteen empirical factors that influence label reading. (As this book was going to press, the new edition was published. See Beverly Serrell and Katherine Whitney, *Exhibit Labels: An Interpretive Approach,* 3rd edition [Lanham: Rowman & Littlefield, 2024].) Also see Stephen Bitgood, "Deadly Sins Revisited: A Review of the Exhibit Label Literature," *Visitor Studies*, Fall 1989 (IV:3): 4–11. Diane F. Cohen, "Words to Live By," *Museum News* 69, no. 3 (May–June 1990); Nancy Tieken, "Take a Long Look," *Museum News* 70, no. 3, 70–72; George Weiner, "Why Johnny Can't Read Labels," *Curator* 6 (1963): 143–56; Don W. Wilson and Dennis Medina, "Exhibit Labels: A Consideration of Content," *History News* 27 (April 1972): technical leaflet no. 60; Ralph H. Lewis, *Manual for Museums* (Washington, D.C.: National Park Service/U.S. Government Printing Office, 1976), 26–27, 121–23, 312–14; William Hayett, *Display and Exhibit Handbook* (New York: Reinhold, 1967), 45–58; P. R. Adams, "The Exhibition," in *The Organization of Museums*, United Nations Educational, Scientific and Cultural Organization, 129–30; James H. Carmel, *Exhibition Techniques, Traveling and Temporary* (New York: Reinhold, 1962), 101–109; Jean Gabus, "Aesthetic Principles of Educational Exhibitions," *Museum* 18 (1965): 16–23; James Gardner and Caroline Heller, *Exhibition and Display* (New York: F.W. Dodge, 1960), 104–11; Neal, *Help!*

54. Beverly Serrell, *Exhibit Labels: An Interpretive Approach*, 2nd edition (Lanham, MD: Rowman & Littlefield, 2015), 178, 190.

55. Minda Borun and Katherine Adams, "From Hands On to Minds On: Labeling Interactive Exhibits," in *Visitor Studies: Theory, Research, and Practice, Volume 4*, edited by Arlene Benefield, Stephen Bitgod, and Harris Shettel (Jacksonville: Center for Social Design, 1992), 115–120.

56. Goode, *Smithsonian Annual Report*, 1895.

57. The Little Free Library project is coordinated by a nonprofit organization whose tag line is "Take a Book. Share a Book." https://littlefreelibrary.org/.

58. Fralin Museum of Art, "The Little Museum of Art," https://uvafralinartmuseum.virginia.edu/program/little-museum-art. The earliest iteration of this museum concept had an open top.

8

To Interpret

For the purposes of this discussion, *museum interpretation* encompasses how museums communicate their message(s) to the public. Interpretation ranges from onsite and online exhibitions to tours and programs, and its chief modality is storytelling. As curator Adina Langer has noted, storytelling "removes limitations caused by rigid assumptions" and erases the invisible barriers that elicit a sense of unbelonging, lack of confidence, or exclusion.[1] Storytelling, as a medium, method, and practice, frees museums. It is a museum's superpower.

The backbone of storytelling in museums can be objects. Through collecting, conserving, or exhibiting objects, museums make judgments, ascribing importance to the objects and the very institutions that contain them. In a sense, museum interpretation is the multilayered process of museums crafting messages—intended and inadvertent—and sharing these with the public. Whether neatly nestled in securely sealed cases or unabashedly advertising senses of smell and sight, objects are the visual cues that can engage visitors in a triangulation between museum, visitor, and object. Thus, visitor engagement is the dialogic process of receiving these messages and responding to them, as well as contributing to their construction. A third word, *immersion*, as in an "immersive exhibit," reflects an additional level of interaction between a visitor and the museum space, collections, or community within their contexts. Or, put another way, think of engagement and immersion as two interrelated processes where museums and visitors contribute to multilayered conversations.

This chapter and Chapter 9 ("To Engage") discuss elements of museum interpretation and facets of engagement. They, along with the final chapter in this section (Chapter 10, "To Serve"), offer an evolving picture of the work of museums through the lenses of interpretation, engagement, and action, historically and today. The emphases here are contemporary ways of understanding museum functions. To begin, though, we will consider the emergence of the term *interpretation in museums* and informal learning settings.

Interpretation Defined

Historian Freeman Tilden defined *interpretation* for the National Park Service in *Interpreting Our Heritage* (1957), a work that remains an important reference for museum staffs and public historians. His six principles provide important guidance for museum practice.[2] Twenty years later, Edward Alexander expanded Tilden's framing and posited that good interpretation contains five basic elements.[3] Whereas Tilden saw interpretation as a means of provocation, which, in turn, led to resource protection, Alexander emphasized interpretation's capacity, as informal education, to incite curiosity through the use of object-based inquiry and sensory perception as part of the learning process. Building upon such work and combining the frames of education and interpretation, the American Alliance of Museums has identified eight standards of education and interpretation for museums. Their list offers characteristics, rather than explicit instructions, on how to approach education and interpretation. Significantly, however, AAM's guidance offers observations on sticky points in terms of diversity of audience and evaluation. For instance, in cases where museums were founded to serve specific interests of a narrowly defined community, some audiences could be excluded—intentionally or not. Using the examples of culture (Swedish Americans), interests (aviation enthusiasts), or genealogy (Daughters of the American Revolution), the AAM standards recognize that museums can identify their own mission and audience. But could museums not serve the broad public, if this audience is too narrowly defined? Moreover, the public, as a whole, supports museums through their tax-exempt status, thus begging the question of whom museums are for. Related, AAM suggests a "systematic, formal, ongoing program of evaluation for exhibits, programs and other interpretive activities, and to use the results of this evaluation to guide improvements."[4] (See Table 8.1.)

In addition to these frameworks for understanding what interpretation is, a rich body of literature, sound advice from professionals working in the field, and current practices are the best resources. Numerous examples provide site-and-content specific guidance on interpretation. For instance, Ken Ames, in *Ideas and Images: Developing Interpretive History Exhibits*, provides eleven guidelines for excellent museum exhibitions. Though written for history museums, they apply to museum exhibitions in any discipline.[5] Ames points out the importance of interpretation; a clear sense of purpose; a reflection of the strength of the museum (whether collections, location, intellectual rigor); understanding of the audience; and evaluation.

An entire book series—INTERPRETING HISTORY—developed by the American Association for State and Local History, offers timely, well-crafted guidance for museums and other cultural heritage institutions. The volumes offer historical scholarship on the topic at hand, while also offering real-world examples of museums and sites that have successfully implemented interpretation of the theme. Notable among the series are Susan Ferentinos's *Interpreting LGBT History at Museums and Historic Sites* and Julia Rose's *Interpreting Difficult History at Museums and Historic Sites.* Others address the untapped potential of museums and historic sites to interpret science, sports, energy, and the environment.[6]

In addition, convenings of scholars and practitioners have helped to reframe interpretation, as in the case of the working group organized by National Council on Public History (NCPH) members in 2019 that focused on a reconsideration of Freeman Tilden's *Interpreting Our Heritage.* Coordinated by Allison Horrocks and Nick Sacco of the National Park Service, the NCPH working group considered Tilden's interpretation principles and thoughtfully considered how they might be revised to meet the needs of twenty-first-century audiences. As part of their exploration, which they called "Interpreting Our Heritage," the working group, and truly all cultural heritage workers who engage directly with the public, desire to promote "inclusive, equitable, and accurate representations of the past."[7]

At odds with this vision are Tilden's language and framing, embedded in the text passages not quoted above. These include passages that refer superficially to visitors as "happy," "wonderfully well-mannered," and "little people" who are seemingly unknowledgeable, empty vessels. The principles were issued in 1957—during the Cold War and in a period of extreme growth in the National Park System with increases in visitation post–World War II. Tilden was also on the cusp of the ten-year program (Mission 66), which expanded visitor services at National Park Service sites. Infrastructure was an important part of that initiative, so that roads, utilities, and amenities could lead visitors to visitor centers chock-full of interpretation. As the first point of contact between visitors and the site, the interpretation at visitor centers and throughout sites on the property became critically important. Tilden responded by narrating a path and practice for the NPS.

While it is easy to be turned off by the language surrounding the principles, they still have merit, for they open up *the possibilities of provocation.* As Horrocks observes, the word *dialogue* never appears in Tilden, though we almost cannot imagine a museum experience *without dialogue.* Further, Hannah Howard articulates that interpretation should be informed by the "communities likely to be most impacted or affected by the interpretation itself." Clearly Tilden got us started with interpretation, but we are now moving beyond, with shared authority and dialogue woven together with the visitor experience. Sara Patton Zarrelli stands on Tilden's shoulder to define twenty-first-century interpretation as "a focus on inclusive presentations that includes multiple perspectives, particularly those previously marginalized, and uses techniques that require participation through demonstration, dialog, or audience generated content to connect the program to current issues. 21st Century Interpretation also places an emphasis on self-mediated experiences and there is a strong focus on getting young people and individuals of diverse cultural and economic backgrounds to historic sites/parks."[8]

Interpretation through Education and Learning

As we have seen throughout the chapters that precede this one, education, information sharing, and the construction of knowledge have been at the forefront of museum practices. They are the building blocks of interpretation. In addition to the work of scholars and historians (Tilden and Alexander), reports and policies bear witness to this association between museums and education. For instance, the *Belmont Report*, commissioned by President Lyndon Johnson and issued in 1969, defined the role of U.S. museums as fundamental educational institutions, complementing libraries and public schools.[9] This formal governmental recognition of museums as educational institutions became a catalyst for innovation in museum interpretation and educational programming, supported by federal education funding and funding from the National Endowments for Arts and Humanities.[10] Twenty years after the *Belmont Report*, the American Association of Museums (AAM) convened a task force on museum education and issued a report calling attention to the need for museums to address interpretation in forthright ways to meet the needs of their diverse audiences. Two elements of that report, *Excellence and Equity: Education and the Public Dimension of Museums* (1992), warrant inclusion here. Just as Tilden and Alexander codified interpretive principles, AAM's task force listed six recommendations relating to what they defined as "learning." These recommendations offer a more institutional framework, reflecting the changing emphasis of U.S. museums from temples to forums; from storehouses to educational centers; from mausoleums to makerspaces.[11] (See Table 8.1.)

In addition to these specific recommendations for excellence in museum practice, the report broadens museum responsibilities to the public, using the very terms of the museum definition adopted by the International Council of Museums (ICOM) in 1995. "*Excellence and Equity* is based on the expanded notion of *public service* and education as a museum-wide endeavor that involves trustee, staff, and volunteer values and attitudes; exhibitions; public and school programs; publications; public relations efforts; research; decisions about the physical environment of the museum; and choices about collecting and preserving. These elements are among the many that shape the educational messages museums convey to the public."[12] While the definition of a museum has changed considerably since then, the broadened commitment to the public underscores the importance of museums to their audiences, in terms of learning and engagement through interpretation—and so much more.

Understanding Learning in Museums

In the United States, as early as the 1920s, museums were seeking to understand both their potential and impact on visitors or learners.[13] AAM's work with Arthur Melton and Edward Robinson in the 1930s elevated the importance of understanding the experiences of visitors in museum galleries.[14] The open education movement of the 1960s attracted museums as educational players. Harvard educator Howard Gardner's catalog of ways of learning, published in 1983, inspired museum educators and provided intellectual support for their efforts to advance the role of learning in the museum setting.[15] Add to this rich intellectual climate in the United States the attention and potential funding from the National Endowments for the Arts and Humanities and federal educational agencies, and educational initiatives within museums were nearly irresistible.[16] Both the rationale and the resources merged.

In the early 1970s in the United States, museums were extending their educational offerings especially for school-age children. Museums offered to supplement classroom education, partnering with the school systems to fully integrate the classroom and museum experiences.[17] Teachers joined the growing ranks of educational staff in museums to create dynamic programs for students. Within

U.S. public education, social studies reforms that emphasized "inquiry" learning and national science curricula that engaged students in hands-on experiments further stimulated museum programs. A national research project into U.S. art museums' educational offerings during the 1973–1974 academic year resulted in a telephone directory–sized report describing and analyzing more than one hundred projects.[18] Regardless of a museum's subject matter, educational offerings had become expected, and *The Art Museum as Educator* chronicled their impressive variety.

Within this rich milieu of educational programs for school students, U.S. museums also pursued innovative adult programs as well.[19] Museums across the disciplines offer hands-on activities, lessons based on historical documents and objects, and experiments in basic scientific laws. Museum learning is no longer limited to didactic exhibitions with complementary lectures and demonstrations. Educational thinkers have stimulated a greater variety in learning opportunities within (and beyond) the museum. Museum educators read and adapted to museum programs the ideas and philosophies of writers Benjamin Bloom, Jerome Bruner, Howard Gardner, Jean Piaget, Mihaly Csikszentmihalyi, and Lev Vygotsky. Today, museum education programs run the gamut from structured, docent-led tours and engagement with historical interpreters to environments where students of all ages pursue their own interests with museum staff (or peer) guidance and maker spaces where exploration and hands-on learning are encouraged. In *Learning in the Museum*, George Hein summarizes what researchers know about learning in museums. He concludes that people learn in museums and museums must allow visitors to "connect what they see, do and feel with what they already know, understand, and acknowledge." Museums ought to aspire to be, thus, "Constructivist Museums"—where knowledge is constructed in the mind of the learner; where learning is made active and engages the visitor; and where the opportunity for learning is made *physically, socially, and intellectually* accessible to the visitor.[20] More recently, the Association for Art Museum Interpretation (AAMI) has outlined five core principles of interpretation that synthesize previous approaches into a tightly woven matrix of accessible and inclusive strategies for online, onsite, and offsite experiences that invite visitors "to shift previously held views and expectations through intentional, respectful, and often playful provocation."[21] While these principles were authored for art interpretation, they are accessible and applicable for all types of museums and deserve close study. (See Table 8.1)

Museums have absorbed and modified the tradition of displaying objects in a rational order—sometimes with explanatory labels and sometimes without—to extend the idea of a museum as a learning lab where visitors become engaged with settings, objects, ideas, performances, conversations, and as a whole, with experiences. They are an integral part of the "learning ecosystem" as defined in a recent report from the Center for the Future of Museums (2014), in which a call was made for museums and schools to collaborate to create a new future for education by investing in the capacity to manage partnerships; by strengthening family engagement; by building learning networks across community institutions; and by leveraging digital learning and collaborative technology.[22] Put simply, museums are a pathway for learning and engagement where visitors anywhere can connect with the larger world—through the collections on view or by interaction with other visitors who are onsite or online.

Interpretive Planning

Interpretation, as a principle and practice, succeeds best when part of an overall plan rather than undertaken as discrete messages disconnected from one another and tethered only to objects in a museum. This process of weaving together narrative threads across multiple objects, an entire exhibition, several galleries, and an entire institution is referred to as *interpretive planning*. Informed by Tilden's and Alexander's principles, as well as re-envisioning of them, interpretive planning in the twenty-first century is used to communicate information but also holds space to allow for self-exploration, discovery, and co-creation on the part of the visitor, while also engendering opportunities for reflection by museum staff as well as visitors.

Table 8.1. Some Approaches to Interpretation, Education, and Learning in Museums, 1957–Present

Author	Focus	Principles of Interpretation, Education, or Learning (see sources)
Freeman Tilden, 1957[1]	Interpretation	Any interpretation that does not somehow relate what is being displayed or described to something within the personality or experience of the visitor will be sterile. Information, as such, is not interpretation. Interpretation is revelation based upon information. But they are entirely different things. However, all interpretation includes information. Interpretation is an art, which combines many arts, whether the materials presented are scientific, historical, or architectural. The chief aim of interpretation is not instruction, but provocation. Interpretation should aim to present a whole rather than a part and must address itself to the whole person rather than any phase. Interpretation addressed to children should not be a dilution of the presentation to adults, but it should follow a fundamentally different approach.
E.P. Alexander, 1977[2]	Interpretation	It seeks to teach certain truths, to reveal meanings, to impart understanding. Thus, it has serious educational purpose. It is based on objects, whether animate or inanimate; natural or man-made; aesthetic, historical, or scientific. It is supported by sound scientific or historical research that examines each museum object, undergirds every program, analyzes the museum's audience, and evaluates its methods of presentation so as to secure more effective communication. It makes use, wherever possible, of sensory perception—sight, hearing, smell, taste, touch, and the kinetic muscle sense. The sensory approach, with its emotional overtones, should supplement but not replace the customary rational avenue to understanding provided by words and verbalization; together they constitute a powerful learning process. It is informal education without the trappings of the classroom, is voluntary and dependent only on the interest of the viewer. It may furnish one with strong motivation to read further, to visit other places, and to seek other ways of satisfying one's newly aroused curiosities.
AAM, 1992[3]	Education	Develop and expand audience research methods that will test and document how people learn in the museum environment. Apply the findings to exhibitions and program development.

(continued)

Table 8.1.   (continued)

Author	Focus	Principles of Interpretation, Education, or Learning (see sources)
		Develop educational experiences for schoolchildren, families, and adults that reflect a knowledge of the different learning styles visitors bring to museums.
		Experiment with exhibition and program strategies and innovative technologies to enhance the capacity of museums to reach a wider audience through exhibitions and programs.
		Assess the effectiveness of exhibitions and programs in an ongoing evaluation process that encourages revision and experimentation to improve the visitor's experience of learning from objects and exhibits.
		Utilize the growing potential for extending the educational role of museums beyond their walls through electronic media, and conduct systematic studies to assess the effectiveness of these resources.
		Establish "learning laboratories" in selected museums for research, experimentation, and dissemination of information about exhibitions and program development, implementation, and evaluation as well as about the special nature of museum learning and museum audiences.
Hein, 1998[4]	Learning	People "learn" in museums. Whether learning is narrowly defined as absorbing specific pedagogic messages contained in exhibits or more broadly defined to include responding to the experience of a museum visit, there can be no doubt that visitors "learn" in museums. People have enriching, stimulating, rewarding, or restorative experiences in museums. They learn about themselves, the world, and specific concepts; they have aesthetic, spiritual, and "flow" experiences.
		In order to maximize their potential to be educative, museums need first to attend to visitors' practical needs; degree of comfort influences the value of the museum experience. Comfort includes orientation, providing amenities, making the museum's agenda clear, and always maximizing the possibility that the intended interactions between the content of the museum and the visitor be as positive as possible.
		People do attend to exhibits—they incorporate the content of museums into the agendas they bring with them, and their social interactions, attention, fantasies, and feelings include, and often focus on, the content of museums.
		People make unique, startling connections in museums.

Table 8.1. *(continued)*

Author	Focus	*Principles of Interpretation, Education, or Learning (see sources)*
		Museums are not efficient places for traditional "school" education, learning specific facts and concepts, because people don't spend enough time and are not there primarily for that purpose.
		Staff should never underestimate the value of wonder; exploration; expanding the mind; and providing new, cognitively dissonant (intellectually shocking), and aesthetic experiences. Museums can do this well, and these are an integral part of "learning."
		For visitors to have a positive experience, their interaction with the contents of the museum must allow them to connect what they see, do, and feel with what they already know, understand, and acknowledge. The new must be able to be incorporated into the old.
		This connection between what visitors bring with them and new experiences is crucial and must be negotiated by each individual whenever new experiences are encountered.
AAM, 2008[5]	Education and Interpretation	The museum clearly states its overall educational goals, philosophy, and messages, and it demonstrates that its activities are in alignment with them.
		The museum understands the characteristics and needs of its existing and potential audiences and uses this understanding to inform its interpretation.
		The museum's interpretive content is based on appropriate research.
		Museums conducting primary research do so according to scholarly standards.
		The museum uses techniques, technologies, and methods appropriate to its educational goals, content, audiences, and resources.
		The museum presents accurate and appropriate content for each of its audiences.
		The museum demonstrates consistently high quality in its interpretive activities.
		The museum assesses the effectiveness of its interpretive activities and uses those results to plan and improve its activities.
AAMI, 2013[6]	Interpretation	Creates multiple pathways for understanding by creating an experience that equally values the visitor, the art object, and the organization's mission.
		Encourages audiences of varying backgrounds, knowledge levels, and learning styles to make relevant connections between art, ideas, and their lived experience.

(continued)

Table 8.1.　(continued)

Author	Focus	Principles of Interpretation, Education, or Learning (see sources)
		Practices socially, intellectually, and physically accessible and inclusive interpretive strategies onsite, offsite, and online.
		Creates learning opportunities that invite visitors to shift previously held views and expectations through intentional, respectful, and often playful provocation.
		Utilizes collaboration, curiosity-driven experimentation, rigorous evaluation, reflection, and skill-building to create meaningful interpretive experiences.

1. Freeman Tilden, *Interpreting Our Heritage* (Chapel Hill: University of North Carolina Press, 1957). Tilden uses the term "man" in principle #5 which has been changed to "person" in this table.
2. Edward P. Alexander, "What Is Interpretation?" *Longwood Program Seminars* 9 (1977): 2–7; "The Interpretation Program of Colonial Williamsburg," 11–12.
3. AAM, *Excellence and Equity: Education and the Public Dimension of Museums* (Washington, D.C.: American Association of Museums, 1992), 17.
4. George E. Hein, *Learning in the Museum* (London: Taylor and Francis, 1998), 54–55.
5. AAM, "Education and Interpretation," in *Standards and Best Practices* (Washington, D.C.: AAM Press, 2008), 59.
6. Association for Art Museum Interpretation, "Art Museum Interpretation," n.d. https://artmuseuminterp .org/about/principles/. The group was formed in 2013. The principles in the chart are value statements that drive their work, as well as demonstrate applicability beyond art museums.

Table prepared by author and extracted from resources cited in the Notes.

Interpretive planning involves developing, organizing, and analyzing content into relevant and engaging messages communicated through storytelling in various modalities—be that exhibition label copy, historical interpretation, guided museum tours, or digital ancillaries. Interpretive planning also requires planning and design beyond the scope of individual exhibitions, and it seeps beyond exhibition development into fundraising, strategic planning, mission definition, and visioning. All these facets contribute to the visitor experience of the featured content.

Interpretation, as one result of interpretive planning, thus, ultimately coalesces around the visitor's experience at the museum. Each party has respective goals: the museum has an interpretive plan that guides it and communicates information to the audience, while the visitor has needs that that he or she seeks to meet by coming to this institution on this day and for this reason.

The Museum Experience

Visitors to museums benefit from an overview of the institution before they start their visits, whether the museum is a large public building or a simple domestic row house. If they understand the nature of the collections, their arrangement, and the setting, they may make choices about what they wish to see and know how to find their way. More and more visitors are using the internet, social media, and exhibition-specific apps to organize their visit. Such resources offer the prospective visitor information on exhibitions and programming along with the important details of travel directions, parking, fees, and museum services. Onsite visitor orientation can be achieved in many ways: a friendly face at the entry or ticket kiosk; a multimedia presentation; or a printed map.

Visitor Experience Opportunities

Visitors may encounter presentations in the museum galleries that add both information and context to the exhibitions. Hands-on desks, art carts, and other opportunities for sounds, smells, and other means to touch reproduction objects and ask questions may engage the visitor in valuable ways to enhance his or her experience. After addressing public programs and historical interpretation, this section looks at virtual reality and augmented reality, briefly, as they will be more fully addressed in the following chapter.

The Tour

Museum tours may be divided into three chief classes—self-guided, in-person, and tech-assisted. The first can be unique and self-defined; the second can be organized by the museum and administered by its staff or volunteers, though as we will see, that needn't be the case. The third is administered by the museum but may be created by a third party. Each of these modes of interpretation can enable visitors to learn new information in ways that appeal to them.

Self-Guided Tours

In the first category, visitors make their way about the museum at their own pace. Printed materials may aid visitors, including a guidebook or a handout that details the museum layout and describes the scope and content of the collections.

In-Person Tours

Personally conducted tours add a valuable human dimension to interpretation and can extend the length of a museum visit.[23] Paid staff members or volunteers, often known as docents, may provide such tours to visitors. What has been viewed akin to the "sage on the stage" approach, guided tours are, in fact, now seen quite differently. Keenly, they provide space. According to museum educator Sharon Vatsky, in-person, guided tours are important to the museum experience, as they have the potential to meet many of the expectations of visitors, including opportunities to "slow down, focus, learn, and most of all, connect with others."[24]

Of particular mention is the new variety of tour promoted by Museum Hack. Based in New York and founded by entrepreneur Nick Gray, the non-traditional museum tour company Museum Hack markets itself as offering experiences at museums in New York City; Washington, D.C.; San Francisco; Los Angeles; and Chicago that are an alternative spin to the traditional tour and customized based on those in the group. Claiming that their tours are "F***ing Awesome," the organization offers "a smart, fun, renegade way to experience museums." The framing is around the less-often-presented, particularized views that resonate with younger audiences and are also smart, fun, and renegade in some way. Their presentation has shifted since their emergence on the museum scene more than a decade ago. They began, in 2011, as a mission of entrepreneur and museum enthusiast Gray, who took it upon himself to start leading museum tours that were against the grain. He called this project "Hack the Met," a way to center and appreciate art by wandering through collections with a new focus.[25] The tours sought to defy expectations of both the tour experience and museums, as institutions with promotions that claim "This Isn't Your Grandma's Museum Tour." Gray brought the idea into fuller view by hiring tour guides and a team of individuals to offer an "un-highlights" tour, as well as "badass bitches" and "big gay" tours as a way to "hack" the museum; hence the formation of the company, Museum Hack.

Catchy titles hook the visitor, while the tours unpack the delight as well as the politics of the museum landscape. For instance, the "Badass Bitches Tour of The Met" is premised upon the under-representation of women in the nation's museums. The tour enables participants to see art "by women who rock, [to] celebrate the accomplishments of modern and historical women, and [to] reveal what's goin' down today." The tour also extends the experience by sharing "actual steps to dismantle the patriarchy" and to empower participants to "leave inspired to change the world." The tour of the American Museum of Natural History offers "DINOSAURS! SCIENCE! ADVENTURE!" in the form of

Audio guides have been a part of the museum tour experience for decades. An early museum audio guide from around 1952 was developed to meet the needs of audiences at the Stedelijk Museum, Amsterdam, for the exhibition *Vermeer: Real or Fake*. Note the sleek design, which museum researcher Loïc Tallon refers to as having the similar appeal as a "1950s version of the iPod."
Photos by Loïc Tallon via Flickr, with publication permission from Loïc Tallon.

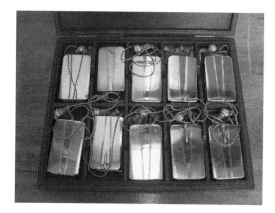

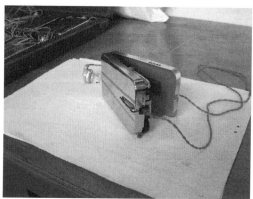
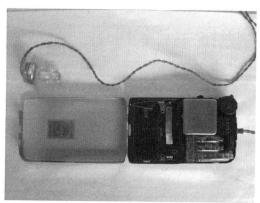

a "brazen expedition" through the halls of the museum with a "maverick tour guide" leading visitors through the "massive 27-building, 1.6 million square foot landmark cultural institution" to learn the science and history of the animals as well as the stories of the "badass adventurers that collected them, and the dirty little secrets that make AMNH like no other museum on earth!"[26] Guides of these tours are "smart, sassy, and fantastic" and know the museums "like the back of their hands," and they make the promise of being "the most fun you've ever had in a museum."[27] The tours are small—with no more than a dozen people—so that everyone can get to know one another, and so the tour can be customized based upon the audience and guide's passion and expertise. Museum Hack also positions an opportunity for thinking about museums as spaces and as institutions worthy of one's time, and a shared commitment to them. Their concept, now, centers museums as institutions. Their offerings include focusing on museums and their collections; curated, themed tours around women or "boy wizards"; and team-building activities that can be sited at museums. In short, they call upon their visitorship to praise and support museums: "When We Believe Museums Are F***ing Awesome. When you stand in a museum, you are literally amongst the greatest collections humanity has created and discovered in our entire existence as a species. Come stand with us, and we'll show you why museums are the greatest institutions on Earth."[28]

Audio guides appeared in U.S. museums by the 1960s, as seen here. The Metropolitan Museum of Art, Acoustiguide counter, *The Great Age of Fresco: Giotto to Pontormo*, September 28–November 15, 1968. *Photo Credit: Image copyright © The Metropolitan Museum of Art. Image source: Art Resource,* NY.

Tech-Assisted Tours

The third category of tour, tech-assisted, may be done on one's own, in a group, or with the aid of a docent. What differentiates it from the other two is the ability to navigate on one's own while also being aware of a prescriptive path. In other words, the tech-assisted tour is similar to a car navigation system in that it offers support, information, and context when needed, but it can also exist without being used. Interesting developments are occurring in this area of interpretation and thus deserve further mention.

As noted earlier (see Chapter 7), tech-assisted tours have existed for more than sixty years. The beauty of these assets is that they may offer multiple levels of information, from basic object identification to interpretation of such details as the object's origins or historical, artistic, or scientific context; period music, to add another sensory element to the experience of viewing; interviews with the creators or other recorded conversations about the objects and their potential meaning; or 3D scans of objects and augmented and virtual reality layers to enable understanding of the object's dimensions and capabilities.[29] Moreover, such digital ancillaries present a range of interpretive material that can be catered to a visitor's interest or to a visitor's preference for breath and depth of knowledge (whether granular or focusing on the "big idea"). Some apps, like ASK Brooklyn Museum, offer a blended approach between the self-guided tour and the docent-visitor dialogue by providing real-time access to staff of the museum to address questions that might go unanswered otherwise ("How should I spend my day at the museum?"). Because this app is very much about having an experience *with art at the Brooklyn Museum*, it works inside the museum only. Apps also offer opportunities to see the museum through another's eyes. Launched in 2016, a new app from SFMOMA (San Francisco Museum of Modern Art) offers "art walks" with the goal of offering voices that reflect the different relationships visitors have with art. Such voices include writer/filmmaker Errol Morris; *99% Invisible*, a web-based show about the overlooked aspects of our designed environment; and social scientist and executive director for Institute for the Future (IFTF) Marina Gorbis; as well as curators. Location-based, the app pushes relevant content to the visitor as he or she encounters a work, rather than requiring persistent entry. The innovation in SFMOMA's app is twofold: using location-sensing technology to identify a visitor's position in the museum, in combination with range-of-tour (or, rather "art walk") possibilities that provide a prismatic approach to the collections—involving the multiplicity of perspectives that are the hallmark of shared authority.

Public Programs

Exhibitions may be brought to life through traditional forms of museum interpretation, such as the lecture and its variations, film screenings, field trips, or special events for affinity groups. Such lectures and programs also may be taken outside the museum walls to other venues or through the web to widen the audiences. To put it simply, the secrets of success of public programs—demonstrations, conferences, workshops, film series, artistic performances, musical events, and the like—demonstrate (1) imagination and thorough planning; (2) careful assessment of the audience's interests and needs; (3) efficient execution, with attention to detail; (4) friendly hospitality shown by all members of the museum staff; and (5) recirculation back into the community. If poorly planned, they may negatively affect the museum's reputation and impact its public support. However, when these events succeed, the museum acquires a following who understand one objective or program—or several of them—in considerable depth. They constitute the kind of preferred support every museum seeks and needs.[30] A casual glance throughout the pages of this volume gives evidence of many successful programs and opportunities for engagement fostered by museums throughout the United States today.

Historical Interpretation

Museum interpretation can be enhanced by actors demonstrating industrial practices, or guiding visitors through the creative process for an artwork. For example, a demonstration of the manufacture of cloth with its carding, spinning, and weaving done by hand or by early machines can be far more enlightening and exciting than a label with illustrations of the process. In the botanical garden, cultivating, harvesting, potting, pruning, and plant-propagating techniques arouse great interest in visitors when they are acted out by live persons.[31]

All these activities involve a high degree of visitor participation, either psychological or actual. They better explain processes; they combine sensory perception with rational analysis; they dramatize collections of objects; and they include the visitor in meaning-making. A basic underlying challenge is that of authenticity. Even if the equipment, processes, and costumes are thoroughly researched, is the demonstrated craft over-romanticized? Are the early industrial demonstrations too neat and clean? Is the tyranny of the machine understood, and what of the social evils of the labor of women and children? In addition, each of these demonstrations or presentations only approaches true authenticity.

Another process of interpretation especially popular in outdoor history museums is that of role-playing by museum staff. Here the interpreter tries to learn everything possible about the historical period and to conduct him or herself as if living then; the interpretation is normally given in the first person. Meanwhile, each one talks with visitors about daily life and chores. This interpretation sometimes involves the visitors and may extend to "live-in" situations where students don period costumes, occupy a historic house or shop, and participate in activities, such as cooking or crafts.

First-person interpretation has an immediacy that makes it appealing to museum visitors. Each of these "dramatic" forms can engage the visitor in very personal ways, placing historical and contemporary issues in a personal setting. For instance, Plimoth Patuxet (Massachusetts) has re-created the seventeenth-century English Village and the Wampanoag Homesite and inhabited these with staff representing historical figures. While the English village is interpreted to the year 1627 and populated with historical interpreters who are role playing, the Homesite is interpreted to the seventeenth century and staffed with modern-day Indigenous people from Wampanoag and other Native Nations. As visitors encounter these "residents" going about their daily chores and livelihood, they can ask questions of their lives and aspirations and learn something of the seventeenth-century worldview. But they are unaware of modern conveniences and contexts (such as the location of the nearest bathroom).[32] The major challenges of these forms lie in the preparatory research, the necessity to "limit" the dramatic license of the actors, and the ability to locate individuals to fill the positions.

Crossover Experiences

Consider the ways in which contexts outside of the museum impact the museum. For instance, after Ken Burns's television documentary *The Civil War* appeared on public television in the early 1990s, attendance at related historic sites dramatically increased. A more informed public arrived at these sites to see for themselves what was represented in Burns's films. Another example of recirculation is visible in recent theater successes and their translation into historic site visits, curation of museum exhibitions, and development of programming. The hit musical *Hamilton*, written by Lin-Manuel Miranda and inspired by the 2004 biography written by Ron Chernow, focuses on the life of Alexander Hamilton, statesman and founding father of the United States. The show debuted in 2015 and has spawned a second resident production in Chicago (2016), a national tour (2017), and a London debut (2017). In speaking of the actors in the play, Miranda noted, "We're telling the story of old, dead white men, but we're using actors of color, and that makes the story more immediate and more accessible to a contemporary audience."[33] And accessible it is—so much so that the "Hamilton Effect" has caused visits to the politician's home to increase by 70 percent in the past year, as have visits to his grave and sites where he lived and worked.[34] In addition, the exhibition *Summer of Hamilton* debuted at the New-York Historical Society in the summer of 2016, featuring works that were displayed in the lobby of the Public Theater when it hosted Lin-Manuel Miranda's musical; Hamilton's writing desk; key documents from his life; and other materials. In addition, professional development opportunities were offered to teachers looking to capitalize on the experience; teachers of social studies classes can enroll at the museum to learn more about Hamilton and the craze surrounding him now—just as it did two hundred years ago. Summer camps and Hamilton-themed parties were also part of the museum's catering to the Hamilton obsession. While having an exhibition on a statesman who lived in the area would not be unusual for the New-York Historical Society, the last one was mounted just over a decade ago—fairly recently, given the scope and content of the museum's collections.[35]

Other examples include the attention paid to the lives of domestic servants and those they serve, coming as a result of the success of the Edwardian-set historical drama *Downton Abbey*. Glensheen Historic Estate, a thirty-nine-room mansion on Lake Superior, has built upon this popularity by developing a "Servants' Tour" focusing on the lives of those who worked at the estate and the spaces they inhabited and knew intimately through that work. Likewise, the Biltmore has developed a "Butler's Tour" as well as an "Upstairs-Downstairs Tour," as has the Richard M. Driehaus Museum in Chicago. A traveling exhibition, *Dressing Downton: Changing Fashion for Changing Times*, has been on view throughout the United States and has drawn visitors to museums that might have gone unnoticed. For instance, at the Driehaus Museum in Chicago, attendance at the exhibition (35,000) has matched its annual attendance (39,000), thus requiring the thirteen-year-old museum to reset an adjacent structure to serve purposes formerly not needed: a temporary gift shop headquarters, a sitting room to await exhibition entry, and a venue for a *Downton*-inspired afternoon tea service. In

Extended realities present opportunities for museums to engage with virtual and augmented worlds and to use these arenas as spaces for interpretation and engagement. In March 2021, visitors at Genesee Country Village & Museum experimented with an augmented reality web application that enabled them to enter an historic structure and, using the camera on their smartphones, to scan an object in the room and "unlock" an augmented reality experience featuring a virtual tour guide.
Photo credit: Koda Drake.

By using a personal device, visitors can trigger enhanced content not visible otherwise.
Photo credit: Koda Drake.

addition, the exhibition was extended twenty-one days (closing on May 29, 2016).[36] Thus, specific museum-centered media complement exhibits and even public programs, thereby extending their reach and expanding the limitations of object labels and casting the net of interpretation even wider.

Extended Reality Experiences

Scholars working across a number of fields (museum studies, computer science, art and design, engineering, and a range of humanities and social sciences) have examined how and why augmented, virtual, and mixed reality have been used in cultural heritage work (from museums, historic sites, and other collections-based institutions). Bekele et al. have identified purposes for their application and use, such as education, exhibition enhancement, exploration, reconstruction, and virtual museums. In these ways, user-centered presentation and access to information and content is important.[37]

The range of approaches encompassed in augmented, virtual, and mixed reality build upon the work of Paul Milgram et al. (1994) who proposed a "reality-virtuality continuum" that defined the range of experiences that could be based in purely virtual environments, purely real environments, or the range in between—whether mediated through a head-mounted device (such as Hololens or Oculus) or monitor-based displays. While their concerns are the technologies behind these mediums, their interest in classifying differences between and among them are useful when considering museum practices.[38] Their framing of how well the medium delivers the information to viewers is useful in terms of what museum visitors may be seeking in their own experiences: knowledge, authenticity, and presence. Ultimately, museum interpretation—whether crafted through analog or digital means—conveys information in a manner that is believable and includes the visitor in that experience.[39]

Moving from museum galleries to other worlds, extended realities are opportunities for museums to engage with virtual and augmented worlds and to use these arenas as spaces for interpretation and engagement. Put simply, virtual reality (VR) is an artificial computer simulation or re-creation. Visitors feel as though they are experiencing *that reality* firsthand. Augmented reality (AR) layers computer enhancements that become more interesting and meaningful through the ability to interact through the blending of digital components with the real world. Augmented reality and virtual reality hold promise for many areas of life, including cultural experiences and museums. Digital discovery zones and centers in museums have been appearing on the stage over the past two decades, with greater and greater capability as maker spaces, and even some with reality interfaces. For instance, at the British Museum, a virtual reality weekend was held in August 2015 to launch a trio of means to explore the British Museum's Bronze Age collections. Using the virtual reality headset devices, visitors could see 3D scans of objects and witness how they would have appeared in their original settings. Using tablets, a similar effect was waged. By stepping into a dome-like canopy, up to five individuals could see the world immersively. While clearly a means of visitor engagement, a key aspect of this project is the presentation of theories relating to the objects' use. Just as historical interpreters transport visitors to a certain moment in time, the VR devices, with the aid of sensory cues, such as birds tweeting or fire crackling, transport the visitor to a rural landscape around the year 3500 BCE. Set in time and given the context, the visitor then is equipped to explore how the objects may have been used in the past.[40] Unlike traditional exhibition development, however, the ancillaries here are nonlinear so that the visitor can interact with each of the items as many times as he/she wishes and may also move about freely.[41]

Taking VR in another direction entirely—as an access platform—in Brooklyn, a VR exhibition and museum was launched in 2015, the Digital Museum of Digital Art, or DiMoDA. The museum is modeled in 3D and accessible to visitors wearing Oculus Rift headsets to approach the museum and enter portals that allow access to the wings of the museum.[42] From the comfort of one's home, VR has become accessible through the Google Arts and Culture initiative. Here, viewers are offered the opportunity to climb inside a painting, for instance, leaving the gallery of Crystal Bridges Museum of American Art in Bentonville, Arkansas, to join nineteenth-century American landscape painter Thomas Cole and poet William Cullen Bryant, who are talking with one another on the edge of a rock in the peaceful Catskill Mountains. In this case, for instance, VR invites visitors to go places where the artist may never have dreamed of: beyond the frame, and *inside* the painting.[43]

Several other examples of tech-infused museum experiences are discussed in the following chapter. Before moving in that direction, let us return to museum and visitor goals. How do museums know if they are succeeding in meeting visitor goals through their interpretation and interpretive plan? To begin to unpack the answer to that question and to conclude this chapter, we will consider visitors by looking at the field of audience research before examining a framework defined as "visitor identity types" and concluding with new research about enhanced well-being.

Researching Audiences and Reaching Audiences

Visitor Studies

Early twentieth-century research studies of museums and their visitors focused on how visitors viewed exhibitions, establishing basic understandings of such things as traffic patterns (visitors turn right when entering a gallery) and label word limits (twenty-five words). As the variety of activities taking place within a museum's galleries (or on its website) has multiplied, museum professionals have become further engaged in knowing, understanding, and meeting the needs of their audiences while also realizing the benefits of communicating with, rather than to, them. A professional field of inquiry called "visitor studies" examines "human experiences within informal learning environments" by collecting and analyzing "information or data to inform decisions about interpretive exhibits and programs." Following strict standards and rigorous research methods of the social sciences, audience researchers, through their work, seek to improve the practices of learning in informal environments.[44] The field is related to a corollary, audience research that shares interests in visitor needs and expectations.

Whatever the term, studies focusing on the visitor experience yield information about the ways in which visitors are engaging with objects, content, interpretation, and programming. Such attention can be gauged onsite and online. Moving from the theory to specific types of evaluation, consider the following approach taken by the Indianapolis Museum of Art, one of the suite of museums known as Newfields in Indiana: "studies on visitor motivation and how people engage with different interpretation approaches to works of art, online visitor segmentation, exhibition and program evaluation, evaluation of interpretive materials, and usability testing." They employ the following methodologies: "comment cards, surveys, timing and tracking, qualitative interviews, and focus groups and visitor panels." In terms of understanding and building audiences, the museum conducts "visitor profile surveys, visitor experience surveys both in general and focusing on target audiences, non-visitor research, and prototype and design testing."[45] In addition to learning from peer institutions, professional networks, such as the Committee on Audience Research and Evaluation (CARE), an affiliate of the American Alliance of Museums, provide a forum for museum professionals and disseminate information about systematic research and evaluation pertaining to museum audiences.[46]

Visitor Identity Types

The interpretive experiences discussed above reflect a shift in museum emphasis from collections to audiences. In the 1980s, U.S. museum evaluators began to study the museum "experience" as a whole, rather than simply focusing on elements of the museum's interpretive offerings, especially specific exhibitions. These evaluations ranged from questionnaires for visitors to complete at the end of their visit to post-visit, face-to-face interviews. Just as with exhibitions, evaluators studied visitors both before and after their museum visits, sometimes using the marketing technique of "focus groups" to gauge visitors' expectations. In 1992, museum evaluators John Falk and Lynn Dierking proposed a way to consider museum experiences from the visitor's perspective rather than that of the museum. They suggested an "interactive experience model" overlapping three elements of a visitor's museum experience: the visitor's personal interests, the social dynamic of the visit, and the museum's physical setting. Building on Alma Wittlin's notion that the best museum exhibitions create dialogues with visitors rather than offering the curator's monologue, Falk and Dierking reflected on how museum visits are, by their very nature, complex events. They determined that visitors learn in different ways and interpret information through the lens of previous knowledge, experience, and beliefs. Further, Falk proposes that visitors arrive at museums, and other sites of cultural interaction, with one or more of the seven identity types: experience seekers; explorers; facilitators; hobbyists; rechargers; respectful pilgrims; and community seekers.[47] Experience seekers seek to mark off their lists of accomplishments, while explorers are driven by curiosity and a generalized interest in the museum or its collection. Facilitators focus on enabling others to engage in learning and interaction (this is a common role taken on by parents and teachers). Hobbyists, also called professionals, associate with the museum and its collection due to a passion or interest of their own. Rechargers see museums as spaces for satisfying emotional, mental, and physical needs through relaxation and the opportunity to "recharge" their batteries—literally and perhaps figuratively. Respectful pilgrims feel an obligation to honor the memory of those represented by the site, while community seekers feel a sense of connection to the museum through heritage, lineage, or other association. In identifying and defining these types, he posits that visitors seek to satisfy identity-related needs—information that museum professionals would be remiss to overlook. Moreover, such research complements the move toward expanding the narrative of each museum and recognizing that one message does not meet the needs of all audiences.

Table 8.2. Well-Being and Museums, Inspired by John H. Falk, 2022

WELL-BEING AND MUSEUMS, INSPIRED BY JOHN H. FALK, 2022

Personal Well-Being	Museums catalyze wonder, interest, and curiosity, all of which foster a sense of personal power and identity.
Intellectual Well-Being	Museums help people more clearly comprehend how their past understandings and activities connect, inspire awe and appreciation for the best of human and natural creation, and, under the best of circumstances, even serve as guides to a better, more informed and creative future.
Social Well-Being	Museums enhance many users' sense of belonging to family, group, and even community, and do so in ways that bestow the user with a high degree of status and respect.
Physical Well-Being	Museums are perceived as safe, healthy, and restorative environments that allow people to gather (physically or virtually), interact, explore, play, and enjoy without fear or anxiety.

Text quoted from John H. Falk, "Why Well-Being Is at the Heart of Museum Experiences," *Alliance Blog*, January 10, 2022, https://www.aam-us.org/2022/01/10/why-well-being-is-at-the-heart-of-museum-experiences/. Table created by author.

Enhanced Well-Being

Museum theorist and scholar of free-choice learning John H. Falk identifies benefits of museum visitation as centering on social well-being—above all else, even learning and identity-formation. In a 2022 blog post for the American Alliance of Museums, Falk stated, "For nearly half a century, I have been thinking and theorizing about museum experiences—why people use museums, what they do during those experiences, and what they take away, including the value they perceive they derive. . . . For much of my career I focused on learning, and more recently identity, but these days I have come to believe that there is an even more basic value that sits at the heart of the museum experience—enhanced well-being. . . . Rather than framing well-being in purely psychological terms, with the primary outcome being happiness or 'life satisfaction,' I argue that well-being is a basic biological process, a mechanism for achieving balance with one's world. In fact, the pursuit of well-being is at the core of what it means to be alive, and the pursuit of human-specific dimensions of well-being are at the heart of what it means to be human."[48] Falk goes on to point out that museums have a function to support well-being, as in the ways discussed in this volume. And, in particular, he asks museums to consider *in what form, in what ways,* and *to what degree* do museum experiences support well-being.

The four areas of well-being that Falk discuss in the post, and in the book from which it's drawn, are: personal, intellectual, social, and physical. To examine these in detail, Falk conducted a small pilot study with 350 museum visitors to six institutions (three in the United States, two in Canada, and one in Finland). Among these, he gathered data that showed that museum experiences at all of these institutions resulted in visitors indicating that these four areas of their well-being were enhanced over the days following their visit (or longer).[49] While not expressly stated in the framing of interpretation (by Tilden, Alexander, or the Association for Art Museum Interpretation), nor in the discussions of education and learning by AAM and Hein, enhanced well-being as an outcome and benefit of museum visitation would surely have pleased each of these authorities. In fact, they promise that interpretation has the capacity to incite provocation (Tilden) and curiosity (Alexander) through the use of object-based inquiry and sensory perception as part of the learning process. The principles proffered by the AAMI provide an open-ended pathway that minimizes the role of the object and situates interpretation around meaningful experiences. Surely all these capacities can be met through twenty-first-century museums.[50]

Notes

1. Adina Langer, editor, *Storytelling in Museums* (Lanham, MD: Rowman & Littlefield, 2022); Adina Langer, "The Stories We Weave: Storytelling in Museums Can Be a Tool of Liberation," *Museum*, March–April 2023: 10–13.
2. Freeman Tilden, *Interpreting Our Heritage* (Chapel Hill: University of North Carolina Press, 1957), 8.
3. Edward P. Alexander, "What Is Interpretation?" *Longwood Program Seminars* 9 (1977): 2–7; *The Interpretation Program of Colonial Williamsburg*, 11–12.
4. AAM, "Education and Interpretation," in *Standards and Best Practices* (Washington, D.C.: AAM Press, 2008), 59–61.
5. Kenneth L. Ames, Barbara Franco, and L. Thomas Frye, *Ideas and Images: Developing Interpretive History Exhibits* (Walnut Creek, CA: AltaMira Press, 1997): 213–24. The eleven points are: 1) Excellence in museum exhibitions extends from an institution's mission statement that reflects a commitment to public interpretation. "Interpretation does not just inform us but pushes us to a deeper and more subtle understanding of some aspect of the world around us. Really interpreting is a difficult and challenging business"; 2) The best exhibitions emanate from a clear sense of purpose or focus. As exhibit teams develop the exhibition—from selecting objects to writing interpretive labels—they must be guided by that focus; 3) First-class exhibitions benefit from what Ames calls "the chaos" of brainstorming among their developers; 4) An excellent exhibition evolves from a dynamic creative process that recognizes and seizes on serendipity; 5) Museum resources must be committed to exhibitions to achieve excellence, and not the least of these resources is time to develop the exhibit; 6) The best museum

exhibitions reflect the strengths of the museum, whether collections, location, or intellectual rigor; 7) Excellent exhibitions acknowledge the "medium" and present the public with nonverbal, sensory experiences. As Ames states it, "The challenge is to help visitors *feel* the interpretation"; 8) Quality exhibitions require talented people, whether museum staff, academic scholars, consultants, or a combination of all. And, as stated above, museum resources must support these qualities; 9) The best exhibitions show that the museum knows their audiences. Ames asks: "Does the exhibition talk to the audience? Lecture? Preach?"; 10) Award-winning exhibitions recognize the processes outlined above and use them to achieve excellence; 11) Evaluation of the process and the product are fundamental to the success of the final exhibition and to the vitality of the museum as an interpretive institution.

6. See the full list of titles, published from 2014 through the present: https://rowman.com/Action/SERIES/_/RLINTERP/Interpreting-History.
7. "Case Statements," *Interpreting Our Heritage in the 21st Century*, 2019, https://interpretingourheritage.com/case-statements/.
8. Allison Horrocks, "Allison Horrocks Case Statement," *Interpreting Our Heritage in the 21st Century*, 2019, https://interpretingourheritage.com/case-statements/allison-horrocks-case-statement/; Hannah Howard, "Hannah Howard Case Statement," *Interpreting Our Heritage in the 21st Century*, 2019, https://interpretingourheritage.com/case-statements/hannah-howard-case-statement/; Sara Patton Zarrelli, "Sara Patton Zarrelli Case Statement," *Interpreting Our Heritage in the 21st Century*, 2019, https://interpretingourheritage.com/case-statements/sarah-patton-zarrelli-case-statement/.
9. *America's Museums: The Belmont Report* (Washington, D.C.: American Association of Museums, 1969).
10. George E. Hein, *Learning in the Museum* (London: Taylor and Francis, 1998), 54–55.
11. *Excellence and Equity: Education and the Public Dimension of Museums* (Washington, D.C.: American Association of Museums, 1992), 17.
12. *Excellence and Equity*, 6.
13. Henry C. Atyeo, *The Excursion as a Teaching Technique* (New York: Teachers College Press, 1939); Marguerite Bloomberg, "An Experiment in Museum Instruction," New Series, no. 8, 40 (Washington, D.C.: American Association of Museums, 1929); Stephen F. Borhegyi, ed., "The Modern Museum and the Community," paper presented at the International Congress of Anthropological and Ethnological Sciences, 1956; Katherine Gibson, "An Experiment in Measuring Results of 5th Grade Class Visits to an Art Museum," *School and Society* 21, no. 5 (1925): 658–62; Benjamin Gilman, "Museum Fatigue," *Scientific Monthly* 12, (1916): 62–74; Grace Fisher Ramsey, *Educational Work in Museums in the United States* (New York: H.W. Wilson, 1938).
14. Edward Stevens Robinson et al., *The Behavior of the Museum Visitor*, New Series, no. 5 (Washington, D.C.: American Association of Museums, 1928); A. W. Melton, *Problems of Installation in Museums of Art*, New Series, 14 (Washington, D.C.: American Association of Museums, 1935); Chandler Screvan, "What Is Formative Evaluation?" in *Introduction to Formative Evaluation* (Washington, D.C.: American Association of Museums, 1974), 59–68.
15. Howard Gardner, *Frames of Mind: The Theory of Multiple Intelligences* (New York: Basic Books, 1985).
16. Hein, *Learning in the Museum*, 54–55.
17. Susan Nichols Lehman and Kathryn Igoe, eds., *Museum School Partnerships: Plans and Programs, Sourcebook no. 4* (Washington, D.C.: American Association of Museums, 1981).
18. Educator Malcolm Knowles coined the term *andragogy*, which means "the art and science of helping people learn," to complement *pedagogy*, which applied to teaching children. Knowles outlined those elements essential to adult learning experiences, and museums quickly adapted them to their programming for both their docents and adult visitors. He argued that successful adult education follows these principles: (a) adults need to know why they need to learn something, (b) they learn best through experiences, (c) they approach learning as "problem solving," and (d) they learn best when the topic is of immediate value. AAM's *Museums, Adults, and the Humanities: A Guide to Educational Programming*, published in 1981, describes the theory and practice of adult education in both classrooms and museums. Newsom and Silver, *The Art Museum as Educator*.
19. Collins, *Museums, Adults, and the Humanities*; Bonnie Sachatello-Sawyer, Robert Fellenz, Laura Gittings-Carlson, Janet Lewis-Mahony, and Walter Woodbaugh, *Adult Museum Programs: Designing*

Meaningful Experiences (Walnut Creek: AltaMira Press, 2002) reflects 1996–1999 study of museums' adult programs.

20. Hein provides a chart of attributes; see George E. Hein, *Learning in the Museum*, 153. On the basic questions related to outlining a constructivist agenda in schools, clubs and organizations that can be applied to museums, see p. 156.

21. Association for Art Museum Interpretation, "Art Museum Interpretation," n.d., https://artmuseum interp.org/about/principles/. The principles date from 2013 to the present and, as of 2024, are displayed on the group's website.

22. Center for the Future of Museums, *Building the Future of Education: Museums and the Learning Ecosystem* (Washington, D.C.: American Alliance of Museums, 2014).

23. Hein, *Learning in the Museum*, 137.

24. Sharon Vatsky, *Interactive Museum Tours: A Guide to In-Person and Virtual Experiences* (Lanham, MD: Rowman and Littlefield, 2023), 8. See also Jay P. Greene, Brian Kisida, Daniel H. Bowen, "The Educational Value of Field Trips: Taking Students to an Art Museum Improves Critical Thinking Skills, and More," *Education Next*, 14:1 (2014): 78–86, which was published online in *Education Next*, https://www.educationnext.org/the-educational-value-of-field-trips/.

25. For an early history of Museum Hack, see Nick Gray, "My Big News: I Sold Museum Hack!" *Nick Gray*, September 28, 2023, https://nickgray.net/sold-museum-hack/; Nick Gray, "How I Learned to Stop Hating and Love Museums," TEDxFoggyBottom, April 2015, https://www.youtube.com/watch?v=6VWPHKABRQA; accessed November 14, 2023.

26. Museum Hack, https://museumhack.com/.

27. Quotes taken from guide Dustin Growick's pitch about tours on the Museum Hack "Bachelorette Party" page. See "Museum Hack Renegade Tours," *Museum Hack*, https://museumhack.com/private-tours/bachelorette-party/, accessed September 20, 2023.

28. https://museumhack.com/.

29. Julia Beizer, "The Pods Have Landed," *Museum News* 84, no. 3 (September–October 2005): 15–17; David Ruth, "Podcast Opens Doors to Richmond National Battlefield Park, *Legacy* 17, no. 5 (September–October 2006): 32–33; Catherine McCarthy, "Cool Technology in a Ranger-Led Tour, *Legacy* 17, no. 5 (September–October 2006): 34–37; Peter Samis and Stephanie Pau, "'Artcasting' at SFMOMA: First-Year Lessons, Future Challenges for Museum Podcasters' Broad Audience of Use," San Francisco Museum of Art, March 2006, www.sfmoma.org; Peter Meng, *Podcasting and VODcasting: A White Paper* (IAT Services, University of Missouri, 2005).

30. Alexander, "What Is Interpretation?" 30–33; Ned J. Burns, *National Park Service Field Manual for Museums* (Washington, D.C.: U.S. Government Printing Office, 1941), 275–79, 297–302; Hal Golden and Kitty Hanson, *How to Plan, Produce and Publicize Special Events* (New York: Oceana Publications, 1966); Tilden, *Interpreting Our Heritage*, 3–10, 26–31; Susan K. Nichols, ed., *Museum Education Anthology* (Washington, D.C.: Museum Education Roundtable, 1984); Susan K. Nichols, ed., *Patterns of Practice* (Washington, D.C.: Museum Education Roundtable, 1992). Each of these volumes provides a wide array of museum-education discussions, both practical and theoretical.

31. Daniel Beysens, "1 Researcher, 1 Exhibit," *ECSITE newsletter*, no. 65 (Winter 2006): 6–7.

32. Until 2020, this site was known as Plimoth Plantation. See Plimoth Patuxet Museums, "Parents' Guide," https://www.plimoth.org/plan-your-visit/helpful-tips-visitors/parents-guide.

33. Lin-Manuel Miranda, as told to Frank DiGiacomo, "*Hamilton*'s Lin-Manuel Miranda on Finding Originality, Racial Politics (and Why Trump Should See His Show)," *Hollywood Reporter*, August 12, 2015, http://www.hollywoodreporter.com/features/hamiltons-lin-manuel-miranda-finding-814657.

34. Robert Simonson, "The *Hamilton* Effect: 8 Unexpected (and Strange) Effects of the Smash Musical," *Playbill*, July 4, 2016, http://www.playbill.com/article/the-hamilton-effect-8-ripple-effects-of-the-smash-musical. In addition, the play saved Hamilton from being removed from the ten-dollar bill. Instead, Andrew Jackson was booted from the twenty-dollar bill. The effect is so great that SoulCycle has chimed in by crafting workout studio offerings, such as "*Hamilton*: A Hip-Hop Theme Ride," that are keyed to the musical and historical figure. See Caryle Wisel, "Hear Ye, Hear Ye: 'Hamilton Workouts Have Arrived in New York City," *Racked*, December 4, 2015, http://ny.racked.com/2015/12/4/9849404/hamilton-broadway-musical-workouts-soulcycle-row-house-nyc.

35. Nicole Levy, "The 'Summer of Hamilton' Is Coming to the New York Historical Society," *DNA Info*, May 16, 2016, https://www.dnainfo.com/new-york/20160516/upper-west-side/summer-of-hamilton-is-coming-new-york-historical-society.

36. Steve Johnson, "*Dressing Downton* Costume Exhibit Is Crowning Moment for the Driehaus Msueum," *Chicago Tribune*, February 3, 2016, http://www.chicagotribune.com/entertainment/museums/ct-dressing-downton-driehaus-ent-0204-20160203-column.html.

37. Mafkereseb Kassahun Bekele, Roberto Pierdicca, Emanuele Frontoni, Eva Savina Malinverni, and James Gain, "A Survey of Augmented, Virtual, and Mixed Reality for Cultural Heritage," *ACM Journal of Computing and Cultural Heritage* 11:2, Article 7 (March 2018), https://doi.org/10.1145/3145534.

38. Paul Milgram, Haruo Takemura, Akira Utsumi, Fumio Kishino, "Augmented Reality: A Class of Displays on the Reality-Virtuality Continuum," *SPIE*, Vol. 2351 (1994), on Telemanipulator and Telepresence Technologies, 282–92.

39. Milgram et al. propose a three-dimensional taxonomic framework for classifying the continuum of "mixed" reality that includes augmented and virtual reality. The model identifies factors that distinguish these systems: Extent of World Knowledge (EWK); Reproduction Fidelity (RF); and Extent of Presence Metaphor (EPM). For the purposes of this chapter, I have associated these with the terms *knowledge*, *authenticity*, and *presence*.

40. The weekend was part of the programming of the Samsung Digital Discovery Centre, which was established in 2009. British Museum, "Virtual Reality Weekend at the British Museum," August 8, 2015, http://www.britishmuseum.org/about_us/news_and_press/press_releases/2015/virtual_reality_weekend.aspx.

41. For more information on the British Museum exploration in VR, its evaluation, and its cross-over into digital collaboration, see Juno Rae and Lizzie Edwards, "Virtual Reality at the British Museum: What Is the Value of Virtual Reality Environments for Learning by Children and Young People, Schools, and Families?" *MW2016: Museums and the Web 2016*, published January 28, 2016, http://mw2016.museumsandtheweb.com/paper/virtual-reality-at-the-british-museum-what-is-the-value-of-virtual-reality-environments-for-learning-by-children-and-young-people-schools-and-families/.

42. Conceived in 2013 by Alfredo Salazar-Caro and William James Richard Robertson, DiMoDA launched in 2015 at the Wrong Biennale and a physical exhibition at TRANSFER in New York. See Lulu Chang, "DiMoDA Is a Virtual Reality Museum That You Don't Want to Miss," November 10, 2015, http://www.digitaltrends.com/cool-tech/dimoda-digital-art-virtual-reality-museum/; www.digitalmuseumof.digital/art.

43. "Virtual Reality: Explore 'Kindred Spirits' by Asher B. Durand | CBVR," Google Arts and Culture, https://artsandculture.google.com/asset/virtual-reality-explore-kindred-spirits-by-asher-b-durand-cbvr/hwHvlJ7NkXnYOg. This experience calls to mind travel writer Bill Bryson's desire to hop into the painting. See *A Walk in the Woods: Rediscovering America on the Appalachian Trail* (New York: Crown Reprints, 2010), originally published in 1998.

44. "Visitor Studies," http://www.visitorstudies.org/glossary-of-terms. Professional organizations have emerged to promote standards and to facilitate research and dissemination. The Visitor Studies Association, founded in 1990, is "dedicated to understanding and enhancing learning experiences in informal settings through research, evaluation, and dialogue." See also Visitor Studies Association, "About," http://www.visitorstudies.org/.

45. Indianapolis Museum of Art, "Audience Research and Evaluation," http://www.imamuseum.org/research/audience-research-evaluation.

46. CARE, http://www.aam-us.org/resources/professional-networks/care.

47. Elaine Heumann Gurian, "Answers to the Ten Questions I'm Most Often Asked," *Civilizing the Museum* (New York: Routledge, 2006) 137–49. John H. Falk and Lynn D. Dierking, *The Museum Experience* (Washington, D.C.: Whalesback Books, 1992), 136–50. Falk and Dierking identify the aims as the following: 1) Each visitor learns in a different way and interprets information through the lens of previous knowledge, experience, and beliefs; 2) All visitors personalize the museum's message to conform to their own understanding and experience; 3) Every visitor arrives with an agenda and a set of expectations for what the museum visit will hold; 4) Most visitors come to the museum as part of a social group, and what visitors see, do, and remember is mediated by that group; 5) The visitor's experience

within the museum includes docents, guards, concessionaires, and other visitors; 6) Visitors are drawn to museums because they contain objects outside their normal experience. Visitors come to "look" in a variety of ways; 7) Visitors are strongly influenced by the physical aspects of museums, including the architecture, ambience, smell, sounds, and "feel" of the place; 8) Visitors encounter an array of experiences from which they select a small number; and 9) The visitor's attention is strongly influenced by the location of exhibits and by the museum's orientation. On the first five categories of the identity-centered approaches, see John Falk, "An Identity-Centered Approach to Understanding Museum Learning," *Curator: The Museum Journal* 49 (2): 151–66; John Falk, *Identity and the Museum Visitor Experience* (Walnut Creek: Left Coast Press, 2009). Two additional approaches were included in Nigel Bond and John Falk, "Tourism and Identity-Related Motivations: Why Am I Here (and Not There)?" *International Journal of Tourism Research* 15 (2013): 430–42.

48. John H. Falk, "Why Well-Being Is at the Heart of Museum Experiences," *Alliance Blog*, January 10, 2022, https://www.aam-us.org/2022/01/10/why-well-being-is-at-the-heart-of-museum-experiences/. Falk posted this in relation to his newest publication at the time: John H. Falk, *The Value of Museums: Enhancing Societal Well-Being* (Lanham, MD: Rowman & Littlefield, for the American Alliance of Museums, 2021). In the quoted material, Falk emphasized enhanced well-being in bold. The emphasis has been removed in the text of this chapter.

49. John H. Falk, "Why Well-Being Is at the Heart of Museum Experiences," *Alliance Blog*, January 10, 2022, https://www.aam-us.org/2022/01/10/why-well-being-is-at-the-heart-of-museum-experiences/.

50. The graphic created by the author of this volume was devised as a supplement for this chapter to show information from John H. Falk, "Why Well-Being Is at the Heart of Museum Experiences," *Alliance Blog*, January 10, 2022, https://www.aam-us.org/2022/01/10/why-well-being-is-at-the-heart-of-museum-experiences/.

9

To Engage

While the previous chapters have set the stage for visitors to enter the museum, this chapter looks at visitor behaviors around museum-centered activities. In short, it looks at how museums foster engagement. First, we will define *engagement* before looking at methods used to engage audiences (both digital and analog), including interactivity, content creation across platforms, the formation of museum communities, varying realities (augmented, virtual, and extended), and artificial intelligence (AI). Each of these approaches will feature recent examples of experiences that have been created to engage visitors.

Engagement Defined

In simplest terms, to *engage* something means to do something or to commit effort. *Museums engage* in collecting, educating, exhibiting, and so on. They take part in these activities. *Visitors engage* in museum-related activities by paying a visit, checking out social media, participating in a tour or workshop, attending a lecture onsite or on Zoom, and so on. However, the term *engage* is also used relative to the impact that the experience has on visitors. Did they enjoy something enough to interact and to immerse themselves? This quality, generally defined as the measure of impact on audiences, is referred to as *visitor engagement*.

As has been made clear in earlier chapters in this volume, museums have their origins in the classical traditions of temples dedicated to the Muses and as repositories of collections initially as storehouses and accumulations of wealth. As visitors entered such spaces to learn, they began, also, to respond to what they saw before them. They began to wonder, to reflect, and, eventually, to interact with the content, the institution, and the people around them. No longer a mere empty vessel awaiting an object, a label, and an idea, visitors bring their own knowledge and experiences to museum visits and, in turn, use those to communicate their likes, interests, and perspectives in and beyond museums.

This new way of thinking about the interaction between a museum and its visitors takes its cues from social media, where "engagement" is measured by interaction with content through clicks, views, comments, likes, shares, and mentions. Social media engagement is fairly easy to measure, however, in that engagement metrics are part of platform analytics. A content creator can see their likes, comments, shares, and impressions. While museums use social media and can, in turn, measure their own social media engagement in Instagram, TikTok, and so on, overall visitor engagement with museums is not confined to social media only. In fact, much of it is tied to audience research undertaken in exhibition and ancillary program creation. As noted in the previous chapter, the field of visitor studies examines visitor experiences within informal learning environments—be that a brick-and-mortar museum or an online space, such as a social media platform or Zoom space. Through careful measure and evaluation of visitor needs, expectations, and interests, museums can strive to create exhibitions and experiences that communicate comprehensible and compelling messages and meet the needs, interests, and desires of their visitors.

The visitor-centered evaluation process, particularly in exhibition creation, begins with knowing who the visitors are, and involves three stages: front-end evaluation, formative evaluation, and summative evaluation. Front-end evaluation studies visitors and potential audiences before the exhibit process begins. It identifies visitors' expectations and knowledge of the exhibit topic. Formative evaluation occurs during the exhibition development process as elements are tested and then revised, affecting label tone and language, object selection and placement, exhibit furniture, and even the exhibit's traffic flow. Summative evaluation, once an exhibition is open to the public, allows museum staff to assess the exhibition's impact and effectiveness; at best, it allows for refinements of exhibition elements based on direct audience feedback.[1]

These evaluation measures are part of a larger framing that relates to design. As museum professional and digital experience designer Barry Joseph explains, six tools are part of the digital design process: audience research, rapid prototyping, public piloting, iterative design, youth collaboration, and teaming up.[2] Part of yielding successful exhibit and content creation requires moving through design thinking strategies in ways that enable museums to try out—even very minimal versions of the final experience—to see how visitors will respond, and then to respond, in turn, to the feedback in order to deliver an experience that will meet the institution's and the visitors' goals. All these inputs, as well as social media engagement, as one indicator contribute to visitor studies and knowledge about visitors more broadly (defined as "audience research").

Consider one example from *The Book of HOV*, an onsite exhibition about musician and rapper Jay-Z at the Brooklyn Public Library in 2023. Eight sections of the library celebrated the Brooklyn native's work through visuals, audio stories, and physical artifacts, including a replica of Baseline Studios, the legendary space where he recorded some of his most influential work. The exhibit is more than objects; it is also a space for engagement, where visitors can interact with the playable turntables and vinyl, as well as a tribute to Jay-Z's philanthropy and social justice work.[3] For the exhibition, the library produced thirteen limited-edition library cards, each one celebrating one of the rapper's

For the exhibition *Book of HOV*, eight sections of the Brooklyn Public Library, across two floors, celebrated Jay-Z's music, philanthropy, and social justice work. In conjunction with the exhibition, the library produced thirteen limited-edition library cards, each celebrating one of Jay-Z's albums. The library cards were wildly popular. Viewed as collectibles, the library cards are readily available for sale on eBay. *Image from eBay listing, https://www.ebay.com/itm/235114661481.*

albums. The library cards were wildly popular, driving a 1,000 percent increase in registrations during the last weeks of July, with a total of eleven thousand new library accounts created in association with the new Jay-Z cards in the first month of the exhibit's run. The drive to collect all thirteen was described as "like Pokémon," as users attempted to "catch" them all.[4] (Fortunately, the exhibition lives online, through the website.[5]) It is a stellar example to help define what engagement is.

Museum visitor engagement, thus, refers to any level of interaction that visitors have with an institution across all of its social media platforms, online content, and onsite experiences. It can be measured through audience research that might include social media analytics, any of the three types of exhibition evaluation measures noted above, as well as observations. Did an exhibition have such long wait times that virtual queues were instituted? Did a hashtag go viral? Did an exhibition incite FOMO (Fear Of Missing Out)? Or did an experience take visitors away from daily life and transport them to places unimaginable? Did vibrant works of art come to life in an immersive experience? These and other experiences as examples of visitor engagement are the focus of this chapter.

Interactivity

Before museums can measure interactivity, they must evidence connectivity, meaning they must bear a relationship to their visitors. While the tradition of taking a collection out beyond its walls is one that extends back to the emergence of French state museums—when Napoleon empowered his ministers to craft exhibitions around Europe, more appropriately today, the transfer and translation of museums happens chiefly through the web and social media.[6]

In the web's early days, the Exploratorium has reached online visitors, others planning museum exhibitions, and teachers in their classrooms to encourage better teaching of scientific principles.[7] The web has made these linkages simple, inexpensive, and valuable to both museum staff and their visitors (both actual and virtual). Designer Tom Hennes describes the potential for these linkages for natural history museums: "Each museum inhabits an important and unique position in such a network, linking to a series of other networks—communities of visitors; educational systems; communities in areas under study, evaluation or protection; nongovernmental organizations; governments; and other museums. Moreover, the museum links them not only to *itself*, but to each other. This is important because those links allow new clusters of individuals and organizations within the aggregated network to interact and share their own knowledge across it. Agency is not driven solely to and from the museum; they can arise spontaneously as well and in many unpredictable, new directions."[8]

Beyond connectivity is interactivity—a back-and-forth flow of connection that serves as a chief measure of engagement. Research focused on interactivity has demonstrated the ways in which museum technologies have improved visitor experiences. For instance, Roberto Ivo Fernandes Vaz, Paula Odete Fernandes, and Ana Cecília Rocha Veiga have demonstrated how digital installations in museums enhance visitor experiences by capturing attention; attracting interest as well as a visit to a museum; communicating the museum collections; and fostering education and learning.[9] As the inaugural chief digital officer of the Metropolitan Museum of Art, Sree Sreenivasan, stated in 2016, "People ask me: What is your biggest competition? Is it MoMA? Guggenheim? Our competition is Netflix. Candy Crush."[10] Thus, rather than seeing one another as competition, museums see other arenas of entertainment and content platforms as their competition.

The Met's website was overhauled entirely in 2016 to simplify and create a platform for spreading digital content across their (at the time) thirty-three million online visitors.[11] Recent statistics from The Met, in fact, show that 91 percent of visitors brought a mobile device with them into the museum. With that kind of knowledge, what choice do museums have but to embrace the use of digital tools for visitor engagement? To that end, museums have employed technology to communicate how museums are more vital than before. Journalist and tech expert Sophie Gilbert has defined some of the meaningful ways museums employ technology to engage audiences: curating for Instagram; augmenting the content through, for example, AR; putting collections online; and presenting born-digital collections.[12]

Academy in Action exhibit, Student Programs Educator and Public Programs Presenter Apriel Coffey viewing Island Innovation section.
Photo by Nicole Ravicchio © 2024 California Academy of Sciences. All rights reserved.

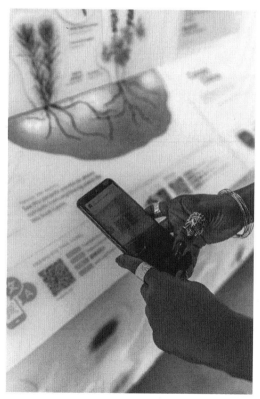

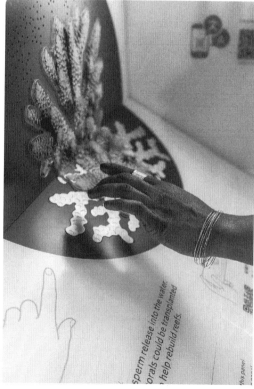

Academy in Action exhibit, Island Innovation interactive.
Photo by Nicole Ravicchio © 2024 California Academy of Sciences. All rights reserved.

While these attributes are manifestations of meaningful muse-tech for the purposes of engagement, they are dated. They are a product of their time: they reflect where museums and the broader field of engagement was in 2016. Because technology is both a tool of engagement as well as a medium, the framing for this chapter is around three key areas: content creation in analog and digital formats; extended realities and immersive experiences; and artificial intelligence.

Content Creation across Platforms

While the previous chapter examined the exhibition process, exhibits are only one avenue of communicating messages and storytelling. Print and digital formats enable the museum to seep beyond its gallery walls and enter the everyday lives of visitors. The following sections address content creation in analog and digital formats, extended realities, immersive experiences, and other analog- and tech-mediated formats.

Museums publish content across a variety of platforms. But museums are not the only creators of museum content. In fact, museum practitioners, consultants, and scholars and students of museum studies are all contributors to content creation of, by, and for museums. Below, a brief glimpse at "traditional" publishing provides a foundation for the expanded universe of content creation platforms, such as web content, podcasts, and social media.

Publications and Resources

Current research and practice in museums reflects an ever-evolving field. Publications appear in immutable, traditional formats such as print publications from professional and scholarly publishers such as Rowman & Littlefield and Routledge. Many of their books are written by museum professionals and scholars and researchers who study the field or collaborate with cultural heritage institutions. Looking online at a publisher website and seeing the new and continuing publications can help readers to discover perspectives from thought leaders in a range of fields, such as collections, collections care, and conservation; education, interpretation, and programs; exhibitions; diversity, equity, inclusion, and accessibility; legal matters; administration and management; marketing and fundraising; as well as museology and museum science. Publications appearing in these books and, also, those appearing in some journals are peer-reviewed, meaning that the content has been evaluated by scholars and professionals in the field who can attest to the academic and/or professional quality of the work.

Beyond the boundaries of peer review, yet also important to providing a space for research, praxis, and scholarship, are websites, blogs, podcasts, and other digital formats. Some of these content creators are also publishers of books and articles, thus blurring the boundaries between print and non-print formats. They are different from books and articles, particularly in their ability to tap in to new ideas and new content without the long timeline of print publication. This doesn't mean, however, that web-sourced content is untrusted: it can come from organizations as well as individuals. For instance, UK-based MuseumNext is an organization focused on museums and their futures through conferences, professional development trainings, and resources, including a blog that shares new approaches to digital, engagement, impact, health, the planet, marketing and fundraising, and opinion pieces. In addition, museum-centric blogs cater to their audience needs, as do YouTube channels where museums post content related to exhibitions, events, and museum operations. This kind of content leads into the myriad ways the digital landscape has become an important part of content creation and visitor engagement.

Digital Content

Podcasts such as *Sidedoor: A Podcast from the Smithsonian* look at collections across the suite of museums in areas such as art and design, history and culture, science, and nature. *Museum Confidential* offers a behind-the-scenes look at museums, as produced by the Philbrook Museum of Art and Radio, Tulsa, Oklahoma. *Museum Archipelago*, produced by interactive museum exhibit creator Ian Elsner, offers fifteen-minute segments focusing on museum spaces around the world and the people who work at them and aim to serve the field.[13] Striving to reach an international audience with podcasts available in English, French, and Spanish, the International Council of Museum's podcast was launched (briefly) in 2022 as *ICOM Voices*, and it relaunched a year later as *Museums and Chill*—a riff on the slang term "Netflix and Chill." The reboot is intended to be more accessible, diverse, and sustainable; by "offering informative and entertaining content, the podcast aims to inspire and entertain our listeners." Recent episodes of *Museums and Chill* include an interview with Kate from the blog/website "Museum Drip"; the rematriation of a Pacific red cedar memorial pole from the United Kingdom to the Nisga'a Nation in Canada; and researcher Helene Chatterjee's commentary about the relationship of museums and culture to health and well-being.[14]

Social Media

Beyond podcasts and other single-direction communication, consider the ways in which museums connect with their visitors through the web and social media. Visitors to museums, as well as offsite fans and aspirational audiences, engage with museums by "friending" the institution on Facebook, following the museum on Twitter (now referred to as "X" since Elon Musk took the helm of the social media giant), watching reel after reel of Instagram stories, and consuming endless hours of clips on TikTok.

The landscape of social media and museums, specifically Twitter, has been analyzed by Alex Espinós in a series of studies from 2013 through 2015 to show that if two people are connected through a third person, chances are they can get connected in the future. Applied to museums, the closure reads: if A follows B, and B follows a museum, M, it is likely that A will eventually follow M. Triadic closure is also related to information spread and trust building—both of which are critical for museums to build in their location-based, geographic communities, as well as their regional, national, and web imprint. Espinós also points out how museums might develop social media strategies by connecting with "big players"—star museums that have thousands of followers who will, then, create triadic relationships for smaller museums. Relevance through activity rather than stagnation and language diversity is used to reach museums outside of English-speaking countries.[15] These findings demonstrate how communication models of museums have changed, as have multiple ways of connecting audiences with museum-related content and means of engaging communities in the sharing of knowledge and construction of co-created content. Communities form around the physical and virtual locus of the museum.

Social media platforms, such as Facebook, Instagram, Twitter, and TikTok have provided a way for museums to immediately connect with their audiences, while also broadcasting in a cost-free platform that enables museums to reach multiple demographics. While TikTok is now taking center stage, we'll return to the notion of "curating for Instagram" to set the stage. To "curate for Instagram" implies thinking about the museum's delivery in a brief format and visitors' reception of (and showing of love for) the museum storytelling on that social media platform. With Instagram, the visuality of the experience is the draw. But is any museum experience "Instagrammable" (i.e., worthy of being attractive or interesting enough to be suitable for posting to Instagram)? While Instagram is dominated by celebrities as well as fashion and fitness influences, the content is visually driven and dominated by beautiful or awe-inspiring people, places, or things. The platform speaks the experience economy through its repository of images, which may include people, places, and products as well as memes and quotes.

For instance, consider the success of the *Rain Room*, a moody gray space illuminated by 528 gallons of water that fall continuously and intermittently halt at a six-foot radius around visitors. Commissioned by Restoration Hardware in 2012 from Random International, a London-based collaborative design studio, and on view from 2013 through 2017 at the Museum of Modern Art in New York and Los Angeles County Museum of Art, as well as several international art venues, the work was created by Florian Ortkrass, Hannes Koch, and Stuart Wood. They undertook several years of research and development that sought to understand how it would feel to be immersed in a rainstorm that would not physically affect someone. Multiple-hour waiting times were no bother to visitors for the opportunity to demonstrate the wonder and awe that can be captured visually—in images and video clips—and shared. As Restoration Hardware CEO Gary Friedman noted, "To us, *Rain Room* is a reflection of creative courage, trust, and a belief that all of us have the ability to affect any environment we choose to step into."[16]

Another example comes from the Smithsonian's Renwick Gallery, a collection of vibrant, room-size installations, by nine artists who were installed throughout the building (which has served various governmental and cultural purposes since its construction in the mid-nineteenth century). After its closure from 2013 until 2015, the inaugural exhibition was framed around the theme of "wonder" and explicitly sought to highlight infrastructure and architectural improvements through the intentional commissioning and display of site-specific installations. Artists created works from bugs; tires; thread; index cards; willow branches; images; a replica of a hemlock tree; marbles; and LEDs. Upon opening the door to the gallery, visitors were struck by the space and the art within it, tagging the museum more than twenty thousand times, thereby demonstrating the exhibition's online success. According to Nicholas Bell, curator-in-charge at the Renwick, the crossover between the museum and its architecture and the installations was intentional: "We wanted people to be very conscious that they are in a museum. . . . The art is meant to draw your attention to the architecture of the space."[17] Such a blowup shows what an effective marketing tool social media can be.

In contrast to Instagram, where "the visual" takes center stage, with TikTok, it's short-format video and a younger demographic. Already with more than one billion downloads, TikTok has a core audience of young people between thirteen and twenty-one years of age. The Metropolitan Museum of Art was among the first museums to engage in TikTok, with a contest created in 2019 to ask viewers to re-create art. Shortly thereafter, they launched a second challenge to create original content inspired by the Met Gala, with the hashtag #MetGalaStyle. In 2020, the Carnegie Museum of Natural History in Pittsburgh, Pennsylvania, launched their TikTok account in early 2020 and grew it to a huge success through joke telling, with punny, collection-related jokes. During the pandemic, as many museums were unable to open their doors, they turned to social media such as TikTok to retain engagement and to fulfill their mission. Also, during the pandemic, the Sacramento History Museum turned to TikTok to connect with their members and the public and found out that their printer, Howard, was a hit. As of December 2023, the museum has 2.6 million followers, with thirty-nine million likes of their short-format video content. This kind of content differs vastly from traditional forms of museum-created content, chiefly in the manner of its presentation: short (less than ten minute) bursts of video format that appears to catch someone in the midst of work, rather than the longer-format YouTube or other platform-based content, which tends to be longer (YouTube has a limit, as of 2022, of twelve hours for video) and more polished.[18]

All these formats, and especially TikTok, have subcultures that provide a niche virtual space for those interested in particular genres or themes. For example, the art historian Mary McGillivray is a TikToker with more than 451,000 followers and more than twelve million likes for her brief explanations and meanderings about museums and art. To put that in context, Mary has more followers on TikTok than the American Museum of Natural History in New York City, which has 322,000 and 6.3 million likes, while Boston's Museum of Science has 161,000 followers and 2.2 million likes.[19]

Aggregation

Before concluding this section, it is worth mentioning content creation through aggregation. Here, Google, rather than an individual museum, stands out as an exemplar with their Arts & Culture suite, which has amplified their online offerings and curated into four portals for visitors: "Explore," "Play," "Nearby," and "Favorites."

- *Explore* enables visitors to look at highlights; arrangements of works by categories (such as art movements, historic events, historical figures, mediums); examinations in a chronological sense—from prehistory to the present—as well as color; engagement with themes, such as virtual museums, Black British music culture, Chinese cuisine and culture, collections by institution, and more.
- *Play* offers games that engage with music, coloring, puzzles, trivia, and crosswords focused on arts and culture. For instance, the digital experience "Artetik: From the Art" uses collections from the Guggenheim Museum Bilbao to create an onsite and online experience.[20] The experience is installed at the museum, as well as online, and it enables visitors to explore how art at the museum may be characterized by other visitors in terms of emotional expression. Words such as *fascination, contemplation, fear, amusement, wonder, curiosity*, and *inspiration* are represented by color bubbles that, upon a tap, are defined and surrounded by images of works from the collection that seem to express that word. The graphic of emotions changes over time, as people interact with the experience and characterize the works before them. Upon selecting a work, information about the work of art, along with real-time data, is presented. For instance, upon selecting Susana Solano's *Jaosokor*, a canoe-shaped armature covered with colorless plastic knotting appears; Artetik conveyed that this work was identified as representing "sadness": sadness represents 4 percent of the emotions reported by the visitors about Jaosokor.[21]
- Nearby, upon allowing access to one's location via Bluetooth, enables viewers to see, on the Map's interface, museums and exhibitions in the area.
- Favorites enables users to save artworks, stories, and collections.

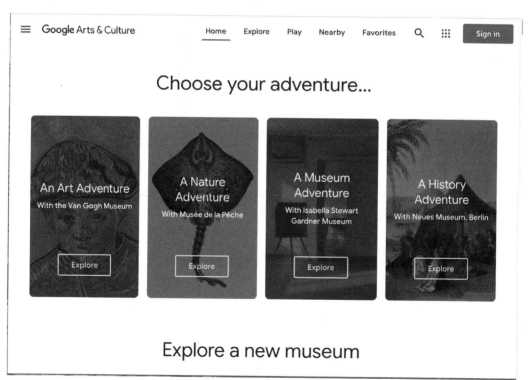

The Google Arts & Culture suite has amplified online offerings and curated four portals inviting visitors into areas entitled "Explore," "Play," "Nearby," and "Favorites." Such tools enable anyone, at the touch of screen, to engage with museums locally, regionally, nationally, and internationally.
Google Arts and Culture, https://artsandculture.google.com/.

Such tools enable anyone, at the touch of screen, to engage with museums locally, regionally, nationally, and internationally.

Museum Communities

As audiences develop agency by visiting or connecting online to museums, as sites, further association is implicit around the museums' collections as well as the associations with one another as enthusiasts, scholars, and professionals. In museums, as in other disciplines and social circles, knowledge and learning occur where communities share an interest for something they do and learn how to do it better through interaction. Such sustained preoccupation has been called, by Etienne Wenger-Trayner and Beverly Wenger-Trayner, "communities of practice," which consist of three elements: a domain, a community, and a practice. [22] Their term offers perspective on loose associations, such as web communities who share a common interest, though their benefits may be applied to the field of museum studies, which, by its nature, triangulates collections, audiences, and the site of the museum. Recently, Wenger-Trayner have furthered their conceptualization by denoting "landscapes of practice," where professionals navigate journeys across and through *multiple* communities of practice. [23] Where do these landscapes exist? What do they look like?

Crowdsourcing

Communities and landscapes of practice can form around collections. For instance, the Smithsonian Institution Transcription Center (SITC) has made efforts in digitizing and transcribing notebooks, diaries, logbooks, albums, specimen labels, and audio recordings to make such materials more accessible. Established in 2013, the SITC has engaged, as of this writing, 83,686 "volunpeers" (that is, volunteers + peers) volunteers have contributed to this project worldwide. [24] (This number of contributors is up from six thousand volunpeers as of the previous edition of this volume in 2017.) Importantly, the term *volunpeer* was coined by Smithsonian staff in 2014 "as a way to more accurately describe our digital volunteers as peers and colleagues in the collaborative work of the Transcription Center." The work exists within a community as part of transcription and review, but also a learning ecosystem surrounding Smithsonian collections, "unlocking and connecting previously inaccessible scientific and historic data, and contributing significantly to the Smithsonian's mission to increase and diffuse knowledge." [25] The Transcription Center volunpeers have contributed to the transcription of nearly 1.3 million pages drawn from the Smithsonian collections.

Such crowdsourcing projects—the term *crowdsourcing* first coined by Jeff Howe in a 2006 *Wired* article focusing on labor and digital technologies—was further elucidated by Mia Ridge, who discusses projects like the Transcription Center as "a form of engagement with cultural heritage that contributes toward a shared, significant goal or research area, by asking the public to undertake tasks that cannot be done automatically, in an environment where the tasks, goals (or both) provide inherent rewards for participation." [26] Before the beta launch of the Transcription Center in 2013 and the fully accessible version in August 2014, the Smithsonian Institution Archives (SIA) embarked on a project aimed to reveal the stories, people, and places embedded in their collections by publishing item-level photographs with "bare-bones" information, or metadata, and asking for help in identifying unknowns. Then, the SIA built campaigns via Flickr Commons, Facebook, and Twitter to highlight collections and bring attention to gaps in information. [27] In both of these Smithsonian-run projects, and countless others, the spirit of the volunteers engaged in this work and the museums who foster connections through collections in a virtual world fulfills the need expressed by John Cotton Dana to involve many in the scholarly work of the museum.

Gameplay

Before exploring how communities also form through tech-mediated museum worlds, a few definitions are in order. First, *augmented reality*, or AR, is one of the suite of "realities" where layering, or augmentation, of the real world is the operational device. AR enhances our perception and understanding of the real world by superimposing virtual information on our view of the world around us; VR, or *virtual reality*, enhances our perception and understanding through the creation of a synthetic world without any real-world presence; while *mixed reality*, or MR, is when real and virtual environments blend. A term used to describe all these realities is XR, or *extended reality*.[28] Related are immersive experiences, which may include AR, VR, or MR. Below, the virtual worlds created by 3D and augmented reality worlds, such as Minecraft, Pokémon Go, and Animal Crossing, are described before moving into a discussion of exhibition-focused uses of XR technologies and games.

Minecraft is a world-building game that emerged in 2009 as a space for players to construct environments out of textured cubes. This 3D-generated world has been coopted by the museum community as well. In 2014, the British Museum posted a call for participants on its website asking visitors to "join a global community building the British Museum in Minecraft." In responding to the query, participants received tasks and challenges that led to the construction of the interior and exterior of the museum. In connecting this endeavor to its status as "a museum of the world, for the world," the museum pointed to this initiative as a community engagement endeavor: "people can engage with the Museum and its collection whether they are visiting London in person on online. Museumcraft will reflect this, so anyone interested can apply to be part of the build." A similar project was also undertaken in 2014 by the Anchorage Museum, which involved families in the construction of *Flat World: Minecraft at the Museum*.[29] Related, Minecraft Education (formerly known as Minecraft: Education Edition) is a platform for using Minecraft in a classroom setting and is keyed to support collaboration and standards-aligned lessons across grades. Virtual environments can be used to learn about history, as well as to re-create museums.

Minecraft has also entered the museum space as its own exhibition. In 2020, *Minecraft: The Exhibition* was organized by the Museum of Pop Culture in Seattle, Washington. The traveling exhibition (still on tour as of 2023) "celebrates the Minecraft phenomenon and looks at the game's impact on our culture and the world. [It] is geared toward players and non-players alike."[30] The exhibition promises opportunities for understanding how the platform can serve as a space for creative expression, community building, and digital citizenship. The platform and the exhibition, in fact, share interests with museums in general. For instance, the exhibition materials indicate that "Minecraft is a platform for creative expression, community creation, and social change" and that the "exhibition highlights the amazing creations and accomplishments achieved with Minecraft, and will inspire visitors to explore, build and create." In fact, it's not a stretch to say that *Minecraft: The Exhibition*, like the online community itself, is personalizeable, as well as inclusive, welcome, and community-oriented. In short, it is like a museum—and what museums aspire to be.

In addition, communities form around, in, and beside Pokémon Go, an app launched in July 2016 that includes the built environment—including museums and heritage centers—and captures the attention of two demographics: young smartphone users and millennials seeking a bit of nostalgia. (For those unfamiliar, Pokémon Go is based upon a series of entertainment media that emerged in the 1990s—a video game, an anime and manga series, and a related trading card game—all of which refer to the fictionalized species of Pokémon, or *Poketto Monsuta*, which translates as "Pocket Monsters"). In the game, players try to catch cartoonish monsters throughout the digital game world. Pokémon Go employs the real world around players as the playing field, rather than an artificial map.

As museum technologist and researcher Blaire Moskowitz has noted, "Pokémon Go's tagline has remained the same as the prior GameBoy iterations. You still want to 'catch 'em all', only this time it's not limited to the virtual world inside the GameBoy." With geolocation and mobile phones, the app knows the user's location, and users seek virtual monsters in public places, such as museums, which are fed to the game through two databases for locations and points of interest. Searching for PokéStops (such as gyms, which seem to be the popular AR [augmented reality] site for museums), people have moved beyond game mechanics to engage in the surroundings and to build community.

Moskowitz explains, "people have even entered the museum and walked around the exhibitions. In large museums, Pokémon will 'live' in one wing, so players are on the lookout for each other to provide helpful hints. . . . But, there are also museums where people are just sitting in the parking lot and not venturing inside. At one small museum, nine people were observed sitting in the parking lot playing Pokémon GO, none of whom entered the museum."[31]

Some museums and sites, such as the United States Holocaust Memorial Museum and Arlington National Cemetery, have made requests of the game's creator to remove their sites from the location database due to the nature of their museums and sites. Some museums are wholeheartedly embracing this new craze. For instance, the International Museum of Art and Science in McAllen, Texas, hosted its first Pokémon Gym Takeover Night in August 2016.[32] Within a few years, some museums, such as the Philbrook Museum of Art in Tulsa, Oklahoma, and the National Geographic Museum in Washington, D.C., offered free and discounted admission for Pokémon Go players. Some institutions strategically incorporated the game into their existing visitor-engagement strategies.

What Pokémon has shown museums is that mobile AR has potential for museums to reach different audiences and, also, to tell new stories to visitors. For instance, given the impossibility of displaying an entire collection (and the number of works in storage), AR could enable institutions to share works not on view, in the museal context. AR could also display a new exhibit experience overlaying a current display. As Sean Magner writes, "With a little bit more investment in a museum's app, a virtual tour could include an AR mode where users could see what other works have been in a hall, superimposed over the current exhibit. Such an update would be almost equivalent to renovating the entire museum, for a fraction of the cost."[33]

The developers behind Pokémon (Niantic) have partnered with the game studio PRELOADED to create a new, device-agnostic software-development kit to do just that: Lightship ARDK. The AR development kit aims to fuse together AR with the real world by using several technologies and tool kits to help beginners create immersive AR experiences.[34] Two museums in London have begun using this technology to create experiences for their audiences. The Science Museum in London created Wonderlab AR, which allows users to look beneath the surface at scientific phenomena. Released in 2022, Wonderlab AR is a companion to the onsite exhibition Wonderlab, which is spread across seven zones in the exhibit space that offer a range of interactive elements. Beyond this space, the app employs a smartphone camera to show the world around us in new ways. For instance, the app displays interactive AR overlays on items in the real world. A jiggling phone booth or a vibrating defibrillator prompt visitors to learn about these technologies in scientific terms.[35]

A second launch with the Lightship ARDK leverages site-specificity of the Tower of London in England, and the platinum jubilee of Queen Elizabeth II in early 2022. For this occasion, twenty million seeds were sown around the medieval moat of the Tower of London, and subsequently they were opened to visitors to enjoy the blooms up close. While the moat around the Tower of London was filled with flowers that brought new biodiversity to central London, visitors around the world were able to see these flowers applied in AR to the world around them with Tower Superbloom AR. This app demonstrates the potential of AR to create an augmented landscape; to illuminate spaces and translate ideas from an historic site to our contemporary landscape is a compelling opportunity for museums to add beauty, whimsy, and history to daily life, beyond their own four walls.[36]

Animal Crossing—a social-simulation game that launched its fifth series in early 2020—merged together sociality, museums, and collections in unexpected ways at the beginning of the COVID-19 pandemic. The multiplayer video game developed by Nintendo for the Nintendo Switch included a museum within its world, as a place where items could be donated. The collections overseen by character-owl Blathers enabled acquisition as well as display of items from players such as insects, fish, fossils, and artwork. The goal of the game was to bring civilization to this deserted land, the eponymous New Horizon of the series, through real-time life simulation. It also had the capacity to document reality and to express unrealized dreams.

Due to its release at the beginning of the lockdown and social-distancing phase of the pandemic, the National Videogame Museum in Sheffield, England, wanted to document the game's release and people's responses to it, as well as its impact during COVID-19. They launched an online exhibit, *Animal Crossing Diaries*, which contained visual and audio interviews from players throughout 2020, who kept track of their progress and reflected on their experience and how it affected them. The museum explains the significance of the game's release, the lockdown of the pandemic, and the importance of documenting and sharing this moment: "While the world was on pause, the island paradises of *Animal Crossing: New Horizons* thrived, welcoming those in isolation with open arms (and paws). The game became a routine part of everyday life. Cancelled plans were reimagined and reprogrammed to the virtual sandy shores of players' islands. For many people unable to socialise in real life, the game became a vital creative space for personal connection."[37] The website containing the records opened in September 2021, and it covered the eighteen months after the game's release.

The social simulation game *Animal Crossing* features a museum where users can donate and view items. During the COVID-19 pandemic lockdown, games like *Animal Crossing* became an outlet for documentation, as in the case of the National Videogame Museum in Sheffield, England. In other cases, players used the platform to simulate museum collections. Here, three dresses created in the game drew inspiration from historic dresses from a museum collection: an orange and blue pioneer dress and two early-nineteenth-century-inspired creations. *Screenshots courtesy of Koda Drake.*

Beyond this historically significant inclusion of *Animal Crossing* as a form of microhistory of our pandemic narratives, the continued use of *Animal Crossing* as a tool of engagement and interaction persists. For instance, through the use of a copying-and-pasting tool within *Animal Crossing*, users can bring collections from museums into the game. Blathers can display the likes of the Metropolitan Museum of Art, the Art Institute of Chicago, or any other open-access collection with a few clicks by selecting an item and using the Nintendo Switch Online app to bring the image into the game. "Using Open Access images from The Met collection, Hans Memling's portraits can hang next to your bed. Fourteenth-century Ottoman tiles could line your bathroom floor. Stroll past some *Views of Mount Fuji* on your morning fossil hunt. You may never get an ironwood kitchenette, but you could certainly have a Van Gogh on your wall."[38] Activities such as this also enable users to diminish canonicity. Users are not constrained or restrained by the library of assets in *Animal Crossing*. As long as a work of art is open access, users can bring it into the world and draw attention to it by curating their own museums—literally and figuratively.

According to researcher Alvina Lai, "the museum in *Animal Crossing* is one stop on a timeline of museums, both in real life and in video games... *Animal Crossing*'s museum reinforces the expectation that, in a museum, there will be a practice of interactive participation and learning, value in collection development, importance placed on unique art and artifacts, and the idea that museums are places of public learning. They are places of research, preservation, and appreciation. In *Animal Crossing*, players can appreciate these ideas as they roam their island, shovel in hand."[39]

The museum in *Animal Crossing* builds on a tradition of museum inclusion in role-playing, simulation games. They have appeared in Uncharted, Skyrim, Bioshock, and Wildstar, for instance. In each of these cases, as researcher Tomas Brown points out, museums are used to drive the story and, on occasion, as devices to communicate information or ideas as well as to give the player a context and/or identity.[40] Such role-playing and gameplay is a form of visitor engagement, no doubt. Could role-playing, identity formation, and representation help us to think differently about museums and our world? Can some of the issues facing museums and the world today, some of which are described in Section III, be broached in game environments?

Exhibition Applications of XR and Immersive Experiences

The Pokémon Company has had partnerships with museums in Japan, such as the Tokyo Metropolitan Art Museum (with trading cards inspired by Edvard Munch's painting Scream, to coincide with the opening of a retrospective of the artist's work there in 2018). More recently, in 2023, the Pokémon Company worked with the National Museum of Nature and Science in Japan to organize a traveling exhibition of fossilized Pokémon.[41]

In the fall of 2023, the Pokémon Universe partnered with Van Gogh Museum in Amsterdam, Netherlands, to create *Pokémon x Van Gogh Museum*. The premise of the exhibit is to draw out the connections that Van Gogh had with Japanese work by displaying six paintings by contemporary creators who have inserted a character from Pokémon into an appropriation of a painting by Van Gogh. Each creator comes from a Pokémon world, be that cartoon, card, or video game. The works include a painting by artist Sowsow featuring Munchlax and Snorlax modeled after *The Bedroom* (1888). All six works are adhered to a temporary wall on the first floor of the Van Gogh Museum in a space that is smaller than the corresponding gift shop, all the more realizing the importance of Pokémon Gogh, perhaps, as a mash-up between the museum and the Japanese card brand. The advertisements for the small exhibit, moreover, draw connections between the old and new: two of the characters (Pikachu and Eevee) are shown through a field of sunflowers before staring up at the sky and seeing the sun and clouds transform into the artist's style. Beyond the draw of the exhibit itself is the commemorative bling: a trading card featuring Pikachu in a gray felt hat (which visitors can claim by filling out an activity booklet clearly designed for small children). The eBay site is now flooded with the cards, with some selling for as much as $2,439. This draw for the commercial item rivals the draw for Van Gogh's works at auction. Perhaps this kind of fanfare purports the ways in which museums can coalesce around the creation of rarity and mechanisms to convert that rarity into cash (at auction).[42]

Another example comes from the Fine Arts Museums of San Francisco, which, in 2024, employs Snapchat's AR technology within a museum context to show how works from the exhibition *Fashioning San Francisco: A Century of Style* might appear on a visitor through mirroring technology. The exhibition at the De Young Museum in the summer of 2024 features more than fifty designers, including pillars of the fashion industry such as Coco Chanel, Christian Dior, and Alexander McQueen, among others. Chief among the engagement strategies is an interactive and adaptive mirror that enables visitors to "try on" works by Yves Saint Laurent, Chinese American Bay Area–based designer Kaisik Wong, and Italian designer Valentino, and to see their own bodies in context.[43] Visitors want to see themselves in the exhibitions, literally (think about how many selfies we take in museums). To combine that ability with the simulation of "trying on" clothing, a new path is charted for museums. In this way, technology affords a simulated experience that is so-fully-collections-centered that it offers an excellent way of thinking about fashion, history, and other exhibit interactives henceforth.

Moving from fantasy, art, and fashion to history, and from AR to VR with a more compelling use of technology, the Shoah Foundation at the University of Southern California directs an effort called *Dimensions in Testimony*. A 3D-interactive, conversational testimony, *Dimensions* is described by the foundation "as an interactive educational tool to permit students far into the future to 'talk' with Holocaust survivors about their life experiences."[44] *Dimensions* presents a collection of interactive biographies that enable people to have a conversation with prerecorded video images of Holocaust survivors and other witnesses to genocide. The media is created through a series of video and audio captures. That is, during the interview process, the individuals sit in the middle of a light stage beneath a half dome latticed with lights and more than one hundred video cameras. Each answers as many as two thousand questions that cover a vast range of subjects. The content is captured and held, awaiting a visitor to ask a question upon encountering the *Dimensions* interface. After introduction of the subject, visitors ask questions of the survivor. Employing natural-language-processing technology, the program matches questions from viewers with the survivor's most relevant response. Over time, the exhibit "learns," and the relevancy rate and speed of the survivor's responses improves. In short, the method has enabled museums to show "interactive biographies."[45]

The Shoah Foundation, and the museums who have been prototyping this project, including the United States Holocaust Memorial Museum (USHMM) in Washington, D.C., and the Illinois Holocaust Museum and Education Center in Skokie, Illinois, foreground the project's authenticity and distance its application of "hologram" or "avatar," which conjure up ideas of sci-fi movies. Each of the sixteen survivors who participated in this project—who were already recorded in oral history "short form"—has exclaimed the depth of this experience in terms of characterizing and presenting a microhistory for audiences in perpetuity to engage with. Researchers have agreed, citing the public understanding of holographic technology as being constructed through movies, rather than documentary. Boswell and Rowland, further, find that the interviews and conversations between visitors and the avatars involve a level of "truthfulness" that is shaped through visitor participation, or engagement. They argue that "performative encounters with the Holocaust have the potential to provide a charged, embodied experience of historical disappearance and loss."[46]

Immersive Experiences

Unlike the previous examples, in which technology has been the vehicle of delivery for the content, this section examines immersive experiences where technology may be involved in some way, most notably through visitor engagement, sharing, and likes. At their core, they are immersive experiences that aim to transport visitors to a new world or other reality. Key to this is the ability to look all around, unfettered and without confinement.

Just as *Rain Room* and *Infinity Mirrors* caused social media buzz, pop-up exhibits have emerged as a new format for museum experiences. They include the Balloon Museum, an installation that bills itself as an exhibition where "air" is the medium. The very premise of the installation is one of visitor engagement; without visitors and their callouts on social media about the experience, the "museum" is simply a room filled with balloons. Yes, the balloons are a key medium of the art installations and soundscapes, all of which are documented on the exhibition website. However, in this space, visitors are keenly the focus of the experience. There is no explicit commitment to communicating "content," but rather, visitors are invited to explore, touch, and share. One of the installations on view in Rome, *Living Forest* by Kateřina Blahutová, featured several trunk-and-limb inflatables each in their own place and illuminated from below (think of holiday inflatables in your neighborhood). The work, though, confronts visitors with the pressing issue of the effects of the global climate situation. In the artist's words, "It is a call to action, to the active participation of the community: through our determination and efforts we can restore the natural landscape in which we live." The work fostered advocacy and action, as well: each donation made during the exhibition period went to support the activities of Fridays For Future, the global climate justice movement started by Greta Thunberg.[47] Other works take on fantastic, invented, and otherworldly subjects, such as Myeongbeom Kim's *Balloon Tree*, which hovers above visitors with a crown of red balloons clustered around the branches of a young tree. The collective Plastique Fantastique's *Tholos* is a large-scale pseudo-dome that takes on an architectural presence. Clearly there is much to see, and much to engage with, as the tagline encourages: "Let's fly: art has no limits." The show, to date, has reached over 2.5 million visitors already worldwide.[48]

Another example of immersion can be grounded in artworks from the past, as evidenced by the exhibition *Chagall, Paris-New York*, which was on view at New York's Hall des Lumières. Here, painter Marc Chagall's lusciously vibrant works of art come to life in a new immersive experience that explores the painter, his works, and their contexts. The immersive exhibition highlights all of Chagall's accomplishments—from painting to theater, costumes, sculpture, ceramics, stained glass, mosaic, and collage—and features a broad range of creatures, circus characters, and illustrative fable stories. The scenes seemingly come to life, dance across walls, and surround visitors.[49]

In addition, technology is used as a premise for content creation, as in the work of the Dutch design studio DRIFT. Based in Brooklyn, New York and Amsterdam, DRIFT was founded in 2007 on the premise of creating experiential sculptures, installations, and performances. The artist founders Lonneke Gordijn and Ralph Nauta have a team of sixty-five artists and designers who use technology "in order to learn from the Earth's underlying mechanisms, and to re-establish our connection to it." Their works illuminate parallels between man-made and natural structures through deconstructive, interactive, and innovative processes, raising "fundamental questions about what life is and explore a positive scenario for the future."[50] Their works have been exhibited or held in the collections of numerous museums, such as the Stedelijk Museum, Victoria & Albert, the Los Angeles County Museum of Art, and The Met. The firm has also created public art experiences, including the release of more than one thousand drones in Central Park in October 2023. *Franchise Freedom*, the kinetic, aerial sculpture that served as a silent art installation, was inspired by bird murmurations, a natural occurrence of synchronized, harmonic, and hustled bird flight.[51]

In 2025, DRIFT will launch a new concept, an immersive museum, in an historic structure in Amsterdam—the Van Gendt Hallen, a series of five factory buildings designed by architect Dolf van Gendt in 1898. Taking cues from London's renovated power station at Bankside in London, which was converted into Tate Modern for the new millennium, DRIFT Museum promises to be a new concept in terms of immersion, but also the effects on visitors by "generat[ing] wonder and emotional responses from our visitors and where they feel more connected to our planet and nature."[52]

In addition, exhibitions have utilized AR and VR to take visitors to other places. At the Dalí Museum, coinciding with the Dream exhibition featuring DALL-E, visitors could take in a VR experience called *Dreams of Dalí*, where three persons at a time, each working independently, could wander a 360-degree virtual world inspired by Dalí's works. Wandering the painting by moving one's head enabled free-range exploration for up to three minutes.

Other examples, beyond the Dalí Museum, of course, abound. For instance, in 2013 an exhibition at London's Somerset House about the singer and artist Björk let visitors have experiences out of the gallery by turning their attention to a deserted beach in Iceland or even inside Björk's mouth while she's performing. A 2015 exhibit at London's Design Museum used hidden cameras to take pictures of people gazing at artworks and then displayed those "portraits" back to the unwitting subjects. In 2021, the Venice Biennale rolled out a satellite program called *Venice VR Expanded*, which offered visitors to the selected museum (Portland Art Museum in Oregon) thirty-five exclusive VR projects viewable through a headset such as Oculus Quest or HTC Vive. Following this collaboration, the museum took the lead in foregrounding VR by launching a new initiative aimed at putting VR in the hands of visitors and allowing them to take it home with them. *VR to Go* offered visitors the opportunity to rent a VR headset preloaded with immersive projects from the museum.[53]

Museums, Data, and AI (artificial intelligence)

Returning to one of the concepts broached at the start of this chapter—interactivity—an assumption was made: interactivity involved human beings. Yet throughout this chapter, we have examined interactions that often involved the use of technology. So, what can be said of museums and artificial intelligence?

By definition, *artificial intelligence* is the broad range of technologies and their applications that involve a number of tools, including machine learning. The result is a tra-digital (traditional + digital) enhancement to the museum experience. An additional tenet of engagement, around having a "museum in one's pocket," involves data and open access. As Sophie Gilbert waxes, "Perhaps one day, some museums won't have a physical presence at all. Instead, they will curate digital exhibitions and change displays quickly to respond to global events in real time."[54] But the collections are not everything: they are a starting point. And they are, in this context, merely data.

Coupled with an API (Application Programming Interface)—which is a set of rules to outline how two machines can talk to one another as if on a call, in the call-and-response format—museum collections are the foundation for ongoing tech-centered engagement. For instance, the Art Institute of Chicago offers access to more than fifty thousand images of works from their collection that are in the public domain or free of copyright. These works are made available through Creative Commons licensing.[55] In addition, the data is available through the API. Further, some tools using the API can provide users with additional levels of engagement that encompass web browsers, video games, voice-controlled home assistants (Alexa), and more. For example, the Getty created an art-generator tool that enables users to add artwork from museum collections to *Animal Crossing*. An L.A.-based company built an extension for the Alexa platform that employs voice commands to take visitors on a virtual tour of a museum. A 3D simulator in a browser window enables viewers to bring works of art into a virtual gallery; an online editor ports over images to yield gifs.[56]

Data and machine learning are used in museum exhibitions such as *Dalí Lives*, an interactive experience created through machine learning–powered video editing of more than six thousand frames to create an algorithm of Dalí's face that was then superimposed over an actor's body. Quotes from Dalí were then synched with a voice actor. The result is a deepfake of "Surreal" proportions, with forty-five minutes of new footage. At the Dalí Museum, visitors stop at the kiosk in the museum corridor on the upper floor and can press the doorbell to beckon Dalí before the conversation begins. In addition to learning about the painter through his own words and a representation of him, the experience fosters awareness, empathy, and curiosity about the past. Factoring in that Dalí died in 1989, before the advent of smartphones, the turns of phrase the artist uses position the visitor in a space that is neither past nor present. Suspended between the two, visitors think of Dalí as somehow present. According to technology journalist, Dami Lee, "Figures in art history often feel like they lived lifetimes ago. But Dalí died in 1989, and standing before visitors in a life-sized kiosk does help bring him into the context of modern life—especially at the end of the experience when he asks visitors if they want to take a selfie."[57]

In addition to unique applications involving machine-learning, earlier applications of visitor-centered, museum-based applications of AI date to 2018, with the launch of Pepper at the Smithsonian. Designed and commercially available in 2014 in Japan, Pepper is part of a class of semi-humanoid robots with the ability to read emotions. Uses of Pepper have been in sports, health care, and consumer applications. In the museum context, however, Pepper has been sited at a handful of institutions, including the Smithsonian (2018–2020) and the Museum of Modern Art in Barcelona in 2021. Six Smithsonian venues deployed the Pepper robots in a trial program as part of an exploration of how the robot could enhance the visitor experience. To be clear, the intent was not to replace humans in the workforce, but rather to give audiences new ways to engage with the museum through conversation-based and screen-based interactions with a robot. In addition to overall exhibit guidance, Pepper aided visitors to the National Museum of African Art in learning Kiswahilli phrases as part of the *World on the Horizon* exhibit. Pepper also performed basic wayfinding functions while attracting

From 2018–2020, six Smithsonian venues deployed the Pepper robots in a trial program as part of an exploration of how the robot could enhance the visitor experience. The intent was not to replace humans in the workforce, but rather to give audiences new ways to engage with the museum through conversation-based and screen-based interactions with a robot.
Source: https://www.si.edu/newsdesk/releases/smithsonian-launches-pilot-program-pepper-robots.

visitors to less-attended gallery spaces. In the case of the Barcelona installation, Pepper proposed a guided tour of the museum after receiving minimal inputs from the visitor. In addition, the robot offered extended information about process, medium, and context that was beyond the scope of the wall labels in the exhibitions, enabling visitors to guide their learning in customize-able ways. With over two months of testing and a sample size of five hundred visitors, the overall interaction rate with Pepper at the Museum of Modern Art was 82 percent, with 92 percent of users expressing a high level of satisfaction with the experience.[58]

An additional example of robot-based museum experiences is the "robot art critic" called Berenson, which debuted in Paris' Musée du quai Branly—Jacques Chirac in 2016. Named after Old Master connoisseur and art critic Bernard Berenson, Berenson the robot was designed by engineer Philippe Gaussier and anthropologist Denis Vidal while seeking visitor responses to works of art. Wandering the exhibition *Persona: Oddly Human*, Berenson expressed his opinions about the art on display in in the exhibition, which examined the "transfer or confusion that exists between human and non-human."[59] Berenson extended the invitation to visitors, then, to respond to the works around them. Berenson was able to analyze the facial expressions of visitors and to sort them into "negative" and "positive" categories. That assessment was then fed into a system that crunched the numbers and arrived at an "overall impression" of the work. If that impression was positive, Berenson would smile and move closer; if it was negative, he would frown and move away. In this way, the robot captured the response of the visitor and amassed a dataset of visitor responses. While Berenson and Pepper were chiefly different in their purposeful engagement with visitors, they both use artificial intelligence (machine learning and natural language processing) to engage with visitors.

Current research at Carnegie Mellon University's Human-Computer Interaction Institute involves the addition of AI to museum exhibits as a means of increasing learning and engagement among youth interacting with science content. Their project uses AI as a virtual guide in an exhibit at the Carnegie Science Center in Pittsburgh, Pennsylvania. They put a virtual assistant, a gorilla named NoRILLA, which stands for Novel Research-based Intelligent Lifelong Learning Apparatus, in the exhibit space. NoRILLA interacted with the visitors, engaged them in questions, and helped them to gain access to additional information, in much the same way as Pepper interacted with Smithsonian guests. One of the lead researchers, Nesra Yannier, sees the system and interaction as an opportunity to deepen learning and provide persistent and consistent support for visitors/learners. Ultimately, NoRILLA seeks to engage these people.[60]

Artistic practice is another way that AI has made its way into the museum experience. DALL-E, the artificial intelligence art app, gives users of the app the opportunity to "create" art. Users feed words into a prompt, from which the computer brings together visuals to create an original photo-realistic presentation of those words. The result is displayed as a "work of art." In 2022, visitors to museums with the app installed could participate as part of a visitor engagement interactive. At the Dalí Museum in St. Petersburg, Florida, when visitors ended their exploration of the exhibition *The Shape of Dreams*, which looks at dreams of Dalí and his fellow Surrealist makers, they headed to one of two three-sided kiosks, where they input words that corresponded to elements of a recent dream. The computer-generated visualization of that dream was flashed upon a multi-panel display, with dreams-capes created by the machine for six visitors. Projected onto the wall of the gallery, the six panels were conjoined into a Dream Tapestry for all in the gallery to see, and to connect with the conversational thread of the exhibit around how dreams have inspired artists for more than five hundred years.[61]

In addition, out-of-gallery, visitor-centric experiences include one of the features of Google Arts & Culture: Art Selfie. Launched in 2018, Art Selfie enabled visitors to take a selfie with their devices, and then (using facial-recognition software) match that with one of the thousands scanned by Google and preselected as looking most similar to the visitor. In the case of DALL-E and Art Selfie, deep machine-learning models are trained on image data to pick up all sorts of minute details not obvious to the human eye, and in the case of DALL-E, create a pastiche from them, or, in the case of Art Selfie, to select the highest percentage of match between the "real person" and an artwork tagged with similar features. Such granular and accurate predictions that would take months of manual analysis to achieve can be done in seconds with machine learning.

A prerequisite to the use of AI, though, is data. Data can also play a role in decision-making in museums. For instance, data from observations of visitors in the gallery (i.e., in the form of formative evaluation or data downloads from Pepper at the Smithsonian) might yield insight relevant to decision-making to assist in exhibition design by predicting the future flow to galleries in exhibitions. These analytics can lead to better design, better visitor experiences, and improved access and safety. In addition, visitor data can be tracked to document how they look at artwork and their behaviors in-gallery to plan space for optimal benefit for visitors.

Thinking about AI, data, and museums more broadly, the "Museums + AI Network" was formed in 2019 by Oonagh Murphy (University of London) and Elena Villaespesa (Pratt Institute) as a space to critically examine current practices, challenges, and opportunities with AI in the UK and the United States. The network aspires to help non-specialists understand the possibilities of AI while also empowering museum professionals to plunge forward and develop project plans and workflows that incorporate AI. Fears of AI persist, however. In poking fun at the thought of AI as part of a standardized museum workflow, *Art In America* posed the question of whether AI might make curators obsolete. Chen and Lampert mused, "Imagine, if you will, that an artificially intelligent robot, let's call it Kunst Lieben Algorithmic Unix System (K.L.A.United States), has been programmed to curate the next Venice Biennale. Rather than spend two years making studio visits around the world, this robo-curator would scan every art periodical, browse gallery and art fair websites, scrape all social media accounts, and linger at parties where it could soberly overhear all the gossip and insider trading. After K.L.A.United States finished crunching petabytes of data and training its neural network, would the resulting exhibition outperform a biennial organized by human curators?" Easily, the alarm was silenced as the author affirms that curators draw on their human qualities of their "eyes" and "hearts," beyond all the research and data, to do their work.[62] Because, as we have seen throughout these chapters, and will continue to witness, museums are about people: they need people as part of that triangulation among the object, institution, and visitor. People, not robots, are at the core of museums, and they are whom museums ultimately serve, as we will see in the following chapter.

Notes

1. Stephen Bitgood, "Deadly Sins Revisited: A Review of the Exhibit Label Literature," *Visitor Studies*, Fall 1989 (IV:3): 4–11; Beverly Serrell, *Exhibit Labels: An Interpretive Approach* (Walnut Creek: AltaMira Press, 1996), 33; John Beetlestone et al., "The Science Center Movement," 8–10, Joaneath Spicer, "The Exhibition: Lecture or Conversation?" *Curator* 37, no. 3 (1994): 185–97; S. Bicknell and G. Farmelo, *Museum Visitor Studies in the '90s* (London: Science Museum, 1993); Judy Diamond, *Practical Evaluation Guide: Tools for Museums and Other Informal Educational Settings* (Walnut Creek: AltaMira Press, 1999).
2. Barry Joseph, *Making Dinosaurs Dance: A Toolkit for Digital Design in Museums* (Lanham, MD: Rowman & Littlefield, for American Alliance of Museums, 2023).
3. Joe Coscarelli, "How a Jay-Z Retrospective Took Over the Brooklyn Public Library," July 14, 2023, https://www.nytimes.com/2023/07/14/arts/music/jay-z-book-of-hov-brooklyn-public-library.html.
4. Callie Holtermann, "How Library Cards Became the Jay-Z Merch of the Moment," *New York Times*, August 15, 2023, https://www.nytimes.com/2023/08/15/style/jay-z-brooklyn-library-cards.html.
5. Roc Nation, "The Book of Hov," https://www.thebookofhov.com/about.
6. At the close of the twentieth century, Marcia Lord, in the journal *Museum International*, reminded us that regardless of a museum's size, through the World Wide Web, museums could reach many more "visitors" than they would ever welcome through their doors. Size no longer seemed important. See Marcia Lord, "Editorial," *Museum International* 51, no. 4 (1999): 3.
7. Ecsite, http://www.ecsite.net.

8. Tom Hennes, "Hyperconnection: Natural History Museums, Knowledge, and the Evolving Ecology of Community," *Curator* 50, no. 1 (January 2007): 106.

9. Roberto Ivo Fernandes Vaz, Paula Odete Fernandes, and Ana Cecília Rocha Veiga, "Interactive Technologies in Museums: How Digital Installations and Media Are Enhancing the Visitors' Experience," *Handbook of Research on Technological Developments for Cultural Heritage and eTourism Applications*, edited by João M. F. Rodrigues, Célia M. Q. Ramos, Pedro J. S. Cardoso, and Cláudia Henriques (Hershey, PA: IGI Global Publisher, 2018).

10. John Paul Titlow, "How a 145-Year-Old Art Museum Stays Relevant in the Smartphone Age," *Fast Company*, February 29, 2016, https://www.fastcompany.com/3057236/how-a-145-year-old-art -museum-stays-relevant-in-the-smartphone-age.

11. Data described in John Paul Titlow, "How a 145-Year-Old Art Museum Stays Relevant in the Smartphone Age," *Fast Company* February 29, 2016, https://www.fastcompany.com/3057236/how-a-145-year-old -art-museum-stays-relevant-in-the-smartphone-age.

12. Sophie Gilbert, "Please Turn on Your Phone in the Museum," *Atlantic*, October 2016, https://www.the atlantic.com/magazine/archive/2016/10/please-turn-on-your-phone-in-the-museum/497525/.

13. Museum Archipelago: https://www.museumarchipelago.com/episodes; Museum Confidential: https:// podcasts.apple.com/us/podcast/museum-confidential/; Sidedoor (Smithsonian): https://www.si.edu/ sidedoor.

14. ICOM, "ICOM Launches Rebranded Podcast: *Museums and Chill*," April 12, 2023, https://icom .museum/en/news/icom-launches-rebranded-podcast-museums-and-chill/.

15. Alex Espinós, "Museums on Social Media: Analyzing Growth through Case Studies," *MW2016: Museums and the Web 2016*. Published January 31, 2016, http://mw2016.museumsandtheweb.com/paper/ museums-on-social-media-analyzing-growth-through-case-studies/.

16. Chi-Young Kim, "Goodbye to Rain Room . . . for Now," *Unframed LACMA*, January 30, 2017, https:// unframed.lacma.org/2017/01/30/goodbye-rain-roomfor-now.

17. Elizabeth Hutchison Hicklin, "The D.C. Art Exhibit That's Blowing Up on Instagram," *Garden & Gun*, February 13, 2016, https://gardenandgun.com/articles/the-d-c-art-exhibit-thats-blowing-up-on-instagram/.

18. The key museums discussed were featured in Tim Deakin, "How Are Museums Using TikTok?" *Museum Next*, December 28, 2022, https://www.museumnext.com/article/how-are-museums-are -using-tiktok/. Guidance on how to develop content for TikTok comes from Seema Rao, "8 Takeways for Museums from TikTok," August 27, 2022, http://museumtwo.blogspot.com/2022/08/8-take aways-for-museums-from-tiktok.html. One of the subcultures on TikTok is art history, such as Mary McGillivray's https://www.tiktok.com/@_theiconoclass.

19. Analytics pulled by the author, December 1, 2023.

20. See Artetik, https://g.co/arts/gwotDQvjkBRHjxBH8. These results were computed from contributions, collected in the Guggenheim Bilbao Museum between 2021 and 2023.

21. https://www.guggenheim-bilbao.eus/en/the-collection/works/jaosokor.

22. Wenger-Trayner, Etienne, and Beverly. "Communities of Practice: A Brief Introduction," April 15, 2015: I define *communities of practice* as "groups of people who share a concern or a passion for something they do and learn how to do it better as they interact regularly." See also Etienne Wenger, Richard McDermott, and William M. Snyder, *Cultivating Communities of Practice: A Guide to Managing Knowledge* (Boston: Harvard Business School Press, 2002).

23. See Etienne Wenger-Trayner, Mark Fenton-O'Creevy, Steven Hutchinson, Chris Kubiak, and Beverly Wenger-Trayner, *Learning in Landscapes of Practice: Boundaries, Identity, and Knowledgeability in Practice-Based Learning* (London: Routledge, 2014).

24. As of January 14, 2016, the "Learn How to Transcribe" note indicates 5,827 volunteers have been a part of this project. See Juilee Decker, "A Note from the Editor," *Collections: A Journal for Museum and Archives Professionals* 12:02 (Spring 2016): 81–83.

25. See Smithsonian Transcription Center, "About," https://transcription.si.edu/about, July 1, 2023.

26. Mia Ridge, "From Tagging to Theorizing: Deepening Engagement with Cultural Heritage through Crowdsourcing." *Curator: The Museum Journal* 56:4(2013): 435–50.

27. See Martin R. Kalfatovic, Effie Kapsalis, Katherine P. Spiess, Anne Van Camp, and Michael Edson, "Smithsonian Team Flickr: A Library, Archives, and Museums Collaboration in Web 2.0 Space," *Archival*

Science 8 (2008): 267–77; Effie Kapsalis, "Making History with Crowdsourcing," *Collections: A Journal for Museum and Archives Professionals*, edited by Juilee Decker, 12:02 (Spring 2016): 191–200.

28. See Mafkereseb Bekele, Roberto Pierdicca, Emanuele Frontoni, Eva Savina Malinverni, and James Gain, "A Survey of Augmented, Virtual, and Mixed Reality for Cultural Heritage," *Journal on Computing and Cultural Heritage* 11:2 (2018), 1–36, DOI:10.1145/3145534.

29. British Museum, "The British Museum in Minecraft," http://museumcraft.tumblr.com/. On Anchorage Museum, see https://www.anchoragemuseum.org/about-us/news/community-archive/minecraft-members-build-museum-one-brick-at-a-time/. Minecraft is also used as an exhibition apparatus. See Matt Kamen, "The Great Fire of London Has Been Reimagined in Minecraft," *Wired*, July 19, 2016, http://www.wired.co.uk/article/the-museum-of-london-is-using-minecraft-to-recreate-the-great-fire-of-london. Minecraft has also been used as inspiration for programs, too, as in the Penn Museum's "Creep Around the Penn Museum" program, which makes connections between tools and materials in Minecraft and those of the museum. See http://www.penn.museum/calendar/event detail/297/creep-around-the-penn-museum-a-minecraft-inspired-program.

30. MoPop, *Minecraft: The Exhibition*, https://www.mopop.org/exhibitions-plus-events/traveling -exhibitions/minecraft-the-exhibition-travelling/.

31. Blaire Moskewitz, "Gotta Visit 'Em All—Pokémon GO in Museums," July 11, 2016, https://blairemoskowitz.com/2016/07/11/gotta-visit-em-all-pokemongo-in-museums/; "Poké It Up: How to Catch Millennials with Pokémon Go at Your Museum," Museum Hack, July 14, 2016, https://museumhack.com/catch-millennials-pokemon-go/.

32. International Museum of Art and Science, http://theimasonline.org/welcome/.

33. Sean Magner, "Museums and Augmented Reality: Lessons from Pokémon Go," https://museum revolution.com/museums-augmented-reality-pokemon-go/, accessed October 20, 2023.

34. Niantic Lightship ARDK, https://lightship.dev/products/ardk/, accessed October 1, 2023.

35. Wonderlab AR, https://play.google.com/store/apps/details?id=com.sciencemuseum.wonderlab &hl=en&gl=U.

36. For more on Tower Superbloom AR, see Lightship AR, "Create a Superbloom in AR: Historic Royal Palaces x PRELOADED," https://www.youtube.com/watch?v=LvWFOK4gAh4.

37. National Videogame Museum, "Animal Crossing Diaries," https://animalcrossingdiaries.thenvm .org/about/, accessed October 1, 2023.

38. The Digital Editors, "Own a Van Gogh . . . in *Animal Crossing*, with The Met's New Share Tool," *The Met*, April 27, 2020, https://www.metmuseum.org/blogs/collection-insights/2020/animal -crossing-new-horizons-qr-code.

39. Alvina Lai, "The Museum in Animal Crossing," *Play the Past*, May 26, 2020, https://www.playthe past.org/?p=6880.

40. Tomas Brown, "The Role of the Museum in Video Games," *Play the Past*, June 6, 2014, https://www.playthepast.org/?p=4717. Brown has examined four game worlds as part of this museum-game dyad: *Uncharted* (2011), with the main character, Drake, beginning his adventure in a museum; *Uncharted 2*, when Drake and a friend break into a Turkish museum; *Skyrim* (2011), an open-world environment where the player achieves a level at which they are invited to the opening of a museum in Dawnstar in the North of the region of the game world, where the museum connotes social power and a sense of place; *Bioshock*, in which museums are used as political devices and institutions for educating about the rapture, and the origins of the land are conveyed (or otherwise manipulated); and *Wildstar* (2014), in which museums are used to communicate about the starting areas, the lore, and the factions. I am grateful for input on this section from my colleague Trent Hergenrader, who researches worldbuilding.

41. The fossilized Pokémon were exhibited at the National Museum in Tokyo, the Mikasa City Museum, the Gunma Museum of Natural History, the Toyohashi Museum of Natural History and the Shimane Nature Museum of Mount Sanbe, among others. See "Pokémon Fossil Museum," https://www .kahaku.go.jp/pokemon/index_en.html.

42. As of November 2023, one Pikachu promo card was listed at three thousand dollars. https://www.ebay.com/itm/374997853768. See also Carl Kinsella, "Pokémon Gogh: What the Viral Mash-Up Between a Museum and a Japanese Brand Reveals About Their Shared Priorities," *Artnet*, October 2, 2023, https://news.artnet.com/art-world/van-gogh-museum-pokemon-exhibition-2370765.

43. Aidin Vaziri, "This S.F. Museum Is Going to Be the First to Use Snapchat's AR Technology," *San Francisco Chronicle*, November 16, 2023, https://www.sfchronicle.com/entertainment/article/snapchat-mirror-de-young-museum-sf-18497305.php. This technology is already in use by retailers, such as Coach and Nike, to give customers an idea of how items will appear on their bodies.

44. The collection of testimonies was initially, in 2016, referred to as "New Dimensions in Testimony," to reflect the iterative, prototype process. Since at least 2018, the project has been referred to as "Dimensions in Testimony." See USC Shoah Foundation, "New Dimensions in Testimony on Display at USHMM," May 11, 2016, https://sfi.usc.edu/news/2016/05/11444-new-dimensions-testimony-display-ushmm.

45. University of Southern California, "What Is Dimensions in Testimony?" https://sfi.usc.edu/dit. The exhibit is/has been on view at the Illinois Holocaust Museum and Education Center; the CANDLES Holocaust Museum and Education Center in Indiana; the Dallas Holocaust and Human Rights Museum; the Holocaust Museum Houston; the Holocaust Museum LA; the Maltz Museum of Jewish Heritage (Cleveland); the Nancy & David Wolf Holocaust & Humanity Center, Cincinnati; the Indiana Historical Society; the Florida Holocaust Museum; Nova Southeastern University; Museo del Holocausto de Buenos Aires; and the Sydney Jewish Museum.

46. Matthew Boswell and Antony Rowland, "Entering Dimensions in Testimony," *Virtual Holocaust Memory* (New York, Oxford Academic, 2023), https://doi.org/10.1093/oso/9780197645390.003.0002.

47. Kateřina Blahutová, "Living Forest," *Balloon Museum*, https://balloonmuseum.world/artworks/.

48. The Balloon Museum, https://balloonmuseum.world/about/; https://www.newyorksocialdiary.com/calendar/balloon-museum-makes-its-u-s-debut-in-new-york-city-this-fall-with-immersive-contemporary-art-exhibition-lets-fly/. The Balloon Museum has been on view in Madrid, Milan, Paris, and Rome; is currently on view in New York City, London, and Naples; and is slated for exhibition in Los Angeles, Miami, and San Francisco, among other cities worldwide.

49. Rossilynne Skena Culgan, Anna Rahmanan, and Shaye Weaver, "Incredible Immersive Experiences to Do in NYC Right Now," *Time Out*, November 3, 2023, https://www.timeout.com/newyork/art/incredible-immersive-experiences-to-do-in-nyc-right-now.

50. DRIFT, "Artists," https://studiodrift.com/drift-artists/.

51. For a review of the experience, and comparisons to Christ and Jeanne-Claude's installation *The Gates*, which was on view in Central Park in 2005, see Roberta Smith, "Flight of the Drones Lights Up Central Park," *New York Times*, October 23, 2023, https://www.nytimes.com/2023/10/23/arts/design/drones-drift-central-park-franchise-freedom.html.

52. DRIFT, "Announcing the DRIFT Museum in Amsterdam," November 7, 2023, https://studiodrift.com/announcing-the-drift-museum-in-amsterdam/. The museum is a partnership with Eduard Zanen, entrepreneur and owner of Gendt Hallen, who stated: "I see it as my responsibility to preserve the building for the future and create a place where entrepreneurship, art and technology come together and where new forms of collaboration emerge. By innovative restoration techniques and repairing rather than replacing it, an energy-neutral national monument is created." See https://driftmuseum.com/.

53. On the Venice Biennale's "Venice VR Expanded," see https://cgsociety.org/news/article/5190/venice-biennales-venice-vr-expanded-returns-to-the-portland-art-museum. On VR to Go, see Chance Solem-Pfeifer, "PAM CUT's 'VR to Go' Program Allows Portlanders to Rent an Oculus Quest Headset Preloaded with Immersive Works," *Willamette Week*, July 13, 2022, https://www.wweek.com/culture/2022/07/13/pam-cuts-vr-to-go-program-allows-portlanders-to-rent-an-oculus-go-headset-preloaded-with-immersive-works/.

54. Sophie Gilbert, "Please Turn on Your Phone in the Museum," *Atlantic*, October 2016, https://www.theatlantic.com/magazine/archive/2016/10/please-turn-on-your-phone-in-the-museum/497525/.

55. The museum makes them available through an API. They request that users include the following caption with reproductions of the images: *Artist. Title, Date. The Art Institute of Chicago*. This information, which is available on the object page for each work, is also made available under Creative Commons Zero (CC0). A download button is included on pages where the artwork is in the public domain. https://www.artic.edu/open-access/open-access-images.

56. Getty Animal Crossing Art Generator, https://experiments.getty.edu/ac-art-generator/; Alexa, open Art Museum, https://flaxen-street-108.notion.site/Alexa-open-Art-Museum-f841e66775644a99a240df9cbf1cb7e3, which is related to Amazon's re:Invent 2018; Virtual Art Gallery, REGL format

of simulating an art gallery in your browser, https://clementcariou.github.io/virtual-art-gallery/; and a gif generator, https://artgif.netlify.app/. For these and more, see Art Institute of Chicago, "Public API," https://www.artic.edu/open-access/public-api.

57. Dami Lee, "Deepfake Salvador Dali Takes Selfies with Museum Visitors," Verge, May 10, 2019, https://www.theverge.com/2019/5/10/18540953/salvador-dali-lives-deepfake-museum.

58. "Smithsonian Launches Pilot Program of 'Pepper' Robots," April 24, 2018, https://www.si .edu/newsdesk/releases/smithsonian-launches-pilot-program-pepper-robots; Kathleen Walch, "AI Revolutionizing the Museum Experience at the Smithsonian," *Forbes* March 26, 2020, https://www .forbes.com/sites/cognitiveworld/2020/03/26/ai-revolutionizing-the-museum-experience-at-the -smithsonian/?sh=167d9b0556fd. See YouTube videos to watch Pepper at work: Smithsonian, Washington, D.C., 2018: https://www.youtube.com/watch?v=AHZ1AhdUS_M; Museum of Modern Art, Barcelona, 2021: https://www.youtube.com/watch?v=RYbtZZ878GQ.

59. On Berenson, see Cait Munro, "Meet Berenson, the Robot Art Critic: Should Art Critics Fear for Their Jobs?" *Artnet*, February 29, 2016, https://news.artnet.com/art-world/robot-art-critic-berenson -436739. The response from the visitor was fed into a neural network simulator called Prométhé. On the exhibit where Berenson was sited, see *Persona: Strangely Human*, https://www.quaibranly.fr/en/ exhibitions-and-events/at-the-museum/exhibitions/event-details/e/persona-36255/.

60. NoRILLA, https://www.norilla.com/.

61. The Dali, "Dream Tapestry," September 20, 2023, https://thedali.org/exhibit/dream-tapestry-2-2/.

62. Chen & Lampert, "Hard Truths: Will Musuems' Digital Plans Make Curators Obsolete?" *Art in America*, May 14, 2020, https://www.artnews.com/art-in-america/columns/artificial-intelligence -art-curators-art-world-advice-1202687166/.

10

To Serve

The first section of this volume examines the history of museums. In this section, the chapters have examined activities that museums do to store, care for, and display their collections. The chapters have also shown how museums strive to meet the needs of their visitors through exhibitions, public programming, tours, and other forms of interpretation and engagement. With this chapter, our attention shifts: whereas in previous chapters, we have assumed the primacy of the object, here we look to people. Attention turns to the ways in which museums serve their communities—be that the neighbors who live near the building, the residents of the city where the museum is sited, or beyond these borders.

To begin, we will turn to the changing concept of the museum, before looking at the role of museums in helping to achieve the United Nations Sustainable Development Goals (SDGs). This chapter also lays the foundation for Section III of this volume, where each chapter examines needs: needs of communities, museum workers, and humanity. Awareness around the role of collections in the history and functions of museums is evident in the research of the United Kingdom–based consultancy Museum Association, which launched its *Collections 2030* initiative in 2018, as a follow-up from their 2005 report on *Collections for the Future*. The association's eleven recommendations focused on changes within museums as institutions; funding and strategic investment within and across the sector; and changes for the profession that would offer guidance on matters such as diversifying the workforce and decolonization practices. A respondent to their survey noted, "Seeing yourself represented in culture is necessary to value and want to participate in it. Strategic collecting from underrepresented groups and additional narratives on existing collections are needed."[1] Clearly, the construction of museums—physically through buildings and collections activities—has become tethered to the role of museums in storytelling and convening communities. Stories are the intangible heritage of museums: they are how visitors navigate the curatorial premise by walking through an exhibition, and they are often how visitors remember their experiences at museums. Stories are the glue that holds exhibitions and experiences together.[2] Storytelling, as we learned in Chapter 8, is a museum's superpower.

Such a construction of museums *conceptually*—as a space for convening, as well as a physical, enterable place with collections—is addressed in the latest definition of *museums* adopted by ICOM in 2022: "A museum is a not-for-profit, permanent institution in the service of society that researches, collects, conserves, interprets and exhibits tangible and intangible heritage. Open to the public, accessible and inclusive, museums foster diversity and sustainability. They operate and communicate ethically, professionally and with the participation of communities, offering varied experiences for education, enjoyment, reflection and knowledge sharing."[3] This changing definition has been part of the history of museums, as it also discloses their changing roles in society.

In the fall of 2021, students at my institution, Rochester Institute of Technology, participated in the creation of a global pop-up exhibition *Hostile Terrain 94*, a participatory project sponsored and organized by the Undocumented Migration Project, a nonprofit research-art-education-media collective, directed by UCLA anthropologist and MacArthur fellow Jason De León. The project draws attention to the humanitarian crisis at the US-Mexico border linked to policies of Prevention through Deterrence. Attendees at workshops I coordinated with my co-organizer, Christine Kray, wrote out the names and identifying information about individuals on toe tags to prepare for the installation. More than 3,200 handwritten toe tags represent migrants who died trying to cross the Sonoran Desert of Arizona between the mid-1990s and 2019. Each toe tag lists the personal information of one such individual: one by one, these tags are geolocated on a wall map of the desert showing the exact locations where remains were found. The exhibition was on view at RIT from October 25, 2021 through January 11, 2022. More information here: https://infoguides.rit.edu/c.php?g=1167470.
Photo credit: A. Sue Weisler.

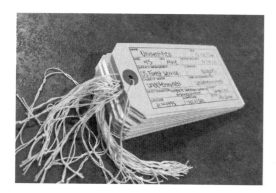

SUSTAINABLE DEVELOPMENT G☼ALS

Museums have the capacity to change, grow, shift, and transform the world around us. As the International Council of Museums (ICOM) has recognized, museums can help contribute toward efforts at global equality by working toward the UN Sustainable Goals (SDGs). They recognize that all countries in the developed and developing world have a responsibility to address all of the goals (items 1-16) and to do so in partnership with one another (goal 17). Exhibitions and events that bring awareness to these concerns, as well as policies and sustainable practices that support the goals, are some of the ways museums can contribute to such efforts. See https://www.un.org/sustainabledevelopment.

The SDG logo and related materials are freely available without the UN emblem. The content of this publication has not been approved by the United Nations and does not reflect the views of the United Nations or its officials or Member States.

The Changing Concept of "Museum"

When Theodore L. Low wrote *The Museum as a Social Instrument* for AAM's Committee on Education in 1942, he advocated that museums make popular education their predominant goal, superior to, but including, acquisitions, preservation, and scholarly study. He opposed having museums confine their attention to the upper strata of society and urged that they vigorously seek to serve "an intellectual middle class." He argued in the same general terms that John Cotton Dana had used in conceiving the Newark Museum as a vehicle for community pride and betterment.[4] In this same spirit, ICOM defined *museums* in 1946 as "all collections, open to the public, of artistic, technical, scientific, historical or archaeological material, including zoos and botanical gardens, but excluding libraries, except in so far as they maintain permanent exhibition rooms."

However, the transformation of many museums in the United States into cultural centers has not been universal. A 1972 Harris Poll asked museum directors to evaluate the two museum purposes most important to themselves, the public, and the trustees, and to identify those purposes most successfully carried out by their institutions. "Encouraging of positive social change" ranked at the bottom of six suggested purposes in the directors' opinions and was ranked as most important by only 6 percent of the directors, 2 percent of the public, and 3 percent of the trustees, and most revealing, this goal was reported as successfully accomplished by only 3 percent of the museums surveyed.[5]

About the same time as the Harris Poll, Brooklyn Museum director Duncan Cameron published his notions of a museum in the journal *Curator* and in the United Nations Educational, Scientific and Cultural Organization's (UNESCO) *Journal of World History*; his thesis was that museums occupy two ends of a spectrum, from "temple" to "forum." He described the temple as representing the "victor's" resting place for spoils, while the forum was the site for engaging in "battles" of ideas. His essay is worth a close reading, as it laid out what has become (and remains) a challenge to museum practice. He asserted that "museums must concern themselves with the reform and development of museums *as museums*. They must meet society's needs for that unique institution which fulfills a timeless and universal function—the use of the structured sample reality, not just as a reference but as an objective model against which to compare individual perceptions. . . . In the absence of the forum, the museum as temple stands alone as an obstacle to change. . . . From the chaos and conflict of today's forum the museum must build the collections which will tell us tomorrow who we are and how we got here. After all, that's what museums are all about."[6] A cursory review of the subsequent years of museum practices suggests that the tensions between temple and forum persist.

As noted in the previous chapter, the American Association of Museums (AAM) convened a national task force to address the roles of museums. Its 1992 report, *Excellence and Equity*, called for museums to attend to their audiences and communities as part of their professional practice. The report concluded with this charge: "The community of museums in the United States shares the responsibility with other educational institutions to enrich learning opportunities for all individuals and to nurture an enlightened, humane citizenry that appreciates the value of knowing about its past, is resourcefully and sensitively engaged in the present, and is determined to shape a future in which *many experiences and many points of view are given voice*" [emphasis added].[7] Cameron's forum emerges as the desirable posture for United States museums, yet the notion of an "enlightened, humane citizenry" smacks of privilege. Why must audiences and communities be "enlightened"? Why would we use that term in spaces that have been framed as informal learning environments? Can museums not be spaces for all?

The American Academy of Arts and Sciences summer 1999 issue of *Daedalus* sought to both define and project current American museum practices. Bonnie Pittman opened the essays with this overarching statement: "Museums are more than the repositories of the past, with memories and objects both rare and beautiful. Museums are cultural, educational, and civic centers in our communities—centers for exhibitions, conservation, research, and interpretation; they are theaters and movie houses, job-training programs, schools and day-care centers, libraries and concert halls . . . forums for their communities."[8] These essays, like Cameron's, suggest that service to audiences trumps the traditional demands of collections and cements the museum solidly within communities. Stephen Weil closes his essay, "From Being about Something to Being for Somebody: The Ongoing Transformation of the American Museum," by noting "that it [the museum] is so potentially open-textured as a destination, so adaptable to a variety of public uses should not—at least in the emerging and visitor-centered museum—be regarded as a defect. Rather, it should be understood as one of its greater glories."[9] In a sense, their discussions extend the thoughts of George Brown Goode, Dana, Low, and Cameron calling for museums to broaden their educational commitment.

In comparing the 1972 snapshot of museums to participatory museums of the early twenty-first century, one might claim that the notion of making museums institutions of popular education, as Low had conceived them, was largely achieved and that efforts have continued to push this definition of a *museum* and further the notion of museums as welcoming, inclusive spaces for all. However, beyond this challenge of old and new, the notion of the forum is not inherently inclusive, for it privileges some views over others. Further, it elides contributions of entire groups through inaccessibility via physical and financial barriers to entry, communication incompatibility (in terms of language and literacy, including American Sign Language), and obstacles presented by the immediate environment (such as a too-stimulating setting).

Museums Movements

Thus, in moving from a definition of a museum as an institution, to the people who comprise it, movements and practices have been underway to challenge the notion of the museum. A fuller discussion of museum movements—advocacy, activism, discussion, and mobilization in the landscape of museums—may be found in Section III. Here, though, are brief introductions to the collectives that have helped shift the needle in defining what museums are and who they are for today.

Museum Hue

Museum Hue was founded in 2014 as a group of millennial Black and Brown (Latino, Asian, Indian, First Nations, Indigenous, Middle Eastern), socially conscious museum and culture workers. The group advocates for mirroring between the diversity of the population of the United States and the audiences and staff of museums. Their goal, according to inaugural strategic director and museum consultant, Monica O. Montgomery, is to work "in partnership with community, so that perceptions will change and museums can truly become welcoming inclusive spaces for all."[10] As an organization, Museum Hue "is dedicated to uplifting the voices of people of color in the arts and culture field by offering tools and resources in a supportive environment. We cultural diversity in the arts ecosystem and create pathways for those who need it most in the sector. Museum Hue works to improve the racial inequity in the field and promote people of color's cultural contributions, artistic practices, and historical narratives."[11] While the organization centers arts organizations, their work is relevant to cultural organizations more broadly. (See more on Museum Hue in Chapter 12.)

Empathetic Museum

Also founded in 2014, The Empathetic Museum seeks to further diversity and inclusion in the museum industry by "using empathy as [their] lens." Comprised of educators, exhibit designers, interpretive planners, and administrators, this consortium of museum professionals seeks change through open dialog about the challenges that face museums and those who work in the field. The group developed and launched the Maturity Model, an assessment tool proposed to "help organizations move towards a more empathetic future." The model identifies five characteristics of an empathetic museum—Civic Vision, Institutional Body Language, Community Resonance, Timeliness and Sustainability, and Performance Measures. Each of the five characteristics identified in the model is defined and elaborated upon in an accompanying rubric to facilitate self-evaluation along a spectrum from regressive to proactive levels of action. By using this tool, individuals and institutions can see where they stand and can highlight areas where change is needed.[12]

Like many of the theories and models developed over the course of the past one-hundred-plus years of professional museum practice in the United States, the Maturity Model builds upon the work of a number of scholars, including Gail Dexter Lord, Ngaire Blankenberg, Gretchen Jennings, Elaine Heumann Gurian, Margaret Middleton, and a number of museum professionals, theorists, commentators, bloggers, and others. They are connected, also, to previous activist movements, such as the Art Workers Coalition (AWC) and a subgroup of this organization led by artists Faith Ringgold and Tom Lloyd, who submitted "13 Demands" to Museum of Modern Art director, Bates Lowry on January 28, 1969. Among the demands were a public hearing on the topic of "The Museum's Relationship to Artists and to Society," the creation of a section of the museum devoted to showing the accomplishments of Black artists, and other demands seeking artists's rights as well as exhibition and display demands. While the AWC's requests may seem a distant need, the notion of inclusion, conversation, and collaboration rings true today. Current chief of archives at MoMA, Michelle Elligott, notes, "The words of Ringgold and Lloyd still prevail upon us, and their actions and activism continue to ring true, affect, and inform us today. Even if the shortcomings of our past do not exemplify our aspirations or expectations, it is important to understand and narrate that past to help us shape a future of progress, inclusion, and hope."[13]

Museums & Race

In 2016, Museums & Race was founded as a direct result of an initial gathering in Atlanta in 2015 as part of the American Alliance of Museums' annual conference. With the hope of challenging and transforming the museum and its people, twenty-four museum professionals convened in January 2016, and the focus of conversation was race and racism in museums. Museums & Race: Transformation and Justice is a movement "to challenge and re-imagine institutional policies and systems that perpetuate oppressions in museums."[14]

Black Lives Matter

Each of the initiatives above occurred after the birth of the hashtag #BlackLivesMatter, which first appeared on Facebook on July 13, 2013, after the acquittal of George Zimmerman, a Florida man who killed a Black teenager in Ferguson, Missouri, in 2012. The post of disbelief and grief, as well as affirmation and "love letter to Black people" on Facebook by Alicia Garza, and the three-word statement that followed by Garza's friend Patrisse Cullors, spawned the BLM movement in the United States and beyond.[15]

Social media–originated movements such as BLM defy traditional top-down, leader-centered movements, and ultimately, the vertical and hierarchical arrangement of museums. To reframe community organizing at the time of BLM as a metaphor for museums, we can see how "the consequence of focussing on a leader is that you develop a necessity for that leader to be the one who's the spokesperson and the organizer, who tells the masses where to go, rather than the masses understanding that we can catalyze a movement in our own community."[16] Instead, movements such as BLM, and the Occupy Wall Street Movement that preceded it, draw attention to the need for change without ever anointing a leader or leadership team. These efforts ignited a spirit of protest through in-person presence (occupying physical space) and dominating social media (occupying digital space). While there are mixed opinions as to the success of Occupy, the efforts did demonstrate "what protest was, and how it could make a difference." Movements such as BLM; #MeToo; and anti-Trump women's marches all have drawn inspiration from Occupy.[17] In this way, movements can be the connective tissue of museums.

Moreover, the summer of 2020 demonstrates, even more fully, the need for museums to serve as faces, spaces, and places. They are sites where communities (*faces*) can convene, that offer *spaces* to reflect, act, and agitate (as well as all the other verbs used to illuminate the chapters in this section) and remain anchor *places* for such communities to convene over time. These places to convene and spaces to heal include museums such as the Jane Addams Hull-House Museum in Chicago, Illinois, located in two of the original settlement house buildings that were part of the social settlement. Founded in 1889, Hull-House Museum positions itself as being "at the forefront of rethinking and transforming museum practice." In 2020, and in partnership with the Museum and Exhibition Studies graduate degree program at the University of Illinois at Chicago, the museum offered a series of museum and social justice programs aimed at welcoming all people in ways they wish to be welcomed. The first in the series looked at the book *Exhibitions for Social Justice*; it brought to light curatorial collaborations from the local area and discussed working with diverse communities to address social change.[18] A second talk in the series looked at the history of art, feminism, and artist-run projects in Chicago through the lenses of collaborative, participatory, and activist history.[19] A third talk moved outward to education by examining how K-12 teachers might use museums to support student exploration while also teaching for social justice by addressing topics such as disability and welcoming all bodies; celebrating queer people's lives and histories; settler colonialism and decolonization; fair workplaces; and Indigenous knowledge.[20]

Additional examples of the work of museums, organized around themes, are the focus of Section III. In thinking about recent and not-so-recent activism in the space of the museum and beyond it, it is apparent that an overarching theme connects many of these recent iterations of the place of the museum in the twenty-first century. Specifically, museums are called upon to be civic leaders and relevant to the societies in which they reside (i.e., "anchor institutions," as defined by Lord and Blankenberg), and they are called to join with other institutions and groups to capitalize upon combined interest and efforts to influence and shape action (i.e., "soft power," as defined by Lord and Blankenberg) and to impact inclusive and empathetic initiatives in museums and elsewhere.[21]

Museums contend with the cultural, political, and economic challenges that face society; yet they also have the capacity to serve society in new ways. Today, we are in the midst of a global refugee crisis with more than one million people moving from political turmoil in Syria, Afghanistan, and Iraq to Germany, Sweden, and other parts of Europe. The relocation of individuals into new environments can leave them longing for familiar cultural contexts first and foremost, and for those who were employed in the museum field previously, for work. In one case, the Prussian Cultural Heritage Foundation, through the project "*Multaka*," which means "meeting point" in Arabic, has begun employing refugees in German society by hiring them as tour guides. "In part, the purpose of the project is get the refugees back into the industries and reignite the passions they had before they were expelled from their countries . . . it can be difficult for migrants with advanced degrees to pursue the high-level careers they had in their homeland. As such, refugees who were in the arts field were excited to be able to jump back into their roles in the community through such an initiative."[22] By offering tours of national museums, the museum professionals are given the opportunity to immerse themselves in another culture while also paying tribute to their own—when they encounter an object from their own civilization. In addition, museums in the Network of European Museum Organizations have begun working individually and in partnership with other organizations to provide skills, education, and employability to migrants, immigrants, refugees, and asylum seekers aged sixteen to twenty-six. Other examples abound. For instance, the British Museum has hosted language centers to teach English to migrants. In addition, a number of programs have been held since 2009 both to diversify staff and governance bodies of museums in Europe and to foster understanding of heritage and identities.[23] Migration is also reflected in museum practices and exhibition content; as Francesca Lanz has noted in her discussion of challenges in representing migration in museums, this involves both the curatorial approaches as well as exhibition settings and practices.[24]

Museums and the United Nations Sustainable Development Goals (SDGs)

Given all these points of contact among museums, visitors, and collections, it is clear that communities of practice have emerged in museums. Due to the expansion of museum practice to include many of the aspects articulated in this chapter, as well as the entire volume, "landscapes of practice" have taken root as museums and their staff become connected to other museums and professionals within the field and beyond it. Museums have demonstrated time and again how they are equipped to address the cultural, political, and economic challenges that face society, as outlined below.

As the International Council of Museums (ICOM) has recognized, museums can help contribute toward efforts at global equality by working toward the UN Sustainable Goals (SDGs).[25] The sixteen goals were adopted in 2015 by all United Nations member states as a framework for peace and prosperity for people and the planet, now and into the future. They ask all countries in the developed and developing world to address all the goals (items one through sixteen) and to do so in partnership with one another (goal seventeen).

The origin of the list of SDGs is the list of Millennium Development Goals aimed at reducing extreme poverty and improving health and education in the Global South (e.g., countries characterized by low income, dense population, poor infrastructure, and political marginalization).[26] The program ran for fifteen years (from 2000 to 2015), during which time it became apparent that the challenges facing these communities were related. Addressing just one challenge was unsustainable. In 2015, a new program, named "Agenda 2030," outlined a vision for pursuing sixteen goals and recognizing a seventeenth goal that saw the importance of collaborating to achieve the goals. The goals are intended to be goals for all, not just for NGOs, governmental organizations, or other institutions. All organizations and communities are called upon to help achieve these goals—together.[27]

Museums are keenly suited to some of the SDGs, especially around the protection and safeguarding of cultural heritage, education for sustainable development, and supporting research and cultural investment. Moreover, museums can help address the challenges facing two areas of focus in the 2030 agenda—people and planet—by addressing poverty, inequality, and marginalization of individuals and communities, and by looking at climate change, energy production, use, and waste.[28]

Explicit concern was made at the International Council of Museums (ICOM) triennial conference in Kyoto in 2019, when the membership approved a resolution that authorized the importance of the United Nations 2030 agenda. The ICOM Resolution notes that "all museums have a role to play in shaping and creating sustainable futures," and they can do this through educational programs, exhibitions, community outreach, and research. To that end, ICOM has used the SDGs as an inspiration for their annual theme for International Museum Day, which is an international effort at celebrating museums and increasing public awareness about the role of museums in society. The event has been held annually since 1953. More recently, the celebration has been held around May 18 and may last a day or longer, depending upon each museum's preferences. Each year since 2020, International Museum Day supports a set of goals, then from the Sustainable Development Goals of the United Nations. In 2023, the focus was on Goal 3: Global Health and Well-Being: Ensure healthy lives and promote well-being for all at all ages, in particular concerning mental health and social isolation; Goal 13: Climate Action: Take urgent action to combat climate change and its impacts, adopting low-carbon practices in the Global North and mitigation strategies in the Global South; and Goal 15: Life on Land: Protect, restore, and promote sustainable use of terrestrial ecosystems, amplifying the voices of Indigenous leaders and raising awareness on the loss of biodiversity.[29] Museums were called upon to emphasize how they address these goals as part of the IMD offerings—thus, tying together the importance of museums on the local, national, and international stage as contributors toward efforts to overcome the interconnected challenges laid out in the UN SDGs.

More generally, how are these areas of concern addressed, whether implicitly or explicitly, by museums? Museums can do this through their regular channels of activities—such as exhibits, education, and other programming—as well as through actions such as policies and procedures. Museums do this by being *in motion*; by *evolving*; and by demonstrating a commitment to growth made possible through *revolution*. Below, the SDGs are addressed in two clusters: people and the environment. Beneath each cluster, the individual SDGs are addressed, with examples of museum exhibitions and programs that show how, intentionally or not, museums can contribute toward global efforts of addressing these needs—one museum and one person at a time.

Part I: People and the SDGs

SDG #1: No Poverty

The first SDG seeks to "end poverty in all its forms everywhere." A single example of such an effort may be found through the work of the nonprofit organization Love Beyond Walls (established in 2011), which has created the traveling, pop-up exhibit *Dignity Museum*. The *Dignity Museum* shares the stories of poverty: those born into poverty and those who became homeless as adults. It seeks to tell their stories, as well as the efforts underway and further needed to help combat these challenges and overcome them. Through interactive technology, exhibits, and visitor reflection, the exhibit utilizes first-person accounts, storytelling, and research to challenge stereotypes about homelessness and poverty; to create empathy through a multimedia experience; and to inspire action toward equality, opportunity, and justice.[30]

This is just one example of an organization based in College Park, Georgia. Where else can we see museums seeking to end poverty? The Queens Museum, in collaboration with two organizations (La Jornada and Together We Can Community Resource Center, Inc.) served meals to up to one thousand families one day a week, and distributed perishable and nonperishable goods during the summer of 2020.[31]

Addressing the SDGs can mean a focus on exhibitions and events, as well as policies and procedures. Such efforts include reduced or free admission to museums. The "Museums for All" program, an initiative of the Institute of Museum and Library Services and administered by the Association of Children's Museums in the United States, enables those receiving food assistance benefits from federal or state programs to access admission to more than 1,200 museums. The program lowers barriers to access through free or reduced admission upon showing their food assistance benefit card and identification. (At the time of this writing, that cost is no greater than three dollars total for up to four people.) Some museums offer free admission; some offer free or reduced admission to more than four people per benefit card.[32]

As Billie Jenkins, poverty proofing coordinator at Children Northeast, writes, museums can help remove such barriers to access and promote opportunities for everyone to enjoy their spaces by focusing on three areas: before the visit; at mealtime; and the onsite experience. Their work centers on asking questions about the experience: How does someone with limited resources feel during their visit to the museum?

Poverty proofing involves a prismatic review of aspects of the visitor experience and reflection on how to improve the experiences for all. Questions to consider include:

- How does the museum address public transportation use? Are links to the schedules on the museum website, along with walking directions from the nearest stop or station? Are the hours flexible for those in shift work who may not be able to attend between 10 and 5 p.m. or such? Are there free opportunities to experience similar offerings to paid experiences, and if so, how are those scheduled?
- What happens at lunchtime? Are there spaces for people to eat food they brought with them? Where can people go if they cannot afford to eat onsite? Are there other options nearby?
- How does your museum experience feel to someone living in poverty? Consider the diversity reflected in the displays onsite. Are donation boxes in obvious or less discreet places, so that any donations—regardless of size—can be made? Are guides and educational materials available for purchase also available in-gallery for free, as browsing copies? Have staff received unconscious bias training?[33]

Answers to these questions can reveal truths about where an institution is in its thinking about poverty, how it might help work toward ending poverty, and how it might strive to meet this SDG, one museum at a time.

SDG #2: Zero Hunger

Goal #2 focuses on three areas: increasing food security (that is, the continual access to food, in contrast to food insecurity, which reflects non-continuous access to food); improving nutrition; and promoting sustainable agriculture. Access to food, and particularly healthy food, is a visitor-centric need, while sustainable agriculture seeks to lessen harms in the food-creation cycle, such as the exploitation of workers and harms to the environment.

Recent work by museums has provided exhibits and events on food justice in their communities, creating avenues for important conversations to take place. Many of these museums are also in urban areas, where food deserts and insecurity can strike the hardest. Exhibits or events that focus on ending hunger appear to serve primarily educational purposes, rather than directly connecting with those audiences who have firsthand knowledge of food injustice as part of their own, lived experience.

The African American Museum in Philadelphia exhibited *Witnesses to Hunger* (2016), which consists of photographs taken by members of the eponymous organization who have themselves experienced food insecurity or who have shared with a family member who has experienced it. In 2019, the New Westminster Museum and Archives in British Columbia, Canada, curated the exhibition *You Are What You Eat*, which focused on food security, sovereignty, food systems, and food literacy. The Hudson River Museum in Yonkers, New York, displayed *Food for Thought: Teen Perspectives on Scarcity and Abundance* that year, with emphasis on teen perspectives (grades nine through twelve) in conjunction with graduate students from the State University of New York, Oneonta, program in museum studies at the Cooperstown Graduate Program. The exhibit featured photographs showing evidence of scarcity and abundance in the region.[34]

Lectures, discussions, and events can center this topic, in addition to exhibitions. In 2020, the National Museum of African American History and Culture in Washington, D.C., offered *A Seat at the Table: A Conversation About Food Equity and Sustainability*. This event enabled attendees to partake in a family-style dinner at the award-winning café at NMAAHC. The event included a moderated discussion that addressed food security and equitability in the context of race, identity, and class. Children's museums, such as Above & Beyond the Children's Museum in Sheboygan, Wisconsin, and Omaha Children's Museum in Nebraska also offered events on the topic of food. Above & Beyond featured the program *Eat, Play, and Grow*, which taught children about gardening and how to identify healthy snacks. Omaha's *Kitchen ABCs* taught children about the basics of cooking, explored foods that might be unfamiliar to children's palates, and shared recipes for home use.[35] The previous two SDGs are related to *SDG #8: Decent Work and Economic Growth*, which seeks to promote sustained, inclusive, and sustainable economic growth, as well as full, decent, and productive employment for all.

SDG #3: Good Health and Well-Being

Goal #3 focuses on measures around ensuring good, healthy lives and well-being—all of which can be addressed in myriad ways, including improved health care overall (as well as mental health), sanitation, and hygiene, as well as greater access to these.

At the ArtScience Museum in Marina Bay Sands, Singapore, attention was paid in 2022–2023 to mental health and well-being. The exhibition *MENTAL: Colours of Wellbeing* is an unusual departure for the museum, which traditionally shows intersections between science and art, often hosting exhibitions on canonical artists with auction caches such as Leonardo da Vinci, Andy Warhol, and Vincent van Gogh. Rather, *MENTAL* features twenty-four interactive exhibits, art projects, and large-scale installations created by a range of makers from artists to scientists to show perspectives on mental health and ways of being. The exhibit also centers the Southeast Asian perspective by exhibiting seven artworks by Singaporean and Southeast Asian artists. Addressing the themes of Connection, Exploration, Expression, and Reflection, the exhibit aims to show how every mental health journey is unique.[36]

The exhibit *Outbreak: Epidemics in an Connected World*, a bilingual English-Spanish exhibition, invited visitors to learn about diseases from both scientific and personal perspectives by centering the work of epidemiologists, veterinarians, and public health workers who collaborate to outrun infectious diseases, such as HIV/AIDS, Ebola virus, influenza, Zika virus, and others. On view from 2018 through 2023 at the Smithsonian Museum of Natural History in Washington, D.C., the exhibit invited visitors to identify and contain infectious diseases, including the COVID-19 pandemic. From mid-June 2020, at the height of the COVID-19 pandemic, online conversations shifted from AIDS and disease vectors in the United States around mosquitoes and ticks to the urgent need of the present, when the webinars began to feature research scientists, federal agencies, and anthropologists "to help put COVID-19 into context and to explore the interconnection between people, non-human animals, plants, and their shared environment." These conversations during the summer of 2020 served an important public service function, as they were convened during the height of competitive and cooperative production of the vaccines, thereby preceding the availability of vaccines by several months.[37]

SDG #4: Quality Education

The UN goals around education are multifaceted and range from expanding higher-education scholarships for developing countries and free primary and secondary education to equal access to quality pre-primary education, as well as the elimination of all discrimination in education so as to achieve universal literacy and numeracy. Ultimately, the goal is to establish inclusive and safe schools for all. Because education undergirds museum functions, it seems that museums have a significant role to play in providing access to information and to provide pathways for informal learning (with, in the most ideal of circumstances, no barrier to entry). In fact, a cursory glance of museum mission statements yields the term *educate*, as well as cognates such as *inspire*, *cultivate*, *understand*, *enrich*, *explore*, *promote*, and *interpret*.

At the Peabody Essex Museum in Salem, Massachusetts, the exhibit *Let None Be Excluded: The Origins of Equal School Rights in Salem* (on view from April 2022 through April 2024), the emphasis is on telling the story of the Salem school committee's decision in 1834 to establish separate schools for Black children from those of White children. Black residents worked tirelessly for a decade to undo this segregation. In 1844, the school committee abolished racially separate schools. Leading the way as one of the first cities to do so, Salem also prompted the Commonwealth of Massachusetts to become the first state to also allow access to education freely. Such exhibitions spotlight the ongoing efforts toward educational equality situated in Salem, but also regionally, thus demonstrating the importance of education. However, the notion of quality education is manifest in the overall operations of museum exhibits, events, and outward-facing experiences for visitors.[38]

As an example, the Eric Carle Museum of Picture Book Art in Amherst, Massachusetts, uses the medium of picture books as methods to teach as well as express emotion. There, the online exhibition *Asians, Everyday* launched in May 2021 in honor of Asian American Pacific Islander Heritage Month and centered the work of twenty-six artists affirming stories of Asian American life. Illustrator and exhibit curator Grace Lin stated that she hoped the exhibit could enable "kids and adults . . . to let go of some of the blame and hate" as a result of seeing the "recognizable humanity in all of our lives," with the result being the possibility of connecting "as familiar friends."[39] In addition, an onsite exhibition, *Facing Fears with Picture Books*, curated by Gabrielle Avena, 2022 Trinkett Clark intern, was on vew in the Reading Library of the museum from July through December 2022 with thirty-seven picture books, divided into three thematic sections: Frightening Folktales, Real-World Worries, and My Friend, the Monster. According to Avena, "The world can be a scary place. In times of uncertainty, picture books can empower readers to keep their courage when life feels frightening. This exhibition emboldens children and caregivers to face their fears together in the safe spaces of picture books. From classic cautionary tales to current social issues, these books will make you gasp in surprise, shriek with delight, and stand tall alongside your shadow."[40] Such an opportunity to read these stories offers opportunities for children and their adults to learn (and face fears) together, as a form of quality education.

SDG #5: Gender Equality

Goal #5 focuses on achieving gender equality and empowering all women and girls. In museums, this work can be done through exhibits and events, as well as in policies—particularly as related to hiring, supporting, and promoting women into positions of leadership.

The exhibit *All Work, No Pay: Women's Invisible Labor* was on view at the National Museum of American History in Washington, D.C., from March 2019 through May 2022. The exhibition and its online counterpart highlighted the historical trajectory of unpaid women's labor in the United States over two centuries. It connected the notions of the "good wife" of the 1770s and the "angel in the house" of the 1830s with the more modern ideas of government programs that positioned running the house almost as a business, with programs such as "household management" and "home economics." Examining the broad history, and peppering these with micro-narratives, quotations about women's work, and analysis of clothing worn to do the work of the house, the exhibit ultimately points to the crux of the issue: economics and the wage gap, as demonstrated by infographics that disclose the differences in pay across occupations.[41]

Such exhibitions, and the many, many exhibitions launched in the United States around the centennial of the ratification of the Nineteenth Amendment in 1920, emphasized the accomplishments toward gender equality while also disclosing the significant work that is yet to be done, as evidenced by the exhibit on invisible labor mentioned above. Even so, the centennial commemorations gave many (though not all) women the right to vote. When the United States was defined through the Constitution in 1787, eligibility requirements for voting were left to each state, rather than universally. From then until the passage of the Nineteenth Amendment, the Constitution only prohibited states from barring voters on the basis of "race, color, or previous condition of servitude." Thus, from the earliest days of the republic through the first decades of the twenty-first century, the movement for women's suffrage involved many women and their supporters, who, finally, transformed constitutional history. The unfinished business remains within our grasp, in the United States and beyond, as do the related efforts to close the gender gap.[42]

Finally, a celebration of gender through the exhibit *Girlhood* at the National Museum of American History situates the possibilities of what gender equality might portend. In five sections, and entirely inspired by color, action, and strength, the exhibit takes its cues from zine culture. The themes are: Education (Being Schooled), Wellness (Body Talk), Work (Hey, Where's My Girlhood?), and Fashion (Girl's Remix), plus seven biographical interactive stories (A Girl's Life).[43] The exhibit companion website showcases many of the objects and stories found in *Girlhood*, enhanced by unique video content and high-resolution, narrated 3D scans. Moreover, this exhibit is one of the rental exhibits from the Smithsonian (Smithsonian Institution Traveling Exhibition Service) from 2023 through 2025, enabling institutions to bring this concept to their communities.

These first five goals are keenly related to *SDG #10: Reduced Inequalities*, which seeks to reduce inequality within and among countries and *SDG #16: Peace, Justice, and Strong Institutions*, which aims to promote peaceful and inclusive societies for sustainable development, provide access to justice for all, and build effective, accountable, and inclusive institutions at all levels.

Single events and exhibits can help organizations to frame inequality and to make progress toward peace and justice. For example, the Minnesota Children's Museum hosted an online event in 2021 called "Reducing Inequality Through the Power of Play," a panel discussion that made the case that playful learning drives growth and development and offered suggestions on how to bring more play into children's lives as a measure of reducing inequalities.[44] The exhibition *Objectively Racist: How Objects and Images Perpetuate Racism . . . and What We Can Do to Change It* at Rochester Museum & Science Center in Rochester, New York, includes images, product packaging, knickknacks, and other objects that help perpetuate individual, institutional, and structural racism. Collected by Mississippi-born, Rochester resident Doug Belton Sr., they were sought as part of his quest for record albums. He perused barn sales and thrift shops outside Rochester, where he moved in 1970. Yet the items are more than ephemera of the past; they disclose racism. After learning about this institution's earlier effort, called *Take It Down*, which transformed a racist carousel panel into an anti-racist educational exhibit, Belton decided to lend his collection for an exhibition to spur and expand conversations with the public about racism. Both the exhibitions and the related events at this institution thus examine how racist caricatures perpetuate individual, institutional, and structural racism and how we can use this imagery as an educational tool to promote social equity.[45]

Entire institutions are framed around peace and justice, in the case of The Legacy Sites, a trio of places in and around Montgomery, Alabama, organized by the Equal Justice Initiative, a non-profit founded by lawyer–turned–civil rights advocate Bryan Stevenson. (The Legacy Sites are also addressed, in less detail, in Chapter 4 of this volume.)

The Legacy Museum, the National Memorial for Peace and Justice, and the Freedom Monument Sculpture Park (opening in 2024) comprise the Legacy Sites, which enable visitors to reckon with racial injustice at the very sites where these events occurred; "on lands occupied by Indigenous people for centuries, in a region that once held the largest population of enslaved Black people and would later become the heart of the Civil Rights movement, the Legacy Sites offer visitors a powerful opportunity to engage with history and begin an era of truth telling."[46] Together, the sites bring place to bear on past, present, and future. According to Stevenson, "We have never acknowledged that we are a post-genocide society. I think what happened to Indigenous people when Europeans came to this continent was a genocide. . . . We said that native people are savages. We created a narrative of racial difference to justify the violence that we imposed on those populations. . . . And it was that narrative of racial difference that made us comfortable with two and a half centuries of slavery. . . . We created a constitution that talks about equality and justice for all that we didn't extend to these populations because we had a narrative of racial difference justifying their exclusion."[47]

The efforts of this museum extend beyond exhibits and a memorial, to also include local initiatives to uncover racial injustice and to reshape the present; the erection of historical markers; racial justice essay contests; and community soil collection at sites of death from racial terror and lynching.[48] The Legacy Sites are clearly doing exceptional work toward peace and justice. However, through efforts large and small, museums can move the needle toward the long arc of justice and make progress toward meeting the SDGs that impact people and their quest for basic needs and equality.

Part II: Our Environment and the SDGs

Shifting from people to the environment, several SDGs consider the environment and our shared responsibility to care for it.

- SDG #6: Clean Water and Sanitation: aims to ensure availability and sustainable management of water and sanitation for all.
- SDG #7: Affordable and Clean Energy: aims to ensure access to affordable, reliable, sustainable, and modern energy for all.
- SDG #9: Industry, Innovation, and Infrastructure: aims to build resilient infrastructure, promote inclusive and sustainable industrialization, and foster innovation.
- SDG #11: Sustainable Cities and Communities: aims to make cities and human settlements inclusive, safe, resilient, and sustainable.
- SDG #12: Responsible Consumption and Production: aims to ensure sustainable consumption and production patterns.
- SDG #13: Climate Action: calls for urgent action to combat climate change and its impacts.
- SDG #14: Life Below Water: aims to conserve and sustainably use the oceans, seas, and marine resources for sustainable development.
- SDG #15: Life on Land: aims to protect, restore, and promote the sustainable use of terrestrial ecosystems, sustainably manage forests, combat desertification, and halt and reverse land degradation and halt biodiversity loss.

The spirit of these goals is to preserve our planet through action and harm reduction. In museums, addressing these goals might take shape through exhibitions and events that highlight the importance of clean water, clean energy, climate change initiatives, and biodiversity. For instance, exhibits focus on communication information about each of these subjects, or they may feature artwork that disclose the dangers of unclean water or show the beauty of clean water. The Brandywine Museum of Art's exhibition *Fragile Earth: The Naturalist Impulse in Contemporary Art* sought to illuminate the beauty of the natural world, and our impact upon it. According to curator Jennifer Stettler Parsons, the artists Jennifer Angus, Mark Dion, Courtney Mattison, and James Prosek "were selected for the profound message their works convey about environmental conservation. They transform natural and non-traditional materials, like insects and found debris, into art in order to make visible the human role in global climate change, and to reveal how our daily choices may endanger our planet's future." In addition to the gallery pieces, artist Prosek created a site-specific silhouette-style mural onsite, highlighting the flora and fauna of the Brandywine Valley in Pennsylvania. Titled *Invisible Boundaries*, the new mural, and a related, earlier work, consider the symbolism of the United States flag in relation to nature. By incorporating fifty images of state animals and the bald eagle, the work illustrates borderless cohabitation: animals inhabit ecosystems independent of geographic boundaries between states or countries.[49] Such a work, perhaps, fully realizes the true vision of the UN SDGs in forming a global community seeking to achieve these goals together.

The exhibition *Slums and Suburbs: Water and Sanitation in the First Industrial City* offered linkages between past events and current crises. On view since 2021 at the Science + Industry Museum in Manchester, England, the exhibit offers "striking parallels between the factors affecting access to clean water and sanitation across the world today and the problems that confronted 19th-century industrial Manchester, the original shock city—a term coined by historian Asa Briggs to describe the rapid and radical change undergone by such cities." An onsite and online exhibition covering nine sections conveys how important water is to our planet and how access to it is not guaranteed. The exhibit moves from description and historical context of deplorable conditions and the reform efforts that upended them to the contemporary by pleading for action today. Citing the importance of vocal protests and campaigns by sanitary reformers and everyday citizens, the exhibit calls on efforts, such as the UN's Water Action Decade, established in 2018, to drive forward its goal of clean water and sanitation for all.[50]

Moving from water to climate and much smaller in scale, a display of art was on view in 2023 in the W. M. Keck Earth Science and Mineral Engineering Museum at the Mackay Mines Building at the University of Nevada, Reno. The exhibit *Where the Wind Blows Wild & Free: Understanding Climate with Science and Art* showcases Nevada's changing climate, without pointing a finger as to its cause.[51]

In some cases, the SDGs and museums align around days of international attention, such as World Water Day (March 22), first designated in 1993. Using the annual event as a starting point, the Metropolitan Waterworks Museum in Boston launched an exhibition in 2017 focusing on bringing awareness about the need for clean water and telling the story of Boston's efforts toward safe and steady supplies of water. In *Thinking About Water: Artists Reflect*, artists focus on environment changes affecting water, as well as deep concerns about the changing status of water in particular areas, as shown by melting glaciers, rising waters, and dry reservoirs. This contemporary art exhibition is situated in proximity to a mammoth hall with three coal-powered, steam-driven water pumps three stories tall. The contrast between the industrial and the aesthetic convey, in different and entirely complementary ways, the urgency of fresh water for Bostonians, and indeed, all of us.[52]

Events at museums—whether related to exhibition content or not—can help foster learning about the environment. For example, the event "Explore Solar Power at NMAAHC" was held at the National Museum of African American History and Culture in Washington, D.C., the first museum on the National Mall designed to reduce the impact on the environment by using renewable energy sources. The museum does this through the use of solar panels on its roof to capture the energy from the sun and convert it into usable electricity. A suite of hands-on activities in September 2018 aimed to teach visitors about solar power and energy production. These experiences were expanded and adapted into a STEM (Science, Technology, Engineering, and Math) as well as STEAM (Science, Technology, Engineering, Arts, and Math) context. This new envisioning, called *Explore More! In STEM: How the Museum Uses Light*, took solar power as a starting point and crossed this content into other aspects of the museum's architecture (including the "Corona" veil surrounding the building) and in relation to Black history and culture. These programs were held in 2023. They were expanded upon for a celebration on October 14, 2023, for Afrofuturism STEAM Day at the museum. For this event, the focus was on how Afrofuturism envisions the future of Black life, "liberated from societal oppression and earthly-bound constraints" and how the museum events "envision the future while peering through the lenses of space exploration, human health, and technology."[53]

In addition to raising interest in climate and our earth through exhibitions and events, actions by museums can speak volumes. For instance, the Nevada Museum of Art seeks to reduce its carbon footprint and energy costs through a "climate action plan" as part of its expansion. In September 2022, amidst the state's warmest September on record, members of the artist collective Fallen Fruit debuted their new public installation, *Monument to Sharing*, in front of the museum. Their work will be the living agricultural installation that is part of a multifaceted museum exhibition scheduled to be completed in 2025. According to artists David Allen Burns and Austin Young of the collective, "*Monument to Sharing* involves planting approximately twenty-one fruit-bearing trees, a berry patch and a series of edible pollinators that the public is welcome to 'harvest,' inviting guests to explore ideas of generosity, agricultural production and the meaning behind 'community.'" The project features more than twenty fruit-bearing trees and other plantings intended to prompt conversations about scarcity, community, and ecology—and provide free food to visitors. The collective began creating interactive installations for a project in Los Angeles for which they created maps of what the artists called "public fruit," or fruit trees that grew over public property.[54] Positioned as part of a sustainability effort at the museum, and a sixty-million-dollar expansion will also see the museum implementing operational changes to reduce its waste and carbon emissions to levels consistent with the Paris Climate Agreement.

Smaller initiatives, such as the Smithsonian's installation of recharge stations on the National Mall in 2022, echo the shapes and functions of plant leaves similar to those found in the Smithsonian Gardens nearby, at the Arts and Industries Building. The gazebo-like installations use photovoltaic (PV) solar panels as the petal tops, creating a multi-purpose structure that can charge devices, run cooling fans, and offer shady rest spots. These spots also provide a way to charge the gardening equipment, including a vehicle and some tools necessary to maintain the surrounding gardens, thus impacting the museum's own use of energy and its goal to reduce its carbon footprint.[55]

Examples of sustainable infrastructure in museums include the use of solar panels, for example, as mentioned above; rainwater collection and graywater reuse systems; high-efficiency HVAC; using recycled materials for building materials; sustainable LED systems and architecture that supports the use of natural light; tri-generation plants, combining heat and power systems to generate heat, cooling, and electricity; and onsite greenhouses, green roofs, and living roofs, as seen at Boston Children's Museum, Boston, and the California Academy of Sciences, San Francisco, California.

Some facets external to museums can aid in achieving some of these SDGs. LEED (Leadership in Energy and Environmental Design) is a globally recognized rating system created by the United States Green Building Council (USBGC) and used to determine the "green"ness of a building. *Green* is the term used to connote sustainability in design, construction, and operation. LEED certification provides a framework for healthy, efficient, carbon-reducing, and cost-saving of green buildings. LEED certifications are provided to buildings with high levels of compliance. To achieve LEED certification, a project earns points by adhering to prerequisites and credits that address carbon, energy, water, waste, transportation, materials, health, and indoor environmental quality.

Further, the USGBC has outlined the ways in which LEED categories can contribute toward meeting the SDGs, not only by saving water, increasing energy efficiency, minimizing carbon emissions (GHGs), and significantly reducing health-harmful air pollutants. They have also gone a step further by articulating extended connections to the SDGs by positioning sustainability and green building practices as related to other SDGs by promoting education, creating jobs, improving health and well-being, and enhancing community resilience. Drawing this point even more finely, the USBGC states that "policymakers, planners, and builders can use LEED and sustainable building practices as strategies for achieving the UN SDGs."[56] Thus, actions that museums can take toward LEED certification can, and do, articulate commitment toward achieving the SDGs.

As this second portion of the exploration of the SDGs shows, the overlap between a number of the SDGs, as well as between exhibit and policy or procedure, discloses a new model for museum work: action-based initiatives that blur boundaries between public-facing and non-public-facing work.[57] For instance, looking at the Nevada Museum of Art example, sustainability, innovation, and infrastructure are not sexy, per se, but when couched between a museum expansion and a compelling public art project, it becomes vastly more interesting, and more integrated to an organization's DNA. The same could be said all of the initiatives discussed above: they are even more interesting and relevant when they can be viewed within the context of ongoing care, concern, and compassion for our local communities and our global world, rather than one-off opportunities that are disconnected from the regular exhibits, events, policies, and procedures of an institution. Perhaps poverty-proofing, described at the head of this chapter, is a good first step toward centering any museum's efforts toward achieving the SDGs.

Clearly, museums serve their communities and the world around us. They can and do address the cultural, political, and economic challenges that face society. They serve. But whom do they serve? Who is serving them? What challenges and opportunities do they face? Where are they headed? These are questions to be explored more fully in Section III.

Notes

1. Museums Association, "Empowering Collections: Report from Collections 2030," 2021, https://www.museumsassociation.org/campaigns/collections/empowering-collections/recommendations -empowering-collections/#. See pages 4–5 for the challenges facing collections: siloed work culture; size of collections, digital access; resources and skills of staff to work effectively with collections and communities; and attention to the growing post-colonial critique of museum collections. The recommendations appear from page 10 onward.
2. John H. Falk, *The Value of Museums: Enhancing Societal Well-Being* (Lanham, MD: Rowman & Littlefield, 2021).
3. International Council of Museums, "ICOM Approves a New Museum Definition," August 24, 2022, https://icom.museum/en/news/icom-approves-a-new-museum-definition/.
4. Theodore L. Low, *The Museum as a Social Instrument* (New York: American Association of Museums, 1942), 20, 29–36; Theodore L. Low, *The Educational Philosophy and Practice of Art Museums in the United States* (New York: Bureau of Publications, Teachers College, 1946). For criticism of Low's thesis and his rebuttal, see Wilcomb E. Washburn, "The Museum's Responsibility in Adult Education," *Curator* 7 (1964): 33–38, and "Scholarship and the Museum," *Museum News* 40 (October 1961): 16–19; Theodore L. Low, "The Museum as a Social Instrument: 20 Years Later," *Museum News* 40 (January 1962): 28–30; Joel J. Orosz, epilogue to *Curators and Culture: The Museum Movement in America, 1740–1870* (Tuscaloosa: University of Alabama Press, 1990), 248–56.
5. *Museums USA* (Washington, D.C.: National Endowment for the Arts, 1973), 25–35.
6. Duncan Cameron, "The Museum, a Temple or the Forum?" *Journal of World History* 14, no. 1, 189–204; Gail Anderson, ed., *Reinventing the Museum: Historical and Contemporary Perspectives on the Paradigm Shift*, 2nd edition (Walnut Creek: AltaMira Press, 2012).
7. *Excellence and Equity: Education and the Public Dimension of Museums* (Washington, D.C.: American Association of Museums, 1992), 25.
8. Bonnie Pittman, "Muses, Museums and Memory," *Daedalus*, Summer 1999, p. 1; Ellen Hirzy et al., *Mastering Civic Engagement: A Challenge to Museums* (Washington, D.C.: American Association of Museums, 2002).
9. Stephen E. Weil, "From Being about Something to Being for Somebody: The Ongoing Transformation of the American Museum: The Ongoing Transformation of the American Museum," *Daedalus*, Summer 1999, 254; Glenn D. Lowry, "A Deontological Approach," in *Whose Muse? Art Museum and Public Trust*, ed. James Cuno (Princeton: Princeton University Press, 2004), 143.
10. Monica O. Montgomery, "Notes from the Field," appearing in the third edition of this volume.
11. Museum Hue, "About Us," https://www.museumhue.org/about-hue/, accessed September 14, 2023.

12. The Empathetic Museum, "About Us," http://empatheticmuseum.weebly.com/about.html; see also Empathetic Museum, "A Metric for Institutional Transformation in Museums," http://www.empathetic museum.com/maturity-model.
13. Michelle Elligott, "From the Archives: Faith Ringgold, the Art Workers Coalition, and the Fight for Inclusion at The Museum of Modern Art," *MoMA Inside/Out*, July 29, 2016, http://www.moma.org/explore/inside_out/2016/07/29/from-the-archives-faith-ringgold-the-art-workers-coalition-and-the-fight-for-inclusion-at-the-museum-of-modern-art. See also Thomas J. Lax's post about MoMA in the age of #BlackLivesMatter: "How Do Black Lives Matter in MoMA's Collection?" *MoMA Inside/Out*, July 9, 2016, http://www.moma.org/explore/inside_out/2016/07/09/how-do-black-lives-matter-in-momas-collection.
14. Museums and Race grew out of a conversation about museums responding to the death of Michael Brown, an unarmed African American teenager, at the hands of police in Ferguson, Missouri, on August 9, 2014. The shooting sparked unrest in Ferguson. Museums and other cultural institutions framed conversations and activities around a larger initiative called #MuseumsRespondtoFerguson, an example of which can be viewed here: https://storify.com/aleiabrown/museumsrespondtoferguson.
15. On the hashtag #BlackLivesMatter, see Monica Anderson, "The Hashtag #BlackLivesMatter Emerges: Social Activism on Twitter," *Pew Research Center: Social Media Conversations on Race*, August 15, 2016, https://www.pewresearch.org/internet/2016/08/15/the-hashtag-blacklivesmatter-emerges-social-activism-on-twitter/; Jelani Cobb, "The Matter of Black Lives," *New Yorker*, March 6, 2016, https://www.newyorker.com/magazine/2016/03/14/where-is-black-lives-matter-headed, accessed September 14, 2023. Cobb documents the use of the words on Facebook by Alicia Garza, a labor organizer in Oakland, and their adoption/response by Patrisse Cullors, an A-based community organizer who replied with the first instance of the hashtag.
16. Quote from Patrisse Cullors appears in Jelani Cobb, "The Matter of Black Lives," *New Yorker*, March 6, 2016, https://www.newyorker.com/magazine/2016/03/14/where-is-black-lives-matter-headed, accessed September 14, 2023.
17. Milkman quoted in James A. Anderson, "Some Say Occupy Wall Street Did Nothing. It Changed Us More Than We Think," *Time*, November 15, 2021, https://time.com/6117696/occupy-wall-street-10-years-later/, accessed September 2023.
18. See Elena Gonzales, *Exhibitions for Social Justice* (London: Routledge, 2019); https://www.hullhousemuseum.org/programs-and-events-at-hullhouse/2020/4/23/elena-gonzales-and-cesareo-moreno, accessed November 1, 2023.
19. See Meg Duguid, editor, *Where the Future Came From* (Chicago: Soberscove Press, 2020); https://www.hullhousemuseum.org/programs-and-events-at-hullhouse/2020/10/22/meg-duguid-where-the-future-came-from, accessed November 1, 2023.
20. See Therese Quinn's book, *School: Questions About Museums, Culture, and Justice to Explore in Your Classroom* (New York: Teachers College Press, 2020); https://www.hullhousemuseum.org/programs-and-events-at-hullhouse/2020/3/19/therese-quinn-about-museums-culture-and-justice-to-explore-in-your-classroom, accessed November 1, 2023.
21. The Empathetic Museum, "About Us," http://empatheticmuseum.weebly.com/about.html; see also Empathetic Museum, "A Metric for Institutional Transformation in Museums," http://www.empathetic museum.com/maturity-model; and Gail Dexter Lord and Ngaire Blankenberg, *Cities, Museums, and Soft Power* (Washington, D.C.: AAM Press, 2015).
22. Shafaq Hasan, "Germany's Art Community Innovates to Integrate Refugees," *Non-Profit Quarterly*, May 11, 2016, https://nonprofitquarterly.org/2016/05/11/germanys-art-community-innovates-to-integrate-refugees/.
23. Network of European Museum Organizations, "Initiatives of Museums in Europe in Connection to Migrants and Refugees," January 2016.
24. See Francesca Lanz, "Staging Migration (in) Museums: A Reflection on Exhibition Design Practices for the Representation of Migration in European Contemporary Museums," *Museum & Society* 14:1 (2016): 178–92.
25. United Nations, "The 17 Goals," https://sdgs.un.org/goals.

26. *Global South* is a political term more so than a geographic one that encompasses Africa, Latin America, the Caribbean, Asia (without Israel, Japan, and South Korea), and Oceania (without Australia and New Zealand).

27. Transforming Our World: The 2030 Agenda for Sustainable Development outlines the seventeen goals and the 169 discrete targets to achieve within each. See https://digitallibrary.un.org/record/1654217?ln=en.

28. This part of the chapter was inspired by a project that I have my students complete, in which they look at museums and the SDGs. Through that assignment, I learned how much students long for museums to do the hard work of the SDGs and how much they enjoy exploring the topics that face the world today, because they are issues that students (not aging faculty) will be called upon to solve, in some way, tomorrow and in the future. I am grateful to all the students in my Fall 2021, 2022, and 2023 Intro to Museums courses who have engaged in conversations with me about the UN SDGs and contributed to this research. I am also grateful to Sydney Arcuri, who initially researched the SDGs in the summer of 2021, and my faculty colleague, Sarah Brownell in the College of Engineering.

29. ICOM, "International Museum Day 2023," https://imd.icom.museum/international-museum-day -2023/the-theme-the-power-of-museums/.

30. See *Love Beyond Walls* and their two initiatives—*Dignity Museum*, which is set up in a shipping container—and *Love Sinks In*, a hand-washing initiative born out of COVID-19 pandemic that brings hand-washing stations to high-traffic areas of unhoused persons. https://www.lovebeyondwalls.org/.

31. https://queensmuseum.org/2020/06/12/la-jornada-and-together-we-can-food-pantry-at-queens -museum/. The museum is located in one of the most culturally diverse areas. The grounds are at the site of the New York World's Fairs in 1939–1940 and 1964–1965. Interestingly, the museum building is the former home to the United Nations (1946–1950).

32. IMLS, "Museums for All," https://museums4all.org/for-visitors/, accessed November 1, 2023.

33. Children North East is a nonprofit based in the UK that serves the needs of children and families. See Billie Jenkins, "Poverty Proofing Museums," *Museum Next*, March 28, 2023, https://www.museum next.com/article/poverty-proofing-museums/.

34. Frank Otto, "Photo Exhibit at African American Museum Will Speak the Truth about Poverty," *Drexel News*, last modified July 22, 2016, https://drexel.edu/news/archive/2016/july/witnesses _dnc_exhibit; "Past Exhibit: You Are What You Eat" (2019), New Westminster Museum and Archives, accessed November 10, 2022, https://www.newwestcity.ca/services/arts-and-heritage/museums -and-archives/sb_expander_articles/1501.php; "Food for Thought: Teen Perspectives on Scarcity and Abundance," Hudson River Museum, accessed November 14, 2022, https://www.hrm.org/exhibitions/ food-for-thought/.

35. Above & Beyond Children's Museum (@ABKIDS), "Eat, Play Grow," Facebook, August 7, 2019, https://www.facebook.com/events/828927924151992/828927950818656/?active_tab=about; "A Seat at the Table: A Conversation about Food Equity and Sustainability," National Museum of African American History and Culture, accessed November 14, 2022, https://nmaahc.si.edu/events/seat-table -conversation-about-food-equity-and-sustainability; "Daily Programming," Omaha Children's Museum, last accessed October 29, 2022, https://ocm.org/programs/daily-programming/.

36. The exhibit has been co-curated by ArtScience Museum in Singapore and Science Gallery Melbourne. See https://www.marinabaysands.com/museum/exhibitions/mental.html. The exhibit was on view from September 2022 through February 2023. Their mission is to "explore where art, science, culture and technology come together." See https://www.marinabaysands.com/museum/about.html.

37. National Museum of Natural History, "Video Webinars," https://naturalhistory.si.edu/exhibits/ outbreak-epidemics-connected-world and https://naturalhistory.si.edu/events/after-hours-programs -adults/video-webinars-outbreak-epidemics-connected-world. The first vaccine was given in December 2020, and it was only available under emergency use until mid-2021. See the FDA News Release, August 23, 2021, https://www.fda.gov/news-events/press-announcements/fda-approves-first-covid -19-vaccine.

38. Peabody Essex Museum, *Let None Be Excluded: The Origins of Equal School Rights in Salem*, https:// www.pem.org/exhibitions/let-none-be-excluded-the-origins-of-equal-school-rights-in-salem. The exhibit was on view from April 2022 through April 2024.

39. Carle Museum, "Asians, Everyday," https://www.carlemuseum.org/explore-art/exhibitions/online-exhibition/asians-everyday. Featured artists include: Nabi H. Ali, Jason Chin, Yangsook Choi, Charlene Chua, Dung Ho, Relicia Hoshino, Melissa Iwai, Aaliya Jaleel, Anna Kim, Julie Kim, Violet Kim, Julia Kuo, Julie Kwon, Khoa Le, Huy Voun Lee, Grace Lin, Ken Min, Joowon Oh, Meenal Patel, Dow Phumiruk, Dan Santat, Anoosha Syed, Taro Yashima, Hyewon Yum, Taeeun Yoo.

40. Carle Museum, "Facing Fears," https://www.carlemuseum.org/explore-art/exhibitions/past-exhibition/facing-fears-picture-books.

41. National Museum of American History, "All Work, No Pay: Women's Invisible Labor," https://americanhistory.si.edu/exhibitions/all-work-no-pay. The exhibit was on view for three years and now exists as an online exhibit. For more information on equal-pay initiatives and information about gender-wage gaps, see the U.S. Bureau of Labor statistics: https://www.dol.gov/agencies/wb/equal-pay-protections.

42. The National Archives exhibit *Rightfully Hers: American Women and the Vote* from May 2019 through April 2022 is also an online exhibit. See https://museum.archives.gov/rightfully-hers.

43. The design featured custom murals and illustrations by artist Krystal Quiles. See Smithsonian National Museum of American History, "Girlhood," https://americanhistory.si.edu/exhibitions/girlhood-its-complicated about the exhibition, and the online exhibit here: https://americanhistory.si.edu/girlhood.

44. Minnesota Children's Museum, November 30, 2021, https://mcm.org/reducing-inequality-through-play/.

45. Rochester Museum & Science Center, "Objectively Racist," https://rmsc.org/exhibits/objectively-racist/.

46. Equal Justice Initiative, "About the Sites," https://legacysites.eji.org/about/.

47. "Transcript: Race in America: Fighting for Justice with Bryan Stevenson," *Washington Post Live*, October 14, 2020, https://www.washingtonpost.com/washington-post-live/2020/10/14/transcript-race-america-fighting-justice-with-bryan-stevenson/.

48. Equal Justice Initiative, "Community Remembrance Project," https://eji.org/projects/community-remembrance-project/.

49. The exhibit was on view from September 2022 until January 2023. See Brandywine Museum of Art, https://www.brandywine.org/museum/exhibitions/fragile-earth-naturalist-impulse-contemporary-art. The exhibit was organized by the Florence Griswold Museum, Old Lyme, Connecticut, in 2019. Working with the curator and the artists, Brandywine curator Amanda Burdan updated the exhibition to include new work by the artists.

50 Science + Industry Museum, "Slums and Suburbs," https://www.scienceandindustrymuseum.org.uk/objects-and-stories/water-and-sanitation.

51. Michelle Werdann, "New Keck Museum Exhibit Opens to the Public," January 25, 2023, https://www.unr.edu/nevada-today/news/2023/keck-museum-new-changing-exhibit.

52. Waterworks Museum, "Thinking about Water: Artists Reflect," https://waterworksmuseum.org/exhibit-catalogs/thinking-about-water-artists-reflect/.

53. National Museum of African American History and Culture, "Explore Solar Power at NMAAHC," https://nmaahc.si.edu/events/explore-solar-power-nmaahc-2. See the list of experiences here: https://nmaahc.si.edu/search?keyword=%22solar%20power%22&sort_by=date_sort; https://nmaahc.si.edu/events/afrofuturism-steam-day.

54. Fallen Fruit was originally conceived in 2004 by Matias Viegener, Burns and Young. Since 2013, Burns and Young have continued the collaborative work. See https://www.nevadaart.org/art/exhibitions/fallen-fruit-monument-to-sharing/.

55. Arts + Industries Building, "Relax, Recharge and Renew Yourself (and the Planet)," https://aib.si.edu/recharge-stations/.

56. United States Green Building Council (USGBC), "Synergies Between LEED and SDGs," November 8, 2022, https://www.usgbc.org/resources/synergies-between-leed-and-sdgs. The website states that the synergies are with Goals 3, 6, 7, 8, 9, 10, 11, 12, 13, 15, and 17.

57. The final SDG is #17, the Partnership for the Goals, which seeks to implement and revitalize the Global Partnership for Sustainable Development, which comprises our collective action.

Introduction to Part III

Museum Aspirations

Each chapter, and this volume as a whole, interrogate issues related to museums today. These chapters examine the contours and nuances of museums in the twenty-first century while analyzing how their existence contests historiographies and hagiographies and fracturing our understandings of history, memory, identity, bias, and representation. The chapters, upon reflection, can help us to pose questions about performing history, memory, identity, and representation, informed by scholar Charles R. Garoian's performance of subjectivity that repositions viewers as participants and enables their agency. By adapting Garoian's notion of "performing the museum" and applying it here, the volume critiques the authorizing and performance of the museum. The volume also serves to critique representations in an effort to produce a space and a subjectivity for the spectator.[1] Third, the volume is linked, inherently, in its efforts of correctives to the "e-race-sure" plaguing and embodied in museums.[2] To begin this examination, let's first look at the notion of institutional genealogy as applied to museums.

Institutional Genealogy

If you encounter this as an unfamiliar term, you might be able to piece together how to define it: the life, ancestry, and path of an institution from birth to today. But how is it uncovered? In the absence of an Ancestry.com for museums, genealogies of institutions are a bit more unspecific. Sure, founders and early trustees can be easily identified, as we have seen throughout this volume. But the stories of the institution along the way—of its practices of inclusion and exclusion, for instance—is a bit more nuanced, if visible at all. An institutional genealogy is "a critical framework for assessing an organization's origins, ancestors and older forms" that is the basis for a metaphor, a method, and a movement, as defined by independent museum consultant Aletheia Wittman, a co-director of Incluseum. Wittman shared her ideas around "institutional legacies" in 2016 before developing it into the Institutional Genealogy framework, which was introduced in December 2020.[3]

For Wittman, genealogy is used as both a *metaphor* and a framework for critique. Genealogy, in this context, and as a construct, enables looking at the roots of cultural heritage institutions to understand organizational pasts and attaching those to one's own sense of self. The *method* of genealogy has five stages or entry points: getting started; taking inventory; synthesis; interpretation; and analysis. The steps are designed to avoid nostalgia and prostalgia (the romanticizing of the future) through visual tools and conversation guides to hold space for conversation and for generation meaning-making and sense of purpose in community. Third, the *movement* of institutional genealogy seeks to gain awareness and use this information as a foundation for moving forward. For Wittman, institutional genealogy offers a starting point for cultivating practices that deepen awareness for and promote engagement with an organization's past. Its audience is museum workers, though the benefits of enacting such a framework will impact all because the purpose lies in facing the inequity and exclusion that persists in cultural heritage organizations and, in turn, doing something about it.[4] In very much the same way, this book, *Museums in Motion*, seeks to examine museum pasts, present, and futures as both a metaphor and a framework.

This section offers perspectives about the roles museums play in the staging of narratives—about individuals, communities, and cultures—as well as the awareness and expression of anxieties and fears. The chapters ask questions about museums and are informed by a dialogic process between the institutions themselves and the myriad of people associated with museums, as visitors, museum workers, and supporters. The chapters present challenges and opportunities. They pose narratives and ask questions about museums, their functions, and their futures.

Change. Evolve. Revolution.

As we have seen throughout the first two sections of this book, museums have demonstrated change over time. But do they evolve? What is the difference?

Change recognizes a shift in thinking from one idea, context, or approach to another. *Evolution* reflects a shift in thinking that may be slow, progressive, or otherwise in a state of motion—always. Evolution can lead to periods of growth, crisis, abandonment, or reinvention—often as a result of a dire circumstance or a drastic shift in thinking. Such periods can be seen as a natural outgrowth of evolution, in the form of *revolution*.[5] And the cycle continues. What incites such shifts in thinking?

What follows in this section are a series of vignettes describing perennial topics that ask for further investigation, rumination, and—ultimately—change, evolution, or another form of action. Undergirding all of these, and the entire scope of this book, is the notion that museums are in motion: they are not stagnant.

To be clear, the notion that museums are in motion and that they can evolve and revolve is not to suggest historicism—a framing that the truth of history unfolds through a chronological narrative that positions the past as an evolution of people and events in a narrative-like fashion in which time seemingly, and logically, unfolds, and that progress it the end result. Rather, humans have agency in defining outcomes, and multiple narratives can simultaneously be told. Museums may be viewed as a product of cyclical time—a shifting back and forth between the past and present, in terms of the collections and their meaning and relevance, as well as the functions of museums, and the roles museums can play in their communities. In addition to realizing a cyclical time, museums evolve in the truest sense of the word: they shift from their rather *simple form* of a treasury, storehouse, and tomb to something much more *complex*. They are enriching and fulfilling *spaces* and *places* where the *faces* of the communities surrounding them can find their *voices*.

Moreover, museums have the capacity to change, grow, shift, and transform the world around us.

How to Read These Chapters

Each of the following chapters contains a series of topics to be intended as vignettes and springboards for conversations about museums today, their aspirations, and their sustainability in the future. The micro-narratives are meant to be starting points for conversations within the classroom or the boardroom. These topics resonate with museums—as institutions and as communities of practice and individuals who work as full-time or part-time staff, freelance specialists and consultants, interns, volunteers, and myriad other professionals who contribute to the ongoing commitment of museums to their communities.

Individually, or in conjunction with the chapters in the previous sections of this book, these vignettes help us to understand where, how, and why we need to apply critical lenses to institutions and articulate how doing so helps us to understand this historical moment and, ultimately, how we might seek resiliency and sustainability for museums and those who make their existence possible. They are aspirations of museums, and all of us.

Notes

1. Charles Garoian, *Performing Pedagogy: Toward and Art of Politics* (Albany: The State University of New York, 1999); Vivian M. Patraka, "Spectacles of Suffering: Performing Presence, Absence, and Historical Memory at U.S. Holocaust Museums," in *Performance and Cultural Politics*, ed. Elin Diamond (London: Routledge, 1996), 89–107, especially 99.
2. On the term *e-race-sure*, see Joni Boyd Acuff and Dana Carlisle Kletchka, "Liberté, Egalité, Fraternité: A Black Feminist Analysis of Beyoncé Performing 'APESHIT' in the Louvre," *International Journal of the Inclusive Museum*, 13, 1(2020): 13–36. Boyd and Kletchka address the recontextualization of Black female bodies as a challenge to the historical erasing and "e-raced," defined as the negated presence or implications of race.
3. Aletheia Wittman, "Creating a Framework for Institutional Genealogy," *Incluseum*, August 20, 2021, https://incluseum.com/2021/08/20/institutional-genealogy-framework/. Her article on institutional legacies was co-authored by another Incluseum co-director. See Rose Paquet Kinsley and Aletheia Wittman, "Bringing Self-Examination to the Center of Social Justice Work in Museums," *Museum*, January/February 2016: 40–45. Additionally, see a post from August 20, 2021, written by Elisabeth Callihan, "Accountability in Practice: Creating a Framework for Institutional Genealogy," *MASS Action*, August 20, 2021, https://www.museumaction.org/massaction-blog/2021/8/20/accountability-in-practice-creating-a-framework-for-institutional-genealogy.
4. Aletheia Wittman, "Creating a Framework for Institutional Genealogy," *Incluseum*, August 20, 2021, https://incluseum.com/2021/08/20/institutional-genealogy-framework/.
5. Larry E. Greiner, "Evolution and Revolution as Organizations Grow," *Harvard Business Review*, May–June 1988, https://hbr.org/1998/05/evolution-and-revolution-as-organizations-grow.

11

Transparency, Openness, and (Land) Acknowledgments

This chapter begins with an address of transparency, openness, and information about collections and their origins. It highlights questions around the ethics of acquisition, deaccession, and looted art. While these topics concern collections, they ultimately reflect human behavior and ethics. In the second section of the chapter, attention shifts, then, to the COVID-19 pandemic and the uptick in calls for transparency and openness related to museum practices, particularly as disseminated through social media accounts and other means, including exhibitions. It concludes as it starts, with a look at virtual museum as method.

Transparency around Collections

Ethics of Acquisition

Museums are becoming more and more concerned about illicit trade in foreign art and archaeological objects—a topic we first examined, even if briefly, in Chapter 6, although a case could be made that many of the museum collections amassed over time are rife with evidence of the steal. Chapters 1–5, for instance, provide some evidence of this. More pointedly, stolen objects smuggled into the United States have turned up in the art market, and have found their way into museums by purchase or through gifts and bequests by private collectors. Museums with anthropological collections urge all museums to take great care in investigating the provenance of objects so as to guarantee that acquisitions have complied with laws protecting the national patrimony of the country of origin. Art museums take reasonable precautions against acquiring objects illicitly exported from foreign lands, but they argue that the primary responsibility for enforcing these laws rests with the countries of origin. They point out that a museum acquiring objects by field collection or excavation could be much surer of their provenance than a museum purchasing objects in the art market or receiving them by gift or bequest.[1]

The United Nations Educational, Scientific and Cultural Organization (UNESCO) in 1970 adopted a Convention on the Means of Prohibiting and Preventing the Illicit Export, Import and Transfer of Ownership of Cultural Property. Under it, each ratifying state would establish an export certificate for important cultural property, and no state would import such property without a certificate. Provision was also made for the return of stolen property to the state of origin. The United States ratified the convention in 1983, and by 2003 a total of one hundred countries were signatories.[2]

An example from the early 1970s and more recent circumstances reveals the complex relationships between museums, dealers, and undocumented property. In 1972, the Metropolitan Museum of Art announced it had purchased for about one million dollars a previously unknown Greek calyx krater of the sixth century BCE made by the potter Euxitheos and the painter Euphronios. The Italian police asserted that the krater had been looted from an Etruscan tomb in 1971. Before its purchase, the museum had inquired about its origin from the dealer, who reported that he had secured it from an Armenian dealer, whose father had acquired the vase in fragments in London in 1920. The situation changed dramatically in February 2006, when the Metropolitan Museum (The Met) and the Italian government agreed to terms regarding the museum's Italian holdings. Then-Met director Phillippe de Montebello explained The Met's plans to return the *Euphronios krater* to Italy this way: "The world is changing, and you have to play by the rules. It now appears that the piece [krater] came to us in a completely improper way—through machinations, lies, clandestine night digging. As the representative of an honorable institution, I have to say no, that is not right."[3] The vessel is now in the collection of the Archaeological Museum of Cerveteri.

Other cases, of course, remain unresolved, as stories of looted objects continue to surface, unfortunately. For instance, the Art Institute of Chicago's collection of South and Southeast Asian art from Nepal, India, and other countries includes a recent gift of more than five hundred items from Marilyn Alsdorf, a local benefactor. The donation led to an exhibition, a flashy catalog, and a named gallery as a tribute to Alsdorf and her late husband in 2008. Of the five hundred pieces, at least twenty-four have questionable provenance, and four of these may have been looted from Nepal and illegally exported.[4] In another example, the Denver Art Museum, in 2022, faced questions as to the origins of artifacts from Cambodia—part of a larger "network of plunder that, over decades, robbed Southeast Asians of a significant part of their art, heritage, and culture." The origin seemed to position a Denver-based scholar of Southeast Asian art working together with an art dealer to hide the means of acquisition. Together they, ostensibly, ran the museum as an illegal artifact "laundromat."[5] As with other cases, the museum features a gallery named in the donor's honor, although the museum has now taken steps to "distance itself" from the donor, thus revealing the nuances and contours of donor and, in Denver's case, consultant relations. These relations, along with ethics and provenance (or, the history of a work from its time of creation to the present day), demonstrate the importance of documentation, transparency, and ongoing research in museums.

World War II and Provenance Research

Beyond the aforementioned examples lies a special category of stolen artifacts: items during the Nazi regime (1933–1945) that were unlawfully appropriated and, oftentimes, forcibly taken from their owners. These paintings, sculptures, other works of art, and objects of worship and material culture were stolen from families, public and private museums and galleries, and religious and educational institutions. (It should be noted that, in other cases, theft, confiscation, transfer of ownership, looting, and pillage were neither the means nor the end: instead, destruction of art and other cultural property also occurred.) To understand how these actions persisted, Marie Malaro includes an instructive example in *A Legal Primer on Managing Museum Collections*:

> In *Menzel v. List*, the Menzels purchased a painting by Marc Chagall in 1932 for about $150 at an auction in Brussels, Belgium. In 1941, when the Germans invaded Belgium, the Menzels were forced to flee the country, and the painting was left behind in their apartment. On their return six years later, the painting was gone, having been taken by the Germans. In 1955, Klaus Perls and his wife, proprietors of a New York art gallery, bought the painting from a Parisian art gallery for $2,800. The Perls knew nothing about the history of the painting and did not question the Paris gallery. Klaus Perls testified that it would have been an "insult" to question a reputable dealer as to the title. Several months later the Perls sold the painting to Albert List for $4,000. In 1962, Mrs. Menzel noticed a reproduction of the painting in a book, which gave List's name as the owner. She requested the return of the painting, but List refused to surrender it. Mrs. Menzel then instituted an action for replevin [return of misappropriated property] against List, and he in turn brought the Perls into the suit, alleging that they were liable to him for breach of an implied warranty of title.... After much litigation, Mrs. Menzel was awarded her painting, and the Perls were ordered to pay List the value of the painting as of the date the painting was surrendered to Mrs. Menzel.[6]

This example gives insight as to how works were acquired, and how they changed hands during the war, and after. In fact, after World War II, effort was made by the Allied Forces to return objects to their owners. Fifty years of some process led two governing museum organizations in the United States—the Association of Art Museum Directors and the American Alliance of Museums—to offer guidance for museums on how to proceed with making information available about collections created before 1946 (after the War had ended) and acquired by institutions after 1932. These dates are important because they reflect the period of activity when objects may have been subject to a change of ownership during the Nazi regime. Artifacts that fall into this period (1933–1945) are referred to as "Covered Objects." A list of Covered Objects is available on the Smithsonian Provenance website. However, inclusion in this database in no way signifies that an object has an uncertain provenance or was unlawfully appropriated; rather, its inclusion, in accordance with the intent of the AAMD-AAM guidance, makes information available to the public in an accessible manner.[7]

In terms of numbers, the AAM has organized a searchable registry of objects in United States museum collections that changed hands over the Coverage Period: their data shows close to thirty thousand works.[8] Also instructive, though not limited to the Covered Objects period, is the Getty Provenance Index, which includes more than 2.2 million records that can be used to establish provenance of a work of art.[9] Such resources are vital to building a better understanding of museums and their histories, as well as their actions over time. For today, the responsibility of the museum community is to strive to identify any material for which restitution was never made. Museum websites offer information on acquisition policies and procedures, as well as general provenance research tools, in addition to institution-specific provenance research efforts. Individual museums and researchers have worked to reconstruct provenance—efforts that have been enriched as new scholarship comes from archival resources, especially records of transactions, including papers from dealers that might anchor an object to a contested period or place.

In addition, international groups of museum organizations and the United States Department of State are working to establish policies to balance the rights of owners with the interests of museums in exhibiting objects lacking fully documented provenance, especially for the years 1933 to 1945.[10] The American Alliance of Museums and the International Council of Museums recognize that the American museum community has been instrumental in the success of the postwar restitution effort. Guidance such as the AAMD Standards and Practices and the AAMD Objects Registry are supplemented by the Getty Research Institute, the Art Loss Register, the International Foundation for Art Research, and the Museum Security Network—all of which provide general provenance research tools.

Turbulent pasts are evidenced in our current landscape whereby the International Council of Museums (ICOM) requests that museums, auction houses, art dealers, and collectors not acquire objects without having carefully and thoroughly researched their origin and all the relevant legal documentation as a means of decreasing illicit traffic in cultural goods. Specifically, in 2013, the ICOM issued a list of Syrian objects as risk—called an *Emergency Red List*, the same term given to endangered species' lists—to alert individuals and institutions seeking collections as to circumstances surrounding acquisition and sale of some cultural artifacts.[11] Such threats to collections remind us of the need for museums to protect and secure collections of all of humanity.

More recently, the Victoria and Albert Museum, in London, launched Culture in Crisis as an initiative to protect heritage at risk through conflict, criminal acts, and climate crises. The international organization aims to support collections and professionals around the world and seeks to bring together those with interests in protecting cultural heritage to work with law enforcement, nationally and internationally, and the British Armed Forces, to develop strategies to prevent the illicit trade of cultural goods and to protect heritage. The project database showcases training programs, documentation and digitization initiatives, funding streams for supporting cultural heritage at risk, and events.[12]

In terms of numbers, as of 2021, the Art Loss Register boasted more than seven hundred thousand items on its loss database, with more than 450,000 searches conducted annually.[13] While the question of provenance may leave an impression of uneasiness when viewing museum collections, individual museums and professional organizations are called upon to act responsibly and proactively and to adopt statements of policy that acknowledge the importance of establishing the provenance of objects to be acquired and exhibited in museums. In order to serve their local, national, and international communities, museums need to demonstrate compassion, care, and concern for rightful ownership and do what is appropriate and lawful to acquire, as well as to release, collections.

Ethics of Dispersal

Just as a museum has a right (and, indeed, a duty) to define its field of acquisition and adopt clear policies relating to accessions, so also it ought to establish principles of disposing of materials that are outside its scope or that it cannot use for exhibition, study, or loan. The difficulty here, however, is that a museum is a public trust and that removal and disposal of objects can lead to public criticism and affect future collections donations.

Deaccessioning is the term used by museums to describe the "outflow" of objects. Author Marie Malaro defines it as "the process used to remove permanently an object from a museum's collection. The definition presupposes that the object in question once was 'accessioned,' that it was formally accepted and recorded as an object worthy of collection status."[14] Generally agreed-upon reasons for this practice are (a) an item does not fit within the museum's "scope of collections," (b) the museum cannot provide proper care for the object, (c) the item is in poor condition, and (d) the museum owns an abundance of like objects. In addition to these reasons for deaccessioning museum objects, museums have used other, less agreed-upon justifications, including lack of storage space, changing curatorial interests, and potential income from an item's sale, sometimes creating a public outcry over these actions.[15]

Many museum objects offer little difficulty if they are deaccessioned. Some museums (especially those dealing with history and science) may even accept objects with the understanding that they may not be accessioned but will be sold or otherwise disposed of for the benefit of the museum. Other objects may have been received years earlier and lie outside a museum's agreed-upon field (for example, taxidermized animals or seashells in a small art museum); if such objects cannot be returned to the donors, no one can reasonably oppose their disposal. Items damaged beyond reasonable repair or actual duplicates also arouse little controversy. Similarly, objects more useful in other collections (for example, Egyptian scarabs in a local history museum) can be placed on long-term loan, given, or even sold to another, more appropriate, museum.

Major problems are encountered, however, when items are sold for financial reasons or traded or sold to upgrade the quality of a collection. Art museums often experience special difficulties because of varying opinions of the importance and monetary value of art objects. Museums follow three general practices in this area. Some museums sell or exchange nothing. A second policy permits sales or exchanges only with other museums or similar nonprofit institutions. The third practice is for the museum freely to sell or exchange works of art to which the museum has unrestricted title in order to refine and enhance its collections.

Museum professional organizations have established within their codes of ethics standards for the use of funds gained from deaccessioning. The Association of Art Museum Directors (AAMD) stated, in 1992, that "Proceeds should be restricted to acquisitions of new works of art." The AAMD's more recent statement (2010) has outlined that deaccessioning is "a legitimate part of the formation and care of collections and, if practiced, should be done in order to refine and improve the quality and appropriateness of the collections, the better to serve the museum's mission." The policy recommends that such funds (and any earnings or appreciation) be tracked independently from other acquisition funds and be used "only for the acquisition of works in a manner consistent with the museum's policy on the use of restricted acquisition funds" and not be used for operations or capital expenses.[16]

The AAM's Code of Ethics (1993) requires that disposals be solely for "the advancement of the museum's mission. Proceeds from the sale of nonliving collections are to be used consistent with the established standards of the museum's discipline, but in no event shall they be used for anything other than acquisition or *direct care of collections*" [emphasis added]. The term *direct care* was first used in this context. The introduction of this term—which has caused confusion for more than twenty years among the museum community—came because of interest among history and natural history museums who argued that their responsibility to care for collections equaled the importance on building collections. Thus, *direct care* replaced language in the code of ethics from 1991 that principled acquisition only, to allow funds for care of collections as well as collection building. The term itself was never defined and remained problematic because museums lacked guidance in their decision-making in this area.

To simplify the understanding of *direct care*, the AAM established a task force that commissioned a field-wide survey to determine how museum professionals from different disciplines define *direct care*, regardless of any practice in use at their institutions. Then, in April 2016, the AAM released a white paper that examined the use of this term with regard to the use of funds realized from the sale of items deaccessioned from permanent museum collections. The paper also provided a matrix intended to aid museums in determining the appropriate use of funds.[17]

The American Association for State and Local History (AASLH) argues forthrightly that "collections shall not be deaccessioned or disposed of in order to provide financial support for institutional operations, facilities maintenance, or any reason other than the preservation or acquisition of collections, collections, as defined by institutional policy" (2012).[18] The International Council of Museums policy (2004) articulates the responsibility of museums and cautions against the use of collections as assets: "Museum collections are held in public trust and may not be treated as a realisable asset. Money or compensation received from the deaccessioning and disposal of objects and specimens from a museum collection should be used solely for the benefit of the collection and usually for acquisitions to that same collection."[19]

However, with the onset of the COVID-19 pandemic, matters regarding deaccession changed dramatically. As museum funding streams dried up, institutions were left scrambling regarding how to afford care of collections, as well as general operating expenses. The Association of Art Museum Directors suspended the imposition of sanctions for violations of its deaccessioning rules, thus permitting museums, for a two-year period, to use proceeds from sales of deaccessioned art for direct care of their collections and the income from those funds for general operating expenses.

Simultaneously, United States museums, in the wake of the extrajudicial killing of Black people, sought to use deaccessioning to change the narrative landscape by actively choosing to sell high-value art and steer the proceeds to acquire works by underrepresented artists. This movement—which writer and art curator Glenn Adamson termed *progressive deaccessioning*—resulted in circuits of sale and consumption that also brought attention to the structural racism that has perpetuated White privilege at the expense of Black lives as well as the institutional racism that has seen the work of underrepresented artists remain so.[20]

The shifting terrain of deaccessioning led the AAMD to vote, in September 2022, to change its policy regarding the use of deaccession proceeds to also include direct care. The term *direct care* refers to "direct costs associated with the storage or preservation of works of art. Such direct costs include for example those for (i) conservation and restoration treatments (including packing and transportation for such conservation or restoration) and (ii) materials required for storage of all classifications of works of art, such as, acid-free paper, folders, matboard, frames, mounts and digital media migration."[21]

Given these differing needs, then, museums ought to design their own disposal procedures based on the highest professional ethics, both in deciding upon the deaccessioning and carrying out the sales or exchanges.

Protecting Collections in Wartime

In all collecting scenarios, context and documentation are key, particularly as the twenty-first century has ushered in threats to collections. As Neil Brodie, director of the Illicit Antiquities Research Centre at Cambridge (UK), has noted: "There are three ways in which wars threaten cultural materials: the most obvious is damage from military attack, but another threat is removal of materials for profit, to fund the war or for propaganda purposes, with the final means perhaps the most disturbing, that of destroying cultural materials to erase ethnic or religious symbols within a society (cultural cleansing)." Are international museum organizations responsible for protecting collections in wartime? As noted in Chapter 6, conflict has impacted collections care over the years. Clearly, collections are at risk, and steps are being taken by international organizations to try to stop, or to highlight, their destruction. For instance, UNESCO has initiated the creation of the "the first virtual immersive reality museum of stolen cultural objects at a global scale"—the Virutal Museum of Stolen Cultural Artifacts. Designed by African artist Francis Kéré, a Pritzer Prize award–winning architect, who is turning his architecture skills to the digital space by conceiving of the museum in the shape of a baobab tree (a tree native to Africa and Australia that also grows in Asia) while also drawing inspiration from Frank Lloyd Wright's design for the Guggenheim Museum in New York. The goal of the space is to raise awareness and eventually to be free of collections—so that no stolen works would be on view.[22]

Individuals have entered this arena, too, as evidenced by the creation of the Museum of Stolen Art. Established in 2023 as a way to document the loss of Ukrainian heritage as a result of the invasion by Russia, which began in 2022, the Museum of Stolen Art sought to "exhibit digital copies of artworks" as a way "to remember, to realize the loss, and eventually to bring home what has survived."[23] While the website is no longer active, articles about the museum are still visible online: together with the landing page of the museum, the Museum of Stolen Art demonstrates the capacity of digital media for documenting theft, loss, and the destruction of cultural heritage. Unfortunately, there remains much work to be done to protect collections—both tangible and intangible heritage—and museum professionals, the institutions where they work, and the organizations of which they are a part must rise to these challenges, perhaps even in collaboration with researchers and innovators outside of museums, to protect our global heritage.

Transparency and Museum Workers: COVID-19 and Open Letters

As noted earlier, the COVID-19 pandemic brought museums to a screeching halt. Yet, as museums were closed to the public onsite due to the pandemic, they "opened up" online and in other ways as they provided space for much-needed services during the pandemic. They also expanded their roles to support their communities and audiences though onsite, limited interaction and virtual content among the diversity of mission, type, and scale across United States museums. These workings were also within the context of the need to confront the global pandemic, the extrajudicial killing of George Floyd, and the injustices elsewhere, including within institutions such as museums.

At a moment when museums face challenges from all sides, what are the major obstacles to systemic change in museums today, and how can they be navigated and overcome? What is at risk in times of institutional instability and transformation?

This section positions questions around transparency as practice, openness, and transformation. It is guided by the notion that museums exist in cyclical time as a constellation between the past, present, and future. Further, it is positioned around the idea that museums can center community narratives, which opens up the possibilities around multi-vocality as a form of transparency and belonging. Such work, though, also has the capacity to reveal truths, harms, and burdens. As philosopher and theorist Walter Benjamin stated, "There has never been a document of culture, which is not simultaneously one of barbarism."[24] The same could be said of museums: museums can simultaneously reflect culture and barbarism. Where do we see this playing out?

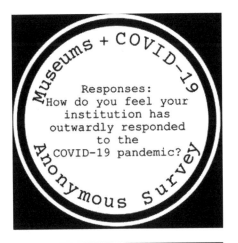
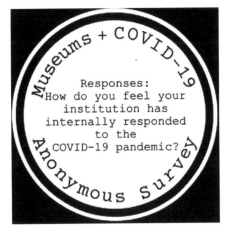

Museums + COVID-19 Responses: How do you feel your institution has outwardly responded to the COVID-19 pandemic? Anonymous Survey

Museums + COVID-19 Responses: How do you feel your institution has internally responded to the COVID-19 pandemic? Anonymous Survey

Museums + COVID-19 Responses: How do you feel your institution is handling calls to commit to anti-racism? Anonymous Survey

Museums + COVID-19 Responses: How has your experience of the museum sector been impacted by the events of this year? Anonymous Survey

At https://covidmuseumsanonymous.wordpress.com/, anecdotes gathered in the summer of 2020 disclosed the impact of the pandemic on museum workers. See discussion on page 255.

Alleging that senior staff at many institutions (primarily art museums) foster toxic work environments of racism, sexism, exclusion, and exploitation, museum workers have begun collectively organizing to articulate their demands for safer and more equitable working conditions, better pay and unionization in some cases,[25] and greater inclusivity alongside the hope for museums that are more robustly diverse and explicitly anti-racist in their programming. The COVID-19 pandemic has exacerbated these tensions, as many museum workers have been furloughed or laid off, and resistance to speaking up has faded in favor of demanding structural change in the museum. When senior-level management has proved resistant, museum workers have gone public, publishing their demands through online outlets and social media. A few examples are described below. It is important to note that these citations are provided as examples to give insight into practice, openness, and transformation in museums at this historical moment, from the murder of Michael Brown in Ferguson, Missouri, in 2014, which led to the movement "Museums Respond to Ferguson," to the open calls to transform toxic workplace culture in museums that mushroomed in 2020.

Calls for change were made in terms of what they collect, whom they hire, and how they cater to their audiences. Each of these arenas unfolds a series of additional questions, such as: what they collect, *and how they collect, and the function of these collections, as far as exhibition, meaning-making, and storytelling*; whom they hire, *and how they treat them*; and how they cater to their audiences, *and how those audiences are made visible in the museum experience.*

Open Letters

In the summer of 2020, the "Open Letter" delivered via social media became the tool of choice for exposing matters of concern at museums, as also in the broader space of activism created during the crisis of racial reckoning.[26] As Aaron Randle noted in his early summary of the Open Letter movement, at the same time of the large protest movement following the murder of George Floyd, workers in the museum world (and mostly the art world) were organizing letters, social media campaigns, and actions as organized protest. Open letters and petitions pulled back the curtain on the Guggenheim in New York City; the Akron Art Museum; the Virginia Museum of Fine Arts (VMFA); the New Orleans Museum of Art (NOMA); the San Francisco Museum of Modern Art; and others. Staff across ranks of front of house, curators, gallery attendants, educators, and others called out the culture of racism within American art institutions. In addition, staff and allies called into question statements of solidarity issued by institutions as too low a bar. For instance, the group VMFA Reform urged the Virginia Museum of Fine Arts in Richmond, Virginia, to do more through their open letter as a Change.org petition: "The Virginia Museum of Fine Arts' institutional response to the Black Lives Matter protests against police brutality failed to critically evaluate the institution's own role in upholding structural racism and other forms of oppression. The VMFA issued a statement of solidarity but did not provide sufficient actionable guidelines or material support for Richmond's Black communities or for the VMFA's Black staff members."[27]

Concerns beyond staff, and in relation to visitors, surfaced as part of the #DismantleNOMA movement. The letter, published on June 24, 2020, states, "In addition to internal racism and bias, there are countless reported incidents of Black school groups, interns and visitors feeling targeted and harassed by white staff while visiting NOMA as recently as February 2020. Front desk associates at NOMA received daily feedback from Black visitors, many 3rd & 4th generation New Orleanians, stating that they have never felt welcomed or represented at the museum. These concerns were brought up in departmental meetings repeatedly and reported to HR only to be buried or dismissed."[28] Their letter, and their follow-up on July 27, 2020, asked for action as well as a call for meeting with the museum. Four days later, the NOMA Board president, Janice Parmelee, patronized their work, stating, "While your concern is appreciated, we must have the time to develop and implement our meaningful plans. Therefore, in response to your recent email, we respectfully decline your invitation to meet. Our progress will be posted periodically on our web site. I, along with our entire board, have every confidence in NOMA leadership and staff for the work they are doing."[29]

Artists heard the group, however, and more than 150 artists amplified the demands for reform and called for art workers "to place strict conditions on their collaborations with NOMA." All the while, the museum issued an anemic response in the form of an "Agenda for Change" in July 2020 that recognized internal and external work to be done. Steps toward progress are recounted on the museum's website in the "About" tab, where the DEI (Diversity, Equity, and Inclusion) report from 2022 is featured. It states, "NOMA is committed to being a welcoming, inclusive, anti-racist institution," as a result of the NOMA Board of Trustees, leadership, and staff beginning to work to address their challenges and opportunities in an "ongoing, long-term, committed process"—a process that, apparently, has seen no action since August 2022. No updates on the website have been made to acknowledge the ongoing nature of their agenda.[30]

Instagram

Open calls for change and the creation (and the persistence) of Instagram handles seek information from individuals witnessing or otherwise experiencing discrimination, harassment, or other workplace harm. Some of these are specific to an institution, such as @ABetterGuggenheim, whereas others serve as aggregators, such as @ChangeTheMuseum, @MuseumWorkersSpeak, @MuseumAsProgress, @fairmuseumjobs, @changetheboard, @cancelartgalleries, and @covidmuseumsanonymous, among others. A handful are discussed below, though readers are encouraged to look online to see the fullness of these social-media pursuits of transparency.

Rather than focus on the critique of a single institution, such as the Guggenheim, which has seen unsettling disclosure on @ABetterGuggenheim recounting racism, sexism, and classism, much of this section will focus on broader movements. However, it is worth noting some of the discussion around @ABetterGuggenheim and to consider how the methods and practices employed there might look with another institution's name in the handle.

According to an investigation by Jasmine Liu of *Hyperallergic*, "Armstrong faced criticism in 2020 from current and former staff organizing under the name 'A Better Guggenheim' for 'nurturing a culture of unchecked racism, sexism, and classism across all departments, levels, and locations.' Among the many complaints listed were that he had displayed a condescending attitude toward Chaédria LaBouvier, the first Black curator to organize an exhibition at the museum. LaBouvier, who curated the 2019 Guggenheim show *Basquiat's 'Defacement': The Untold Story*, later called that experience 'the most racist professional experience of my life.'"[31] Two years earlier, shortly after the story of LaBouvier broke, @ABetterGuggenheim reported, "Armstrong has called himself a steward of the institution. His actions show that he is, instead, a steward of the toxic, inequitable structures we seek to uproot."[32] Since that time, the museum has hired Mariët Westermann, the vice chancellor of NYU Abu Dhabi in the United Arab Emirates and the first woman director of the entire Guggenheim Museum group, not solely the Manhattan entity. Even the announcement of the new director recalled moments of crisis and accountability for the museum: Westermann assumes leadership of an institution "still healing from a period of turmoil . . . an "inequitable work environment that enables racism"; the removal of the Sackler name in 2022 after protesters called attention to that family's ties to the opioid crisis; the fight for a union contract; and a protest inside the museum that left the main entrance temporarily closed. Recently, the Guggenheim temporarily closed its entrance on Fifth Avenue after a protest inside the museum denounced Israel's military airstrikes in Gaza in the fall of 2023.[33] It appears, however, at the close of 2023, that the majority of the work of @ABetterGuggenheim has shifted to another platform or died down.

In contrast to @ABetterGuggenheim, with 197 posts and 3,500 followers, @ChangeTheMuseum is going strong with nine hundred posts and 52,700 followers, as of November 2023. @ChangeThe Museum sees its role as "pressuring US museums to move beyond lip service proclamations of anti-racism by amplifying tales of unchecked racism."[34] Specifics, as to institutions, are given, while simultaneously allowing the poster to maintain anonymity. Abuses of leadership and lack of support for hiring candidates from diverse backgrounds, and diversity, equity, inclusion, and belonging have been the subject of numerous posts. Excerpts from a few posts are shared below, without confirmation of proof, as is the method maintained by the channel operators.

On November 2, 2023, the following post was made: "While the abuses of the leadership team at the Worcester Art Museum are stunning (age, racial and gender discrimination, gaslighting, harassment, and bullying, the list goes on) perhaps the most disheartening element is the dozens of staff members, including curators, conservators, and DEAI specialists who have stood by and enabled years of abuse. I wonder if they will ever feel safe enough to raise their voice."[35] On September 25, 2023, the following post was made: "The Guggenheim prides itself on collecting artwork and presenting shows of overlooked and marginalized artists. But then why not have your senior curatorial staff reflect these core values? . . . In 2019 the Guggenheim hired its first full-time black female curator, it is now 2023, more than 5 years later and we only have 2 Black female curators, 1 Asian female curator, 2 Latin curators, one female and the other male, and over 10 white curators, 90% of which are female. Do better, you had the opportunity to hire two BIPOC and/or POC senior curatorial staff but yet you chose to repeat history, the very one you claim to dismantle."[36]

Beyond art museums, science museums have also been subject to scrutiny, as have university museums. On September 25, 2023, the following post was made: "The Great Lakes Science Center tries hard to show itself as a bastion of STEM diversity and equality, but behind the scenes there's a staggering culture of exclusivity and sexism. . . . GLSC pretends to be the future of STEM, but maybe it's a bit too accurately a portrait of the STEM industry as it is."[37] On November 23, 2022, the following post was made: "Over the last three years, 50 of the 100 full time employees at the Penn Museum have left. . . . Lower and medium level staff have no room for growth, professionally or with their salary, and the DEIA efforts have been increasingly performative. At least the 3 deputy directors have received promotions over that period. Coincidentally, those three are frequently cited as reasons for staff departures. Staff increasingly realize that the only way for things to improve is to escape."[38]

Posts have also borne the weight of systemic racism and fear over how change might unfold with leadership coming from within privilege. On March 1, 2021, the following post was made: "I identify as BIPOC and attended a top public university to obtain my bachelors and masters in art history + art education. I didn't realize this until years later but I was a diversity checkmark box for the program. . . . At my most recent museum job, I was given way too much work at one point during the pandemic when I had many personal issues going on (as many of us had), and suffered 3 mental breakdowns in the span of 2 months. . . . This is all to say that I'm leaving the field and never looking back. I value my mental health, professional goals, and personal future so I can make a better life for myself and my family. I'm sick of working 2 jobs, 60 hrs a week just to get by. Wake up, museums. Talent is leaving."[39] Professionals who stay in the field are also worried about its future. On November 2, 2020, the following post was made: "I am a POC Conservator who has witnessed and experienced countless moments of microaggression and subconscious bias since entering this field. . . . The majority of professionals in this field come from similar racial, social, and economic backgrounds, yet they are the stewards of our collective heritage (which has proven to privilege only certain histories and narratives). Now they are involved in molding DEI initiatives and trying to create structural change, when they were the ones who helped maintain the status quo in cultural institutions for generations. I am afraid of my colleagues everyday and what good they *think* they are doing now and will pat each other on the back for later."[40]

Concerns about abuse of power, and its outlay in the visitor experience, at the expense of museum staff well-being are also expressed in posts. One pointed to a tech-based experience that was not functioning as intended. "Two of the interactives that used facial recognition had difficulty registering black faces. Instead of sharing this information openly and taking advantage of an opportunity to talk about how tech is biased, the project lead forced black staff and interns to spend hours having their faces repeatedly scanned so the technology could improve (incremental improvement)."[41]

Posts have also drawn attention to non-personnel concerns and have pointed to where meaningful change can occur. For instance, on October 13, 2021, a post brought to attention use of the term Indian princess in teaching resource materials from the National Portrait Gallery. "The National Portrait Gallery still has a classroom resource where they refer to Pocahontas as an 'Indian princess.' I wonder if NMAI knows or was even consulted before the Portrait Gallery did this? How many students have been told by Portrait Gallery educators that Pocahontas was an Indian princess?" The post provided the link to the online resource. At some point between then and now, the curriculum online has removed this reference and, further, utilizes original place names in the description. Whether or not the museum knew of the Instagram post or not, steps are being taken toward inclusivity in very real ways.[42]

Demands are voiced for results from such calls for change and promises made by all museums. On July 8, 2021, a post requested the progress made to date: "Over a year ago, museums made a promise, albeit fumbled, to do better for their BIPOC employees after the murder of George Floyd. So many of us feared and knew this would yield close to no results. . . . Progress made is always progress celebrated, of course. But when that progress still comes at the cost of overworked and underpaid employees who carry the load to see these projects manifest for the glory of the heads of the institution all the while knowing there has been little to no attempt to connect with our needs or daily concerns, they become hollow. . . . Change comes from the top, is that where the true focus of your work ends up landing?"[43]

While these are only a handful of the thousands of posts collectively made on the volunteer-run, anonymous feeds, even these raise questions as to the ethics of sharing and managing such a site. Where is the accountability? At @ChangeTheMuseum, when posts were critically received, erasure of posts and subsequent scrubbing of the site attempted to "undo" the harm of the original posts, while also silencing the very discourse and transparency that the handle seeks to model and call for within museums.

@MuseumWorkersSpeak offered a digital space for museum workers/activists "interrogating the relationship between museums' stated commitments to social value and their internal labor practices."[44] The group formed at American Alliance of Museums in 2015, where the conference theme was "The Social Value of Museums: Inspiring Change." The organizers of the "rogue" session used the forum as a way to bridge the disconnect between the field's increasing commitment to addressing social inequality and initiating civic dialogue and the silences around internal practices, including hiring, leadership, and working environment of museums. Inspired by Paulo Freire's critical pedagogy,[45] the group dialogued and arrived at a set of action points to enact change. One of these involves supporting underpaid staff financially by establishing a "relief fund" that sought radical redistribution "in which individuals leverage whatever privilege they can to support their peers who have been disposed of by museums." By securing donations from individuals within and beyond the museum community, the group dropped five-hundred-dollar gifts into the bank accounts of as many museum workers as they could, as a demonstration of radical trust and solidarity. Between the fund launch date of May 13, 2020, and August 14, 2020, the collective received over six hundred applications and have raised over seventy thousand dollars, distributing funds to twenty recipients per drawing each time they reached a ten-thousand-dollar fundraising milestone.[46]

Other Platforms

An alternative was provided by @covidmuseumsanonymous, an online repository established and managed during the summer of 2020. The intent was to record "in the moment" anonymous accounts of museum activities around the COVID-19 and BLM. The responses were gathered through a Google Form, linked in the @CovidMuseumsAnonymous, and archived at the "Journal of the Plague Year" international archive launched by academics, public historians, and communities of volunteers in March 2020.[47]

Anecdotes were posted only once, on August 5, 2020, before the two organizers realized the burden was too great to continue trying to manage the survey collection, data sharing, and archiving while also simultaneously managing themselves to get through the pandemic. However, the single data dump did provide feedback from ninety participants, with charts and graphs indicating employment role/position; department; number of staff; country; and size of city where the institution was located. The four open-ended questions navigated museum responses outwardly, internally, calls to commit to anti-racism, and the impact on the museum sector overall. Though short-lived, this hashtag was intentionally unlike the other social-media efforts in their reporting and calling out, striving to bring awareness and to deposit a moment in the historical record, with the hope of effecting change. However, the organizers also acknowledged the stress of the pandemic and the related institutional and racial crises. On the website, they note, "This is a stressful and difficult time for many of us in the museum and gallery field. See the bottom of the page for a list of mental health and support resources."[48]

Reports of workplace realities may be gleaned from other forums, including the online job community Glassdoor, which promotes itself as the place "where work talk gets real." Though simultaneously, once entered into the platform, a cautionary note to "Be respectful. You're posting in a Bowl™—an anonymous community with real people—so keep it professional." And "Honor your agreements. Remember your confidentiality agreements and don't share sensitive information."[49] Upon entering the site, and after offering a review or salary of their current or previous employers, users are permitted to read reviews of companies. A cursory look at some museums disclosed information about the workplace. For instance, on October 11, 2023, a manager of a museum posted the following as "cons" of the work environment at the museum where they were employed: "Hierarchy, only senior level management is seen as competent. Anyone else is treated terribly, no matter how many years of experience, degrees, etc. Bullying, especially by senior level management. No HR department, so don't bother complaining or trying to better situations, they will always come back to bite you! Pay is insultingly little. Not much to recommend. Advice to Management: Clean house, and hire less power-hungry, egotistical people."[50]

Worker-led mobilizing has been situated within blogs and newspaper reporting. More recently, it been examined within a scholarly context. In the fall of 2022, Margaret Middleton and Jamie Hagen published an article, "Worker-Led Feminist Mobilizing for the Museum of the Future," where they examined museums as a site of transformative activism in the United States and the UK; they looked at layoffs coexisting with other long-standing social-justice issues within the institutions where they worked. In seeking answers about transformation, Middleton and Hagen state that change "requires looking more concretely at where the power of museums as institutions lies by addressing sexism and racism directly, while also confronting the legacies of colonialism." They "recognize the COVID-19 pandemic as just one of many overlapping experiences of crisis, acknowledging the interlinkages between the economic, political and social dimensions of the struggle for social justice."[51]

Beyond Open Letters: Expeditions, Exhibits, and Action

The Natural History Museum, launched by the activist art collective Not An Alternative in September 2014, began as a performative art intervention taking the form of a traveling, pop-up museum that seeks to illuminate and combat "greenwashing." Calling for transparency around funding and ethics in sponsorship and donor relations, their efforts around sponsorship escalated in 2015, when they released an "open letter" to museums from the scientific community that questioned the association between money and museums. Particular attention was drawn to David H. Koch, a board member, major donor, and exhibit sponsor of the Smithsonian National Museum of Natural History and the American Museum of Natural History. His empire, Koch Industries, is one of the greatest contributors to greenhouse gas emissions in the United States; Koch funds a large network of climate change-denying organizations that together pose a threat to the continued preservation of our shared, natural heritage. The letter pointed to bilateral association, such that when Koch sponsors institutions, these museums are also sponsoring Koch. The 148 signatories called for action: "we believe that the only ethical way forward for our museums is to cut all ties with the fossil fuel industry and funders of climate science obfuscation."[52]

Their work connects "current events and social movements to the histories of ecology, science and museums, the legacy of colonialism, and ongoing concerns about natural and cultural heritage."[53] Themes include greenwashing; science activism, environmental justice, and water conservation; and Indigenous ways of relating. A key facet of their work may be defined as the "Red" Natural History Museum, a facet that emphasizes care for Indigenous land, culture, and practice.

The Natural History Museum approaches its work in terms of exhibitions, expeditions, and actions—all of which have onsite and virtual elements. One exhibit, for example, saw a partnership between the Natural History Museum and the House of Tears Carvers of the Lummi Nation to create "Whale People: Protectors of the Sea." The film installation and its companion three-thousand-pound orca whale totem tell the story of today's environmental emergency of fossil fuel pollution and industrial development which places collective natural and cultural heritage at risk.[54]

Expeditions include the 2021–2022 project to carve a totem pole from Washington state to Washington, D.C., to raise awareness about Indigenous sacred sites. Called the "Red Road to D.C.," the act involved master carver Jewell "Praying Wolf" James and others creating a twenty-five-foot pole

The Natural History Museum approaches its work in terms of exhibitions, expeditions, and actions—all of which have onsite and virtual elements. Actions include the open letter, as well as petitions to return place names of Indigenous lands, to re-Indigenize the land. Such efforts at re-Indigenizing the place names stands in contrast to the term *de-colonizing*, where *de-* means "from" or "again," such that the focus becomes the second part of that word: *colonizing*, to the extent that the repetition of colonizing can cause further harm. Here, Nicholas Galanin's *Indian Land*.
Ted Drake (CC-BY-ND-2.0-flickr), https://thenaturalhistorymuseum.org/re-indigenize-place-names-on-public-lands/.

that would make its way to the National Mall to serve as a reminder "of the promises that were made to the first peoples of this land and waters" and as a call to "share in their responsibility to safeguard the sacred sources of life—Earth, water and sky."[55]

Actions include the open letter, as well as petitions to return place names of Indigenous lands, *to re-Indigenize the land*. Such efforts at re-Indigenizing the place names stands in contrast to the term *de-colonizing*, where *de-* means "from" or "again," such that the focus becomes the second part of that word: *colonizing*, to the extent that the repetition of colonizing can cause further harm.[56] In this vein, the Natural History Museum launched a letter campaign in April 2022 supporting the effort, led by interior secretary Deb Haaland, as part of the Department of Interior's broader movement to remove derogatory and offensive names from federal lands, including national parks, rivers, and other geographic features. Further, the Museum asked for signatures to encourage further action that would not only rename landmarks, but also give the authority for naming to the Indigenous Nations whose lands were dispossessed in order to give access to the public through the federal government.[57]

Since its debut a decade ago, the Natural History Museum has evolved into an organization that questions the existence of museums themselves, stating, "we do not need bigger and better mausoleums; nor do we need more durable fortresses to protect our most treasured landscapes and cultural objects. We need to turn museums inside out, to transform them into resources that support the life that runs through everything—inside, beneath, and beyond their walls."[58]

Land Acknowledgments and Normalizing Decolonizing Principles

Land acknowledgments are a traditional custom that dates back centuries in many Indigenous communities. Today, land acknowledgments are used by Indigenous and non-Indigenous peoples to recognize that Indigenous communities were the original stewards of the lands on which we now live. They also acknowledge the long span of human history that has existed on a particular site, including contemporary Indigenous populations. Land acknowledgments are valuable forms of respect and verbal witness to the past and present. They can serve as verbal embodiments of anti-colonist and anti-racist practices. These statements are commonly communicated orally or through sign language at the opening of public events or found in print on organizational websites.

However, land acknowledgments by non-native people have often been called meaningless or performative.[59] By stating this claim is not to suggest that we should not do acknowledgments, but rather that they "should be motivated by genuine respect and support for Native Peoples. Speaking and hearing words of recognition is an important step in creating collaborative, accountable, continuous, and respectful relationships with Indigenous nations and communities." In addition, researchers Theresa Ambo and Theresa Rocha Beardall suggest the term *rhetorical removal* for the use of language (in their study of land-grant universities) that selectively erases Indigenous peoples. Ambo and Beardall call for the intentional address of colonial legacies of violence and indication of material support for Indigenous students and Native peoples.[60] There are contingencies of enacting land acknowledgments in settler institutions, such as museums. Understanding and connecting land acknowledgments to the broader arc of museum work and learning about museums requires ongoing work, not a simple placement of words on a website or a statement to be read at the beginning of an event.

Indigenous scholar and museum professional Amy Lonetree examined historical and contemporary museum practices more than a decade ago (2012) and shared how museums can pull back on settler-focused narratives and integrate Indigenous epistemologies, refute stereotypes, and thoughtfully represent and reflect the Native American past and present in visual and verbal museum exhibit development and museum practices. In charting out paths forward, Lonetree presents a critical and decolonial museum practice that inspires justice and recognition of Indigenous life.[61]

Building upon a foundation of Lonetree and others,[62] museum studies scholar Laura Phillips has drawn attention to one of the end goals of decolonizing work in museums, universities, and beyond as the opportunity for White settlers to "understand *how* and *what* we need to give up and, more importantly, *give back*." Alongside decolonization is re-Indigenation, which Phillips describes as "to make and hold space for Indigenous people to live, work, create, and be—in their own way, not expected to conform, perform, explain, or curtain their Indigeneity for the institution." Phillips makes this claim known because, in her view, museums have authority in society and "must use this to enact change, starting with visibilizing the ongoing colonialism around us."[63] Part of this work necessitates multi-vocality as a means of challenging colonial structures in museums and realizing curated spaces as open rather than closed, as a "'forum' for society rather than a 'temple' for an authorized few."[64]

Of keen interest for this volume and our immediate audience is decolonizing and Indigenizing, as part of the coursework developed by Phillips, as the focal point without the mention of these two terms in the course title "Curatorial Practice." Phillips has taught a graduate-level museum studies course at University of Toronto and a career development course aimed at museum professionals via Museum-Study.com. These approaches are integrated and embedded into the course and smoothly integrated in ways that reflect a shift from the separation of these courses into their own discrete offerings that are, often, electives in curriculum.

The seamlessness and incorporation of anti-colonizing and re-Indigenation as themes and subjects in courses where they are not the topic, but, in fact, the process, calls to mind the call for normativity issued by museum scholar Ross Parry, whose work focuses on digital heritage and the notion of the "postdigital museum"—a stage of development in which it doesn't make sense to separate the digital from other facets of museum work.[65]

Decolonize This Place (DTP)

The movement Decolonize This Place was born out of a residency at New York City's Artists Space Books & Talks series in the fall of 2016,[66] bringing together movements in a nonprofit residency for organizing, activism, and art-making. DTP brings together individuals and groups, where artists and cultural workers are playing leading roles, engaged in social movements. They organize around "decolonization, not only of the mind, but of land, institutions and social relationships, [which] has emerged as a sweeping imperative across contemporary political struggles."[67] At the core of their process is a weekly program of public events that center six lines of action: Indigenous Struggle, Black Liberation, Free Palestine, Global Wage Workers, De-Gentrification, and Dismantle Patriarchy.[68] Many of the participants have been organizers of other groups and actions, thus demonstrating the importance and persistence of activism within and about museums. Other organizations with similar interests are numerous, including Liberate Tate, an artist collective that fought for years to end BP's sponsorship of Tate Museums (which eventually occurred in 2016, five years after their open letter to then-director of Tate Nicholas Serota); G.U.L.F., a subsidiary of Gulf Labor Artist Coalition, a group fighting for the labor rights of migrant workers building the Guggenheim Museum in Abu Dhabi; NYC Stands with Standing Rock Collective, a group of Indigenous activists and supporters who resist the construction of the Dakota Access Pipeline, which threatens traditional and treaty-guaranteed Great Sioux Nation territory; and several others.[69] Each one of these issues, and others, highlights big concerns for our country, for humanity, and for our planet. Activists look to museums as spaces to make their voices heard.[70]

However, DTP has been also been criticized for their methods in targeting museum board members and associated executives and inciting calls for violence. For example, in 2019, their protest traveled from the Whitney Biennial to the home of the vice chair of the Whitney Museum, Warren Kanders, where they left a larger-than-life-sized tear gas canister, reflecting upon his ties to a company that manufactures the tear gas used as a weapon against asylum seekers at the United States-Mexico border.[71]

One of DTP's most public-facing events occurs with regularity at the American Museum of Natural History in New York City, as Anti–Columbus Day Tours with three (or more) requests: to remove, rename, and respect. At issue is the statue created in 1940 by James Earle Fraser of Theodore Roosevelt, the twenty-sixth president, shown on horseback and supported by two mostly nude figures, one Black and one Indigenous. Second, DTP calls for New York City's mayor and City Council to rename "Columbus Day" as "Indigenous People's Day" to honor the land and forebears, the Lenape, and the more than one hundred thousand Indigenous people who live on that land today. Third is the museum's display and interpretation of objects. DTP organizer Marz Saffore points out the marginalization of African people through the displays that are designated "Hall of African Peoples," in contrast to the methods used to identify other sections of the museum and their exhibits. Further, the group asks why Indigenous, Asian, Latin American, and African cultural artifacts reside in the AMNH, in the realm of nature and science, whereas European (and in particular Greek and Roman counterparts) are housed in the Metropolitan Museum of Art. The group questions the perspective of interpretation in specific examples, as well, citing the rings on the cross-section of an ancient California Sequoia tree felled in 1893 for its labels with dates from Eurocentric history, such as Christopher Columbus's "discovery" of the Orinoco River rather than from the history of the peoples who lived here already. DTP states, "In a decolonial museum, these dates would tell a different story and different histories. It would acknowledge Indigenous life in the forests of California, the clear-cutting of Redwood trees by agricultural speculators," and so on.[72]

Some efforts of DTP, and their allies, have been successful. On January 20, 2022, the statue of Roosevelt was removed from outside of the American Museum of Natural History.[73] The museum's attempts at contextualizing the monument since the work of DTP began in 2016 focused on balancing the accomplishments of Roosevelt with the message of the statue today, noting "the statue itself communicates a racial hierarchy that the Museum and members of the public have long found disturbing." The museum articulated the relationship between the concerns around this one work and museums writ large: "We recognize that more work is needed to better understand not only the Statue, but our own history. As we strive to advance our institution's, our City's, and our country's passionate quest for racial justice, we believe that removing the Statue will be a symbol of progress and of our commitment to build and sustain an inclusive and equitable Museum community and broader society."[74]

DTP organizer Saffore is one of many who call for more action: "While many United States museums have made moves toward what the field calls 'diversity, equity, and inclusion,' it's critical that we move past identity politics. . . . It's not enough to hire an Indigenous curator. It's not enough to have one Black person on your board. Museums as we know them have to be abolished."[75]

Restitution

According to journalist and consultant Adrian Ellis, restitution claims center around four types of activity:

- Early museum acquisitions for the assembly of museums in the eighteenth through the twentieth centuries
- Appropriations made during periods of war and civil unrest (Nazi-era acquisitions; Taiwan's holdings of collections from mainland China)
- Historic ethnographic collections, such as human remains of Indigenous persons
- Contemporary looting (Italy, China, and other locations)[76]

As such, there is no single solution on how to handle questions of provenance, ownership, and possession. Restitution matters require answers deliverable after the long and hard work of provenance research; crowdsourced databases with information on works; and legal research keyed to specific instances or cases.

Hollywood movies have shown that restitution is a thread of interest, even among the public. In 2018, the Marvel Cinematic Universe franchise of movies released *Black Panther*, which examines the rise to power of the fictional, isolationist African nation of Wakanda. In one scene, the character N'Jadaka/Killmonger steals a Wakandan artifact from a London museum (called "The Museum of Great Britain" and seemingly intending to portray the British Museum) as one step in his plan to challenge T'Challa/Black Panther and to launch a global revolution. As museum studies researcher Casey Haughin noted, museums have something to learn from this movie, first by acknowledging that Killmonger's anger and the experience can be read as "a magnification of museum practices in the modern world" that deny presence and agency to people of color. Haughin further notes that museums need to "listen to communities and communicate openly with their audiences to see how to adapt their practices and make the institution a place that is relevant and respectful for all visitors."[77] Calls for life imitating art, as in museums taking cues from movies, have yielded few results, however, as recent history has demonstrated the ability of museums to deny truths and opportunities for change.

The Bizot Group & Universal Museums

For example, a group of thirty museum directors from major U.S. and European art museums[78] issued a statement in 2002 that affirmed the need for collections from all over the earth to be assembled and shown in single venues—the notion of the "encyclopedia" or "universal" museum. This subset of museum administrators belonged to a loosely organized body of decision-makers engaged in discussions about large-scale, often traveling, exhibitions. Formed as the "International Group of Organizers of Large-Scale Exhibitions," they became known as the "Bizot Group," after Irène Bizot, a former museum director who organized the first meeting of the group in 1992.[79]

At issue was the potential return of cultural heritage to the countries of origin, such as the Parthenon Marbles claimed from the Louvre and the British Museum; the Pergamon Altar claimed by Turkey; the Forbidden City artifacts, now in Taiwan, claimed by China; the Benin bronzes claimed by Nigeria; and pre-Columbian artifacts claimed by Mexico. Neil MacGregor, then-director of the British Museum, communicated the concern in the museum group regarding the proposed loss of their museum collections by framing the backstory to the creation of the document: "There was grave alarm at the way Greece was applying political pressure over the Marbles and the idea that one Western country could build a museum to house objects belonging to another."[80]

In authoring the *Declaration on the Importance and Value of Universal Museums*, the museum administrators point out that repatriation has been a topic of discussion for several years, and that each case should be considered on its own. However, the document goes on to defend museums as owners, protectors, and caretakers, as well as homes for the items where others can come to see them. These responsibilities, in their view, outweigh any claims to ownership. The document goes on to see museums as agents of change, as the objects "have become part of the museums that have cared for them, and by extension part of the heritage of the nations which house them." Moreover, the superiority of the museum-centered context, for which their institutions are responsible, connotes a sense of privilege: "We should not lose sight of the fact that museums too provide a valid and valuable context for objects that were long ago displaced from their original source."[81]

The declaration goes on to point out the way in which museums serve all. They have universal collections for universal visitors: "We should acknowledge that museums serve not just the citizens of one nation but the people of every nation. Museums are agents in the development of culture, whose mission is to foster knowledge by a continuous process of reinterpretation. Each object contributes to that process. To narrow the focus of museums whose collections are diverse and multi-faceted would therefore be a disservice to all visitors."[82]

What is presented as a way to share collections and maintain collections intact "for all," is, in fact, a harsh, immutable, and culturally insensitive framing that issues a challenge to the concept of the twenty-first-century museum as a space of relevance, understanding, agency, and thoughtful meaning-making. Such an approach denies restitution.

Restitution is aimed at returning works, though it is more than a transfer of a physical object. Objects in many contexts are not mere things: they are extensions of living and dead bodies that have been dis-associated from their immediate context. As such, restitution also requires political work and diplomacy toward enabling countries to register claims and to assert sovereignty. An example of ongoing discussions over the restitution of thousands of artifacts is the subset referred to as "Benin bronzes," created in West Africa, looted in the late nineteenth century, and residing in museums in the United States and Europe. Alongside the truth of the looting of these works are decolonialist (or anti-colonialist), anti-racist, and anti-harm practices being undertaken by scholars, professionals, and museums that seek truth through more accurate and complete histories and interpretation of museum collections that are fuller and more inclusive.

Brutish Museums

Perhaps the most notable journey from falsity to truth uncovering is told by Dan Hicks, curator of world archaeology at the Pitt Rivers Museum at Oxford. Hicks's book *The Brutish Museums* (2020) traces a violent event in colonial history and the meaning and effect of public display of works gathered from the sacking of Benin in February 1897.[83] The book burst on the pop culture stage as part of an invitation by Black rapper M.C. Hammer to engage in a conversation about the book on the viral, invitation-only, audio-only app platform @Clubhouse in March 2021.[84] For four hours, Hammer and

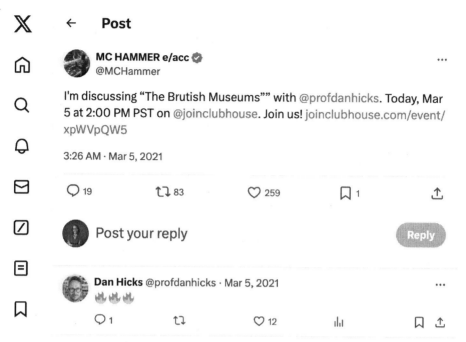

Tweet by MC Hammer about Dan Hicks, curator of world archaeology at the Pitt Rivers Museum at Oxford, who authored *The Brutish Museums* (2020), an examination of a violent event in colonial history and the meaning and effect of public display of works gathered from the sacking of Benin in February 1897. The book burst on the pop culture stage as part of an invitation by Black rapper, M.C. Hammer, to engage in a conversation about the book on the viral, invitation-only, audio-only app platform @ Clubhouse in March 2021.
See https://twitter.com/MCHammer/status/1367753444572815363.

Hicks discussed restitution, and engaged in a discussion beyond Hicks's reach or his institution's—a measure of success according to Hicks: "Hammer regularly has conversations with his enormous base on Twitter, which includes a lot of young African Americans who really care about this issue but are not normally part of the conversations with museums." This was only one visit of his fifty-date virtual book tour, thus demonstrating the interest in this subject by audiences in the United States, Europe, and Nigeria.[85]

However, the book and its meteoric rise were not subject to praise only, as Nigel Biggar noted in the British publication *The Critic*. For Biggar, the book is "typical of the 'decolonising' movement" with its anti-Western counter-narrative. He also sees in it an abuse of data in order to manufacture its narrative.[86] In the publication *Law & Liberty*, Michael Mosbacher takes issue with Hicks's proclamations about museums—like the Pitt Rivers: that institutions that hold such collections are engaged in a continual practice of harm and violence against the cultures that created the objects. Mosbacher eschews Hicks's claim that museums are enablers of "the militaries-corporate-colonialist model" and engines of White supremacy rather than seeing museums as places where the public can "discover different and remote cultures." Mosbacher also takes issue with Hicks's plea to return the bronzes to Nigeria, leaving absences dappling the museum landscape, a claim similar to that of the Bizot group. In short, Mosbacher asks whether museums can survive such evidence of "colonial guilt."[87]

Returning to the book and its subject: in it, Hicks describes the violent past surrounding objects looted as a result of the sacking; the objects are on display or held in at least 161 museums and galleries in North America and Europe. One of the largest collections of these is at Hicks's own institution, begging the question: Are museums like the Pitt Rivers just neutral containers, custodians of a universal heritage, displaying a common global cultural patrimony to an intergenerational public of millions each year? Hicks states the contention of this book is that as long as museums continue to display sacred and royal looted objects, "they will remain the very inverse of all this: hundreds of monuments to the violent propaganda of western superiority above African civilizations."[88]

Brutish Museums is about sovereignty and violence and about resisting this racist legacy of museums today. While it addresses the British reckoning with the brutishness of Victorian colonial history, *Brutish Museums* is also about making pasts visible in museum collections, beyond a single institution. A key to this is realizing and assuming archaeological thinking—that photographs of artifacts and the items themselves are not "frozen in time," but they are, in fact, "ongoing durations." They are not stills, but they are extensions of colonial violence, meaning, therefore, that "museums are devices for extending events across time: in this case extending, repeating and intensifying the violence."[89]

Hicks ascribes to his own institution the status of "brutish museum," which, along with other anthropology museums, allowed itself "to become a vehicle for militarist vision of white supremacy through the display of the loot of so-called 'small wars' in Africa." The purpose of the book is to change the course of these museums, to redefine them as public spaces and sites of conscience, places to begin practical steps toward cultural restitution.[90]

In Hicks's telling, museums are places of violence, where said violence "is repeated every day that restitution and reparations do not move ahead." He has noted how "inverse histories" function to upend the narrative, telling of how objects came to be in museums and can, rather, silence the histories of loss and death associated with objects that have been taken from their context and shown in museums in this manner, a field he has defined not as "object biography" (or the life history of an object), but as *necrography*, and its root knowledge base, as *necrology*.[91]

Importantly, Hicks situates the issue of decolonization with the approaches of scholars, researchers, curators, and the entire enterprise of the museum to tell of an object's history, albeit in a limited fashion. These approaches ignore the potential continued life of an object, had it stayed *in situ*. Hicks cites a trio of framings with Arjun Appadurai's formulation of the "social life of things" (1986), Bruno Latour's model of "actor-networks" (1993), and Alfred Gell's recasting of artworks as indexes that distribute the agency of artists, as part of the "relational texture of social life" (1998), and combine these with framings of museums as anthropological, "world culture," and ethnological.[92] Woven into these contexts is the objectification and cultural dispossession of material culture, of objects that once had homes within context and now are re-cast in museums. But institutions today must act. Hicks notes, "Our purpose must be to redefine the purpose of the anthropological museum . . . away from being a space of representation and towards what Hannah Arendt called a 'space of appearance'—in which curatorial authority is actively diminished and decentered while their expert knowledge of collections is invested in and opened up to the world."[93]

Hicks brings into focus the role museums have in telling the history of violence and subjugation, as well as dispossession. In citing the preface to the major 2007 traveling show *Benin: Kings and Rituals*, co-authored by James Cuno from the Art Institute of Chicago, and the directors of three other museums (Museum für Völkerkunde Wien—Kunsthistorisches Museum in Vienna, in cooperation with the National Commission for Museums and Monuments, Nigeria; the Ethnologisches Museum—Staatliche Museen zu Berlin; and the Musée du Quai Branly, Paris), Hicks points out their problematic framing around the good of museums in sharing these collections, as if they served no purpose prior to being taken: "*From our twenty-first-century perspective* the military action *seems* unjustifiable; however, *we must recognise the role* it played in bringing these works of art to *far broader attention*"[94] (emphasis mine).

No.

Rather, as we have seen throughout this book, it is *from our twenty-first-century perspective* that, in fact, *museums are called upon* to move past such simplistic justifications of violence and dispossession. They need to, in the words of Deborah Mack of the Smithsonian, "reckon with our racial past."

Our Shared Future: Reckoning with Our Racial Past

At the Smithsonian, a multi-pronged, multimedia initiative, *Our Shared Future: Reckoning with Our Racial Past*,[95] is underway to celebrate, contextualize, and make meaning of collections in ways that do not preserve them in amber nor draw out a distance from us today. Rather, they compel us to look, study, examine, question, and wonder. *Our Shared Future* is a collaborative, multidisciplinary platform to explore how race has informed each of our lives, regardless of our individual racial or ethnic identity. Drawing on the breadth of the Smithsonian's research, exhibitions, and collections, the online content explores the complicated history and legacy of race and racism in our communities and institutions.

According to Deborah Mack, director of this initiative, "These objects were selected because they tell meaningful stories, to help us learn more about the complicated history and legacy of race and racism, while also humanizing the stories that have helped build a more equitable, shared future." At the National Air and Space Museum, 3D digital scans of objects include clothing and sculpture that tell dramatic stories of achievement and are inspiring to experience. For instance, Patrice Clark Washington's uniform helps to tell her story from her aeronautical degree and working at United Parcel Service as a flight engineer, both of which set the stage for her promotion in 1994 to the captain of a major U.S. airline, the first woman of African descent to do so. Another item is the bronze bust by Eddie Dixon of Eugene Jacques Bullard, the first and only Black combat pilot in World War I, who rose to the rank of second lieutenant posthumously by the United States Air Force, in 1994. Through this exhibit, Mack states an overall aim and ambition "to grow engaged, intergenerational communities of learners and doers."[96]

NAGPRA and the New Duty of Care

As part of efforts to become better stewards of collections, be more inclusive, and express care toward communities and audiences, museums must realize the need *to let go* of collections as part of a decolonization or anti-colonization practice.

Returns of cultural heritage to source or descendant communities are only one component in the complex process of decolonizing museums. This concept of "decolonization" in the academy and the museum guides this book's context to mean the process of reducing or removing colonial structure and influence to the greatest extent possible. It should be noted, though, that a preferred term has become hypervisible more recently, that of *re-Indigenation*, meaning the return to Indigenous context as ways of knowing, holding, seeing, relating, and understanding.[97]

Within the context of Indigenous collections, and in particular Native American collections, the context is human—for the items are not *merely* objects. They are human remains and burial belongings.[98] They reflect, most intimately, lineal descent. They also call upon us to imagine the circumstances by which they were removed: disruption of custodial care, brutal excavation of burial sites, removal from familial context, and deposition beyond the sites at hand. Within this specific context, then, the term for a return of goods—whether the act of *repatriation* literally means the act of returning to the "fatherland," or *rematriation*, as in the return to the "motherland"—acknowledges a human context along with the land. Repatriation and rematriation seek the return of belongings as well as human remains to Native land, literally and figuratively, through return and reburial.

To be clear, collections are only one facet of repatriation, In the United States, these are mandated through legislation such as the Native American Graves Protection and Repatriation Act (NAGPRA), which focuses on human remains and burial belongings. On November 16, 1990, President George Bush signed into law the Native American Graves Protection and Repatriation Act, a law known as NAGPRA, which established processes and procedures for museums and other institutions to return human remains, burial objects, and other items to "Indian tribes" and "Native Hawaiian organizations." Since 1993, the Department of the Interior has published rules relating to the actions carried out, including a 1995 update; the civil penalties rule in 2003; the future applicability rule in 2007;

the disposition of unidentified human remains rule in 2010; and the disposition of unclaimed cultural items in 2015. The 2023 rule, enacted in 2024, was drawing from a 2022 proposal to "clarify and improve upon the systematic processes for disposition or repatriation of Native American human remains and cultural items."[99] In these contexts, *human remains* means any physical part of the body of a Native American individual, whereas the term *cultural items* refers to any burial object, sacred object, or object of cultural patrimony according to the Native American traditional knowledge of a lineal descendant, Indian tribe, or Native Hawaiian organization.[100]

As of the fall of 2023, approximately ninety-six thousand human remains are still held by museums and other collecting and research institutions in the United States.[101] The parameters of the new Duty of Care enacted in 2024 governs the holding and display of Native American cultural items: federal regulations require museums to obtain consent from tribes before displaying or performing research on any of these materials. The new law forced the hand of museums: to close or remove from display cultural objects, an effect designed to quicken the pace of returns, authorizing a five-year clock for preparing all human remains and related funerary objects for repatriation, and to grant more authority to tribes throughout the process. The new Duty of Care notes that "throughout these systematic processes, museums and Federal agencies must defer to the Native American traditional knowledge of lineal descendants, Indian Tribes, and Native Hawaiian organizations" thereby inverting the authority of the culture over that of the institution.[102]

The update to the law required action: across the United States, exhibits were de-installed, and cases were covered. At the American Museum of Natural History in New York City, two galleries were closed (the Eastern woodlands exhibition as well as the Great Plains), and several other display cases featuring Native American cultural items were covered. These actions, according to American Museum of Natural History president Sean Decatur, were part of a new initiative, a "new approach to the stewardship" of the museum's human remains collections. Decatur noted, "While the actions we are taking this week may seem sudden, they reflect a growing urgency among all museums to change their relationships to, and representation of, Indigenous cultures. The Halls we are closing are vestiges of an era when museums such as ours did not respect the values, perspectives, and indeed shared humanity of Indigenous peoples. Actions that may feel sudden to some may seem long overdue to others."[103]

Cementing the new approaches of museums today, Decatur further added that museums are at their best "when they reflect changing ideas."[104] Fortunately for us, they are evolving beyond the premise of captured, purchased, or otherwise acquired goods. Fewer and fewer are the realities of yesteryear, captured in the musings by Holden Caulfield, the protagonist in J.D. Salinger's *The Catcher in the Rye*, who revels in the stasis of displays at the American Museum of Natural History: "The best thing, though, in that museum was that everything always stayed right where it was. Nobody'd move. You could go there a hundred thousand times, and that Eskimo would still be just finished catching those two fish, the birds would still be on their way south, the deer [sic] would still be drinking out of that water hole. Nobody'd be different. The only thing that would be different would be you."[105]

Extended Reality as a New Frontier: Virtual Museums and Digital Repatriation

Digital Repatriation

One path forward is in digital repatriation—whether that means creating a duplicate or surrogate of the original material and leaving the original with its source community or retaining the original in the museum collection (the former is preferred, clearly, as part of a de-colonial practice). However, as Hannah Alpert-Abrams and others have noted, no one community claims ownership of materials. Alpert-Abrams takes cues from Jeannette Bastian, whose framing of post-custodial archiving introduces the possibility of reproduction, in some form, as a solution in cases when multiple communities lay claim to tangible cultural heritage.[106] In archives and librarianship, thus is the notion of reprography, or the replication of historical records through light-based or photographic methods, such as photocopiers. However, if we broaden the definition of *reprography* to include digital means, such as scanners, then reprography gives way to digital surrogacy and, ultimately, digital repatriation.

Several examples throughout this book, and beyond, illustrate careful, thoughtful, and reasoned approaches to technology and digital initiatives. One example is the Ur of Chaldees Project at the British Museum, which demonstrates the capacity of collaboration that aims to reunify—through digital means—material from the ancient Mesopotamian city of Ur, to bring together the information, and to open it up to the public for access, use, and study.[107]

In the late 2010s, Eric Hollinger, tribal liaison with the Repatriation Office at the Smithsonian National Museum of Natural History,[108] worked with Indigenous communities in the United States to repatriate tribal belongings through 3D replication. Through collaborative efforts, Hollinger has been able to scan repatriated items and archive them digitally, as well as find ways to tell the story about the repatriation of belongings and the original roles they had in their communities. This initiative, begun at the 2017 Tlingit Sharing Our Knowledge conference in Sitka, Alaska, was the first museum-led 3D replication of repatriated sacred belongings and could prove precedent-setting for cultural institutions and Indigenous groups.[109]

Other digital repatriation projects may involve language restoration and preservation, as well as a variety of disciplines, including performing and visual arts, anthropological, linguistic, and comparative literature studies.[110] Further, the use of 3D modeling tools (such as Autodesk Maya and Blender) and animation engines (such as Unity and Unreal Game Engine) can foster the creation of entire environments, leading to the creation of a virtual museum.

Virtual technologies such as non-fungible tokens (or NFTs)[111] can also center conversations around calls for action. For example, artists Chidirim Nwaubani and Ahmed Abokor established an art collective operative, Looty, in 2021 with the goal of "relooting" items. They operate by using LiDAR technology to digitally record stolen artifacts and render them in 3D. The surrogates are available through blockchain technologies using NFTs, in this case, as replicas of the original works. With Looty, the goals are threefold, using technology to: call attention to the items still held by museums; make it easier for anyone to acquire a surrogate; and encourage study and inquiry about the items. Their acts are called "digital heists" that seek to "restitute the knowledge" about cultural artifacts that are captive in museums. By digitally rendering, and then "freeing" the content and placing it online, others who do not have access to the item can gain it through replicas, through exhibitions of digital works, and as AR surrogates on location from where the objects originated. According to Dan Hicks, mentioned earlier, this form of restitution acknowledges urgency as well as agency, stating, "There is a new generation, it seems, who are not willing simply to wait for the cogs to turn at the glacial pace at which museums often operate." Their work shows that the artifacts are "not dead," but that they are "a living part of culture."[112]

In 2022, for instance, for their first content "drop," Looty created and auctioned a series of Benin bronzes drawn from museum collections.[113] They also took scans of the Rosetta Stone in the British Museum in order to liberate it digitally by using location-based augmented reality to put the stone near its original site in Egypt in 2023.[114] Their efforts are documented on their website and exercise clarity of vision. According to Nwaubani, the power is in the object, not the surrogate: "Let's at least get the power of digital in our own hands, for us to be able to tell that story, rather than leave it up to museums to then start representing things digitally, and then own that narrative."[115]

Virtual Museums as Method

As librarian and information science scholar Paul F. Marty noted more than fifteen years ago in his evaluation of museum websites and visitors, museums would do well to adopt a visitor-centered approach when developing digital resources, as "information technologies," as they were called at the time of the article (2007), have "changed the way museum visitors approach museums and their resources."[116]

Over the decade that followed, museums took their own approaches to going digital. Having a digital presence could mean one of three things: a computerized surrogate of something that exists in real life; content that was created for an online audience in mind (whether or not it was replicating actual born-paper content was important, though not essential); and born-digital content that only existed online. These approaches could mean *a digital reproduction*, such as a digital photo, of an object from the collection; *online exhibition content*, such as an exhibition introduction or other extended content; and *born-digital content*, such as social media posts.

Today, in 2024, we think beyond digital and, instead, to virtual. Virtual content implies a simulated experience, created through digital means. Think of this analogy: square is to rectangle *as* virtual is to digital. All virtual museums are digital; but not all digital museum practices are virtual.

Of course, during COVID-19, both digital and virtual content were essential to museum engagement. In particular, virtual tours took center stage as a way for people to connect with their museums, and ones they never even knew about, during lockdown. For the purposes of this immediate discussion, however, virtual museums can play a role in repatriation, restitution, and re-Indigenation. An excellent example of this is the UNESCO and INTERPOL collaboration to create the first virtual museum to combat illicit trade of cultural artifacts. The museum will be designed by an architect and build upon the existing database of stolen artifacts to display fifty-two thousand items in immersive 3D representations, each with detailed information about their history and cultural significance. Additionally, local connection to the objects will be included by incorporating stories and testimonies from the communities to which these artifacts belong.[117] Slated to open in 2025, UNESCO's virtual museum with 3D renderings of stolen artifacts is an exciting example of how we might consider the possibilities that await us with this new potential of virtual museums and museum transparency, openness, and the way forward.

Notes

1. Ann Zelle, "Acquisitions: Saving Whose Heritage?" *Museum News* 49 (April 1971): 19–26; the International Foundation for Art Research (IFAR) Reports maintains a database for stolen art that encompasses these categories: fine arts, decorative arts, antiquities, ethnographic objects, Asian art, and miscellaneous objects; Russell Chamberlin, *Loot! The Heritage of Plunder* (New York: Facts On File, 1983).
2. UNESCO agreements (1983, U.S. signatory); Stephen E. Weil, *Making Museums Matter* (Washington, D.C.: Smithsonian Press, 2002).
3. Metropolitan Museum of Art, *Report on Art Transactions* (New York: Metropolitan Museum of Art, June 20, 1973), 23–24; Karl E. Meyer, *Plundered Past* (New York: Atheneum, 1973), 86–100; Bonnie Burnham, *The Art Crisis* (London: Collins, 1975), 137; John L. Hess, *The Grand Acquisitors* (Boston: Houghton Mifflin, 1974), 141–51; Metropolitan Museum of Art, *The Euphronios Krater: A Report to the Members of the Corporation*, March 7, 1974; Thomas Hoving, *The Chase, the Capture: Collecting at the Metropolitan* (New York: Metropolitan Museum of Art, 1975), 40–56; Deborah Solomon, "Stolen Art," *New York Times Magazine*, February 19, 2006; Peter Watson and Cecilia Todeschini, *The Medici Conspiracy* (New York: Public Affairs, 2006), 327–28.
4. Elyssa Cherney and Steve Mills, "She Was the Queen of Chicago's Arts Community. But Her Collection Now Means Trouble for the Art Institute," *Crain's Business*, March 20, 2023, https://www.chicago business.com/arts-entertainment/art-institute-chicago-nepal-looted-art-concerns.
5. "Editorial: The Denver Art Museum Must Address 'Looted' Scandal," *Denver Post*, December 12, 2022, https://www.denverpost.com/2022/12/12/denver-art-museum-dam-art-antiquities-looted/. The scholar was Emma C. Bunker, and the dealer was Douglas Latchford. Together they operated a decades-long illicit art scheme. Her validation and scholarship helped to legitimize his looted collection. By securing works from Latchford for the museum's collection and/or exhibition, the museum validated his illicit behavior, even if unknowingly.
6. Malaro, *A Legal Primer*, 75.
7. See Smithsonian Institution, "About the Covered Objects Database," https://smithsonianprovenance.si .edu/about-covered-objects-database.

8. See AAM, Nazi-Era Provenance Internet Portal, http://www.nepip.org/. According to the 2001 American Association of Art Museum Directors report, *Art Museums and the Identification and Restitution of Works Stolen by the Nazis*, about one thousand items held by American museums require further study regarding their provenance during the Nazi era.

9. Getty Research Institute, "Collecting and Provenance Research," https://www.getty.edu/research/tools/provenance/.

10. See *AAM Guidelines Concerning the Unlawful Appropriation of Objects during the Nazi Era*, 1999, amended 2001; see also AAM's resources here: https://www.aam-us.org/programs/ethics-standards -and-professional-practices/unlawful-appropriation-of-objects-during-the-nazi-era/. Lynn H. Nicholas, *The Rape of Europa: The Fate of Europe's Treasures in the Third Reich and the Second World War* (New York: Vintage, 1994); Stephen E. Weil, "The American Legal Response to the Problem of Holocaust Art," *Art, Antiquity and Law* 4, no. 4 (December 1999): 285–300.

11. International Council of Museums, "Emergency Red List of Syrian Cultural Objects at Risk," 2013, http://icom.museum/resources/red-lists-database/red-list/syria/.

12. See Culture in Crisis, https://cultureincrisis.org/ and https://www.vam.ac.uk/info/culture-in-crisis/.

13. See Art Loss Register, https://www.artloss.com/. Art Loss is based in the UK. A committee of ICOM, the International Committee for Museum Security, it was founded in 1974. This group concerns itself with matters of museum security in general, as well as cultural property provenance, whereas the Museum Security Network was established in 1996 as an online forum for cultural property protection professionals. See https://groups.google.com/g/museum_security_network/about.

14. Malaro, *A Legal Primer*, 138; Evan Roth, "Deaccession Debate," *Museum News* 69, no. 2 (March–April 1990).

15. Miller, "Guilt Free Deaccessioning"; S. Weil, "Deaccession Practices in American Museums," *Museum News*, February 1987, a comprehensive review of museum deaccessioning practices with detailed references to good practices; Iain Robertson, "Infamous Deaccessions," *Museums Journal* (March 1990): 32–34.

16. Association of Art Museum Directors, *AAMD Policy on Deaccessioning*, June 9, 2010.

17. AAM, "Code of Ethics for Museums, adopted 1991, amended 2000, http://www.aam-us.org/resources/ethics-standards-and-best-practices/code-of-ethics; AAM, "Required Elements for Core Documents," http://www.aam-us.org/resources/assessment-programs/core-documents/documents; AAM, Task Force on Direct Care, Updates 2015, http://aam-us.org/resources/ethics-standards-and -best-practices/direct-care/direct-care-task-force.

18. AASLH, "Statement of Professional Standards and Ethics," June 2012. See "Historical Resources," item D.

19. ICOM, "Code of Ethics" adopted in 1986 and revised in 2004. The code has been translated into thirty-eight languages and is available freely on the ICOM site. See http://icom.museum/the-vision/code-of-ethics/2 museums-that-maintain-collections-hold-them-in-trust-for-the-benefit-of-society -and-its-developme/. See also "Museum Collections: Deaccessioning," a bibliography compiled by the UNESCO-ICOM Museum Information Center. Published in 2010.

20. Glenn Adamson, "In Defence of Progressive Deaccesioning," *Apollo*, October 26, 2020, https://www.apollo-magazine.com/deaccessioning-and-diversity-us-museums/.

21. "AAMD Policy of Deaccessioning," August 28, 2023, https://www.aam-us.org/wire/aamd/aamd -policy-on-deaccessioning/. AAMD, "Membership of AAMD Approves Change to Deaccessioning Rule, Bringing Policy in Line with American Alliance of Museums (AAM) and Financial Accounting Standards Board (FASB)," September 30, 2022, https://aamd.org/for-the-media/press-release/membership-of-aamd-approves-change-to-deaccessioning-rule-bringing. The new rule was approved with 109 of 199 eligible votes in favor. A total of 130 votes were cast.

22. See Adam Schrader, "UNESCO Has Teamed Up with Interpol to Build a Virtual Museum of Stolen Cultural Artifacts," *Artnet*, October 13, 2023, https://news.artnet.com/art-world/unesco-virtual -museum-stolen-cultural-objects-2374871; the UNESCO press release noted, the use of the museum as a tool has helped "to raise awareness on the illicit trafficking and the importance of protecting cultural heritage among the relevant authorities, culture professionals and the general public, notably young generations . . . and to represent a catalyzing moment among the international community who has made

continuous efforts over the years to put the illicit trafficking of cultural objects on the policy agenda." See UNESCO, "Information Meeting on the Virtual Museum of Stolen Cultural Objects," October 3, 2023, https://www.unesco.org/en/articles/information-meeting-virtual-museum-stolen-cultural-objects.

23. In the previous edition of this book (third edition, 2017), the term *Museum of Stolen Art* was used for a virtual space for display of stolen art created by Ziv Schneider and launched in 2015. This digital intervention archived lost works, including those destroyed as a result of looting in Afghanistan and Iraq, as well as works that have been stolen (including the famous Gardner Museum heist from 1990). Its website is no longer active. See Laura Feinstein, "Tour a Virtual Museum Housing Art Stolen or Destroyed by Conflict," March 9, 2015, *Good*, https://www.good.is/articles/tour-a-virtual-museum -that-houses-art-stolen-or-destroyed-by-terror. It does not appear as if this museum is related to the Museum of Stolen Art, https://www.museumofstolen.art/en, which was established as "a digital space for saving and documenting Russia's crimes against Ukrainian culture." The Ukraine-focused museum's website is also no longer active: https://www.spatial.io/s/Museum-of-stolen-art-64ff49f19ab28d7dd ccd73d6?share=0. Yet its release on October 11, 2023, and its continued, even if inactive, digital presence, remain visible, digital reminders of the power of documentation.

24. Walter Benjamin, "On the Concept of History," Gesammelten Schriften I:2. Suhrkamp Verlag. Frankfurt am Main, 1974; translated by Dennis Redmond, 2005, https://www.marxists.org/reference/ archive/benjamin/1940/history.htm. This translation uses "culture" while others use "civilization": "There is no document of civilization which is not at the same time a document of barbarism." Benjamin wrote on historicism, as well as collections. He is perhaps best known for his essay "The Work of Art in an Age of Mechanical Reproduction," which looks at mechanical printing methods and their role in reducing the work as a result of the loss of the "aura," or trace of the artist. Benjamin was also a collector himself, having written an essay on his personal library called "Unpacking My Library."

25. For information about unions and organizing, see Catherine Wagley, "Museum Workers Across the Country Are Unionizing. Here's What's Driving a Movement That's Been Years in the Making," *Artnet News*, November 25, 2019, https://news.artnet.com/market/union-museum-analysis-1714716; Eric Morse, "Why Employees at the Philadelphia Museum of Art Are Unionizing," *Art Museum Teaching*, July 17, 2020, https://artmuseumteaching.com/2020/07/17/why-employees-at-the-philadelphia-museum -of-art-are-unionizing/; Sarah Cascone, "The Tenement Museum's Union Filed a Complaint with the Labor Board After the Institution Laid Off 80 Percent of Unionized Staff," *Artnet News*, July 31, 2020, https://news.artnet.com/art-world/tenement-museum-union-files-unfair-labor-complaint-1898799; and Billie Anania, "Art Museums in the U.S. Are Facing a Reckoning," *Jacobin*, October 25, 2020, https:// jacobinmag.com/2020/10/us-art-museums-workers-organizing-racism-unions.

26. I am grateful to colleagues Janet Marstine, Ceciel Brouwer, Stephanie Brown, Sarah Chicone, Laura-Edythe Coleman, Rosanna Flouty, Chelsea Haines, Jennifer Kingsley, Jessica Luke, and Heidi Lung, as well as Alexa Cummins, Sydney Yaeger, Will Neer, and Megan Villa, for their thoughtful conversations around censorship, self-censorship, and open calls to transform toxic workplace culture in museums. These were held in the summer/fall of 2020. See https://msnconversations.wordpress.com/.

27. Aaron Randle, "'We Were Tired of Asking': Why Open Letters Have Become Many Activists' Tool of Choice for Exposing Racism at Museums," *Artnet.com*, July 15, 2020, https://news.artnet.com/ art-world/museum-open-letters-activism-1894150. The Guggenheim's curatorial staff called out the museum's practices in their letter and ongoing expressions of concern, outrage, and dissent. Taylor Dafoe, "The Letter, Signed Only by the Museum's 'Curatorial Department,' Calls on the Museum to Make Its Workplace More Equitable," *Artnet.com*, June 23, 2020, https://news.artnet.com/art-world/ guggenheim-curatorial-staff-letter-1889290. The Akron Art Museum's activities are chronicled by @ aam_accountable, https://www.instagram.com/p/CB28EwAFznD/. See also Sam Lefebvre, "SFMOMA Staffers Condemn 'Racist Censorship' and Institutional Inequities in Letter Calling for Change," *Art News*, June 23, 2020, https://www.artnews.com/art-news/news/sfmoma-protest-letter-1202692108/, and the original letter posted to @xsfm0ma on June 23, 2020: https://www.instagram.com/p/CBx-Eu6wgM4n. Former employees of the New Orleans Museum of Art accused the institution of racism and hypocrisy as part of the "plantation-like culture" at the historic property Greenwood. See Alex Greenberger, "Alleging 'Plantation-Like' Culture," Former Workers Accuse New Orleans Museum of Art of Racism and Hypocrisy," *ARTnews*, June 24, 2020, https://www.artnews.com/art-news/news/

new-orleans-museum-of-art-racism-open-letter-1202692299/. VMFA Reform posted on Change.org on June 21, 2020, https://www.change.org/p/alexander-nyerges-director-of-the-virginia-museum-of -fine-arts-demand-that-the-vmfa-support-their-staff-and-black-indigenous-and-people-of-color -bipoc. In 2020, the Museum Education Roundtable started digital spaces for museum workers to share their perspectives, called "Dear Museums," https://www.museumedu.org/dearmuseums-a -call-for-submissions/. They encourage museum workers to "take inspiration from PostSecret (https:// postsecret.com/) or @OverheardMuseum to express what you want to communicate to museums in this moment."

28. #DismantleNOMA, "Open Letter to the New Orleans Museum of Art," June 24, 2020, https:// sites.google.com/view/dismantlenoma/collective-statement?authuser=0.

29. "Response from the NOMA Board," July 31, 2020, https://sites.google.com/view/dismantlenoma/ board-response?authuser=0.

30. NOMA, "DEI Progress Report," https://noma.org/about/dei-progress-report/.

31. Jasmine Liu, "Guggenheim Museum Director Richard Armstrong to Step Down," July 8, 2022, https:// hyperallergic.com/746338/guggenheim-museum-director-richard-armstrong-to-step-down/.

32. @ABetterGuggenheim, August 17, 2020, https://www.instagram.com/p/CEAaqNtFytE/?hl=en &img_index=1. The full post reads: "It has become apparent that @guggenheim Director Richard Armstrong not only was aware of the mistreatment @lalabouvier [Chaédria LaBouvier] faced, but also contributed to the harm. When LaBouvier attempted to escalate reports of her experience to his attention, he refused to meet with her without @nespector, despite the clear conflict of interest. Meanwhile, he is noted to have concurrently shown 'deference' to a different collaborator; an examination of this disparate treatment must take into account differences in gender and race. When Armstrong finally met with LaBouvier, he was combative and dismissive. This behavior is not isolated. Video from a 2019 panel shows Armstrong deriding the perspective of a Director at a fellow NYC institution. Even after this disturbing exchange, during which he mocks her, he remains confrontational. Paired with LaBouvier's account of his blatant disrespect toward her in their meeting, a pattern of condescension becomes apparent. Yet, he shows respect to some, reportedly treating the aforementioned collaborator with such a level of favoritism that Spector stated Armstrong was incapable of defending the institution. Video clips reveal that Armstrong's views are contrary to the core values of A Better Guggenheim: he believes museums in their current state are already fully democratized and that expertise-based hierarchies are unimpeachable. Furthermore, his views on unions—namely that he does not want to work with anyone with 'limited experience in the museum field'—explain why the museum has yet to negotiate a contract with our unionized colleagues. Armstrong has called himself a steward of the institution. His actions show that he is, instead, a steward of the toxic, inequitable structures we seek to uproot."

33. Robin Pogrebin, "Guggenheim Selects Director, First Woman to Lead the Museum Group," *New York Times*, November 20, 2023, https://www.nytimes.com/2023/11/20/arts/design/guggenheim -director westermann-abu-dhabi.html.

34. The channel is here: https://www.instagram.com/changethemuseum/?hl=en; information, including the link to submit a story, may be found here: https://linktr.ee/changethemuseum. The recent posts include the questioning of why museums are not releasing statements regarding the attacks during the Israel-Hamas war that began with Hamas' attack on Israel on October 7, 2023. The post read, "I find the silence of museums and museum professionals on the genocide in Gaza terrifying, disgusting, and nonetheless, unsurprising. All of the surface level land acknowledgements, DEAI 'efforts,' and posturing doesn't mean anything when it actually comes to taking a stand." The post was made on November 20, 2023, and as of November 22, it has garnered more than three thousand likes/support. See @ChangeTheMuseum, https://www.instagram.com/p/Cz3qBgRsdri/?hl=en.

35. @ChangeTheMuseum, November 2, 2023, https://www.instagram.com/p/CyvygQaxxkJ/?hl=en.

36. @ChangeTheMuseum, September 25, 2023, https://www.instagram.com/p/CxnWLZFr0T-m/?hl=en&img_index=1. The full post reads: "The Guggenheim prides itself on collecting artwork and presenting shows of overlooked and marginalized artists. But then why not have your senior curatorial staff reflect these core values? Why only hire junior-level curatorial staff as BIPOC and POC? Who are by the way severely underpaid and have not been able to reach their union agreement despite years of effort. The Guggenheim is always talking about their DEAI initiatives but fails to actually complete

anything concrete. In the past 5 months, the Guggenheim has hired two white female curators but believes that showing exhibitions and collecting works of BIPOC and POC artists resolves these massive and obvious internal inequalities. They believe it is enough to have our stories shown, that it is enough for them to be narrators of our lived experiences. They believe we are only valuable to be seen and not heard. What is the point of showing and collecting these works if you do not allow those who have lived these experiences to tell their stories? Do better. In 2019 the Guggenheim hired its first full-time black female curator, it is now 2023, more than 5 years later and we only have 2 Black female curators, 1 Asian female curator, 2 Latin curators, one female and the other male, and over 10 white curators, 90% of which are female. Do better, you had the opportunity to hire two BIPOC and/or POC senior curatorial staff but yet you chose to repeat history, the very one you claim to dismantle."

37. @ChangeTheMuseum, July 20, 2023, https://www.instagram.com/p/Cu8BOkXs3OE/?hl=en &img_index=1. The full post reads: "The Great Lakes Science Center tries hard to show itself as a bastion of STEM diversity and equality, but behind the scenes there's a staggering culture of exclusivity and sexism. Women on the front lines who bring up safety concerns (we frequently transport combustible and corrosive chemicals in our personal vehicles with no safety measures), they downplay the risk, but when a man mentions the same, it's taken seriously and talks begin about a work van. When middle managers commit microaggressions against our (exceptionally few) PoC, leadership turns a blind eye. The VP of STEM Learning is renowned for his passive aggression, keeps disabled employees down, regularly pushes out talented women, 'forgets' to approve promised raises, and holds no regard for anyone outside the C-suite. Pretty sure he doesn't know our names. Our President is a woman who seems nice but she's either complicit in the behavior or is completely shielded from it by her VPs, we don't know because she never talks to us. Not for lack of trying, we follow proper channels and report to HR but our massively overburdened HR person can only do so much. GLSC pretends to be the future of STEM, but maybe it's a bit too accurately a portrait of the STEM industry as it is."

38. @ChangeTheMuseum, November 23, 2022, https://www.instagram.com/p/ClTw5BhrmVQ/?hl =en&img_index=1. The full post reads: "Over the last three years, 50 of the 100 full time employees at the Penn Museum have left. And that doesn't include the high turnover departments like visitor services, catering or the gift shop, many of whom were furloughed during the first part of the Pandemic. Staff who have remained during those three years have faced a difficult environment featuring multiple international scandals, a partially successful union campaign against the monolithic U of Penn and a prolonged director change. Lower and medium level staff have no room for growth, professionally or with their salary, and the DEIA efforts have been increasingly performative. At least the 3 deputy directors have received promotions over that period. Coincidentally, those three are frequently cited as reasons for staff departures. Staff increasingly realize that the only way for things to improve is to escape."

39. @ChangeTheMuseum, March 1, 2021, https://www.instagram.com/p/CL5ozmWFsxT/?hl=en. The full post reads: "I identify as BIPOC and attended a top public university to obtain my bachelors and masters in art history + art education. I didn't realize this until years later but I was a diversity checkmark box for the program. And throughout my studies, I had white professors cheering me on and making me believe that I could really make a difference in students' lives. However, the reality is that I think they just wanted me to enter the field because of my ethnic identity. I've been a professional in the museum field now for the past 5 years and I cannot tell you how many instances of elitism, racism, bias, and overall inconsideration is given to museum professionals from higher-ups. At my most recent museum job, I was given way too much work at one point during the pandemic when I had many personal issues going on (as many of us had), and suffered 3 mental breakdowns in the span of 2 months. Instead of being met with compassion and understanding, I was given more work. I haven't had a day off since last summer and even then, I felt stressed and guilty for taking the time off to give myself grace. I am so overworked, underpaid, and undervalued. I wish someone had knocked some sense into my brain and convinced me to dive into a less-niche field, but my family had no idea what I was doing. Can't blame them because they don't spend much time in museums to begin with. The museum is not accessible for people of color. This is all to say that I'm leaving the field and never looking back. I value my mental health, professional goals, and personal future so I can make a better life for myself and my family. I'm sick of working 2 jobs, 60 hrs a week just to get by. Wake up, museums. Talent is leaving. And those who stay are either overworked or undervalued. And if you don't feel it yet, it'll hit you. Hard. Don't settle for less, y'all."

40. @ChangeTheMuseum, November 2, 2020, https://www.instagram.com/p/CHG5IxWlzfJ/?hl=en&img_index=1. The full post reads: "I am a POC Conservator who has witnessed and experienced countless moments of microaggression and subconscious bias since entering this field. I do not wish to recount specific instances publicly as they already haunt me every day. The majority of professionals in this field come from similar racial, social, and economic backgrounds, yet they are the stewards of our collective heritage (which has proven to privilege only certain histories and narratives). Now they are involved in molding DEI initiatives and trying to create structural change, when they were the ones who helped maintain the status quo in cultural institutions for generations. I am afraid of my colleagues every day and what good they *think* they are doing now and will pat each other on the back for later."

41. @ChangeTheMuseum, July 29, 2021, https://www.instagram.com/p/CR6p3zjF3J4/?hl=en&img_index=1. The full post reads: "I was part of the team that launched an integrated art and technology space at a mid-west art museum. Two of the interactives that used facial recognition had difficulty registering black faces. Instead of sharing this information openly and taking advantage of an opportunity to talk about how tech is biased, the project lead forced black staff and interns to spend hours having their faces repeatedly scanned so the technology could improve (incremental improvement). There was no public discussion, internal or external, of how our tech was flawed and contributed to the continued marginalization of black people in digital spaces."

42. @ChangeTheMuseum, October 13, 2021, https://www.instagram.com/p/CU-J4sqFFgJ/?hl=en; Smithsonian National Portrait Gallery, "Pocahontas (c. 1595–1617), https://npg.si.edu/learn/classroom-resource/pocahontas-c1595%E2%80%931617, accessed November 22, 2023.

43. @ChangeTheMuseum, July 8, 2021, https://www.instagram.com/p/CR6p3zjF3J4/?hl=en&img_index=1. The full post reads: "Over a year ago, museums made a promise, albeit fumbled, to do better for their BIPOC employees after the murder of George Floyd. So many of us feared and knew this would yield close to no results. What's worse was knowing these institutions would prioritize exhibitions and public programs over listening and answering the call of their employees[.] While significant progress is needed in these areas, and awareness of how they serve the public is incredibly important, they're also the most visible facing parts of a museum. They're what an institution can point to as what they've done in response. When priorities lie in the most visible part of what a museum has to offer and employees are still lacking communication, results, or promise of how their daily lives and concerns will change for the better it is almost impossible to view these things as anything but self-serving to the institution's reputation. Progress made is always progress celebrated, of course. But when that progress still comes at the cost of overworked and underpaid employees who carry the load to see these projects manifest for the glory of the heads of the institution all the while knowing there has been little to no attempt to connect with our needs or daily concerns, they become hollow. I wish they'd do better for us. Even the ones who think they are. Change comes from the top, is that where the true focus of your work ends up landing?"

44. MuseumWorkersSpeak operates on email, Facebook, Twitter/X, Instagram, and their website: https://sites.google.com/view/museumworkersspeak/home, which has links to all their contact methods. They also compiled a resource page that included articles about their work, sites, and social media channels. As of November 2023, their Instagram had thirty-four posts, the most recent from April 2022.

45. Freire's pedagogy is discussed in light of UN SDG #4 in John Corbett and Manuela Guilherme, "Critical Pedagogy and Quality Education (UNESCO SDG-4): The Legacy of Paulo Freire for Language and Intercultural Communication," Language and Intercultural Communication, 21:4 (2021), 447–54.

46. The fundraising occurred on GoFundMe, https://www.gofundme.com/f/museum-workers-speak-relief-fund.

47. In full disclosure, I was one of two organizers of @covidmuseumsanonymous, and I co-ran the blog and form. I also was among the initial organizers and steering body of the digital repository of COVID stories, A Journal of the Plague Year (JOTPY), https://covid-19archive.org/s/archive/page/whoweare. In the final chapter of this volume, I examine in more detail JOTPY as a lens for teaching and museum studies.

48. COVID Museums Anonymous, https://covidmuseumsanonymous.wordpress.com/survey-results/. It is also worth mentioning that publications such as Marc Brackett's Permission to Feel is a potential resource for understanding how emotional intelligence can help museum workers—and all of us—move toward well-being. See Marc Brackett, Permission to Feel: Unlocking the Power of Emotions to Help Our Kids, Ourselves, and Our Society Thrive (New York: Celadon Books, 2019).

49. See Glassdoor log-in and account creation portal: https://www.glassdoor.com.
50. See Glassdoor reviews. To preserve anonymity of the review, full URL available upon request: https://www.glassdoor.com/Reviews/Employee-Review-....-RVW80864561.htm, October 11, 2023.
51. Margaret Middleton and Jamie J. Hagen, "Worker-Led Feminist Mobilizing for the Museum of the Future," *European Journal of Women's Studies*, 29:4 (2022), 593–617. The quoted material occurs on page 594.
52. Natural History Museum, "An Open Letter to Museums from Members of the Scientific Community," March 24, 2015, https://thenaturalhistorymuseum.org/open-letter-to-museums-from-scientists/. See also Elizabeth Merritt, "The Limits of Neutrality: A Message from the Natural History Museum," *Center for the Future of Museums Blog*, April 23, 2015, https://www.aam-us.org/2015/04/23/the-limits-of-neutrality-a-message-from-the-natural-history-museum/.
53. Their framing into themes and projects appears on their NHM.TV page: https://thenaturalhistorymuseum.org/nhm-tv/.
54. See Natural History Museum, "Exhibitions," https://thenaturalhistorymuseum.org/explore/exhibitions/.
55. Dana Hedgpeth, "Native Americans Are Transporting a 5,000-Pound Totem Pole to D.C. from the Pacific Northwest," *Washington Post* June 19, 2021, https://www.washingtonpost.com/dc-md-va/2021/06/19/native-american-totem-pole-washington/.
56. In my thinking of re-Indigenizing, I am greatly influenced by the work of Brooke Smiley, "Re-Indigenizing Land," *Indigenous Performance Productions*, September 13, 2022, https://www.indigenous-performance.org/post/re-indigenization-a-return-to-land-hire-native. Here, she tells how the term *re-Indigenizing* offers a value system led through language that is supportive, rather than "speaking from actions of violence," which "can be retraumatizing and confusing . . . exhausting and deeply disconcerting, unsupportive of where to start in the rebuild." Also important are Anahí Naranjo, "Decolonizing to Re-Indigenize," *Columbia Oral History*, November 14, 2019, https://www.indigenousperformance.org/post/re-indigenization-a-return-to-land-hire-native, and Kekek Jason Stark, Autumn L. Bernhardt, Monte Mills, and Jason A. Robison, "Re-Indigenizing Yellowstone," *Wyoming Law Review* 22:2 (2022): Article 7, https://scholarship.law.uwyo.edu/wlr/vol22/iss2/7.
57. Haaland noted, "Words matter, particularly in our work to make our nation's public lands and waters accessible and welcoming to people of all backgrounds. Consideration of these replacements is a big step forward in our efforts to remove derogatory terms whose expiration dates are long overdue." See Alejandra O'Connell-Domenech, "DOI Moves Toward Final Steps to Remove Derogatory Name from Federal Lands," *Hill* July 22, 2022, https://thehill.com/changing-america/respect/equality/3571151-doi-moves-toward-final-steps-to-remove-derogatory-name-from-federal-lands/. On the petition, see https://thenaturalhistorymuseum.org/re-indigenize-place-names-on-public-lands/.
58. See Natural History Museum, https://thenaturalhistorymuseum.org/about/ and https://thenaturalhistorymuseum.org/action/.
59. See Nerida Blair, "Lilyology as a Transformative Framework for Decolonizing Ethical Spaces within the Academy," in Jo-Ann Archibald, Jenny Bol Jun Lee-Morgan, and Jason De Santolo, *Decolonizing Research: Indigenous Storywork as Methodology* (London: Zed Books, 2019), 203–23; Dylan Robinson, Kanonhsyonne Janice C. Hill, Armand Garnet Ruffo, Selena Couture, and Lisa Cooke Ravensbergen, "Rethinking the Practice and Performance of Indigenous Land Acknowledgement" *Canadian Theatre Review* 177 (Winter 2019): 20–30. https://doi.org/10.3138/ctr.177.004. Moreover, in developing a practice around land acknowledgments, however, Laura Phillips had remarked on the ways in which unpacking the language students used, such as "traditional lands of," proved problematic, as well as emptily performative. See Laura Phillips, "Teaching Decolonizing and Indigenizing Curatorial and Museum Practices," *Museum Worlds: Advances in Research* 10 (2022): 114.
60. The body of literature on land acknowledgments is vast. On one example and meaningful explanation, see National Museum of the American Indian, "Honoring Original Indigenous Inhabitants: Land Acknowledgement," https://americanindian.si.edu/nk360/informational/land-acknowledgment. On critique of them, see Theresa Ambo and Theresa Rocha Beardall, "Performance or Progress? The Physical and Rhetorical Removal of Indigenous Peoples in Settler Land Acknowledgments at Land-Grab Universities," *American Educational Research Journal* 60:1 (2023): 103–40; Heather George, "This Is Not a

Land Acknowledgement," *Collections* 18(1), 3–4. Ambo and Beardall refer to "land-grant universities" as "land-grab universities." See also, Theresa Stewart-Ambo and K. Wayne Yang, "Beyond Land Acknowledgment in Settler Institutions," *Social Text* 39:1 (March 2021): 21–46. Ambo and Yang have situated the notion of "beyond" as a framework, for the political strategies that push "into the beyond of Indigenous futurity, decolonial sovereignty, and land relationships that are already integral to Indigenous protocols." For this, Ambo and Yang draw from Chelsea Vowel's formulation, "Into the Beyond," and framing around hosts, guests, and invaders, and a relationship built around reciprocity.

61. Amy Lonetree, *Decolonizing Museums: Representing Native America in National and Tribal Museums*, First Peoples, New Directions in Indigenous Studies (Chapel Hill: University of North Carolina Press, 2012).
62. See also Karen Coody Cooper, *Spirited Encounters: American Indians Protest Museum Policies and Practices* (Lanham: AltaMira Press, 2007); Patricia Penn Hilden, *From a Red Zone: Critical Perspectives on Race, Politics, and Culture* (Trenton: Red Sea Press, 2006); Peter Morin, "My Life as a Museum, or, Performing Indigenous Epistemologies." In *Embodied Politics in Visual Autobiography*, edited by Sarah Brophy and Janice Hladki (University of Toronto Press, Scholarly Publishing, 2014), 137–52; Linda Tuhiwai Smith, *Decolonizing Methodologies: Research and Indigenous Peoples* (London: Zed Books Ltd, 2012).
63. Laura Phillips, "Teaching Decolonizing and Indigenizing Curatorial and Museum Practices," *Museum Worlds: Advances in Research* 10 (2022): 112–31, DOI:10.3167/armw.2022.100109. Phillips discusses a graduate course, as well as a "Decolonizing Museums in Practice" (DMIP) course that is keyed to emerging professionals and mid-to-late career staff at institutions. For this course, the goals are to identify and understand limitations of the Enlightenment inheritance of museums and to share strategies on internalizing decolonizing and Indigenizing principles. On page 113 of the article, from which the trust argument is made, Phillips further cites Coco Fusco, "Deaccessioning Empire," *New York Review*, February 25, 2021, and Maya Chung and Coco Fusco, "Decolonizing the Museum," *New York Review of Books*, February 6, 2021.
64. Laura Phillips, "Teaching Decolonizing and Indigenizing Curatorial and Museum Practices," *Museum Worlds: Advances in Research* 10 (2022): 118.
65. See Ross Parry, "The End of the Beginning: Normativity in the Postdigital Museum," *Museum Worlds* 1(2013): 24-39.
66. The group's origins are connected with activist Alicia Boyd's proclamation at the Brooklyn Museum on May 7, 2016, where she urged action against the museum for its role in gentrification, relocation, and greed. She declared, "Every black community is under attack!" and gave a protest at *This Place*, a photography exhibit at Brooklyn Museum showing Israel and the West Bank, at which the group chanted "Decolonize This Place!" See Michelle Chen, "Gentrification and Occupation at the Brooklyn Museum," *Nation*, May 11, 2016, https://www.thenation.com/article/archive/occupying-museums/.
67. Artists Space, "Decolonize This Place: September 17–December 17, 2016," https://artistsspace.org/exhibitions/decolonizethisplace#announcement. See also the list of announcements of events during the residency, including "Decolonize This Museum," https://artistsspace.org/programs/decolonize-this-museum.
68. DTP, "Movement Space," https://decolonizethisplace.org/movement-space. The group originally centered the first five agendas, and have added "dismantling patriarchy" since 2016. The events include assemblies, trainings, skill shares, readings, screenings, meals, and healing sessions.
69. Stanley Reed, March 11, 2016, "BP to End Sponsorship of Tate Museums," https://www.nytimes.com/2016/03/12/business/energy-environment/bp-to-end-sponsorship-of-tate-museums.html; Gulf Labor Artist Coalition, https://gulflabour.org/.
70. An article by Mark Sundeen put it best: "Two of our country's biggest issues, racism and climate change, have collided on a North Dakota reservation." See Mark Sundeen, "What's Happening in Standing Rock?" *Outside*, May 12, 2022, https://www.outsideonline.com/outdoor-adventure/environment/whats-happening-standing-rock/. See https://nycstandswithstandingrock.wordpress.com/.
71. Alex Greenberger, "'We Will Come Back': Decolonize This Place Leads Protest at Whitney, Marches to Controversial Board Member's House," *ARTnews*, May 17, 2019, https://www.artnews.com/art-news/news/we-will-come-back-decolonize-this-place-leads-protest-at-whitney-marches-to-controversial-board-members-house-12590/.

72. Quote from Saffore may be found in Brian Boucher, "People Are Calling for Museums to Be Abolished. Can Whitewashed American History Be Rewritten?" *CNN*, July 12, 2020, https://www.cnn.com/style/article/natural-history-museum-whitewashing-monuments-statues-trnd/index.html. A number of the posters and zines created by DTP are available for download: https://decolonizethisplace.org/downloadable-materials. The quoted material about the Sequoia can be found in the "Anti-Columbus Day Tours of AMNH 2016–2019 Reader," which also includes updates through 2021, https://decolonizethisplace.org/s/Anti-AMNH_Actions-2016-2021_ReaderSpread_4Website.pdf.

73. Adela Suliman, "Theodore Roosevelt Statue Removed from Outside New York's Museum of Natural History," *Washington Post*, January 20, 2022, https://www.washingtonpost.com/nation/2022/01/20/theodore-roosevelt-statue-new-york/. The public request from the museum for the statue's removal was posted on June 21, 2020; though the statue is owned by the City, the Museum provides interpretation and context. See "AMNH Requests the Equestrian Statue on Central Park West Be Moved," Press Release, June 21, 2020, https://www.amnh.org/about/press-center/amnh-requests-statue-removal. Further, it is important to note that several other "namings" and commemorations of Roosevelt persist. The two-story memorial includes the Central Park West entrance, the Rotunda, and the Memorial Hall. https://www.amnh.org/exhibitions/permanent/theodore-roosevelt-memorial.

74. For context, the museum created this website: https://www.amnh.org/exhibitions/addressing-the-statue/today; the quoted material about addressing the statue may be found in the special onsite and parallel online exhibit, *Addressing the Statue*, from July 16, 2019 through January 23, 2022 (just after the removal of the monument), https://www.amnh.org/exhibitions/addressing-the-statue. The initial press release requesting the removal and citing it to the museum's work may be found here: https://www.amnh.org/about/press-center/amnh-requests-statue-removal.

75. Brian Boucher, "People Are Calling for Museums to Be Abolished. Can Whitewashed American History Be Rewritten?" *CNN*, July 12, 2020, https://www.cnn.com/style/article/natural-history-museum-whitewashing-monuments-statues-trnd/index.html.

76. These four areas are noted by Adrian Ellis in "Museum Inaction on Restitution Is Undermining Public Trust," *Art Newspaper*, October 31, 2005, https://www.theartnewspaper.com/2005/11/01/museum-inaction-on-restitution-is-undermining-public-trust.

77. Casey Haughin, "Why Museum Professionals Need to Talk About Black Panther," *Hopkins Exhibitionist*, February 22, 2018, https://jhuexhibitionist.wordpress.com/2018/02/22/why-museum-professionals-need-to-talk-about-black-panther/.

78. Institutions signing the Declaration include: the Art Institute of Chicago; the Cleveland Museum of Art; the J. Paul Getty Museum, Los Angeles; the Solomon R. Guggenheim Museum, New York; the Los Angeles County Museum of Art; the Metropolitan Museum of Art, New York; the Museum of Fine Arts, Boston; the Museum of Modern Art, New York; the Philadelphia Museum of Art; and the Whitney Museum of American Art, New York, in the United States, along with the British Museum, London; the Louvre, Paris; the Bavarian State Museums, Munich; the State Hermitage Museum, St. Petersburg; the State Museums, Berlin; Opificio delle Pietre Dure, Florence; the Prado Museum, Madrid; Thyssen-Bornemisza Museum, Madrid; and Rijksmuseum, Amsterdam. The document and list are available online in an article by Martin Bailey for the Art Newspaper. See Martin Bailey, "We Serve All Cultures, Say the Big, Global Museums: World's Leading Institutions Release a Declaration on Restitution," *Art Newspaper*, December 31, 2002, https://www.theartnewspaper.com/2003/01/01/we-serve-all-cultures-say-the-big-global-museums-worlds-leading-institutions-release-a-declaration-on-restitution.

79. Bizot was director of the Réunion des Musées Nationaux.

80. See Martin Bailey, "We Serve All Cultures, Say the Big, Global Museums: World's Leading Institutions Release a Declaration on Restitution," *Art Newspaper*, December 31, 2002, https://www.theartnewspaper.com/2003/01/01/we-serve-all-cultures-say-the-big-global-museums-worlds-leading-institutions-release-a-declaration-on-restitution.

81. See Martin Bailey, "We Serve All Cultures, Say the Big, Global Museums: World's Leading Institutions Release a Declaration on Restitution," *Art Newspaper*, December 31, 2002, https://www.theartnewspaper.com/2003/01/01/we-serve-all-cultures-say-the-big-global-museums-worlds-leading-institutions-release-a-declaration-on-restitution.

82. See Martin Bailey, "We Serve All Cultures, Say the Big, Global Museums: World's Leading Institutions Release a Declaration on Restitution," *Art Newspaper*, December 31, 2002, https://www.theart newspaper.com/2003/01/01/we-serve-all-cultures-say-the-big-global-museums-worlds-leading -institutions-release-a-declaration-on-restitution.

83. Dan Hicks, *The Brutish Museums: The Benin Bronzes, Colonial Violence and Cultural Restitution* (London: Pluto, 2020). Part of Hicks's argument sees mis-truth in the telling that the punitive raid by the British, which led to the removal of these items, was retaliation for the killing of seven British officers who were attacked during an expedition by James Phillips, who led a party of military along with African porters to the kingdom of Benin. They were attacked, after which the British launched a punitive expedition.

84. @profdanhicks, February 24, 2021, https://twitter.com/profdanhicks/status/136491954025000 5509?lang=en. On February 24, Hicks announced the session to be held on Clubhouse on Friday, March 5. The Clubhouse app has a veil of exclusivity itself, by being an invite-only application. That sense of selectivity and entitlement is something museums are known for; it seems very antithetical and counter to Dan Hicks's own principles. But its emphasis on audio-only, long-format conversation in an equitable fashion was more compelling a fit. By 2023, the Clubhouse had downsized, laid off 50 percent of its employees, and it was looking to reinvent itself.

   Also, for a range of responses to the book's central premise and broader contexts, see Dan Hicks's provocation posed on February 21, 2021, in *British Art Studies*, with ten scholars and practitioners responding. See Dan Hicks, "Necrography: Death-Writing in the Colonial Museum," *British Art Studies*, Issue 19, https://doi.org/10.17658/issn.2058-5462/issue-19/conversation; https://www .britishartstudies.ac.uk/index/article-index/death-writing-in-the-colonial-museums/article-category/ conversation-piece.

85. Jack Grove, "'Hammer Time' Professor: For Diverse Audiences, Try New Platforms," *Times Higher Education*, March 16, 2021, https://www.timeshighereducation.com/news/hammer-time-professor -diverse-audiences-try-new-platforms. In this article, Hicks championed Hammer's use of these platforms, hoping that more academics would try out "more egalitarian and democratic" tools. He also wrote widely for the *Guardian*, the *Telegraph*, and *Art Review*, among other publications. He has appeared on TV, radio, podcasts, and other media formats talking about *The Brutish Museums*. The tour included events hosted in Lagos, New York, San Francisco, Berlin, Paris, Aarhus, Brussels, Frankfort, and Lisbon.

86. Nigel Biggar, "Whites and Wrongs: Review of Dan Hicks, *The Brutish Museums*," March 18, 2021, *Critic*, https://thecritic.co.uk/whites-and-wrongs/.

87. Michael Mosbacher, "Can Museums Survive Colonial Guilt?" *Law Liberty*, July 8, 2021, https://law liberty.org/book-review/can-museums-survive-colonial-guilt/.

88. Dan Hicks, *The Brutish Museums: The Benin Bronzes, Colonial Violence and Cultural Restitution* (London: Pluto, 2020), 3.

89. Dan Hicks, *The Brutish Museums: The Benin Bronzes, Colonial Violence and Cultural Restitution* (London: Pluto, 2020), 13, 15.

90. Dan Hicks, *The Brutish Museums: The Benin Bronzes, Colonial Violence and Cultural Restitution* (London: Pluto, 2020), 4.

91. Dan Hicks, *The Brutish Museums: The Benin Bronzes, Colonial Violence and Cultural Restitution* (London: Pluto, 2020), 33.

92. Arjun Appadurai, "Introduction: Commodities and the Politics of Value," in Arjun Appadurai, editor, The Social Life of Things: Commodities in Cultural Perspective (Cambridge: Cambridge University Press, 1986), 3–63; Bruno Latour, We Have Never Been Modern, translated by Catherine Porter (Cambridge, MA: Harvard University Press, 1993); and Alfred Gell, Art and Agency: An Anthropological Theory (Oxford: Clarendon Press, 1998), 26.

93. On page 36, Hicks cites Hannah Arendt, *The Origins of Totalitarianism* (Cleveland: Meridian Books, 1958), 199–212.

94. Christian Feest, Jean-Pierre Mohen, Viola König, and James Cuno, "Preface," *Benin Kings and Rituals: Court Arts from Nigeria* (Ghent: Snoek, 2007), 17.

95. Smithsonian Digitization Program Office, "Our Shared Future: Reckoning with Our Racial Past," was launched in 2021, and is ongoing. For more information, see https://oursharedfuture.si.edu/.

96. Smithsonian Institution, "Our Shared Future: Reckoning with Our Racial Past," https://oursharedfuture.si.edu/race/.

Chapter 11

97. See Brooke Smiley, "Re-Indigenizing Land," *Indigenous Performance Productions*, September 13, 2012, https://www.indigenousperformance.org/post/re-indigenization-a-return-to-land-hire-native.

98. Museum holdings of Indigenous items may be referred to collections in the broadest sense. However, terminology varies, as evidenced by the newest NAGPRA law (2024). Comments on the law from members of the public, including Native American tribes, referred to the items removed from the ground as "burial property," see page 86463, comment NPS–2022–0004–0123 in Office of the Secretary, Interior, Section I: Background of "Native American Graves Protection and Repatriation Act Systematic Processes for Disposition or Repatriation of Native American Human Remains, Funerary Objects, Sacred Objects, and Objects of Cultural Patrimony," December 13, 2023, as deposited in the Federal Register Vol. 88, No. 238, https://www.federalregister.gov/documents/2023/12/13/2023-27040/native-american-graves-protection-and-repatriation-act-systematic-processes-for-disposition-or.

99. Office of the Secretary, Interior, Section I: Background of "Native American Graves Protection and Repatriation Act Systematic Processes for Disposition or Repatriation of Native American Human Remains, Funerary Objects, Sacred Objects, and Objects of Cultural Patrimony," December 13, 2023, as deposited in the Federal Register Vol. 88, No. 238, https://www.federalregister.gov/documents/2023/12/13/2023-27040/native-american-graves-protection-and-repatriation-act-systematic-processes-for-disposition-or. With this proposed rule, ninety days of open comments were permitted, and are browsable here: https://www.regulations.gov/document/NPS-2022-0004-0001/comment. Comments came from anonymous individuals, thoughtful undergraduate students, Native American tribes and elders, the National Native American Boarding School Healing Coalition, and leaders of major institutions, including the Field Museum of Natural History, the Denver Museum of Nature and Science, and the Robert S. Peabody Institute of Archeology at Phillips Academy in Andover, Massachusetts; and professional organizations, such as the Society for American Archaeology and the Association of Art Museum Directors.

100. For more on the terminology of NAGPRA, see https://www.nps.gov/subjects/nagpra/glossary.htm.

101. See page 3 of the report by the National Park Service, "National NAGRPA Program: Fiscal Year 2023 Report," National Park Service reporting for October 1, 2022–September 30, 2023.

102. Office of the Secretary, Interior, "Native American Graves Protection and Repatriation Act Systematic Processes for Disposition or Repatriation of Native American Human Remains, Funerary Objects, Sacred Objects, and Objects of Cultural Patrimony," December 13, 2023, as deposited in the Federal Register Vol. 88, No. 238, https://www.federalregister.gov/documents/2023/12/13/2023-27040/native-american-graves-protection-and-repatriation-act-systematic-processes-for-disposition-or.

103. Decatur's statement to the museum, dated January 26, 2024, is here: https://www.amnh.org/about/statement-new-nagpra-regulations. He also acknowledges an interest in communicating the changes to visitors "to help them understand the changes they will begin to see in our galleries and the considerations that are shaping changes to our collection practices and the evolving presentations of Indigenous cultures at the Museum." Decatur's statement on stewardship, dated October 12, 2023, is here: https://www.amnh.org/about/human-remains-stewardship.

104. This quote of Decatur's appears in Julia Jacobs and Zachary Small, "Leading Museums Remove Native Displays Amid New Federal Rules," *New York Times*, January 25, 2024, https://www.nytimes.com/2024/01/26/arts/design/american-museum-of-natural-history-nagpra.html.

105. J.D. Salinger, *The Catcher in the Rye* (Boston: Little, Brown, 1951), 157–58 (Chapter 16).

106. Hannah Alpert-Abrams, "Facsimile Return: On the Replicative Exchange of Colonial Documents." Conference Presentation, Society for the History of Authorship, Reading, and Publishing, July 2019, https://halperta.com/public%20speaking/SHARP191/. Jeannette Bastian referred to solutions with reprography long before 3D scanning and printing emerged as ways of working fluidly in museums and archives. Bastian has coined the term *community of memory* to refer to the practice of creating records as requiring the subjects and creators of records as active participants in the process. See Jeannette A. Bastian and Ben Alexander, editors, *Community Archives: The Shaping of Memory* (London: Facet, 2009).

107. See Gareth Brereton, Duygu Camurcuoglu, Birger Ekornåsvåg Helgestad, and Jonathan Taylor, "The Ur of Chaldees Project: A Virtual Vision of Woolley's Excavations at Ur," in Juilee Decker, editor, *Technology and Digital Initiatives: Innovative Approaches for Museums* (Lanham, MD: Rowman & Littlefield, 2015).

108. The National Museum of the American Indian Act (NMAIA), 20 U.S.C. §80q (Public Law 101–85) was passed in 1989, and amended by the NMAI Act Amendment of 1996 (Public Law 104–278), which included additional return criteria as established with the Native American Graves and Repatriation Act of 1990 (NAGPRA). The NMAIA requires the Smithsonian to return, upon request, Native American human remains, funerary objects, sacred objects, and objects of cultural patrimony to culturally affiliated federally recognized Indian tribes. The Repatriation Office was established in 1991 to implement the statutory requirements of the National Museum of the American Indian Act, which asserts the right of Native American, Alaska Native, and Native Hawaiian peoples to determine the disposition of culturally affiliated human remains, funerary objects, sacred objects, and objects of cultural patrimony currently in the collections of the Smithsonian Institution.

109. Eric Hollinger, "Digital Age Repatriations of Tribal Objects," Penn Museum, November 14, 2018, https://nais.sas.upenn.edu/events/digital-age-repatriations-tribal-objects. The video is available on YouTube: https://youtu.be/CL7ypXVhCkA?si=hBaFulab9w9OibnK. See also Eric Hollinger and Nick Partridge, "Is 3D Technology the Key to Preserving Indigenous Cultures?" *Smithsonian Magazine*, November 29, 2017, https://www.smithsonianmag.com/blogs/national-museum-of-natural-history/2017/11/29/3d-technology-key-preserving-indigenous-cultures/.

110. Some early resources on digital cross-over into archaeology, digitization, and the re-creation of virtuality include: Colleen L. Morgan, *Emancipatory Digital Archaeology*, unpublished dissertation, Department of Anthropology, University of California-Berkeley, 2012; Juan A. Barceló and Florencia Del Castillo, editors, *Simulating Prehistoric and Ancient Worlds* (Berlin: Springer-Verlag, 2016); Peter Der Manuelian, *Digital Giza: Visualizing the Pyramids* (Cambridge: Harvard University Press, 2017); Chiara Piccoli, *Visualizing Cityscapes of Classical Antiquity: From Early Modern Reconstruction Drawings to Digital 3D Models* (Oxford: Archaeopress, 2018); Erik Champion, *Critical Gaming: Interactive History and Virtual Heritage*, Digital Research in the Arts and Humanities Series (Aldershot: Ashgate Publishing, 2015); Erik Champion, editor, *The Phenomenology of Real and Virtual Places* (New York: Routledge, 2018); and the journal *Digital Applications in Archaeology and Cultural Heritage*.

111. It's worth noting that NFTs have not quite made it into the art world, or the museum world more broadly, although several articles and posts have been written about them, including Tim Deakin's "Museums and NFTs: What's the Opportunity, Who's Doing it Best, and Why Question Marks Remain," *Museum Next*, July 19, 2022, https://www.museumnext.com/article/museums-and-nfts/.

112. Hicks is quoted in Farah Nayeri, "A 'Digital Heist' Recaptures the Rosetta Stone," *New York Times*, August 11, 2023, https://www.nytimes.com/2023/08/11/arts/looty-rosetta-stone-benin-bronzes.html.

113. See Looty's site, https://www.looty.art/. Amah-Rose Abrams, "Meet Looty, a New Project That Infiltrates Museums, Makes NFTs from Stolen Objecs, and Sells Them to Fund Young African Artists," *Artnet*, May 25, 2022, https://news.artnet.com/art-world/looty-nfts-digital-restitution-of-stolen-objects-2121054. For the Benin Bronzes, the highest price for an NFT at auction was two thousand dollars, a portion of which is used for grants to African artists.

114. Chantel Tattoli, "A High-Tech Heist at the British Museum," *New Yorker*, April 17, 2023, https://www.newyorker.com/magazine/2023/04/24/a-high-tech-heist-at-the-british-museum.

115. Farah Nayeri, "A 'Digital Heist' Recaptures the Rosetta Stone," *New York Times*, August 11, 2023, https://www.nytimes.com/2023/08/11/arts/looty-rosetta-stone-benin-bronzes.html.

116. Paul F. Marty, "Museum Websites and Museum Visitors: Digital Museum Resources and Their Use," *Musuem Management and Curatorship* (March 2008): 81–99.

117. Christina Petridou, "Francis Kéré to Design UNESCO's First Virtual Museum of Stolen Artifacts," *Design Boom*, October 16, 2023, https://www.designboom.com/architecture/francis-kere-unesco-virtual-museum-stolen-artifacts-interpol-10-16-2023/. African artist Francis Kéré will design the structure in the shape of the baobab tree (a tree native to Africa and Australia that grows also in Asia) while also drawing inspiration from Frank Lloyd Wright's design for the Guggenheim Museum in New York.

12

Labor, Equity, and Inclusion

Recently, a meeting with my colleague Fran Flaherty, head of the Dyer Arts Center at the National Technical Institute for the Deaf, was an opportunity to brainstorm with staff from a local museum who were seeking ideas on how to include and welcome Deaf and Hard-of-Hearing visitors. After rattling off a few ideas, Fran suggested that by centering the interests of Deaf communities—reflecting minority visitorship at this institution—and considering their needs *first*, the programming could, in fact, still meet the needs and interests of all. By flipping the script and considering the Deaf and H/H first, and by positioning these communities at the center of all actions, the museum could practice, what she called, "radical inclusivity."[1] Such an emphasis, it seems, could also extend to all museum activity. For "who visits museums?" is as important a question as "who works in museums?" So we begin this chapter with the notion of "radical inclusivity" before moving into our address of labor, equity, and inclusion. How is "The Work"—both of museums and of inclusion—to be done?

Labor and Pay Equity

According to the 2015 Mellon Foundation/Association of Art Museum Directors demographic report of art museum staffers,[2] 72 percent of art museum staffers that year were non-Hispanic White, while only 28 percent belonged to historically underrepresented groups. These numbers varied from department to department: curatorial offices tended toward more White staffers while janitorial and service tended toward higher numbers of non-White staffers. With the 2018 and 2022 surveys, the study has revealed gradual progress toward a fuller representation of women and people of color. In 2022, the number of persons of color rose 36 percent. The data for that report was gathered from 328 museums in North America from February to April 2022, with records reported for over thirty thousand individuals. Even so, data also show that progress has been uneven, with certain positions remaining overwhelmingly and disproportionately White, and limited gains overall among staff members who are Black or Indigenous.

Information about demographics and diversity may be found through survey data from the past decade, and they give insight into the miniscule progress in diversity at some museums. But data is only numbers, a snapshot. The intent with surveys such as this is to show progress, as well as the work yet to be done, with a baseline against which to measure progress.

Concerns about labor, pay secrecy, and simultaneous interest in pay equity are ongoing in museums. In terms of pay "secrecy"—put simply, it's against the law. The National Labor Relations Act, passed by Congress in 1935, states that private-sector employees have the right to engage in "concerted activities for the purpose of collective bargaining or other mutual aid or protection"—activities that the National Labor Relations Board says includes discussion of pay.[3]

Continuing the theme of the last chapter, it's worth noting that calls for transparency have also been made by organizations, such as the Mountain-Plains Museum Association, that require that any job or internships include monetary pay. Individual organizations—for instance, the Corning Museum of Glass in Corning, New York—decided to begin posting their salary and wage offerings as

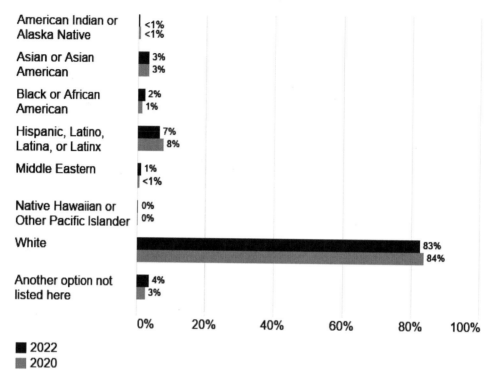

American Indian or Alaska Native: <1% (2022), <1% (2020)
Asian or Asian American: 3% (2022), 3% (2020)
Black or African American: 2% (2022), 1% (2020)
Hispanic, Latino, Latina, or Latinx: 7% (2022), 8% (2020)
Middle Eastern: 1% (2022), <1% (2020)
Native Hawaiian or Other Pacific Islander: 0% (2022), 0% (2020)
White: 83% (2022), 84% (2020)
Another option not listed here: 4% (2022), 3% (2020)

■ 2022
▨ 2020

Surveys can share perceptions as well as realities. In 2022, as follow-up from a 2020 survey, museum directors at 328 institutions representing over 30,000 individuals completed a survey for the American Association of Museum Directors from February to April 2022. The data was compared, as outlined in this and the following images. In this case, as in 2020, more than 80 percent of directors identify as White. Directors that identify as Hispanic are the next most represented, making up 7 percent of the sample. The racial and ethnic composition of museum directors is similar at academic museums and municipal museums. This figure appears in the report, Figure 24, page 44.

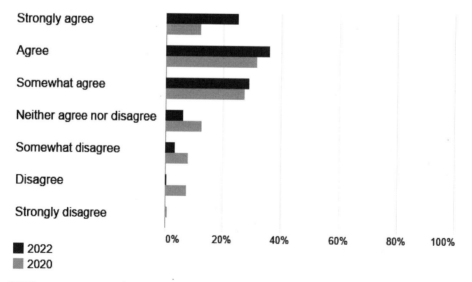

Strongly agree
Agree
Somewhat agree
Neither agree nor disagree
Somewhat disagree
Disagree
Strongly disagree

■ 2022
▨ 2020

In the 2022 survey, museum directors felt they had well-developed strategies for improving equity, diversity, inclusion, and accessibility for its employees. The chart above shows the percentage of directors that selected each agreement level, 2022 and 2020. This figure appears in the report, Figure 6, page 18.

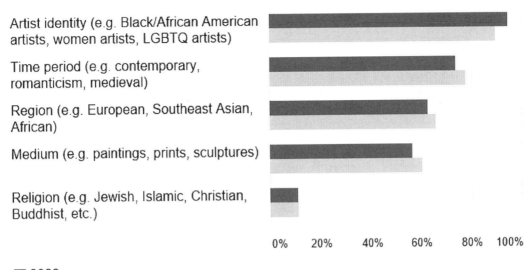

Artist identity (e.g. Black/African American artists, women artists, LGBTQ artists)

Time period (e.g. contemporary, romanticism, medieval)

Region (e.g. European, Southeast Asian, African)

Medium (e.g. paintings, prints, sculptures)

Religion (e.g. Jewish, Islamic, Christian, Buddhist, etc.)

0%   20%   40%   60%   80%   100%

■ 2022
▨ 2020

In the 2022 survey, museum directors considered these factors when considering to acquire works for their collection. The chart above shows the percentage of directors that selected each agreement level, 2022 and 2020. This figure appears in the report, Figure 7, page 19.

part of a longer-term strategy and a multipronged approach to DEI in April 2022. Later that year, in November 2022, the American Alliance of Museums began requiring salaries for positions posted.[4] But that achievement had been several years in the making through letter-writing campaigns, publicly accessible spreadsheets showing salary transparency, and outright calls for change.

A membership organization, the National Emerging Museum Professionals Network, an outgrowth of the American Alliance of Museums' Emerging Professionals Network, began advocating for salary transparency, not only for truth in advertising but also as part of the second measure of refraining from asking for salary history, as that can stigmatize those who have worked "under" their wage band or who have been underpaid. In May 2022, a petition to AAM president Laura Lott asked AAM to require salaries on their job board. They built out a platform for their advocacy around their already-completed work, including letter-writing campaigns to regional museum associations, seeking commitment to post salaries on job announcements for greater transparency, among a number of reasons.[5] That effort resulted in a spreadsheet that disclosed what organizations required salary postings.[6] The co-president of NEMPN announced on August 16, 2022, that their goal had been achieved with AAM's decision to require salaries on job listings. Sierra van Ryck de Groot noted, "This did not happen without all of our voices and the work of so many who advocated for this work before us."[7]

To demonstrate enormous pay disparities, especially among lower-level staffers and other museum employees, a crowdsourced salary spreadsheet has been created.[8] Inspired by a graduate student and contingent faculty collective, a keynote address by curator Kimberly Drew in 2019, and the nonprofit POWarts (Professional Organization for Women in the Arts),[9] organizers called upon museum staff at all levels to share their salaries anonymously. They also called upon others to research and report (through tax forms and publicly accessible data sources, such as federal employee salaries). A snapshot of that spreadsheet revealed 3,323 salaries (as of 2022) reported along with designation as to hourly, part-time, or contingent; benefits; years of experience; and so on. Clearly at the top of the spreadsheet, alongside instructions, is the intent: "the point of the survey is proactively coming together in a spirt of transparency and collegiality, and offering some (but not complete, perfect) insights into our field."[10] (It is important to note that the anonymously crowdsourced spreadsheet has been relaunched by NEMPN in 2022.)[11]

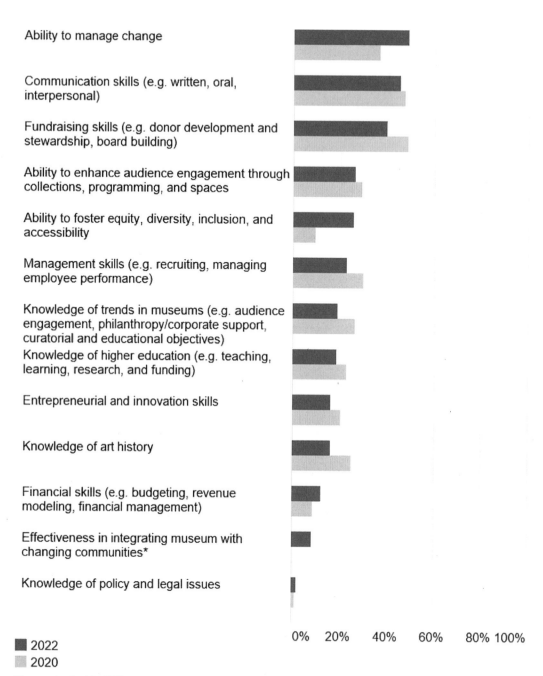

Ability to manage change

Communication skills (e.g. written, oral, interpersonal)

Fundraising skills (e.g. donor development and stewardship, board building)

Ability to enhance audience engagement through collections, programming, and spaces

Ability to foster equity, diversity, inclusion, and accessibility

Management skills (e.g. recruiting, managing employee performance)

Knowledge of trends in museums (e.g. audience engagement, philanthropy/corporate support, curatorial and educational objectives)

Knowledge of higher education (e.g. teaching, learning, research, and funding)

Entrepreneurial and innovation skills

Knowledge of art history

Financial skills (e.g. budgeting, revenue modeling, financial management)

Effectiveness in integrating museum with changing communities*

Knowledge of policy and legal issues

0% 20% 40% 60% 80% 100%

■ 2022
　2020

*Item not asked in 2020

Results showed that, in the 2022 survey, a larger percentage of art museum directors in the aggregate recognized the ability to manage change as a key competency for their work. Thirty-five percent of respondents reported managing change as a key competency in 2020, but this increased to nearly 50 percent in 2022, making it the leading competency for directors in this cycle of the survey. This figure appears in the report, Figure 1, page 9.

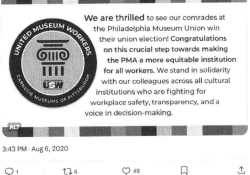
To resist the impact of the COVID-19 pandemic on museum staff and the related lack of transparency, museum employees began turning to unions in greater numbers than ever. Above, two Tweets celebrate the vote to unionize at the Philadelphia Museum of Art.
Source: https://twitter.com/PMA_Union/status/1291450419349270528.

William S. Rubin seated at pamphlet table, during "New York Art Strike." May 22, 1970.
Digital Image © The Museum of Modern Art/Licensed by SCALA/Art Resource, NY.

Visitors at pamphlet table during "New York Art Strike." May 22, 1970.
Digital Image © The Museum of Modern Art/Licensed by SCALA/Art Resource, NY

The earliest example of museum unionization is the early 1970s, when employees at the Museum of Modern Art held strikes in 1971 and 1973, the latter shown here. Staff strike. Adrienne Mancia (center). The Museum of Modern Art, New York. 1973. PASTA and Protests. The Museum of Modern Art Archives, New York. (PA340).
Digital Image © The Museum of Modern Art/Licensed by SCALA/Art Resource, NY.

The context of the data and the conversations around salary that have been spawned as a result of this survey are important to note. The calls for salary transparency were put in place to seek a path toward a fairer and more equitable sector, especially for emerging professionals. Those goals were brought into sharper focus during the COVID-19 pandemic, as museums struggled. According to data gathered for the American Alliance of Museums,[12] museums in the United States locked their doors to the public for an average of twenty-eight weeks starting in March 2020 because of the pandemic. Museums reported from December 2021 through early 2022 that they experienced an average of 62 percent of their normal, pre-pandemic, attendance.

Relatedly, museums began to lay off staff members, and the reality that layoffs disproportionately affected workers of color while leaving massive executive salaries relatively untouched. circulated among workers, further demonstrating how those with lower pay were likely to be people of color.

Unionization

With the impact of the COVID-19 pandemic on museum staff and the related lack of transparency, museum employees began turning to unions in greater number than ever since 2020. The interest in unions and labor organizing has been occurring on college campuses, as noted above, and at Starbucks locations as well as Amazon warehouses (both established in 2021).[13]

The idea of organized labor around museums is not new: the earliest example of unionization is the early 1970s, when newly unionized employees at the Museum of Modern Art held strikes in 1971 and 1973. Employees at the Metropolitan Museum of Art, the Brooklyn Museum, the American Museum of Natural History in New York City, the Milwaukee Public Museum, and the Detroit Historical Society are represented by the American Federation of State, County & Municipal Employees, and are served by the Cultural Workers United union.[14] In addition, unions have been formed from coast to coast and areas between since the pandemic: in New York City (Whitney Museum of American Art, the New Museum, the Tenement Museum, and the Guggenheim Museum); in Seattle at the Frye Art; at the Museum of Tolerance and the Museum of Contemporary Art in Los Angeles; in the Boston area at the Museum of Fine Arts and MASS MOCA (the Massachusetts Museum of Contemporary Art); at the Milwaukee Art Museum; and at the Philadelphia Museum of Art. Some museums have organized with sister unions. For instance, the Carnegie Museum Workers in Pittsburgh, Pennsylvania, voted in favor of joining the United Steelworkers Union in late 2020.[15]

However, unions are by no means commonplace in museums. In 2021, they reached a high point of 14.8 percent of their industry,[16] as museum employees continue to cite conditions that are untenable: minimal wage increases, draining resources, lack of transparency from top administrators, and mass layoffs and furloughs. Calling this state one of "crisis mode," employees at more than thirty museums in the United States are in the process of unionizing, as of the fall of 2023.[17]

Internships and Labor

In the United States, museum studies internships have been "a thing" for sixty years.[18] By definition, they are supervised, structured environments where undergraduate and graduate students can connect their classroom learning with real-life experiences. The internship experience is intended to be meaningful and practical while also giving students the opportunity for career exploration and development.

The Department of Labor offers guidance on employee or volunteer status of interns. The Fair Labor Standards Act indicates that the "primary beneficiary test" can be used to determine whether an intern or student is, in fact, an employee under the FLSA. Criteria is used, such as type of training, connection to academic degree coursework, duration of commitment, and the intern's role as complement to other paid staff, among others.[19]

Some internships are paid, while far more are unpaid. While it is up to the individual to apply for and accept an internship, unpaid internships (in particular) pose issues particularly.

The National Emerging Museum Professional Network (NEMPN) continues their advocacy to end unpaid internships. In 2021, they launched a "Sweatober" campaign to fund previously unpaid internships and to encourage others to do the same.

First, they devalue the work. As Elizabeth Merritt, founding director of the Center for the Future of Museums, noted in 2014, an ethical concern emerges by offering unpaid, non-academic internships that do real work and are not primarily for the benefit of the intern. In short, the work becomes valueless. If working without pay is the only path to access an opportunity, then the fair market value of that position values the labor at zero.[20]

Second, requiring applicants to work for free restricts the field to those who can afford to do so. Therefore, unpaid internships (particularly, though a case could be made for any internship) require privilege in order to participate. Unpaid internships indirectly privilege those who can afford to work for free. They can also expose employees to exploitation. As Incluseum contributor Joseph Gonzales states: "In my experience as a museum professional and museum studies professor, those who self-select to be in the museum field have access to an economic 'safety net' that allows them to take the financial risk of educating themselves and/or taking on volunteer and low-paying skill and social capital building experiences to allow them access to increasingly better (paying) positions in museums. There is a class dynamic to working in museums that both transcends and intersects with racial and ethnic status. A student from a poor or working-class background might feel dissuaded from choosing a low-paying professional job, especially if they are thinking about supporting their family in the future. Furthermore, if an emerging professional has to think about student loans, middle-class amenities, children, etc., then opting for a museum job without a family, partner, or other means to supplement their income is a conscious decision to struggle financially."[21]

A vigorous discussion is underway among members of the museum community regarding unpaid internships, and their implications for the diversity of museum professionals, now and in the future. Led by @MuseumWorkersSpeak and the National Emerging Museum Professional Network, a growing number of advocates are calling for changes to ensure that all candidates have access to internships and jobs in the field. As museologist Nicole Ivey has noted, "The current trend of the obligatory unpaid museum internship makes the pathway to museum employment less accessible for workers without means."[22]

Indeed, internships offer valuable training, experience, and networking opportunities to new professionals. If internships are a pipeline to employment, changes need to be made, beyond simply paying interns.

One important step is to welcome all applicants, particularly those who do not see themselves represented in museum work and leadership. Related is the aspiration to fund all internships. (Fortunately, some internship and employment opportunities built around workforce development and diversity, equity, and inclusion have seed money from foundations, such as the Mellon Foundation or the Getty, to help fund these positions.)

A second step is to develop position descriptions that honor and value a range of methods for meeting particular criteria. As museum scholar Porchia Moore has stated, "On the one hand we are saying that we acknowledge that the pipeline needs work and yet if someone appears ready and willing to do the work, we penalize them for not possessing a traditional or formalized education and accompanying skillsets or experience when in fact their different skillsets and knowledge base is what makes them uniquely qualified. This is not a lowering of standards but a realistic attempt to recalibrate museums at the same time as leveling the playing field."[23]

A third step is to consider the benefits and drawbacks of virtual internships (what is reasonable to expect and what it is possible to provide). Related, seek guidance about volunteers and internships to provide the best possible experience. For instance, the American Alliance of Museums and the American Association for Museum Volunteers (AAMV) share their expertise with onsite museum internships, and relatedly, volunteering. These documents are a helpful starting point for all internships, regardless of modality. For instance, the Standards and Best Practices for Museum Volunteer Programs by the AAMV indicates thirteen guidelines, and it indicates that these are not requirements, but rather suggestions for consideration. These cover the topics of orientation, training, communication, supervising, evaluation of/by volunteers and staff, recognition/reward for their work, recordkeeping, and risk management.[24] At the American Alliance of Museums' annual meeting in 2016, a session on internships was hosted and offered insight as to current challenges, many of which are noted above.[25]

A fourth step is to provide micro-internships—short-term, paid projects for college students that are available throughout the year and can help students explore opportunities beyond their college major and learn highly generalized, transferable skills.[26] They also provide ways for organizations to set clear deadlines and parameters for hosting an intern, and even extending their term of engagement.

Guidance for Internships

While there is no manner to retrieve holistic information about internships in museums, a review of one program in particular gives insight on how internships can positively impact the museum field.

The Getty Multicultural Undergraduate Internship program was established in 1993—a moment not unlike today, as noted in the 2020 report of the program. It was "a period of profound awakening about systemic racism and its impact on people of color. The beating of Rodney King and the resulting civil unrest in 1992 brought widespread visibility to deep-seated inequities in Los Angeles and generated a city-wide reckoning on race." The Getty Foundation director at the time, Deborah Marrow, believed deeply that the foundation could begin to address diversity and equity within the visual arts. She worked with the staff to develop the internship program that has, recently, been renamed in her honor as the Getty Marrow Undergraduate Internship Program.[27]

The program offers paid summer internships at museums and visual arts organizations in Los Angeles for undergraduates from underrepresented backgrounds. Since 1993, the program has supported 3,200 interns with a fourteen-million-dollar budget. Interns were placed at 175 local arts institutions, including the Los Angeles County Museum of Art and the Hammer Museum; culturally specific organizations, such as the California African American Museum; and community-based organizations, such as Self Help Graphics & Art.

The program collected data over the past twenty years, releasing a report in 2020 that found persistent engagement among the cohort with arts and museums. The report identifies six components that make the internship a comprehensive, educational, and rewarding experience. These include:

- Diversity: inviting participation from undergraduates from underrepresented groups with an interest in the arts, but with no prior experience required);
- Scale: varied positions at a broad range of museums and visual arts organizations;
- Substance: meaningful projects that make the experience significant;
- Compensation: stipends that make participation financially viable;
- Networking: peer-to-peer networking to provide a sense of belonging for historically excluded groups; and
- Mentoring: access to dedicated supervisors and other professionals.[28]

In sum, good internships provide clear position or project descriptions for the experience; orient the student to the organization, its culture, and staff; offers feedback to the student; and allows the student to offer feedback to the organization. Moreover, internships can create pathways to mentor, train, and amplify the voices of students from a range of disciplinary, cultural, economic, social, and educational backgrounds. Ultimately, whether paid or unpaid, internships can lead to more welcoming, equitable, and sustainable museums.

Inclusion

According to the Strong Families Network, part of a national organization that prioritizes queer, trans, Black, Indigenous, and other peoples of color, four out of five people living in the United States do not live behind the picket fence imagined as the "ideal home" a generation ago. Their lives "fall outside outdated notions of family, with a mom at home and a dad at work." Advocating that "all families matter," Strong Families sees the trend of family definition—"across generation, race, gender, immigration status, and sexuality—as a powerful and promising development for the United States"[29] Museums have responsibilities to include families and individuals in their exhibitions, programming, and approaches. Four initiatives have promoted work in this area, with more to be done.

Published in 2016, and updated in 2019, the *LGBTQ Welcoming Guidelines*, developed by the LGBTQ Professional Network of the American Alliance of Museums, offers specific practices to ensure LGBTQ sensitivity and inclusion. In addition, Margaret Middleton, an exhibit developer and designer, has developed a *Family Inclusive Language Chart* (launched in 2014) to enable museum

THINK OF A TIME YOU DIDN'T FEEL WELCOME.

A multidisciplinary group of professionals created the "Welcoming Guidelines" to align industry best practices with creating welcoming environments in museums for visitors, staff, and volunteers. The document is indexed to AAM's core standards and functional areas. A glossary and bibliography offer more information.
Copyright protected, American Alliance of Museums, Washington, D.C. Reprinted with permission. For more information, visit www.aam-us.org. Material designed by The Design Minds, Inc. (www.thedesignminds.com).

professionals to examine language and word choice in order to be inclusive of the twenty-first-century family.[30]

In addition, an organization called the Incluseum seeks to advance "new ways of being a museum through critical discourse, community building, and collaborative practice related to inclusion in museums." Founded in 2012 and facilitated and co-directed by thought leaders Porchia Moore, Aletheia Wittman, and Rose Paquet, the Incluseum is an online community fostering practice-based projects that provide a forum for expertise and conversation around inclusion and social-justice efforts in museums through workshops, trainings, exhibits, advisory positions, and publications. The website provides information and links to publications that serve as important resources for anyone interested in new ways of thinking about museums. Through collaborative practice, community building, and consulting, the Incluseum is meant to build a space for community, to be a resource for research and practice, to dialogue, and to weave together digital and offline "engagements to catalyze 'next practices.'" Of particular mention is the bibliography of critical print and online resources to anchor discussions while also drawing connections to initiatives beyond the museum field. In addition, their recent publication, *Transforming Inclusion in Museums: The Power of Collaborative Inquiry* (2022), offers a new model for understanding inclusion grounded in museum workers' efforts to test the limits of inclusion. Throughout the volume, readers are invited to reflect on their own experience and to expand on new ways of thinking about inclusion in museums.[31]

Museum Hue

As noted in Chapter 10, Museum Hue is a membership organization based in New York dedicated to advancing Black, Indigenous, and all people of color in the cultural field, primarily the arts. Coming up on their ten-year anniversary, their mission has shifted from acknowledgment and visibility to community building, professional development, illumination, and mentorship.

Founding strategic director Monica Montgomery defined the composition and history of Museum Hue in the previous edition of this book (2017) as "a group of millennial black and brown (Latino, Black, Asian, Indian, First Nations, Middle Eastern) socially conscious museum and culture workers, who came together to hold space for ourselves and our peers, unapologetically make our presence felt in museum spaces, and counter false narratives that we were 'hard to find.'"[32]

Montgomery called out the need to press ahead, regardless of what the institutions and culture fostered: "We started Museum Hue in September 2014, after realizing we cannot wait for the sector, to rediscover us, we cannot wait for Black History Month for people of color to be in vogue. We have to be self-reliant and solutionary, iterating ideas and collaborating with willing allies to generate jobs and bolster agency via self preservation. We know through our lived experience that people of color are more than qualified to lead institutions, but are frequently overlooked, ignored, undermined, and left out of the conversation and the spheres of influence where hiring decisions are made. . . . Museum Hue has become an agent of change in a largely stagnant industry. We are doing the work because it needs to be done and because our museums deserve a chance to be greater."[33]

Today the organization is a hub for employment, professional and peer-to-peer mentorship, as well as research. Museum Hue's leadership is working hard to advocate for BIPOC arts professionals through substantiated research. In addition to hosting events onsite and online for members and the public, as well as managing a job board for members, Museum Hue collects and shares data and information to illuminate cultural organizations of color. Examples include HueArts NYC (New York City) and Hue Arts NYS (New York State), as well as Hue Museums National Map, which connects and amplifies more than 150 museums created and led by BIPOC cultural workers across the United States. The map connects to a database with information about the history, location, and significance of the institutions for visitors, as well as for the field, by hoping to build a stronger network among the organizations.

The data gathering and reflective analysis by Museum Hue also points to unique challenges BIPOC-led arts organizations and museums face, despite their increasingly important and unique roles in preserving culture, traditions, and histories of communities of color. As executive director Stephanie Johnson-Cunningham characterized this shift, the organization has evolved and now undertakes critical thinking about how the organization can assist in ways to change (or evolve or move) the field.[34]

Facing Change: Collections, Staff (and Boards), and Audiences

Diversity, equity, and inclusion work is best when centered on the triad of museum collections, people employed by museums to serve the communities, and museum audiences. The American Alliance of Museums, in 2017, issued a report, *Facing Change: Insights from AAM's DEAI Working Group*, and launched a three-year program to develop museum board members from underrepresented groups (2019–2022) in partnership with the Ford, Alice Walton, and Mellon Foundations. The name of the report is inspired by author and public intellectual James Baldwin, whose guidance for writers in 1962 remains relevant today: "not everything that is faced can be changed; but nothing can be changed until it is faced."[35]

The Working Group on Diversity, Equity, Accessibility, and Inclusion (DEAI), comprised of twenty museum professionals, undertook the following tasks:

- identified current DEAI activities in the field,
- understood key challenges, issues, and opportunities related to promoting DEAI,
- learned how other sectors have successfully overcome DEAI challenges,
- identified steps that museum professionals can take to advance DEAI, and
- outlined opportunities for collaboration and further work.[36]

The report serves as a starting point, with vocabulary and principles to guide museum professionals. The key takeaways are:

- Every museum professional must do personal work to face unconscious bias,
- Debate on definitions (DEAI) must not hinder progress,
- Inclusion is central to the effectiveness and sustainability of museums,
- Systemic change is vital to long-term, genuine progress, and
- Empowered, inclusive leadership is essential at all levels of an organization.[37]

At bottom is the call to seek and sustain diversity as a path to relevance that requires re-inventing the museum. The call and response are both wrapped up in privilege, that is, the privilege to tell these stories, as explained by Working Group co-chair Dr. Johnnetta Betsch Cole: "If your museum is large or small, old or young, famous or not yet famous, the need for seeking and sustaining diversity in your museums . . . has never been greater. If we are to be relevant in this ever-changing world, to stay artistically and financially viable, all of our museums must boldly—indeed, bodaciously—commit to rethinking about what takes place in our museums, to whom our museums belong and who the colleagues are who have the privilege of telling important stories through the power of science, history, culture and art."[38]

Other collecting and memory institutions also began, in 2017, to strategize and mobilize to effect change. Archives, and archival studies as evidenced in the work of library and information science faculty member Michelle Caswell, have taken steps toward helping students enrolled in academic programs to "identify the ways in which white privilege is embedded in archival institutions and to collectively strategize concrete steps to dismantle white supremacy in their own archival practice."[39] Caswell explains how the election of Donald Trump as president of the United States in 2016 provided an opportunity to pull back the curtain on matters of importance and to tie those to archives and archival practices. At hand was White supremacy as the underlying cause of a Trump presidency[40] and how to dismantle it through anti-racist behavior. By confronting the current event in the moment, and using it as a springboard for reflection and, ultimately, action, Caswell moved toward the practice of *liberatory memory work* in her introductory archival course, "Archives, Records, and Memory." *Liberatory memory work*, as defined by Gould and Harris, is "premised on the need to work with the past, to insist on accountability, to acknowledge and address pain and trauma, and to reveal hidden dimensions of human rights violations—these are key to preventing a recurrence" with the aim of releasing societies "from cycles of violence, prejudice and hatred and instead to create vibrant and conscious societies that strive to achieve a just balance of individual and collective rights."[41] For Caswell, archival activism—that is, documenting social movements as they happen; building participatory systems that empower marginalized communities; expanding representational practices; and encouraging use of materials to inspire contemporary activism—are no longer enough. Caswell, instead, calls for more radical interventions to build "liberatory archival imaginaries."[42] Modeling behaviors of critique and resistance can empower students to "disrupt the status quo of oppression" in archives, and by extension, museums.

The status quo of oppression is also centered in the work of scholar and practitioner Gracen Brilmyer, who uses disability studies and queer theory to illustrate power and authority within archives and archival theory, as well as to draw attention to archival and museum absences of disability.[43] Brilmyer describes their early work looking for the presence of disabled people at the World's Fair in Chicago (1893) and situates important observations around how collections are constructed, processed, described, organized, and made accessible.[44] Their research examines how they have experienced "looking for disabled people in history—the feelings of longing, excitement, sadness, and loss that occur" and how their "experiences in archives are shaped by [their] experiences with disabled communities—how activism, advocacy, and community have all shaped [their] identity and [their] understandings of disability."[45] In this way, Brilmyer articulates a *crip provenance*—recalling that in museum contexts, *provenance* refers to the story of a work from its creation to the present day. For Brilmyer, such a provenance emphasizes *people* (creators, subjects, archivists, and other stewards); *systems* (those that created records and fostered the continuation of said methods); *materials* (those present in the record for the item itself and those parallel histories and practices that enable discussing disability and ableism); and *space* (as in the effective ways in which accessibility is interwoven). And, also, for Brilmyer, such a provenance draws "attention to absences, messiness, and the impossibility of knowing a complete disability history." In this way, then, disability is possible to discuss, even if only through its acknowledging the reality of its absence from the record.[46]

Clearly Caswell, Brilmyer, and others mentioned throughout this chapter aspire toward the "radical inclusivity" noted at the head of this chapter—and so much more. But how can change be sustained? That requires funding, and so we conclude our chapter with a discussion of money.

Funding Belonging

Philanthropic foundations that have, often, supported museum work are now prioritizing work that centers marginalized communities, as well as those who have prioritized re-Indigenization. For instance, the Mellon Foundation funds areas of work in museums, universities, and other organizations that "contribute to a more connected, creative, and just society" by supporting ideas, programming, and initiatives that center arts and culture, higher education, humanities, and public knowledge. In addition, the foundation supports initiatives that show how "the arts and humanities can move our interconnected communities closer to justice." These areas of work are not exclusive to museum funding, although intersections with museum work are apparent.[47]

Foundations like Mellon have also recognized that a way forward for museums, in the work of Belonging, requires greater support and collaboration. In May 2023, Mellon and three national funding partners (the Alice L. Walton Foundation, the Ford Foundation, and Pilot House Philanthropy) launched a new initiative, Leadership in Art Museums. The five-year program situates eleven million dollars toward a focus on leadership roles (curators, conservators, collections managers, community engagement staff, educators, and others) to "advance racial equality." Nineteen institutions in the United

States were chosen as part of this first cohort of funding and were granted funds to create, revamp, or otherwise conceive of positions that will be sustained by the institutions and, in turn, will enable them to advance their work in a manner that is inclusive of communities of color, including Black, Latinx, Indigenous, Arab, Asian, and Pacific Islander communities.[48] Such an initiative—while only one effort—offers a model for others, as well as hope for those who are empowered to be the change they want to see: to undertake liberatory memory work and to realize the vision of radical inclusivity.

Notes

1. Dyer Arts Center, home to a permanent collection of artwork by deaf and hard of hearing artists and allies, is located on my home campus of Rochester Institute of Technology. This meeting with Fran Flaherty and museum guests occurred on February 8, 2024. At this meeting, Fran suggested the term *radical inclusivity* for this Bakhtinian approach of inversion—considering the needs of the minority as if they were the majority.
2. The three surveys from 2015, 2018, and 2022 are available here on the Mellon Foundation website: https://www.mellon.org/report/aiding-the-evolution-of-art-museums-to-reflect-the-diversity-of-our -country. A direct link to the 2022 report is available here: https://sr.ithaka.org/publications/art -museum-staff-demographic-survey-2022/.
3. National Labor Relations Board, National Labor Relations Act is also cited NLRA or the Act; 29 U.S.C. §§ 151–69, https://www.nlrb.gov/guidance/key-reference-materials/national-labor-relations-act. The website describes the act as protecting "workplace democracy by providing employees at private-sector workplaces the fundamental right to seek better working conditions and designation of representation without fear of retaliation." While the clear intent is unionization, general employee protections are implicit.
4. See statement on Mountain-Plains Museums Association, which identifies their Board of Directors unanimous vote on September 11, 2018, requiring this information: https://mpma.net/Job-Bank-Forum. Karol Wight, "Salary Transparency in Job Postings: One Museum's Journey," *AAM Blog*, September 23, 2022, https://www.aam-us.org/2022/09/23/salary-transparency-in-job-postings-one-museums-journey/. AAM's requirement for posting defines the necessary work to be done: "Effective November 15, 2022, the salary field on job postings shared on AAM's JobHQ will be required. We know that salary transparency practices can't thoughtfully take place overnight or in isolation. It requires a critical look at current practices and, for many, the collaboration and approval of parent organizations, boards, and other entities. With this advanced notice, we urge museums to begin making the policy reviews and changes, benchmarking, and compensation studies required to holistically implement these important practices." https://aam-us-jobs.careerwebsite.com/.
5. NEMPN, "Salary Range on Museum Job Postings Letter Writing Campaign," https://nationalempnet work.org/salary-range-on-museum-job-postings-letter-writing-campaign/. They cite inspiration from Vu Le, "When You Don't Disclose Salary Range on a Job Posting, a Unicorn Loses Its Wings," *NonprofitAF*, June 1, 2015, https://nonprofitaf.com/2015/06/when-you-dont-disclose-salary-range-on-a-job -posting-a-unicorn-loses-its-wings/.
6. NEMPN, "Equity in Pay + Pay Transparency Accountability Tracker," https://airtable.com/app4fJqf42 uXCbto5/shrnUHFzPpFsGZ0cb/tblMKOpHYIlxmT2oJ. NEMPN worked with forty-three museum associations from 2016–2019 on this effort.
7. See update/victory at the foot of the petition, https://www.change.org/p/the-future-of-museums -includes-salary-transparency-aam-must-commit-to-equity-for-all-museum-workers-and-showthe salary.
8. The submissions were viewable here: https://docs.google.com/spreadsheets/d/14_cn3afoas7N hKvHWaFKqQGkaZS5rvL6DFxzGqXQa6o/edit#gid=0. The spreadsheet began in June 2019, and it was open during the early days of COVID. See Zachary Small, "Museum Workers Share Their Salaries and Urge Industry-Wide Reform," *Hyperallergic*, June 3, 2019, https://hyperallergic.com/503089/museum -workers-share-their-salaries-and-urge-industry-wide-reform/.
9. CUNY Adjunct Project, https://cunyadjunctproject.org/mission/, has existed since 1994, but specifically the campaign launched in 2017 called "Toward a Just Contract"; it used written material, including data and testimonials from adjuncts and teaching fellows, to explain the current conditions and need for

change. See https://issuu.com/cunyadjunctproject/docs/justcontract. Also important were Kimberly Drew's keynote, https://www.aam-us.org/2019/05/28/aam2019-keynote-kimberly-drew/; and the POWarts salary survey released in 2019, https://www.powarts.org/; https://www.powarts.org/powartsurveys; and resources, https://www.powarts.org/powarts-salary-survey-resources.

10. Salary Transparency Spreadsheet, https://docs.google.com/spreadsheets/d/14_cn3afoas7NhKvHWaFKqQGkaZS5rvL6DFxzGqXQa6o/edit#gid=0. The sheet has been archived, and possibly visualized, and it has been made accessible through Tableau, a data visualization platform, according to the National Emerging Museum Professionals Network: https://public.tableau.com/app/profile/m.mandula/viz/shared/2K8ZTWT8P. As of this writing, the data was not accessible on that site.

11. NEMPN, "Urge AAM to #ShowTheSalary on Their Job Postings," May 23, 2022, https://www.change.org/p/the-future-of-museums-includes-salary-transparency-aam-must-commit-to-equity-for-all-museum-workers-and-showthesalary.

12. See American Alliance of Museums, "National Snapshot of COVID-19 Impact on US Museums," February 8, 2022. Data gathered by Wilkening Consulting, https://www.aam-us.org/2022/02/08/national-snapshot-of-covid-19-impact-on-united-states-museums-fielded-december-2021-january-2022/.

13. Megan K. Stack, "Inside Starbucks' Dirty War Against Organized Labor," *New York Times*, July 21, 2023, https://www.nytimes.com/2023/07/21/opinion/starbucks-union-strikes-labor-movement.html.

14. AFSCME, "Museum and Cultural Instructions," https://www.afscme.org/about/jobs-we-do/museums-and-cultural-institutions. The AFSCME Cultural Workers United works in conjunction with the federated labor unions of the AFL-CIO. For a list of their recent accomplishments, see https://www.culturalworkersunited.org/node/158517/rss/1.

15. United Museum Workers, "Frequently Asked Questions," https://www.umwpgh.org/frequently-asked-questions.html.

16. According to the Union Membership and Coverage Database, which tracks labor activity, 14.8 percent were unionized in 2021, up from 13.3 percent in 2020. In 2022, the last year of reporting, the number dipped to 13.8 percent (reflecting 12.8 percent of employees in comparison to 13.1 percent of employees in 2021 and 13.2 percent of employees in 2020). See Barry Hirsch, David Macpherson, and William Even, "Union Membership and Coverage from the CPS (Current Population Survey)," https://www.unionstats.com/.

17. See Mark Guarino, "'We Are in Crisis Mode: Museum Workers Are Turning to Unions over Conditions They Say Are Untenable," *Washington Post*, November 4, 2021, https://www.washingtonpost.com/entertainment/museums/museums-workers-unionizing/2021/11/03/d4655ee8-2863-11ec-9de8-156fed3c81bf_story.html.

18. The Cooperstown Graduate Program was established in 1964 as the first grad program in the United States designed to train students to work in history museums. One of the tenets of this program, from the beginning, has been applied learning, which, at first, was not characterized as an internship, but akin to it. Internships are required of students at CGP, and many other graduate (and undergraduate) programs. A list of museum studies programs may be found on the National Emerging Museum Professionals Network page: https://nationalempnetwork.org/directory-museum-studies-programs-us/. The international list is hosted by American Alliance of Museums, http://ww2.aam-us.org/resources/careers/museum-studies-programs.

19. Department of Labor, "Fact Sheet #71: Internship Programs Under the Fair Labor Standards Act," January 2018, https://www.dol.gov/agencies/whd/fact-sheets/71-flsa-internships.

20. Elizabeth Merritt, "Po-tay-to Po-taa-to: On Unpaid Internships," October 28, 2014, https://www.aam-us.org/2014/10/28/po-tay-to-po-taa-to-on-unpaid-internships/.

21. Incluseum, "Michelle Obama, "Activism," and "Museum Employment Part III," *Incluseum*, November 6, 2015, https://incluseum.com/2015/11/06/michelle-obama-activism-museum-employment-part-iii/.

22. Nicole Ivey, "The Labor of Diversity," *Museum* (January/February 2016): 36–39, http://ww2.aam-us.org/docs/default-source/resource-library/the-labor-of-diversity.pdf?sfvrsn=0. The entire issue of *Museum* is dedicated to "Diversity in the Museum Workplace."

23. Incluseum, "Michelle Obama, "Activism," and "Museum Employment Part III," *Incluseum*, November 6, 2015, https://incluseum.com/2015/11/06/michelle-obama-activism-museum-employment-part-iii/.

24. American Association for Museum Volunteers, "Standards and Best Practices," https://aamv.org/Standards-and-Best-Practices.

25. Omar Eaton-Martinez, Herbert Jones, Megan Millman, and Richard Harker, "Embracing the Power of College Interns as Volunteers," AAM Session, May 26, 2016, https://aamv.org/College-Students-as-Interns.

26. Rakshitha Arni Ravishankar, "It's Time to Officially End Unpaid Internships," *Harvard Business Review*, May 26, 2021, https://hbr.org/2021/05/its-time-to-officially-end-unpaid-internships. While Ravishankar was discussing for-profit internships, the takeaway about micro-internships is relevant for museums.

27. The Getty Foundation, Getty Marrow Internship Program Impact Report, 2020, 3, https://www.getty.edu/interns-2020/report/.

28. The Getty, "Getty Marrow Program," https://www.getty.edu/projects/getty-marrow-undergraduate-internships/, the Getty Foundation, Getty Marrow Internship Program Impact Report, 2020, 9, https://www.getty.edu/interns-2020/report/. Some findings include: 32 percent of intern alumni surveyed work in the arts. The Getty Marrow internships bring individuals from underrepresented groups into arts careers: among alumni not working in the field, 40 percent report that their current job relates to the arts, and 46 percent have worked in the arts in the past. Ninety-two percent of alumni working in the arts attribute their career paths to their internships for students who want to pursue careers in the arts; undertaking multiple internships gives them the skills and experience to do so. Thirty-nine percent of alumni who had two internships, and 50 percent of alumni who had three or more internships, work in the arts, compared to 30 percent who had one internship.

29. Strong Families, "What We Do," http://strongfamiliesmovement.org/what-we-do.

30. The LGBTQ Welcoming Guidelines are available here: https://indd.adobe.com/view/b3e67357-2f62-4809-b757-17813aadeb13. The Family-Inclusive Language Chart is available here: http://www.zazzle.com/magmidd.

31. The Incluseum, "About," https://incluseum.com/about/. As quoted in https://incluseum.com/, the new publication draws attention to a quote from Quinn as to the tenth anniversary of Incluseum and pondering what an "'insurgent museum project' can tell us about inclusion and the future of museums." The source quote by Quinn is not locatable, other than its citation as "Quinn, 2016, p. 11" on the website.

32. Edward P. Alexander, Mary Alexander, and Juilee Decker, *Museums in Motion: An Introduction to the History and Functions of Museums* (Lanham, MD: Rowman & Littlefield for the AASLH, 2017), 18–19.

33. Edward P. Alexander, Mary Alexander, and Juilee Decker, *Museums in Motion: An Introduction to the History and Functions of Museums* (Lanham, MD: Rowman & Littlefield for the AASLH, 2017), 18–19.

34. "With Data-Driven Research, Museum Hue Advocates for Equality and Representation into New York's Art and Cultural Organizations," *Side of Culture*, April 5, 2023, https://sideofculture.com/2023/04/museum-hue/.

35. James Baldwin, "As Much Truth As One Can Bear," *New York Times*, January 14, 1962, Section 7, part 1, pages 1, 38.

36. Nicole Ivy, "Introduction," *Facing Change Report*, 2018, 2. These bulleted points of the group's charge are explored in detail in the report.

37. American Alliance of Museums, *Facing Change Report*, 2018, 7–11.

38. American Alliance of Museums, *Facing Change Report*, 2018, 7.

39. See Michelle Caswell, with graphic design by Gracen Brilmyer, "Teaching to Dismantle White Supremacy in Archives," *Library Quarterly: Information, Community, Policy* 87, no. 3 (July 2017): 222–35. https://doi.org/10.1086/692299.

40. Asserting that White supremacy is the underlying cause of the election is not to discredit the role of misogyny, but it is, rather, to argue of the interaction between race and gender in complex, complicated ways. Caswell also reminds us that the majority of White women voted for Donald Trump. See Ronald W. Cox, "Trump's Ponzi Scheme Victory," *Class, Race, and Corporate Power* 4(2) 2016: article 5; Michael Eric Dyson, *Tears We Cannot Stop: A Sermon to White America* (New York: St. Martin's, 2017).

41. Chandre Gould and Verne Harris, "Memory for Justice," *Nelson Mandela Foundation*, 2014: 4–5.

42. Michelle Caswell, "Inventing New Archival Imaginaries: Theoretical Foundations for Identity-Based Community Archives," in *Identity Palimpsests: Ethnic Archiving in the U.S. and Canada*, edited by Dominique Daniel and Amalia Levi (Sacramento: Litwin, 2014).

43. Gracen is self-defined as a "white, queer, non-binary (they/them), Disabled person." Their work is informed by their own experience as a disabled person and their work in natural history museums where they digitized millions of specimen. See http://gracenbrilmyer.com/about.html. With Caswell, Brilmyer designed a poster focused on "Identifying & Dismantling White Supremacy in Archives," available here: http://gracenbrilmyer.com/dismantling_whiteSupremacy_archives_WHOLE.pdf.

44. Gracen M. Brilmyer, "Toward a Crip Provenance: Centering Disability in Archives through Its Absence," *Journal of Contemporary Archival Studies* 9: 3 (2022), https://elischolar.library.yale.edu/jcas/vol9/iss1/3. Brilmyer notes 1893's claim of "savage" cultures on display, and later, in 1904's fair in St. Louis, where "defectives" were on display. See also James W. Trent, "Defectives at the World's Fair: Constructing Disability in 1904," *Remedial and Special Education* 19:4 (July/August 1998): 201–11, https://doi.org/10.1177/074193259801900403.

45. Gracen M. Brilmyer, "Toward a Crip Provenance," 16.

46. Gracen M. Brilmyer, "Toward a Crip Provenance," 19.

47. The Andrew W. Mellon Foundation, based in New York City, has funding priorities of arts and culture; led by Elizabeth Alexander, it has emphasized funding priorities as dismantling systemic racism, centering multi-vocality, and raising Indigenous and other sorties. https://mailchi.mp/mellon/b0jty8a87r?e=31dbe44c7a. The presidential initiatives include: Imaging Freedom ("artistic, cultural, and humanistic work that centers the voices and knowledge of people impacted by the US criminal legal system"); Puerto Rico ("Puerto Rico's vibrant artistic, cultural knowledge, and memory ecosystems, and the individuals who work within them, both on the archipelago and in the diaspora"); and the Monuments Project ("commitment to transform the nation's commemorative landscape by supporting public projects that reflect the breadth and complexity of American stories and communities"). See https://www.mellon.org/grant-programs/presidential-initiatives.

48. Mellon Foundation, "New Investments for More Diverse Leadership in Art Museums," May 3, 2023, https://www.mellon.org/news/new-investments-for-more-diverse-leadership-in-art-museums.

13

Antiracism, Belonging, and Coalition-Building

The concept of anti-racism[1] has been defined by scholar Ibram X. Kendi as effort put toward dismantling racism. Kendi is careful to distinguish between "not racist" and "anti-racist," noting that racist and anti-racist are not fixed identities. Where "not racist" is a term and identity of denial, "anti-racist" is an active behavior to see and realize people as *inherently equal*. To be an anti-racist, according to Kendi, "is a radical choice in the face of history, requiring a radical reorientation of our consciousness. . . . And, like fighting an addiction, being an antiracist requires persistent self-awareness, constant self-criticism, and regular self-examination."[2]

The anti-racist movement in museums, as an avenue of activism,[3] was spawned in 2020, with museum professionals among those suggesting a path forward. Art scholar and curator Kimberly Drew noted, "Watching museums like the British Museum and the Met—institutions with historic ties to colonialism—use a slogan rather than admit to their own roles in the 'race problem' ignites a desire for a more holistic investigation of museums not only as homes for art and culture, but as entities with both the buying power and the political ties to make a lasting impact on life beyond this uprising."[4]

Curator Taylor Brandon noted the disconnect between social media posts and a lack of action—the so-called Slac-tivist (as in slacker + activist) approach: "Performative gestures like social media statements in solidarity with Black life do nothing when Black staff are being treated unfairly. Yes, you have the work of a Black artist on your wall, but do you have staff that are a representation of that and can speak authentically to the cultural nuances of said work? Are that same staff equitably paid? Are they listened to and cared for? Do roles for them exist outside of educational and community engagement departments? A complete overhaul is in order that centers Black voices until museums are abolished. A lot of people won't agree with me, but I would like to envision a future without museums and large cultural institutions. History and Black scholars have been telling us that reform is often more harmful. In the meantime, the leadership of these spaces need to be working towards equity and better working conditions for Black staff."[5]

Key to these critiques of the institution of "The Museum" is the realization that museums do not see themselves as active participants in systemic racism and racist practice. By not seeing racism in their own history and practice, museums struggle to see how to understand what they have done, continue to do, and can seek to stop doing. Outside of The Museum, other organizations, such as the Sierra Club, recognize their past, seek to distance themselves from it, and want to do better. In July 2020, the group announced an end to their "blind reverence to a figure who was also racist" and situated the need to tell truths about the past and how they are moving toward work that is anti-racist and reparative. Executive director Michael Brune called upon the organization to follow the actions of those who are engaged in taking down monuments and memorials: "It's time to take down some of our own monuments, starting with some truth-telling about the Sierra Club's early history. That will be followed by posts on how we've had to evolve on issues of immigration and population control, environmental justice, and Indigenous sovereignty. We will also devote a post to a discussion of how the Sierra Club is working to center the voices of people we have historically ignored, so we can begin repairing some of the harms done."[6]

Some institutions, such as the Nelson-Atkins Museum of Art in Kansas City, Missouri, are using their museums as a lens through which to view race, representation, identity, and belonging in America. A five-part series launched in January 2022 paired local poet Glenn North with museum staff and community members to tell complex stories about what an art museum can mean to a community. Further, the series evidences how listeners can see the museum and its campus through another's perspective. According to Jocelyn Edens, interpretation and digital engagement associate at the Nelson-Atkins Museum, the project is built around conversation and co-creation in seeking visitor responses. A Frame of Mind grapples with the impact of the museum's architecture and neighborhood on visitor experience, monuments designed from settler colonial perspectives, racial representation in museums, and how museums have the power to build and construct new stories. Building upon previous museum initiatives in co-creation when a process to connect with a local advisory group to help shape an interpretive strategy that included community-written labels, multivocality became the framework here.[7] In this podcast, storytelling becomes the work of many, not a select few. The team from the museum sought to "unearth" experience of the past and present through archival sources and interviews that yield the participatory and co-creative methodology.[8]

In addition to podcasts, the audio medium has been developing in museum visits since the earliest days of the 1952 Stedelijk Museum audio guide, which utilized wireless transistors.[9] (See Chapter 8.) Today, such audio tours enable visitors to choose their own adventure. For instance, the Minneapolis Institute of Art offers a suite of audio tours keyed to one of four areas: museum overview tours; special-exhibition-related content; point-of-view tours, such as collections that center women, African American art, LGBTQ+ pride, Native American heritage, and Hispanic heritage; and themed topics such as felines, Barbie, or music in the galleries.[10]

Outside of art, museums, and the outdoors, science is not immune. Ruth Tyson, a Black employee of the Union of Concerned Scientists, noted the disconnect between promise and reality. In penning her resignation letter–turned–open letter to the organization, Tyson cited three areas of concern (Black death, Black silencing, and Black fugitivity) as directly in opposition to affirmations of Black life. Recalling her three-year stint that saw her move from being one of four BIPOC employees in a cohort of a fourteen-person team to being the last one standing, Tyson evidenced ideas but little action toward anti-racism: "As if anti-racist work were something you could just sprinkle on top."[11]

Museums Respond to Ferguson

As Margaret Middleton and Jamie Hagen note, the extrajudicial killing of Michael Brown in Ferguson, Missouri, launched action by way of a "Joint Statement from Museum Bloggers and Colleagues on Ferguson and Related Events"[12] on December 14, 2014, which called upon museums to "reflect on their internal oppressive practices and actively demonstrate their roles as change agents fully embedded in our nation's social, educational, and cultural infrastructure." As Aleia Brown, co-founder of #MuseumsRespondtoFerguson and #BlkTwitterstorians, and Adrianne Russell, museum educator and consultant, have noted, Black institutions and Black museums forged paths in social action and protest. Citing the Schomburg Center for Research in Black Culture and the Hampton University Museum, among others, their institutional assertions of Blackness "as humanity and worthy of being documented and presented to the public was incredibly subversive in the late nineteenth century" and they suggest that these institutions and their work can be held up as a model for twenty-first-century concerns within and beyond the museum. They state, "We believe there is a need for contemporary museums to look to centuries-old Black institutions to navigate our current racial climate."[13] Several examples of anti-racism and anti-colonialism and other forms of activism and movements are examined in this chapter. Before examining these, it is important to look at the way museums are perceived and whether they are (or can be) neutral.

Museums Are Not Neutral

A recent report, Museums and Trust 2021, confirms that the public considers museums as highly trustworthy—ranking second only to friends and family, and more trustworthy than certain facets of the private and public sectors, including researchers, the government, corporations, and social media.[14] Even so, awareness in the museum profession and transparency about actions and how museums may communicate or foreground a specific point of view refute neutrality. In fact, if *neutrality* is defined as "the state of not supporting or helping either side in a conflict,"[15] then museums cannot be neutral.

In 2017, museum educator and change leader Mike Murawski and art historian and cultural organizer La Tanya Autry used the phrase "museums are not neutral" as part of an online exchange about their lived experiences highlighting the myth of individual and institutional "neutrality." They joked that they should print a T-shirt with that saying—and they did! What started as a three-week campaign has resulted in the sale of thousands of T-shirts that have raised funds for social-justice charities and nonprofits while also joining together individuals who see museums as being part of the problem, and the solution, too.[16]

Seeing someone with a T-shirt (or mug or other merch) pulls people together through a shared interest and identity as change makers. Those involved in the movement, within and beyond museums, are students, faculty, staff, researchers, and the public—all are dedicated to dismantling racism and oppression in museums. As Autry noted, "Wearing the T-shirt is, as one student termed, 'a walking

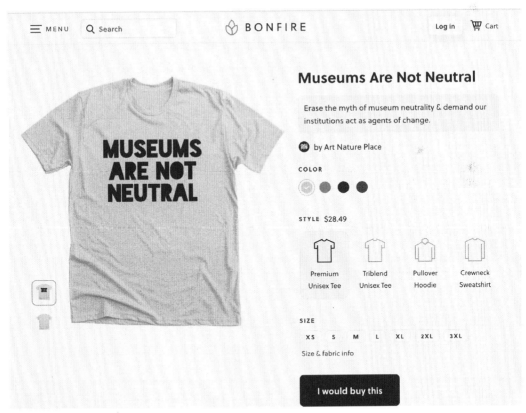

Museum educator and change leader Mike Murawski and art historian and cultural organizer La Tanya Autry used the phrase "museums are not neutral," claiming they should print it on a T-shirt. The statement, and accompanying swag, started a movement.
Screencap from https://www.bonfire.com/museums-are-not-neutral-2022/.

Google News   🔍   museums are not neutral

Home   For you   Following   News Showcase | U.S.   World   Local   Busines

MuseumNext°

Can Museums Be Neutral Or Should They Take A Stance?

Jan 9, 2023

ICOM

"Museums do not need to be neutral, they need to be independent" - International Council of Museums

Dec 6, 2019

ideastream

moCa Curator La Tanya Autry Advocates Museums Are Not Neutral

Jan 31, 2020 • Carrie Wise

The hashtag #MuseumsAreNotNeutral persists in the news, on social media, and otherwise.
Screencap created via Google News Search, November 2023.

exhibition' [because] the emphatic statement often leads to impromptu discussions about the histo-ries and roles of museums."[17]

As Murawski noted, the movement is about individuals and institutions: "Acknowledging that museums are not neutral is a meaningful and urgent step toward gaining awareness of the powerful role that these forces play within these institutions. It is a crucial step toward recognizing one's own role in questioning it, interrupting it, and being a part of taking transformative action to replace it." Autry added that *the movement highlights ways to reject the status quo*: "Our initiative spotlights actions for change and exposes how the claim of neutrality fosters unequal power relations, and Museums Are Not Neutral became my way to inform people that I reject the status quo. It's one of my tools for improving the museum field, and it is now a global community."[18]

Autry and Murawski also note that they are standing on the shoulders of giants: their work is building on the activism work of many others, including the founders of "Museums Respond to Ferguson" Twitter chat in 2014 started by Adrian Russell and Aliyah Brown and the work of MASS Action, from 2016 on. Other voices continue to contribute to the discussion, including Nathan *"mudyi"* Sentance, a Wiradjuri librarian and museum professional from New South Wales who runs the blog "Archival Decolonist." Sentance, in fact, argues that museums and other memory institutions need to challenge perceptions about neutrality, because, in fact, they have never been neutral. Ever.[19]

Together, and on their own, these and many other voices in activism call for museums to respond and to take action to non-neutrality and injustice. In response to the movement, activism, and the hashtag #MuseumsArtNotNeutral, the American Alliance of Museums acknowledges that museums need to cultivate a deeper understanding of what visitors and staff think about museums, especially around neutrality, or lack thereof. They offer a report on audiences and inclusion as one path forward (in 2021).[20] Though together, we have to ask if neutrality is something that can ever be achieved by museums at all.

MASS Action

Looking at the idea of transformation, the collaborative group MASS Action (Museum As Site for Social Action) was established around 2015.[21] According to one of the co-founders, Eileen Callihan, the group was born out of need: "That's where I saw an opportunity. If our museums are only held back because we lack the tools to do the work and the roadmap to move forward, then let's give people the tools and the roadmap! There are many colleagues out there doing good work, so this project could aggregate what they are doing; we could put that all together in a toolkit, share it widely with the field, then everyone will have what they need to get to work."[22] The group met online before convening in-person in 2016, yielding a toolkit,[23] as well as a process for change.

Beyond this initial resource, the collaborative convenes together, scrapes data, and creates resources for use by all. Their aim is to pose questions for individuals and institutions:

- What is the role and responsibility of the museum in responding to issues affecting our communities locally and globally?
- How do the museum's internal practices need to change in order to align with, and better inform, their public practice?
- How can the museum be used as a site for social action?

The work of MASS Action seemed even more critical a few years later, as they developed a study to examine museum mission statements; proclamations against racism and for greater diversity, equity, and inclusion; and the actions they pursue. Their baseline data-gathering in late 2020 analyzed 1,088 museums in the United States in terms of their websites and social-media posts to determine their general approach to anti-racism and how this commitment aligns with their actions. Of the 1,088 examined, just over half (572) made a racial equity–related statement on their website or social media, while 512 did not.[24] In reviewing this information about these institutions, MASS Action affirmed the importance of museums being held accountable across six arenas, as defined below.

1. Acknowledgment: Does the statement acknowledge the organization's complicity in and perpetuation of racism as an institution, including examination of museum history (and impact on staff, as well as community)?
2. Structural Analysis: Does the statement provide specific institutional examples of racist and non-inclusive practice by the museum?
3. Actions: Does the statement give examples of actions the institution will take to address the above-described racist/non-inclusive practices?
4. Desired Outcomes: Does the statement articulate desired outcomes of anti-racist/inclusive actions? These are key to setting measurable goals so that the institution can gauge its progress in anti-racism and equity work.
5. Deadlines: Does the statement provide estimates of how and when anti-racist/inclusive actions will occur? Deadlines create transparency around commitments and ensure collective accountability to actions.
6. Financial Investment: Does the statement commit any funding to the achievement of the above?[25]

By using these six criteria as the lenses through which the statements were evaluated, they critically evaluated each institution's commitment to anti-racism, and how a stated commitment aligns with actions (or doesn't). As a transparency and accountability campaign, the data and contextualization are intended as a flashpoint of a moment in time, as well as a starting point for examination and dialogue about how museums can and do commit to anti-racism.[26]

In addition, guidance comes from beyond the United States, and thoughtfully before COVID-19 and the summer of 2020. Based in the U.K., the Museums Association convened a conference with more than one thousand individuals in 2018–2019 focused on the role of collections, the role of museums, and changes to museum practice. Called "Collections 2030," the initiative identified the significant role that collections can have in empowering people "to be active participants in our society, giving them the insight and tools they need to design solutions to contemporary problems, challenge injustice and create stronger communities. In practice, this means democratising museum collections—promoting co-curation, co-production and participation."[27] Though organized before the movement of 2020, their recommendations remain an important starting point for change:

1. A culture change in museums and collections practice by enabling "all staff to work with collections and communities to share their expertise in both areas"
2. A proactive approach to the democratization and decolonization of museums
3. A focus on reinterpretation of out-of-date displays

Black Lives Matter

The extrajudicial killing of George Floyd in May 2020 sparked mass protests in Minneapolis–St. Paul and beyond. His death also sparked sustained preoccupation with the Black Lives Matter (BLM) movement. The demonstrations were responding to police brutality, systemic racism, and systematic injustice. These events were underway during the global pandemic and as museums were tottering between serving as virtual hubs expressly and reopening in the summer of 2020 after closure since March's lockdown.

Institutions responded in a variety of ways. First and foremost, many acknowledged the death of Floyd on social media. The Walker Art Center in Minneapolis responded by stating they would no longer contract the services of the police department for their special events until the Minneapolis Police Department "implements meaningful change by demilitarizing training programs, holding officers accountable for the use of excessive force, and treating communities of color with dignity and respect. Enough is Enough. George Floyd should still be alive. Black Lives Matter."[28]

Addressing the situation in a rather more anemic manner, some institutions issued statements about equality, without mentioning BLM. Such pronouncements, like those from the Getty, SFMOMA, and the Museum of Modern Art, among many others, expressed concern but overtly refused to mention George Floyd. Apologies and additional posts appeared, though not before attention to the approach was drawn. Scholar, curator, and former manager of The Met's social media noted, "It's telling that many museums that choose to show work about Black subjectivity are deeply silent right now."[29]

Open letters were crafted and shared as a way to call out one's own field. For instance, Chris Anagnos, head of the Association of Art Museum Directors, identified a sharp contrast between vision and action, noting: "We have dabbled around the edges of the work, but in our place of privilege we will never live up to the statement that 'museums are for everyone' unless we begin to confront, examine and dismantle the various structures that brought us to this point. . . . I think our field has an obligation to do a better job engaging with these issues."[30]

The statements of support, though, were called into question almost universally, with wonder as to whether anything would change institutionally. New York–based curator Antwaun Sargent posted the following critique on Twitter in the early days of the protests: "The museums posting 'black lives matter' now are the same ones who have participated in the social death of black folks . . . do black lives matter on your curatorial team or board? do they matter in your collections and shows?"[31] He further noted that museums should have to "earn the right" to use the phrase *BLM*.

Museums went on to affirm commitments to Diversity, Equity, and Inclusion (or some other variation of Diversity, Equity, Inclusion, *and Accessibility*, or Diversity, Equity, Inclusion, *and Belonging*) initiatives as steps their institutions have taken. For instance, by refocusing attention on the Black Lives Matter (BLM) movement, museums and other cultural organizations issued public statements as noted above, and they began to take some action by curating their collections to center the contributions of Black people, for instance, highlighting the work of Black writers, artists, and scientists.[32] Nevertheless, open letters, other calls, and responses to some efforts taken continued to see greater transparency and indications as to how the senior staff would be held accountable (such as actionable goals).

Museum Innovation

Museum scholars Haitham Eid and Robert R. Janes, in their analysis of museums,[33] state that such institutions have both a need and a desire to reflect upon their practices and adopt innovative approaches in order to meet their civic responsibilities. They believe that museums, as civic institutions, have a moral duty to take action to make the world a better place.

The social responsibilities of museums is not a new concept, of course, extending back to the days of John Cotton Dana and the Newark Museum before moving forward to include the writings of Stephen Weil, Elaine Heumann Gurian, Robert R. Janes, Emlyn Koster, Richard Sandell, and Lois Silverman, among others, who are committed to enhancing the meaning and relevance of museums. For Eid and Janes, however, at the heart of this charge to better the world lies the concept of social innovation, which is "the process of developing and deploying effective solutions to challenging and often systemic social and environmental issues in support of social progress. . . . Solutions often require the active collaboration of constituents across government, business, and the nonprofit world."[34] It isn't the responsibility of museums, solely, to effect change in museums.

Moreover, the pre-pandemic calls for change in museums emphasized the role of museums as agents for social change, or museums as social innovators. As Eid and Janes point out, this shift in thinking of the institution as an innovator positions the museum purposefully: it turns "static objects and distant histories into forces of good that helps elevate communities and advance environmental and social justice causes."[35]

As museums aspire to transform themselves into the realm of social agency and advocacy, a shift in museum practice is essential. While accessibility, engagement, immersion, and participatory experiences remain important and still have a vital role to play in museum work, new models to fulfill the new purposes are required. Among these are glimpses into leadership and staffing. To this end, data has been gathered to demonstrate the lack of diversity in leadership[36] more holistically. For instance, in 2015 the Andrew W. Mellon Foundation and Ithaka S+R, published the Art Museum Staff Demographic Survey to quantify the lack of representative diversity in professional museum roles.

This notion of effecting change in museums being the responsibility of many is at the core of many movements and groups. Some, like SHIFT (established in 2014), professed the good of shared authority, horizontal leadership, and professional collectives as a new learning, and leadership, model that enables all participants to lead, learn, lend support, and follow.[37] The premise behind SHIFT was the creation of "a collective of cultural workers engaging in critical reflection and accountability in order to shift their practices as educators, administrators and artists toward an anti-oppressive feminist paradigm."[38] In addition, in the MASS Action toolkit's chapter on "Inclusive Leadership," guidance is offered for inclusive leaders on how to empower all levels of a museum organization to create a more equitable paradigm.[39]

Coalition building is part of Museums and Race, which challenges institutional policies and systems that perpetuate oppression in museums. In 2016, Museums & Race: Transformation and Justice was formed as a movement to challenge and reimagine institutional policies and systems that perpetuate oppressions in museums.[40] Chief among their initiatives are dialogues and ciphers. Two years later, the group developed the M&R Report Card, a tool that can be used to scrutinize museums about policies and practices surrounding diversity, equity, inclusion, and representation.[41] Museums may seek counsel with Museums and Race in addition to utilizing the downloadable Report Card as a first step in their anti-racist journey and their path to concrete structural change. On this last point, it is important to note how the group has conceived of self-evaluation as a method for community of practice.

Museums and Race has also been engaged in action-oriented activism. On June 1, 2020, after learning of the death of George Floyd, they released a statement of solidarity that acknowledged complicity of museums in systemic racism. Their statement called upon every person in the United States to counter hate, oppression, and systemic injustice by actively working to dismantle the oppression facing Black Americans and to fight against anti-Blackness. Their statement calls upon "museums to step forward with those who are already fighting, cast off their chains of inaction, and find some way to make a difference in the field, for museum workers, and in support of dismantling white supremacy in all institutions for the good of their communities, their institutions, and their nation."[42] Museums and Race identified three actions that can be taken by individuals and institutions:

- Lift up Black voices and center the experiences of Black people;
- Learn and embrace anti-racist policies and practices that dismantle anti-Black oppression; and
- Engage with groups such as their organization and Museum Hue, MASS Action, Museums Art Not Neutral, and others to do the work that is needed for transformation.

Ultimately, through the report card, statement of solidarity, and other practices, Museums and Race sees their work as forging a community of practice, a conceptualization defined by Etienne Wenger-Trayner and Beverly Wenger-Trayner, who have defined such communities as having three elements—a domain, a community, and a practice. As noted in an earlier chapter, a community of practice offers perspective on knowledge and learning where communities share an interest in something they do and they learn how to do it better through interaction.[43] The extended term, *landscapes of practice*,[44] offers a metaphor for how professionals navigate journeys across and through multiple communities of practice—an additional articulation that speaks to the current state of engagement in DEI work. *It's no longer islands, but intersections.*

Community Engagement and Muscle Memory

Museums need to do better to be anti-racist. Part of that work can be done through community engagement and repeated practice—that is, muscle memory. As Joanne Heyler, founding director of the Broad Museum in Los Angeles, stated, in 2020: "Museums are facing a reckoning on many, many fronts. But particularly on the front of anti-racism, we are engaged internally with active and authentic and genuine conversations about how to be better as an anti-racist institution, and how to confront those pieces of the art world and the museum world that consciously and unconsciously work against those goals." Her suggestion is for museums to develop "muscle memory" around community engagement. "You have to know or learn the community that is going to be impacted by what you're presenting. And then you've got to go talk to those communities. This is a lot of work. Then after you do all of that work, you are probably going to make a decision that's not going to make everybody happy. . . . Talk to everybody. Not just the art people, not just the obvious people—try to reach out to absolutely everybody."[45] Importantly, Heyler also noted the importance of diversifying the workplace: "Museums also need to get creative in how they recruit. Museums who rely on search firms need to not accept a pool of candidates that's not diverse. . . . Until the pipeline that leads right into museums is truly healthy—and by healthy, I mean inclusive and diverse, which it isn't yet, to be blunt—you've got to look at other professions and other industries where parallel job titles and responsibilities are more diverse and go recruit in those places."[46]

Music historian and curator Nwaka Onwusa curated *It's Been Said All Along: Voices of Rage, Hope, and Empowerment* at the Rock and Roll Hall of Fame and Museum in Cleveland, Ohio, in 2020, as a response to extrajudicial killing of Black people and the ensuing protests for racial equality post-George Floyd. The interactive exhibit is viewable online: https://artsandculture.google.com/story/1QUB08nha4E7yQ. *Courtesy of the Rock and Roll Hall of Fame.*

Moving from the community and looking inside the walls of the institution, George Sparks of the Denver Museum of Nature & Science noted, "It's an interesting exercise to walk into the building and look for the humans and see how they're portrayed. The donor wall is almost all white people. And if you want to find somebody of color, they're in the dioramas with Indigenous people represented. When somebody of color comes into the museum, they recognize pretty quickly if there aren't many staff around who look like them. And what do the scientists look like, versus the people who are on the front line selling them tickets? Or in the advertising, or the materials asking them to buy a membership? Or, personally, my job?"[47]

By contrast, music historian and curator Nwaka Onwusa curated *It's Been Said All Along: Voices of Rage, Hope, and Empowerment* at the Rock and Roll Hall of Fame and Museum in Cleveland, Ohio, in 2020 as a response to extrajudicial killing of Black people and the ensuing protests for racial equality post–George Floyd. The exhibit featured an onsite presence on the lower level of the galleries with artifacts and digital interactives enabling visitors to hear music and learn more about the artists, their work, and their legacies. The exhibit is also online, marking the first time that an exhibit was mirrored onsite and online. As curator Onwusa noted, she drew upon the full catalog of artists to connect past and present as a way of drawing out what music—specifically rock and roll—is. "The artists highlighted in the exhibit eloquently celebrate and touch on notes of rage. It's only a sampling, because there are so many voices who have spoken out about injustice through their music, through their actions, through being on the front lines. . . . That's where I feel like I'm also there to help clarify what rock 'n' roll is. What it means. What is the feeling. What it represents. Who it represents, and how it represents the rebel in all of us."[48]

Framing Systemic Racism

As noted elsewhere in this volume, the Smithsonian has utilized digital technologies, in particular 3D scanning, in order to make collections available to the public for the purpose of telling more diverse stories. That initiative, *Our Shared Future: Reckoning with Our Racial Past*, is part of a multipronged effort that seeks to frame systemic racism, to help the public understand what it is, and to determine how to identify it and affect change. The work is arranged around six pillars: race and wellness; race and wealth; race and place; race, policy, and ethics; race beyond the United States; race, arts, and aesthetics. Each of these topics is introduced with an "Explainer Video" that offers a background of about three minutes before linking to any number of Smithsonian collections. The 3D files are fully moveable through the online viewer, and they are downloadable as well, enabling anyone to pop the file into a 3D printer and reproduce a surrogate of the museum object. Some pillars also include links to the Smithsonian podcast *Sidedoor*. In addition, the site links out to events from across the Smithsonian, such as the Native Cinema Showcase, an annual celebration in November that offers the best in Indigenous film.[49]

Other initiatives from the Smithsonian include Recovering Voices (RV), a collaborative program of the National Museum of Natural History, the National Museum of the American Indian, the Center for Folklife and Cultural Heritage, and the Asian Pacific American Center working in conjunction with communities around the world to revitalize and sustain endangered languages and knowledge. Established in 2009, the program aims to develop effective responses to language and knowledge loss through research, collaboration, and assistance with knowledge revitalization.[50]

Funding of important exhibitions that help to "flip the script" on what we have learned about American history can also help foster anti-racist museum work. For example, the National Endowment for the Humanities (NEH), in its commitment to telling broader narratives of who we are as a country, as we move toward the semiquincentennial (250th anniversary), is funding public humanities work such as exhibitions to give museum visitors opportunities to see new narratives before them that are more diverse and reflect perspectives that have been underrepresented in large-scale exhibitions. This resists the claim on static history offered by photographers such as Edward Curtis, a non-Native artist who catalogued "the vanishing race" and, in so doing, furthered the misperception that Native Americans were disappearing into history. The exhibition *In Our Hands: Native Photography, 1890 to Now* at the Minneapolis Institute of Arts "flip[s] the script" of the Curtis narrative by showcasing Native photographers. The show was created "with, by, and for Native people." In addition, expanding narratives that are more authentic and representative include *Making Her Mark: A History of Women Artists in Europe, 1400–1800* at the Baltimore Museum of Art (Fall 2023), which featured more than two hundred works of art that reflect a range of mediums including paintings, sculpture, devotional works, embroidery, metal work, ceramics, furniture, and more.[51]

Openness through Open Access

Museums may see a path forward through Open Access—or, more pointedly, transparency through digitization, access, and policies. In August 2023, the British Museum announced that about two thousand items of their collections, were lost or missing. The chair of Museum Trustees, George Osborne, announced that the museum was "the victim[s] of an inside job by someone, we believe, who over a long period of time was stealing from the museum and the museum put trust in. There are lots of lessons to be learnt as a result of that, the member of staff has been dismissed by us. The objects have started to be recovered." The announcement of missing items was followed by a plan to digitize the entire collection—a Herculean task that is half complete to date—as well as plans for differentiated access, including enhanced access to view collections by appointment and stricter rules for access to more secure areas ("strong rooms"). These efforts have been called a way forward with "openness and transparency."[52]

Perhaps, in some ways, the British Museum is far behind other institutions. For instance, *Apollo* magazine published a list of institutions with open access to works that are out of copyright, in 2020. It includes the Art Institute of Chicago, the Cleveland Museum of Art, Harvard Art Museums, the J. Paul Getty Museum in Los Angeles, The Met, millions of images from the national archives in the Library of Congress, and others. Internationally, the list includes the Belvedere, Vienna; Kunstmuseum, Basel; the Museum of New Zealand, Te Papa Tongarewa, Wellington, New Zealand; Národní galerie Praha in Prague, Czech Republic; the Statens Museum for Kunst, Copenhagen, Denmark; and more.[53]

Institutions, such as The Met, also provide datasets about their collections through the software developer hosting platform GitHub. There, users may find data about 470,000 works in the collection, with the associated media located on the Open Access page of The Met.[54] Further, access to extensive collections and related media are available through the Smithsonian Institution's Open Access hub, which invites online visitors to "download, share, and reuse millions of the Smithsonian's images—right now, without asking." The portal makes nearly five million digital assets in 2D and 3D available from across their twenty-one museums, nine research centers, libraries, archives, and the National Zoo.[55]

These provisions for open access came not as a result of a seemingly scandalous loss (or wonders of the whereabouts) of collections. As the former chief digital officer of the Met Museum, Sree Sreenivasan allayed fears that if the art was available online, visitors would not come to the museum. In fact, the opposite was true, as he claimed in 2016, the museum needed to embark upon efforts to share their work, distinctively to draw audiences in. This is not to suggest that The Met had an attendance problem, of course—the institution sees more than six million visitors per year. But rather, providing access is another means of access: The Met's digital initiatives aim to make sure online access can enhance the enjoyment of art, rather than detract from it.[56]

Online efforts can also foster transparency through research. For instance, the Cleveland Museum of Art is one of several museums that host a Provenance Research Project online, fostering awareness of the ongoing curatorial research that looks at the history of a work's ownership. As a subpage off the museum's main website, the Nazi-era provenance research site presents background, methodology, and disclosure of 373 works of art in European paintings collection and the eighty-six in the museum's European sculpture collection that either have gaps in their provenance or that were known to have

Data visualizations created in 2020 by Pratt Institute graduate student Anna Size detailing the diversity of collections at the Museum of Modern Art (MoMA). The institution was founded in New York City in 1929. Size points out the museum's mission ("Central to The Museum of Modern Art's mission is the encouragement of an ever-deeper understanding and enjoyment of modern and contemporary art by the diverse local, national, and international audiences that it serves") and asks if, over the past century of its existence, and among the more than two hundred thousand works, if the museum practices its values. The visualizations show acquisitions by gender; gender representation of artists reflected in where they are held across departments; acquisitions by country; and number of artworks by country. *Courtesy Anna Size. See https://public.tableau.com/app/profile/anna.size8574/viz/ RepresentationinMoMAsCollectionsStory/Story1.*

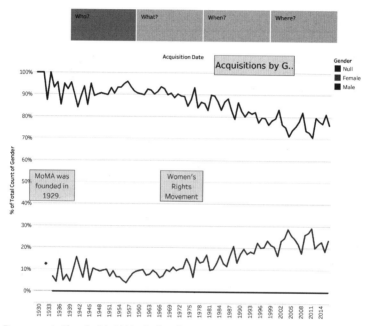

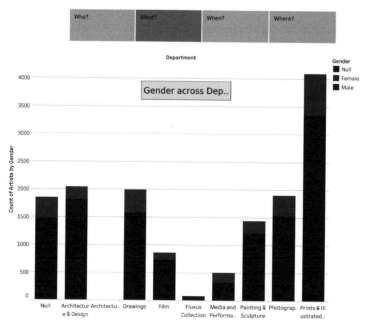

Representation in MoMA's Collections

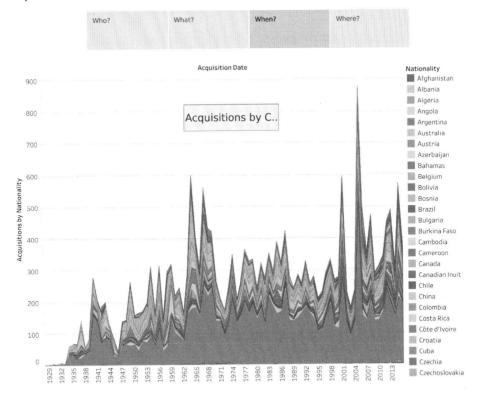

Representation in MoMA's Collections

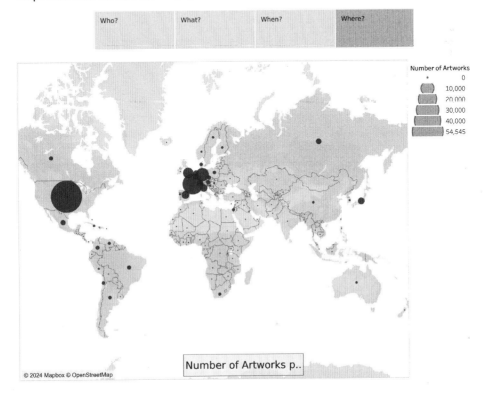

been confiscated by the Nazis in the early twentieth century. While the project is ongoing, the disclosure is one step toward greater accountability of this institution, among many others. Other museums, particularly in the United States, are also engaged in this work, as is the International Foundation for Art Research (IFAR), a not-for-profit educational and research organization that concerns itself with art theft and ownership.[57]

Thus, whether well-entrenched in digitization and open access work or just beginning, it is clear that the incorporation of digital practices, meaningfully and with intention, is one of many strategies that can, ultimately, lead to greater accountability within and beyond museums.

Collections That Reflect Diversity

The publication *ARTnews* has produced a list of the top two hundred collectors in the art world annually since 1990. The list's early days came on the heels of record-breaking sales at auction in the 1980s, followed by a recession in the 1990s. Beyond the transactional nature of collecting, collectors can show supports of artists and institutions, all the while balancing the care and stewardship of their own collections. Collectors, as shown through the earlier pages of this volume, have been perceived as interested individuals—perhaps, even, hoarders—storing works for themselves, and perhaps a museum who might, in the future, receive the collections through bequest of donation. However, the act of collecting is much more nuanced, particularly now, as institutions seem to diversify their collections. Collector and museum trustee Rodney Miller stated the importance of this work: "We all benefit from having all voices heard, and we should all do our part to make that happen."[58] Art collector and philanthropist Batia Ofer uses her collection to highlight feminist artists and to advance understanding of marginalized communities, social justice, and climate change concerns. She stated, "My collection methodology is deliberate, intentionally weaving connections and contrasts. . . . It is my aspiration to maintain a collection that remains vibrant, ever-evolving, and attuned to the current zeitgeist."[59]

Calls for change, however, have also been afoot for some time. The American Alliance of Museums (AAM) championed an initiative called *Facing Change*. At the annual meeting in 2019, Kippen de Alba Chu, board dhair, American Alliance of Museums, reminded attendees that how we see concerns and how we face situations—as individuals and as institutions—are informed by ourselves and our assumptions. He stated, "The way I see something is one way of seeing; the way I feel about someone is the way I feel; the way I remember an event is my memory of that event." She stated that the initiative and DEAI needs to be "sold" on people, noting that "the process of change is iterative. It requires inordinate amounts of patience, and it is extremely inefficient, but we can all easily recognize when there is a lack of leadership."[60]

To conclude, we can look to curator and Black contemporary art scholar Kimberly Drew, whose keynote at the AAM conference in 2019 posited, "I have always felt better when I have an opportunity to engage and learn with people; I am not a person who wants to be in homogenous spaces at all for any reason. I am always intrigued and empowered in spaces where I feel like there's many different narratives in the room. I think it is partially because there is always an opportunity to learn, but there is also an opportunity to be quiet, too. Because I think when you are the only person who is representing, or assuming to represent, a particular identity, you have to be so much louder. Right? And so how can we create a better orchestra symphony cacophony of sounds so that it's not just this dull murmur and then you're rolling through like a band. Because it's a lot of work."[61] Drew also sees the value in calling upon youth and artists to effect change. In an op-ed piece in *Teen Vogue* on June 2, 2020, she wrote, "For far too long, people across the globe have suffered due to the direct effects of colonialism, patriarchy, state violence, and so much more, but it is our art and creativity that have helped us to communicate our collective rage."[62]

Communication can lead to action, as museums aspire toward anti-racism, belonging, and coalition-building. As such, they can demonstrate they are *in motion*.

Notes

1. The term *anti-racism* is examined in Ibram X. Kendi's *How to Be an Antiracist* (New York: Random House, 2019).
2. Passages from Kendi's book. See also Ericka Taylor, "Ibram X. Kendi Says No One Is 'Not Racist.' So What Should We Do?" *NPR*, August 15, 2019, https://www.npr.org/2019/08/15/751070344/theres-no-such-thing-as-not-racist-in-ibram-x-kendis-how-to-be-an-antiracist.
3. For resources on museum activism, see Museum Activism and Social Justice (Fall 2020), https://docs.google.com/document/d/144CK_0UstimnQ4kuv5sSWyWKOR6kCCaXJyEHh-G8pyI and many of the named collectives in this section of the book.
4. Kimberly Drew, "What Should a Museum Look Like in 2020?" *Vanity Fair*, August 24, 2020, https://www.vanityfair.com/culture/2020/08/what-should-a-museum-look-like-in-2020.
5. Brandon quoted in Kimberly Drew, "What Should a Museum Look Like in 2020?" *Vanity Fair*, August 24, 2020, https://www.vanityfair.com/culture/2020/08/what-should-a-museum-look-like-in-2020.
6. Michael Brune, "Pulling Down Our Monuments," July 22, 2020, https://www.sierraclub.org/michael-brune/2020/07/john-muir-early-history-sierra-club.
7. This co-creative process was used for label writing in the 2019 exhibition 30 Americans: Race, History, Identity, Beauty, which presented American experiences as visualized by Jean-Michel Basquiat, Rashid Johnson, Kerry James Marshall, Mickalene Thomas, Hank Willis Thomas, Kara Walker, Carrie Mae Weems, and Kehinde Wiley. See Nelson-Atkins, *Museum of Art*, "30 Americans," https://nelson-atkins.org/exhibitions/30-americans/.
8. Jocelyn Edens, "Introducing a Frame of Mind: A New Podcast Takes a Hard Look at Race in America Through the Lens of the Nelson-Atkins Museum of Art," February 11, 2022, https://incluseum.com/2022/02/11/podcast-looks-at-race-in-america-nelson-atkins/.
9. Loic Tallon, "Holland, Amsterdam, Stedelijk Musuem," https://www.flickr.com/photos/27591534@N02/albums/72157617021503629/.
10. See the Minneapolis Institute of Art offerings: https://mobile.mia.yourcultureconnect.com/experiences, which includes an audio guide to the new exhibition, *In Our Hands: Native Photography, 1890 to Now*.
11. Ruth Tyson, "An Open Letter to the Union of Concerned Scientists: On Black Death, Black Silencing, and Black Fugitivity: An Affirmation of Black Life from a Concerned Black Human," https://docs.google.com/document/d/132Ow3_FYcTQdc73pyAe0V_IloIzq4nktYpZ-V4MZRTY/edit.
12. The statement may be found on the Incluseum website dated December 22, 2014: https://incluseum.com/2014/12/22/joint-statement-from-museum-bloggers-colleagues-on-ferguson-related-events/.
13. Museum consultant Adrianne Russell and historian Aleia Brown began using the hashtag #MuseumsRespondtoFerguson "to push museums and public historians to more thoughtfully engage race, racialized spaces and the history of state sanctioned violence." See Kami Fletcher, "#MuseumsRespondtoFerguson: Interview with Aleia Brown and Adrianne Russell," African American Intellectual History Society, September 29, 2016, https://www.aaihs.org/museumsrespondtoferguson-an-interview-with-aleia-brown-and-adrianne-russell/.
14. See Museums and Trust Report, available online https://www.aam-us.org/wp-content/uploads/2021/09/Museums-and-Trust-2021.pdf. Previous reports analyzing museum and the public's trust in them are listed on the American Alliance of Museum's website: https://www.aam-us.org/2021/09/30/museums-and-trust-2021/.
15. Definition from *Oxford Languages* via Google, December 1, 2023, https://www.google.com/search?channel=frsc&client=firefox-b-1-d&q=neutrality.
16. Mike Murawski, "Museums Are Not Neutral," *Art Museum Teaching*, August 31, 2017, updated July 2020, https://artmuseumteaching.com/2017/08/31/museums-are-not-neutral/. See also, La Tanya S. Autry and Mike Murawski, "Museums Are Not Neutral with Movement Co-Founders La Tanya S. Autry and Mike Murawski," interview by Paul Ferber, Monument Lab, Episode 26, May 14, 2020, https://monumentlab.com/podcast/museums-are-not-neutral-with-movement-co-founders-la-tanya-s-autry-and-mike-murawski.

17. La Tanya Autry and Mike Murawski, "Museums Are Not Neutral: We Are Stronger Together," *Panorama: Journal of the Association of Historians of American Art* 5:2 (Fall 2019): https://journalpanorama.org/article/public-scholarship/museums-are-not-neutral/.

18. Quotes from Murawski and Autry appear in Mike Murawski, "Museums Are Not Neutral," *Art Museum Teaching*, August 31, 2017, updated July 2020, https://artmuseumteaching.com/2017/08/31/museums-are-not-neutral/.

19. Nathan's blog, research, and practice focus on First Nations knowledges, languages, and histories. See https://archivaldecolonist.org/. On the point of neutrality, see Nathan Sentance, "Your Neutral Is Not Our Neutral," *Archival Decolonist*, January 18, 2018, https://archivaldecolonist.org/2018/01/18/your-neutral-is-not-our-neutral/.

20. Wilkening Consulting and American Alliance of Museums, *Audiences and Inclusion: A Primer for Cultivating More Inclusive Attitudes Among the Public* (Washington, D.C.: Wilkening Consulting and AAM, 2021). See https://www.aam-us.org/2021/02/09/audiences-and-inclusion-primer/.

21. The history is recorded by Elisabeth Callihan as the introduction to the MASS Action Toolkit published in 2017, which is available here: https://incluseum.com/2018/07/23/an-introduction-to-the-mass-action-toolkit-from-the-co-founder/.

22. Callihan points to a December 2014 museum bloggers' statement urging museums to respond to the crisis in Ferguson, which spawned the hashtag #MuseumsRespondToFerguson. A meeting the following year at AAM Atlanta in 2015 saw a convening (#MuseumWorkserSpeak) that also demanded action from museums to turn the social justice lens inward.

23. The tool kit was produced in the fall of 2017, and is available online: https://www.museumaction.org/resources.

24. The data is available here: https://docs.google.com/spreadsheets/d/1u--B15_Rf2v5yMoa59QI-JtqiV8eHyTtqbcJ00Ezou-g/edit#gid=863135589, which also links to all statements, organized by state: https://drive.google.com/drive/folders/1PJSzEZ5JT8rGAEIeANCq4Fxp_NQ_PZBV.

25. The criteria and links to data are available online. See MASS Action, "Museums and Anti-Racism: A Deeper Analysis," October 30, 2020, https://www.museumaction.org/massaction-blog/2020/10/30/museums-and-anti-racism-a-deeper-analysis.

26. As of the fall of 2023, the Twitter, Instagram, and website of MASS Action have stalled, with the latest blog posts from 2021 on institutional genealogy and calls to support the Museum Workers relief fund @MuseumAction, March 30, 2022, https://www.instagram.com/p/Cbu42ExrqJF/, and Museum Advocacy Day 2022, https://mwad2022.carrd.co/. The group's website and resources as well as data remain profoundly useful.

27. Museums Association, "Recommendations: Empowering Collections," 2019, https://www.museumsassociation.org/campaigns/collections/empowering-collections/recommendations-empowering-collections/#. The complete brochure from the program may be found here: https://media.museumsassociation.org/app/uploads/2020/06/11085829/MS1681-Empowering-collections__v8.pdf.

28. @WalkerArtCenter, June 3, 2020, https://twitter.com/walkerartcenter/status/1268224866303512576.

29. Kimberly Drew posts on Twitter/X as @museummammy. Her Tweet is quoted in Alex Greenberger and Tessa Solomon, "Major U.S. Museums Criticized for Responses to Ongoing George Floyd Protests," June 2, 2020, https://www.artnews.com/art-news/news/museums-controversy-george-floyd-protests-1202689494/.

30. Christine Anagnos, "Message from the Executive Director [of the AAMD]: Black Lives Matter," June 1, 2020, https://aamd.org/for-the-media/press-release/message-from-the-executive-director-black-lives-matter.

31. @Sirsargent, June 2, 2020, https://twitter.com/sirsargent/status/1267809646355587072.

32. IMLS, "Understanding the Social Wellbeing Impacts of the Nation's Libraries and Museums," 2021, 9.

33. Haitham Eid and Richard R. Janes, editors, *Museum Innovation: Building More Equitable, Relevant, and Impactful Museums* (London: Routledge, 2021).

34. Sarah A. Soule, Neil Malhotra, and Bernadette Clavier, "Defining Social Innovation," Stanford Graduate School of Business, https://www.gsb.stanford.edu/experience/about/centers-institutes/csi/defining-social-innovation. For more on museums and social innovation, see Haitham Eid's *Museum Innovation and Social Entrepreneurship: A New Model for a Challenging Era* (London: Routledge, 2019), and Robert R. Janes and Richard Sandell, *Museum Activism* (London: Routledge, 2019).

35. Haitham Eid and Melissa Forstrom, "Introduction," Haitham Eid and Richard R. Janes, editors, *Museum Innovation: Building More Equitable, Relevant, and Impactful Museums* (London: Routledge, 2021), 2.

36. It should be noted that the increase in number of positions in museums dedicated to providing strategic guidance in addressing DEI (Diversity, Equity, and Inclusion) is not alone an indicator of success or promise. Also, the American Alliance of Museums (AAM) announced, on February 2, 2017 (around 110 years after its founding), the appointment of its inaugural director of inclusion, Dr. Nicole Ivy.

37. Notes from American Alliance of Museums 2016 Session "Professional Collectives as New Leadership Models," presented by SHIFT (the collective). The presentation in New Orleans was made by Becky Aleman, Keonna Hendrick, Stephanie Johnson-Cunningham, PJ Policarpio, and Paula Santos of SHIFT.

38. See Keonna Hendrick, "About," https://keonnahendrick.squarespace.com/.

39. MASS Action "Toolkit," 2017, https://www.museumaction.org/s/TOOLKIT_10_2017.pdf.

40. The twenty-four attendees and participants in the initial convening are listed here: https://museumsandrace.org/history-of-museums-race/participant-list/.

41. The Museums and Race Report Card is available in PDF and Word, as well as English and Spanish, https://museumsandrace.org/2023/05/15/museums-and-race-report-card-now-in-word/. The categories are: governance, funding, representation, responsiveness, resources, transparency, and accountability. Within each, the team evaluates themselves over the past year—to celebrate excellence, challenge mistakes, and identify areas of growth.

42. The full statement is here: https://museumsandrace.org/2020/06/01/museums-race-statement-of-solidarity/.

43. See Etienne Wenger, Richard McDermott, and William M. Snyder, *Cultivating Communities of Practice: A Guide to Managing Knowledge* (Cambridge, MA: Harvard Business School Press, 2002), 1.

44. See Etienne Wenger-Trayner, Mark Fenton-O'Creevy, Steven Hutchinson, Chris Kubiak, and Beverly Wenger-Trayner, *Learning in Landscapes of Practice: Boundaries, Identity, and Knowledgeability in Practice-Based Learning* (New York: Routledge, 2014).

45. Joanne Heyler was one of four directors interviewed in this piece: See Victoria L. Valentine, Constance Grady, and Jen Trolio, "Plight at the Museum," *Vox*, November 20, 2020, https://www.vox.com/the-highlight/21545993/broad-museum-african-american-coronavirus.

46. Joanne Heyler was one of four directors interviewed in this piece: See Victoria L. Valentine, Constance Grady, and Jen Trolio, "Plight at the Museum," *Vox*, November 20, 2020, https://www.vox.com/the-highlight/21545993/broad-museum-african-american-coronavirus.

47. George Sparks was one of four museum directors interviewed. See Victoria L. Valentine, Constance Grady, and Jen Trolio, "Plight at the Museum," *Vox*, November 20, 2020, https://www.vox.com/the-highlight/21545993/broad-museum-african-american-coronavirus.

48. Nwaka Onwusa was one of four museum directors interviewed. See Victoria L. Valentine, Constance Grady, and Jen Trolio, "Plight at the Museum," *Vox*, November 20, 2020, https://www.vox.com/the-highlight/21545993/broad-museum-african-american-coronavirus. Nwaka Onwusa served as chief curator at the Rock and Roll Hall of Fame from 2020–2023, when she became creative director at the Hip Hop Museum, slated to open in the Bronx in late 2025. See uhhm.org.

49. The pillars are defined here: https://oursharedfuture.si.edu/about/our-pillars; the Smithsonian podcast is here: https://www.si.edu/sidedoor. Events are held in conjunction with the Smithsonian initiative, many of which are online and onsite at the museum. An exception is the convening "Museums Advancing Racial Justice" in St Paul, Minnesota, in April 2024, at the Science Museum of Minnesota, the institution that organized the exhibition *RACE: Are We So Different?* in 2007, which went on a national tour at sixty cultural institutions. The Science Museum of Minnesota (SMM) has a long history

of facilitating learning opportunities focused on dismantling systems of oppression and creating equitable change. See https://new.smm.org/marj. For the film festival, see https://new.smm.org/marj.

50. National Museum of Natural History, "Recovering Voices," https://naturalhistory.si.edu/research/anthropology/programs/recovering-voices.

51. For information on "In Our Hands," see https://new.artsmia.org/stories/in-our-hands-turns-the-camera-around-puts-native-photographers-in-control; for "Making Her Mark," see https://artbma.org/exhibition/making-her-mark-a-history-of-women-artists-in-europe-1400-1800/press. The latter show travels to the Art Gallery of Ontario in the spring of 2024.

52. Steven McIntosh, "British Museum Was Victim of Inside Job, George Osborne Says," *BBC*, October 18, 2023, https://www.bbc.com/news/entertainment-arts-67144607.

53. "Open Access Image Libraries—A Handy List," February 18, 2020, https://www.apollo-magazine.com/open-access-image-libraries-a-handy-list/. In addition, some collections have been shared with Wikimedia Commons. See the National Gallery of Art, Washington: https://commons.wikimedia.org/wiki/Commons:NGA.

54. The Met Museum's open access dataset may be found here: https://github.com/metmuseum/openaccess, while the images may be found here: https://www.metmuseum.org/art/collection. As of this writing, Github has the data for 470,000 works, while The Met collections media reflect 490,000 works.

55. Smithsonian Institution Open Access, https://www.si.edu/openaccess.

56. John Paul Titlow, "How a 145-Year-Old Art Museum Stays Relevant in the Smartphone Age," February 29, 2016, https://www.fastcompany.com/3057236/how-a-145-year-old-art-museum-stays-relevant-in-the-smartphone-age.

57. See Cleveland Museum of Art, "Nazi-Era Provenance," https://www.clevelandart.org/art/collections/nazi-era-provenance. Other museums engaged in this work include The Met, https://www.metmuseum.org/about-the-met/policies-and-documents/nazi-era-provenance-research; the Museum of Modern Art, https://www.metmuseum.org/about-the-met/policies-and-documents/nazi-era-provenance-research; and the Art Institute of Chicago, https://www.moma.org/collection/provenance/. A list of museums engaged in this work in the United States and abroad is featured here: https://www.metmuseum.org/about-the-met/provenance-research-resources/museum-provenance-research-projects.

58. Maximilíano Durón, "The Changing Face of Collecting: An Introduction to the 2022 Edition of the ARTnews Top 200 Collectors," *ARTnews*, October 5, 2022, https://www.artnews.com/art-news/news/top-200-collectors-issue-2022-introduction-1234641726/. An exploration of Miller's earlier colleting was captured in an interview with Rute Fine, curator at the National Gallery of Art, in 2014: https://www.nga.gov/audio-video/audio/collecting-african-american-art-x1.html.

59. Maximilíano Durón, "What Even Is a Collector These Days? An Introduction to the 2023 Edition of the ARTnews Top 200 Collectors List," *ARTnews*, October 17, 2023, https://www.artnews.com/art-news/news/top-200-collectors-issue-2023-introduction-1234682610/.

60. Kippen de Alba Chu, "Introduction to Keynote, AAM 2019," May 28, 2019, https://www.aam-us.org/2019/05/28/aam2019-keynote-kimberly-drew/.

61. Kimberly Drew, "Keynote, AAM 2019," May 28, 2019, https://www.aam-us.org/2019/05/28/aam2019-keynote-kimberly-drew/. Drew served as social media manager of The Met and now curator at Pace Gallery. She started her blog, BlackContemporaryArt on Tumblr, in 2011 and amassed a survey of five thousand artists, some of which were transferred into her edited anthology, *Black Futures*, which was published in 2020. See *Black Futures*, edited by Kimberly Drew and Jenna Wortham, New York: Penguin Random House, 2019.

62. Kimberly Drew, "Kimberly Drew's Book 'This Is What I know About Art' Drops Educational Gems," *Teen Vogue*, June 2, 2020, https://www.teenvogue.com/story/kimberly-drew-this-is-what-i-know-about-art-book.

14

Risk Taking, Risk Aversion, and Leadership

Prior to the COVID-19 pandemic, the Institute of Museum and Library Services (IMLS) began an examination of social well-being (positive social health) as measured through ten dimensions from 2018–2020 in every county in the United States. These ten social well-being dimensions included economic well-being, ethnic and economic diversity, housing opportunities, institutional connection, cultural assets, school effectiveness, health access, personal health, and personal security. These dimensions were used to identify associations between the presence and usage of libraries and museums and multiple dimensions of social well-being. Then, twelve libraries and twelve museums in the United States were selected as sites for measuring social well-being during the study period. In 2021, the IMLS issued a report focused on the "social well-being impact" of libraries and museums in the United States.[1] From the outset, the report notes the role of libraries and museums as spaces of informal learning, creativity, and empathy: "Local libraries and museums are actively involved in animating social and institutional connections that catalyze the creativity, ingenuity, and empathy within their communities in ways that promote personal and social wellbeing. These unique features of libraries and museums make them critical institutions to advance ongoing efforts to promote inclusion and equity for historically underrepresented populations, particularly residents of color."[2]

Some of the interviews were gathered during the height of the first year of the pandemic, the summer and fall of 2020, seeking to understand: how their institutions were responding to the pandemic; the greatest challenges they were facing in terms of service delivery and sustainability; the opportunities they perceived for what lay ahead; and how their institutions were responding to the elevated awareness of racial inequality in American society.[3]

Museums experimented with traditional methods while experimenting with new or previously niche technologies. For instance, they prepared "takeaway" or "DIY" activities that individuals and families could enjoy, including coloring sheets and puzzles, as well as takeaway kits that could be used to supplement the online learning K-12 students were enduring. Some museums pivoted to virtual platforms, as explained below, both to connect audiences with content, but also to engage people and build a sense of community.

Pivoting

The COVID-19 pandemic impacted every kind of institution. With even the most heavily endowed and publicly funded museums dependent upon admission ticket sales, income at museums evaporated. Museums faced the hurdle of economic struggles from the pandemic. But this was not new—as the financial recession of 2008 had revealed the vulnerabilities of museum revenue; they were reliant upon visitation and onsite purchases, such as membership, admissions, and store and restaurant profits, in addition to external support from financial contributions, government allocations, or foundation gifts.[4]

In the seemingly "early days" of the pandemic, museums registered a sense of responsibility to engage with their audiences, and they did so by bringing content online in a variety of ways. As Tim Ritchie, president of the Museum of Science in Boston, explained: "Within a couple of weeks, we were spinning up what now we would call 'minimum viable products.' . . . It was not that great at first. But people were hungry [for it], and they tuned in."[5]

Of course, the revenue loss is only part of the concern, with museums being forced to take cost-cutting measures, including the layoff of employees. The ASTC (Association of Science and Technology Centers), for example, gathered data from March 2020 through June 2021, and has conservatively estimated a loss of one billion dollars in revenue from museums.[6] Throughout the pandemic, museums and their associations pleaded with the federal government and grantors to support museums due to the impact of the pandemic on the institutions and their abilities to enact their missions and serve their audiences. A series of applications and pleas were made, including a multi-party-authored letter sent on January 12, 2022, on behalf of the American Alliance of Museums (AAM), the American Association for State and Local History (AASL), the American Public Gardens Association, the Association of African American Museums (AAAM), the Association of Art Museum Directors (AAMD), the Association of Children's Museums (ACA), the Association of Science Museum Directors, the Association of Science and Technology Centers (ASTC), and the Association of Zoos and Aquariums (AZA). Their letter, while asking for an opportunity to seek funding through a particular funding stream, ultimately pointed out the significant role that museums played during the pandemic as "essential community infrastructure." Museums performed a variety of roles that positioned them as "crucial to their communities' resiliency during the pandemic—from supporting vaccination to hosting food distribution."[7]

The role of museums was made abundantly clear, and their letter serves as evidence of all of the functions—and more—that museums fulfill. They wrote: "During the COVID-19 pandemic, museums across the country are contributing to the ongoing education of our country's children by providing lesson plans, online learning opportunities, and drop-off learning kits to teachers and families. They are using their outdoor spaces to grow and donate produce to area food banks, as well as maintaining these spaces for individuals to safely relax, enjoy nature, and recover from the mental health impacts of social isolation. They provided access to childcare and meals to families of health care workers and first responders, have donated their PPE and scientific equipment to fight COVID-19, and are serving as vaccination centers."[8]

Programming during COVID-19

The California Academy of Sciences in San Francisco turned its program called NightLife—a regular Thursday night event that charged from ten to twenty dollars for admission to the museum and billed as a space for "Creatures + cocktails. Music + movements. Science + spectacle. Culture grows in the dark"—into a free weekly online program called NightSchool. The first event was streamed on YouTube on April 2, 2020, and it aimed at giving an interactive event featuring scientists, artists, and musicians, including Nigel Sussman, a featured scientific illustrator who masterfully drew a hammerhead shark with an audience watching and commenting in real time. Bringing together fantasy and science, Nigel drew a shark with a cocktail, spinning tunes on turntable in the galaxy. This hilarious fiction had the audience's attention and engagement. Viewer Brett Chavez chimed in with a call out to the shark's potential name: "DJ Sharkie, serving the smoothest beats in the galaxy." Others commented on the reality of COVID. Commenter LW stated, "You should give him a N95 mask," and Jessica Chow noted, "If a shark wore a N95 mask how would it look." The question caught Nigel's attention, and he complied, giving the shark PPE (personal protective equipment) of his own, though he points out that an N95 wouldn't fit on a hammerhead shark and would pose challenges with filtration underwater.[9] Streamed on YouTube, with archived programs viewable online through a playlist, the new offering of NightSchool has remained an opportunity in addition to its antecedent, which has resumed. Clearly focusing on different objectives, modalities, and purposes, NightLife and NightSchool speak to the ways in which museums saw new roles for themselves during and after the pandemic.[10]

Museums were also well-suited to address the need for clear, science-based information about the COVID-19 pandemic. Collaborating with scientists on staff and nearby medical experts at Brown

NightLife & Friends: A Virtual Event

California Academy of Sciences   🔔 Subscribed ∨   👍 203   👎   ↪ Share   ✂ Clip   ⊞+ Save   ⋯
225K subscribers

During the pandemic, the California Academy of Sciences in San Francisco turned its program called NightLife into a free weekly online program, dubbed NightSchool. During the first installment on April 2, 2020, Nigel Sussman, a featured scientific illustrator, masterfully drew a hammerhead shark with an audience watching and commenting in real time. Bringing together fantasy and science, Nigel drew a shark with a cocktail, spinning tunes on turntable in the galaxy. This hilarious fiction had the audience's attention and engagement. Viewers chimed in with comments throughout this segment and during the rest of the show. Archived episodes are available on YouTube. This and other programming by the museum, including NightLife and NightSchool, speak to the ways in which museums saw new roles for themselves during and after the pandemic.

Screencap from YouTube video with permission of California Academy of Sciences.

University, the Museum of Science in Boston interviewed public health expert Dr. Ashish Jha, posing more than five hundred questions about the pandemic. Using these questions and answers as the basis, they worked with the company StoryFile to create a conversational video AI interactive that allows viewers online the opportunity to "Ask a Virtual Expert" by posing questions about the coronavirus and getting a response keyed to their question.[11] Other institutions responded by having "explainers" about the virus. In addition, some institutions used their websites to communicate how staff share their expertise through research related to the virus.[12]

Like other industries, museums have shown their resilience post-COVID, as well as their adaptability. According to Steven Snyder, president and CEO of San Diego's Fleet Science Center, COVID has enabled museums to show how nimble and agile they are and how they can truly serve their audiences: "We need to double down on this idea of wanting to respond at all times to what the community needs. . . . It's also a proof of concept that we're not locked to our building. Science centers never have been."[13]

Adding to the shifting parameters for museums, Smithsonian Institution secretary Lonnie Bunch noted changes in approaches that would still yield onsite visitors. As former director of the National Museum of African American History and Culture, the newest Smithsonian to have opened prior to the pandemic, Bunch was aware of the need to temper excitement to be onsite. There he implemented a ticket-method that helped to control crowds. Now, timed tickets are much more common in an effort to control crowds while also enabling connection with others in museum galleries again. Seeing a positive effect of these efforts, Bunch also reflected on the museum's learnings in the eight months since the pandemic began. "By making the crowd smaller, we really are enriching the visitor experience. At the Smithsonian, you tend to have to elbow your way around to see something. But now, while it means that fewer people will see an exhibit—although we can really replicate a lot of that virtually—the in-person visitor experience will be even better."[14]

George Sparks, head of the Denver Museum of Nature & Science, a six-hundred-thousand-square-foot natural history museum, stated the broader vision that museums would need to take post-COVID, in terms of factoring in audiences across technology. In remarking upon the museum's responsiveness to the community and vice versa, he noted that by November 2020, the museum had reached one hundred thousand different devices digitally with programing around science and policy. He also reported on the museum's use of appreciative inquiry to learn from their audiences and to build exhibit content, context, and experiences in community: "With appreciative inquiry, you go to the communities and try to gain their trust by just listening and figuring out, what are they really good at? What do they value? And how do we build upon that? Once you make that transition, that's a really big shift. And as part of that shift, our communities feel comfortable coming here because they see their fingerprints on what we're doing."[15]

Institutional Change through Partnership

Museums are respected and valued, as reports from American Alliance of Museums, the Institute of Museum and Library Services (IMLS), and others note. A review of museum data files[16] or a scan of their websites will point readers to numerous data points and executive summaries as to the value of museums in their communities—even pre-pandemic. For instance, in 2016, the Institute of Museum and Library Services (IMLS) embarked on a new Community Catalyst Initiative (CCI) "to elevate the capacity of museums and libraries to collaborate with local partners and advance common goals related to the health and vitality of the communities they serve." These initiatives included grant making and technical assistance; developing a field-level "theory of change" to show how museums and libraries promote positive change in their communities; and supporting research about museums and libraries and social well-being. A key message from the report is evidence that museums and libraries engage with "community concerns and visions through their programmatic activities and strategic partnerships."[17]

As we saw in Chapter 7, audience-centered institutions have renewed the work of John Cotton Dana, Elaine Heumann Gurian, and Stephen Weil, and they have fostered a new generation of leaders, among them Nina Simon, from the Santa Cruz Museum of Art & History, who ushered in a movement to listen to the community, to open their doors to new visitors, partners, and experiences, and to change. In seven years, the museum increased its attendance by nine times, membership by three times, and budget by four times, while also reflecting more diversity. It became *of*, *by*, and *for* the community of which it was a part: Santa Cruz County.[18] That museum, and other museums as well, were demonstrating their capacity to transition—to be about *somebody*, in the words of Stephen Weil, and to be *of*, *by*, and *for* all.[19]

As a direct result of the transformation of this single institution, and thinking of the Santa Cruz Museum of Art & History as its incubator, Nina Simon launched an initiative called "Of/By/For All," as a distributed network of individuals working to "connect, strengthen, and accelerate inclusive practices around the world" in 2018. The result was a suite of three pilot projects involving museums,

OF/BY/FOR ALL provides resources, such as a free tool to help organizations take action, both externally and internally, during times of crisis. Other resources include a community issue exhibition toolkit. *Courtesy OF/BY/FOR ALL, https://blog.ofbyforall.org/tools/a-framework-for-action.*

libraries, performing arts organizations, parks, community centers, health centers, and cultural centers working toward community involvement. Out of these three waves of activity, and relying on feedback along the way, the Change Network was born as an "ecosystem of activists, artists, and changemakers" seeking to work in partnership and engage communities. Their role is to help make civil and cultural organizations become more inclusive.[20]

Such examples point to new ways of thinking about change and how museums might learn from these practices and the embrace of non-hierarchical structure, collaboration, and community. As noted earlier in this volume, in the address of social movements, and in particular Occupy, according to marketing scholar Sonya Grier, membership in such activist groups "was broad enough to capture all the associations the American public could generate at the time. . . . Even absent a unifying strategic action plan, Occupy Wall Street had the legs to spread to different societal groups in a way that continues to the present."[21]

Many other examples of distributed networks and thought leadership are included in this chapter and throughout this third part of the book. In addition, it's worth noting that leadership is not a cookie-cutter quality that someone possesses.

Institutional Change through Leadership

Insight about leadership may be gleaned from a Zoom gathering held during the early days of COVID (May 20, 2020) with the Museum Studies Network, a professional network of the American Alliance of Museums. This was the second such gathering launched during the pandemic that I coordinated that focused on reading and books. It seemed everyone had time to read or longed to have time to read as a diversion.

This session was moderated by museologist Laura-Edythe Coleman, who was joined by panelists Melanie A. Adams (director of the Smithsonian Anacostia Community Museum), Dina Bailey (CEO of Mountain Top Vision), Mike Murawski (founding editor of ArtMuseumTeaching.com and the co-producer of #MuseumsAreNotNeutral), and Richard Urban (then digital asset manager and strategist at the Corning Museum of Glass). Their suggested readings (gathered at the end of this chapter) are prompts on the topic "Leadership Books for Highs and Lows." The recording is available online.[22]

Coupled with the book list, and the topics covered in this section of the book, we may ask: What kind of leadership is needed in museums today? Certainly, leadership with agility, resilience, and the ability to lead, follow, and be in community during times of crisis.

Testing Leadership: Censorship and Self-Censorship

Secretary of the Smithsonian Institution Lonnie Bunch has articulated the function of museums as beyond collections, but a space where wisdom, knowledge, and communication can be fostered—all the while reflecting the United States. In November 2020, he stated this by referencing the will of museums and their role in communities: "Museums need to recognize that it's not enough to be a place of beauty. We have to be a place of insight. We've got to be a place that gives people tools to help them grapple with the challenges of today, whether it's helping people grapple with race, or a better understanding of the power of science. The biggest challenge is making sure museums reflect America. Museums say they believe in that. I do not believe all museums have the will to make the changes they need to make. It's the will." Importantly, Bunch noted that museums cannot become community centers, "but they ought to be at the center of their communities."[23]

How do museums do this in times of crisis?

An example is the calculated postponement of an exhibition focused on the work of Philip Guston (1913–1980), a Canadian-American, Jewish artist, featuring more than 150 of his paintings and drawings over his fifty-year career. Organized by the National Gallery of Art, Washington; the Museum of Fine Arts, Boston; Tate Modern, London; and the Museum of Fine Arts, Houston, the exhibit *Philip Guston Now* included twenty-four works referred to as the "Klan paintings" that depict a figure covered by a white hood that appears to be a garment reminiscent of the Ku Klux Klan.[24]

The museums authored a joint statement outlining the postponement until 2024, "until a time we think that the powerful message of social and racial justice that is at the centre of Philip Guston's work can be more clearly interpreted." Immediately, controversy ensued from artists and art critics who simultaneously saw the decision as a cowardly move, shifting away from engaging with challenging works of art (in the case of the former), and a necessary step back during double pandemics of COVID and the racial justice protests that began in the summer of 2020 and continued in the United States and beyond (in the case of the latter).

The key reason for the postponement was further interpretation and contextualization in light of the current moment. However, as Mark Godfrey, a curator at Tate Modern in London who co-organized the exhibition, noted, Guston made images of Klansmen in 1930 "to draw attention to their horrific activities" and later in the 1960s to comment on evil, when blatant or in disguise.[25] Godfrey found the decision "extremely patronizing"[26] to audiences because it assumes that they are not able to understand and appreciate the nuance of Guston's works—an act that caused him to be suspended by, and eventually to part ways with, the museum.[27]

It seemed, however, that artists "got" the work and banded together to express their discontent with their decision. Led by art critic and author Barry Schwabsky and artist Adrian Piper, a group of artists, critics, and scholars penned an open letter within hours of the announcement. It was distributed via email with the *Brooklyn Rail*, after which it began racking up signatures from artists, curators, and dealers, climbing from one hundred to twentyfold. The letter, in short, admonished the museums for their decision to postpone the Guston show. It took issue with the reason for postponement, noting: "Rarely has there been a better illustration of 'white' culpability than in these powerful men and women's apparent feeling of powerlessness to explain to their public the true power of an artist's work—its capacity to prompt its viewers, and the artist too, to troubling reflection and self-examination. But the people who run our great institutions do not want trouble. They fear controversy. They lack faith in the intelligence of their audience. And they realize that to remind museum-goers of white supremacy today is not only to speak to them about the past, or events somewhere else. It is also to raise uncomfortable questions about museums themselves—about their class and racial foundations. For this reason, perhaps, those who run the museums feel the ground giving way beneath their feet. If they feel that in four years, 'all this will blow over,' they are mistaken. The tremors shaking us all will never end until justice and equity are installed. Hiding away images of the KKK will not serve that end. Quite the opposite. And Guston's paintings insist that justice has never yet been achieved."[28]

Perhaps the rush to cancel proved to be untenable self-censorship. For whereas censorship in museums involves the suppression of ideas by any entity that has the power to do so, self-censorship is the suppression of ideas by an individual during the creative process or an institution during the exhibition development process. It can be more difficult to identify as it often blends into the work process.[29]

As art critic Jerry Saltz reported in *Vulture*, the act of postponement was both right and wrong. Questioning the censorship of these works, and not others, Saltz asks, "Each of these museums probably has things on their walls and in their halls right now that are as disturbing and contestable as the Guston paintings. If the show went on as planned, and the works produced the protests its curators apparently expect, presumably the institutions would feel obligated to state, 'We will remove those works and no longer exhibit such art that perpetuates racist, sexism, xenophobia, and ideologies that promote hate and pain.' This sets a bad precedent." He also points to the artist's daughter, Musa Mayer, who called upon the paintings as important at this historical moment of the national reckoning on race in 2020. "These [Klan] paintings meet the moment we are in today. The danger is not in looking at Philip Guston's work, but in looking away." Isn't this what museums are to do, in the twenty-first century: to ask questions and to ask audiences to confront issues today?[30]

The controversy, postponement, and open letter drew much attention, with press coverage in the *New York Times*, the *New Yorker*, the *Washington Post*, the *Art Newspaper*, *Artnet*, and on CNN, as well as on podcasts.[31] Within a few weeks of the initial announcement and joint letter from the organizing museums, the decision was made to move the date of the postponement to 2022, rather than 2024. The postponement took into account the surging racial justice protests across the country and the possibility that twenty-four of the Guston works featuring imagery of the Ku Klux Klan risked being "misinterpreted" and needed to be better contextualized for the current political moment, and thoughtfully approached.

Further, the director of the National Gallery of Art said that the exhibition is part of a larger, broader series of actions on behalf of her museum, and part of that is not having a White artist explain racism. In an interview with Julia Halperin of *Artnet* (October 6, 2020), director Kaywin Feldman stated, "I would stress that I'm absolutely committed to doing this exhibition and I believe in Philip Guston. I'm not sure that I would argue that the public needs a white artist to explain racism to them right now. That, combined with the meager track record that the National Gallery has of showing and engaging artists of color, makes it difficult that one of our first major exhibitions about racism is from a white perspective."[32] Yet, the decision to delay the retrospective was called out as self-censorship fueled by fear of controversy, even as the institutions countered that the museums were still committed to the exhibition.

The exhibition did go on view at the MFA Boston in mid-2022, with stops at the four locations through early 2024. At the National Gallery, attention was drawn in the online summary of the show: "As Guston contemplated his complicity in the injustices of his time, he made 'self-portraits' of artists in Klan hoods in works such as *The Studio* (1969)."[33]

This case study illuminates potential issues in self-censorship, as in this case where the pressure to self-censor seemed to stem from risk aversion. To address this, museum studies scholar Janet Marstine proposes the concept of "craftsmanship" to understand how practitioners might negotiate self-censorship: it presents the ethical navigation of censoring pressure as a skill to be nurtured and honed and acknowledges one's agency.[34] Self-censorship is not synonymous with controversy, however. Nor is it meant to signal the diminishing of voices. It is intended to be a signal to commit to working thoughtfully and inclusively, even if at a different timetable than initially established.

Other Examples of Postponement or Cancelation

But, as Tim Schneider points out in *Artnet*, it is "impossible to perfectly safeguard any artwork or idea from criticism. No matter how much time you take, you could *always* have done more. And this inconvenient truth is precisely what worries me so much about how this episode is now poised to play out in the culture sector."[35] Schneider also connects the postponement with evidences of recent missteps between museums and their exhibitions and publics: the 2017 Whitney Biennial, where White artist Dana Schutz portrayed Emmett Till in her painting *Open Casket*; Sam Durant's installation at the Walker Art Center in Minneapolis in 2017, which references the largest mass execution of Indigenous people in Mankato, Minnesota, in 1862; Mexican American artist Vincent Valdez's paintings of Klan and burning mattresses, respectively in *The City I* and *The City II*, on view at the Blanton Museum of Art at the University of Texas, Austin, in 2018 (after being postponed for a year); and Afro-Latino artist Shaun Leonardo's exhibition of charcoal drawings of police killings of Black and Latino boys and men, *The Breath of Empty Space*, was canceled by MoCA Cleveland in 2020.[36]

Thinking about each of these examples, and many others perhaps, it is easy to question the boundaries of censorship and self-censorship. There are no easy solutions on what to do and how to move forward. The exhibition of these works and the controversies surrounding them demonstrate the importance of working with artists and, when possible, including them in engagement with community members ahead of exhibition openings and to frame artwork without censoring the artist's vision.

In the case of Sam Durant's *Scaffold*, which ignited protests among Dakota Sioux activists in Minneapolis, it seemed as though, according to journalist Andrea K. Scott, that "Durant and the Walker's [then-director Olga Viso] have conceded in heartfelt open letters this week . . . that they failed to imagine an audience for 'Scaffold' that wasn't white."[37] The work was dismantled and burned, in conversation with the artist.

The museum posted an open letter outlining the museum's intent to move forward and acknowledgment of its missteps to *The Circle*, a Native American publication devoted to news and arts. Director Viso established a route of communication between community members, the artist, and the museum. The following week, the Walker announced that *Scaffold* would be dismantled that day, and the wood would later be burned, at another site, in a private Dakota ceremony. Viso resigned from her position as executive director of the Walker Art Center soon after. In 2019, the center launched an open call directed at Native artists for a public art commission to be located at the Minneapolis Sculpture Garden or the Walker grounds. Angela Two Stars was commissioned to create a piece for the space—an act that was one of many part commitments made by the museum to Dakota elders during the mediation process that led to the removal of Durant's sculpture.[38]

Such unfolding of events show how collections—in this case, public art—do not transcend time and place, thus calling upon museums (as institutions) to think critically and specifically about the works they put on view. Groundwork must be done, as well as connection, as well as awareness of the positionality of the artists, the institutions, and their leadership.

Flourishing in Museums

As made clear in this chapter, risk taking, risk aversion, and leadership are critical to museum work. Done well, these facets set museums up to survive, and even to thrive. But is something greater possible—for "to thrive" assumes (perhaps merely) growth or development? Can museums truly *flourish*—for "to flourish" means to grow—and do so impressively, successfully, and with enthusiasm?

Such robust activity requires involvement of all—not solely the executive team or upper leadership—and also an interweaving between reflection and practice. *Flourishing* is an approach that is neither top-down nor bottom-up; nor is it 360-degrees. Developed and presented in Kiersten F. Latham and Brenda Cowan in 2024, the "Flourishing Museum Framework" offers a model for reflection and practice around six themes: courage, transformation, care, optimism, gratitude, and delight.

Cornerstones of the framework are principles of abundance-thinking and strength-based appreciative inquiry, much like the framework that George Sparks mentioned above, in using appreciative inquiry to learn from their audiences and to build exhibit content, context, and experiences in community. The same approach can be used *within* the museum and *for* the museum. Together with the concept of flourishing, models for leadership, collaboration, and sustainability emerge.[39]

In this spirit of reflection and flourishing, this chapter ends with a look back at the first edition of this very book. Published in 1978, and authored by Edward P. Alexander (see his biography at the close of this book), *Museums in Motion* displayed "the self-awareness that comes from contemplating where we are and how we got to be that way."[40] At that time, the field of museum studies was in its early days. Each subsequent edition of *Museums in Motion* in 2008, 2017, and now in 2024, has continued to reflect on museums, where they are, and how they got to be this way. With this revision, in particular, the chapters in this book have laid a foundation for reflecting on museums and positing a future for them.

So, take this notion of flourishing with you, into the final chapter of this volume, and into the work of museums. Bring with you the courage, transformation, care, optimism, gratitude, and delight you possess. They are *your assets* that *you give* to others: in sum, they are *our assets*, which comprise our shared museum communities.

Supplement to Chapter 14: Book List

Museums responded to COVID, and so did Museum Studies courses, undergraduate programs, and graduate programs. Faculty and professionals found community in the Museum Studies Network of the American Alliance of Museums, where the group organized a series of three talks and open to all. The first, held on March 25, 2020—within two weeks of the COVID-19 lockdown beginning in the United States—was called a "shelfie," as a quasi-*porte manteau* of "shelf" and "selfie" and aimed to look at our ubiquitous bookshelves. (Yes, eyeing someone's bookshelf as part of their Zoom backdrop was a "thing" during COVID!).

This inaugural webinar offered a discussion of museum studies resources, including but not limited to, books and other traditional publications, as well as other resources such as blogs and websites. A second session was held several weeks later (May 20, 2020) and aimed to share leadership books for highs and lows. The lists of the books from these sessions are included here as a way of sharing what museum professionals, leaders, and changemakers read. They are not endorsements, but merely a starting point for your own exploration.

The following texts were recommended by panelist and attendees during an online gathering of museum studies faculty and community on March 25, 2020:

AASLH Technical Leaflets.
Adair, Bill, editor. *Letting Go?: Sharing Historical Authority in a User-Generated World.* Walnut Creek: Left Coast Press, 2011.
Adair, Joshua G., and Amy K. Levin. *Museums, Sexuality, and Gender Activism,* 2020.
Alexander, Edward P., Mary Alexander, and Juilee Decker. *Museums in Motion: An Introduction to the History and Functions of Museums.* Lanham, MD: Rowman & Littlefield, for the AASLH, 2017.
Ames, Kenneth L., Barbara Franco, and L. Thomas Frye. *Ideas and Images: Developing Interpretive History Exhibits.* Walnut Creek, CA: AltaMira Press, 1999.

Anderson, Maxwell Lincoln. *Antiquities: What Everyone Needs to Know*. New York: Oxford UP, 2017.

Baldwin, Joan H., and Anne W. Ackerson. *Women in the Museum: Lessons from the Workplace*. New York: Routledge, 2017.

Brooks, Geraldine, and Edwina Wren. *People of the Book* (fiction). New York: Viking, 2008.

Buck, Rebecca A., Jean Allman Gilmore, and the American Association of Museums. *MRM5: Museum Registration Methods*. Washington, DC: AAM Press, American Association of Museums, 2010.

Coles, Robert. "The Art Museum and the Pressures of Society." *On Understanding Art Museums*, edited by Sherman E. Lee. Englewood Cliffs, NJ: Prentice Hall, 1975, 185–202.

Duncan, Carol. "Civilizing Rituals: Inside Public Art Museums." London: Routledge, 1995.

Fraser, Andrea. *2016 in Museums, Money, and Politics*. Cambridge: The MIT Press, 2018.

Graff, Garrett M. *The Only Plane in the Sky: An Oral History of 9/11*. Waterville: Thorndike Press, 2020.

Gurian, Elaine Heumann. *Civilizing the Museum: The Collected Writings of Elaine Heumann Gurian*. London: Routledge, 2007.

Hamburger, Jeffrey F. *Nuns as Artists: The Visual Culture of a Medieval Convent*. Berkeley, Calif.: University of California Press, 1997.

Harrison, Victoria S., Anna Bergqvist, and Gary Kemp. *Philosophy and Museums: Essays on the Philosophy of Museums*. Cambridge: Cambridge University Press, 2016.

Hein, Hilde S. *Museum in Transition: A Philosophical Perspective*. Washington, D.C.: Smithsonian Institution Press, 2000.

Jones-Rogers, Stephanie E. *They Were Her Property: White Women as Slave Owners in the American South*. New Haven: Yale University Press, 2020.

Karp, Ivan, and F. Lavington. *Exhibiting Cultures: The Poetics and Politics of Museum Display*. Washington, D.C.: Smithsonian Institution Press, 1991.

Kirshenblatt-Gimblett, Barbara. *Destination Culture: Tourism, Museums, and Heritage*. Berkeley, Calif.: University of California Press, 2009.

Laszlo, Christopher, Judy Brown, John Ehrenfeld, Mary Gorham, Ilma Barros-Pose, Linda Robson, Roger Saillant, Dave Sherman, and Paul Werder. *Flourishing Enterprise the New Spirit of Business*. Stanford, Calif.: Stanford Business Books, an imprint of Stanford University Press, 2014.

Laudun, John. *The Amazing Crawfish Boat*. Jackson: University of Mississippi Press, 2016.

Lee, Ingrid Fetell. *Joyful: The Surprising Power of Ordinary Things to Create Extraordinary Happiness*. New York: Little, Brown Spark, 2020.

Lubar, Steven D. *Inside the Lost Museum: Curating, Past and Present*. Cambridge: Harvard University Press, 2018. https://doi.org/10.4159/9780674982901.

Oldfield, Molly. *The Secret Museum*. New York: Harper Collins, 2013.

Putnam, James. *Art and Artifact: The Museum as Medium*. London: Thames and Hudson, 2009.

Schwarzer, Marjorie. *Riches, Rivals, and Radicals: A History of Museums in the United States*. Lanham, MD: American Alliance of Museums, 2020.

Silverman, Lois H. "Taking a Wider View of Museum Outcomes and Experiences: Theory, Research and Magic." *Journal of Education in Museums* 23 (2002): 3–8.

———. "Visitor Meaning-Making in Museums for a New Age." *Curator: The Museum Journal*, 38:3 (1995): 161–70.

Simon, Nina. *The Art of Relevance*. Santa Cruz: Museum 2.0, 2016.

Stewart, Susan. *On Longing: Narratives of the Miniature, the Gigantic, the Souvenir, the Collection.* Durham; London: Duke University Press, 1993.

Trouillot, Michel-Rolph, and Hazel V. Carby. *Silencing the Past: Power and the Production of History.* Boston, Massachusetts: Beacon Press, 2015.

Tucker, Marcia, and Liza Lou. *A Short Life of Trouble: Forty Years in the New York Art World.* Berkeley: University of California Press, 2010.

Turkle, Sherry. *Evocative Objects Things We Think With.* Cambridge: MIT Press, 2007.

Weil, Stephen. *Making Museums Matter.* Washington, D.C.: Smithsonian Institution Press, 2002.

Weil, Stephen E. *Rethinking the Museum and Other Meditations.* Washington, D.C.: Smithsonian Institution Press, 1990.

Weschler, Lawrence. *Mr. Wilson's Cabinet of Wonder: Pronged Ants, Horned Humans, Mice on Toast, and Other Marvels of Jurassic Technology.* New York: Vintage Books, 1996.

Zakim, Michael. *Ready-Made Democracy: A History of Men's Dress in the American Republic, 1760–1860.* Chicago: University of Chicago Press, 2005.

This second list of books and resources was mentioned during an online gathering of museum studies faculty and community on May 20, 2020.

Behave, Team Dynamics. https://podcasts.apple.com/us/podcast/behave/id1462437275.

Bjergegaard, Martin, and Cosmina Popa. *How to Be a Leader.* New York: Picador, 2016.

Brown, Brené. The Call to Courage | Netflix Official Site. (n.d.). https://www.netflix.com/title/81010166. Retrieved May 17, 2020.

Brown, Brené. *I Thought It Was Just Me (But It Isn't): Making the Journey from "What Will People Think?" to "I Am Enough."* New York: Gotham Books, 2007.

Brown, Jennifer. *How to Be an Inclusive Leader: Your Role in Creating Cultures of Belonging Where Everyone Can Thrive.* Oakland, Calif.: Berrett-Koehler Publishers, 2019.

Chödrön, Pema. *When Things Fall Apart: Heart Advice for Difficult Times* (20th anniversary edition). Boulder, Colorado: Shambhala, 2016.

Colonna, Jerry. *Reboot: Leadership and the Art of Growing Up.* New York: Harper Business, 2019.

Cooper, Brittney C. *Eloquent Rage: A Black Feminist Discovers Her Superpower.* New York: St. Martin's Press, 2018.

DiAngelo, Robin. *White Fragility. Why It's So Hard for White People to Talk About Racism.* Boston: Beacon Press, 2018.

Empathetic Museum Maturity Model. (n.d.). http://empatheticmuseum.weebly.com/maturity-model.html. Retrieved May 19, 2020.

Haga, Kazu. *Healing Resistance: A Radically Different Response to Harm.* Berkeley, Calif.: Parallax Press, 2020.

Hurston, Zora Neale. *Their Eyes Were Watching God.* New York: Perennial Classics, 1998.

Leadership Matters. (n.d.). https://leadershipmatters1213.wordpress.com/. Retrieved May 17, 2020.

Murphy, Kate. *You're Not Listening: What You're Missing and Why It Matters/* New York: Celadon Books, 2020.

Noble, Safiya Umoja. *Algorithms of Oppression: How Search Engines Reinforce Racism.* New York: New York University Press, 2018.

Patterson, Kerry, Joseph Grenny, Ron McMillan, and Al Switzler. *Crucial Conversations: Tools for Talking When Stakes are High* (2nd ed.). New York: McGraw-Hill, 2011.

Revisionist History, Season 3, Episode 7. (n.d.). http://revisionisthistory.com/episodes/27-malcolm-gladwell-s-12-rules-for-life. Retrieved May 17, 2020.

School of Life. *On Confidence.* School of Life Press, 2016.

Sinek, Simon. *Start with Why: How Great Leaders Inspire Everyone to Take Action.* New York: Penguin, 2017.

Zaki, Jamil. *The War for Kindness: Building Empathy in a Fractured World* (First Edition). New York: Crown, 2019.

Notes

1. See Michael H. Norton, Mark J. Stern, Jonathan Meyers, and Elizabeth DeYoung for the IMLS, "Understanding the Social Wellbeing Impacts of the Nation's Libraries and Museums," 2021, https://www.imls.gov/publications/understanding-social-wellbeing-impacts-nations-libraries-and-museums.
2. IMLS, "Understanding the Social Wellbeing Impacts of the Nation's Libraries and Museums," 2021, 2.
3. IMLS, "Understanding the Social Wellbeing Impacts of the Nation's Libraries and Museums," 2021, 6.
4. Founding director of AAM's Center for the Future of Museums, Elizabeth Merritt stated, "They [museums] didn't have a very resilient financial model or deep pockets that could carry them through a crisis like this." See Victoria L. Valentine, Constance Grady, and Jen Trolio, "Plight at the Museum," *Vox*, November 20, 2020, https://www.vox.com/the-highlight/21545993/broad-museum-african-american-coronavirus.
5. Emily Anthes, "How Science Museums Reinvented Themselves to Survive the Pandemic," *Science News*, June 4, 2021, https://www.sciencenews.org/article/science-museums-online-exhibits-education-coronavirus-covid-pandemic.
6. ASTC, "Weekly Attendance and Operations Survey: Year-in-Review Aggregate Report," 2. The report is available on the ASTC site: https://www.astc.org/astc-news-announcements/a-year-of-data-on-science-center-attendance-and-operations-provides-signs-of-hope/. The survey collecting used a baseline survey from 2019 operations as a benchmark. Once an institution submitted this data, they could participate in the weekly survey for the collection of data on the onsite attendance, facility status (physical site being closed or open during COVID), and program offerings.
7. Laura Lott, John Dichtl, D. Casey Sclar, Vedet Coleman-Robinson, Christine Anagnos, Keni Sturgeon, Christofer Nelson, Bonnie Styles, and Dan Ashe, Letter to "The Honorable Nancy Pelosi; The Honorable Charles Schumer; The Honorable Kevin McCarthy; The Honorable Mitch McConnell," January 12, 2022. This letter was a request to renew SVOG (Shuttered Venue Operators Grant) funding, which did not happen. However, their partnership in authoring the letter and their description of the contribution of museums is useful.
8. Laura Lott, John Dichtl, D. Casey Sclar, Vedet Coleman-Robinson, Christine Anagnos, Keni Sturgeon, Christofer Nelson, Bonnie Styles, and Dan Ashe, Letter to "The Honorable Nancy Pelosi; The Honorable Charles Schumer; The Honorable Kevin McCarthy; The Honorable Mitch McConnell," January 12, 2022. This letter was a request to renew SVOG (Shuttered Venue Operators Grant) funding, which did not happen. However, their partnership in authoring the letter and their description of the contribution of museums is useful.
9. California Academy of Sciences, "NightLife & Friends: A Virtual Event," April 2, 2020. https://www.youtube.com/live/UjTxUQzMsUg?si=yrKkUkOFBDE4Cy4h.
10. As of November 2023, there are ninety-two videos on the playlist, available here: https://youtube.com/playlist?list=PLS14biAqBAtGNwvFxHGET8a4SVH03ruR1&si=iUerpcy2XpWDEvJp.
11. The interactive may be accessed here: https://virtualexhibits.mos.org/covid-conversations/. For more on the technology employed, see StoryFile, https://storyfile.com/.
12. See American Museum of Natural History, "The Science of COVID-19," https://www.amnh.org/explore/covid-19-science. For instance, curator Nancy Simmons, at New York's American Museum of Natural History, served as part of a group using modeling methods to predict unrecognized wildlife host species

for viruses related to SARS-CoV-2 that will help prioritize future sampling for emerging viruses. Several other listings are online.

13. Emily Anthes, "How Science Museums Reinvented Themselves to Survive the Pandemic," *Science News*, June 4, 2021, https://www.sciencenews.org/article/science-museums-online-exhibits-education -coronavirus-covid-pandemic.

14. Lonnie Bunch was one of four museum directors interviewed. See Victoria L. Valentine, Constance Grady, and Jen Trolio, "Plight at the Museum," *Vox*, November 20, 2020, https://www.vox.com/the -highlight/21545993/broad-museum-african-american-coronavirus.

15. George Sparks was one of four museum directors interviewed. See Victoria L. Valentine, Constance Grady, and Jen Trolio, "Plight at the Museum," *Vox*, November 20, 2020, https://www.vox.com/the -highlight/21545993/broad-museum-african-american-coronavirus.

16. For data files, see IMLS, Museum Data Files, updated in 2018: https://www.imls.gov/research- evaluation/data-collection/museum-data-files. Earlier data may be found online at https://catalog .data.gov/dataset/museums-universe-data-file-mudf-fy-2013 and https://data.world/imls/museum -universe, though it is not available and maintained by IMLS.

17. IMLS, "Community Catalyst Initiative," https://www.imls.gov/our-work/priority-areas/community -catalyst-initiative.

18. Of/By/For All, "Our Story," https://www.ofbyforall.org/our-story.

19. Stephen E. Weil, "From Being about Something to Being for Somebody: The Ongoing Transforma- tion of the American Museum," *Daedalus*, 128:3 (Summer 1999): 229–58.

20. Of/By/For All "Approach," https://www.ofbyforall.org/approach.

21. James A. Anderson, "Some Say Occupy Wall Street Did Nothing, It Changed Us More Than We Think." *Time*, November 15, 2021, https://time.com/6117696/occupy-wall-street-10-years-later/.

22. I am grateful to my collaborators Janet Marstine, Stephanie Brown, Sarah Chicone, Laura- Edythe Coleman, Rosanna Flouty, Jennifer Kingsley, Jessica Luke, and Heidi Lung. https://youtu .be/hljr_Wjcf1M?si=5Kp3bFd3gllrwqOf and https://youtu.be/ToZwcR64xXA?si=uCriY8xWF lvZKlfH. The resources and all links are available here: https://www.aam-us.org/2020/08/06/ museum-studies-network-inaugural-online-gathering-msn-shelfie/.

23. Lonnie Bunch was one of four museum directors interviewed. See Victoria L. Valentine, Constance Grady, and Jen Trolio, "Plight at the Museum," *Vox*, November 20, 2020, https://www.vox.com/the -highlight/21545993/broad-museum-african-american-coronavirus.

24. The original schedule for the show was: June 2020 at the National Gallery of Art in Washington, then the Museum of Fine Arts, Houston, then to Tate Modern in London, and finally, the Museum of Fine Arts, Boston in 2021. The exhibit opened two years later, not four, with the following venues: Museum of Fine Arts, Boston, May 1–September 11, 2022; Museum of Fine Arts, Houston, October 23, 2022–January 15, 2023; National Gallery of Art, March 2–August 27, 2023; and Tate Modern, London, October 5, 2023–February 25, 2024. For the current dates, see https://www.nga.gov/exhibitions/2023/ philip-guston-now.html.

25. The works were *Drawing for Conspirators*, 1930; a mural, *The Struggle Against Terrorism*; and later works painted after "he watched scenes of police attacking anti-war demonstrators at the Democratic Convention in Chicago in 1968. . . . [He] was appalled by the rightward turn in America and wanted to reflect on White supremacy: how evil is concealed by hoods, how evil might succeed through its banal- ity. But he also felt compelled to imagine himself behind the hood. Can one be White in America and remain untarnished by such forces, he asked." @markgodfrey1973, September 25, 2020, https://www .instagram.com/p/CFjVJxsF4ph/?img_index=3.

26. @MarkGodfrey1973, https://www.instagram.com/p/CFjVJxsF4ph/?img_index=7. Further, God- frey cheered when Musa gave more than two hundred works by Guston to the Met Museum, https:// www.instagram.com/p/CmKU9TclNy1/?ref=lonijames.com.

27. Sarah Cascone, "Tate Has Suspended Curator Mark Godfrey for Openly Criticizing Its Decision to Postpone the Philip Guston Show He Co-Organized," *Artnet*, October 28, 2020, https://news.art net.com/art-world/mark-godfrey-suspended-tate-1918726. "Respected Curator Mark Godfrey Will Leave Tate Modern Following His Blow-Up with the Museum Over Its Postponed Philip Guston Show," *Artnet*, March 11, 2021, https://news.artnet.com/art-world/mark-godfrey-leaving-tate-1950948. A

spokesperson for Tate stated that he was leaving as part of a voluntary layoff program, which was related to pandemic-related revenue losses and the need to downsize 12 percent of the staff. Godfrey accepted the offer to downsize, which was open to all staff.

28. "Open Letter: On Philip Guston Now," *Brooklyn Rail*, September 30, 2020, https://brooklynrail.org/projects/on-philip-guston-now/. The *Rail* is an independent journal covering New York City.

29. I am grateful to colleagues Janet Marstine, Ceciel Brouwer, Stephanie Brown, Sarah Chicone, LauraEdythe Coleman, Rosanna Flouty, Chelsea Haines, Jennifer Kingsley, Jessica Luke, and Heidi Lung, as well as Alexa Cummins, Sydney Yaeger, Will Neer, and Megan Villa, for their thoughtful conversations around censorship, self-censorship, and open calls to transform toxic workplace culture in museums. These were held in summer/fall 2020. See https://msnconversations.wordpress.com/.

30. Jerry Saltz, "4 Museums Decided This Work Shouldn't Be Shown. They Are Both Right and Wrong. Fear Postponed a Philip Guston Retrospective. A Reckoning Must Follow," *Vulture*, October 1, 2020, https://www.vulture.com/2020/10/museums-decided-philip-gustons-work-shouldnt-be-seen-why.html.

31. Some responses to the postponement include (in chronological order): Tim Schneider, "The Gray Market: Why the Delay of 'Philip Guston Now' Will Backfire on the Entire Culture Sector (and Other Insights)," *Artnet*, September 28, 2020; https://news.artnet.com/news/philip-guston-now-postponement-1911180; Jason Farago "The Philip Guston Show Should Be Reinstated," *New York Times*, September 30, 2020, https://www.nytimes.com/2020/09/30/arts/design/philip-guston-shows-open-letter.html; Alex Greenberger, "Philip Guston's KKK Paintings: Why an Abstract Painter Returned to Figuration to Confront Racism," *ARTnews*, September 30, 2020, https://www.artnews.com/feature/philip-gustons-kkk-paintings-history-meaning-1234572056; Oscar Holland, "Artists Slam Decision to Postpone Exhibition of Philip Guston's KKK Paintings," *CNN*, October 1, 2023, https://www.cnn.com/style/article/philip-guston-kkk-art/index.html; Trenton Doyle Hancock, Mark Thomas Gibson, Jacolby Satterwhite, Tschabalala Self, and Gary Simmons, "Artists Speak Against the Postponement of 'Philip Guston Now,'" *Frieze*, October 2, 2020, https://www.frieze.com/article/artists-speak-against-postponement-philip-guston-now; Martha Schwendener "Why Philip Guston Can Still Provoke Such Furor, and Passion," *New York Times*, October 2, 2020, https://www.nytimes.com/2020/10/02/arts/design/guston-painter-career.html; Gareth Harris, "Directors of Tate and the National Gallery of Art Defend Controversial Decision to Delay Philip Guston Show," *Art Newspaper*, October 4, 2020, https://www.theartnewspaper.com/2020/10/04/directors-of-tate-and-the-national-gallery-of-art-defend-controversial-decision-to-delay-philip-guston-show; Paul Carter Robinson, "Philip Guston Postponed: Curator David Anfam Speaks Out," *Artlyst*, October 6, 2020, https://artlyst.com/news/philip-guston-postponed-curator-david-anfam-speaks-out-paul-carter-robinson/; Peter Schjeldahl, "Philip Guston and the Boundaries of Art Culture," *New Yorker*, October 12, 2020, https://www.newyorker.com/magazine/2020/10/19/philip-guston-and-the-boundaries-of-art-culture; Ben Davis, "The Strongest Reactions to the Philip Guston Show's Postponement Misses Two Key Points. Here's What They Are—and Why They Matter," *Artnet*, October 15, 2020, https://news.artnet.com/news/philip-guston-now-cancellation-1914529; Sebastian Smee, "The Philip Guston Controversy Is Turning Artists Against the National Gallery," *Washington Post*, October 16, 2020, https://www.washingtonpost.com/entertainment/museums/philip-guston-exhibition-postponement/2020/10/16/930d74a4-0ef5-11eb-8a35-237ef1eb2ef7_story.html; Barry Schwabsky, "Don't Hide the Art of Philip Guston," *Nation*, October 30, 2020, https://www.thenation.com/article/culture/guston-national-gallery/; Glasstire (Texas Visual Art podcast), "Art Dirt: Is Philip Guston Right for Now?" *Glasstire*, November 8, 2020, https://glasstire.com/2020/11/08/art-dirt-is-philip-guston-right-for-now/.

32. Julia Halperin, "Why Did the National Gallery Postpone Its Guston Show? The Museum's Director Says the Public Doesn't Need a 'White Artist to Explain Racism' Right Now," *Artnet*, October 6, 2020, https://news.artnet.com/art-world/kaywin-feldman-philip-guston-interview-1913483.

33. *Philip Guston Now* includes the largest reunion of paintings from his pivotal Marlborough Gallery show—in total twelve of the original thirty-three paintings shown.

34. *Curating Under Pressure: International Perspectives on Negotiating Conflict and Upholding Integrity*, edited by Janet Marstine and Svetlana Mintcheva, part of the Museum Meanings Series (London: Routledge, 2020).

Chapter 14

35. Tim Schneider, "The Gray Market: Why the Delay of 'Philip Guston Now' Will Backfire on the Entire Culture Sector (and Other Insights)," *Artnet*, September 28, 2020, https://news.artnet.com/news/philip-guston-now-postponement-1911180.

36. On each of these controversies, see the coverage by *Artnet*, among others. Lorena Muñoz-Alonso, "Dana Schutz's Painting of Emmett Till at Whitney Biennial Sparks Protest," *Artnet*, March 21, 2017, https://news.artnet.com/art-world/dana-schutz-painting-emmett-till-whitney-biennial-protest-897929; Sarah Cascone, "After Outcry from the Dakota Nation, the Walker Art Center May Dismantle a 'Traumatizing' Gallows Sculpture by Sam Durant," *Artnet*, May 30, 2017, https://news.artnet.com/news/walker-controversy-sam-durant-scaffold-974612; Sarah Cascone, "Artist Vincent Valdez Made a Painting So Provocative This Texas Museum Waited a Year to Unveil It. Now It's a National Sensation," *Artnet*, July 23, 2018, https://news.artnet.com/art-world/vincent-valdez-kkk-panorama-blanton-1320290; and Sarah Cascone, "'We Failed': A Cleveland Museum Apologizes for Cancelling an Exhibition on Police Brutality Without Consulting the Artist," *Artnet*, June 9, 2020, https://news.artnet.com/art-world/moca-cleveland-apologizes-cancelling-shaun-leonardo-exhibition-1882671.

37. Andrea K. Scott, "Does an Offensive Sculpture Deserve to Be Burned?" *New Yorker*, June 3, 2017, https://www.newyorker.com/culture/cultural-comment/does-an-offensive-sculpture-deserve-to-be-burned.

38. Alicia Eler, "A 'Healing' Work Celebrating Dakota Culture Takes the Place of 'Scaffold' in Minneapolis Sculpture Garden," *Star Tribune*, October 7, 2021, https://www.startribune.com/healing-work-celebrating-dakota-culture-takes-the-place-of-scaffold-in-minneapolis-sculpture-garden/600104570/.

39. Kiersten F. Latham and Brenda Cowan, *Flourishing in Museums: Towards a Positive Museology* (London: Routledge, 2024). The chapters in the edited volume demonstrate how and where flourishing is made visible, and provide evidence that museums today can flourish.

40. See W. T. Alderson, "Foreword" in *Museums in Motion: An Introduction to the History and Functions of Museums* (Nashville: AASLH, 1978), xi. Alderson earned his Ph.D. in history at Vanderbilt University and served as senior archivist at the Tennessee State Library and Archives. He served as former of the American Association of State and Local History, director of the museum studies program at the University of Delaware prior to Edward P. Alexander, who authored the first edition of this book, *Museums in Motion*, in 1978. Alderson also served as director of the (Margaret Woodbury) Strong Museum in Rochester, New York, before heading up Old Salem in Winston-Salem, North Carolina. His entire work world revolved around historical perspective and museum studies, much like Ed Alexander's.

15

Sustainability, Empathy, and Collecting

To conclude, we again return to the definition of *museum* approved by ICOM in 2022: "A museum is a not-for-profit, permanent institution in the service of society that researches, collects, conserves, interprets and exhibits tangible and intangible heritage. Open to the public, accessible and inclusive, museums foster diversity and sustainability. They operate and communicate ethically, professionally and with the participation of communities, offering varied experiences for education, enjoyment, reflection and knowledge sharing."[1] Clearly, the chapters in this volume, especially the previous few chapters, have offered vignettes that emphasize how museums do all this and more. Museums are institutions where transparency, anti-racism, anti-colonialism, and belonging are valued, as are labor and equity, along with risk-taking, sustainability, and empathy. Museums are, indeed, about people: who we are, where we have come from, and where we are going.

Key to this self-awareness is, simply, *the self*. For in keeping with Stephen Weil's assessment that museums shifted from being *about something* to being *for somebody*, the past decade has shown how museums are pivoting away from objects and toward people; away from specific, unidirectional narratives and toward bidirectional engagement and multi-vocality. As the director of Museum Hue, Stephanie Johnson-Cunningham, has noted, culturally specific museums are an incredible model of responsive care *because community care is at their center*, as opposed to collections. In addition, Smithsonian secretary Lonnie Bunch has called upon museums to be at the center of their communities.

As we have seen with the vignettes in this final third of the book, making the museum more human-centered and open to varied experiences, reflection, and knowledge sharing *is not* solely about visitors. Movements such as @MuseumWorkersSpeak, @ChangeTheMuseum, and #Museums ArtNotNeutral, among other calls for change, as well as labor, equity, and transparency movements, draw attention to the needs and rights of museum workers—the very people who put the Institution at the center for their communities. As visitors to museums seek self-care, so, too, do museum staff. For visitors, museums perform all the functions we have learned about in the earlier chapters of this book, in deed, and they also can function as places of retreat, relaxation, learning, and fun for visitors. Museum workers are in need of self-care, too, as they have always been, only now are their calls for care and change are being made publicly through movements noted above—and their calls are being acknowledged and addressed.

Museums are "letting go" of authority and sharing it with their neighbors, communities, and audiences, as well as traditional knowledge bearers and those with lived experience. Museums are also opening up opportunities for crowdsourcing and co-creation. Perhaps, too, museums as institutions and places of work can "let go."

What are museums? What are their histories? How do they function? Whom are they for? The answer to each of these is the same: museum are *of, by*, and *for* all of us.

To wrap up this discussion, this chapter focuses on community-created collections during times of crisis and, more recently, the COVID-19 pandemic. The chapter then asks who is not represented in museums and acknowledges continued silences before questioning whether museums can even persist at all. Rather than abolishing them entirely, we need to "un-fix" them. Or, perhaps they already are: they are *in motion*.

As part of this discussion, we have wound a series of narratives around museums and collections—they've oscillated from being the focus of museums to *not* being the focus—we end this book with a note about the actual *act* of collecting, especially collecting in times of crisis (i.e., rapid-response collecting). This meandering path back to collections is, rather, intentional, not to privilege objects, but to privilege *the stories they tell*, as we will explore below.

Rapid-Response Collecting

Museums and archives have documented crisis as part of their efforts to reflect their communities, audiences, and the world around them. One such example is the COVID-19 pandemic, an event that will be familiar to readers, with a university-led initiative to catalog the pandemic, as detailed below. However, a few brief comments will help situate the challenge and opportunities with rapid-response, or immediate, collecting.[2]

Artifacts tell stories. According to anthropologist Daniel Miller, objects "continually assert their presence as simultaneously material force and symbol. They frame the way we act in the world, as well as the way we think about the world."[3] To understand the past, we have to understand the artifacts of the past. In the midst of a crisis, artifacts are often left at the site of tragedy, a phenomenon known as "immediate" memorializing a facet of loss that situates the site in a similar way that cemeteries are conditioned: a space for public acknowledgment of tragedy, loss, and mourning.[4] Those boundaries are blurred at sites of tragedy, and as a result, the impulse to collect the materials that are left onsite becomes an important part of the storytelling around the event.

Museum professional Deborah Tulani Salahu-Din has examined the intersection between rapid-response collecting and museum mission. The social unrest in Baltimore, Maryland, after the death of twenty-five-year-old Freddie Gray while in the custody of the Baltimore Police Department led to peaceful protests-turned-rioting in the city. This series of events spurred the Smithsonian's National Museum of African American History and Culture (NMAAHC) to begin acquiring artifacts and archival materials associated with the city's social protest and civic engagement activities. While this collection process was being done prior to the museum's opening in 2016, the acquisitions were informed by adherence to the museum's guiding principle that connects objects to the human experience. They tell a story of the moment.[5]

Pam Schwartz, Whitney Broadaway, Emilie S. Arnold, Adam M. Ware, and Jessica Domingo have recounted the experience of collecting after the Pulse Nightclub Massacre in Orlando, Florida, on June 16, 2016, leaving forty-nine people murdered and sixty-eight people injured. Material tributes poured in, in tangible and intangible formats, leaving the museum staff of Orange County Regional History Center as caretakers of documenting, collecting, grieving, and healing the community through the "One Orlando Collection Initiative." Drawing upon the collected items enabled the museum curator (Schwartz) to identify objects that simultaneously "both broke and mended" her heart. Some of these were incorporated into the *One Year Later: Reflecting on Orlando's Pulse Nightclub Massacre* exhibit at the museum.[6]

Several other examples of rapid-response collecting exist. To explore the function that such efforts fill, and how they can serve as indicators of museum practice in the twenty-first century, we will look at one example, the COVID-19 pandemic archive, a digital museum of documenting, collecting, grieving, and healing.

Rapid-Response Collecting during COVID-19

In the spring of 2020, as I was teaching a course on visitor engagement and museum technologies, my undergraduate students and I were tapped in to this purpose as we researched, classified, and tested digital technologies and also created our own public-facing experiences using any number of

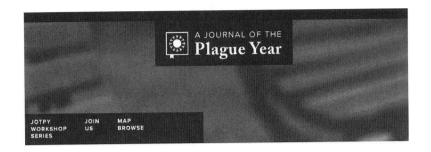

Items

| Created | ⌄ | Descending | ⌄ | SORT |

2022-09-22

Anthony

Explains about the warzone in the emergency department doing good during those times to bring people together in the community and a hero being honored by the state of colorado for all his work .This was submit to the house of representatives and this story has been shared in schools such as fredrick highschool by students who look up to him thank you

2020-03-11

The Effect COVID-19 Had on me.

I was a freshman in high school when we had the first COVID outbreak. I remember when my mom had to explain to me what was going on. It happened so fast I was just a confused and scared kid. Then I found out we had to go online. I missed a big part of my freshman and sophomore year of high school because of COVID. I lost contact with a lot of my friends. It was a very rough time not just for me, but also my parents. It was a very big change. I want to say the time sucked, but I try to think of the positives that came out of it. By one being I got a lot closer with my family. We were always close, but through COVID we only had each other. So, I try to think of the positives that happened throughout the

@ Save   t Post   ✉ Email   </> Get embed code

Global Pandemic Map

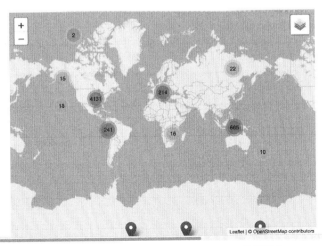

A rapid-response collecting initiative called *Journal of the Plague Year* (JOTPY) was undertaken from 2020–2022; it is the largest digital archive devoted to recording experiences of the COVID-19 pandemic and the wider historical and cultural moment of the pandemic. JOTPY is focused on international collaboration, ethical practice, and iterative digital humanities methods.

technologies. As we departed for Spring Break, students were well on their way to devising our second visitor experience—developing digital ancillaries to pitch to a local museum for use as part of their exhibition celebrating the centennial of woman suffrage. Instead of returning to our campus, computer labs, software, and the thought leadership among our collaborators, we were thrust into isolation, both in the physical sense, but also in terms of our learning community.

The COVID-19 pandemic and lockdown had begun.

No longer working as a cohort of twenty-nine on campus with tech and access within reach, we were individuals aspiring to realize our collective project vision, which would have been more fully defined upon our return from the break.[7] In short, our project with the museum was truncated significantly.

I still wanted the students to have some digital experiences, and I needed to be mindful of meeting them where they were—geographically, technologically, emotionally, and socially. One of the "new assignments" I developed—as I reworked my syllabus to move from an onsite, hands-on, project-based course to a course tethered to a pandemic and adapted for disparate technological access among our cohorts—involved the emerging pandemic archive, as a collaboration among several faculty, staff, and graduate students at a handful of universities. I was part of this emergent community of collaborators seeking to document the pandemic as it was occurring. Enter the *Journal of the Plague Year*, or JOTPY, archive.[8]

Returning to my course and students, I anchored the practice of community co-creation, documentation, and co-curation in developing an assignment for my course that would center the students' experiences and the archive—which is, ultimately, a museum. My goal with the assignment was to retain some spirit of the aforementioned project (content creation and digital deploy) and larger course learning outcomes while also affording students the ability to work independently. Called simply "COVID-19 Archive," the assignment tasks were threefold: 1) review the site and make observations on user experience, both in terms of interface and content; 2) create five entries that would become items in the publicly accessible archive; and 3) appraise the value of the archive as an entirety.

Students were asked to spend time on the JOTPY site and to assess its usefulness. This part of the assignment was self-guided; students could view and peruse as they wished. Then, students gathered images of five items concerning COVID-19, social distancing, closures, or ways their worlds had been impacted. After creating or capturing images, the students cataloged each item by identifying or assigning a title along with a description, date, type of item, and its location of origin. Twenty-three students completed the assignment, depositing the items and a sheet about each item to our course management system.[9] After examining the site, creating content and cataloging it to minimal standards, the students shared their experiences during our weekly Zoom meeting and wrote a response to the assignment, which they shared on our course discussion board.

The student responses reflected how comfortable they felt scrolling the site and, in turn, creating content for it. They enjoyed looking at the entries and seeing how others had characterized their experiences. With its short-form descriptions and inability to comment, JOTPY was unlike the politicized dregs of social media or the ego-deflating viral trends of TikTok. It offered, rather, useful, visual, short-form documentary narratives of life during the pandemic, an historic event they themselves were also experiencing. Many students also approached their own documentation and cataloging as if it were exhibition label copy writing. Students could apply what we had learned about writing label copy and preparing content for an interested reader to their immediate task of documenting their own experiences and writing for a public-facing audience who is unfamiliar to them though curious for information.

In terms of the archive in its entirety, students acknowledged its historical value, commenting upon its unique ability to document a range of experiences from traumatic and fearful to joyful and productive. As one student wrote, "This site is essentially a collective diary, something that will be priceless for later historians. I think looking at previous examples in history, like documentation surrounding World War I and II, that people will not realize the importance of an event until they are several years well-removed from it."[10] Interestingly, while several students curated content that reflected personal isolation, separation, anxiety, and fear after being extricated from their semester and their campus community, none of the students wrote about isolation as a result of viewing the archive. In other words, viewing the archive, creating content for it, and reflecting upon the experience enabled each of them to find community among the archive. One student went so far as to characterize the archive's value as empathetic, as well as documentary.[11]

Importantly, this assignment enabled students to articulate the shift between viewers or visitors as audiences and viewers or visitors as participants, which is one of our course learning outcomes that coheres with the embrace of museum studies and public history toward shared authority, community-curation, and inclusion.[12] While this learning objective is embedded as part of a number of assignments, its import here is particularly relevant and encouraging as a number of students found the site and the experience to be therapeutic in one way or another, as a way to put attention toward documentation and contributing to a new-found community.[13]

On a personal level, the assignment helped me to remain connected to my students, to empathize with them, and to understand their range of authentic, unique experiences. I was able to spend time reading about the experiences of my international students who shared the difficulties and frustrations of being unable to reach family while simultaneously comparing the news reports from the United States and China; students moving back home and contending with siblings, daycare, and additional work responsibilities to help make family ends meet; digital diversions, such as shopping and *Animal Crossing*; and localized practices, such as putting a stuffed animal in your window (this was "a thing" I learned from my student who went back home to the Boston area!). While I have designed viewer and visitor experiences for audiences whereby empathy is one of many aspirations, I had not anticipated that this COVID-19 archive assignment could provide the same for me. An embarrassment of riches for which I remain grateful, the assignment offered the finest proof that digital practices can forge community.

Finally, in terms of meaning-making as part of the visitor engagement and experiences, it is easy to dismiss the JOTPY—an Omeka-based, item-level content management system—as irrelevant when contrasted with the exciting range of possibilities that can foreground meaning-making and, perhaps, forge authenticity and empathy. However, in much the same way that technology-fueled, immersive experiences can provide pathways for empathy, so can exploring, creating content for, and reflecting upon the JOTPY. In this way, this assignment became a way to move, as museum scholar Stephen Weil stated, "from being *about something* to being *for somebody*."[14] Even though my students and I were geographically separated, together we tiptoed away from the act of curating objects (*something*) and fully charged our way into the process of joining a community (*somebody*) that shared in the collective experience.

Museum Silences

After seeing the ways in which museums can be about *somebody*, it is important to think about who is not represented in museums. The term *archival silences* refers to "a gap in the historical record resulting from the unintentional or purposeful absence or distortion of documentation."[15] Many who have written about this subject have pointed to Haitian historian Michel-Rolph Trouillot and his questioning of what is left out and what is recorded. For Trouillot: "Silences enter the process of historical production at four crucial moments: the moment of fact creation (the making of sources); the moment of fact assembly (the making of archives); the moment of fact retrieval (the making of narratives); and the moment of introspective significance (the making of history in the final instance). . . . Rather, they help us understand why not all silences are equal and why they cannot be addressed—or redressed—in the same manner. To put it differently, any historical narrative is a particular bundle of silences, the result of a unique process, and the operation required to deconstruct these silences will vary accordingly."[16]

The concept of archival silence has overlaps with allied fields that include museum studies. Consider how museums display "silence." Consider how the presences and absences are embodied in what we see in collections and what we don't see; what we see in exhibitions, and what we don't see; what is told in stories, and what is not told. Institutions—not just archives but also museums and other memory work sites—collect objects and facts that are thematized, processed, and presented. They are not neutral, nor are they natural. They are constructions.[17]

It may be, perhaps, that we need to collectively adopt methods of collection—whether of tangible or intangible heritage—defined by museum curator and historian Julius L. Jones who has defined *"temporal disorientation"* as a way to capture and document the everyday. Borrowing from *spatial disorientation*, defined as the condition that aviators face when they cannot interpret altitude or airspeed relative to a point of reference, Jones defines the condition of *temporal disorientation* as rendering the time since an event meaningless. One's sense of time depreciates and, instead, the knowledge, memory, and material of an event would emerge immediately. Communities would recognize an event as historically significant as close to the moment as possible.[18] By extension, then, in authorizing temporal disorientation, museums might help to fill voids and "archival silences" before even allowing them to take shape.

Abolishing Museums or, Rather, Unfixing Them?

Reflecting on the call from DTP organizer Marz Saffore to "abolish museums," the act of abolishing museums seems entirely unrealistic, as does the call for "Death to Museums," originated in a 2019 issue of the journal *FWD: Museums*, produced by the graduate program in museum studies at University of Illinois-Chicago.[19] The issue sought to ask questions about museums and their future—reminder, this is pre-pandemic.

- Do museums need to change to avoid their death?
- Do museums need to die in order to change?
- Are museums under attack?
- If so, by whom and to what end?

The journal team, under the direction of Therese Quinn, expressed discontent, noting "the idea of the museum as a cold, aloof, and stuffy mausoleum needs to come to an end." Their issue title-turned-mantra was a call to action, a stated need for change, and "an alert that cultural institutions held in public trust are at risk and need protection."[20]

After the launch of the publication, the pandemic erupted, as publication team members June Ahn, Rose Cannon, and Emma Turner-Trujillo and others were transitioning from graduate students in a museum studies program to emerging professionals in an ecosystem of calamity from the pandemic. Taking inspiration from their journal issue, Ahn, Cannon, and Turner-Trujillo were among several organizers of Death to Museums, the movement.

The organizers saw renewed relevance in their journal theme "at a moment when museums are crumbling before our very eyes." They were careful in their articulation about death, noting that "the idea to destroy museums comes not from a place of hate, but we do question whether they are redeemable in their current form. We want to galvanize the collective power of museum workers driving toward radical change. So that death to museums can become a platform to brainstorm new ways to push the field forward."[21] Though their website has gone dark, the five sessions from August 2020 through January 2021 are available on YouTube, in a deep-cut manner that lays bare the anxieties and concerns of emerging museum professionals and others in the early days of the pandemic, and the return to work in January 2021 for many in the field.[22]

"Unfixing" Museums

Rather than abolishing, perhaps the path forward lies in "un-fixing" them. To un-fix means to undo *fixity*, which is defined as "the state of being unchanging or permanent."[23] By extension, "un-fixing" implies removal from the tethers, re-invention, and seeing a new reality, and realizing a new future.

For museum futures, there is no single approach for all museums. The latest tally of United States museums given by the Institute of Museum and Library Services gave a number of more than thirty-five thousand, which is more than the number of Starbucks and McDonald's in the United States combined.[24] That data was gathered in 2014 and serves as the best estimate (unfortunately no such tally has been done in the United States more recently, though a great deal of data has been presented about the impacts of COVID-19 on museums, in the short term). Mamie Bittner of IMLS notes that that many of these institutions, particularly in small towns and rural areas, are historical societies and history museums. They serve an important function in the lives of the community, particularly when it comes to informal learning—the extended and hands-on learning that children and adults can engage with, outside of the classroom. She notes, "We are in love with our history—at a very grassroots level we care for the histories of our towns, villages and counties. . . . These museums are the community institutions that are the cornerstones of this informal learning."[25] Clearly, the importance of museums to their communities cannot be overstated.

As pillars of their communities, each museum or similar institution has its own history and function as tied to its mission. But do they reflect their *entire* community? Are they still relevant? As shocking as these questions may appear to be, they need to be asked. Where do we turn for answers?

We can learn from other arenas, namely public art, especially the monuments and memorials that bedeck villages, towns, and cities across the United States: around forty-eight thousand, according to the latest data available from Monument Lab, the Philadelphia-based think tank and community convener.[26] Monument Lab offers methods for engaging in conversation such as creative arts practice, data scraping, guidebook creation, and other forms of resource creation and granting of access and pathways to foreground inclusion and belonging. Such activities can be undertaken by students and learners of all ages, culture bearers, researchers, scholars, practitioners—everyone in a community can be invited to participate in the process of publicly sourcing ideas about monuments and memorials.

An example of such engaged practice is Monument Lab's Public Iconographies Map program. Over the summer of 2019, they gathered 750 illustrated maps featuring over one thousand places in St. Louis, Missouri. From these hand-drawn iterations, a re-created map was made, featuring commonly drawn landmarks on the maps, places that have been erased or demolished from the landscape, and opportunities where monuments might be realized. Called a "residency," the program culminated with a stakeholder engagement and the release of a map publication that visualized the research team's findings.[27] This publication and the dataset undergirding it offer a micro-narrative of the lived experience of communities, their monuments, and their awareness of what is missing from the cultural landscape.

On a larger scale, the aforementioned National Monument Audit, undertaken in 2020–2021 analyzed fifty thousand conventional monuments from every U.S. state and territory. It sought information about what is present and what is absent. The audit is the first part of a multi-phase program by the Mellon Foundation to "transform the way our country's histories are told in public spaces and ensure that future generations inherit a commemorative landscape that venerates and reflects the vast, rich complexity of the American story."[28]

The report from the audit opens with the words of orator and abolitionist Frederick Douglass, who denied the possibility for monuments to evidence a full truth. The quoted passage reads: "Perhaps no one monument could be made to tell the whole truth of any subject which it might be designed to illustrate."[29] Could the same be said of museums?

Evidence to illustrate Douglass's point about monuments is woven throughout the report, which noted that the monument landscape is "overwhelmingly white and male" along with data about the top fifty persons depicted, the percentage of these who enslaved other people (50 percent); the percentage of whom were Black or Indigenous (10 percent); and the percentage of whom were women (6 percent).[30] The report critiques the messaging of monuments and memorials, as if they were a text in the ways that this series of essays has also demonstrated. For instance, the audit shows the ratio of monuments reflecting war to peace is 13:1; war to love is 17:1; and war to care is 59:1.[31]

The report from the National Monument Audit also issues four calls to action for monuments and memorials framed around:

- reimagining commemoration;
- engaging in a "reckoning with monumental erasures and lies";
- building a new understanding of how monuments function; and
- shifting representation that is more full and reflective of the United States.

The report asks us, as a nation, to take steps toward creating a monument landscape that acknowledges a fuller history of this country. The report asks for evolution, embracing the idea that monuments *must* change and by seeking ways to repair and reimagining "how history lives with us every day."[32] Superbly researched, data-driven, and yet still accessible, the audit is a profound state of the field that offers very clear, actionable items—a path forward.

What can we glean from the report in terms of museums—all of them in the United States, large and small and of every type? Adjusting the calls for action from the report to the space of museums, we can ask questions about museums and their futures.

- Can we reimagine museums?
- Can we engage in a "reckoning with museum erasures and lies"?
- Can we build a new understanding of how museums function?
- Can we shift representation and storytelling that is more full and reflective of the United States?

Other publications from Monument Lab provide structured methods for carrying out these calls, for instance, in offering guidance for engaging with monuments and, also, museums.[33] Interspersed with quotes from scholars and artists, the ten-page guide *Monument Lab Field Trip* (2020) offers four points of departure for investigating historical monuments and asking questions about art and social justice. The guide defines a *monument* as "a statement of power and presence in public" before moving on to an investigation of monuments in one's city, town, or neighborhood that frames practices of observations as well as fact-finding onsite by looking at markers, signs, or inscriptions. The same is true for museums—they reflect power and presence in the public. Moving into observation, the guide asks readers to draw the monument and its environs before asking about the feelings that the monument evokes as well as speculation about its history and the omission of some perspectives from the monument's narrative. The third part of the guide asks readers to "unfix" the ideas we have inherited about monuments, to think beyond who is represented on a monument's base to conceive of their associations (good and bad), before asking readers to record their thoughts about the layers of history, people, and events that are linked to the monument's site. The final section asks readers to propose a new monument that represents something or someone "that matters to you and your community."[34] With each of these four starting points, we can insert "museum" for "monument" as a point of departure for how to think about museums—where they have come from, and where they are going.

A second guide from Monument Lab focuses on museum field trips (2022) and asks readers to investigate questions about learning and to propose ideas for making museums less exclusive and more inclusive spaces—very much in the same way that the guide focused on monuments and memorials seeks to make public space and the built environment of monument and memorials more

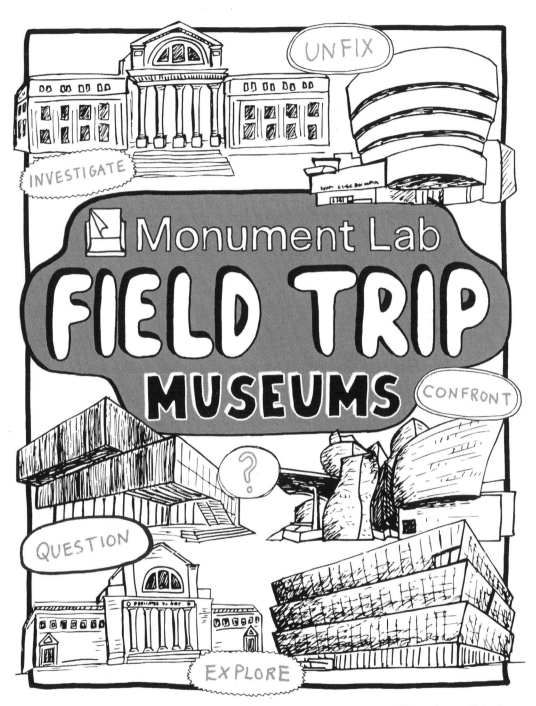

Monument Lab worked with Mike Murawski and Bryna Campbell of Art Nature Place, along with La Tanya S. Autry, to produce a guide that focuses on museum field trips. It asks readers to investigate questions about learning and to propose ideas for making museums less exclusive and more inclusive spaces. *Courtesy Monument Lab and Art Nature Place.*

accessible, less exclusive, and truly more meaningful. Referencing activism of "Decolonize This Place," "Museums Are Not Neutral," and "Museum Workers Speak,"[35] the task here, again, is to "unfix" through investigation and activities. Drawing upon the same paradigm of reflect, draw, speculate, and realize, the museum guide also draws out the idea of stories, themes, and narratives within constructed spaces: galleries or rooms within a museum offer information through labels, text, and videos, but they also offer—implicitly and explicitly—stories, themes, and topics. The guide also recognizes the labor across the institution as a preface to understanding whether the space feels welcoming and accessible and how it might represent power.[36]

By weaving together approaches to "unfix" monuments and memorials and museums, we can carry the lessons forward of the chapters within this volume, and our own, lived experiences. By seeing museums as lenses through which to view the fullness of who we are as communities, and what we value for keeping and exhibiting in museums, we can examine critical issues about the world around us, including race, memory, and the legacies of war, power, and subjugation. We can begin or, optimistically, continue efforts of diversity, equity, inclusion, and belonging. We can dismantle the idea of museums as representations of power, entitlement, possession, control, and authority to offer, anew, opportunities to "unfix" their meanings and interpretations.

Collectively and individually, we have the opportunity to pose and answer questions about museums and what they say about who we are and what we value. We can demonstrate how they are, truly, *in motion*. In doing so, perhaps we can add another verb to the list of functions of museums: *to be kind*. Museums can aspire to be kind to themselves, their visitors, and their collections: they can reaffirm the triangulation around museum-visitor-object previously defined in this discussion of museum histories and functions to also inform their aspirations.

Notes

1. International Council of Museums, "ICOM Approves a New Museum Definition," August 24, 2022, https://icom.museum/en/news/icom-approves-a-new-museum-definition/.
2. On rapid-response collecting and COVID-19, see Jeffrey Brodiem, "September 11: Collecting for the National Postal Museum," *NMAH Blog Post*, September 11, 2011, https://americanhistory.si.edu/blog/2011/09/september-11-collecting-for-the-national-postal-museum.html; Mark Cave and Stephen M. Sloan, eds., *Listening on the Edge: Oral History in the Aftermath of Crisis* (New York: Oxford University Press, 2014); Richard J. Cox, *Flowers after the Funeral: Reflections on the Post-9/11 Digital Age* (Lanham, Md.: Scarecrow Press, 2003); Lisa P. Nathan, Elizabeth Shaffer, and Maggie Castor, "Stewarding Collections of Trauma: Plurality, Responsibility, and Questions of Action," *Archivaria* 80 (Fall 2015): 89–118; Mark Tebeau, "A Journal of the Plague Year: Rapid-Response Archiving Meets the Pandemic," *Collections* 17:3 (2021): 199–206; Brenda Tindal, "K(NO)W Justice K(NO)W Peace: The Making of a Rapid-Response Community Exhibit," *Public Historian* 40:1 (February 2018): 87–96; "TPH Rapid Response | National Council on Public History." Accessed June 18, 2018. http://ncph.org/history-at-work/tag/tph-rapid-response/.
3. Daniel Miller, *Material Culture and Mass Consumption* (Oxford: Blackwell, 1987), 105, as quoted in Steven Lubar and Kathleen Kendrick, "Looking at Artifacts, Thinking about History." In *Artifact and Analysis: A Teacher's Guide to Interpreting Objects and Writing History*, edited by Kendrick Kathleen (Washington, D.C.: Smithsonian Center for Education and Museum Studies and the National Museum of the American History, 2001), https://smithsonianeducation.org/idealabs/ap/essays/looking.htm.
4. On memorials, see Harriet F. Senie, *Memorials to Shattered Myths: From Vietnam to 9/11* (New York: Oxford University Press, 2016).
5. Deborah Tulani Salahu-Din, "Documenting the Black Lives Matter Movement in Baltimore through Contemporary Collecting: An Initiative of the National Museum of African American History and Culture," *Collections* 15:2–3 (2019): 101–12. The article also includes a list of recommendations for acquiring materials associated with contemporary issues.

6. Pam Schwartz, Whitney Broadaway, Emilie S. Arnold, Adam M. Ware, and Jessica Domingo, "Rapid-Response Collecting After the Pulse Nightclub Massacre," *Public Historian* 40:1 (February 2018), 105–14. Quote on page 109. The Pulse Memorial Foundation has organized an interim memorial onsite.

7. I have written about this teaching experience in truncated form for the National Council on Public History. See Juilee Decker and Cheryl Jiménez Frei, "Adapting and Finding Meaning In Uncertain Times: Teaching the JOTPY Archive," *History@Work*, September 24, 2020, https://ncph.org/history-at-work/teaching-the-jotpy-archive/.

8. *A Journal of the Plague Year* can be found here: https://covid-19archive.org/s/archive/page/Share. As with any project, some students in the course had familiarity with the platform; others did not. Some of the students in the course were familiar with Omeka from other courses they had taken with me, such as Cultural Informatics. See https://ritarchives.omeka.net/exhibits.

9. These items, along with my contributions, and twenty-three stories from our student government association were gathered and will be uploaded to the site in the coming weeks.

10. Koda Drake, discussion post, April 12, 2020.

11. Sven Patterson, discussion post, April 15, 2020: "Being able to keep up to date through a crowdsourced service, as well as being able to empathize with others in the situation that you are in are incredible resources to have for many people."

12. While the student posts were largely biographical, the posts made by students could function as source for a form of autoethnography that gives scholarly voice to personal experience. Such highly personalized accounts draw upon the experience of the author/researcher for the purposes of extending sociological understanding. By beginning with a personal story, autoethnographers combine auto- (self), -ethno- (the sociocultural connection), and -graphy (the application of the research process) to varying degrees.

13. As one student put it, "While the social isolation and act of quarantining may be intimidating for many, this opportunity to share specifically about life changes due to the virus may prove therapeutic in the immediate moment." See Courtney Barber, discussion post, April 12, 2020. Philip Rust also commented, "There is something therapeutic about sharing your experience with others and this offers an outlet in this trying time," discussion post, April 12, 2020.

14. Stephen E. Weil, "From Being about Something to Being for Somebody: The Ongoing Transformation of the American Museum," *Daedalus* 128:3 (Summer 1999): 229–58.

15. See Society of American Archivists, "Archival Silence," *Dictionary of Archives Terminology*, https://dictionary.archivists.org/entry/archival-silence.html.

16. Michel-Rolph Trouillot, *Silencing the Past: Power and Production of History* (Boston: Beacon Press, 1995), 26–27. In thinking about archival silences, see also Rodney G.S. Carter, "Of Things Said and Unsaid: Power, Archival Silences, and Power in Silence," *Archivaria*, September 25, 2006; David Thomas, Simon Fowler, Valerie Johnson, editors, *The Silence of the Archive* (London: Facet Publishing, 2017).

17. Borrowing from Trouillot, 48.

18. Julius L. Jones, "Black Digital Pasts & Reflections on Black Digital History and Museums: Julius Jones and Nile Blunt in Conversation," Rochester Institute of Technology, April 4, 2023, https://www.rit.edu/events/reflections-black-digital-history-and-museums-julius-jones-and-nile-blunt-conversation.

19. See "Death to Museums 2019," *FWD:Museums Journal*, https://fwdmuseumsjournal.weebly.com/death-to-museums-2019.html.

20. "Publication Team 2019," *FWD:Museums Journal*, https://fwdmuseumsjournal.weebly.com/death-to-museums-20191.html. Therese Quinn is director of Museum and Exhibition Studies at UIC.

21. Death to Museums, "An Introduction to Death to Museums," September 5, 2020, https://www.youtube.com/watch?v=9brEbjbnnls. They cite Tunde Wey, a New Orleans–based activist, artist, and chef, who asks: "Can you renovate a burning house? Can you renovate a single room in a burning house?"

22. See Death to Museums on YouTube, https://www.youtube.com/@deathtomuseums2242.

23. Definition from *Oxford Languages* via Google, November 25, 2023, https://www.google.com/search=fixity.

24. Christopher Ingraham, "There Are More Museums in the U.S. Than There Are Starbucks and McDonalds—Combined," *Washington Post*, June 13, 2014, https://www.washingtonpost.com/news/wonk/wp/2014/06/13/there-are-more-museums-in-the-us-than-there-are-starbucks-and-mcdonalds

-combined/. Of the roughly twenty-five thousand museums with income data in the file, fifteen thousand of them reported an annual income of less than ten thousand dollars on their latest IRS returns.

25. Christopher Ingraham, "There Are More Museums in the U.S. Than There Are Starbucks and McDonalds—Combined," *Washington Post*, June 13, 2014, https://www.washingtonpost.com/news/wonk/wp/2014/06/13/there-are-more-museums-in-the-us-than-there-are-starbucks-and-mcdonalds-combined/.

26. Kriston Capps, "What Counting Every Monument in the U.S. Adds Up To," *Bloomberg*, October 1, 2021, https://www.bloomberg.com/news/articles/2021-10-01/mapping-every-public-monument-in-the-u-s.

27. See "Public Iconographies: St. Louis, MO," January 2019–August 2020, https://monumentlab.com/projects/public-iconographies. This page has links to assets such as transcribed maps, inventory of places, gallery of all scanned maps, and data.

28. Monument Lab, "National Monument Audit, 2021, is downloadable here: https://monumentlab.com/projects/national-monument-audit. The audit was undertaken from October 2020 through December 2021 and was produced by Monument Lab in partnership with the Andrew W. Mellon Foundation.

29. Monument Lab, "National Monument Audit," 2021, 3. In fact, Douglass critiqued Thomas Ball's Emancipation Monument, in that same letter to the editor of the D.C.-based paper, *National Republican*, because it did not show the rights of formerly enslaved persons. Douglass exclaimed, "What I want to see before I die is a monument representing the negro, not couchant on his knees life a four-footed animal, but erect on his feet like a man." With the monument created in Douglass's honor by Stanley Edwards, that vision was achieved nearly twenty-five years later, in 1899. See Frederick Douglass, "A Suggestion: To The Editor of the National Republican," *National Republican*, April 19, 1876, 4.

30. Monument Lab, "National Monument Audit," 2021, 17.

31. Monument Lab, "National Monument Audit," 2021, 21.

32. Monument Lab, "National Monument Audit," 2021, 29.

33. See Monument Lab, "Publications," https://monumentlab.com/publications.

34. Monument Lab, "Monument Lab Field Trip," July 2020, https://monumentlab.com/publications/monument-lab-field-trip. The PDF was designed and illustrated by Mike Murawski and Bryna Campbell.

35. Decolonize This Place, https://decolonizethisplace.org/; Museums Are Not Neutral, https://www.museumsarenotneutral.com/; Museum Workers Speak, https://sites.google.com/view/museumworkersspeak/about-museum-workers-speak.

36. Monument Lab, "Monument Lab Field Trip: Museums," June 2022, https://monumentlab.com/publications/monument-lab-field-trip-museums. The PDF was designed and illustrated by Mike Murawski and Bryna Campbell.

Index

VR (virtual reality) 183, 185, 189, 190, 195, 206, 210, 211, 212, 218. *See also* AR (augmented reality). *See also* XR (extended reality)

Vygotsky, Lev, 178

Waller, Robert, 133, 135, 137, 148, 149
Washington Monument, 21, 68, 69, 77
Weil, Stephen, x, 161, 224, 303, 318, 331, 335
Whitney, Gertrude Vanderbilt, 22, 25, 35
Whitney Museum of American Art, 19, 22, 275, 285

Wiley, Kehinde, 21, 92, 311
Wittman, Aletheia, 241–243, 288
World's Fair(s) 10, 17, 20, 47, 48, 49, 50, 54, 63, 65, 69, 70, 109, 126, 153, 290, 294
Wunderkammer, 4

XR (extended reality), 189, 201, 206, 209, 265. *See also* AR (augmented reality). *See also* VR (virtual reality)

zoos, 57, 105, 110, 111, 112, 122, 123, 316

About the Author

Juilee Decker, Ph.D., is professor of history at Rochester Institute of Technology, where she directs the Museum Studies/Public History program and co-directs the Cultural Heritage Imaging Lab. She earned her Ph.D. from the joint program in art history and museum studies at Case Western Reserve University/Cleveland Museum of Art. She serves as editor of the peer-reviewed journal *Collections* (SAGE). You may find her at https://juileedecker.com/ or email her at jdgsh@rit.edu.

In Memoriam

EDWARD P. ALEXANDER, 1907–2003

On a snowy January day in Madison, Wisconsin, members of the State Historical Society gathered to say good-bye to Alice and Ed Alexander as they prepared to move to Williamsburg, Virginia, to join the staff of Colonial Williamsburg (CW). The party was planned, presents wrapped, and speeches written, but there was one hitch. Alice was blocks away at University Hospital, where daughter Mary Sheron was making her entrance. That spring, the Alexanders, including Anne, John, and Mary (in a laundry basket) drove south to Williamsburg, Virginia.

Edward Alexander seems to have done it all in terms of history museums. In the 1930s and 1940s, he led the New York and Wisconsin state historical societies. He brought to Colonial Williamsburg a commitment to intellectual rigor in public interpretation, relying on his academic background in U.S. history. He was elected president of the American Association of State and Local History (AASLH), the third in the association's history, and he was the president of the American Association of Museums (AAM) in the 1960s. On his retirement from CW in 1972, he described his departure this way: "I left my office at the Goodwin Building on a Friday and the next Monday I faced my Museum Studies students in a classroom at the University of Delaware." He was sixty-five years old and was establishing a new museum studies program.

As I wrote and rewrote additions to this volume, I was striving to be the engaging storyteller that Dad was. One of his former students described reading his text as "having a chat with Dr. Alexander." His books, *Museums in Motion: An Introduction to the History and Functions of Museums* (1979), *Museum Masters: Their Museums and Their Influence* (1983), and *The Museum in America: Innovators and Pioneers* (1997), remain basic texts on museum professionals' shelves. The last was published when he was ninety years old.

In his lifetime, Edward P. Alexander was appropriately honored for his contributions to museum practice with the Katherine Coffey Award (Northeast Museums Conference), the Award of Distinction (AASLH), and the Distinguished Service Award (AAM). He is listed on the AAM's Centennial Honor Roll.

—Mary Alexander
written for the Second Edition of *Museums in Motion*, 2008

In Recognition

MARY ALEXANDER

Mary Alexander authored the second edition of *Museums in Motion* and passed the baton to me to usher in the third edition. Mary, as was her father, is a consummate scholar and professional who has laid an important foundation in museum studies through her work. Mary has worked in and for Washington-area history museums for the past four decades. She has been a museum educator, assistant director, leader of the Common Agenda for History Museums project for the American Association for State and Local History, and administrator of the Museum Assistance Program of the Maryland Historical Trust. She is co-author with George Hein of *Museums: Places of Learning* (1998), and in 2008, she revised the first edition of this volume. Mary holds a BA in history from Beloit College, and an MA in education from the University of Connecticut.

While her and her father's names are no longer on the cover of this book, I want to acknowledge their work and to express gratitude in having the honor and privilege of continuing their work, and also making it my own.

While I never had the opportunity to meet Edward, I have met Mary over email. So I will close with a little anecdote about that introduction. In short, it's how I found out Mary's thoughts on my revision to her and her father's book.

On Saturday, April 17, 2017, I opened my laptop to find an email from Mary Alexander. *The* Mary Alexander.

Gulp.

It read: "You can imagine my trepidation when I received the new edition. Now that I've reviewed it, I'm thrilled with your approach. I look forward to meeting you someday soon."

Exhale.

Thank you, Mary, for being who you are, for taking the time to send a brief email to me, to introduce yourself and to connect. I wanted to make this known to all readers of this book to share, also, the importance of kindness and taking time to connect with others, even if you do not know them. For this reason, I consider Mary a mentor to me. And I am forever grateful.

—Juilee Decker
written for the Fourth Edition of *Museums in Motion*, 2024